Clinical Psychology

Clinical Psychology

Integrating Science and Practice

Arthur Freeman

Stephanie H. Felgoise

Denise D. Davis

John Wiley & Sons, Inc.

Library of Congress Cataloging-in-Publication Data:

Freeman, Arthur, 1942–
  Clinical psychology : integrating science and practice / by Arthur Freeman,
Stephanie H. Felgoise, Denise D. Davis.
       p.   ;   cm.
  Includes bibliographical references.
  ISBN 978-0-471-41499-5 (cloth : alk. paper)
  1. Clinical psychology.   I. Felgoise, Stephanie H.   II. Davis, Denise D.
III. Title.
  [DNLM: 1. Psychology, Clinical.   2. Mental Disorders—diagnosis.   3.
Mental Disorders—therapy.   4. Psychotherapy—methods.   WM 105 F855c 2008]
  RC467.F74   2008
  616.89—dc22
                                                              2007011146

Printed in the United States of America.

10 9 8 7 6 5 4 3 2 1

CONTENTS

There is an old saying that "the more things change, the more they stay the same." This is true for the field of clinical psychology. Despite the enormous changes and developments in applied practice over the past 30 years, clinical psychology remains firmly connected to its scientific foundations. Clinical psychologists have made significant contributions to the growing fund of empirically based methods and strategies used in mental health applications today. Through their commitment to the integration of science and applied practice, clinical psychologists have helped to raise the qualitative standards of mental health care, expand the range of those who have access to care, and lower overall costs of care by developing targeted interventions that are effective and efficient.

Perhaps the most important psychology course taught is the basic introductory course. It stimulates interest, provides basic grounding; and establishes the foundation for future work. Successful academic and professional advancement in graduate work in clinical psychology is built on these same tenets. The course that introduces clinical psychology sets the tone for graduate training. Whether you are the teacher or the student in such a course, a comprehensive, realistic, yet interesting introductory text is an essential tool in this challenging endeavor.

Much has been said about the importance of integrating science and practice in clinical psychology; yet few texts illustrate the actual workings of this process. Our goals in offering the present text are threefold. First, we want to provide beginning graduate students with a comprehensive introduction to the field of clinical psychology. This text is intended to build an appreciation of clinical psychology's richness and historical significance and its leadership in the scientific development of methods and techniques for clinical assessment and intervention. Throughout the book, we emphasize clinical psychology as a vital force in today's health care practice. The model that we use throughout the text is the biopsychosocial systems model of understanding human behavior. We direct students toward developing critical thinking skills that are applied in the context of this interactive model, rather than endorsing any single theoretical orientation.

Second, we offer students a detailed look at basic clinical tasks and skills that are the nuts and bolts of a practitioner's work. We explain things from the ground up, so that the student can integrate the scientific, theoretical, and practical underpinnings of their applied tasks. This will prepare the student to acquire more detailed and specific information in later courses on research methods, ethics, cultural diversity, assessment, psychotherapy, and other specialized, advanced practice skills. Clinical cases and vignettes are used liberally throughout the text to illustrate, emphasize, and help the student conceptualize professional, scientifically grounded clinical encounters. In reading this text, students can gain a vivid picture of what the work of a clinical psychologist really looks like. Because so many case examples are used, it is important to note that this book is expressly intended as an educational resource for the training of professional psychologists. All our case material is disguised and presented in composite form so that no specifically identifiable person is discussed. We sincerely hope that the tone of all case material communicates respect for the dignity of those whom we intend to serve.

Finally, we strive to make the life of a clinical psychologist more readily visible and perceptible through a variety of methods and illustrations throughout the text. We offer an overview of different fields of clinical psychology and describe different subspecializations that are possible career directions. We draw a descriptive picture of six contemporary, well-known colleagues as they share details of their work life. In these "day in the life" portraits, we see some important variations in what occupies the psychologists' time, how they integrate science and practice, and also how they live their lives and care for their personal selves and their families. In addition, we devote an entire chapter to an enormously important but often neglected subject—practitioner self-care. We specifically include the term *ethics* in the title to this last chapter because it is fundamental to the concept of self-care for the psychologist, but ethical fundamentals are woven throughout the book.

We hope you will find this text to be user-friendly. As much as possible, we have attempted to engage the student reader as a direct participant in our discussion. We frequently ask questions, or direct the reader to reflect, explore, or consider the concept at hand. We draw on illustrations or examples that are likely to resonate with the students' own life or personal experience. We do this throughout the material, as one might raise such issues in the course of teaching a class, rather than just listing questions for further thought at the end of a didactic chapter.

Every chapter begins with at least five learning objectives so that students have a structure and anticipatory focus for their reading of that material. The overall text is divided into four main sections. Part I contains introductory material (Chapters 1 through 4). Part II includes four chapters on assessment methods and techniques, and Part III, six chapters pertaining to intervention strategies, techniques, and common challenges. In Part IV, we focus on what every clinician needs to know, emphasizing ethics, self-care, and positive psychology.

In Chapter 1, the reader takes a journey through the ages, as the historical backdrop for the political and social development of clinical psychology comes alive in a uniquely vivid way. In Chapter 2, the professional culture and subcultures of today's clinical psychologist are detailed. Chapter 3 presents an overview of the vast topic of cultural diversity and the scientific concepts and practical strategies that are important in culturally competent practice. In Chapter 4, the student is introduced to basic research concepts in an easy-to-understand and digest format. Chapter 5, explores why people become clients and introduces the basic classifications of psychopathology via the *DSM* system. Part II, Chapters 6, 7, and 8 form an assessment trio where the goals, types, and purposes of clinical assessment are described, the biopsychosocial systems model for understanding human behavior is introduced, the application of scientific methods and approaches to data gathering in the assessment process is articulated, and finally the logistics of actual assessment procedures are explained and illustrated.

Proceeding to Part III, readers learn about the importance and basic strategies of case conceptualization (Chapter 9), followed by a discussion of the nuts and bolts of collaboration, treatment alliance, and effective treatment planning (Chapter 10). An extended illustration of interventions including strategies that are systemic or interpersonal, affective, cognitive, and behavioral is offered in Chapter 11. Chapter 12 focuses on the process of change; how to understand it, foster its development, evaluate it, and communicate about it. In Chapter 13, the traditional notions of resistance receive a more contemporary consideration as impediments to change. Concluding Part III is Chapter 14, a comprehensive discussion of termination strategies and tactics suitable for today's demanding practice environments. Finally, in Part IV, the reader is directed to think about self-care as a "need to know" topic. In Chapter 15, the reader encounters the topics of burnout, personal responsibility, and the use of positive psychology to mediate stress and facilitate well-being.

Although this may sound a bit scarier than it is, the authors of this text have among them *nearly* a century of experience as clinical psychologists. They have had the pleasure of learning from and working with many of the masters in the field and knowing these eminent contributors over long periods of time. The authors of this text are qualified by advanced degrees, postdocs, diplomates, past presidencies, memberships, chairmanships, fellowships, authorships, and well-stamped passports. An integration of teaching, research, and clinical practice aptly describes the past, present and future of our combined careers in this exciting field.

Many hearts and hands have helped this book come to fruition. First and foremost, Tisha Rossi and Isabel Pratt, our editors at John Wiley & Sons, have been amazingly patient and supportive. A heartfelt "thanks for sticking with us" barely begins to express our gratitude for their efforts. Sweta Gupta, editorial assistant at Wiley, has been a whiz at smoothing out our jagged edges and helping us spot our missing pieces. We also want to collectively thank our anonymous reviewers for excellent feedback on earlier chapter drafts. A special thanks to our colleagues, Ron Fudge, Gayle Iwamasa, Anne Kazak, Sam Knapp, Chris Royer, and Patti Resick, for giving us a glimpse into their lives as clinical psychologists, and allowing us to share that glimpse with our readers. Each of us has personal thanks to offer as well.

I have been fortunate, if not blessed throughout my career. I have somehow managed to be in the right place at the right time to cross paths with some of the foremost clinicians in our history. As a graduate student, I heard Carl Rogers speak many times, drove Rollo May home from a meeting, debated with Joseph Wolpe, collaborated with Mike Mahoney on several projects, and had the opportunity to spend time with Albert Ellis, Kurt Adler, and so many others.

As an adolescent, and at various points through my adult years, I had the chance to be helped by the late Dr. Emanual F. Hammer. Manny was the clinician's clinician. Well trained, superb teacher, erudite, well versed in theory and research, empathic, and kind. What I am today as a clinician, I can easily trace back to my emulation of his model of what a clinical psychologist should be. To my teachers, mentors, students, and patients, I owe a debt of gratitude. They have taught me so very much about the human condition and what is needed to help others effectively cope.

Two of my very fortunate discoveries have been Drs. Denise D. Davis and Stephanie H. Felgoise. I met Denise over 25 years ago at a symposium at APA. She has become a superb clinician, colleague, collaborator, coauthor, and friend.

Several years ago as chair of the Department of Psychology at Philadelphia College of Osteopathic Medicine (PCOM), I had an opening for an assistant professor. I called Drs. Art and Christine Nezu at Drexel University and asked if they had a recent graduate who might be interested in the position. They recommended Stephanie Friedman, now Felgoise. Stephanie is now Vice-Chair of the Department, Director of the Clinical Psychology program, an ABPP diplomate, and Associate Professor. These two younger generation women represent and will be part of the bright future of clinical psychology. Drs. Aaron T. Beck and Albert Ellis have been supportive and magnificent models and mentors. I could not have achieved what I have without them. My children and grandchildren are sources of great joy and encouragement. Finally, my wife Sharon is a superb clinician, personal consultant, partner, supporter, colleague, coauthor, coeditor, and best friend.

—A. F.

First and foremost, emphatic thanks are extended to my coauthors and colleagues, Dr. D. Denise Davis and Dr. Art Freeman, whose collaboration made the writing of this book exciting, challenging, and an enriching experience. Thank you to student-colleagues Talya Hammer, Catherine McCoubrey, Leslee Frye, and Sara O'Neal for their dedicated and tireless efforts in searching the literature, fine-tuning chapter edits, and compiling references for inclusion in this book. Dr. Robert DiTomasso offered support, encouragement, and flexibility that allowed time for chapters to be written. He and Dr. Art Freeman have created a fabulous department of psychology in an already wonderful, collegial, stimulating, and family-oriented environment at PCOM. Work on the self-care chapter was enhanced by many conversations with Dr. Bruce Zahn regarding student self-reflection, self-care, and impairment in the context of our Student Progress Evaluation Committee and NCSPP attendance, in addition to the discussions we had with Drs. Diane Smallwood and Taka Suzuki in committee work surrounding these important topics. The prior and ongoing mentorship provided by Drs. Art and Christine Maguth Nezu, and their problem-solving model have been monumentally influential on how I think critically, scientifically, broadly, and ideographically about clinical psychology as a science and practice. Their work's influence on the research, assessment, and self-care chapters are evident.

My love, thanks, and appreciation are always due to my sisters and my parents. Their support, encouragement, friendship, and role-modeling of courage, achievement, and dedication to helping others have always been central to my success. My fabulous children, Benjamin and Elizabeth, are the most wonderful daily reminders of reasons for self-care and what is most important in life; they offer the innocent perspective of how to enjoy life to its fullest. Lastly, and of most significance, is the ongoing thanks to my best friend and husband, Glenn; with his help and support anything is possible. Thanks for help with this book during many late nights.

—S. F.

Many thanks to friend, mentor, and colleague Art Freeman for inviting me to participate in this valuable and challenging project. I am grateful for our dozens of years of collaboration on various projects, and for his encouragement and inspiration. It was certainly a pleasure to become acquainted with

Stephanie Felgoise over the course of writing this book. Both Art and Stephanie brought a very special wisdom and perspective to our shared task of explaining the integration of science and practice. I deeply appreciate having had this opportunity to learn from both of them.

Special thanks to my student colleagues Monica Franklin and Hollister Trott, and former-student-now clinician Christopher Mosunic, for insightful comments and helpful suggestions on health psychology, working with diversity, and the case of Doris (Chapter 3). My wonderful consultation group; Kirsten Haman, Laurel Brown, and Dotty Tucker, have provided much encouragement and many discussions on details of treatment and termination. I hope they know how much I value and appreciate their contributions. Steve Hollon's leadership in developing a cadre of clinicians committed to integration of science and practice provided vital collegial support. Thanks, Steve. I would also like to acknowledge the community of psychologists at Vanderbilt University (including our adjunct clinical faculty!) who represent and inspire excellence in all aspects of science and practice. And finally, but certainly not least, thanks to Charlie for taking care of everything and keeping a steady rhythm.

—D. D.

PART

1

INTRODUCTION

The History, Politics, and Social Environment of Clinical Psychology

1

Chapter

This chapter sets forth our theme of integrating clinical science and clinical practice. We discuss the philosophical and practical or applied aspects of clinical psychology and place clinical psychology in perspective relative to the historical, social, gender, cultural, and scientific environments in which it was created and in which it and we, as clinical psychologists, exist.

Our model is based on clinical psychology as a general treatment model, with the clinical psychologist serving as a primary care practitioner: the "psychological family doctor." This chapter also delineates the direction and plan for the book.

Learning Objectives

At the end of this chapter, the reader should be able to:

- List five historical markers in the conceptualization and treatment of clinical phenomena.
- Identify three scientific eras that have influenced the development of clinical psychology.
- Describe the contemporary organizational environment of the field of clinical psychology.
- Explain the concept of the clinical psychologist as a primary care practitioner.
- List at least 10 learning objectives for reading the chapters ahead.

Mary, a doctoral-level psychologist, was at a party where the hostess introduced her to someone by saying, "This is Mary. She's a psychologist." The other person smiled and said, "Whoops. I better be careful what I say so you won't be analyzing me." Mary's response was that she was not a clinical psychologist, but an experimental psychologist working on aspects of language acquisition in chimpanzees.

It is of more than passing interest to know that many people who hear the word *psychologist* assume that the person so identified is a clinical psychologist. Many people use variations of the term *psychology* to denote motivation ("I am really psyched for that date"), readiness ("I am psyched for that exam"), intimidation ("I really psyched him out"), or a person who appears to be out of touch with reality or with societal norms ("That guy is really psycho"). The range of psychology applications and practice is discussed in Chapter 2. In this introductory chapter, we discuss the history and development of clinical psychology as a practice, a science, and a treatment; and we place clinical psychology in perspective relative to the historical, social, gender, cultural, and scientific environments from which it emerged.

Writing a text such as this one takes a great deal of thought and discussion among the authors. We have had to decide what to include, what to exclude, and how to present the material in as scientific, readable, and useful way as possible. We have, between us, over a century of experience, first as students and then as university faculty members and practitioners. We are aware of the challenges in developing a text. Will it hold your interest? Will it allow your instructor to elaborate on the ideas we present? Will it provide the requisite information? The latter two points are in fact relatively easy to fulfill. To keep you interested is a much harder job. For this reason, we have decided to talk to you directly and to think of you as one of our students.

The clinical psychologist, in the simplest definition, works in a clinical setting, with clinical populations, and uses clinical interventions. But what does that mean? Clinics are usually for people needing treatment of one sort or another. A look at a hospital directory might list the hours of operation for the spine clinic, the asthma clinic, the well-baby clinic, or the mood clinic. That is where you would expect to find clinical psychologists. Although this has been true for much of the existence of clinical psychology, the appellation of *clinical* has now been affixed to other terms such as clinical health psychology, clinical child psychology, or clinical neuropsychology.

The notion that people have emotional problems is not new. That some people act unacceptably within their social or family group and are thought to be deviant from their fellows is, instead, an ancient belief. Rather than dazing (or amazing) you with the historical or prehistorical experience of psychology, we have decided to make it easy.

We are going to take you for a ride on an incredible magic carpet. Not only can it fly though the air, it allows you to board without going through a metal detector. Second, it can travel through time so that we can view many experiences, circumstances, and situations. Third, it renders us invisible so that we can observe others and not be seen. Fourth, it is soundproof so that we can discuss what we are seeing without being heard. Fifth, if, for any reason, our trip is interrupted, you can climb aboard again and take up where you left off. Sixth, this magic carpet has a universal translator that allows us to listen in to what is going on in front of us. Finally, it will safely return us to our starting point. Please note that no snacks will be served on this flight so before embarking, collect your favorite snacks to take along.

A Flying Carpet Tour of Clinical Psychology

If you are safely aboard, our first stop is prehistory. We can feel the heat. We are on a plain in Africa. A formerly social and well-adjusted member of the tribe has been howling at the moon, attacking other members of the tribe, and having uncontrolled seizures or other acts against the best interest of the tribe, clan, or group. He has been caught and subdued by other members of the tribe and has been rendered unconscious by being forced to drink a potion the tribal healer has concocted from herbs and flowers. The healer is about to perform a surgical procedure still used today, called *trephining.* She is using sharpened flints to bore a hole in the person's skull to release the demons and spirits that have been trapped there. Releasing the demons should relieve the patient of their "possession."

Although we might expect the patient to die from what we see as a barbaric operation, skulls dating back thousands of years have been found with holes drilled in the skull, and the regrowth of bone indicates that the person survived. Scientists think that the holes were drilled to release demons that inhabited the individual causing aberrant behavior. In other cases, the clan healer might simply offer potions made from roots, barks, or leaves of plants as prescriptions for various disorders. Some combinations of drugs calmed the angry patient, and others likely energized the inactive individual. What we now call "folk" remedies were the earliest attempts at dealing with the broad range of illnesses, including those that we now label as psychological disorders. If we listen carefully, we might hear the healer give the man's wife a bag of herbs and leaves, and instruct her to brew a tea with them when the man awakens from his surgery.

If you will hold on tight, we are going to move on to ancient Greece. Before we fly into the office of a healer, there are some things that you need to know. The Greeks posited that there were four basic elements; fire, water, earth, and air. As all persons were constructed of these elements, their balance within the body was of major importance. Each element would correspond with a particular characteristic that would create a *humor* within the body: fire = blood humor; earth = black bile humor; water = yellow bile humor, and air = phlegm humor. Fire, of course, was hot. Water was wet. Earth was dry, and air was cold. The particular humoral mix could be seen in the person's personality and behavioral style. These ideas seem quaint to us today, but we still refer back to them. An angry person is said to be "hot-blooded" or to have a "fiery temper." The old term for depression, *melancholy,* stems from the terms *melan* (black, as in melanin) and *choli* (bile, as in colon). Melan + Coli = melancholy. We may describe someone as *phlegmatic,* meaning "subdued."

In the quarters of the ancient Greek healer, we have an opportunity to watch a treatment. The healer is assessing the patient's humoral mix and will then prescribe a treatment. The patient reports that he is often angry, and the anger involves him in physical fights with family, friends, and even strangers. The healer is recommending bloodletting as the treatment of choice to lower the force of the blood humor that is obviously creating the problem. The patient lies on a couch and the healer cuts into the patient's arm and blood flows copiously into a bowl held by the healer's assistant. When the healer has seen enough blood flow, she will stanch the bleeding with folded linen and pressure. The patient will then rest. Other treatments might include enemas to relieve the excess of black bile, forced purging or the use of emetics for yellow bile, or compression of the chest for too much air.

If you found that scene a bit unpleasant, be forewarned that the next stop may be even more visceral. We are now in medieval France. We are flying over a walled town, and in the middle of the town square workers are preparing for an execution. They are piling branches and wood around a stone column. Set high in the column is an iron ring. We are all thinking the same thing. They are planning on burning someone to death. There, off to the right we can see a woman being dragged toward the post. We can hear the charges against her being read.

Fortunately our carpet allows us to understand medieval French. The prisoner was found guilty of practicing the black arts, witchcraft. The court, a church court it seems, has sentenced her and two other women to be burned as witches. Her hands are tied to the iron ring and her feet secured. She is gagged so she cannot say anything or cast a spell. A torch is lit. I think it is time for us to leave this place.

In the Middle Ages, the church developed as an arbiter of both what is normal and what is abnormal, and then offered "cures" for the abnormal behavior. These cures ranged from prayer and meditation to exorcism and execution. The inquisition brought with it the beating, flogging, burning, hanging, and drowning of those suspected of trafficking in the black arts. Interestingly, those black arts included healing and midwifery. If a town was unfortunate enough to have a disease manifestation such as the plague, it was considered the work of witches. Only a concerted search for the witches and their immediate eradication could cleanse and heal the community.

Our next stop is going to be the seventeenth-century town of Salem, Massachusetts. We think that you know what we will find. We are in a courtroom. As you can see, everyone is dressed just like the Pilgrims in the pictures of the first Thanksgiving. This, however, is no celebration. A woman is dragged into the courtroom and brought before the two judges. The charges against her involve witchcraft. The accusers are three teenage girls who report having seen the woman muttering "spells" and having a conversation with her cat. Some of the woman's neighbors testify that they, too, saw her "acting strangely," though other townspeople testify that she is a harmless person who caused no problems for anyone.

At that moment, we see something incredible. The teenage accusers fall to the floor of the courtroom and seem to be having spasms and convulsions. They point to the woman as they are doing it. Amazingly, the girls' behavior is entered as "evidence" against the woman and she is pronounced a witch and sentenced to burn. We would later learn of the death of several women based on the report of these teenage girls. Interestingly, when it was decided to stop using the girls' behavior as evidence, the girls' spasms ceased.

Our next stop on this magic carpet is outside Paris on a sunny Sunday afternoon. The year is about 1785. It is before the French Revolution, and the wealthy and elite of Paris are obvious. We can see carriages arriving, and well-dressed men and women are emerging from the carriages. It seems that their destination is a mental hospital called *Salpetriére.* The visitors do not seem intent on seeing a relative who might be residing in this particular hospital, but rather they are strolling along and viewing the inmates as if visiting a zoo. We can see some inmates posed in postures that they seem to hold for exceedingly long periods. Other inmates are playing with pieces of wood. A woman is cradling a rag as if it were a baby. The onlookers delicately cover their noses with perfumed handkerchiefs to block the odor coming from feces-encrusted inmates, rotting food, and inadequate hygiene facilities. Servants are setting a picnic lunch for some of the sightseers . . . far away from the hospital building.

A quick trip over the English Channel takes us to an English hospital for lunatics: St. Mary Bethlehem, also known as the Bethlem Royal Hospital. Coming from within the walls of this building we hear the rumble of human voices. Some are shouting, some are crying, and some are making noises that we cannot interpret. When we hear the cacophony, we think that this place sounds as if it is out of control. It seems to exist without any sense of order. There is confusion and uproar everywhere. It is, in fact, pure *bedlam*—a contraction of the hospital's name still used to denote what we are witnessing. Bedlam is the uncontrolled and confusing events and actions we see in the midst of crises. We see visitors touring the hospital who, like their Parisian counterparts, are laughing and mocking the residents. Some are even carrying long poles to prod the patients and make them angry within their cages so that they will react with outrage and produce a better "show." The guardians of these patients do nothing to protect their charges.

We fly back to eighteenth-century Paris and stop at the salon of a physician, Dr. Franz Anton Mesmer. He was born in 1734 and died in 1815. He was credited by some as having accidentally discovered the idea of group therapy. Mesmer argued that health or illness was a result of the harmony or discord between the bodily fluids and the planets (e.g., "lunacy" was a result of the gravitational pull of the moon). He later redefined his theory and suggested that harmony or discord within the individual was a result of some distortion of the internal magnetic fields.

Let's observe Mesmer at work. Several patients are sitting around an oak tub, and the "magnetic fluid" is sending magnetic forces through iron bars that patients are holding as extensions from the tub. Mesmer is walking around and speaking soothingly and quietly to the patients. He lays his hands on them and evaluates the balance of their magnetic fluid. Some of the patients in his treatments appear to faint or swoon and others seem to sit transfixed during their treatment. We would later learn that in the spirit of the time, scientific support was deemed to be the mark of any treatment. After an investigation by the Paris Academy of Sciences, Mesmer's model of treatment was found to be without merit and the academy would not support it. Although Mesmer later died in obscurity, his name lingers far beyond his treatment to describe someone who is *mesmerized* as being fixed on an object or in a trancelike state.

We now fly ahead to Vienna in the early twentieth century, where a young neurologist has been building quite a reputation for himself. Dr. Sigmund Freud, frustrated at not getting the faculty appointment that he so badly wanted in the Department of Neurology at the University of Vienna, is about to give a lecture. He has abandoned his academic quest and has started a practice to treat patients who have what he calls "nervous disorders." Freud has not yet come to the podium and we can hear comments and discussion by members of the audience. "I'm aghast at some of the things that I heard about him," commented a lawyer. "Well, he writes rather nicely, but some of his statements are a bit, how shall I say this? Over the edge," responded an accountant sitting nearby. A businessman commented, "His work is unsavory, at the least." A fourth commented, "Well, he is one of us, so we should listen respectfully."

Freud comes to the stage and is introduced as the speaker of the evening. The president of the Vienna lodge of B'nai B'rith, a group of Jewish professionals, presents Freud and his topic: *The Interpretation of Dreams.* We can only wonder what Freud has done or said to make it so difficult for him to get a hearing on this subject from his medical colleagues. He has sought to go to the people for this presentation. The group listens to his presentation, but by the shakes of their heads, and the shared smiles, they are finding his presentation of dreams as the "royal road to the unconscious" a bit much.

Let's get back on our carpet and take a quick trip forward. World War I has broken out, and we are in an army recruitment center in 1917. Recruits are being given a test to determine their abilities and aptitude. The results of the tests will help in placing the soldiers where the military can gain the greatest value from their contributions. Two officers are discussing the testing program. "Darn shame this test. What they need to do is fight. Just courage and a gun is what they need. They'll do what we tell them to do just like before, and heaven help them that doesn't do what we tell them." The second officer responds that he had experiences in Cuba some 20 years earlier with soldiers who appeared to understand instructions, but were later killed. "We need to build a core of competent, intelligent soldiers and more intelligent officers. Maybe this way of selecting them will make a difference."

The second officer does not know how prophetic he is. Binet's work will be the basis for the Army Alpha and the Army Beta tests in years to come. The Army Alpha and Beta tests were standardized measures for screening large numbers of people to optimize recruit placement. These tests identified aptitudes and skills to determine which positions in the military would be suitable for an able recruit. Each test served the same purpose, but the Beta test could be administered to individuals who did not speak English as a primary language. The fact that all individuals could be examined with these assessments became significant not only for military recruiting purposes at the time but also for clinical applications after the war.

Hold on. We leave again and head for England. It is 1938 and we are observing an old man speaking into an early wire recording machine. He speaks slowly and deliberately because of the prosthesis in his mouth. His speech is somewhat muffled but we can make out his English. It is Sigmund Freud speaking of his career:

I started my professional activities as a neurologist trying to bring relief to my neurotic patients. Under the influence of an older friend [Josef Breuer] and by my own efforts I discovered some important new facts about the unconscious, insight, the role of instinctual urges, and so on. Using these new findings, I developed a new science, psychoanalysis, a branch of psychology as a new method for the treatment of the neurosis. I had to pay heavily for this bit of good luck. People did not believe in my facts and thought my theories unsavory. In the end I succeeded in acquiring pupils and bringing up an international psychoanalytic association. But the struggle is not yet over.

He stops for a moment and then says, "Sigmund Freud." We know that he died of cancer the following year. It must make us thoughtful that by his own words, Freud saw psychoanalysis as part of what we would call clinical psychology.

Next we travel to the United States. It is 1944, and we are looking in on a military strategy meeting at the Pentagon in Washington, DC. The Army is pondering what to do about World War II soldiers suffering from combat fatigue. (In World War I, it was called *shellshock*.) "We need to be able to do something with these boys," declares a colonel. Wearing the insignia of the medical corps, he argues for more psychiatrists for both field hospital work and behind the lines. The brigadier general asserts, "If they are doctors, we need them to be cutting and patching these kids up to save their lives. I am less worried about their mental health if they have shrapnel in their gut." A major tentatively raises his hand. "What about the possibility of using psychologists to deal with the psychological problems? They are not physicians but they have studied about helping people with psychological problems." "Where would we find them?" asked the colonel. "I can contact several universities and see who might be available," replied the major. "Do it," commands the general.

Our next stop is at a coffeehouse in Witwatersrand, South Africa. It is the early 1950s. A young psychiatrist is discussing an idea with another colleague. "It seems obvious. If patients are anxious, they have great difficulty being relaxed. If they are relaxed it is hard to be anxious. What if we can teach anxious patients to relax? Wouldn't that ease their problem?" His colleague shook his head. "Dr. Wolpe, don't be foolish! You are a trained psychoanalyst. You know that the anxiety is a symptom of the underlying conflicts. Sure, we can remove the anxiety for a moment or two, but it will return. Even if we help to remove the anxiety about one situation, it will only return in another symptom. Besides, the complexity of the anxiety disorders cannot be explained in so simple a paradigm." We can only smile knowing the enormous impact that Joseph Wolpe had on his generations of students and thereby on millions of anxious patients.

Back to the Future

At this point, we come back and land our magic carpet. The rest of the history of clinical psychology belongs in today's world. The associations, organizations, divisions, meetings, certifying bodies, and philosophies of practice are contemporary.

Yet in the practices, publications, and missions of these institutions, we see the historical influence of the people, events, and scientific eras that have shaped the field of clinical psychology.

Major Organizations Concerned with Scientific Practice

Major organizational bodies relevant to the professional culture of clinical psychology include the American Board of Professional Psychology (ABPP), the American Psychological Association (APA), and the Association for Behavioral and Cognitive Therapies (ABCT). Each of these organizations has specialty subdivisions that reflect the growing complexity of clinical psychology. Established in 1948, the American Board of Examiners in Professional Psychology (now shortened to American Board of Professional Psychology), offers advanced certification of competency in a subspecialty of clinical psychology. These specialties include clinical psychology, clinical child and adolescent psychology, and clinical neuropsychology.

Founded in 1892, the American Psychological Association (APA) is the largest worldwide association of psychologists. With approximately 150,000 members, the APA offers a vast number of programs and initiatives, including 56 numbered divisions or special interest groups that focus on particular topics. Clinical psychologists are often affiliated with the following APA divisions: Clinical Psychology (12), Psychotherapy (29), Psychoanalysis (39), Psychologists in Independent Practice (42), and Society of Clinical Child and Adolescent Psychology (53). There are many other divisions that the clinical psychologist might be interested in joining. For additional information, see www.apa.org.

APA Division 12—Clinical Psychology

APA members who belong to this division are active in practice, research, teaching, administration, and study in the field of clinical psychology. Graduate students in APA approved or regionally accredited doctoral programs may become student affiliates. Members and student affiliates may also join one or more sections of the division: Section II: Clinical Geropsychology; Section III: The Society for a Science of Clinical Psychology; Section IV: Clinical Psychology of Women; Section VI: Clinical Psychology of Ethnic Minorities; Section VII: Emergencies and Crises; Section VIII: Association of Psychologists in Academic Health Centers (APAHC); Section IX: Assessment; and Section X: Graduate Students and Early Career Psychologists.

APA Division 29—Psychotherapy

APA members who also belong to this division share in fostering collegial relations among APA members who are interested in psychotherapy. This division stimulates the exchange of information about psychotherapy, encourages the evaluation and development of the practice of psychotherapy, educates the public about the service of psychotherapists, and promotes the general objectives of the APA.

APA Division 39—Psychoanalysis

This division encompasses the diversity and richness of psychoanalytic theory, research, and clinical practice. The nine sections within Division 39 represent members' broad interests: (I) Psychologists-Psychoanalyst Practitioners; (II) Childhood and Adolescence; (III) Women, Gender, and Psychoanalysis; (IV) Local Chapters; (V) Psychologist-Psychoanalysts' Clinicians; (VI) Psychoanalytic Research Society; (VII) Psychoanalysis and Groups; (VIII) Section on Family Therapy; and (IX) Psychoanalysis of Social Responsibility.

APA Division 42—Psychologists in Independent Practice

This APA membership division deals with psychological services in all independent practice settings and advocates on behalf of consumers of these services. Through its committees and task forces, it promotes quality and accessibility. The division also provides a forum for issues affecting independent practice at the APA convention and at the annual Practice Development Conference.

APA Division 53—Society of Clinical Child and Adolescent Psychology

This group of APA represents psychologists who are active in teaching, research, clinical services, administration, and advocacy in clinical child psychology. The division has established research and professional service awards, including an annual student research award and also sponsors publications describing graduate programs and clinical internships that provide specialized training in clinical child psychology. The division also supports task forces on the development and evaluation of evidence-based treatments for childhood disorders and coordinates efforts for dissemination of information about evidence-based services.

Association for Behavioral and Cognitive Therapies

The Association for Behavioral and Cognitive Therapies (ABCT; formerly the Association for Advancement of Behavior Therapy) was founded in 1966. The founders were among the elite of behavior therapy, but many mainstream psychologists considered the ABCT to be a radical splinter group.

Although ABCT draws members from various mental health disciplines (psychiatry, social work, psychiatric nursing, counseling), the bulk of the approximately 5,000 member organization comprises clinical psychologists who share a fundamental interest in integrating science and practice. Their mission is to relieve human suffering by designing, testing, developing, and disseminating culturally sensitive methods that work, based on the latest scientific advancements (www.abct.org). Advancement of empirically based practice was the original momentum for the founding of this organization. Over time, scientific developments have led this group toward focusing on cognitive innovations and discoveries, and the name of the organization was officially changed in 2004. Because cognitive-behavior therapy is based on broad principles of human learning and adaptation, it can accomplish a wide variety of goals. The therapy has been applied to issues ranging from depression and anxiety to the improvement of parenting, relationships, and personal effectiveness.

Training Philosophy in Clinical Psychology

In 1949, at the request of the newly formed Committee on Accreditation of APA, the National Institute of Mental Health (NIMH) sponsored a conference in Boulder, Colorado, to discuss the development of standards for training in clinical psychology. This conference was, in effect, a step in the government's initiative to tap the resources of psychology for the WWII effort, circa 1944 Washington, DC. Although some clinical psychology training programs were in existence at the time, the content, length, format, requirements, and missions varied. All the programs were housed in university departments, but some were in graduate schools of arts and science and others were in schools of education.

The government connection was a boon to the development of clinical psychology. The Veterans Administration (VA) and the NIMH offered training funds for internship sites. The ideas and protocols developed at the Boulder conference became known as the "Boulder Model" for clinical training. The participants at the conference agreed that the minimal training must include a PhD, thereby placing psychologists squarely in the midst of their academic colleagues in other disciplines. Psychologists were to be scientists and therefore would be trained to be competent in research as well as the development of clinical skills and competencies. This dual emphasis resulted in the notion of the clinical psychologist being educated and trained as a scientist-practitioner.

The Boulder conference established the following parameters for doctoral training in clinical psychology:

- Boulder-model programs in clinical psychology award the PhD degree.
- The appropriate location for clinical psychology training is a university department, usually in a faculty of arts and science, not in a separate school that is part of a university (e.g., law, medicine, dentistry) or in a free-standing school (e.g., many schools of medicine).
- The program can be one of several programs within an academic department.
- Clinical psychologists are to be prepared for work in both the academic world and the practice world.
- The APA Committee on Accreditation provides an approval and accreditation for training programs in clinical psychology. The accreditation process, though meticulous and sometimes arduous to complete, has made the designation "APA accredited" the gold standard for clinical psychology programs.
- The PhD programs require a research-based dissertation as a requirement for the completion of the degree.

- To provide maximum funding through grants, fellowships, and scholarships, small numbers of carefully selected students are admitted.
- Limiting the number of students facilitates maximum mentorship of students, as the goal is successful training of every student accepted for admission.

The scientist-practitioner model was questioned by many practicing clinicians. As early as the 1960s, the scientist-practitioner emphasis was under scrutiny. As an alternative approach to training, the California School of Professional Psychology was founded by Dr. Nicholas Cummings in 1969. Cummings, a former president of APA and a behavioral science entrepreneur, worked with the California State Psychological Association to develop a PhD program that more strongly emphasized the applied clinical aspect of clinical psychology. Cummings, who is president of the Foundation for Behavioral Health and Chairman of the Nicholas & Dorothy Cummings Foundation, Inc., was the founding CEO of American Biodyne (MedCo/Merck, then Merit, now Magellan Behavioral Care), the first U.S. behavioral managed care company. Dr. Cummings has also founded four campuses of the California School of Professional Psychology, the National Academies of Practice, the American Managed Behavioral Healthcare Association, and the National Council of Professional Schools of Psychology. Cummings has advanced the view that clinical psychologists should be trained to be knowledgeable consumers and contributors to research, but that this is secondary to skill development for clinical interventions.

The issues raised by Cummings and others led to a second major conference on training philosophy held in 1973 in Vail, Colorado, and the proceedings of this conference became known as the "Vail Model." The Vail conferees endorsed different principles from those endorsed by the conferees at the earlier Boulder conference, leading to an alternative training model (D. R. Peterson, 1976, 1982). Psychological knowledge, it was argued, had matured enough to warrant creation of explicitly professional programs along the lines of professional programs in medicine, dentistry, and law. These professional programs were to be added to, not replace, Boulder-model doctoral programs. Further, it was proposed that different degrees should designate the scientist-practitioner role (PhD; emphasis on the term scientist) from the practitioner-scholar role (PsyD—Doctor of Psychology; with emphasis on the term practitioner).

The Vail conference asserted the following parameters for doctoral training in clinical psychology:

- Vail-model programs in clinical psychology award a Doctorate of Psychology degree, referred to as a PsyD.
- Vail-model programs can be housed in three types of organizational settings. They are found in a psychology department that is part of a university setting. They are also found in a university-affiliated professional or psychology school that may be part of a university. Or, they exist as independent, freestanding schools of professional psychology. The latter programs are not affiliated with universities; but rather are independently developed and staffed.

- These professional training programs focus primarily on clinical practice and less on research, but graduates should know how to do research and how to appropriately access and use research to inform their clinical practice.
- Professional schools can be not-for-profit or for-profit institutions and several schools of professional psychology are affiliated in a network of freestanding professional schools. These schools offer doctoral programs in clinical psychology, and graduate work in counseling and master's level programs.
- PsyD programs are responsive to the market demands for clinical services in their enrollment policies and procedures. Compared with PhD programs, they will enroll as many as three times the number of incoming doctoral candidates per school (Mayne, Norcross, & Sayette, 1994). Over time, this will create greater numerical parity in psychologist graduates from scientist-practitioner programs.

The differences between clinical PhD and clinical PsyD programs are quantitative, not qualitative. The primary disparity is in the relative emphasis on research. Boulder programs aspire to train producers of research who will work within academic settings and agencies. Vail programs train consumers of research and individuals who will be the therapists and supervisors of therapists in community agencies. The clinical opportunities for licensure and practice are similar for students in both programs.

Several studies demonstrated that initial worries about stigmatization, employment difficulties, and licensure uncertainty for PsyDs have never materialized (Hershey, Kopplin, & Cornell, 1991; D. R. Peterson, Eaton, Levine, & Snepp, 1982). Nor are there discernible differences of late in employment except that the research-oriented, PhD graduates are far more likely to be employed in academic positions and medical schools (Gaddy, Charlot-Swilley, Nelson, & Reich, 1995).

In terms of application and acceptance rates, PsyD programs average 141 applications and 53 acceptances, but there are significant differences as a result of institutional location (Norcross, Sayette, & Mayne, 2002). Freestanding programs, on average, receive twice the number of applications as university department programs (with university professional schools in between). Similarly, the freestanding programs accept significantly more of the applicants than both types of university-based programs. The average acceptance rate for PsyD programs is 40% to 41% (i.e., 4 out of 10 applicants to a PsyD program are accepted). By contrast, the average acceptance rate for clinical PhD programs is 11% to 15% (i.e., 1 or 1.5 out of 10 are accepted).

Student Characteristics

The educational and demographic characteristics of PsyD and PhD students are similar, but there is an interesting trend across the field. Seventy percent of all clinical psychology doctoral students are now women, and about 20% are members of ethnic or racial minorities. The one difference between programs is that students in PsyD programs are far more likely to have master's degrees already (and tend to be older) than PhD students who typically come right from undergraduate programs. About 35% of incoming PsyD students possess a master's degree, compared with about 20% in PhD programs (Norcross et al., 2002).

Licensure in Clinical Psychology

It has been said that when psychologists are under attack we circle the wagons and shoot at each other. To some, this might seem to be the state of affairs in obtaining the privilege to practice psychology through state licensure. Each state board of professional psychology maintains its own requirements. Some use the title "Clinical Psychologist" (e.g., Illinois, which has the designation of licensed clinical psychologist). Indiana uses the term "Health Service Provider in Psychology" as the designation for independent practice, and Pennsylvania has a generic psychology license. The state boards also set minimum requirements (e.g., graduation from an APA accredited program). Some states require a test on ethics, others an essay examination in research, and others an oral examination before a committee of the board. Some states accept ABPP diploma status as a credential, whereas others ask that membership in the National Register be a credential for admission to the board process.

However, the good news is that there is a definite trend toward establishing more consistency and continuity in professional credentialing standards across states. It only makes sense that professional mobility serves the best interests of the public. With appropriate checks and balances to address the times when such mobility might be a risk to the public (e.g., an unscrupulous practitioner is running away from his or her latest mistakes and seeking a new venue for exploitive or unprofessional practices), qualified providers will be able to practice in different locations as their lives and interests may take them to new places. To learn more about licensure and credentialing matters, including the option to "bank" one's credentials for mobility across states and future needs, consult the Association of State and Provincial Psychology Boards (www.asppb.org).

The Practicing Role of a Clinical Psychologist

What is most important for you, our students, is that clinical psychology is constantly changing. By the time you have completed your graduate work (either PhD or PsyD), the field will have evolved beyond what we describe in this text. Areas such as clinical health psychology, almost unknown a decade ago, have become a major emphasis for clinicians. We work with physicians in health care settings; lawyers in forensic settings; aerospace specialists, who look at behavior in space; and the military, who want to ameliorate the consequences of training, battle, and homecoming from war.

Today's practicing clinical psychologist is a primary care provider and can be likened to a family doctor who treats a variety of problems. Ideally, there is no stigma to consulting a clinical psychologist. The clinician offers help with many challenges in living such as child-rearing issues, school-related problems, interactions with medical services (pain management, medication compliance), substance abuse problems, issues in dealing with aging parents, and the full range of emotional and behavioral disorders. This primary care function does not mean that every individual enters therapy. Instead, the psychologist may provide brief consultations (1 to 3 meetings), short-term treatments (3 to 20 visits), or extended intervention as appropriate. A professional relationship with the psychologist may extend over many years and include multiple family members. The clinician is a continuing psychological resource, to be consulted on an "as needed" basis.

Preview of the Text

The following chapters in Part I detail the foundation of clinical psychology. In Chapter 2, the activities of a clinical psychologist are described in greater detail. Rather than focusing on a single area, we describe the overall professional culture and its subspecialties. We detail the similarities and differences between clinical psychology subspecialties such as community psychology, health psychology and behavioral medicine, neuropsychology, forensic psychology, pediatric and child clinical psychology. The emphasis is on the common elements and relationships of clinical psychologies. In addition, we offer a glimpse into the lives of contemporary colleagues to provide perspective on living and working as a clinical psychologist.

Chapter 3 emphasizes the importance of understanding cultural differences and similarities when working with diversity. We first define cultural diversity and describe how it can impact—both positively and negatively—our clinical formulations and interventions. Becoming a sensitive and aware clinician is essential. We explore many psychological processes that influence our perceptions of culture and diversity, and we offer practical suggestions for integrating what we know about cultural variables into the context of what we do in clinical settings.

In Chapter 4, we discuss clinical research and outcome assessment in a highly understandable format. The importance of empirical support for clinical psychology is discussed. We describe and discuss various research models including experimental, quasi-experimental, observational, and case study designs. The question of how we know which treatments are effective is explored as we describe an outcome assessment framework for clinical practice.

Chapter 5 explores why (or how) people become patients. What brings them in? What are they looking for? How has their life circumstance evolved into one that now is maladaptive at its best and pathological at its most severe? There are at least 12 common "d" words that describe why people seek therapy. The individual, family, or couple may be: *d*iscomforted, *d*iscontented, *d*istressed, *d*isabled, *d*ysfunctional, *d*isconnected, *d*ispirited, *d*isgusted, *d*istraught, *d*issatisfied, *d*yscontrolled, and *d*isorganized. This first clinical chapter will discuss the broad issues of psychopathology and adaptation that affect the client's general functioning and quality of life, health, and well-being.

To best understand psychopathology, we use the multiaxial diagnostic systems of *DSM-IV-TR* (American Psychiatric Association, 2000) and of *ICD-10*. An individual is rarely totally pathological or incapacitated. To clarify this issue, we discuss the interaction of function and psychopathology and how we determine the point at which "normal" behavior becomes pathological. Finally, we discuss the specific treatment goals of therapy. Are we working to help the client "feel better," or is our goal to help the client to "get better?"

In Part II, "Basic Techniques for Clinicians," we begin our discussion of clinical issues. (This is really what you came for, isn't it?) Basic techniques are considered in two main subsections covering assessment and intervention.

The next three chapters cover the foundation of clinical intervention—the clinical assessment. The reader becomes firmly grounded in the scientific approach to clinical practice, where the forming of hypotheses and the collection of data are essential for everything we do. In Chapter 6, we introduce the purpose and goals of clinical assessment, the types of assessments, and the biopsychosocial model for understanding human behavior. This model directs us to look at the biological/physiological/neurological correlates of behavior as well as the psychological and social/environmental elements.

In Chapter 7, we continue the scientific approach to assessment, starting with an explanation of a data-oriented model. Our discussion focuses on structuring the assessor's critical thinking to be the best consumer of available information, including scientific information on different assessment devices. Using the scientific method to approach assessment gears the clinician toward hypothesis testing, taking an operational approach to targeted domains, and using a multimodal, multimethod, time-series assessment, as appropriate.

Chapter 8 continues the discussion of data collection strategies and tools, taking a closer look at how to build an assessment protocol, how to decide what needs to be assessed, and how to integrate clinical assessment into clinical practice. We discuss the use and integration of psychological assessment tools including clinical interviews, psychological testing, observation, report of significant others, report of other professionals, and self-report. A problem-solving approach to clinical decision making and assessment is emphasized to assist clinicians in the assessment and treatment process.

Part III addresses the "how to" of psychotherapy. The key issue to be mastered is that of case conceptualization (i.e., building models for understanding the client and developing appropriate interventions).

In Chapter 9, we focus on developing effective treatment conceptualizations. The highest order skill for the clinician is to develop a treatment model or conceptualization. We both define and describe the conceptualization process and describe how the treatment conceptualization informs the treatment plan throughout therapy.

Chapter 10 explains the next step in therapy, developing the treatment plan. We emphasize setting collaborative goals as well as developing and maintaining the therapeutic alliance or productive working relationship. Any relationship is filled with pitfalls and problems. The therapeutic relationship is no different. We identify the requirements of the therapeutic relationship, describe techniques for relationship building, and outline some benchmarks of a good working relationship.

It is hard to build a house without tools. It is equally difficult to build a therapy without specific methods or tools. In Chapter 11, we discuss specific methods or tools of intervention that you can add to your psychotherapy skills repertoire. These methods are grouped according to interpersonal or systems interventions, affective interventions, behavioral interventions, and cognitive interventions.

Chapter 12 involves understanding, facilitating, and evaluating change. We begin by exploring the basic principles of change and the concept of motivation to change. We then look at change in terms of dynamic stages, which helps us to better understand the many variations in how clients actually make progress toward their goals. Next, we return briefly to the topic of assessment as we discuss the measurement of change in therapy. Barriers to measuring change in applied clinical contexts are explained, along with ways to overcome these barriers. Finally, we illustrate the mechanism of communicating about change with clients, agencies, families, and cooperating professionals.

Next, we take a troubleshooting approach in our discussion of resistance and impediments to change in Chapter 13. There are several areas of impediment or resistance to change. These include how the patient can be a source of therapeutic impediment, how the therapist can be a source of therapeutic impediment, how the environment can be a source of therapeutic impediment, and how the psychological disorder can be a source of therapeutic impediment.

Therapy should not be viewed as a life sentence. In Chapter 14, an effective termination strategy is presented. We illustrate seven types of termination, on a spectrum from positive to unprofessional. We then explain the professional standards of care for competent termination. In addition, 10 applied skills for an effective termination are detailed.

In Part IV, Chapter 15, we discuss a frequently avoided but critically important topic. Few careers can be as taxing as clinical psychology. We are dealing with the feelings, actions, problems, traumas, and miseries of others. There is great weight in what we say and do because our actions have life-altering effects. In this chapter, which focuses on caring for yourself and your colleagues, we describe therapist burnout. As we consider ways to use positive psychology in our quest to thrive personally and professionally, we provide access to information on self-care ideas and resources that include the scientific knowledge generated in our own field.

The Fields of Clinical Psychology

2

Chapter

You have likely decided to pursue graduate studies in clinical psychology because you are curious about people. You are probably interested in learning how and why people think, behave, learn, make decisions and judgments, and interact with others the way they do. What accounts for the differences between and among people? Is it biology? Is it environment? Is it culture? Or is it a combination of variables? You may wonder why some people function well within their environments and among coworkers, family, and friends; whereas others have difficulty in similar environments. Perhaps you want to formally investigate more specific questions relating to these topics, or you plan to consume information established in the psychology literature so that you can help people be comfortable with themselves and others. Clinical psychology is a broad umbrella term for the substantive field of psychology that addresses such questions.

Learning Objectives

At the end of this chapter, the reader should be able to:

- Describe the elements of a clinical psychology.
- Identify the common elements of the clinical psychologies.
- Discuss the importance of a constant interchange of ideas between clinical science and the application of that science.
- List at least five fields or specialties of clinical psychology.
- Discuss the ethical obligations specific to declaring a specialty in clinical psychology.

The American Psychological Association's Society of Clinical Psychology (Division 12) defines the field as follows:

> *The field of Clinical Psychology integrates science, theory, and practice to understand, predict, and alleviate maladjustment, disability, and discomfort as well as to promote human adaptation, adjustment, and personal development. Clinical Psychology focuses on the intellectual, emotional, biological, psychological, social, and behavioral aspects of human functioning across the life span, in varying cultures, and at all socioeconomic levels (APA, n.d.-b).*

Within this definition lie the common threads that tie together the many specialties of this greater field. A closer look at each aspect of this description throughout the chapters in this book magnifies the fantastic array of opportunities for individuals trained in clinical psychology and highlights the necessity for decision making throughout your graduate training. The goal of this chapter is not just to give you a bird's eye view of the field of clinical psychology, but also to help you begin your journey into that field.

Becoming a clinical psychologist is much more complex than just graduating from a doctoral program (and that alone is no small accomplishment). Becoming a clinical psychologist requires acculturation to the profession, and its norms, mores, and customs. Acculturation is defined as "a set of internal psychological outcomes including a clear sense of personal and cultural identity, good mental health, and the achievement of personal satisfaction in the new cultural context" (Berry & Sam, 1997, p. 299). Becoming an ethical psychologist adds another layer to the acculturation process (Handelsman, Gottlieb, & Knapp, 2005) and is even more challenging because the ethical guidelines for practice are sometimes ambiguous. Navigating in a new culture of an ethical clinical psychology can initially feel like navigating in a strange land.

This book approaches the field of clinical psychology from your perspective—someone who wants to be a part of this field. Thus, we first aim to guide you in the understanding of the field of clinical psychology, broadly defined. Chapter 2 begins with a basic description of the core components: science, theory, and practice. It orients readers to the focus of clinical psychology, and the themes that are the underpinnings of each specific chapter that follows. The remainder of this chapter introduces the many career paths clinical psychologists may take, explains how to gain credentials, experience, and expertise, and tells you where to find more information about the topics that interest you. Leaders and exemplars in the field offer their perspectives on particular areas of specialty and provide recommendations for preparing yourself to jump in. The descriptions are meant to inspire, interest, and encourage you to talk to practicing professionals throughout your training so that you can make a well-informed decision about the specialty that best suits you. Training credentials and pertinent ethical principles are described in detail.

Elements of a Clinical Psychology

Science

Clinical psychology has foundations in biological, physical, and social sciences. Research and investigation in these areas have contributed to the understanding of human functioning at various independent and interacting levels: the mind-body connection; intellectual functioning; emotional processing; behavior; and the interactions of biological, social, and psychological systems. Science refers to any knowledge that is based on investigation of relevant phenomena by empirical methods.

Empirical methods are methods such as observation or experimentation that are used to identify, study, and test objective phenomena. Naturalistic observation refers to systematically studying a (clinical) phenomenon in its naturally occurring environment, without interference, manipulation, or influence by the investigator. Experimental techniques entail manipulating (influencing, controlling) persons, their environment, or some aspect of their biological, psychological, behavioral, or social behaviors. Such observations and experimentation help scientists understand antecedents, consequences, maintaining variables, and related variables to the phenomena being studied.

Empirical methods, either naturalistic or experimental, usually rely heavily on operational definitions and replicable techniques that allow for verification of findings and are grounded in the *scientific method*. The scientific method is a core component of a scientific psychology, similar to most sciences. The scientific method has four components: guiding question, hypothesis, experiment or observation to collect data, and interpretation of results from the experiment. Later in this book, we discuss the scientific approach to assessment and treatment of persons with clinical problems related to cognitive and behavioral excesses and deficits. Also, more specific empirical methods and techniques used in clinical psychology are discussed in chapters on clinical research methods, outcome assessment, clinical assessment, and evaluation of change.

Theory

Clinical psychology, like other specialties in psychology, draws on many theories of personality, individual "normal" and abnormal behavior, family systems, memory, gender differences and feminist perspectives, development, learning, culture, and other areas of human functioning. A theory is defined as "a general principle formulated to explain a group of related phenomena" (Chaplin, 1985, p. 467). Theories can generally not be proven, and thus, they do not become facts, although scientists often seek to show support for theories.

The difficulty in proving a theory is that human behavior is subject to individual nuances that lead to some exceptions to a particular theory. This does not mean that a theory does not hold true in the majority of situations, or that the theory is no longer useful in generally understanding human functioning. Support for theories can be easy to find, whereas evidence against a particular theory may be more difficult to objectively demonstrate. If you had a theory that persons of your body weight and height could open a 200-pound steel door by throwing themselves at the door and you could do so freely, you would be supporting your theory. Supporting your theory that the door could not be opened by this technique would be more difficult to demonstrate without raising many questions. If you threw your body against the door but could not open it, you could suggest that you were incapable of opening the door; however, there could be many other reasons you were unable to open the door besides your height, body weight, and technique. Can you think of some of these reasons? Motivation, effort, force (drawing on physics), location where your body made contact with the door, and many other possible reasons could explain your lack of success. Also, you could not prove this theory to others because somewhere in the universe might exist someone of your height and weight who could exercise the same technique and successfully open the door. As such, you could again lend support to your theory (that persons of your height and weight can open a 200 pound steel door by throwing your body into it), but you could not prove this statement as fact.

A large part of what clinical psychologists do and believe about human functioning and behavior is based on theory—some that is empirically supported, and much that is not. Some specialties within the field of clinical psychology rely more heavily than others on empirically supported or validated theories and practices. Clinical psychologists and psychologists-in-training are encouraged to adopt a scientific skeptic's approach to literature, practice recommendations, and scientific outcome studies that are produced within the greater field as well as their subdisciplines or specialties. In fact, laypersons also should be inquisitive and skeptical of theories, practice recommendations, and published studies from any discipline or field—psychology or others—to ensure they are wise and discriminating consumers of reputed facts on the information highways. Such thinking might mitigate the influence of talk-show guests, television or radio hosts, and advice-giving newspaper or magazine columnists when they share theories with little to no scientific merit. The following subsections define the tenets of clinical psychology.

Practice

Practice, quite simply, usually refers to psychologists putting their knowledge and skills into use. The practice of clinical psychology may take the form of teaching clinical psychology foundations, theory, or practice; supervision or training (of psychologists, trainees, other health or mental health professionals, laypersons, teachers, police officers, etc.); administration; assessment and treatment; program evaluation/research; and consultation. Some of these roles distinguish clinical psychologists from nondoctoral practitioners or other health and mental health care professionals. Research on mental health issues, treatment, and best practices is most often accomplished by doctoral-level psychologists and is a core component of clinical psychology practice that differentiates these experts from others in different fields and professions. Likewise, persons with master's degrees may perform some roles and functions of clinical psychologists, but are limited in what they can do compared with doctoral-level

clinical psychologists (teaching doctoral-level courses, providing independent
assessment and treatment without supervision from a licensed psychologist).
Discussion of these differences is beyond the scope of this chapter, and since
state laws differ, interested readers are directed to the rules and regulations of
practice for their respective states.

The American Psychological Association and other publishers offer journals specific to the roles and functions that represent different areas of clinical
psychologists' practice. Journals such as *Professional Psychology: Research and
Practice; Health Psychology; Clinical Psychology: Science and Practice; Clinical Psychology in Medical Settings; Journal of Personality Assessment;* and *Rehabilitation Psychology* illustrate the integration of science and theory in the application or practice
of the various roles for clinical psychologists. Reviewing a few issues of these
journals might pique your interest in a particular area of clinical psychology
and provide insight into how science and theory influence practice.

Integrating the Elements

Some clinical psychologists focus their work on a specific defining aspect of the
field such as their scientist training. They concentrate on scientific investigation
of clinical phenomena and choose to spend little or no time in clinical/patient-care practice. Other clinical psychologists, though trained in scientific techniques, are solely practitioners and do not engage in scientific investigation at
all. There are even some theoreticians who philosophize, publish, promulgate,
and teach about clinical phenomena, without producing scientific work or engaging in clinical practice. Clinical psychology benefits from professionals who
focus on specific aspects of the disciplines and also from those who attend to the
science, theory, and practice of psychology, as related to clinical phenomena.

We advocate for clinical psychologists to maintain awareness of developing theories, cutting-edge science, and best practices, regardless of their professional work. The American Psychological Association's and licensing boards'
support and expectation of continuing education for clinical psychologists increase the likelihood of achieving this goal. Those who can balance and integrate these aspects of the field, no matter what their specialty may be, benefit
from the vast array of knowledge available to alleviate clients' maladjustment
and distress, and increase prosocial and positive functioning, consistent with
the field's mission.

The mission statement of APA's Division of Clinical Psychology highlights
the purpose for clinical psychologists' integration of science, theory, and practice: to understand, predict, and alleviate maladjustment, disability, and discomfort and to promote human adaptation, adjustment, and personal development.
Throughout this book, the scientific, theoretical, and practical approaches to the
understanding and prediction of human behavior are highlighted; specifically,
chapters on clinical research and assessment are designed to deepen your understanding of these concepts. The purpose of alleviating maladjustment, disability, and discomfort differentiates clinical psychology from other disciplines
within psychology, such as industrial/organizational psychology or developmental psychology. Industrial/organizational psychology focuses on industrial
problems concerning employee practices, working conditions, and employment

rewards and response costs; industrial psychology might also include aspects of business such as marketing, advertising, and the military (Chaplin, 1985). Developmental psychology focuses on human development, maturation processes, experiences throughout the life span and their effects on later functioning. Developmental psychologists mostly focus on understanding, theorizing, predicting, and explaining such life events, rather than producing and implementing interventions for behavior change or alleviating suffering, maladjustment, or disability. In disciplines like these—in contrast to some aspects of clinical psychology—the focus is not in patient care or individual practice. Yet, child clinical psychologists would incorporate the learning of developmental psychologists in their thinking about their patients or research.

Promoting Human Adaptation, Adjustment, and Personal Development

It is important to note that clinical psychology focuses not only on positive aspects of human behavior and functioning but also on maladaptive behavior, psychopathology, and personal and interpersonal problems. As stated in Division 12's mission, the field strives to recognize, increase, and facilitate prosocial functioning, positive adjustment, and personal development. Some clinical psychologists work exclusively on primary prevention (prevention of disease or illness in susceptible persons); others concentrate on social skills training for social competence, life skills coaching in areas such as time management, and optimizing persons' quality of life, even in the absence of problematic situations, stressors, or clinical problems.

In 2000 and 2001, the inception of the *Journal of Positive Psychology* and several other articles in the *American Psychologist* (Fredrickson, 2001; Lyubomirsky, 2001; Masten, 2001; Schneider, 2001; Sheldon & King, 2001) introducing "positive psychology" intended to reorient or remind psychologists across disciplines that highlighting positive aspects of human functioning instead of deficits or weaknesses is important in clinical work and scientific research. Sheldon and King (2001) define positive psychology as the "scientific study of ordinary human strengths and virtues"; emphasis is on the average person and on effective functioning. They argue that the positive psychology movement contrasts with traditional negative bias found in many aspects of psychology. In addition to examples from evolutionary and economic psychology, the authors illustrate clinical psychology's focus on psychopathology, and social cognitive psychology's attention to biases, negative judgments, and errors in thinking. The Division 12's mission statement for clinical psychology states that "promoting human adaptation, adjustment, and personal development" is a goal. Clinicians in their daily practice should strive to attend to and incorporate knowledge from this pertinent aspect of the field. Positive psychology is discussed further in Chapter 15 of this book, "Self-Care and Ethics: Applying the Techniques of Positive Psychology."

A Focus on Multiple Dimensions of Human Functioning

Clinical psychology recognizes the multidimensional nature of human functioning. To evaluate intellectual, emotional, biological, psychological, social and behavioral aspects of human functioning as independent components would provide a narrow and likely inaccurate view of an individual or persons. Therefore, a multidimensional approach to research, assessment, treatment, and understanding of individuals, person-environment, and person-person relationships is required. Throughout this book, we highlight the multidimensional approach to understanding people, their strengths, weaknesses, excesses, and deficits. In clinical psychology, the various facets of human functioning are studied across the life span, and within the context of various cultures and socioeconomic levels. Where possible, these distinctions are illustrated.

Training Qualifications and Ethics Regulations

Training and qualifications such as coursework, certificate or degree requirements, and years and type of experience differ for various specialties. Description of each specialty's requirements is beyond the scope of this chapter. There are, however, basic qualifications that are common to all clinical psychologies, which include a bachelor degree, a doctoral degree, and predoctoral internship. Postdoctoral supervised training and licensure are optional for some careers that are not oriented toward independent service delivery. Continuing education credits are another state-legislated requirement of all licensed professionals. Board certification distinguishes specialists from general practitioners, and this credential is discussed. The APA Ethics Code is critical to self-regulating one's professional activity and testimony of specialty, so relevant principles in the Code are described.

Doctoral Degree

Individuals must obtain their doctoral degree to be eligible to become a clinical psychologist. Master's degrees are often awarded during the course of doctoral training, and some terminal master's degrees are granted in the field of clinical psychology. However, the master's degree does not permit the use of the title "clinical psychologist," nor does it allow for independent practice specifically in this field. (Master's level therapists can earn some licenses that are titled "counselor," or something similar.) To become a clinical psychologist requires training in a Doctor of Philosophy (PhD), a Doctor of Psychology (PsyD), or a Doctor of Education (EdD) program focusing on applied clinical psychology. The American Psychological Association accredits programs in psychology, and this accreditation is critical to ensure one's doctoral degree will likely transfer from state to state and be accepted by state licensing boards. There are, however, excellent programs that are not yet eligible for APA accreditation because they are new or do not intend to train practitioners and deem this certification unnecessary. Applicants should always inquire about APA status and the limits to licensure and practice in the local and distant areas if a program is not accredited. The most common doctoral training programs, PhD, PsyD, and EdD, are described to clarify the similarities and differences in the degrees and career options available.

Doctorate of Philosophy (in Clinical Psychology)
A PhD program typically follows the Boulder Model of training to produce scientist-practitioners on graduation. The Boulder Model is so named after the seminal conference held in Boulder, Colorado, in 1949 that defined the research-practice emphasis desired in PhD programs. PhD programs are usually housed in university settings. Fewer students are accepted in these programs than in PsyD or EdD programs because students are usually required to work in a faculty member's research lab for the duration of their graduate training and are paid a stipend or tuition remission for doing so. PhD programs traditionally emphasize research training more than practitioner-oriented programs. The core belief in the Boulder Model of training is that clinical psychologists must be *producers* of research and science to be skilled users of research and current knowledge. Thus, the exchange between practice and research is deemed critical to advance the field. However, the degree to which any program prepares individuals for careers in any of the subspecialties or for research, teaching, administration, or clinical work varies greatly.

PhD programs are typically designed to be completed in an average of 5 to 7 years postundergraduate degree. Some require the completion of a terminal master's degree and some field experience prior to admission. Entrance into doctoral programs is very competitive. Acceptance may be even more competitive than most medical schools since there are often only a few seats available and many competitive applicants for each entry class.

Doctorate of Psychology in Clinical Psychology
The PsyD programs ascribe to the Vail Model of training. This model was so named after a 1973 meeting that was funded by the National Institute of Mental Health (NIMH) to explore the alternative training models that would accommodate the changing needs and demands of society. A doctoral level alternative to the PhD, the PsyD, was endorsed. This training model prepares individuals to be practitioner-scholars. The National Council of Schools and Programs of Professional Psychology (NCSPP) put forth a recommended core curriculum for professional psychology training programs that includes the following competencies: Relationship, Intervention, Assessment, Research and Evaluation, Consultation and Education, and Management and Supervision (R. L. Peterson et al., 1992), and Diversity was later added. The PsyD programs, while needing to justify their curriculum to meet APA standards, do not have the same governing curricular guidelines.

Unless you have enrolled in a PsyD program, you may be surprised to learn that PsyD graduate students have coursework and some requirements in research as well. Many aspiring psychologists erroneously believe that research skills differentiate PsyD from PhD graduates. This may be true to some degree for career paths and training emphasis, but it is inaccurate to say that PsyD students do not acquire research skills. The type of research that is commonly conducted differs, although this is not necessary. The research of PsyD students frequently involves studying "local science," or examining phenomena in clinical practice or the community, more than benchmark research of underlying psychological processes and principles. Qualitative research and case studies are common methodologies for completion of a PsyD dissertation study, whereas quantitative observational and outcomes research might be more common in scientist-practitioner training programs.

Doctorate of Education

Doctorates of Education (EdD) are recipients of degrees that focus on counselor education. Most psychologists with an EdD work in school or educational settings, but some also work in agency counseling or community counseling settings. EdD psychology programs typically have less emphasis on research than psychology programs, and typically less coursework and practical experience in psychological assessment, intervention, and psychopathology. Assessment skills gained are often more psychoeducational and occupational, instead of focusing on personality or psychopathology. However, EdD students are usually eligible to compete for internships in clinical psychology, in which case they can gain assessment and intervention skills, and subsequent requirements necessary for independent practice.

Predoctoral Internship

All doctoral programs leading toward qualification as a clinical psychologist require a predoctoral internship training year prior to awarding the doctoral degree. Clinical psychology predoctoral internships are full-time programs for 1 year, or part-time programs for 2 years, in which students function as a practicing psychologist under the supervision of a licensed psychologist. Students often leave their home base training program to seek supplemental or altogether new training in a clinical practice of their choice. Predoctoral internships occur in any of the various settings previously discussed, or in a combination of settings. Interns may specialize in a particular area of patient care (e.g., severe mental illness, acute care), or seek general training. Predoctoral internships should have weekly seminars and didactics, and ongoing supervision of all professional activities. This training experience usually is the culmination of the doctoral degree, unless outstanding dissertation work needs to be completed.

Most programs permit or encourage students to seek internships through the Association of Psychology and Postdoctoral Internship Centers (APPIC). This national organization lists qualified internship and postdoctoral training sites, and serves to match sites with applicants according to a two-way ranking system. It is one of the predominant affiliations that clinical psychologists recognize as certification that a predoctoral training program is of sufficient rigor and breadth in experience. The APA also accredits internships, and training in an APPIC or APA-accredited internship is essential for licensure in many states, or for obtaining some academic jobs. A challenge in the field is that there is a national shortage of APA-accredited internships compared with the number of graduate students in need of training. Some policymakers in the field, therefore, advocate granting degrees and making the internship year a postdoctoral, postdegree requirement.

Postdoctoral Fellowships and Postdoctoral Training

On completion of the doctoral degree, the doctoral degree recipient is ready to practice psychology, right? This is not exactly the case. Graduates of doctoral programs who want to practice clinical psychology must obtain supervised postdoctoral training to be eligible for state licensure. Postdoctoral fellowships or internships can be similar to predoctoral internships; few of them, however, are part of a regular postdoctoral training program and they are not regulated by the degree-granting institution. The number of hours required, or what constitutes appropriate training experiences, varies by state. Fulfilling this training requirement can be a challenge because graduates may have outstanding debts to pay from graduate school, and the income earned by most postdoctoral fellows or interns is substantially less than that of a regularly practicing professional. Postdoctoral fellows need supervision and may be limited in their ability to bill fully for services. However, if you were to ask graduates of doctoral programs if they would want to skip their postdoctoral training year and immediately become solely responsible for their work, many would say "no!" There is much to learn about practicing as a clinical psychologist, whether it is how to write research grants, how to enlist oneself on insurance panels or market a private practice, or how to obtain privileges in a neighborhood hospital. The postdoctoral training year transitions graduates into their role as a full professional by teaching them essential skills through apprenticeship and training, and initiates a career-long practice of peer consultation and support.

Licensure

Each state controls and regulates the privilege to practice psychology. Licensure is an individual qualification that is obtained through state regulatory boards. Practitioners must be licensed to practice independently and use the title "psychologist." Licensed psychologists must meet the following minimal requirements: (a) a doctoral degree in a psychology or psychology-related field, (b) 1 year of predoctoral supervised clinical work, (c) 1 year of postdoctoral supervised clinical work, (d) a passing score on the national standardized exam (the Examination for Professional Practice in Psychology, or EPPP), and (e) any state mandated standardized, written, or oral examination on state law and professional ethics. Licensure is a quality control mechanism that ensures the minimum standards have been met for the privilege of calling oneself a psychologist.

Licensure only regulates the use of the title "psychologist," not "clinical psychologist" or "clinical health psychologist," or even "forensic psychologist." Licensure is general, and the description of one's practice is self-regulated and dictated by the legal and ethical standards set forth by the state and profession. Essentially, the psychologist is held responsible for "truth in packaging." One must be qualified as competent on the basis of training, education, and experience to offer either general or specialized psychological services. Thus, calling oneself a clinical psychologist requires appropriate licensure as a psychologist, and credentials in clinical psychology (doctorate, internships, and postdoctoral training). This quality control mechanism and state regulations are in place to protect the public from unqualified practitioners putting themselves forward as something they are not, and ensuring that those who are psychologists meet the minimal standards set forth at the time of licensure and throughout their tenure in the field. Those who engage in unqualified practice, either by misusing the title or misusing a method or procedure due to incompetence, negligence, or willful disregard of the law can be subject to legal sanctions for unprofessional conduct.

Continuing Education

State licensing boards mandate psychologists to complete a certain number of continuing education credits per license cycle (usually 2 years). Continuing education requirements were developed to ensure that psychologists maintain some degree of currency with movements and training in the field. Almost all states require some portion of the continuing education requirement to include ethics workshops or training. What constitutes credit varies to allow scholars, practitioners, and researchers to obtain credits in their area of expertise. In Pennsylvania, individually publishing a research article counts for 10 continuing education credit hours; the credit for coauthoring an article is calculated by dividing 10 hours by the number of authors.

Teaching classes, attending workshops, completing online courses, turning in quizzes from current research articles, or at-home study can all count toward continuing education credit in most states. State boards randomly audit individual psychologists to ensure compliance with this law. Review requires psychologists to produce their continuing education certificates and verification of fulfilling the requirements.

Board Certification

Psychologists can and are encouraged to seek certification or a diploma in one of the specialties recognized by the American Board of Professional Psychology (ABPP).

This board is independent of the American Psychological Association, but was incorporated with their help in 1947. This governing body protects the public by ensuring and certifying individuals' qualifications and skills to deliver services and practice within a designated specialty area. According to ABPP, a specialty area is a "defined area in the practice of psychology that connotes special competency acquired through an organized sequence of formal education, training, and experience" (ABPP, n.d.). The ABPP awards diplomas, resulting in one becoming a "diplomate," based on a thorough review of credentials (doctoral training, license, appropriate internship and postdoctoral training), self-statement, work samples, and an oral examination by existing board members.

ABPP recognizes the following specialties through Member Boards: child and adolescent psychology, cognitive and behavioral psychology, clinical psychology, clinical health psychology, clinical neuropsychology, counseling psychology, family psychology, forensic psychology, group psychology, psychoanalysis, rehabilitation psychology, school psychology, and organization and business. While board certification to date is only sought by approximately 10% of licensed psychologists, it is becoming more important for financial reimbursement from insurance companies, reciprocity between state licensing boards, and distinction among colleagues in an ever-growing competitive profession. Outside the field of psychology, medical and forensic colleagues perhaps are most likely to look for this credential when collaborating, referring to, or seeking psychologists.

Respecialization

Psychologists who want to shift the focus of their practice after completing their training are expected to seek necessary education, training, consultation, or supervision from others with the desired expertise. For complete respecialization, psychologists can enroll in formal training programs to complete portions of a clinical degree that pertain to their area of interest. Psychologists may choose to do additional practicums or internships or take relevant coursework in neuropsychology if their original training was in clinical child psychology. Some programs may award certificates of respecialization, but the preparation to shift or designate focus in one's practice is largely self-governed by following the ethics code.

Ethics Guidelines

An old adage suggests, "A wise man knows what he knows, and knows what he doesn't know." This could not be truer than in the self-evaluation and self-promotion of one's clinical abilities in psychology. By-and-large, clinical psychology is a self-regulated field to the extent that practitioners must meet the minimal competency standards for training qualifications and emotional well-being necessary for practice in their designated area. Emotional well-being is discussed in detail in Chapter 15, and therefore, only competence in training is addressed here.

Competency in psychology is accomplished by completion of doctoral training, supervised postdoctoral hours, licensure, and continuing education credits. The monitoring of a person's competency or skill becomes a more diffuse process following licensure. Becoming a licensed professional offers a high degree of independence, even among those who work in a hierarchical organization such as a hospital or clinic where there may be quality oversight through various mechanisms. To protect the public from clinicians who might allow their skills to erode or become obsolete by failing to keep up with new developments, the state regulatory boards generally mandate a certain amount of regular continuing education for all health-related professionals as a minimum effort for maintaining competence. So, if psychologists have a current license and complete the requisite number of continuing education credits, they are theoretically competent to practice as they see fit, within the guidelines of the American Psychological Association's Ethics Code (2002). But to truly become and remain competent, professional psychologists must acquire a great deal of specialized knowledge, clinical experience, and a strong set of skills for self-control and self-regulation.

Specialties in Clinical Psychology

Specialists in clinical psychology focus their careers on working with a particular age group or diagnosis, with a specific population, in a select setting, or with emphasis on a type of therapeutic modality, or stage of intervention. Some combination of these parameters can also be chosen to create unique and valued specialties. Examples of these specialties are described, and those that are most common are highlighted with descriptions of associated organizations, and professional groups, and by snapshots of days in the life of professionals practicing in their fields.

Specialties across the Life Span

To think of any major mind-body function or aspect of psychology across the biopsychosocial model in reference to a 5-year-old versus a 50-year-old, most would agree that even similar functions and processes are different between the two. Communication, thought and reasoning processes, expression and experience of emotion, physical responses to stressors, social relations, perception and experience of one's environment, and even the types of psychopathology manifested differ across the life span. Clinical psychologists need to be experts in normal and abnormal psychological human functioning for the population with which they work. Although some psychologists adopt a generalist approach that allows them to work with patients across the life span, these professionals likely have other limits to their practice because they cannot address the gamut of all issues for all patients. Three specialties that are recognized within the field are *clinical child and adolescent psychology, pediatric psychology,* and *clinical geropsychology.*

The focus of the specialty in clinical child and adolescent psychology, as described by the mission statement of Division 53 of the American Psychological Association, is on the scientific, training, practice, and professional aspects of "furthering knowledge, welfare, and mental health of children, youth, and families" (Masten, 2001). Child psychologists often have more expertise in behavioral analysis; assessment and intervention; intellectual assessment; play therapy; and milieu or home-based evaluation than general practitioners. Child psychologists can maintain any theoretical orientation in their practice of therapy or scientific research. However, behavioral assessment and intervention are preferred approaches for many child problems and disorders.

The Association for Behavioral and Cognitive Therapies (ABCT) has Special Interest Groups (SIG) that bring together professionals who subdivide the specialty of clinical child and adolescent psychology even further. Relating to child and adolescent psychology, ABCT's Special Interest Groups include "Parenting and Families"; "Cognitive Behavioral Therapy in School Settings"; "Child and School Related Disorders"; "Child Maltreatment and Violence"; and "Child and Adolescent Anxiety." Child and adolescent psychologists can choose to focus on any and all aspects of clinical psychology as previously defined (science, theory, practice). Child and adolescent psychologists may work in a large variety of settings, such as academic institutions, psychiatric facilities, administrative organizations, or private practice. Some child psychologists work in hospital settings and focus on the health, physical illness, and well-being of children and adolescents and are typically classified as "pediatric psychologists."

The Society of Pediatric Psychology was founded in 1968, and is a division of the American Psychological Association (Division 54). Scientists and professionals practicing pediatric psychology focus on health care of children, adolescents, and their families. Practitioners of pediatric psychology work in interdisciplinary settings such as family medicine practices, children's hospitals, developmental clinics, academic settings, or traditional child psychology venues. Pediatric psychology is actually a subspecialty of behavioral medicine and health psychology, and perhaps represents the interface between health psychology and clinical psychology focusing on children, adolescents, and families. Pediatric psychologists work to address such issues as coping with chronic illnesses, behavioral change for prevention or maintenance of child or adolescent weight gain/loss, preparation for surgical or medical procedures, psychological development of children who have chronic or acute medical illnesses, head traumas, or physical disabilities. Clinical and research areas of interest may focus on crises, prevention, assessment, intervention, maintenance, or all those issues. Professionals in this field also address children or adolescents within the context of their family, and aid parents and siblings in coping and adjusting to the identified patient's needs, lifestyle, or psychological changes. Pediatric psychologists often offer services to these constituents directly as well. Dr. Anne Kazak is a nationally and internationally known pediatric psychologist. She shares her perspectives on the field and her career in Box 2.1.

Box 2.1 Highlights of a Contemporary Clinical Psychologist

Anne Kazak, PhD, ABPP

Dr. Kazak is a graduate of University of Virginia, predoctoral intern at Yale University School of Medicine—Connecticut Mental Health Center, licensed psychologist in Pennsylvania, and Board Certified in Family Psychology by the American Board of Professional Psychology.

Dr. Kazak is a member of numerous organizations: American Psychological Association (Fellow—Divisions 12, 38, 43, 44, 54); Society for Research in Child Development; American Family Therapy Academy; Association of Medical School Psychologists; Association for Cognitive and Behavioral Therapies; International Society for the Study of Traumatic Stress; Society of Developmental and Behavioral Pediatrics; Pennsylvania Psychological Association; and the American Psychosocial Oncology Society. She obtains her continuing education credits through attendance at these conferences, and stays informed with the literature through annual memberships to psychology, medical, and multidisciplinary journals. In addition to those she edits, she reads the following journals regularly: Journal of Consulting and Clinical Psychology, Professional Psychology, Clinical Psychology, *and* Health Psychology; Families, Systems and Health, Pediatrics, Journal of Traumatic Stress, Journal of Clinical Oncology, *and* Pediatric Blood and Cancer. *She provides the following overview of her exciting niche and career.*

I am a clinical psychologist whose work is at the intersection of pediatric and family psychology. I am a professor in the Department of Pediatrics at the University of Pennsylvania and Director of the Department of Psychology and Deputy Director of the Behavioral Health Center at the Children's Hospital of Philadelphia (CHOP). CHOP is a large, academic pediatric center. In my current position, I spend one third of my time in administration (overseeing a department of approximately 60 doctoral level psychologists and collaborating with others through our academic medical center to develop and sustain behavioral programs) and two thirds in a variety of research and mentoring activities with local, national, and international foci. My lab is currently organized around two federal research grants from the National Cancer Institute addressing the development of interventions for children with cancer and their families. I also serve as a mentor to postdoctoral fellows, and psychologists and pediatricians. I do not see patients at the present time. Currently, I am the editor of the *Journal of Family Psychology* and a past editor of the *Journal of Pediatric Psychology*. And I am active nationally in the American Psychological Association (APA), now as past president of the Society of Pediatric Psychology (SPP) and chair of an APA task force on Evidence Based Practice for Children and Adolescents.

A Day in the Life of Dr. Kazak

I get up between 6:00 and 6:30. I'm usually the first one up and initiate the morning routines for our Rhodesian Ridgeback (Bella) and cat (Moxiefe). I eat breakfast with my partner (Chris) and 4.5-year-old son (Sam), catch a bit of news from the newspaper or the television and pack lunch. At some point before leaving for work, I generally peek at my e-mail. I drive to work (about 30 minutes door to door), sometimes dropping Sam off at preschool.

My day at work is split between research and administrative responsibilities. I'm usually at work between 8:00 and 8:30 and leave between 5:00 and 5:30. I generally do not take time for lunch unless I am having a business lunch. It's difficult to say what a typical day is like because they are quite variable, some spent more in administrative responsibilities and others more focused on research or mentoring. There is a lot of time at home spent on work, on evenings and weekends. Some typical examples during a workday include:

- *Meetings with other staff about administrative matters related to the Department of Psychology or the Behavioral Health Center:* These may include discussions of programmatic and/or budgetary planning, staff recruitment, development and review of policies or topics such as planning around space or other resources, quality improvement, or regulatory issues. There are often conversations that might be broadly described as "problem-solving," whether around a clinical issue and a specific patient situation, or to figure out how to best accomplish goals related to projects and initiatives.

- *Meetings with research staff to review projects and detailed discussions about study progress and difficulties encountered in projects:* Our clinical research involves the development and delivery of clinical services to patients and families, so these sessions may include review of tapes of sessions and discussions of our impressions of the treatments and their impact. Depending on the phase of a project, we may also be reviewing results and discussing next steps for data analysis.

I enjoy writing and value this as one of the most important aspects of my professional life. Often there is at least one manuscript in preparation and/or a grant that is being written or revised. I am also frequently reading and editing work that is being written collaboratively with others or papers from trainees. In order to facilitate the process of writing, I take occasional days for working at home. These days, with less distraction, are critical to my productivity. It's also common that I come into the office for a couple of hours on Saturday mornings to write.

The process of running a research lab and conducting research entails meetings and materials to review related to potential new projects and collaborations. It's not unusual, to attend a meeting with a group of potential collaborators, anticipating the submission of a new grant proposal or exploring ideas for collaborative efforts. Related to this category of activity, I'm also commonly addressing questions from people at CHOP, nationally and internationally about research projects and potential collaborations. More and more conference calls are used to facilitate collaborations across institutions. It's also common to meet with mentees to discuss projects or professional development issues. And, research has administrative activities, so phone calls with our business administrator or completion of paperwork related to grants is also common.

As a journal editor, I work with my journal assistant to assure that submitted manuscripts are entered properly through the electronic journal management system, that reviewers are identified and assigned to papers and that we can track the flow of papers through the editorial process. I am almost always carrying with me the materials to write at least one editorial letter. There are also publishing deadlines to meet in order to produce each issue of the journal and numerous questions, some easy, some more complex, from authors and reviewers that I answer almost everyday.

E-mail is a key component of all of my activities. The amount of e-mail can be considerable and involves "conversations" about many administrative issues from many individuals in the Hospital and information about research studies and questions from team members. I'm "copied" on many conversations which helps keep me informed about a variety of issues of concern. Nationally, I receive e-mail from a variety of listservs and communications from people around the world about research projects and other national activities.

I usually pick up Sam at his babysitter's. I'm a runner and try to run in the neighborhood several nights a week before dinner, if it fits with everyone's schedules and plans for the evening. We eat dinner as a family, often with a friend joining us. After dinner, we relax and play. I'm often back on the computer later in the evening, mostly doing e-mail, journal work, and finishing up some work from the day. I'm usually relaxing and settling down for the night by 10.

Dr. Kazak Provides the Following Recommendations for Persons Interested in Joining Her Field

There will be many opportunities in child health. A strong grounding in clinical, child, and family psychology during training is important as is seeking out experiences in pediatric settings. A breadth of experiences is important, including skills in clinical services, research and teaching. People with the ability to be flexible, who can work as members and leaders of teams, and those who can readily see opportunities that transcend traditional disciplinary boundaries will continue to be very competitive in pediatric psychology.

Clinical geropsychology maintains the same general mission as all fields of clinical psychology with intention to further develop science, practice, and theory. This subspecialty focuses on the mental health of older adults and psychological service delivery for them. Section 2 (Clinical Geropsychology) of the Society of Clinical Psychology (Division 12 of APA) is an organization dedicated to furthering this mission.

The meaning of the term *older adults* has changed over time, as general life expectancy and the population of older individuals have increased. Now, psychologists have come to address different adult populations as the "young old" for persons aged 65 to 74 years, "old old" for persons aged 75 to 85 years, and "oldest old" for persons aged 85 years and older (Santrock, 1999). These distinctions are helpful in recognizing that different cohorts of individuals might have similar experiences within groups, but not across groups.

In comparison to younger adults, the psychological care of older adults coinciding with normative or age-expected life events often requires greater attention to medically related problems, medication use and compliance, medication or substance abuse, differential diagnoses (e.g., Alzheimer's disease versus Depression), neuropsychological phenomena, systemic issues (e.g., nursing or assisted home care, family involvement; insurance), and death and dying issues. Generational experiences (cohort effects) and age-related cultural variables are also critical considerations for the optimal care of this population. Since older adults have increasingly become a more prevalent population in the workforce and in the care for younger generations, attention to these issues as they relate to older adults' beliefs and cohort experiences also require psychologists to have specialty knowledge and sensitivity.

Empirically based protocols for the treatment of many psychological disorders are geared toward the general adult population. Research not specifically targeting senior adults tends to focus on persons between the ages of 18 and 65: 18 as a lower limit to avoid difficulties in obtaining informed consent; 65 as upper limit probably because this is the age of retirement and a marker for differential experiences between those older and younger. Also, it had been assumed that psychotherapeutic interventions for older adults do not need to differ from those of the average population (Thorp & Lynch, 2005), but practitioners find this not to be true. Clinical geropsychologists have dedicated much effort to the modification of protocols intended for younger adults, and the development, testing, and validation of new assessment tools and techniques, and interventions for older adults. More work is needed in this area. Also, topics such as the impact of social support, methods and location of treatment delivery, and patient and therapist variables related to the treatment and care of older adults need further exploration (Thorp & Lynch, 2005). Research on caregivng has also expanded to investigate the impact of senior adult spouses caring for their partners as well as caregivng issues specific to adult children, family members, and professionals.

Specialties by Disorder

Many practitioners and researchers specialize their practices by focusing on populations of individuals who have their psychological disorders or intervention needs in common. In community mental health centers and primary care facilities, this practice is not always feasible; but in private practices and academic research, this tends to be the norm rather than the exception. Niche practices can help practitioners secure a continual stream of referrals, and help researchers make a significant impact in the identification, assessment, treatment, or advancement of theory for a target group.

The *Diagnostic and Statistical Manual of Mental Disorders* (*DSM-IV-TR*; American Psychiatric Association, 1994) made categorization of individuals discrete to distinguish between types of problems experienced by patients, although many patients have coexisting disorders and problems. Practice directories, training directories, and associations tend to index psychologists' expertise according to *DSM* disorders and additional subgroups. Some psychologists primarily treat individuals with mood disorders, whereas others predominantly work with patients who have personality disorders. Psychologists may specialize in substance abuse, sexual dysfunctions, developmental disabilities, or neuropsychological disorders. In Box 2.2, Dr. Ronald Fudge, the Director of Substance Abuse Services in a metropolitan VA hospital, explains his roles, responsibilities, and recommendations for this area of clinical practice and research.

Box 2.2 Highlights of a Contemporary Psychologist

Ronald C. Fudge, PhD

Dr. Fudge holds a doctoral degree from University of Georgia, and master's degrees from University of Bridgeport and Princeton University (psychophysiology). His predoctoral internship was in the New Jersey state psychology internship program, and his postdoctoral training was in Detroit, where he continued psychophysiology and biofeedback training and research. He is currently licensed in the state of New York, and is an active member of the American Psychological Association and the Association for Behavioral and Cognitive Therapies. While Dr. Fudge subscribes to Cognitive and Behavioral Therapy, *and the* Journal of Consulting and Clinical Psychology, *he has access to a vast library of substance abuse journals and other relevant titles in his workplace. He routinely attends APA and ABCT conferences, and occasionally attends conferences of the Association of Black Psychologists, and other meetings in New York City. Dr. Fudge explains his roles and responsibilities in his position as Director of Substance Abuse Services in a VA Hospital.*

My current position is the Director of Substance Abuse Services in a metropolitan VA hospital. Substance abuse services include a residential program for individuals with severe addiction problems and moderate or chronic medical issues. There is also an intensive outpatient program that includes evenings and weekends, a methadone maintenance clinic, a community outreach program located in several venues throughout New Jersey, and a consultation and liaison service within the medical specialty hospital. As Director, I am responsible for a staff of 25 people that include administrative assistants, Psychologists, Psychiatrist, Internists, a physician assistant, rehab techs, nurses, and social workers.

Job responsibilities and duties are wide ranging and at times challenging. As Overall Director, I am responsible for program development and supervising the provision of services. While a considerable amount of time is dedicated to administrative and related services, I also provide clinical oversight and supervision. Since the "buck" stops at my desk, final clinical decisions are my responsibility. I also chair interdisciplinary team meetings, supervise intakes, and act as community liaison in public affairs. It is also part of my role as administrator to determine, monitor, and maintain the quality of services. I also serve as the Mental Health Program Analyst ensuring the maintenance of departmental standards.

Probably the most enjoyable part of the position aside from direct clinical services is the provision of supervision and training for Psychology and Social work interns, Medical Students, and Residents. When time permits, I have provided supervision and collaboration on research and dissertation projects.

What makes the job most interesting is the challenge of serving a diverse population with a wide variety of issues both prior to and as a result of substance abuse. Their problems are often complicated by medical issues either as a result of substance use or from other causes. The challenge comes in affecting their lives in a very short period of time. Regardless of misconceptions about substance abuse, marked psychological and physical changes do result from treatment. The diverse etiologies and variety of people with substance abuse problems call for a wide variety of clinical skills.

What Does Dr. Fudge Find to Be His Biggest Challenges in His Specialty or Position?

Substance abuse is closely related to the economy and the individual's perception of their place in society. In trying to provide treatment we are often faced with the interaction of poverty, childhood, and sexual abuse, racism, and the vagaries of economics.

I have often seen patients make major changes in their life only to be faced with the hopelessness of their previous environment. It is difficult for some in this society where some live very well and others have nothing and little hope for any change. When you add in the devastating effect that substance abuse has on the physiognomy, permanent positive change is extremely difficult.

What Does Dr. Fudge Like the Least about His Area of Specialty or Current Position?

As an administrator I am often faced with the sometimes contradictory goals presented by the clinical needs of the client population and the administration and economic concerns of the organization. While it is not always the case that these two interests diverge, it occurs often enough to be a source of regular irritation. Additionally, there is in substance abuse a conflict between the traditional view of substance abuse treatment, which is often based on experiential considerations, and the application of more empirically tested interventions. I have been fortunate to have a fairly enlightened staff that is open to almost any approach. In some other facilities, there is what amounts to open warfare over treatment philosophy and goals.

A Day in the Life of Dr. Fudge

Dr. Fudge enjoys a full day beginning at 5 A.M. until he retires at 11 P.M. The bulk of his professional work occurs between 7 A.M. and 4 P.M. In addition to his responsibilities detailed previously, his day includes a 30- to 50-minute commute to or from work, coaching several nights a week, household duties and family time, and time to practice music, read, and "veg" in front of the "tube."

Dr. Fudge Provides the Following Recommendations for Persons Interested in Joining His Field

First, I think that one should have a thorough understanding of the physiology of addiction, particularly the long-term effects of addiction and abuse. As new research on addiction and substance abuse emerges, the role of neurological changes needs to be incorporated with behavior change. An awareness of a societal bias against substance abusers is also important. There is a broad-based view that substance abusers are either weak willed, or deficient in some way that allows them to become addicted to drugs. Many in mental health often feel that working with substance abusers is the bottom of the barrel.

Second, a more than passing acquaintance with medicine is something that a well-trained psychologist needs, especially in substance abuse. After 27 years in the field, I feel that psychologists need to have a better background in physiology and a familiarity with the psychological effects of medical problems. This should include enough lay medicine to understand basic lab values and the behavioral consequences of medications and abnormal conditions. Anyone in the field should have enough of a medical vocabulary and understanding to follow most medical charts. A medical dictionary and *Physician's Desk Reference* should be part of the psychologist's library.

Many organizations coalesce their members around particular mental health disorders or clinical health psychology topics. There are national organizations that focus on science, theory, and practice surrounding one or more diagnostic category: Anxiety Disorders Association of America, the Association for the Treatment of Sexual Abusers, the Association for the Advancement of Mental Retardation, the Society of Behavioral Medicine, and the Treatment and Research Association (TARA) for Personality Disorders. This is only a small sampling of the specialties categorized in this way. The Association for Behavioral and Cognitive Therapies (ABCT) has Special Interest Groups (SIGs) in the organization that also have organized interested members around diagnostic categories, in addition to other categories. A sampling of the SIGs include the following: Addictive Behaviors, Anxiety Disorders, Child and School-Related Issues, Developmental Disabilities, Insomnia and Other Sleep Disorders, Obesity and Eating Disorders, Schizophrenia and Other Serious Mental Disorders. There are Divisions in the American Psychological Association that focus on diagnostic groups (e.g., personality, addictions) as well; however, these groups may not focus exclusively on the criteria of clinical psychology. Associations relevant to specialties in clinical psychology can be found in the Appendix (p. 53).

Clinical Health Psychology

Clinical psychologists whose distinct focus is on physical health problems and the maintenance of physical health specialize in clinical health psychology. This specialty attends to the interface between behavior and health. Clinical health psychologists adopt a biopsychosocial model of health and illness and believe that attention to the mind-body relationship is critical to physical and mental well-being. This field aims to apply scientific knowledge to "the promotion and maintenance of health; the prevention, treatment and rehabilitation of illness and disability; and the improvement of the health care system" (APA, 1997). Services are provided to families, individuals, and the organization of health care systems. Hospitals, medical practices (primary care and specialty practices), nursing homes, outpatient clinics, and rehabilitation centers are settings in which clinical health psychologists might work.

Clinical health psychologists could ascribe to any theoretical orientation. Most research in this field, however, promotes cognitive and behavioral approaches to resolving, stabilizing, minimizing, or preventing problems. Most service is delivered in short-term individual psychotherapy, consultation, psychoeducation, or group formats. Services are also likely to be developed through multidisciplinary collaboration or coordination of care. Organizations that advance clinical health psychology practices and research include ABCT's Special Interest Group in Behavioral Medicine, the Society of Behavioral Medicine, and APA's Division 38, Health Psychology.

Clinical health psychologists are involved in physical health care in research and clinical endeavors. They may help with any of the following problems: behavioral and psychological risk factors for disease, illness, or injury; psychological factors secondary to disease, illness, or injury; somatic presentations of psychological disorders; and behavioral and psychological aspects of medical procedures such as surgery, chemotherapy, and dental work in need of attention because of the way psychological phenomena are thought to impact physical health, or vice versa (Golden & Felgoise, 2005). Areas in which clinical health psychologists have had significant impact on the fields of medicine and health care include obesity and eating disorders, oncology, HIV/AIDS, gastroenterology, cardiology, organ transplant, surgery, pain management, smoking and respiration (asthma, chronic obstructive pulmonary disease [COPD]), sleep medicine, and fertility and sexual functioning. In fact, clinical health psychology has made inroads in helping people deal with illness and maintenance of health for all organ systems. Services are also often provided to family members who are either caring for persons with medical illnesses or are affected by their loved ones' health status.

Clinical Neuropsychology

Clinical neuropsychology is another specialty that warrants specific discussion when considering focal areas in terms of disorder. Clinical neuropsychology can be classified under the umbrella of clinical psychology, but is also recognized as a specialty of psychology (APA's Division 40) in its own right. Clinical neuropsychologists often differentiate themselves from clinical psychologists although some engage in both general clinical psychology and neuropsychology practice.

Clinical neuropsychology focuses on the scientific study of "brain-behavior relationships, and the clinical application of that knowledge to human problems" (APA, Division 40, www.div40.org/body.html). The mission of the APA Division of Clinical Neuropsychology is to "promote the use of scientific research to develop its knowledge base and clinical techniques," and to develop and promote "quality standards of professional training and practice" (Barr & Cole, 2007). Division 40 broadens the focus on neuropsychological phenomena beyond clinical psychology to include interdisciplinary interest from other aspects of psychology (i.e., cognitive, school, forensic, developmental, clinical rehabilitation, physiological psychology). Within the field of clinical psychology/clinical neuropsychology, a specialty of *behavioral neuropsychology* has emerged. Horton (1979) defines behavioral neuropsychology as follows:

> *Essentially, behavioral neuropsychology may be defined as the application of behavior therapy techniques to problems of organically impaired individuals while using a neuropsychological assessment and intervention perspective. This treatment philosophy assumes that inclusion of data from neuropsychological assessment strategies would be helpful in the formulation of hypotheses regarding antecedent conditions (external or internal) for observed phenomena of psychopathology. (p. 20)*

Clinical neuropsychology requires specialized training in addition to that of general clinical psychology or clinical health psychology. Many doctoral training programs offer neuropsychology tracks or concentrations that include specialized coursework, practica, and research experiences. Clinical neuropsychologists focus on assessment and diagnosis; behavioral neuropsychologists emphasize problems of management, retraining, and rehabilitation (Horton, 2005). Patients who suffer from strokes, degenerative diseases (e.g., Alzheimer's disease, Huntington's chorea), traumatic brain injury, or neurological problems secondary to other medical problems or treatment (e.g., chemotherapy) are typical clients of the clinical neuropsychologist. These specialists practice their profession in many settings: private practice, hospitals, rehabilitation centers, nursing homes, and interdisciplinary outpatient clinics. Christopher Royer, PhD, a neuropsychologist and Division Director of Psychology and Neuropsychology at his facility, describes his work as a clinician, administrator, supervisor, and professor in Box 2.3.

Box 2.3 Highlights of a Contemporary Psychologist

Christopher Royer, PhD

Dr. Royer is a neuropsychologist working in a rehabilitation center in Central Pennsylvania, and also as a half-time core faculty member in a doctoral program in clinical psychology at the Philadelphia College of Osteopathic Medicine. A graduate of Widener University's PsyD Program in Clinical Psychology, he holds a Certification of Neuropsychology specialty training from this institution. Dr. Royer is a Pennsylvania Licensed Psychologist, and a member of the American Psychological Association and Pennsylvania Psychological Association. His journal of choice is Archives of Neuropsychology.
Reflecting on his favorite and most challenging aspects of his clinical practice, he shares the following thoughts.

There are two components that are truly rewarding in this specialty. First, it is a great opportunity to use psychological and neuropsychological assessment techniques to understand the person with a wonderful breadth of data. I look forward to difficult diagnostic questions and using psychological instruments to help me tease out these problems. Secondly, working with individuals who have medical conditions is highly rewarding. There are so many areas to intervene, and patients learn new ways to cope, manage their illnesses, and become empowered with using behavioral strategies rather than more passive medical treatments.

The biggest challenges are never related to the patient, but always in the business arena. That being said, working with patients who have potential bias, such as workers' compensation claims and other litigation, offer the most difficult challenges.

What Does Dr. Royer Like the Least about His Area of Specialty?

There is a great deal of need to educate the professional and lay community about how psychology interacts with the body and with medical practice. While I really enjoy this process, it feels, at times, as if the community, particularly in this area of the country, is less ready to accept a behavioral approach that is so weighted in terms of the physical manifestations of illness.

A Day in the Life of Dr. Royer

My days are quite varied, which is part of my continued enjoyment of this career. In addition to my clinical work, I teach half time, and there are responsibilities that go with that obligation which take up more or less of my time depending on the day or week.

Typically, my family wakes up around 6:30 a.m. We try to do as much the night before to be ready for the next day so that the family can get those few extra minutes in the morning. Typically, I will try to review my personal e-mail in the morning, while holding my clinical and school accounts until later in the day. After getting everyone fed, we take my 15-year-old son to school. On a day with reasonable weather, I will walk with my 11-year-old daughter to school, and then on to work (about 1.9 miles). I am visually impaired and I do not drive, so on bad-weather days, my wife will do a lot of transporting. My wife is a part-time visiting nurse, so my 5-year-old will go to preschool on those days.

Upon arriving at work, my first order of business is to review the mail and referrals from the day before. As the director of the office, I have to ensure that business flows. I take time to check work e-mail as well. Often in the morning, I will meet and interview a testing referral and then get them started with an intern for the actual testing. I then see two therapy patients before lunch. About 85% of my patients have medical issues, and often they are able to come in during the day, as unemployment is a big part of medical problems. I use a variety of behavioral and motivational interviewing techniques to help patients cope with their illness and life circumstances. At 11:30, I eat a quick lunch and meet with the intern (doctoral student from Philadelphia College of Osteopathic Medicine; PCOM) to see how the testing is going and make any mid-course corrections in the protocol. I then review my school e-mail and try to do some callbacks. The afternoon tends to be a mix of therapy clients, pain evaluations, disability evaluations, dictating time, callback time, or consultation time for the hospital. My office is located in a medical rehab and long-term acute care setting, and we consult with inpatients on a daily basis. Depending on the day, the last hour is either given to dictation or calls. Two days per week, I meet with the intern for formal supervision, although a lot of that occurs during the week. One afternoon per week, I leave a bit early to teach class. I teach graduate students from the PsyD Program in Clinical Psychology program at PCOM. In Harrisburg, there is a distance learning site to accommodate students in central Pennsylvania.

Evenings are also variable, and sometimes unpredictable. When there is school work to be done (reading papers, dissertations, etc.), that is the time. Otherwise, I try to keep as much work as possible at work, as family time is extremely important to all of us. Dinner is together, and then homework gets done. We have a large room where we all congregate to talk, play games, go online, watch movies, and so on. At some point, e-mail is attended to again. Growing older, sleep is a nice end to the day!

Dr. Royer Provides the Following Recommendations for Persons Interested in Joining His Field

Working with the medical population is a fantastic niche to be in. The need is great and there is quite a bit of unexplored territory in terms of identifying and validating effective assessment and treatment strategies. For those considering neuropsychology or health psychology, I would only caution that these are really entire fields of knowledge and require a large amount of training in order to become competent. Finding graduate and postgraduate specialty tracks allows one to really immerse oneself in the field.

Specialties by Personal Characteristics

Sometimes clients seek to find clinical psychologists who specialize in assessment or treatment of mental health problems in persons from identified minority groups. Some persons from gay, lesbian, transsexual, or transgendered communities, feminists, those who hold spirituality or a specific religion as central to their identity, or persons with diverse cultural backgrounds may prefer to obtain psychological services from persons who identify themselves as having expertise in their area. Specializing in clinical psychology for persons with such characteristics is often accomplished in less formal ways than that of other specialties in that there are few programs with separate training tracks for specific populations. However, all training programs should emphasize cultural awareness and respect for individual diversity, and the importance of culturally minded knowledge, skills, and professional attitudes.

Psychologists who become experts in the assessment, diagnosis, or treatment of one or more minority groups likely do so by focusing their research (dissertation or postdoctoral work), literature review, clinical skills training (workshops, practica, internship, supervision), consultation, and clinical practice on working with such populations. There are Special Interest Groups in the ABCT organization that recognize these important specialties: African Americans in Behavior Therapy; Asian American Issues in Behavior Therapy and Research; Hispanic Issues in Behavior Therapy; Masculinity and Mental Health; Native American Issues in Behavior Therapy and Research; Spiritual and Religious Issues in Behavior Change; Study of Gay, Lesbian, Bisexual, and Transgendered Issues; and Women's Issues in Behavior Therapy. Likewise, the

Society of Clinical Psychology (APA Division 12) has two pertinent sections that bring professionals together to discuss, study, and further some of the topics discussed here: Section 4: Clinical Psychology of Women, and Section 6: Clinical Psychology of Ethnic Minorities. Gayle Iwamasa, PhD is a seasoned professional who has had tremendous impact on the field of clinical psychology through her leadership in national organizations (ABCT, APA) and publications on multicultural competence. Her career embraces clinical, academic, and professional activities, as described in Box 2.4.

Box 2.4 Highlights of a Contemporary Psychologist

Gayle Iwamasa, PhD

Dr. Iwamasa holds a master's degree in psychology and a doctoral degree in clinical psychology from Purdue University. Her predoctoral internship and postdoctoral training took place at University of California—San Francisco, School of Medicine, Department of Psychiatry. She interned in major rotations in short-term inpatient services, psychiatric emergency services, short-term cognitive behavioral therapy, and long-term psychodynamic therapy. She is an associate professor at DePaul University in Indiana, and a licensed psychologist and health service provider in psychology in Indiana. She also maintains a private practice conducting clinical assessments and psychotherapy. Dr. Iwamasa has held numerous leadership positions in national organizations, including the Association for Behavioral and Cognitive Therapies, Asian American Psychological Association, and the American Psychological Association, and has published and consulted widely on multicultural competencies. Dr. Iwamasa highlights her most and least favorite aspects of her career.

What Does Dr. Iwamasa Like the Most about Her Area of Specialty?

I don't do the same thing all the time. I teach undergraduate and graduate students, conduct cognitive behavioral therapy, conduct psychological evaluations, supervise master's level therapists and doctoral students, conduct research in areas of my interest, and do consulting within and outside of psychology.

What Does Dr. Iwamasa Like the Least about Her Area of Specialty?

Since I like to do a lot of things, being able to say no to projects that I'd like to do is difficult. What I like the least as a faculty member are the numerous meetings, as a therapist—too much paperwork!

Dr. Iwamasa Provides the Following Recommendations for Persons Interested in Joining Her Field

Get as much training as you can while you are in school, as once you get out, you'll realize just how much you don't know and wish you did! Once your job and personal life demands fill your day, you might not have the time and money necessary to pursue as much education and training as you'd like.

Dr Iwamasa recommends two journals of primary interest to her: *Cognitive and Behavioral Practice,* and *Cultural Diversity and Ethnic Minority Psychology.* Dr. Iwamasa strives for personal and professional balance, values her friendships and prioritizes her family. She relies on e-mail to accomplish much of her leadership and professional work, and it also allows her to stay connected with friends and colleagues nationally and internationally.

Specialties by Stage of Intervention

Viewing psychological and biopsychosocial problems along a continuum from the trigger of a problem through its extinction splinters the discipline of clinical psychology into additional subspecialties. Clinical psychologists' practices may be concentrated in the areas of prevention, crisis management, trauma response, acute- or long-term intervention, and rehabilitation. Sometimes the focus on these areas of practice is dictated by practitioners' employment setting (e.g., psychiatric emergency center, partial hospitalization program, rehabilitation hospital). Clinical psychologists who are primarily researchers, scholars, or academicians may select any of these stages of intervention for further study on particular populations. Persons interested in pediatric clinical psychology might investigate approaches to primary prevention of obesity. Or, clinical psychologists might focus on the immediate crisis of experiencing, or psychological sequelae to surviving natural disasters such as Hurricane Katrina in New Orleans, Louisiana.

Prevention

Primary prevention generally refers to interventions or attempts to reduce the probability that a mental or physical health problem will develop. Clinical health psychologists who teach stress management and coping skills workshops to employees of a large corporation may help prevent the development of anxiety or depressive disorders and subsequent time lost from absenteeism. Likewise, counseling children of impending divorcees may moderate potential negative effects from parental separation.

Secondary prevention focuses on the early identification and treatment of an existing disease (Llewelyn & Kennedy, 2003) or mental health disorder. Recognizing a child's weaknesses in the classroom and timely diagnosis of attention deficit disorder may increase the likelihood that the child will receive necessary services to compensate or deal with those problems. Clinical psychologists aim to help clients minimize negative intrapersonal, social, and occupational consequences resulting from psychological stressors or disorders.

Crisis Management and Intervention

Crisis management and intervention may be necessary at the individual, familial, societal, or even national level. On a personal or family level, clients might experience a crisis caused by a sudden death or suicide in one's family; one's own self-mutilating behavior or drug overdose and presentation to an emergency room; or domestic violence, rape, sexual harassment, or natural disaster (e.g., fire or flood). Some of these events lead clients to appear in acute care settings, whereas others are recipients of outreach efforts by mental health professionals. Societal or national crises might include terrorism, hate crimes, bombing, open firearms in schools, or other similar events. Clinical psychologists who have specialized training in crisis management and trauma intervention would be called to action for these clients. The intervention or support given within the immediate time following the event is likely to differ greatly from therapy rendered months after the occurrence. Clinical psychologists with specialty in crisis and trauma intervention know when and how to intervene. The Association for Behavioral and Cognitive Therapies has Special Interest Groups (SIGs) that focus on crisis and trauma topics: Disaster and Trauma, and Child Maltreatment and Family Violence. The Society of Clinical Psychology (APA, Div.12) also has a section (7) for professionals interested in furthering knowledge, training, and clinical services for "Clinical Emergencies and Crises." Dr. Patricia Resick, a clinical psychologist, is renowned for her work in trauma and crisis response. An innovator and pioneer in this area, Dr. Resick is a past president of ABCT (2003 to 2004) among many other impressive accomplishments. She shares a sample of her workday and her perspectives on this area of research and practice in Box 2.5.

Box 2.5 Highlights of a Contemporary Psychologist

Patricia Resick, PhD

Dr. Resick, a Missouri licensed psychologist, obtained her doctoral degree at the University of Georgia. Her predoctoral internship training took place at the Middlesex Hospital Medical School in London, and at the VA in Charleston, South Carolina. Since her specialty in trauma response did not exist, her early experiences in the field came through volunteer work as one of the first rape crisis counselors in the United States. In this position, she was "on call" and went to the emergency room if a rape victim was brought to the hospital. Postdoctoral fellowships were not required at the time her degree was granted, so she took her first position as an assistant professor at the University of South Dakota. Dr. Resick shares her experiences and insights about her career working in trauma response.

Dr. Resick is an active member in the American Psychological Association, the Association for Behavioral and Cognitive Therapies, and the International Society for Traumatic Stress Studies. Her journals of choice include Journal of Clinical and Consulting Psychology, Journal of Applied Psychology, Behavior Therapy, Cognitive and Behavior Therapy, Journal of Traumatic Stress, *and* Psychology of Women Quarterly.

What Does Dr. Resick Like the Most and the Least about Her Area of Specialty?

I have never been bored by my area of specialty. When I began, nothing was known about the effects of trauma on symptoms and functioning, natural recovery or how to treat these symptoms. Over the past 3 decades, we have learned a great deal, but there is still much to be learned. I find the topic endlessly fascinating and believe that the topic is important.

Regarding my job position, I love the people I work with. They are smart, hardworking, full of ideas, and dedicated to quality research and clinical work. In my current position at the National Center for PTSD, I have the potential to have an impact on improving the quality of care given to those who have served our country and been harmed by this service, veterans with Posttraumatic Stress Disorder.

What I like the least is that the VA is a very large health care system and a very large bureaucracy. There are, what feels at times, unnecessary restrictions, rules, and repeated trainings. Sometimes it seems like I fill out so many productivity reports that it actually interferes with my productivity.

What Does Dr. Resick Find to Be Her Biggest Challenges in Her Specialty or Position?

Our biggest challenge is to continue producing quality research and excellent care when resources are becoming stretched under current national circumstances.

A Day in the Life of Dr. Resick

5:30 A.M.	Wake up.
7:00	Leave for work (my husband and I commute together and we listen to a book on tape).
8:00	Arrive at work.
8:15 to 9:00	Check and respond to overnight e-mail and prepare for meetings.
9:00 to 11:00	Work on a PowerPoint presentation for a conference later in the week (interrupted by e-mail, people dropping in to ask questions, and a phone call).
11:00 to 12:00	Take a conference call about a book I am coediting.
12:00 to 1:00	Eat lunch at desk while working on responding to e-mail.
1:00 to 2:00	Take conference call with other Directors of the National Center for PTSD. We talk about Director's recent visit to VA Central Office in Washington and our new efforts to respond to veterans with PTSD, outreach to military sites.
2:00 to 2:30	Junior staff member stops by to get some feedback on a revision of a grant proposal.
2:30 to 3:00	Check more e-mail and spend a few more minutes on presentation.
3:00 to 4:00	Discuss group therapy supervision by way of conference call. Therapists from two sites of the national center for PTSD are on the phone discussing the use of cognitive processing therapy (CPT) for their clients.
4:00 to 5:00	Discuss local CPT supervision. Staff members, postdoctoral fellows, and interns attend.
5:00 to 5:30	Check last e-mails and close up for the evening.
5:30 to 6:30	Drive home. We discuss our days and then listen to more book on tape.
6:30 to 7:30	Prepare and eat dinner.
8:00 to 9:00	Exercise.
9:00 to 11:00	Clean out and respond to e-mail while watching TV.
11:20	Bed.

As you can tell, I do a lot of my work on e-mail. I work on projects with many people at different sites, edit manuscripts, answer questions, file reports, and do many administrative duties. E-mail saves us from having as many meetings, but I read and respond to about 150 e-mails a day.

Dr. Resick Provides the Following Recommendations for Persons Interested in Joining Her Field

Before deciding, get some volunteer experience with traumatized populations such as at a rape crisis center, domestic violence program, or victim assistance agency. Make sure that you can handle hearing about traumatic events without being overwhelmed by the stories. If you think you might be interested in research, do the same—get some experience at your university, or at another research program.

At the national level, the American Psychological Association organized the Disaster Response Network (DRN) through local and regional psychological associations in 1992 to provide a mechanism through which psychologists can volunteer to respond to local and national disasters and other traumatic events. Through this organization, psychologists came together to aid Americans in coping with the Oklahoma City bombing, Hurricanes Andrew and Katrina, 9/11, and other events. This volunteer network provides pro bono services to communities affected by trauma, crisis, and disaster, and provides access to disaster mental health training for its members. The DRN collaborates with other organizations that serve the same purpose of providing support during these events. Its primary function is to participate in joint activities with the American Red Cross (APA, 2006).

Acute or Long-Term Intervention
Some may argue that acute and long-term intervention describes the bulk of what most clinical practitioners do, so therefore, they may not constitute specialties within the field. However, those who practice in emergency room settings, psychiatric hospitals, or partial programs would argue that the skills used in these settings differ from those used in others. In acute psychiatric settings, psychologists' practices might emphasize diagnostic skills, assessment and referral practices, and crisis intervention. Clinicians must write reports quickly and efficiently, and be skilled at working with a wide variety of clients and other health care professionals. Clients who use acute psychiatric services are diverse in mental health status, psychological problems, and other personal characteristics.

Long-term interventions could pertain to the practice of psychodynamically oriented psychotherapy, treatment of severely mentally ill or developmentally disabled individuals, or interventions geared toward persons with personality disorders, multiple clinical diagnoses, or pervasive difficulties. Given the movement in health care toward brief psychotherapy, a specialty in long-term interventions is least likely to classify many psychologists today. It is more likely that practice in a particular setting (e.g., psychiatric hospital) or with a particular population (e.g., schizophrenic patients) would dictate who uses long-term treatment interventions most often.

Rehabilitation
Rehabilitation psychology is operationally defined this way by Division 22:

> *[T]he study and application of psychosocial principles on behalf of persons who have physical, sensory, cognitive, developmental or emotional disabilities. . . . Rehabilitation psychologists work to foster personal and social growth of individuals with disabilities using a perspective that emphasizes the whole person and optimal use of assets. Rehabilitation psychologists pursue goals of improving rehabilitation practices and changing environments to broaden opportunities available to persons with disabilities in social relationships, employment, education, community and leisure activities. (Scherer et al., n.d.)*

Psychologists specializing in rehabilitation psychology with training in clinical psychology may work with spinal-cord injured patients, persons with Lou Gehrig's disease (amyotrophic lateral sclerosis), traumatic brain injuries, or developmental disabilities, as examples. Their practice may be in medical settings, academic institutions, political positions, administration, or community services. Careers in rehabilitation psychology can take the form of clinical practice, research, teaching, or administration. Again, many specialties of clinical psychology overlap in the populations addressed, services provided, or settings involved. For example, similarities between clinical health psychology and rehabilitation psychology are evident, although there are some distinct differences between these two fields in their missions.

Division 22 of APA is dedicated to rehabilitation psychology. The purpose of this division is to "bring together all APA members interested in the psychological aspects of disability and rehabilitation, to educate the public on issues related to disability and rehabilitation, and to develop high standards and practices for professional psychologists who work in this field" (APA, n.d.-c). In working toward this mission, clinical psychologists join colleagues from public policy psychology, developmental psychology, health psychology, community psychology, physiological psychology, and other fields. It is possible and likely that neuropsychologists and clinical health psychologists practice within the field of rehabilitation psychology.

Specialties by Therapeutic Modality

In most doctoral training programs in psychology, students are taught about psychopathology and well-being, and about individual assessment and treatment of children and adults. Assessment is a core component of clinical psychology that differentiates the abilities of psychologists from other mental health professionals. Some psychologists do evaluations and assessments as the staple practice of their profession. Assessments are critical to all treatment planning, but are often required for forensic purposes, educational assistance programs, supplemental insurance evaluations, disability determinations, and differential diagnosis, to name a few. Not all clinical psychologists maintain competency in objective and projective testing, and therefore, they, too, rely on colleagues with this expertise.

Doctoral-level elective courses in graduate programs often are available in group, family, or couples therapy although few doctoral programs in clinical psychology directly offer extensive specialty training in these treatment modalities. Psychologists establish their expertise in providing group, family, or couples therapy through some didactic training, but largely develop their skills through supervised clinical experience. Typically, psychologists who deliver treatment in groups, family, or couples therapy do so for specific populations in which they specialize: medically ill, relationship satisfaction, depressed individuals, and others.

Specialties by Settings

Graduate training is usually general in that it prepares graduates to practice psychology in a variety of settings for diverse populations. As many psychologists' careers develop, their competencies are likely to expand within their specialty area, and fade in others. Psychologists who practice in outpatient community mental health might have completely different philosophies about note-taking, client retention, and treatment planning than academic psychologists who typically treat volunteer clients as part of their research programs. A greater contrast might be found by comparing clinical psychologists who are employed in hospital settings with those who work in the forensic arena. These two groups of psychologists tend to have different knowledge bases, competencies, and practices. Thus, psychologists are likely to follow professional literature and conferences that pertain to their daily activities and are less likely to maintain awareness of distal practices. The following is a list of common settings in which clinical psychologists work: inpatient mental health facilities, outpatient private or community mental health practices, inpatient/outpatient medical settings (hospitals, physician or holistic health care practices), corporate settings, educational/academic settings, forensic settings, research settings, or political settings. The roles and functions of clinical psychologists in these settings differ extensively. Yet, science, theory, and practice are common themes in all subspecialties of clinical psychology and can be applied or explored in any of these settings.

Forensic Psychology

Clinical forensic psychologists dedicate their career to focusing on the interface between law and psychology, and the application of theory, principles, and research from both disciplines. Forensic psychologists work within prison systems, in private practices, academic settings, legal settings, or government. Educating the public and both professions about law and psychology is also a critical role for these specialists.

Assessment is often a core component of forensic psychology practices. Forensic psychologists may conduct assessments to evaluate child or senior-adult custody cases, to determine competency to stand trial or be one's own guardian, or to assess fitness for duty. Within the court system, these psychologists are involved in jury selection and providing expert testimony. The Federal

Bureau of Investigation (FBI) also seeks clinical forensic psychologists in profiling criminals, and carrying out governmental work requiring expertise in clinical psychology. Applied forensic intervention practice might involve psychotherapy for persons remanded to treatment by the courts, such as sex offenders or professionals with addictive disorders. In addition, forensic psychologists often become involved in helping with state and national legislation of licensure and other field-related policies.

Like other specialties in clinical psychology, forensic psychologists hold academic appointments and conduct research on topics interfacing psychology and the law. Psychologists with expertise in forensic psychology often teach ethics courses and specialty topics regarding decision making, law, and clinical populations. Training in forensic psychology is achieved either through specialty track training in a clinical psychology doctoral program, or by acquiring a doctorate in clinical psychology and a separate law degree. Some training programs offer joint degrees in law (JD) and psychology (PhD or PsyD). The APA Division 41 is the American Psychology-Law Society, and is dedicated to the "understanding of law and legal institutions, the education of psychologists in legal matters and law personnel in psychological matters, and the application of psychology in the legal system" (APA, n.d.-a). Dr. Samuel Knapp maintains a unique position in the field of forensic psychology, but the impact of his work reaches across all practice areas of psychology. Highlights of his daily practice are exhibited in Box 2.6.

Box 2.6 Highlights of a Contemporary Psychologist

Samuel Knapp, PhD

Dr. Knapp holds a master's degree in psychology from Indiana University of Pennsylvania (1976), and a doctorate from Lehigh University (1982). His predoctoral internship training was at the Lehigh University Counseling Center. Dr. Knapp's practice of forensic psychology is unique in that he works for the Pennsylvania State Board of Psychology.

Dr. Knapp is a member of numerous organizations: American Psychological Association—Fellow; Division 29 (Psychotherapy); Division 31 (State, Provincial, Territorial Psychological Associations); Division 36 (Religion and Psychology); Asian American Psychological Association; Pennsylvania Psychological Association (PPA); and Society for Ethics Across the Curriculum.

He attends annual conventions of the American Psychological Association and the Pennsylvania Psychological Association, and subscribes to numerous professional publications to stay abreast of the literature: Professional Psychology: Research and Practice; Ethics and Behavior; International Journal of Religion and Psychology; Ethics and Across the Curriculum; Scientific American: Mind; *and* Psychotherapy: Theory, Research, Practice, Training. *Dr. Knapp strives for balance in his life by walking his dogs, enjoying relaxing activities with his wife and his adult children, or reading science fiction.*

Here he shares some of his favorite aspects of his job, as well as its greatest challenges.

What Does Dr. Knapp Like the Most about His Area of Specialty?

The job responsibilities that I like most include direct consultation with members on legal and ethical issues, writing articles, and working with specific committees.

Consultation/Education/Committee Work

Some of the programs developed by the State Board of Psychology include the creation of an article bank of common professional and ethical problems encountered by our members that are placed on the PPA web site. We have also published a book, *Pennsylvania Law and Psychology* (now in its fourth edition) that graduate programs often use.

We have a comprehensive program of continuing education, especially in the areas of ethics and professional issues. These include small-group collaborative learning programs, small group interactive programs in specialties (such as psychologists working in child custody areas, in college counseling centers, with religious professionals, in prisons or correctional facilities), and a small group decision-making program where we have collected pre- and posttest data on the respondents and are currently analyzing the data to determine if the CE program led to an actual improvement in ethical decision-making ability. In addition to their didactic value, these small group workshops help psychologists get to know other psychologists and help create a sense of community.

With assistance of the PPA Ethics Committee, we have created a series of home studies on ethics that is designed to cover the range of common ethical issues encountered by psychologists. In my role, I also consult with PPA members by helping to problem-solve and answering over 2,000 e-mails and 1,000 phone calls annually regarding ethical questions or dilemmas.

The perspective we take in ethics education is "positive ethics," whereby we try to use ethics to help psychologists reach their highest level of performance, as opposed to merely avoiding disciplinary sanctions. I am fortunate to have a "gaggle" of colleagues who share this perspective and who write and teach with this orientation.

Articles

I also write articles for the *Pennsylvania Psychologist*. I try to make these articles down to earth and relevant for practicing psychologists. On my own time, I write articles for professional publications (I have about 100 peer-reviewed articles so far). Sometimes I adapt materials from my personal writing for publication in the *Pennsylvania Psychologist* and vice versa.

What Does Dr. Knapp Find to Be His Biggest Challenges in His Specialty or Position?

The biggest challenge is dealing with insurance and managed care companies. The patient protection laws are weak and there are many loopholes by which patients are denied the benefits they were promised in their contracts. I spend a lot of time with members (and also government agencies and insurers) on insurance and reimbursement issues.

Summary: Making the Right Choices for You

Clinical psychology, a specialty within the overarching field of psychology, also has many subspecialties. Clinical psychologies have a common interest in the integration of science, theory, and practice with the mission of advancing the field for the betterment of the profession and society. A key facet to all specialties within clinical psychology is the constant interchange of ideas between clinical science and the application of that science. Thus, scientist-practitioners, practitioner-scholars, educators, administrators, and all others who hold true to clinical psychology need to stay abreast of current literature, movements in the field, government and politics related to the specialty areas, and feedback from clients who use clinical psychology services and information.

In this chapter, the practices of clinical psychologists have been magnified to illustrate how specialized the subfields of clinical psychology have become. With so many choices, and so many overlapping missions and purposes, how do you make sense of it all? How do you choose a career path? If you are a doctoral student, you may soon be asked to name your dissertation topic, which will associate you with a particular expertise. In master's training, your clinical experiences and supervision during graduate school may dictate what jobs you can acquire when you complete your degree. Which way should you go? Which way should you turn on this winding and expansive road of clinical psychology? This summary can help you understand your options among the many subdisciplines described in this chapter.

First, by selecting your graduate training program, it is likely that you have chosen or will soon focus on a particular theoretical orientation from which you will learn to conceptualize clients, hypothesize about research questions, or interpret the thoughts and behaviors of persons you encounter. You have already begun to define your expertise in clinical psychology. As you progress through your training, many of your courses will delve into life span issues, psychopathology, ethics, cultural and individual diversity, research, and perhaps assessment and intervention. Which courses have excited you the most or you are most looking forward to? As you work through each course, use paper assignments as opportunities to learn about patient populations or practice settings that you may not be discussing at length in class. Or, if you are already a practitioner, think about the clients who have interested you the most or piqued your curiosity. What do you find yourself wanting to learn more about? This is where the specialties begin to develop.

For some, psychopathology in the form of severe mental illness or Axis II personalities is most fascinating. For others, no one patient population stands out—the diversity of mental health issues, perhaps among the general community, is most intriguing. One psychologist-in-training gears practicum and internship choices toward working exclusively with schizophrenic patients and creates a dissertation on a particular nuance of treatment for these individuals. For another trainee, the medical setting and working with physically ill individuals might seem to be her true calling. This individual might seek diversified training opportunities to prepare to work with a variety of patient populations in hospitals, outpatient, or primary care settings.

Thus far on this journey, perhaps you have selected a patient population or setting for practice. Within these choices lie many more. Do you have the stamina to make a difference in a crisis situation, to help minimize the impact of a traumatic event? Do you excel in establishing long-standing personal relationships that could aid in complicated long-term treatment of persons who may not otherwise trust people they encounter? Where do you think you are likely to make a difference?

Many psychologists develop expertise around particular techniques and skills, such as stress management and relaxation training, meditation practices, self-control strategies, cognitive restructuring, or contingency management. The skills you develop may also dictate the career you create for yourself. Some techniques and skill sets are geared more toward a specific setting than toward others, or toward particular patient populations rather than others. This is yet another aspect of training to consider.

As you reflect on this chapter, you may recognize that there are many ways to select your specialty areas within clinical psychology, if you choose to specialize at all. To come up with a plan for your future career, you may want to consider which modality (individual, couples, family, groups) of treatment you most enjoy. Is there a particular population (e.g., children, adults, senior adults, medical patients, underserved immigrants) to which you hope to dedicate your work? Are there certain human pathologies that you would most like to learn more about? Finally, in what setting do you believe you are most likely to thrive? You will find the answers to these questions in bits and pieces of your experiences along the way as you continue your training journey. If you attend to these guideposts along the way, you will find your direction. Remember that the answers are not mutually exclusive, nor are the careers in the subspecialties. Many paths run parallel or concurrent. Many psychologists have fulfilling careers by retaining generalist practitioner skills in assessment and intervention for the service of diagnostically and individually diverse clients. Clinical psychologists commonly hold teaching, administrative, clinical, and research positions in one stage of their career. The beauty of a career in clinical psychology is that your choices are almost endless!

Appendix: Professional Societies in Clinical Psychology

Academy of Psychological Clinical Science
http://w3.arizona.edu/-psych/apcs/apcs.html

American Academy of Pain Management
http://aapainmanage.org

American Association of Marriage and Family Therapy
http://aamft.org

American Board of Forensic Psychology
www.abfp.com

American Psychological Association (APA)
http://apa.org

American Psychological Society
www.psychologicalscience/org

Association for Behavioral and Cognitive Therapies
www.aabt.org

Association of Black Psychologists
http://admin@abpsi.org

Association for Death Education and Counseling
www.adec.org

Association for the Psychotherapy of Schizophrenia
www.schizophrenia-help.com/menu.html

Cognitive Neuroscience Society
www.cogneurosociety.org

Council of Teachers of Undergraduate Psychology
www.indiana.edu/-iuepsyc/CTUP.html

Eating Disorders Association
http://edauk.com

Federation of Behavioral, Psychological and Cognitive Sciences
www.am.org/federation

International Association of Applied Psychology
www.iaapsy.org

International Association for Cross-Cultural Psychology
www.fit.edu/CampusLife/clubs-org/iaccp

International Society for the Study of Dissociation
www.issd.org

International Society on Infant Studies
www.isisweb.org

National Association of Cognitive and Behavioral Therapists
http://nacbt.org

National Mental Health Association
http://nmha.org

Society for Personality and Social Psychology
www.spsp.org

Society for Research in Child Development
www.srcd.org

Society for the Teaching of Psychology
http://teachpsych.lemoyne.edu/teachpsych/div/divindex.html

Working with Cultural Diversity

3

Chapter

We live in a society that comprises many cultural elements, yet our clinical assumptions are often based on information from limited subgroups or limited contexts. What we know about human behavior frequently lacks a broad cultural framework. To be effective with an increasingly diverse population, our clinical interventions need to be grounded in cultural dynamics. This begins with sensitivity to culture as a primary psychological and social variable. By increasing our consciousness and studying the workings of culture, we can open the door to deeper understanding and more effective interventions in our pluralistic society.

Learning Objectives

At the end of this chapter, the reader should be able to:

- Understand the importance of cultural context.
- Describe current patterns and future trends among major population groups.
- Understand common terminology related to culture, ethnicity, and diversity.
- Recognize key cognitive and social processes that shape cultural dynamics.
- Understand the ways that culture is incorporated into personal identity.
- Describe the ethical foundations of culturally competent practice.
- List four important action strategies for building cultural competence.

A clinical case example illustrates various points throughout the chapter.

Clinical Example: Doris (Vignette 1)

Doris is a 45-year-old African American woman who is married, has two children, and holds an administrative position in a large academic institution. Despite a demanding schedule, her lifestyle is sedentary, and she is not involved in any systematic form of exercise. Although her employer has a sophisticated employee wellness program that includes various opportunities for health improvements and even financial incentives for wellness efforts, she does not take advantage of these options. In fact, Doris seems to avoid attending to her health. She went for a medical checkup a few years ago only because persistent headaches were interfering with her work. In this evaluation, it was discovered that she had hypertension (high blood pressure) and Type II (adult onset) diabetes.

Her physician prescribed antihypertensive medication and dietary management of the diabetes. The doctor noted several important health risks in addition to her lack of exercise: a high fat diet; smoking; a family history of hypertension and heart disease; and a body mass index (BMI—a measure of her overall body weight in proportion to her height) greater than 30, classifying her as obese. He encouraged her to stop smoking and lose weight, and insisted that she have a follow-up consultation with a diabetes management clinic.

Doris initially complied with taking the antihypertensive medication, but she was inconsistent in adhering to the medication regimen. She also complied with the recommendation for the diabetes clinic consult. During her first visit, she talked briefly with a diabetes health care team that included a physician, a nurse practitioner, a nutritionist, a social worker, and a psychologist. They encouraged her to begin regular exercise, to develop a plan for smoking cessation, to modify her diet according to the guidelines offered by the nutritionist, and to return for regular follow-up visits at the diabetes clinic to monitor her progress. Doris appreciated their kindly manner, but did not follow through on any of their suggestions, and did not keep any follow-up appointments.

Can you suggest why Doris made the two office visits but did not engage in the recommended behavioral changes or follow-up visits? Do you think that any aspect of culture might have played a role in this outcome? We discuss Doris periodically throughout the chapter to illustrate the interaction between culture, clinical and behavioral problems, and the methods and strategies of intervention.

Cultural Competence as Fundamental Practice

In the revisions of the APA Ethics Code for psychologists published in 2002, the notion of competence in understanding and working with cultural differences in both clinical and research settings went from aspiration to a specifically detailed standard for expected professional conduct (APA, 2002, 2.01 [b]). This standard recognizes that an understanding of factors associated with age, gender, gender identity, race, ethnicity, culture, national origin, religion, sexual orientation, disability, language, or socioeconomic status may be essential for effective implementation of service or research. Other ethical principles emphasize that respect for others' rights and dignity (APA, 2002, Principle E), justice and equality of service to all persons (Principle D), and the safeguarding of the rights and welfare of those directly and indirectly affected by our work (Principle A) are essential aspirations for all professional decisions and judgments in the field of psychology.

Understanding cultural context should not be marginalized as an optional or special interest pursuit, but instead valued as a basic component of professional competence. Cultural context is important in clinical work because cultural variables affect the validity of assessment and diagnosis, the applicability of research results, the quality of a therapeutic alliance, the development of a treatment plan, and the overall effectiveness of treatment delivered. Traditional psychological services are often inadequate for members of ethnic minority groups, particularly in terms of cultural and linguistic fit (S. Sue, 1998). At the same time, we have a growing multiethnic population in the United States (Aponte & Crouch, 2000; U.S. Census Bureau, 2001).

The notion of cultural competence incorporates knowledge, skills, and attitudes. S. Sue (1998) defines cultural competence as "the belief that people should not only appreciate and recognize other cultural groups, but be able to effectively work with them" (p. 440). In this chapter, we cover population trends, terminology, and cultural processes to help you recognize differences, and summarize some key strategies for working effectively with cultural variables in a clinical setting.

The Diverse People of the United States

The people of the United States are becoming an increasingly varied population in terms of ethnic and cultural heritage (see Figure 3.1). Demographic trends based on the population composition as of the 2000 U.S. Census predict that by the middle of this century (2050), the Caucasian majority will shrink to 50%, with other racial/ethnic groups comprising the remaining 50% in varying degrees. Currently, approximately 67% of the U.S. population is identified as White. Although categories overlap to some extent as individuals may report

Figure 3.1

United States Demographic Composition in 2000

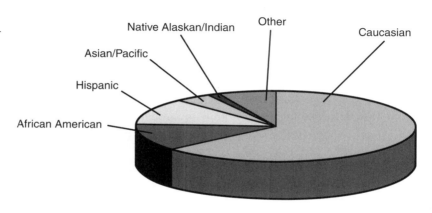

more than one racial affiliation, the breakdown of the remaining 33% is as follows: 13% African American, 13% Hispanic, 4.5% Asian/Pacific Islander, 1.5% American Indian or Alaskan Native, and 7% of some other race (APA, 2003; U.S. Census Bureau, 2001). There also appears to be an increasing birthrate of biracial individuals, as 42% of those who endorsed more than one race in the 2000 census were under the age of 18.

Historically, the United States has been a country with a significant White majority, with African Americans comprising the largest minority, and other racial/ethnic groups having much smaller presence. Now, there is greater diversity, and in the future we can expect even more heterogeneity among the people. Beyond increasing racial and ethnic variance, we also expect more age variance, as longevity increases. Now, approximately 12% of the population is age 65 or older, but that is expected to grow to 21% by mid-century. There will also be a corresponding increase in the oldest ages, with those 85 and beyond comprising 5% of the population, compared with 1.5% as of the year 2000 (Armas, 2004, as cited in "Whites' Majority Steadily Shrinking," 2004).

Clinical science and practice has significant challenges ahead in understanding and relating to diverse clinical populations and appreciating the possible social and personal implications of these broad cultural shifts. We can reasonably anticipate that tensions, challenges, and opportunities will be embedded in this increasingly heterogeneous society. The environment as we now know it will be significantly changed, although we cannot fully predict the impact of those changes. Clinicians now entering the field, including those who will complete their training in the years between 2010 and 2020, will be the providers working with this changing population over the bulk of their career as we progress toward the predicted patterns of 2050. Major population trends to anticipate are summarized in Table 3.1.

As the population changes, we may also see corresponding shifts in the clinical problems that precipitate a referral to psychological treatment. This may be particularly true for problems that disproportionately affect certain groups. There are many potential examples of problems associated with population groups such as persons who are elderly, disabled, homeless, and gay/lesbian. Whether these problems are adequately conceptualized and treated depends in part on the social impact of these concerns and the visible advocacy on behalf of the minority group affected. Culturally sensitive research can help us to pinpoint relevant factors that influence the onset, maintenance, or out-

Table 3.1 **Major Demographic Trends Expected between 2010 and 2050**

- The very elderly (over 85) will more than double in number.
- Those over age 65 will grow to more than 20% of the population.
- A young biracial cohort will contribute to significant growth in ethnically blended cultures.
- The Caucasian majority will continue to shrink.
- Other racial/ethnic groups will increase in varying degrees.

come of pressing clinical and behavioral problems, and thus increase the effectiveness of our interventions.

Common Terminology

Defining terms and concepts is important in establishing a systematic approach for training, research, and development of a common understanding (see Table 3.2). As outlined in the APA Multicultural Guidelines (2003), the terms of culture, race, ethnicity, multiculturalism, and diversity should be delineated for clear and consistent use. *Diversity* is the most encompassing term, referring to the multiple aspects of a person's social identity—race, ethnicity, language, sexual orientation, gender, age, disability, economic status, education, religious/spiritual affiliation, and other social roles. When we describe these aspects of a person's social identity, we are describing the individual's social diversity. The term *multiculturalism* is often used interchangeably with diversity to refer to the dimensions relevant to identity. In the APA Guidelines, however, the term is used precisely and refers to interactions between racial or ethnic groups in the United States. In this chapter, we follow this distinction and discuss the *diverse* aspects of individual clients and encourage *multicultural* experiences as a means of increasing cultural competence.

Although the term *race* is formally defined as a genealogical line (*American Heritage*, 1994), psychological observers have noted that biological racial categories and phenotypic characteristics have more within-group variation than

Table 3.2 **Common Terminology for Working with Diversity**

Term	Meaning
Diversity	Multiple aspects of personal/social identity (race, ethnicity, language, sexual orientation, gender, age, disability, economic status, education, religious/spiritual orientation, social roles)
Multicultural	Variables relevant to personal/social identity; interchangeable with diversity
Race/ethnicity	Group heritage of common and distinctive features; consensual definition lacking
Ethnocentricism	Belief in superiority of one ethnic group, usually one's own
Culture	Belief systems and value orientations that shape a way of living through norms, practices, customs, organizations, psychological processes, and social institutions
Psychological acculturation	Learning the beliefs, values, and practices that characterize a new culture and determining a personal degree of acceptance or identification

between-group variation, and that a consensual definition of race does not exist (Helms & Cook, 1999). A definition of race within the field of psychology is a socially constructed category to which individuals are assigned on the basis of physical characteristics such as skin color (APA, 2003). Similarly, *ethnicity* does not have a consensus definition. APA Guidelines refer to ethnicity as "the acceptance of the group mores and practices of one's culture of origin and the concomitant sense of belonging," (p. 380). The Guidelines also note that individuals with multiple ethnic identities may operate with different salience at different times. Similarly, the *American Heritage Dictionary* (1994) defines "ethnic" as a group heritage of common and distinctive racial, national, religious, linguistic, or cultural features. Of note in this context is the common term *ethnocentricism,* which is the belief in the superiority of one's own ethnic or other culturally based group compared with other ethnic or other culturally based groups.

Finally, *culture* is defined as the belief systems and value orientations that influence customs, norms, practices, psychological processes, organizations, and social institutions (APA, 2003, p. 380). Culture includes a way of living and viewing the rest of the world that is influenced and shaped by historical, economic, ecological, and political forces. As Triandis (1995) aptly states, "Culture is to society what memory is to the person" (p. 341). It specifies ways to think about self and social behavior that produce functional designs for living. As Kaschak (1992) points out, culture includes the rules for perception and organization of experiences, both interpersonal, and intrapersonal. Thus, the meaning of any experience or practice is embedded within the context of culture. Cultural socialization helps to determine the salience of experiences related to the *private* self (thoughts related to traits, states, or actions of oneself, or what "I" see); the *public* self (thoughts related to the view of oneself from a generalized other or what "they" see of me); or the *collective* self (thoughts about what a group of specific others think, such as what "the family" or "my colleagues" think of me). Persons raised in the culture of East Asia, for example, will pay more attention and think more often of their collective self than people with a European or North American background (Triandis, 1995).

Although there are many variables within a culture, all individuals have a cultural heritage, and an ongoing cultural identity. A person who has contact with another culture may experience *psychological acculturation,* or the internal modification of beliefs, values, and other aspects of behavior as a result of this interaction. This modification is typically an uneven process where beliefs or values and behaviors do not shift in a uniform manner, but rather through a series of interactions, highly influenced by acculturation attitudes and strategies (Berry, 1995). Both self and culture are dynamic, ever-changing across time and different environments, moving toward complexity when acculturation is effective, and shifting back toward simplification when complexity becomes very high or unworkable (Triandis, 1995).

An appreciation of diversity will help us better understand individual differences, both within and between groups. Culture is a mechanism that shapes individual and group identity by systematizing the beliefs and values that organize and direct perceptions, thoughts, actions, and indeed the very definition of self and reality for its constituents. Cultural belief systems, value orientation, and common practices are, in turn, shaped by history, politics, economics, and the interaction of all these forces. As individuals are exposed to and become involved with different groups, they will likely experience psychological acculturation, where they develop some understanding and accept or adopt characteristics of the new group, including the salience of a private, public, or collective self. Multicultural experiences thus contribute to the diverse aspects of anyone's social identity. To be effective as clinicians, educators, and scientists, we need to be familiar with these diverse aspects of identity (APA, 2000a). Both race and ethnicity are socially constructed ways of grouping large numbers of people. In reality, most racial or ethnic categories incorporate many individual differences within the group, so that we must use great caution in considering any cultural generalizations on this basis. It is relevant, however, to consider racial and ethnic identity in a context of cultural diversity (Table 3.2).

Attunement to Cultural Diversity in Clinical Context

Many current resources emphasize two primary perspectives on culture in the context of clinical practice: knowledge of one's own cultural heritage and varying social identities, and knowledge of other cultures (APA, 2003, p. 378; see also Hansen, Pepitone-Arreola-Rockwell, & Greene, 2000; Hays, 2001). An understanding of yourself provides grounding in internal awareness of culture and its influence on perceptions and values, as well as recognition of your stimulus value to others and the potential limitations or even biases in working with differing cultures. Knowledge of other cultures can reduce limitations or potential biases although this is a volitional process and will not happen automatically with a bit of information or slight exposure.

Ask yourself to think about at least one cultural institution and its practices that you believe had a significant impact on your childhood or adolescence. Maybe you will think about growing up in a military family and how that affiliation affected your geographic mobility and your sense of patriotism and service. Or you might think about your ethnic background and how your family connected with various social activities and events associated with this ethnicity. Maybe you continue to treasure and practice these traditions. Perhaps the educational system was a prominent aspect of your cultural development, and you spent long hours studying to achieve academic success. You worried about your performance, but your excellent grades were highly rewarded, and your family made a major fuss over your graduation.

Do you think that your experiences with this particular cultural institution and its practices fostered your sense of belonging and self-esteem, or did they lead you to question your place or value in the broader society? How did these experiences shape the person that you know yourself to be today? Now ask yourself to consider just how this particular experience might affect your reactions to someone with a different personal history and different values. If you are devoted to your extended family and your client shrugs off a family reunion as being "unimportant and too much trouble," would you label that person as schizoid or interpersonally impaired? If you have a close involvement with a religious institution, do you tend to view others with casual religious practices as having poorly formed character? How might your own experiences affect the way that you filter or interpret someone else's "story" that is either similar or different from your own?

Our attunement to cultural diversity begins with the recognition that all people are multicultural, all interactions are cross-cultural, and all experience is perceived from a cultural perspective (APA, 2003). In the clinical setting, the patient's culture can influence the development and maintenance of the presenting problem, how the therapist perceives the problem, how the patient copes, assets and barriers that will influence treatment, and the degree of collaboration and rapport. To further understand how culture affects our judgments and interpersonal interactions, let's take a closer look at the psychological and social processes that are relevant to cultural dynamics.

Cognitive and Social Processes

A basic psychological process in how we organize information about our world and experience is by reducing information into manageable chunks. The application of this cognitive process to social interactions was originally conceptualized by Allport (1954) in his social categorization theory. To make sense out of a highly complex and dynamic social world, people use the normal process of information chunking to create categories into which they can sort people. Then they associate various characteristics, preferences, and tendencies with particular categories and groups. Categorization appears to be an automatic, largely nonvolitional process that serves several useful purposes, including fast and efficient use of cognitive resources (Fiske, 1998), and a means by which we locate and define ourselves within a complex social landscape (J. Turner, 1987). However, the advantages of speed and orientation are often offset by significant issues of accuracy and notable resistance to change.

Easily noticeable characteristics, especially those that are visible or physical features of the person quickly create summary impressions. The summary impression is then perceived as predominant or prototypic aspects of the category, forming a stereotype (Wade & Tavris, 2000; Worchel, 1999). This stereotype will persist, even when disconfirming information is available (Kunda & Thagard, 1996). Behavior is then interpreted and judged through the filter of the stereotype, further reinforcing the cognitive aspects of the existing category, particularly when there is some motivation to confirm the stereotype (Kunda & Sinclair, 1999). Arbitrary inferences may occur, especially concerning motivations of the categorized person, even if these inferences are inaccurate for one, some, or most people or situations.

Stereotyping effects typically refer to judging an individual on the basis of an expectation for the group or category, such that the person is assimilated into category membership (Biernat, 2003). Exceptionally tall people are frequently assumed to have both skill and passion for playing the game of basketball. If you attend a national basketball tournament or a professional game, where the players indeed do have skill and passion, you will also likely notice the remarkable height among this group. A survey of tall high school seniors would probably yield a wide range of interest, motivation, and skill concerning basketball. Yet most of those tall seniors would probably be familiar with the basketball stereotype, having been routinely asked about their interest or involvement in the sport.

Biernat (2003) further explores how stereotypes affect judgments in other ways, including shifting subjective standards when behavior contrasts with stereotyped expectations. Staying with our basketball example, this shift based on category stereotypes would occur when a relatively small player receives surprised congratulations for scoring a three-point shot, because he is "pretty good for a short guy." The subjective judgment of "good" is shaped by the contrast with the stereotyped expectation that skillful basketball players are exceptionally tall. According to Biernat, these stereotypic effects have a potentially significant impact on the standards to which stereotyped groups are held, the evaluations they receive, and the behaviors that others display toward them. Consider further how different cultural dimensions may interact in applying stereotypes. Persons of color, especially African Americans, may be stereotyped as superior at basketball. Women, however, are stereotyped as less athletic than men. Thus, if one imagines a superior basketball player, chances are—based on stereotypes—that an image of a tall, African American male would come to mind. When considering potential interests or talents of a petite Asian woman, stereotypes could affect our judgments to the extent that we might put basketball at the end of a long list of options, if we even considered it at all.

An important social aspect of the categorization process is the separating of categories into in-groups and out-groups (Fiske, 1998; Hornsey & Hogg, 2000; Tajfel & Turner, 1986; J. Turner, Brown, & Tajfel, 1979). In identifying with different social groups to create an internal social identity and corresponding sense of place and position in the world, we automatically sort social groups into categories of "us" and "them." This identification can happen easily and quickly, often on the basis of visible group membership characteristics (Atkinson & Hackett, 1995; D. W. Sue & Sue, 1999) and as soon as it does, predictable biases become operative (Wade & Tavris, 2000). First, there is a tendency to give favor to our in-group over the out-group. Second, we tend to exaggerate differences between groups and similarities within our group and to magnify the consistency of those relationships (e.g., "we" are *better and very different* from "them," and we are consistently better, while they are consistently inferior; Fiske, 1998; Hewstone, Rubin, & Willis, 2002). Reactions to our in-group versus an out-group consistently show greater trust, more cooperation, greater generosity, and higher value (Brewer & Brown, 1998; Hewstone et al., 2002). The differences may not be as significant or consistent as we think they are, but our reactions tend to be highly consistent with our judgments.

Strong in-group affiliation has been associated with a greater degree of prejudice toward outsiders (Swim & Mallett, 2002), a serious concern when the distribution of power and resources is considered (APA Guidelines, 2003). In-group affiliation is strengthened in competitive situations, but with notable psychological risks. Competition can make people feel insecure and anxious, even if they are winning, and angry and frustrated if they lose. It can decrease work motivation, and promote jealousy and hostility toward rivals (Wade & Tavris, 2000). In-group members of a majority group may legitimize discrimination toward out-group members of a minority group on the basis of perceived differences that are often simply a function of the categorical split between the groups. Prejudice, a negative stereotype with strong associated affect, will likely increase when people worry about their incomes and stability of their communities and perceive themselves to be in direct competition with another group for economic resources.

Implications, Risks, and Risk Management

Social categorization has profound implications, particularly in competitive situations. We know that categorization is a normal cognitive process and an aspect of the important executive function of constructed judgment. As clinicians and researchers, we learn critical thinking skills that emphasize the importance of both confirming and disconfirming information when forming judgments about individuals or groups. However, the human interactions brought into therapy by our clients are not typically characterized by careful, critical thought processes. Even having a conscious endorsement of egalitarian beliefs does not necessarily mean that one is free from unconscious stereotypes about groups (Greenwald & Banaji, 1995). Our challenge is to bring a deliberate thought process into the clinical interaction so that we can more fully recognize the influences of social categorization within the client's struggles and attempts at solution.

We all have multiple social identities, some visible and others more private. We all make judgments and inferences on the basis of categories of social identity, especially the most visible ones. And we are all influenced by the in-group/out-group categorization process. As noted by APA (2003, p. 385) "membership in one group helps to shape perceptions not only of one's own group but also of other groups. The links between those perceptions and attitudes are loyalty to and valuing of one's own group and devaluing the other group." Further, persons of racial or ethnic minority background comprise an out-group for most psychologists (APA Guidelines, 2003). Issues of competition, particularly for vital resources, can trigger a hazardous situation of polarization based on group membership, increasing the possibility of prejudice and discrimination.

A starting point for mitigating the risks of social categorization in clinical situations is the clinician's own commitment to control automatic biases. This is possible by following professional recommendations to establish motivation, information, and appropriate mood (APA Guidelines, 2003; Fiske, 1998). "Color-blind" approaches that minimize or ignore group differences have been found to be ineffective and may increase stereotypes or perpetuate intergroup inequalities (Brewer & Brown, 1998; Macrae & Bodenhausen, 2000; Wolsko, Park, Judd, & Wittenbrink, 2000). Instead, "ongoing development of one's personal and cross-cultural awareness, knowledge, and skills is recommended," (APA Guidelines, 2003, p. 384). Awareness of attitudes and values is the first step, especially awareness of attitudes of preference for within-group similarity, and negative perceptions of out-group members. Exposure to other groups is important if it includes empathy and recognition of the different perspectives (Finlay & Stephan, 2000; Galinsky & Moskowitz, 2000; Pettigrew, 1998) and actively increases tolerance and trust of racial and ethnic groups (J. Greenberg et al., 1992; R. M. Kramer, 1999) while directly recategorizing "us versus them" to a concept of "we" (Gaertner & Dovidio, 2000).

Greater knowledge of and contact with different cultural groups in a context of empathy, understanding, and valuing should also include appreciating what it is like to be a member of a culturally stigmatized group (Crocker, Major, & Steele, 1998; Major, Quinton, & McCoy, in press). External events such as acts of prejudice and discrimination trigger internal emotional and cognitive processing of these experiences, activating schema for value and social status. These events might occur episodically, randomly, or predictably, and without regard to whether they are recognized as discrimination by the target, or by observers such as a therapist.

Discrimination is real, yet it is seldom "as real" to those for whom it is an infrequent or distant event. Members of stigmatized groups live with the specter of stereotype threat, or the constant possibility that their behavior will be found consistent with negative stereotypes, regardless of the accuracy of this judgment. Further, the broader cultural hierarchy is an inescapable stress, in the sense that individual members cannot change the position of their own stigmatized group, and they cannot deny that a social hierarchy exists.

Clinical Example: Doris (Vignette 2)

Doris has some notable health risks and problems. Is it possible that in-group and out-group dynamics affected Doris' response to the health care professionals?

As a member of a minority group and a person with only a high school education, Doris may have been intimidated by the all-Caucasian, highly educated and powerful medical team. As an African American, Doris is a member of a group that, for a variety of reasons, is apprehensive about placing trust in the health care system. The brief and directive recommendations of the team, although well-intentioned, implied a lack of understanding or concern for Doris and her particular frame of reference. She knows many people in her community who smoke and have hypertension, diabetes, and obesity, and thus she does not grasp the urgency of her health risks. It is easier to dismiss the medical recommendations that come from sources she does not necessarily trust, especially when she has much anecdotal evidence that people live with these problems all around her and nothing bad

seems to be happening to them. Doris might be more attuned to the perspective of her collective self (what her family and community think of her) than to her private self (what she thinks and feels) or to her public self (what "they" think she should do), but the team appealed mainly to her private self.

The medical team, on the other hand, may have assumed that Doris did not care about her size or health and was unwilling to change. They may have exaggerated her acceptance of her obesity and diabetes based on a stereotype, since both conditions are so prevalent in her African American cohort (www.cdc .gov). Given limited resources (their time), they may have automatically decided to discharge her with a few quick recommendations to preserve the resources for other patients who might accept guidance more readily.

How could the team have been more effective? We return to the discussion of Doris in subsequent sections on effective strategies for practice.

Individuals in a Cultural Context

Some theoretical models of identity development specific to racial and ethnic minority groups have emphasized conceptualization of stages of cultural integration (see Atkinson, Morten, & Sue, 1998; Berry & Sam, 1997; Helms, 1990; Parham, 2001; Ruiz, 1990). In contrast to members of a majority group whose positive identification with their culture may develop automatically, members of racial and ethnic minority groups have a more challenging psychological acculturation. They may initially value other groups (the dominant culture) and devalue their own culture. In further development, they may move to valuing their own group and separating from the dominant culture. Eventually there may be some integration of value for both groups, with a sense of belonging to the minority group. When resolution of these issues is insufficient, members may become estranged or marginalized from one or both groups.

Although other perspectives present alternatives to a stage model of minority identity (e.g., Oetting & Beauvais, 1990–1991; Oyserman, Gant, & Ager, 1995; Thompson & Carter, 1997), it is essential to recognize that cultural forces affect identity development, and in turn influence beliefs, emotions, behavior, interaction styles, coping strategies, and further experiences within a person's social environment. Beginning with the genes and the socialization passed along by parents, the initial bricks in the wall of identity are marked by cultural features and references (Worchel, 1999). This cultural identity is an ever-changing process.

Other situational social factors may influence the prominence of a cultural identity at any given point as well. The power, prestige, and success of the group, the perception of costs and benefits associated with group membership, and the opportunity to connect with an orderly and well-defined set of social practices may increase the salience or importance of a cultural identity, particularly if a person is experiencing a crisis or some major life event (Worchel, 1999). In negotiating the turbulent experience of marital dissolution, a common response is to increase affiliation with a religious organization or church, often the church associated with one's upbringing. When "Mrs. Jones" is no longer Mrs. Jones, at least she knows she's still a Christian, and can count on the support of her "faith family." An apt metaphor is offered by Worchel (1999) to describe the stabilizing functions of cultural identity. "Our ethnic identity, then, lies like a dog, sleeping by the hearth, waiting to spring up when a personal or collective crisis confronts us" (p. 46). Further, turning to the ethnic group during times of transition or personal crisis ensures that there will always be someone to preserve the continuity of the group. Being a member of a cultural group provides security and protection, particularly if it is a dominant group.

Various personality theorists have described normal personal development as the striving to be individual, special, and independent along with striving to be included within a group and to have a secure social identity or sense of belonging (see, e.g., Brewer, 1991). Integrating or balancing one's sense of being unique as well as being part of a social order is certainly influenced by the larger culture or social environment and how personal identity is constructed within the culture. Both types of striving, to be an individual and to belong to a social group can be expected but will likely vary in the framework of relevant cultural influences.

Although the construct of culture is admittedly a fuzzy one, it can be related to the specific psychological functioning of the individual through specific cultural themes or syndromes. In particular, the cultural theme of *individualism-collectivism* has been successful in describing systematic cultural variations that affect individual behavior, attitudes, norms, values, goals, family structure, and sense of self (Triandis, 1996; Vandello & Cohen, 1999).

Western culture, including the United States, is largely individualistic; it values separate persons whose identity is based on their personal attributes or accomplishments: what they do. People are motivated to develop attributes that make them distinct and special, such as intelligence, beauty, talents, or skills. Entry into social relationships or groups is often based on the person's unique or special contributions. Competition takes place between individuals, and affiliation or acceptance into a group is based on individual merit.

In individualistic cultures, in-groups validate the self-worth of their members and to some extent meet social needs, but individuals try to minimize or control their dependence on the in-group. The view of self emphasized is that of private experiences and thoughts related to being a solo entity. Your happiness is not dependent on what "they" think of you, but rather on being true to your own voice. Personal comfort, satisfaction, and achievement are important, and a lack of inner harmony is viewed as problematic. Both inner disharmony or confusion and a lack of distinction may be sources of anxiety or despair. Individualism may allow loose boundaries for social identity, with people moving in and out of groups relatively easily, meeting new people, forming or disbanding relationships as needed, and making personal choices about which affiliations to select and which to discard. However, many options for group involvement can lead to confusion and a sense of alienation. Individualistic cultures exchange compliments frequently, and emphasize fairness and equity in structuring interactions. Individualists also tend to see themselves as having access or relative proximity to sources of power.

In contrast, more collectivist cultures of the East and traditional cultures of Africa and Latin America emphasize external relationships such group membership and socialization to the expectations of either a specific group or the generalized other. The role that one has within a group, and how well one serves the group in that role is key to personal identity, rather than unique personal achievements or interests.

The view of self is a collective one, characterized by perceived appraisals from the perspective of significant others. The family is usually the most important in-group, but coworkers, religious affiliates, or scientific colleagues may also form important in-groups. Although the definition of the in-group may shift, collectivist cultures are organized to protect the integrity of the in-groups, and they may be unwilling to respect or cooperate with members of an out-group. Boundaries between in-groups and out-groups may be clear and unyielding. Social behavior is more affected by the in-group versus out-group distinction within collectivist cultures, particularly in small, tight in-groups such as the family, and when the in-group norms are highly associated with important rewards and punishments (e.g., a paycheck).

Anxiety is caused by in-group disharmony or public conduct that observers perceive as improper. Competition may be fierce, but it takes place between groups such as families. Avoidance of conflict helps to maintain in-group harmony, and self-denial or suppression may be used to assist conformity. Those in collective cultures not only will do what is expected even if it is noxious, but will adjust their perceptions to see burdens as enjoyable or advantageous. Long hours may be spent cooking special foods for a family gathering, even when the cook dislikes the food or has other pressing tasks; yet this effort may be viewed as pleasant and worthwhile rather than tedious. Teens or other family members may be expected to serve the needs of the family, perhaps by providing child care or working in a family business, even if it interferes with their personal plans or preferences. In-groups may also perceive their own norms as universally valid, a form of ethnocentricism (Triandis, 1995).

The individualism-collectivism theme is more than just tradition, as these varying dimensions likely serve important social functions for stabilizing and preserving a culture under certain conditions. Both individualist and collectivist elements are present in all cultures, but in different combinations (Vandello & Cohen, 1999). Findings by Triandis (1996), indicate that when the society is affluent, heterogeneous in its people, and complex in offering a multiplicity of choices, then individualism will be higher. Loose boundaries and rules are functional and serve to minimize friction between members, where the context of persons and options is more elaborate or diverse. When a society has fewer resources, is more homogeneous, has less social mobility or choices available, or needs members to be interdependent to survive or live in close proximity, then norms will be more tightly imposed. Secure boundaries and rules also serve to minimize friction between members when options are limited.

Thus, the overall context of the culture plays an important role in how individual members design a balance between internal experience, personal identity, and their external involvements and social identity. Without an understanding of this critical context, we run the risk of overemphasizing individualistic assumptions and failing to appreciate social perspective as an operative and functional basis of personal identity. Our increasingly diverse patient populations will include those whose personal identity is more *allocentric* than *idiocentric,* terms that refer to individuals who carry the values of a culture of collectivism versus individualism (Triandis, 1995).

Persons who are allocentric may be high on conformity and emphasize interdependence, empathy, and respect among in-group members (Marin & Marin, 1991). Behavioral intentions of persons who are allocentric are likely to be most affected by cognitions that relate to the benefit of their culture. A study of Hispanic (collectivist culture) versus non-Hispanic (individualistic culture) persons revealed notable between-group differences in attitudes that could affect smoking cessation. Allocentric persons cared more about how smoking would affect the health of others, set a bad example for children, or bother others with bad smells. Individualistic persons, on the other hand, were more concerned with the physiological effects of withdrawal from cigarettes (Marin, Marin, Otero-Sabogal, Sabogal, & Perez-Stable, 1987).

Clinical Example: Doris (Vignette 3)

As an African American and a highly committed member of her church, Doris is likely to be more allocentric, evaluating herself and her experiences from the perspective of others in her affiliated groups. She takes her role as a teacher in the church very seriously and wants to do whatever is needed to serve this community. It may be culturally consistent for her to subordinate her personal goals to the needs and directives of her community and the community leaders.

These observations suggest that Doris might be more responsive to considering how her smoking negatively impacts those in her environment, as opposed to emphasizing only the effects on her personal health and comfort. She might be concerned about the cost of smoking as it affects her family budget or her contributions to the church, and she might worry about offending her pastor with smoke-breath at the Wednesday night fellowship dinner. She might also be especially reluctant to give up the camaraderie of taking a smoke break with her friends and colleagues. These hypotheses, though, need to be tested for relevance by discussion and exploration with Doris.

Discussion Exercise

As an exercise in considering how cultural context informs our hypotheses about patient beliefs, norms, expectations, sources of conflict and possible solutions, consider the following examples of two persons going through an experience of separation and divorce after 8 years of marriage, with no children involved.

The first patient, Ms. A, has a master's degree and a successful career as a nurse administrator. She initiated separation and divorce proceedings due to her spouse's irresponsible financial behavior, including gambling debts, and a lack of sexual intimacy. Ms. A attributes the low sexual intimacy to her own long-harbored questions about her sexual orientation, but she mostly avoids thinking about this because of the associated anxiety. She considers herself to be a good friend and an excellent nursing supervisor, as well as a healthy, smart person with sophisticated tastes and interests. She is loosely active in a faith community, and currently attends a divorce support group at her church. She experiences discomfort in her free time at home on nights and weekends when she misses the physical presence of another person. She complains of loneliness and pessimism about the possibility of future remarriage or any sort of relationship. The holidays are particularly difficult, so she assigns herself extra work shifts to both cover the schedule and fill in her time.

The second patient, Mr. B, has a college degree and works in his family-owned business. He is living separately from his wife, which is a relief from the strain of daily interactions with her, but he feels tortured by the possibility of divorce. For at least 3 generations, he and his family have been prominent members of a tightly organized faith community that regards divorce as unacceptable. The rules of this faith dictate adherence to specific behavioral norms, and sanctions of eternal damnation in hell for violation of those rules. Mr. B's spouse was also sexually distant and financially irresponsible, spending and causing debts that threatened the family business. When Mr. B's father learned of the financial threat to his business, he insisted, in a loving but firm way, that Mr. B should do "whatever it takes" to remedy the problem and avoid bringing the stigma of failure on the family name. Furthermore, it was considered Mr. B's responsibility to control his wife's behavior. No matter how miserable he might feel about the long hours of work, the financial strain, the lack of marital intimacy or the degree of marital conflict, divorce was not an option in their family or religious community. Meanwhile, Mrs. B initiated divorce proceedings. Mr. B complained of feeling hopeless and worthless as a person, and he was preoccupied with fear of an afterlife in hell. Despite his inner turmoil, he forced himself to go to work and attend church and family functions because it was expected by others.

How does the cultural context of beliefs, rules, norms, group affiliation, and perspective on self-image shape the particular experiences of Mrs. A and Mr. B? Are they allocentric or idiocentric? What risks or advantages might be associated with each cultural perspective? What do you think would bring either of them into therapy? What sort of interventions might be helpful? Would you have an easier time working with one or the other?

Culturally Sensitive Practice

Culturally sensitive practitioners are aware of the diverse aspects of their own cultural identity, limits of experience, and stimulus value to others. They understand the cognitive and social processes that shape our judgments and behaviors, and recognize salient cultural differences. In this section, we outline some basic strategies for building and maintaining cultural sensitivity in applied clinical practice.

You do not necessarily need an entirely new repertoire of clinical skills for each and every culture, but rather the ability to see the patient's cultural context, and to appropriately adjust, modify, or develop assessment and interventions practices to be both valid and useful (APA Guidelines, 2003; Bernal, Bonilla, & Bellido, 1995; S. Sue, 1998). It is the therapist's responsibility to speak with the client in a way that accurately taps their worldview and reaches into their cultural framework.

With assessment techniques, practitioners must keep in mind the fairness and linguistic understandability for specific individuals, as well as the reference group for valid test interpretation. Culture-specific therapy may include nontraditional interventions, including strategies or additional helpers in the process of healing. A therapist working with a Native American population might participate in a "sweat lodge" experience with the tribal elders to gain their trust and then enlist the elders as participants in certain therapeutic interventions with members of the community.

There is a large continuum of possible adjustments that you might make to accomplish a culturally sensitive practice. It is easy to be overwhelmed at the thought of understanding and appropriately responding to the vast array of potential cultural variables. This sense of being overwhelmed can already be activated in the beginning practitioner who is just developing basic clinical skills. And this sense can expand as you delve into the literature and find a burgeoning number of lists, requirements, and tasks to master as part of the notion of cultural competence (Hansen et al., 2000; Hays, 2001; LaRoche & Maxie, 2003; Matthews, 1997; Stuart, 2004; Tanaka-Matsumi, Seiden, & Lam, 1996). There is no mistaking the reality that clinical practice is a complex endeavor, with potential for harm in mislabeling behavior, misdiagnosing problems, misdirecting treatments, and disrespecting those seeking help. Further, traditional models that form the basis of most clinical training are, in their Eurocentric, White, middle-class male focus (see APA Guidelines, 2003; Strickland, 2000), at best only partially adequate for serving the increasingly diverse population. To cope with these notable demands, we turn first to a basic grounding in sound ethical reasoning.

Ethically Based Interventions

Ethical grounding of culturally sensitive practice begins with the principles of beneficence, nonmaleficence, justice, and respect for human rights and dignity. These principles are a foundation for sound practice with *all* clients. We suggest that practitioners use a series of questions to self-monitor their practice in appropriately conducting treatment amid the vast possible array of cultural issues that may confront the provider at any given point in time.

- *Beneficence:* Is this patient (or couple or family) benefiting from treatment? Are salient cultural expectations taken into consideration in measuring possible benefits? Is the provider working toward goals that are both important to the patient and consistent with his or her cultural affiliations? Is the provider using methods and strategies that are a good fit for the patient's culture? Are there other treatment or community resources that may better serve their interests?

- *Nonmaleficence:* Is this treatment plan free of potential harm to the patient? Are issues of cultural risks, including challenges to cultural norms, given sufficient consideration as potential sources of stress and possible harm? Is the provider alert to possible personal biases that could affect the therapy relationship and cause some interpersonal harm to the patient?

- *Justice:* Is this patient receiving fair access to treatment resources and quality service? Has the tendency to categorize this patient as a member of an "out-group" affected clinical judgment in any way?

- *Respect for human rights and dignity:* Is the provider alert to possible stereotypes in working with this patient? Has the provider appropriately discussed relevant issues with the patient so that he or she may have adequate informed consent to treatment? Have alternative resources and procedures been discussed? Has the provider taken the time to provide a sufficient rationale for treatment that targets specific, culturally based variables such as risk factors?

In essence, culturally sensitive practice is an ethically based practice in which care for the patient is the highest priority, and significant effort is made to ensure benefit, respect, justice, and protection from harm.

Professional Boundary Issues

An area of clinical practice that challenges both novices and veteran practitioners is maintaining the boundaries of appropriate behavior in a professional context. There is some difference of opinion among those in the profession as to what constitutes a "boundary" and is appropriate or inappropriate practice (Helbok, Marinelli, & Walls, 2006; Pope, Tabachnick, & Keith-Spiegel, 1987). Questions of boundary violations inevitably come up when adapting interventions to a patient's culture, a course of action that might include using nontraditional interventions, involving community leaders or helpers in the intervention, or personally participating in culture-specific activities (APA, 2003, p. 392).

Is it a boundary violation to invite the head of the family to participate in the treatment of a family member when the family is from a collectivist culture? Do you violate the patient's boundaries by declining to involve pertinent family members? Do you violate proper therapeutic boundaries by participating in a culturally important ritual with members of the patient's community to better understand their culture and to gain trust and rapport? What if the patient wants to introduce the therapist to family at large, so that they will know and trust him? Should the therapist accept an invitation to a family event in the interest of culturally sensitive practice? Is the acceptance of a token gift a boundary violation, or conversely, is it the refusal of the gift that is the boundary violation? Does age or disability status make a difference in determining proper therapy boundaries?

These complex questions require a sensitive reasoning of each instance, and judgment based on individual situations. A boundary violation might occur if any or all of the following consequences result from the provider's decisions or actions: (a) It causes the therapist to lose objectivity with regard to the patient; (b) it exploits the patient in any way; and (c) it disrupts or derails the ongoing treatment (Younggren, 2004).

It is incumbent on therapists to consider issues such as diagnosis, level of functioning of the patient, and local standards and practices when considering the impact of their actions. Consultation with other qualified professionals, especially those who might be cognizant of the relevant cultural norms and practices, is also an important step in supporting one's reasoning as far as adapting clinical methods (Younggren & Gottlieb, 2004). Under no condition could an action that would violate basic standards of care be rationalized as a cultural adaptation if it causes the therapist to lose objectivity, exploits the patient, or disrupts ongoing treatment. Engaging in sexual intimacy with the patient would always violate these standards, no matter what the cultural standard. On the other hand, a therapist might participate in a cultural ritual with the leaders of a community, such as the Native American sweat lodge previously mentioned, and this would not necessarily violate any of the basic standards of care.

Consultation with colleagues on cultural matters should be done tactfully and in the context of a broader collegial or professional relationship. If possible, consult with colleagues on the basis of their clinical or research experience in working with the population of interest, or their expressed interest in the culture. In a survey of ethnic minority therapists, some reported the experience of being viewed as an "expert" on their particular ethnic group as a positive one, whereas others found it insulting that they would be perceived as helpful only on matters of ethnicity (Iwamasa, 1996). Consultations with colleagues who are just as unfamiliar with the culture of interest may result in further confusion, and perhaps misapplication of standards of care.

Therapists need to assess their own boundaries of competence when working with a particular population and be alert to circumstances where an understanding of cultural factors is essential for effective service, as noted in Ethical Standard 2.01 (b) (APA, 2002). This standard also holds that therapists must obtain relevant training, experience, consultation, or supervision as necessary, or make appropriate referral. Thus, in dealing with matters of age, gender, gender identity, race, ethnicity, culture, national origin, religion, sexual orientation, disability, language, or socioeconomic status, we must seek enough information and consultation or supervision to provide competent service that is beneficial and not harmful to the patient, or help locate more appropriate, alternative resources.

Four Action Strategies

Good intentions are just that, unless there is a clear action plan for behavioral implementation. Although it is beyond the scope of this chapter to thoroughly delineate cultural competence in practice (see LaRoche & Maxie, 2003; Stuart, 2004; S. Sue, 1998), we offer the following four recommendations for building and maintaining clinical skills in the cultural domain.

Action Strategy One: A Personal Cultural Inventory

First, take a personal cultural inventory, and periodically update it. Knowing yourself and your primary identifications is the foundation for understanding your assumptions, values, and possible biases, as well as comprehending your potential impact on others. Cultivating awareness of your own cultural identity is a vital step in countering ethnocentricism or the tendency to generalize your own worldview as an assumed perspective. By acknowledging and accepting yourself as a person with a particular point of view that is grounded in certain cultural dimensions, you become more practiced in recognizing the importance of cultural identity in yourself and others.

There are many different ways to explore your cultural identity. A thorough approach is detailed in Hays (2001) with multiple dimensions summarized in the acronym ADDRESSING. This stands for the cultural influences of *a*ge and generational influences, *d*evelopmental or acquired *d*isabilities, *r*eligion and spiritual orientation, *e*thnicity, *s*ocioeconomic status, *s*exual orientation, *i*ndigenous heritage, *n*ational origin, and *g*ender. This thorough approach offers a broad overview of cultural identity and helps the therapist discern any specific dimensions that may be particularly salient.

Other broad questions may be useful in exploring your personal cultural inventory. How would you describe yourself in terms of cultural identity? What comes to mind as important in describing you, at this point in time? Do you think that your values and priorities are more allocentric or individualistic? What are the groups or communities that are or have been important to you? Do you place high value on your group affiliations or are you loosely tied to these commitments?

For a simple exercise to assess your perspective, complete 20 sentences that begin with the stem "I am . . ." This is a method used by researchers to assess cultural perspectives of the self (e.g., Higgins & King, 1981). Once you have completed the list, review each item to see if there is a reference to a social group (e.g., I am a mother; I am a native Floridian), a generalized public perspective (e.g., I am viewed as responsible), or a private statement (I am hard-working). Social references suggest an allocentric perspective, and private self responses suggest individualistic perspective, with public perspective being relatively infrequent (Triandis, 1995).

What elements of your cultural identity do you think have the most impact on your professional role? When patients meet you for the first time, what will strike them about you as a person? Remember, qualities are not static, but are perceived from the perspective of the other person. The therapist's personal impact is perceived by the client in terms of similarities and differences. What do your potential patients want to know about you to make an informed choice about working with you, and accepting your influence? Are you willing to answer inquiries about personal matters, and if so, how will you address issues of differences?

Although answering patient inquiries is influenced by the theoretical approach taken and the case conceptualization, the principles of informed consent and respect for patient autonomy suggest that it is important to address patient concerns directly and early in treatment, and support the patient's right to choose providers, even if this results in being rejected. Cultural sensitivity also helps us to better understand why the patient asks these questions. An individualistic person might be more concerned with inquiring about your degrees and where you went to school. This feels culturally consistent to an individualistic therapist, who easily answers such questions and views them as appropriate. On the other hand, an allocentric person might not be highly concerned with your degree, but places trust in you on the basis of your affiliation with an important group or the recommendation of a respected authority.

Common areas of cultural inquiry from patients include parental status (do you have children of your own?), religious orientation (Are you a Christian? Are you Jewish? What is your attitude toward Muslims?), sexual orientation or appreciation of different orientations (Are you heterosexual? How do you deal with gay or lesbian people?), socioeconomic status (Do you understand what it is like to have a low or high income?), or simply willingness to disclose basic personal information (e.g., where you grew up). By carefully and selectively sharing some of this personal information (in the context of professional conduct), the therapist might establish an "in-group" bond with the patient, a fundamental step in developing trust and rapport. However, beginning therapists should be aware that effective self-disclosure in a clinical setting requires considerable judgment and skill. One must learn to strike a balance between the extremes of sharing too much information and stonewalling the patient's attempts to be informed about the clinician's experience and possible sources of bias. As you are learning the skills of therapy, caution and restraint in self-disclosure is the best beginning posture. Gradually, you can learn how to provide limited information for the sole purpose of serving the patient's best interests.

These sorts of questions can be viewed as a welcome invitation by the patient to form a relationship, not as threats to your competence. No one can represent all cultural variations, or be fully conversant in aspects of different cultures. If you are clear in knowing your own cultural identity, have an appreciation of its possible impact with patients, and understand how to maintain the boundaries of your professional role, you will likely be more confident in discussing questions raised by the patient. An appreciation of important cultural variations can also help you effectively understand the importance of the question from the patient's point of view.

In instances where you may differ from the patient's cultural preference, but you believe that you have competent skills for helping him or her, you can address the underlying issue of trust with a statement of reassurance. The following is a response to an inquiry about your family status:

> *I am married, but do not have children of my own. However, I do have experience in helping families with troubled teens, and I am committed to offering my skills and perspective to you in dealing with your current family issues. If you're willing to give it a try, we can see if you feel comfortable and can benefit from our work together. However, if you would prefer to work with someone who is also experienced as a parent, I will be happy to provide you with the names of other qualified providers.*

If there are cultural differences between yourself and your patient, it is important to ask yourself whether you have the emotional or intellectual competence to accept the patient. If not, how will the patient's best interests be served? In some instances, you may decide that you can acquire enough intellectual competence through some additional continuing education. This may be most adaptive when there are no significantly better alternative resources, and cultural issues are not directly relevant to the presenting problem. This could occur when a patient seeks treatment for panic attacks, and also happens to be gay and Christian and is not struggling with either of these identities. However, if you are not sure you have the emotional or intellectual competence for working with someone of a particular group, even if that is not a presenting issue, then responsible case management would indicate referring the patient to alternative resources.

Determining the patient's best interest in matters of cultural difference or similarity with the therapist should also include a collaborative element. Even though it may be uncomfortable to bring it up, this decision deserves the patient's direct involvement. The important element is to convey openness to recognizing and discussing differences as they may matter to the patient, *without making assumptions* about the patient's perspective. This means not assuming that the patient considers it difficult to work with you, because of a cultural difference, or would be either comfortable or uncomfortable in discussing the matter. The following is an example of how to open such a discussion:

My goal is to be as helpful to you as I possibly can, and to address anything that might affect our working productively together. As part of getting to know each other, I would like us to be open about any questions or concerns that come up. There are always differences between people in terms of cultural background, and sometimes that matters, sometimes not. If there are differences between us that you think might matter, or be worth discussing, would you be willing to talk about it? Likewise, if we find common ground, let's try to take note of that. How does that sound to you?

The discussion of cultural differences does not always proceed gently. There may be strong affect associated with both the cultural difference, and the power difference between patient and therapist. These combined elements will make some patients more submissive while others may become highly defensive and emotionally reactive to the therapist. They may present a barrage of questions about your background or qualifications, or judgments of your competence. Although such reactions may feel like an attack, they can, if handled empathically, lead into a productive discussion of cultural differences. An African American patient in family therapy reacted to the Caucasian therapist's attempts to engage her in discussion of parenting issues by angrily exclaiming, "I'm sick and tired of you White bitches trying to tell me how to raise my kids." This was a clear opportunity for the therapist to pursue discussion of the racial difference issue, and to learn more about the patient's perspective. To counter with either anger or defensiveness would entirely lose this opportunity.

Clinical Example: Doris (Vignette 4)

Let's return to our consideration of Doris. If Doris's medical team had taken their own personal cultural inventory, they might have been more alert to some of the perceived differences between themselves and their patient. All members of the team were fairly young (under 45 years of age), and they represented a traditional power structure of a Caucasian male (the physician) being assisted by a group of Caucasian females. Further, they all had a slender body size and tended to organize experience from an individualistic perspective.

A greater cognizance of these cultural differences as having some potential impact on the interaction with Doris might have helped the team realize the crucial importance of taking time to develop trust and rapport, helping Doris to see herself as an actual participating member of the team and not just another case on a long list. They might have been more successful in gaining her involvement by getting to know her as a person and allowing her to get to know them before dispensing advice on how she should change. Instead, they expected her to have assumptions that matched their own about valuing individual health and taking personal responsibility for maintaining health, and they misjudged her readiness to change. No one took the time to inquire about Doris's perceptions of the team and possible barriers that might affect her ability to trust and relate to them.

Action Strategy Two: Continuing Education

For the second action strategy, continue to seek new information and learn about beliefs, values, and practices of various cultures and subcultures. There are many experiential ways to come into contact with cultural diversity. Seek opportunities to get to know people who are members of groups that are different from your own. Expose yourself to reading materials that represent a wide range of audiences. Participate in an event or gathering that represents an opportunity to share in the practices of a certain culture or group, even if it is not something you are particularly inclined toward.

This approach can take on a superficial cast if not done in a spirit of openness to seek new information. Eating dinner at the Chinese buffet is not a particularly strong exercise in cultural diversity. However, you can make an effort to interact with individuals of Asian descent when the opportunity presents itself. By taking an interest in the *people,* you can find the opportunity to better understand possible aspects of a culture. A snippet of exposure does not create expertise, but it is a beginning.

For a simple exercise, again take an inventory, this time a quick one. During any given day, how many times do you have contact with someone of a racial or ethnic background different from your own? Include incidental contacts such as people you might easily speak to in passing. How many of those contacts do you see as an opportunity for learning something about cultural experiences different from your own? Do you speak to the Egyptian cab driver? Do you allow yourself to learn anything about his experience as someone of Arab descent? Perhaps challenge yourself to learn something new about someone else's cultural experience at least once a week or more. If you are Christian, ask a Jewish friend if you can participate in her Seder supper. Go ahead and talk about the differences in Jewish and Christian customs. Some information may seep in through sheer exposure, but it is much more likely to be a culturally informative experience if you make it a point to learn something related to the person's cultural background.

Scholarly or academic forms of continuing education on cultural diversity are key aspects of the second action strategy. Culture can be a continuing education theme or topic to which you return again and again throughout the course of a career. Scholarly literature that informs our clinical work within various cultural contexts is very useful and increasingly available (see Appendix 3.1). Where specific guidelines exist (APA, 2000a, 2002, 2004), it is important to become familiar with those guidelines and to keep a reference copy handy for review and consultation as needed. Books on the topic of multicultural practice (e.g., Aponte & Wohl, 2000) as well as texts related to issues concerning particular populations or groups (e.g., Adams, 1995; Boyd-Franklin, 2003; Helms, 1990) can expand your cognitive or intellectual grasp of cultural matters as they may affect patients.

There is a growing list of journals devoted to the study of diversity (see Appendix 3.1). Empirical studies concerning certain cultural populations also appear with some frequency in other topical journals (e.g., Bernal et al., 1995; Nilsson & Anderson, 2004). In addition, selected web site resources may provide useful summary information about mental health issues and other matters related to specific cultural groups. The United States Department of Health and Human Services offers a detailed report from the office of the Surgeon General concerning culture, race, ethnicity, and mental health. In addition to independent reading, many excellent workshops or continuing education seminars offered by professional organizations provide opportunities to keep expanding your externally developed knowledge base (see Appendix 3.1 for more resources).

This recommendation for ongoing learning also merits a caveat of recognizing the impossibility of ever completing the task (LaRoche & Maxie, 2003). Students delving into material concerning different broad cultural groups often have a similar initial reaction of realizing the group actually comprises many subgroups. Arab Americans might have family originating from any of 20 or more countries with significant Arab populations (Erickson & Al-Timimi, 2001). Further, approximately two-thirds of Arab Americans were born in the United States, as there have been at least three waves of Arab immigration, beginning in the 1880s. With this scratch to the surface of the Arab culture, we begin to see the possible complexity, even before considering religion, acculturation stresses, or educational standing.

We must seek information so that we are not completely culture ignorant, yet recognize that superficial knowledge will not result in an overall competence. The risk of a little superficial knowledge, without recognizing its limits, could be overgeneralization and treating a patient as a member of a class or category. Instead, we hope that knowledge gained from studying about a group can be used to inform hypotheses about specific people. Given the vast array of cultures and cultural combinations and permutations, we recognize the need to have a strategy of openness and caring about each unique client, combined with curiosity about cultural influences. To attempt to present ourselves as knowledgeable about all cultures can only be a pretense, and one that violates the values of honesty and genuineness that are expected in psychotherapy (Wohl, 2000).

Clinical Example: Doris (Vignette 5)

The diabetes team that worked with Doris was a top-notch group of health professionals who were diligent in their ongoing continuing education. After their consultation with Doris, several members of the team attended the annual conference of the Society of Behavioral Medicine. While there, they heard a presentation on the concept of religious health fatalism as it affects members of the African American faith community (Franklin, Schlundt, & Wallston, in press). They learned about the importance of religious affiliation in the African American community and how certain beliefs about faith and health may substantially affect subsequent health-related behavior. This provided the team with some ideas to explore with Doris concerning culturally based beliefs and attitudes affecting her response to their interventions. Doris might hold the belief, "I don't need to try to improve my health because I know it is up to God." Or, "If God wants me to have better health, He will provide."

Action Strategy Three: Beware of Cultural Cookbooks

Continuously seeking new information leads us directly to the third action strategy, which is to beware of the simplicity of cultural cookbooks. A person is not simply a product of a singular cultural group. Social categorization is an automatic process that aims to simplify the world, but with significant risk of overgeneralization. As you go about gathering more information about cultures, be sure to look for information that is consistent *and* inconsistent with group practices or norms.

In clinical work, it is especially important to suspend preconceptions about patients based on cultural background, and to recognize that patients may indeed be quite different from others in the group in which they appear to belong (Cardemil & Battle, 2003). No individual person is a living representation of all aspects of a culture, and no culture is so homogeneous that all generalizations apply to all members (Wohl, 2000). Sometimes the recognition of possible divergence from expected cultural patterns is a significant clinical issue, and can give rise to important personal exploration. If patients are Hispanic, that does not automatically mean they will be Catholic. If they are Hispanic and Catholic, that also does not mean that their distress is necessarily related to difficulties in family relations. Hispanic and Catholic cultures are traditionally collectivist-oriented, yet it may be that the educational and economic aspects of the patient's culture are the salient issues and the clinically significant concern revolves around trying to succeed in a highly competitive environment.

For each patient, find out how demonstrated distress may or may not be related to ethnic or cultural issues. We might expect that in times of relative stress, crisis, or transition, the patient's sense of belonging to some identified cultural group will be salient. The person who does not have a sense of belonging, or who seems to have lost the belief in belonging is likely to be in the greatest degree of distress. It may be that changes in the patient's life have caused corresponding changes in cultural associations, or rendered a previous association more tenuous or even nonexistent.

Clinical Example: Doris (Vignette 6)

Doris eventually made her way back to the diabetes clinic after being urged to do so by her primary care physician. She returned to the PCP because of vision changes and tingling in her hands and feet, symptoms that scared her. The doctor said this was peripheral neuropathy caused by her diabetes. After Doris met with the team, the psychologist scheduled an extended visit so they could take an in-depth psychosocial health history. This step allowed the team to better understand Doris and her health needs, to explore the ambivalence Doris seemed to have about making changes, and to discuss specific ways that culture affected her health problems.

During this history taking, it became clear that Doris was concerned that her body size detracted from her appearance, even though she did not view extreme thinness as the only attractive form. She was indeed concerned with the health risks related to obesity. However, she also endorsed many beliefs

(continued)

Clinical Example: Doris (Vignette 6) (Continued)

characteristic of religiously based health fatalism. Her ambivalence about taking action was affected by these fatalistic beliefs, as well as the tension between the perspective of her in-group and priorities of her community, and the team's expectation of a substantially individualist focus on her health needs.

Thus, the psychologist advised the team to encourage Doris to view her weight management as an important contribution to her family. They provided specific information to her on the mechanisms of health impairment in obesity and diabetes. This helped Doris see the connection between these two conditions and others in her family who

eventually died from the medical consequences. By helping her to understand how diabetes could cause breakdown of the vascular system that would harm her heart, kidneys, and nervous system, the team helped Doris realize that the disease progression was not inevitable. To specifically address her religiously based fatalistic beliefs, the team might also suggest that perhaps God was providing this information to help her improve her health. They could gently guide her toward resolving the tension between her commitment to her social affiliations, and her need to attend to her personal health.

Action Strategy Four: Keep a Multidimensional Focus

Finally, keep the *multi* in multicultural, remembering that all persons are multidimensional. There are many aspects of a cultural identity, and full understanding of a client cannot happen if we assign too much weight to one or two cultural variables. For example, one of the most common cultural misconceptions encountered among young clinicians in training is the belief that all older persons are more alike than they are different. This automatic reaction is based on assigning too much weight to a single cultural variable (age) and assuming that the out-group is highly similar in composition, and less desirable as a group.

In fact, there are more differences between age groups than not. Older adults as a group are more heterogeneous than other age groups (APA, 2004; Crowther & Zeiss, 2003; Nelson & Dannefer, 1992). Brief reflection usually makes clear how this stereotype of similarity of all older people is just that, a stereotype. In a group of persons at age 75, you are likely to find a notable range of cognitive functioning and possible clinical symptoms, physical health and mobility, emotional well-being, social engagement and access to friends, economic status, daily living circumstances, and responsibilities including employment and the care of grandchildren or other dependents. Compared with clinical trainees at age 25, there are far more differences within the elder group. And these differences can reflect degrees of greater rather than lesser desirability compared with those of the younger group. Many elders have plentiful free time, high economic status, comfortable living arrangements and freedom from responsibility, close connections with loved ones, good physical health, stable emotional well-being and a strong sense of life satisfaction. A multidimensional perspective is required for understanding someone in either group, with an appreciation of how the magnitude of differences may vary within groups.

Cultural affiliations may shift or change across a life span. Our culture is heterogeneous, with boundaries that are to some degree loose or fluid. Given the complexity of our society, there is also a general expectation of cultural adaptability or change to meet the demands of varying circumstances. However, both internal and external barriers affect psychological and social shifts in cultural participation. Boundaries that should be open, or appear to be open may in fact be only semipermeable. Emotional and behavioral stress associated with encountering and crossing cultural boundaries is an important clinical consideration.

A minority student from a low-income, single-parent family attends a competitive college preparatory academy. His mother feels strongly that this opportunity will provide many advantages for her son's future, yet she endures constant ridicule from her coworkers for all the time, effort, and expense required to support his full participation in school activities. The support offered by the in-group of other parents at the academy may be good, it may be marginal, or the atmosphere may be downright hostile to this scholarship student. Internally, the student may wish to both please his mother, and gain access to the world of privilege in the academy, yet feel guilt over the growing distance from old friends, his neighborhood culture, and the emotional and financial strain on his mother.

Clinical Example: Doris (Vignette 7)

Let's revisit why Doris did not respond immediately to the recommendations of the diabetes team. Her actions were both similar and dissimilar to what might be expected just on the basis of her age, race, and gender. First, she had the sense of mistrust in the health care system that may be common among African Americans. However, she did not hold the attitudes of large body size acceptance that others expected based on her age and race. She had a strong religious affiliation that might have been predicted by her race, but religious affiliation alone does not explain her response to the first diabetes consult. Rather, her religious fatalism is the psychological component that most affected her health-related behavior.

The prevalence of certain health conditions and behaviors within her culture may have had notable impact on her thinking. The salience of seeing diabetes, hypertension, and obesity as common among her friends and family needed to be acknowledged by the team as a perspective different from their own. For the team, these were serious conditions that merited significant time and attention. For Doris, these conditions were just part of everyday living, and health deterioration was a matter of God's plan. Finally, as an allocentric person, Doris was particularly conflicted by the expectation that she invest more time and energy attending to a personal choice when she believed that her community did not think this was a necessary or important use of her time or resources.

Summary

In a complex society with many options as ours, openness, understanding, flexibility, and self-awareness are key elements of working with cultural similarities and differences. In conducting psychotherapy, it is likely that we encounter people who are adjusting or revising their cultural identity as they progress through their lives, encountering inevitable changes in opportunities and circumstances. Facilitating this process can be a fulfilling challenge.

Instead of trying to ascertain fixed aspects of the patient's cultural identity based on group stereotypes, and trying to alleviate distress by creating a better fit with this given identity, we can embrace the notion of cultural identity as an ongoing process. Psychotherapy offers a protected relationship where cultural limits and opportunities are acknowledged and explored. The role of the therapist can be likened to that of a guide who helps the patient sort out the cultural pressures and options impinging on psychosocial adaptation. In an ethically grounded practice, understanding the multiple dimensions of culture is vital to understanding and effectively helping our diverse clientele. Culturally attuned practitioners take a personal cultural inventory and periodically update it. They are careful about self-disclosure, but respect the client's right to be informed about the therapist's cultural influences. Culturally attuned practitioners continually seek new information about various cultures and subcultures, but avoid the oversimplicity of cultural cookbooks. Instead, they maintain a multidimensional perspective on culture and its many implications.

Appendix: Resources for Emerging Information on Diversity

Journals

Journal of Multicultural Counseling and Development
Cultural Diversity and Ethnic Minority Psychology
Journal of Immigrant Health
Journal of Cross-Cultural Psychology
Minority Health Today

Web Sites

www.cdc.gov
www.surgeongeneral.gov/library/mentalhealth/cre/

Clinical Research and Outcome Assessment

4

Chapter

Because science and practice are two cornerstones of clinical psychology, clinical research and outcome assessment can be considered as the building blocks of clinical practice. Various research methods are used in clinical psychology, including case studies and qualitative research designs. The objectives of clinical research are twofold. The first objective is to build a scientific foundation for understanding normal and abnormal human behavior or psychopathology. The second objective is to determine which interventions are effective in changing or adjusting problematic behavior and emotional disorders, and under what conditions these interventions are known to be effective. The quality and usefulness of any clinical intervention is directly tied to the quality of its empirical support.

Learning Objectives

At the end of this chapter, the reader should be able to:

- Describe the importance of empirical validation or support for clinical interventions.
- Explain the differences between experimental, quasi-experimental, and observational designs.
- Describe the pros and cons of single-subject designs and case study research.
- Differentiate between empirically validated, empirically supported, well-established and probably efficacious therapies, and evidence-based therapy.
- List the pros and cons of manualized practice protocols.

Having gained an appreciation for the many specialties in the field of clinical psychology, the variations in degrees and requirements for practitioners in this field, and individual and cultural diversity in the practitioners and consumers of clinical psychology, you should begin to wonder what techniques, treatments, and protocols are available to clinicians for helping people with clinical needs. How do consumers, clients, or patients, know what type of therapy to seek? How can insurance companies justify paying for mental health services or verify that therapy is effective? How does the field substantiate itself compared with other alternative therapies for alleviating suffering and improving psychological well-being?

This chapter reviews a sample of empirical research strategies used to test clinical therapies and techniques for a broad range of populations and disorders. The generalization of clinical research to clinical practice is explored, with descriptions of empirically supported treatments, evidence-based practice, and manually driven therapies. Pros and cons of these developments are addressed, and the field's means of dissemination is reviewed. Future chapters explore how clinicians develop a treatment plan and select certain techniques from among the standardized treatments and protocols.

Clinical Research and Research Methods

Research in clinical psychology spans the gamut of research methods, designs, and adherence to general principles of science. Investigations vary from use of *highest-constraint* to *lowest-constraint* methods, with a wide range of strategies and techniques between these two artificial anchors. Numerous research methods are covered in research courses you will take, so only those relevant to outcomes research are described here. High-constraint research refers to methods and designs in which the conditions, variables, and participants are scrupulously screened and selected for specific traits or characteristics desired by the researcher to isolate what is being studied from any possible confounds, or undesired interference in the study. Quantitative *experimental and quasi-experimental designs* are categorized as varying degrees of highest constraint research. These are the research designs you probably most often think of because pharmaceutical companies and other funding agencies provide financial support for treatment outcome studies using these designs, and therefore, radio and newspaper advertisements seeking participants are plentiful (e.g., "Are you feeling sad, blue, hopeless, depressed . . . the University of Somewhere is conducting a study to test a new medication to help you. Please call to see if you qualify.").

Lowest constraint research describes studies that use methods and designs where the investigator—while creating little if any interference—observes conditions, variables, and participants in natural surroundings or circumstances. Examples of lower constraint research include *observational, correlational,* and *archival* studies. When participants complete a packet of questionnaires based on personal characteristics or experiences, but do not enroll in any interventional program, such studies exemplify this type of research. Similarly, reviews of insurance company information that compile statistics of the types of patients who have positive outcomes in psychotherapy is archival (lower constraint) research. The case study, which is classified as lower constraint research, has recently gained more attention in the research and practice of clinical psychology because of its potential for significantly affecting systematic treatment selection. In line with this research, practitioner-scholars advocate for the development of *local clinical science*. In this approach, clinicians adopt an outcomes-focused treatment and apply research methodology to their evaluation of practice on a case-by-case basis. The aggregate of case-based data acquired through practice would then inform other clinicians and researchers about the effectiveness of treatment interventions with clients who are not screened for uniformity in their presentations or for control of confounding variables in settings or treatment.

Some biases exist about which types of research are more scholarly or meritorious, but the knowledgeable psychologist recognizes that the *goal* of the research dictates the design and methodology chosen, and that almost all methodologies have their limits and flaws. The choice of research design and methodology should be made by using honed critical thinking and rational decision-making skills toward achieving the goal of answering research questions.

Clinical psychologists whose work crosses the research-practice spectrum can appreciate the need for bridging the gaps between the two subspecialties of the field. True scientist-practitioners recognize the important contributions made by clinicians and researchers, and the current limitations of both areas of practice. The following basic explanations of several research designs are helpful in understanding the subsequent review of where the field stands in applying research to practice, and having practice inform research in the service of human psychological welfare. While the decision-making skills to be employed are beyond the scope of this chapter, the problem-solving model of clinical decision making (A. M. Nezu, Nezu, & Lombardo, 1999) can be useful for considering clinical problems and choosing relevant research applications to evaluate them, or for selecting empirically validated or evidenced-based methods for use in practice.

Research Designs

Experimental research ("true research") and *quasi-experimental research* are families of designs that are typically used in research laboratories or research clinics with large numbers of participants, comparison groups, and multiple data collection points (pretreatment, posttreatment, follow-up time frames). They involve a high degree of input, manipulation, and selection of participants, or control of environmental, treatment, therapist, and participant characteristics. These designs are often used to determine cause and effect in examination of two or more *independent* and *dependent* variables.* *Random selection, random assignment,* and *control groups* define the differences between experimental and quasi-experimental research and other research designs. *Randomized controlled trials (RCTs)* are often the basis for discovering empirically supported treatments, as defined later on. Researchers randomly select and assign participants to experimental conditions (e.g., treatment groups, exposure to different environmental stimuli) and compare those who get a dose of the experimental variable with those who do not. In this way, researchers can draw conclusions about the relationships between variables that investigators observing individuals independent of each other cannot. The influence these parameters have on controlling the threats or confounds to the interpretation of the results is significant, but not without criticism.

Experimental designs employ random selection when feasible, and random assignment as a defining feature. Quasi-experimental designs use random selection often to the extent that experimental designs do, but the population, setting, or other features of the independent variable prohibit random assignment. Random selection and random assignment represent different aspects of research methods and procedure, and have different implications for interpreting the outcomes. Students and those new to research often confuse these terms, and therefore, a careful explanation follows.

Random Selection
Random selection requires that each participant in an overall population has an equal chance of being selected. How the population is defined is the key to determining the likelihood of employing random selection. Selecting a random sample from the population of clinical child psychologists would require identifying and potentially recruiting all clinical child psychologists for a given study. This would mean that psychologists from all over the world would need to be identified (with credentials and training being equivalent), and then a random sample of this population would be selected. For most studies, based on feasibility due to budget and logistics among other reasons, the likelihood of a true random selection of this population would be unrealistic. Simply determining the equality of degrees and training across cultures would be a tremendous task. As such, psychology studies typically use a *convenience sample* restricted by such things as geographic location, accessibility, or volunteer sta-

---

* Independent variables are the *input* variables, or the variables that the investigator chooses to exist in an expected and determined way. Examples of independent variables include race, gender, therapy type (e.g., psychopharmacology, cognitive-behavioral therapy, family therapy), years of training, or degree of depression (mild, moderate, severe). Dependent variables are the *output* variables, or the variables that are expected to be affected by the input variables. These are the variables the researchers are watching to see if and how they change as a result of the independent variable. Independent and dependent variables are often thought of as part of an "if/then" statement. For example, "*If* severely depressed persons engage in cognitive-behavioral therapy (CBT), *then* they will experience a decrease in depression and increase in quality of life following therapy, compared with (*if*) severely depressed persons who do not engage in CBT. Therapy is the independent variable that is selected by the researcher; quality of life and post-treatment depression (or changes in depression scores) are the dependent variables.

tus. If, however, the population of "clinical child psychologists" was further defined as "Pennsylvania licensed clinical child psychologists in Philadelphia," and you were a researcher living in that area, random selection might be more feasible. You could verify a list of qualified psychologists from the state regulatory board licensure rosters and would need to establish some inclusion and exclusion criteria to determine who is a child psychologist, and what constitutes practice in Philadelphia. The selection method would then require giving each psychologist an equal chance of being chosen for the study. This latter scenario is potentially feasible on a limited budget and time schedule.

Random Assignment
Supposing that you now have selected people to participate in your research study, how will you decide who gets what treatment, by whom, or when? Or, how will you decide which therapist will conduct therapy for which individuals or groups? In true experiments (experimental design), participants would be randomly assigned to each of the experimental conditions. This means that each participant (already selected to participate in the study-at-large) has an equal chance of being placed in any of the experimental conditions. So, if you were testing the differences between cognitive-behavioral therapy and nondirective supportive psychotherapy, ideally each participant would have a 50/50 chance of being assigned to one of these conditions, and this assignment would occur essentially by a method similar to flipping a coin. Thus, the independent variable lends itself to a true experimental design.

If you are comparing the impact of cognitive-behavioral therapy on treating generalized anxiety disorder in persons who have a significant other (spouse or partner) with those who do not, you cannot randomly assign your participants to groups. The characteristics of your sample will dictate which group they are in—they either come to therapy having a significant other, or they do not have a significant other. Thus, the independent variable is not randomly assigned. There is no variation in each participant's likelihood of being in a particular group—they are either in it, or they are not. In quasi-experimental research, therefore, investigators are studying the cause and effect of independent and dependent variables, but the study is created, in part, around existing conditions or characteristics of the participants, the setting, therapy conditions (e.g., therapist characteristics), or other features of the independent variable already in place. The design is still experimental because cause and effect is being studied, and there is manipulation of some aspect or at least one independent variable; in the preceding case, the investigator is manipulating therapy condition.

There are many variations to experimental and quasi-experimental designs with regard to sampling techniques (e.g., how participants are selected), type of comparison groups to be used against what is being studied (e.g., comparing your treatment to no treatment, or to a different kind of treatment), methods to minimize sources of artifacts and bias, types of variables being investigated, and even the components of the study that identify the potent factors of an intervention. The interested reader is referred to research methods textbooks (e.g., Kazdin, 2003) for more detail.

Observational study designs are a lower-constraint type of research than experimental designs, but also with high yield of information. As with the experimental and quasi-experimental designs, researchers can often identify cause and effect from variables studied with this methodology, but the researchers' role is to observe rather than to affect or intervene with the variables. Observational designs examine naturally existing variables (e.g., height, personality disorder), or variables that result from naturally occurring circumstances (meaning the investigator does not create them, e.g., pregnancy, trauma experience, medical disorder).

Observational designs can answer numerous research questions. These designs may be used as precursors to treatment outcome studies to support the need for intervention development, or for posttreatment studies to observe populations' functioning or well-being over time. Likewise, treatment efficacy (whether the treatment works in regular settings or circumstances) studies might utilize observational studies because interventions may be evaluated in their natural settings, without manipulation of treatment variables, therapist variables, or patient variables. For this type of study, it would be important to follow up on an empirical finding that a particular intervention works under ideal laboratory settings. Benefits of observational designs are that multiple variables can be considered simultaneously because there is less of an attempt to control for all confounding variables (e.g., noise or distracting factors) in a study. Observational designs might be less expensive than employing experimental designs, and more information may be obtained as to how well the treatment will generalize to applications in real world settings.

Qualitative research studies are another form of lowest-constraint research designs. Qualitative studies have a different purpose and result than quantitative research, yet they are both empirical approaches to obtaining new knowledge. Instead of summarizing findings about relationships between variables based on large groups of participants, qualitative research aims *to expand and broaden the understanding of a particular topic or phenomenon.* Such studies usually depend on a small number of participants or groups of participants (interviewing each group as one participant) and are not typically hypothesis driven. Qualitative research often takes the form of semi- or unstructured interviews to investigate a rare or poorly understood condition, experience, or circumstance, individualized responses to given circumstances, or something typically deemed personal or private (e.g., use of spiritual guidance). Perhaps, the focus is on aspects of a person's thoughts, feelings, or behaviors that require elaboration rather than on concise responses to pencil-and-paper tests. Interviews allow for in-depth responses by participants that might not otherwise be acquired. Data takes the form of narratives, stories, or even words used. Data is typically analyzed by a collaboration of interpreters or by software used to analyze words or phrases that summarize the gist of materials.

Although different from quantitative methodology, qualitative research uses legitimate methodology and is a "systematic, replicable, and cumulative" approach to research (Kazdin, 2003, p. 329). Qualitative research can help develop a particular theory, or to identify variables important to study using quantitative methods. Interviews with amyotrophic lateral sclerosis (ALS) persons and their caregivers helped determine relevant aspects of quality of life (QOL) for this population to be included in a later-developed QOL instrument (Simmons et al., 2006).

The possible roles for qualitative research in treatment-outcome studies and empirically validated treatment are several. Qualitative research may be used to understand patient-client relationships and their impact on treatment, patients' experience of therapy, and how therapeutic lessons are or are not integrated into daily functioning. Perhaps interviews with patients might reveal what they deemed important in treatment. Likewise, qualitative study of therapists' experience delivering empirically supported treatments or their decision making during this process would likely enhance our understanding of treatment implementation. There are many other places for qualitative research in the examination and development of empirically supported treatment, some of which can be found in the literature and journals exclusively publishing qualitative studies, such as in *Qualitative Health Research, Qualitative Research,* and *Qualitative Research in Psychology.*

Compared with large-sample experimental group designs and small-scale qualitative research studies, *single-subject designs* describe another important research methodology. Single-subject designs and case studies are useful venues for studying the responses of individuals (or single collective groups of individuals) to assessment or treatment, and can provide valuable information toward development or evaluation of treatment-outcome research. Case-based research is discussed later in this chapter. Although single-subject designs are sometimes criticized for lack of generalization, there are benefits and reasons for studying people individually.

Single-subject experimental designs, such as ABAB designs, multiple-baseline designs and changing criterion designs, maintain the same methodological rigor of experimental group designs. Research employing single-subject methodology examines the causal effects of independent variables on dependent variables, but looks at these relationships within one individual (or *single* group or *single* society, referred to as a "single case" from this point forward) rather than between groups of individuals exposed to different conditions. Instead, the single case may be exposed to various conditions at different times (e.g., first, a nutritional counseling program; second, an exercise regimen; third, a weight management support group), or to the same conditions at various time points (e.g., alternating 6 weeks of group weight management participation with 6 weeks of self-monitoring). The distinguishing characteristics of single-subject designs include continuous assessment and use of different phases.

Continuous assessment is defined as "observations on multiple occasions over time prior to and during the period in which the intervention is administered" (Kazdin, 2003, p. 274). Continuous assessment usually includes a *baseline assessment* that describes the observations made about the independent and dependent variables prior to any intervention or purposeful influence by the researcher. Baseline assessment is critical to making predictions about what might or might not occur as a result of introducing the independent variable(s). *Different phases* refers to the "different periods of time (several days, weeks) in which a particular condition (baseline or intervention) is implemented and data are collected" (Kazdin, 2003, p. 274). Thus, the continuous monitoring and evaluation of the independent and dependent variables allow critical changes to be detected, and permit the researcher to distinguish whether the changes in the dependent variables occurred subsequent to the introduction of the independent variables. The different phases allow for different interventions or independent variables to be introduced while being monitored, and therefore, for cause and effect to be determined. In fact, if you are an empiricist at heart, or have knowledge of cognitive-behavioral psychology, you might begin to wonder how this methodology differs from best practice in applied clinical psychology. Stay tuned for the answer to this question.

In ABAB designs, treatment and assessment are alternated to monitor changes that occur in the dependent variable as a result of introducing or discontinuing an intervention. In multiple-baseline designs, several dependent variables are monitored for an extended period before introducing treatments or interventions and monitoring their impact. If a behavioral modification plan is designed to stop child tantrums, the child's behaviors in school, home, and perhaps in the company of babysitters are monitored. The intervention might first be introduced in one setting, while all three circumstances continue to be monitored. The clinician or researcher continues to look for changes in the behaviors to see if the modification plan is directly impacting the behaviors. The child may discontinue tantrums only in the environment where the plan is in place, or perhaps the impact generalizes to other settings as well. In such multiple-baseline designs, the intervention may be tested across settings, across behaviors (so first tantrums are targeted, then aversive eating behavior, and finally perhaps an increase in prosocial behavior is monitored). In more complicated designs, multiple baseline designs can be tested across participants (see Kazdin, 2003, pp. 283–285 for more details).

Changing criterion designs monitor exactly what is inferred. Relationships between independent and dependent variables are studied, and the goal is to show that "behavior changes in increments to match a performance criterion" (Kazdin, 2003, p. 286). The independent variable, or treatment/intervention/consequence, continues to change (i.e., more/less reinforcement/punishment/consequence) after each goal is met (desired increase or decrease in behavior is exhibited). While quantitative data is likely collected during single-subject research, it is analyzed by visual inspection methods rather than by statistical analyses.

The previous descriptions are oversimplified, and there are many other single-subject designs. The goal here is to give you at least some sense of what is described in research articles reviewing treatment efficacy or effectiveness based on the single-subject designs. But, why use single-subject designs if interpretation is subject to visual inspection, and therefore to researcher bias? Why use this methodology if the ability to generalize the findings to others is possibly limited?

The benefits of single-subject designs are several. First, unique treatments, characteristics, or conditions can be studied in single-subject designs, whereas large *N* studies may not be feasible due to limited access to participants (by virtue of incidence) or the cost of such implementation. An example might be a single-subject design to study the impact of a new anger management therapy with hypertensive patients (Wilner, 2004). In this situation, known elements of different cognitive-behavioral therapies were combined with close medical monitoring of the patients' blood pressure to evaluate if this type of therapy would be effective in reducing anger, lowering blood pressure, increasing problem-solving skills, and improving overall quality of life. Because aspects of this treatment were tested empirically with other populations, modifications based on this sample's needs could be considered and close evaluation by the clinician and patients' physicians allowed for fine-tuning the intervention based on individual needs. The important concept here is that all other explanations for change in anger and blood pressure could be ruled out and any changes could be attributed to the intervention. This is the essence of internal validity, and one of the key elements to experimental designs. Once success is met on a small-scale study, and researchers can determine what elements of a treatment should be included, added, or taken away, larger studies can be conducted more cost-effectively. Thus, single-subject designs share some of the credibility of larger experimental studies while allowing more specificity in addressing the issues at hand and can serve as a precursor to larger studies.

Single-case studies are also important to study the implications of having or treating rare conditions. It is likely less common to attract a large sample of schizoaffective patients with panic disorder, diabetes with resulting nerve damage, and asthma to study the modification of an empirically validated treatment for panic disorder without comorbid difficulties. With both medical conditions compromising relaxation treatment, and the psychological disorder needing to be accounted for, empirically testing the results of thoughtful clinical decision making could be important to inform other clinicians of what worked and did not work in such a situation. If such research is not conducted, independent clinicians must continue to rely on trial and error, without systematically knowing what about the therapeutic interventions is helpful or not. Further discussion of case-based research is provided later in this chapter.

The limitations of single-subject designs, even in the cases described here, are significant and need to be carefully considered in deciding on the goal of research to be designed and implemented. Although cause and effect may be relatively clear in most of the designs and for the purposes described, single-subject designs typically cannot distinguish what role the participant's or the therapist's characteristics played in the outcome. So, if hypertensive patients benefited from the newly designed cognitive-behavioral treatment, was it distinctly because of the treatment? Or, was there something about the energy level and dedication of the therapist, or the receptivity and motivation of the patient that made the treatment particularly successful? These questions cannot be answered without replication of the studies with new therapists or patients, or in larger group designs. Yet, many would argue that large group designs also require replication, since their results are based on averages of changes in dependent variables and individual changes are usually not reported.

Relevance of Single-Case Design

Earlier we posed the question, "How does single-subject research methodology differ from best practices in applied clinical psychology?" It is now time for your answer and a comparison of these two applications. Relevant to the practice of clinical psychology, the data collected and outcomes generated by this family of single-subject designs are exactly the type of information sought by behavioral health care agencies and insurance companies to justify payment for treatment, or verification of the outcome of therapy. Because the design of cognitive behavioral therapy relies on systematic and ongoing assessment, monitoring of progress, and follow-up on outcomes, it is often well accepted by behavioral health care insurance companies for treatment of many common problems. Later chapters illustrate methods of assessment and treatment that could be used for therapy as well as in single-subject design research. The important difference between research and therapy, when a distinction needs to be made, is that research aims to further knowledge about a particular phenomenon (intervention, condition, behavior), and therapy aims to advance the well-being of an individual. Thus, the desired outcome in research is for the greater good of psychological science and its consumers; the desired outcome for therapy is for the better health of the individual and those directly affected by him or her.

Case studies refer to "the intensive study of the individual" (Kazdin, 2003, p. 267). As in single-subject designs, *individual* can refer to one person, one group, one society, and so on. In contrast to single-subject designs, depending on how case studies are operationally defined, they may not be methodologically rigorous, and are usually not based on quantitative data. Case study authors provide specific, detailed anecdotal and contextual information, and the biases of the writer's perspective or interpretations. Their goal often is to explicate the intricacies of a particular phenomenon, to reflect on the action taken under specific circumstances or, perhaps, to illustrate the information leading to the development of a theory. This description may sound similar to that of the qualitative study, but qualitative designs require preplanned methodology, are replicable, and are analyzed systematically, often by more than one individual, to achieve consensual validation. Thus, studies based on qualitative methodology differ significantly from case studies, although they both rely on narratives, detailed explication of constructs, and possibly qualitative analysis.

The relevance of case studies to clinical psychology is that often people present with unique and unexplained behaviors, personality patterns, or coping styles that are not documented as disorders or common occurrences, and best treatments for these individuals are not always evident. Case studies highlight individuality and the relative success (or lack thereof) of the approach taken by the author. These anecdotes can be useful for contemplating the approach to a similar person. While single-subject designs require preplanned methodology and prospective study, case studies, as defined here, are often written retrospectively and are usually not replicable due to their unstructured or unsystematic methods of information gathering and reporting. So, generalization and even the validity of the outcomes reviewed are often questioned and sometimes questionable. Confusion in the literature can occur when case studies are defined more broadly to include single-subject designs or other systematic methodology.

The value of case studies has been acknowledged widely in the clinical psychology field. Some journals (e.g., *Clinical Case Studies*) are solely dedicated to case studies, as are others to single-subject designs. Case studies can be viewed as a jumping-off point for new ideas, hypotheses, theories, and political action (e.g., the anecdote of one person's negative experience of ageism in adoption might lead to further explanation of general practices and state legislation on the issue, if relevant). Therapy techniques can be developed in response to recognizing unique phenomena that might have significant attributes relevant to a subset of a population or individuals sharing similar characteristics. Kazdin (2003) also explains the value of case studies that offer counterinstances, or examples of when a known and accepted therapy *does not* work. Furthermore, Kazdin argues the motivational and persuasive value of case studies as both a value, and as a stimulus for more systematic and controlled research. Claims made that classical music played during exam preparation enhanced an individual's performance significantly from being a "C" student to being an "A" student might be so compelling to readers that some consumers will instantly invest in new music collections, whereas investigators (and production companies!) will jump to their computers to write new research protocols to study the veracity of such claims using experimental designs. Thus, the persuasive ability might be somewhat concerning when not critically examined (such as testimonials for fad diets), but the generation of more research helps to keep cause and effect, and scientific truth and fallacy in balance.

Methods Summary

Research of any kind is not perfect. Researchers face the challenge of answering their questions and examining their hypotheses under optimal circumstances that allow cause and effect to be determined, and allow their results to be generalized to others. Sometimes this means that quantitative research is conducted with very selective population samples under highly controlled environments, and sometimes this means selecting a diverse sample and examining their behaviors or responses to changes in the independent variables (treatment) under conditions as similar to "normal" as possible. There is much grey in between, and cultural considerations, replicability, feasibility, and the goals of the research all need to be considered.

Qualitative studies allow more latitude because hypotheses are not clearly formed at the outset, but rather, questions guide the studies' development. Concepts are expected to be expanded, and the results are not necessarily predictable. Single-subject research designs follow in the complexity of the experimental and quasi-experimental designs, and are further limited by the small sample included. However, their return for answering research questions and advancing treatment developments and modifications can be outstanding. Case studies offer a unique contribution to treatment development in their nonmethodological approach to exploring new ideas and concepts in the context of anecdotal reports of individual experiences. The advancement of clinical science and the expansion of empirically validated, empirically supported, and manually driven therapies rely on the combination of the methodologies and studies described so far in this chapter. As we turn to examine the range of treatment options available for clinicians' use, and how they are categorized, studied, and disseminated, your understanding of the complexity of research and methodologies should allow you to understand why the application of scientific techniques to the study of human behavior and behavioral change (broadly defined—thoughts, feelings, actions) is so challenging.

Therapeutic Interventions: Are They All the Same?

The 1990s saw health care reform through the management of care, and mental health professionals were called to task to justify their practices, services, and outcomes. This has also been true of medical practitioners, but issues directly relating to medicine are not addressed here. Since clinical psychology both thrives and suffers from grand diversity in theory and practice, the ambiguity of what constitutes "good therapy" highlighted many questions and called for action from the field. When a field is as wide as mental health care or even clinical psychology, bringing a profession to consensus is a difficult task.

Imagine you had to organize a discussion about therapeutic best practice for treating a depressed young adult who has not been attending work for the past 3 weeks. Your discussion group consists of three psychologists you knew from your undergraduate training in a room with three of your graduate professors. Then you asked volunteers from yet a different theoretical prospective to join the discussion. Would you gain agreement on steps to take? Maybe, but it is more likely you would not. Now, offer the same group the opportunity to design treatment for a personality-disordered adult. Would the consensus come easily? It is highly unlikely that it would. Even with the most clear-cut diagnoses and problems, individual differences among the clients and the therapists would cause variation in treatment plans. How, then, was the field to come to an agreement on what to support in the face of external challenges? Surely there was a need to rely on the research literature. Yet, research is more popular among some specialties of therapy (e.g., cognitive-behavioral therapy) than others (e.g., long-term psychoanalysis), and therefore, even this approach was likely to yield varying responses.

Empirically Supported and Probably Efficacious Treatments

To revert back to the beginning of the movement, the demands from third-party payers and the public spawned the development of a task force under Division 12 (Clinical Psychology) of the American Psychological Association and the leadership of David Barlow. The purpose of the Task Force on Promotion and Dissemination of Psychological Procedures was "to consider methods to educate clinical psychologists, third party payers and the public about effective psychotherapies" (APA Division of Clinical Psychology, 1995, p. 3). The task force delineated two categories of therapies, "Well-Established Treatments," and "Probably Efficacious Treatments." The terms "empirically validated treatments" and "well-established treatments" are often used interchangeably. Sometimes "empirically supported treatments" refers to the well-established treatments, and sometimes to those in the probably efficacious group. The criteria for each of these categories are listed in Table 4.1. Note the inclusion and roles of "experimental designs," "case studies," and "single-subject designs." The lists of treatments meeting the criteria outlined in Table 4.1 were established on the basis of empirical evidence published in peer-reviewed literature. The 1995 list of well-established and probably efficacious treatment was ex-

Table 4.1 **Criteria for "Well-Established" and "Probably Efficacious" Treatment, According to the APA Division 12 Task Force**

Well-Established Treatments	Probably Efficacious Treatments
1. Group studies by different investigators demonstrating efficacy by (a) showing superiority to pill, psychological placebo, or another treatment, or (b) demonstrating equivalency to an established treatment with adequate statistical power ($n = 30$/group)	Two studies showing treatment is more effective than a waiting-list control group; or
2. A large series of well-designed single case studies compared with a 1(a) treatment and demonstrating efficacy, with	Studies otherwise meeting the well-established criteria 1, 3, and 4; or
3. Treatment manuals, and	At least two good studies demonstrating effectiveness but flawed by client sample heterogeneity; or
4. Clear specification of client samples.	A small series of single-case design studies otherwise meeting the well-established treatment criteria 2, 3, and 4.

Source: Task Force, 1995, *APA Division of Clinical Psychology*, p. 3.

panded to include additional treatment protocols in 1998 (see Table 4.2). Although the attempt to classify and list effective therapies was a noble starting point, it was met with much controversy.

Cognitive-behavioral therapy as a paradigm and specialty in clinical psychology is known to be a short-term approach to therapy that is based on treatment manuals for techniques and agendas. Other long-term therapies that rely more on process-oriented topics and analysis-based interactions are less amenable to description in a manual and replication. Experimental and quasi-experimental designs, almost by definition, require manualized treatment and operationally defined interventions to evaluate effectiveness. Without a manual, the independent variable in experimental designs would not be systematically delivered or measurable to determine its impact on the dependent variable (patient change). Thus, cognitive-behavioral therapies were said to be overrepresented in the lists of established and efficacious treatments, and other therapies were not well represented (Levant, 2004).

Although the intention of the task force was to educate others about existing therapies and their credits, perhaps the unintentional consequence was that some therapies were assumed to be ineffective or not valid versus not validated or lacking evidence because empirical evidence was not available. Third-party payers, laypersons, and perhaps some clinicians may have

Table 4.2 **Well-Established and Probably Efficacious Treatments as Defined and Listed by the Division 12 Task Force**

Well-Established Treatments	Probably Efficacious Treatments
Beck's cognitive therapy for depression	Applied relaxation for panic disorder
Behavior modification for the developmentally disabled	Brief psychodynamic therapies
Behavior modification for enuresis and encopresis	Behavior modification for sexual offenders
Behavioral therapy for headache and irritable bowel syndrome	Dialectical behavior therapy for Borderline Personality Disorder
Behavioral therapy for male and female sexual dysfunction	Emotionally focused couples therapy
Behavioral marital therapy	Habit reversal and control techniques
Cognitive therapy for chronic pain	Lewinsohn's psychoeducational treatment for depression
Cognitive therapy for Panic Disorder (with or without agoraphobia)	
Cognitive-behavioral therapy for Generalized Anxiety Disorder	
Exposure treatment for phobias (agoraphobia, social phobia, simple phobia, and PTSD)	
Exposure and response prevention for Obsessive Compulsive Disorder	
Family therapy for Schizophrenia per Hogarty or Falloon	
Interpersonal therapy for bulimia	
Klerman and Weissman's interpersonal therapy for depression	
Parent training for Oppositional Defiant Disorder	
Systematic desensitization for simpl phobias	
Token economy programs	

Source: Task Force, 1998, *APA Division of Clinical Psychology.* Reprinted with permission.

dichotomized existing therapies prematurely, setting unrealistic expectations that all therapies must be categorized as empirically validated or empirically *un*supported. This dichotomy might restrict trade or consideration of available treatments, which ultimately does not serve the best interests of scientific inquiry or service to the public.

A Closer Look at Manuals

So what is a manual exactly? Some people think of treatment manuals as cookbooks, and this is one of the biggest criticisms of the format. "If your client has agoraphobia, turn to page 15 for instructions on what to do. Worried thoughts? Please turn to page 21." Therapy would sure be a lot easier if treatment decisions and implementation were so straightforward. Even the best manual cannot address all the nuances of individual differences, but manuals should provide specific information about the parameters of the treatment. A manual should indicate for whom the treatment is appropriate. Has research shown that the treatment is more or less effective with a certain age or ethnic group? Has it been tested with heterogeneous samples, or is that a recognized caution? What should be done if the patient has comorbid psychological disorders? In what sequence should the treatment be delivered? Is it contraindicated or acceptable if the client is also taking psychotropic medications or medications for medical illnesses?

What are other useful ingredients in treatment manuals? Many manuals contain session-by-session objectives, goals, and homework assignments. It is helpful when manuals indicate what diagnostic criteria should be used to determine the emphasis of the treatment delivery. Scripts and handouts for clients also help maximize reliability and transfer of information from the therapist to clients. Handouts might include bulleted or expansive explanations of information discussed during a therapy session, worksheets to practice skills learned in therapy, or record sheets that provide a format for between-session data collection by the client on thoughts, feelings, behaviors, interactions, or other information. Some manuals provide sample explanations therapists can use to approach client issues, and others provide analogies or perhaps even mnemonics to aid in comprehension or retention of information for the patient. Troubleshooting guides, pertinent decision-making questions, and examples of how treatments can be modified for nontraditional therapy settings, persons with different characteristics than those who participated in validation of the manual, or perhaps, tips on how to modify treatment for delivery in a different modality (e.g., group, couples) are all helpful sections that might be included. With the use of technology, treatment manuals are also now incorporating web-based information, online exercises, and other resources. Some manuals include a compact disk with clinical forms that purchasers can use in their personal practice. The many benefits of manualized treatment seem obvious from the description of their text. Just the time savings for creating patient handouts and resource guides is a significant benefit.

If all the preceding information is provided in a manual, then you might wonder why clients could not use such books as self-help tools. The truth is that many self-help books include much of the same material as some treatment manuals. For a small subset of the mental health consumer population, self-help books might be sufficient to change problematic thinking or behaviors. For many, however, lack of motivation, feelings of desperation, or the impairment the disorder has caused in home, work, or social environments is too significant to be treated without professional help. Likewise, if treatment manuals are so inclusive and precise, why is there controversy in the field about their use? Shouldn't any professional be able to read a manual and deliver its contents effectively? Perhaps you have begun to identify some of the potential criticisms of manualized treatments. The following discussion alerts you to some of these possible limitations.

The Science in the Practice and the Practice of the Science

In reality, what we know from the literature is that the scientific validation of therapies is still immature. Many therapies have not yet been tested, and those that have been are tested with a restricted sample (those with pure diagnoses and no comorbid diagnoses, which is actually atypical in mental health clients; homogeneous groups lacking ethnic and cultural diversity) and often in artificial environments (university-based settings versus community-based clinics or private practices). Given these limitations, the generalization of findings from empirical studies is also restricted. This argument is not to discredit the scientific integrity of existing research on manualized treatments and techniques. It is intended to highlight the limits of our knowledge about what works and what does not work for specific disorders in persons with varying individual characteristics, in varied settings, delivered by a wide range of therapists with varying talents, characteristics, and abilities.

In fact, some research (Lambert & Barley, 2001, as cited by Levant, 2004) suggests, "Specific techniques (namely, those that were the focus of the Division 12 Task Force report) accounted for no more than 15% of the variance in therapy outcomes" (Levant, 2004, p. 221). More of the variance in therapy outcomes (as much as 30%) was explained by the characteristics and relationships between therapists and clients (Levant, 2004) and factors common to all therapies (warmth, genuineness, positive regard), including helping patients to confront or face problems (Weinberger, 1995). These statistics resulted from the Task Force on Empirically Supported Therapy Relationships, which was developed in 1999 by John Norcross, then president of Division 29 (Psychotherapy) of the American Psychological Association.

So, if evidence indicates that therapy is generally effective, that some approaches are more effective than others but the difference explained is only approximately 15%, should treatment be restricted to empirically validated protocols or manual-based therapies from the Division 12 task force list? Third-party payers would certainly have an easier time deciding what is valid for reimbursement if therapy decision making was that simple. However, Reisner (2005) astutely points out, "Much can be said for actuarial decision making, (but) it is the therapist who decides, moment to moment, when to talk and when to listen, what technique to use and why, and as Linehan (1993) discusses, when to accept and when to encourage change. A technique or set of techniques cannot substitute for a therapist's judgment or make the therapist more empathic or caring" (p. 10 of online version).

Treatment manuals cannot teach therapists how to think, when to challenge a client, or when to gently sit back and observe the interpersonal dynamics of the session as the therapy unfolds. Therapists' styles vary greatly, as they probably should. Thus, use of humor may be appropriate and effective for one therapist-client dyad at a given moment, and not for another dyad or at another juncture. Manuals cannot adequately teach clinicians how to engage in the common factors of treatment, or convey the importance of implementing the strategies of the manual in a common factors context.

The combination of best practice techniques, clinical skills and judgment, and therapist's characteristics are critical elements in successful therapy. Some of these ingredients can be manualized and taught systematically, others cannot. Many therapies have been tested by randomized clinical trials and experimental designs, and many therapies have yet to be evaluated in this way. The field has recognized that only a subset of therapies for a subset of disorders has been examined in these ways. This does not mean that only these therapies are empirically valid for use, or that randomized clinical trials are the only way to evaluate therapies. From these realizations evolved the application of the medical terminology, "evidence-based medicine" to that of psychological treatments and practice.

Evidence-Based Practice and Case-Based Research

In the beginning of this chapter, the argument was made that multiple research designs contribute to the advancement of clinical psychology through developing and evaluating treatment options. Scholars (Edwards, Dattilio, & Bromley, 2004) promulgating a holistic model of the development of clinical knowledge illustrate how practitioners', scholars', and researchers' work interface for the development of theory, treatment, randomized clinical trials (RCTs), and empirical tests of these treatments, and case-based refinement of empirically supported treatments. Evidence-based practice results from consideration and integration of these knowledge sources. Therefore, evidence-based practice is more than just the use of empirically supported treatments. Sackett, Rosenberg, Gray, Haynes, and Richardson (1996) define evidence-based practice as, "the conscientious, explicit and judicious use of current best evidence in making decisions about the care of individual patients, [which] means integrating individual clinical expertise with the best available external clinical evidence from systematic research" (p. 71). According to Edwards et al. (2004), this requires consideration of experimental literature and case-based research.

Edwards et al. (2004) assert that clinical practice and science are "partners" (p. 590) in the development of clinical knowledge. According to their model, clinical practice includes case-based clinical observations, supervision, and professional discussion based on theoretical principles and science, and it results in refinement of clinical theory, development of constructs and hypotheses, and new science. Sharing case-based observations through case conferences and publications is encouraged so that other perspectives can be openly solicited. *Case-based research* in this model is broadly defined to include single-subject designs that use qualitative or quantitative strategies, generated prospectively or retrospectively. Numerous case-based observations together may lead to development of new clinical treatment models. These can then lead to treatment manuals to be tested in RCTs that, in turn, allow clinical treatment models to be scrutinized according to scientific principles and research methodology, and often yield additional experimental studies. According to this model, the studies inform or challenge applied clinical theory, which, in turn, should influence and inform clinical practice. What develops from these reciprocal interactions is "evidence-based medicine" and advancement of clinical psychology knowledge. Edwards and colleagues appear to have resurrected and applied the defined "scientist-practitioner model" of training to the actual science and practice of clinical psychology. Their connection of the subfields of clinical psychology is masterful in helping readers understand how the pieces of the clinical psychology jigsaw puzzle may fit together.

As you are discovering your niche in clinical psychology and are beginning to ground yourself in a pattern of thought about your potential role in the field, the discussion of evidence-based medicine and case-based research might seem obvious and simple. Certainly, the model seems clear, so perhaps the controversial aspects of this model are not. If this is where you find yourself, take a moment and enjoy your perspective.

Many researchers argue against the proposed model or those similar to it, because of all the arguments provided earlier in the chapter against case studies and single-subject designs. However, those in favor of case-based research, and those who appreciate that theory can be grounded (Strauss & Corbin, 1994) or steeped in case example, also suggest that operational definitions can be developed and generalizations can be made from a compilation of case-based data. Some argue that researchers undervalue case-based data and tend to minimize the significant problems associated with RCTs and experimental designs. After all, the data generated by experimental study of clinical therapies is often based on self-report results of pencil-and-paper instruments that have widely varying degrees of reliability and construct validity. In fact, the instruments used to obtain the data provide a another whole source of bias, restriction of information, and error. But that story is for another day.

These arguments can give you a flavor of the challenges that face clinical psychology in today's search for best treatment practices. There is plenty of material in the literature that criticizes or defends case-based research or that criticizes or defends experimental designs, RCTs, and quantitative research strategies. Perhaps we should be mindful of Edwards et al.'s (2004) quote of Kiesler's (1981, p. 213) work stating, "all research is flawed . . . scientific progress results from repeated empirical attacks on a problem . . . no single study . . . is worth much in and of itself."

Summary

Many educators, scientists, and clinicians would agree that we should not throw out the baby with the bathwater. Efforts to empirically validate the methods used in psychotherapy are critical to the advancement, acceptance, and development of the field of clinical psychology, but they do not provide the total answer. Likewise, clinical practice, experience, and consideration of individual case studies are significant to the advancement of the field in theory development, and evaluation of treatments supported by randomized controlled trials to persons with individual differences. Yet case studies cannot stand alone.

Consideration of manuals and their role in treatment and treatment outcome studies was highlighted. Treatment manuals are highly valued, and yet their flaws and limitations are readily recognized. Manuals provide a basis for which third-party payers can anchor their expectations for treatment plans and payment, and the general population can develop an appreciation for techniques in the field. Manualized treatments permit easier implementation of experimental designs, and these designs give clearer pictures of what works in ideal settings, with ideal patients, and optimally trained clinicians. From there, additional data need to be collected, perhaps through single-subject designs and case-based research, to learn how the manualized treatments can be varied effectively and for whom the treatments can be successful. Qualitative studies can detail the therapist's and client's participatory experiences in manualized treatments and their reactions to the ingredients under surveillance.

Criticisms of treatment manuals include the possible unreliability of their implementation without proper training and experience. Furthermore, if manualized therapies solved the mystery of variation in treatment response, it is likely that computers could be equally effective in delivering therapy, and we know that is not reality. So, we need to learn more about client and therapist differences, variable presentations of disorders and conditions, and how all these factors interact.

This chapter aimed to increase awareness of research methodologies in clinical psychology, and their use in treatment evaluation. Awareness of the issues in empirically supported treatments and case-based research may translate into more conscious practice and attention to decision making as you progress in your graduate studies and careers. We have much further to go on this journey. The information in this chapter suggests the complex issues the field is addressing, and from where opinions evolve.

Why People Become Patients

5

Chapter

You may have heard, "Everyone can profit from therapy," or "Everyone *needs* psychotherapy." Neither of these is correct. Not everyone needs psychotherapy nor can everyone profit from the experience. What then makes a person decide to become a patient or client? Who actually might need therapy? In this chapter, we explore the reasons a person seeks or gets referred for psychotherapy.

Learning Objectives

At the end of this chapter, the reader should be able to:

- List the 12 most common reasons that people seek psychological help.
- Explain at least four differences between normal and abnormal behavior.
- Describe the multiaxial diagnostic systems of *DSM-IV-TR* and *ICD-10*.
- Discuss how psychopathology and functional behavior are connected.
- Identify disorders that are usually first diagnosed in childhood.
- Describe the difference between major symptomatic disorders and personality disorders.

Edward was very worried about germs and possible contamination. When he washed his hands (which he did several times a day), he washed with a stiff scrub brush and a special germicidal soap. He would wet his hands, soap them, scrub them, rinse them and then soap, scrub, and rinse several more times.

Alice was always scanning for danger. She rarely saw anything dangerous, but she was always on her guard. She looked at people's faces for some hint of danger. She would scrutinize their bodies without any sexual interest, looking for hidden weapons. She watched for body language that might signal the person was a terrorist.

Tim appreciated his job. He worked alone, lived alone, and only saw other people about once every 3 months when he had to deal with them to restock his pantry. He preferred his books, classical music CDs, and online activity.

Sonia loved attention. She bought outlandish outfits knowing that this attire would make everyone stare at her. At one point, it was a skimpy bathing suit that was so daring, everyone was startled when she wore it. At other times, she wore outfits that covered her body from head to toe in a garish mix of colors.

Eric was a perfectionist. He did not accept "close" to perfection as an acceptable conclusion of any task. He believed that he could not just be near the mark, but must always be right on the mark. He demanded of himself and others that perfection was the only acceptable goal.

None of these people came for therapy, at least not for the preceding behavioral patterns. None of these people saw the need to change what they did. Edward was a surgeon, Tim was the caretaker of a lighthouse, Alice was in charge of airport security at a large metropolitan airport, Sonia was an actress, and Eric was a neurosurgeon.

Understanding Why People Become Patients

At least 12 common *D-words* describe the reasons people seek therapy. These include the individual, family, or couple being *D*iscomforted, *D*iscontented, *D*istressed, *D*isabled, *D*ysfunctional, *D*isconnected, *D*ispirited, *D*isorganized, *D*istraught, *D*issatisfied, *D*yscontrolled, and *D*isgusted. All these descriptive terms refer to mood states that are unpleasant and perhaps frightening to the person experiencing the mood and possibly to those around him or her. Not only is the mood or affective state an inherently aversive experience, these states can preclude or interfere with other moods and interactions that would be more beneficial. Imagine that you are thinking about going to a party, but you feel generally dispirited and disconnected. Perhaps you will find just the antidote to those feelings at the social function. Or it may be that you scarcely notice who or what is going on around you because of your negative preoccupation. As a result, you interact poorly and tend to turn others away. Others mutter about your "weird" attitude and behavior. When "D-word" moods are prolonged, the impact on a person's general functioning and quality of life and health can be enormous.

Describing Normal versus Abnormal Behavior

The operational definitions of normal and abnormal may be a function of time, culture, geography, or style. If one were to wear an exceptionally brief bathing suit, it might be viewed appreciatively on the French Riviera, but would be unacceptable in another country. In some groups, wearing a garment that exposes any part of the body would be considered inappropriate or even illegal. A bathing suit that would be acceptable according to today's standards might have gotten someone arrested 40 years ago at the very same beach.

Speaking in tongues, seizure-like body movements, and drooling might be labeled as abnormal in one setting and as religious fervor in another. Is the correct interpretation of this behavior religious rapture, psychological decompensation, or neurological problems? Although an operational definition for abnormal is essential to understanding psychopathology, we must admit from the beginning that we are stuck. There are a multitude of definitions that are based in culture, philosophy, religion, or politics. Szasz (1984, 1988, 1997) saw the term and the construct of mental illness as a way for society to control its members. Those who did not conform to the demands and expectations of the dominant society were seen as mentally ill. Probably the best example of Szasz's idea would be in countries that see their political system as perfect and unassailable despite visible and contrary data. Anyone, therefore, who is dissident to their country's "perfect system" must be (by definition) mentally ill. They would then need to be immediately placed in a secure psychiatric facility to have their "illness" treated.

We have come a long way from assessing people as being possessed by demons to explain their behavior. We recognize biological, sociological, and psychological reasons for behavior that deviates from the societal norm. None of these explanatory models can offer a total answer. As is often the case, numerous combinations and permutations of factors explain behavior. Behavior may be caused or influenced by biogenetic factors, the genotype. The observed behavior is identified as the phenotype. There may be environmental and social factors that impact and impinge on the individual, the sociotype.

Problems emerge when a person's behavior noticeably interferes with what they are trying to do. What gets noticed in one setting may be easily and quickly overlooked in another. One of the caveats that we offer in any discussion of psychopathology is that there may not be a single standard that transcends all people, at all times, in all circumstances. With every individual, we have to take great care to evaluate that individual's strengths, coping abilities, and personal attributes, in addition to problems and problem areas.

It is negative behavior, or behavior that has a negative outcome, that most often brings someone into psychotherapy. Simply, the behavior is causing problems both within the person and with others. Individuals who are very dependent may gather people around them who provide care. They may not perceive this as a problem nor would they see depending on others as negative. If, however, they lose their support system for any reason, then their dependence may have a negative effect because they feel abandoned. Individuals often come with the complaint that they need to get their lives together, get their head together, or take control of their life.

Among the most important diagnostic factors is the ability of the individual to develop and use a broad range of actions and reactions. Over time, each of us develops and maintains a repertoire of reactions to various internal and external stimuli. The person with a limited repertoire of behaviors is more likely to have a difficulty that triggers one of the 12 D-word moods. They try to use the same responses in most situations no matter whether the responses fit.

If life for an individual is very limited and tightly controlled, this may not be a problem. For example, in the military, what one wore (a uniform), how one wore it, when one wore it, and the proper care of that uniform would be set out by rules, custom, and regulations. A person with a limited repertoire may be very adaptive as long as the situation remains the same. When life changes, or when circumstances demand a greater variety of responses the same person may not effectively cope.

Kenneth, aged 66, sought therapy because of his depression. He reported that he had been depressed for most of his life. On several occasions, he had sought therapy and after varying amounts of time, had terminated it when he felt less depressed. When questioned by his current therapist as to whether he had ever been happy, he quickly replied, "Yes, when I was drafted into the army at age 18. I was sent to Europe in 1958. It was wonderful!" When asked what made it wonderful, Ken replied, "It was so easy to live there. I never had to worry about what to wear, what to do, where to eat, what to eat, where to live, or even when to get up and when to sleep. It was the perfect life." When asked if it was always like that, Ken replied, "No. There was a time when several of us were told to go to a town in Germany to help build a school. We were told to wear *civvies* so as not to stand out too much. I hated that. We lived in a local hotel and ate at various restaurants. I never knew what to wear or what to order. The other guys made fun of me because I wore the same thing every day." Ken had limited internal resources.

Some individuals might have perceived Ken's assignment as wonderful. For some, living at a hotel as opposed to a barracks was heaven. Having a private room and bath as opposed to community living and latrines was wonderful. They could eat at any restaurant and choose their meals without having to pay for them as opposed to eating in a mess hall. For Ken, this was torture and he could not wait to return to his unit and to the army regimen. Because of a limited repertoire of different choices and actions, his behavior became ritualized and compulsive. Even when his actions did not produce the desired results, he continued to act in the same way. He would even complain about how he longed to return to the unit, which his buddies simply did not understand.

Related to the compulsive nature of such behavior is that these individuals are inflexible in dealing with problems and with people. When invited to try a different approach to coping with problems, their likely response is that they have always done it in the same way and are reluctant or insistent that they should not have to change what *they* do. Again, even when their approach does not work, they maintain the same inflexible approach.

On returning to civilian life, Ken studied electrical engineering, and over the years he was moderately successful. His work was not conceptual or innovative. Rather, it involved technical production of models designed by others. Being told what to do was what he wanted. Did this style contribute to his depression? Or, was the major factor in his depression the reality that the world cannot always be regular and predictable?

For other individuals, the difficulty stems from their manner of approaching interpersonal or intrapersonal difficulties. Their approach to problem solving may be described as "thoughtless." By thoughtless, we do not mean that they cannot or do not think or that they are necessarily cognitively challenged.

Rather, their behavioral responses appear to be "automatic." Essentially, their lives operate in a stimulus-to-response mode. Having always responded in a particular manner, they continue to do so, even if the situation warrants a different response. They do not seem to make choices but try to make one size fit all.

Lisa had always been shy. She avoided situations where she would be the center of attention. She had always managed to remain in the background in classes and now at her work. When offered a promotion with a sizable salary increase, Lisa was torn. Should she accept it or stay "safe" in the background. Her life circumstances required that she earn more money to help pay for her mother's medical care. She accepted the position, but after 3 weeks was called into her supervisor's office and told that she could not keep her office door closed and communicate with her staff via e-mail. She had to have weekly staff meetings, and interact with her staff. The ensuing anxiety brought Lisa to seek therapy.

For some individuals, their actions are often so noticeable to others that the individual gets marked and colored by their own behavior. Probably the simplest example is driving according to the speed limit. Many people accept as a fact that driving no more than 5 miles over the posted speed limit is okay. By what authority is this okay? Has anyone ever seen in writing, a rule that says any driver can exceed the speed limit by 5 miles without penalty? Likely not! The myth comes from the personal experience we have all had of driving 5 miles over the posted speed without repercussions. However, if we drive 10 or more miles over the speed limit and pass all those driving only 5 miles over the speed limit, we are more noticeable. Subsequent to being noticed, we may face censure, anger, retribution, and revenge. We may, in fact, be forced to pay a fine by the agents of our society, the criminal justice system.

This leads to the next factor, the individual's behaviors, thoughts, and feelings being extreme. What is most likely seen as "normal" is behavior, thoughts, and feelings that tend to be moderate. It is wonderful to feel good, but it can become euphoria that leads to dangerous actions.

Susan, aged 20, sought therapy because of her anxiety. She announced to the therapist that she wanted to be cured of her anxiety. She reported that it kept her from sleeping, interfered with her school performance, negatively impacted her social life, and made relating to peers difficult. The problem with trying to rid Susan of all her anxiety was that it might leave her amotivational. Too little anxiety and there may not be motivation to study. Too much anxiety could interfere with studying and with memory. Ideally, to become normal, Susan would move her anxiety from the extreme to a more moderate point. There will always be people at the extremes of the normal curve. The majority of individuals are between −1 and +1 standard deviations.

The issue of adaptation is another key concept. How adaptive are people to their environment and situation? The person who seeks clinical services is more likely to experience some form of maladaptive behavior. Sometimes actions or thoughts that worked at some earlier point in life stop working or the new situation calls for a shift in thinking, action, or affect. Using Piaget's idea, adaptation is an interaction between assimilation and accommodation. Assimilation refers to the incorporation of new information into existing schemas (using old schemas in new situations). This helps to give the world some predictability and context. Accommodation involves the alteration of an old schema to account for new information. This allows an expanded understanding of the world.

Another problem may emerge when individuals are in tune with a small subpart of the larger community. They may have no problems as long as they stay in their small community. It is when they are at odds with the larger community that they come to our attention. The subculture may be the family, the neighborhood, the town, or the local community. Children who have been reinforced for not speaking and for using hand signals and grunts at home to get what they desire will not be treated the same way once they go to school, but will be expected to speak and participate in the life of the class.

Paul was born and raised in a small ethnic enclave in a large eastern city. He spoke his parents' native language at home and with his friends and neighbors. He went to a parochial school in his neighborhood and attended his local parish church which was also an ethnic church. After graduating from high school, he went to a state college at some distance from his home. He chose the college because of its excellent program in his area of interest. After one term, he was so upset and unhappy that he left the school, and later he enrolled in a small college near his home. Although it did not have the program that he wanted, he stayed through to graduation and chose another area of specialization because he felt comfortable with the culture of the smaller college.

Large parts of maladaptive patterns may be self-consonant. That is, these individuals may not see their behavior as abnormal. They may see their problem as the ill will or negative behaviors of others. Their sentences often begin with, "If only *they* . . ." People who see their behavior as reasonable and appropriate, despite evidence to the contrary, will not only avoid therapy, but may have great difficulty when forced to be involved in therapy.

Evan was a tenured college professor who had earned a doctorate in history from a prestigious university. He was infamous among the students for his veiled sexist comments and innuendos in his classes. Many colleagues, male and female, had asked him to be careful with his comments inasmuch as they could be taken as harassment. After he made a particularly egregious comment, his behavior was finally reported and a grievance was filed. He denied any negative intent and tried to dismiss the grievance as the product of "poor sports," "people without a sense of humor," or the college administration pandering to the "God of political correctness." After an investigation, he was placed on administrative leave and told that he would have to participate in several months of weekly one-on-one sexual harassment counseling. At the end of that time, the counselor would report back on the result of the counseling. After the counseling was completed, the counselor reported that in every session, Evan insisted that he had done nothing wrong, that he was unfairly being singled out for punishment by a "radical, lesbian, feminist cabal" at the college. He was fired for cause, and after some legal interaction, left the college.

The final two pieces relate to the areas of concern or conflict. The interpersonal issues are those issues that affect others. For the sake of our discussion, we can group problems into interpersonal (between the individual and those in that individual's surroundings) and intrapersonal (problems that are troubling for the individual). There is a bidirectional influence between the interpersonal and intrapersonal domains. If an individual who experiences depression may be sad and filled with self-loathing ("I'm worthless. I would be better off dead."), this depression may also influence others in the family ("I hate to be with you when you're like this. I feel so helpless to do anything.").

Some of the intrapersonal issues are experiences such as being discomforted by feelings, thoughts, or experience ("I try to avoid driving over bridges. I can do it if there is no other way, but I would drive 10 miles out of my way to avoid driving across a bridge."). We may feel discontented. We view our lives or experience and ask, "Is this all that there is?" We may be distressed by internal or external stimuli ("I am lost since my girlfriend left me. I wander around with no direction.").

When the experience is severe, we may become disabled. This might be seen in an individual's functioning decreasing to a point of no apparent function ("I just cannot get out of bed. I lie there for hours."). This is both quantitatively and qualitatively different from the intrapersonal experience of being dysfunctional where the individual's usual level of function is decreased ("I just have to push myself to get anything done. I get it done, but it is so hard.").

Sometimes the intrapersonal issue is feeling disconnected from people and experiences that surround us. ("I was at the party and people were trying to be friendly but it felt as if I had a wall up."). At times, we may feel dispirited. ("I try and try to do well but nothing that I try seems to work."). We may experience danger and great anguish and feel distressed ("I just know that some great calamity will fall on me."). When we cannot figure out what direction to go in, or when we are doubtful about what to do, we may feel distraught ("What shall I do? I can't stay, and I can't go, I'm stuck in the middle."). There are times that we are dissatisfied with our present experience. ("I want more!"), or disgusted with the actions of others or the turn of affairs (I can't stand her; this just makes me sick!). When we do things that we know are negative and for which we will pay a price, we may be dyscontrolled ("I know that the drinking is no good for me but once I start, I can't stop."). Finally, we may be disorganized ("Everything that I need to do is spread across six continents, and I can't seem to get my act together.").

These mood experiences are more the norm than the exception. We have all had these moods in some form, at some time, for some duration, with some impact. Again, we need to delineate between those problems that are part of living and development and those that bring someone to the attention of the medico-legal system. Specifically, what will bring that individual in to see a clinical psychologist?

Biological Perspectives

In what seems to us in the twenty-first century to be a rather quaint and interesting idea, the phrenologists of the eighteenth century "discovered" that certain attributes of personality or general functioning could be localized in the brain. The more that a particular faculty was exercised, it would, like a muscle, grow and show up as it pressed against the skull to raise bumps. Similarly, an underused faculty would atrophy and result in a depressed area of the skull. For example, reach back to the base of your skull. Is there a bump or a depressed area? This is the area identified by phrenologists as "amativeness." If you have a large bump in this area you can be phrenologically certain that you are high on amativeness. Or, possibly low on that faculty. Contemporary terminology labels amativeness as sexuality, defined as attraction to and attractiveness to others for sexual purposes. You might want to assess that again.

The biological view looks at brain function in terms of brain structures, brain circuitry, and brain chemistry. The interaction of the brain with the endocrine system, the autonomic nervous system, the sensory input systems, the muscles, digestive tract, and respiratory system is well known to us. Terms such as "nervous stomach," "a case of nerves," "heartache," "butterflies in the stomach," or "nervous twitch" are familiar to us. We understand these descriptive metaphors for the effect of emotion and cognition on our bodies. A cognitive therapist may ask about the thoughts in your head, a Gestalt therapist might ask for the feelings in your heart. The emotions are, however, more related to the hypothalamus, the cortex, and the limbic system. The amygdala, part of the limbic system, serves the function of evaluating a stimulus for its emotional valence.

The frontal lobes of the cortex control abstract thought, focus of attention, the ability to plan and sequence behaviors, and social adjustment, and some aspects of personality. Individuals who sustain frontal lobe damage may have great difficulty in controlling their verbal or motor behavior, possibly being aggressive with very slight provocation. Postinjury, previously shy and inhibited individuals may become grandiose and inappropriate. Previously reluctant or unable to step forward, they now may demand center stage. They may say socially inappropriate things, tell off-color jokes, and generally have a personality change. This change is not reversible, and the social controls that were previously coded and controlled by the frontal lobes seem to be turned off.

The technique of prefrontal lobotomy was once used as a means of controlling behavior. This involved cutting the connection between the right and left frontal lobes. The desired reaction was to make excited and out-of-control patients less excitable and more easily controlled. The result of calming was not always achieved and what occurred more often was a "flattening" of the emotions. This technique is rarely used today for controlling behavior, though it has been used for seizure activity that cannot be controlled by medication.

Similarly, individuals with damage to the temporal lobes of the cortex that result in uncontrolled electrical output that we label as seizures may act in antisocial ways, without recognition or memory of the acts.

"What a rush! We were doing 95 miles per hour, and the road was clear and straight. It was incredible!" The rush that we experience is a rush of adrenaline. This hormone released by the adrenal glands pours into the bloodstream and causes a release of glycogen (energy material), and increase in respiration (increased oxygen for metabolism), an increase in heart rate (to get the glycogen and oxygen around the body as quickly as possible). Again, our emotional state can be both caused by and cause an emotional interpretation.

Sociological Perspectives

It is extremely rare that anyone lives in a social vacuum. We live within the social contexts and communities of family, church, school, and peers. Each context overlaps and interacts with others, to a greater or lesser degree. We act on social context, and that context forms the myriad social schema that direct our behavior. It is not within the framework of this text to fully describe and discuss these social issues. (For a broader explication of this issue, the reader is referred to the following texts: Bowers, 2000; Brugha, 1995; Cockersham, 1999; Dubin & Fink, 1992; Horvitz & Scheid, 1999; and Tausig, Michello, & Subedi, 2003). We know that the social context that a person lives within can both pressure and support individuals and families. Social disorganization and community breakdown undoubtedly play a significant role in the development and exacerbation of abnormal or disturbed behavior. Moving to a new town, a new region of the country, or to a different country can significantly impact how someone feels and how those feelings are interpreted by the community. Even within a broad community, views of behavior may differ broadly. For example, the Jones brothers, Jim and Joe, go to a local pub every night for a few beers. They are also known for their loud and raucous discussions regarding such esoteric topics as, "Who was the best quarterback in history?" or "What third baseman had the highest batting average of all time?". More often than not, the discussions end in a wresting match and an occasional bloody nose. Regular customers at the pub have learned to ignore the Jones brothers and step over their wresting bodies. After the wresting, they usually take time for another beer. However, the Jones brothers were invited to a wedding in an elegant hotel and were arrested when their wrestling was deemed inappropriate.

Societies often place a stigma on those whose behavior is deviant or aberrant from the larger group (even our use of terms like *deviant,* and *aberrant* are stigmatizing). Dubin and Fink (1992) state, "Mental illness was once thought to be related to being possessed by demons. In more recent times such concepts are no longer prevalent. Patients with mental disorders continue to be viewed as constitutionally weak, dangerous, and responsible for their own plight" (p. 1).

In the classic 1957 musical, *West Side Story* (written for the stage by Arthur Laurents and which became a film in 1961), the lyrics to "Gee, Officer Krupke" (music by Leonard Bernstein and words by Stephen Sondheim) describe the various problems that might lead to the delinquent behavior of a gang member and how different societal spokespersons react to this adolescent behavior. (The song is sung by gang members to the police officer on the beat, Sergeant Krupke.) The gang members variously blame: parental use of drugs and alcohol, lack of love by parents, child abuse, family member's gender confusion, deprivation of love and material possessions at home, parental spousal abuse, lack of work and career opportunities, and political factors.

Added to this are the views of various mental health professionals, for example, a psychoanalyst views them as needing a career, a social worker believes that incarceration would be best along with vocational training, and a judge views the adolescents as deprived. Society's message to the adolescents is stated in the conclusion of the song:

> We're no good!
> We're no good!
> We're no earthly good!
> Like the best of us is no damn good!

Social disorganization and community breakdown undoubtedly play a significant role in the development and exacerbation of abnormal or disturbed behavior. Although it is beyond the scope of this chapter to offer a review of community factors, we need to acknowledge the vast impact of social and community stress as well as the mediating effects of social and community support.

Psychological Perspectives

The psychological perspective on normal behavior is rooted in theoretical models of personality. The psychodynamic perspective may differ markedly from the behavioral perspective which may differ markedly from a Jungian position. Rather than try to recapitulate a lecture in personality theory, we can say that the psychological perspective comes from the way in which the individual processes the stimulus cues, both internal and external. If you were walking down the street and saw a very huge dog sitting in the middle of the sidewalk with its lips drawn back in a snarl, what would you do? If you are a trained animal handler you might react by continuing on your way speaking softly and calmly to the dog. If you were frightened of animals you might run away. A simplified description of your reaction could be summarized by the following equation: *Risk versus Resources equals Response*. Risk is your perception of the danger to you. Resources are your perception of your abilities to adaptively cope with the perceived risk. Your response is a product of that ratio.

Are our reactions a result of deeply held beliefs? Probably so! Are these beliefs hidden away in the dark recesses of our unconscious? Maybe so! Are we destined to repeat the mistakes of the past unless and until we resolve the conflicts and drives that spur our action? Probably not! Why the lack of certainty? There are ideas, thoughts, beliefs, needs, expectations, attributions, and explanations that are not easily available to awareness. We simply do not think of them. They may still have an active role in why we do what we do, what maintains our behavior, and how we can change what we do. For example, why are we depressed? One psychological perspective is that it relates to how we view ourselves, our world, and what we predict to be the future effect (cognitive behavioral view). Another widely accepted perspective is that it relates to experiences and perceptions of loss of love objects (object relations view).

The essence of the psychological perspective on why people become patients is that we all experience a series of life events from which we derive some meaning that subsequently influences our thoughts, actions, and feelings. This meaning, however it is derived, can precipitate any of the D-Word states that trigger the quest for therapeutic intervention.

Patients versus Clients

The terminology to denote a person seeking or being part of a psychotherapeutic collaboration has shifted with the political winds. Is the person in therapy properly termed a patient, a client, or a consumer? Are there differences or is it a matter of "a rose by any other name would smell as sweet"? Terms in vogue to describe an individual seeking or involved with mental health services include "patient," "client," "customer," "survivor," and "consumer."

There have been many concerns about referring to an individual as a patient because doing so places that individual in a "sick," or "disabled," role (Sharma, Whitney, Kazarian, & Manchanda, 2000). A study by Meuser, Glynn, Corrigan, and Baber (1996) suggested that no single term was preferred by the users of mental health services. Of their study population, 45% preferred the term "client," 20% preferred the term "patient," 8% preferred the term "consumer," and 27% either had no preference or preferred another term. In a replication of the Meuser et al. study, Sharma et al. (2000), found that among providers of mental health services, 68.4% preferred the term "patient," 26.5% preferred the term "client," and .5% preferred the term "consumer." Among service recipients, 54.8% preferred the term "patient," 28.8% preferred the term "client," 7% preferred the term "survivor," and 2.8% preferred the term "consumer." What is clear from these studies is that there is no clear preference for terms used by providers or recipients of mental health services. The conclusion of both studies is that there is a need for an early, frank discussion between therapists and their "service recipients."

Specific Types of Problems

People who are anxious or depressed will likely try different remedies in their attempt to feel better. Some of them sleep, some shop, some incessantly talk on the telephone. Some will try to feed their troubles and make them go away with double-fudge rocky road mocha ice cream. Other people will avoid the obvious, seeking their answers in cyberspace, and still others will use drugs or alcohol to relieve the pain or discomfort. When and if these "solutions" stop working, there are problems. Even if the "solutions" work to reduce the upset or depression, the solutions may become the new problem.

Codifying Psychopathology

Over the years, there have been many attempts to develop and maintain a standard coding system for mental problems. The two systems that are used are the system developed by the World Health Organization entitled the *International Classification of Disease* (*ICD*), and the system developed by the American Psychiatric Association entitled the *Diagnostic and Statistical Manual of Mental Disorders* (*DSM*). Presently, *ICD* is in its tenth edition (*ICD-10*, 1997), and the *DSM* is in its fourth edition, having recently published an edition that revised much of the descriptive text (*DSM-IV-TR*, 2000).

DSM is used as the convention in the United States and several countries around the world. *ICD* is more widely distributed and used in many countries throughout the world. When the two are compared, there are many similarities but also several differences. These differences appear in the terms and titles used for disorders and also for some of the criteria.

In the "bad old days" of the diagnosis of psychological problems, it was both easier and harder to diagnose a person's problem(s). It was easier because there were no clear rules, criteria, or terms. Clinicians could "mix and match" theoretical, descriptive, and diagnostic terms. It was harder because there were no clear rules, criteria, or terms. Clinicians could easily make up their own diagnoses, mix and match terms, and not easily communicate their diagnosis to another clinician. *DSM-I* (1952) states, "There resulted a polyglot of diagnostic labels and systems, effectively blocking communication and the collection of medical statistics" (p. v). The New York Academy of Medicine sponsored a conference in March, 1928 that developed a trial edition of a standard nomenclature that was published in 1932. By 1948 the system was in turmoil inasmuch as the Armed Forces, the Veterans Administration, and the civilian standards were different. Not substantively so, but different enough that a patient going from the Army to the VA and then to a civilian hospital might carry different labels.

In 1948, The World Health Organization published *the International Statistical Classification of Diseases, Injuries, and Causes of Death* in two volumes. This included not only psychiatric disorders, but all medical disorders. For all classification systems, the ability to record, code, and classify disorders into set categories was important for studying prevalence of the manifestation of the disorder across groups.

In *DSM-I* (1952), all mental disorders were divided into two major groups:

1. Those in which there is a disturbance of mental function resulting from, or precipitated by, a primary impairment of the function of the brain, generally due to a diffuse impairment of brain tissue; and

2. Those which are the result of a more general difficulty in adaptation of the individual, and in which any associated brain function disturbance is secondary to the psychiatric disorder (p. 9).

DSM-I covered the definition of terms for all disorders in 31 pages (pp. 12–43). *DSM-II* (1968) was published as a collaborative effort with WHO, which had published the eighth edition of *ICD*. By 1968, the definition of terms was 38 pages in length. *DSM-II* offered greater specificity and attempted to clarify some basic concepts. As a point of comparison, we can examine the *DSM-I* diagnosis termed "Sociopathic Personality Disturbance." Individuals in this category were described as, "ill primarily in terms of society and of conformity with the prevailing social milieu, and not only in terms of personal discomfort and relations with other individuals. However, sociopathic reactions are very often symptomatic of severe underlying personality disorder, neurosis, or psychosis, or occur as the result of organic brain injury or disease. Before a definitive diagnosis in this group is employed, strict attention must be paid to the possibility of the presence of a more primary personality disturbance; such underlying disturbance will be diagnosed when recognized. Reactions will be differentiated as defined below." (p. 38). This was then followed by the categories of *Antisocial Reaction*, referring to people who are "always in trouble," *Dyssocial Reaction*, "individuals who manifest disregard for the usual social codes," and *Sexual Deviation*, "such as homosexuality, transvestitism, pedophilia, fetishism, and sexual sadism" (pp. 38–39).

Both *DSM-I* and *DSM-II* were based in psychodynamic theory. As a definition for Psychoneurotic Disorders, *DSM-I* states, "The chief characteristic of these disorders is *anxiety* which may be directly felt and expressed or which may be unconsciously and automatically controlled by the utilization of various defense mechanisms (depression, conversion, displacement, etc.)" (p. 31). *DSM-II* (1968) uses the exact wording as a definition of the term *Neuroses* (p. 39).

With the publication of *DSM-III* in 1980, the profession had done away with the term neurosis. The new term was *disorder*. The disorders were no longer defined in the psychodynamic light of expressions of anxiety, but rather as criteria that were more behaviorally based. Each disorder now had a series of criteria that limited the freedom for clinicians to interpret and adjust the categories. For the first time, clinicians had to stay with the criteria sets as defining a particular disorder. The definitions of disorders now ran from page 35 to page 335, a total of 300 pages, or roughly 10 times the number of pages devoted to definitions in the previous text.

Another important change in *DSM-III* was the idea of diagnosing an individual on five separate axes. This multiaxial diagnosis allowed the clinician to identify and code, "aspects of the environment, and areas of functioning that might be overlooked if the focus was on assessing a single presenting problem." (p. 23). The five axes were

- Axis I Clinical Syndromes
- Axis II Personality Disorders
- Specific Developmental Disorders
- Axis III Physical Disorders and Problems
- Axis IV Severity of Psychosocial Stressors
- Axis V Highest Level of Adaptive Functioning in the Past Year

Conditions not attributable to a mental disorder might still be a focus of attention or treatment and would be coded with a descriptive "V Code."

To continue our comparison, Antisocial Personality Disorder is defined in *DSM-III* (1980) as, "a Personality Disorder in which there are a history of continuous and chronic antisocial behavior in which the rights of others are violated" (p. 318). The definition no longer includes sexual deviation. Homosexuality is only diagnosed when it is ego-dystonic (the individual is unhappy or displeased with his or her homosexuality).

In 1983, *DSM-III* was revised as *DSM-III-R*. The reason for this rather rapid revision was that, "the data were emerging from new studies that were inconsistent with some of the diagnostic criteria." In addition, there were "many instances in which the criteria were not entirely clear, were inconsistent across categories, or were even contradictory" (p. xvii). In *DSM-III-R*, the criteria sets (definitions now take up 336 pages, another 10% increase), Antisocial Personality Disorder is now defined as, "a pattern of irresponsible and antisocial behavior beginning in childhood or early adolescence and continuing into adulthood" (p. 342).

When *DSM-IV* was published in 1994, the definition of terms had swelled to an astounding 650 pages. The description of Antisocial Personality Disorder is the same, though some criteria differ from *DSM-III-R*.

Finally, *DSM-IV-TR* was published in 2000. The criteria sets are generally unchanged but there is a substantial revision of the descriptions, features, cultural, age, and gender differences, associated features, prevalence, course of the disorder, familial pattern, and differential diagnosis. The definition of terms covers 703 pages. Now we have good news and bad news. The good news is that there will continue to be increasing specificity in succeeding volumes of *DSM* throughout your career as a psychologist. *DSM-V* is due in 2012. Given the continuous size increase, the bad news is that the sheer weight of *DSM* in the future will surely cause major muscle strain.

The Range of Disorders

DSM is an evolving concept and document. The students reading this book will, in the course of their career, likely meet several revisions of the manual. We cannot, in the context of this chapter offer an in-depth discussion of the broad range of mental disorders. For an excellent view or review of psychopathology, see Kring, Davison, Neale, and Johnson(2006).

To acquaint the reader with why people become specific kinds of patients, we offer the fledgling clinician an overview of the current diagnostic nomenclature and its categories of psychopathology.

Before we begin, we want to emphasize three points. First, not everyone will fit neatly into a single category or diagnostic group. Second, we are emphasizing the disorders that are most commonly seen in clinical practice. The *DSM* has many, many more that are unusual or even rare. A fuller description and diagnostic markers for these disorders are the purview of another course in psychopathology or advanced abnormal psychology. Finally, and by far the most important consideration is for the student to be aware of the most dreaded and dreadful emotional or mental disorder that has ever been observed. It is simply called "The Student's Disease." Generally, it is first manifested in the undergraduate years during the Introductory Psychology course when studying the chapter on abnormal psychology. It is often exacerbated in the later undergraduate years or early graduate years when taking a course specific to psychopathology. It is at this point that the disease strikes with its full weight. The student see him or herself (or some significant other) in every diagnostic category. They become upset (or obsessed) with having diseases that will likely render them incapacitated in a short period of time. As you go through the next pages, BEWARE!

Disorders Usually First Diagnosed in Infancy, Childhood, or Adolescence

Mental Retardation

You have likely heard someone demeaning the intellectual capacity of other persons by calling them morons, idiots, or imbeciles. What are presently insults were once legitimate categories for delineating levels of mental retardation. Likewise even the term *retardation* has come to have a pejorative meaning, as in the slang term "You're a RE-tard."

DSM requires three conditions for the diagnosis of mental retardation. First, the individual must have significantly subaverage intellectual functioning: (an IQ of approximately 70 or below). This score should be derived from an individually administered IQ test rather than a group testing. The second requirement for this diagnosis is far vaguer. It requires that the individual have concurrent deficits or impairments in present adaptive functioning (the person's effectiveness in meeting the standards expected for his or her age by his or her cultural group) in at least two of the following areas: communication, self-care, home living, social/interpersonal skills, use of community resources, self-direction, functional academic skills, work, leisure, health, and safety. There are many other disorders that might also lead to or cause impairment in adaptive function. The final factor is that the origin of the problem was during the developmental period, prior to age 18. The following groupings are ranges, rather than a single number, because each individual cannot be assigned a single descriptive number.

The following ranges are based on the degree of severity reflecting the assessed level of intellectual impairment:

317   Mild Mental Retardation: IQ level from 50–55 to approximately 70

318.0 Moderate Mental Retardation: IQ level 35–40 to 50–55

318.1 Severe Mental Retardation: IQ level 20–25 to 35–40

318.2 Profound Mental Retardation: IQ level below 20 or 25

319   Mental Retardation, Severity Unspecified: when there is strong presumption of Mental Retardation but the person's intelligence is difficult or untestable by standard testing instruments.

Mental retardation is coded on Axis II.

Learning Disorders

A common problem seen in consultation with children and adolescence has to do with their performance in their "work"—the acquisition of basic academic skills. These problems include reading disorders, mathematics disorders, disorders of written expression, developmental coordination disorder, expressive language disorder, mixed receptive language disorder, and phonological disorder.

In all cases, the individual's performance is measured by individually administered standardized tests. The individual's performance on standard measures is found to be substantially below the age or grade level expected, given the child's chronological age, measured intelligence, and age-appropriate education.

The previously noted problems significantly (and this is a key word) interfere with the person's academic achievement, the individual's activities of daily living that require the particular skills being evaluated, or the individual's social interactions. Finally, if there is a sensory deficit, the difficulties that the individual has are in excess of those usually associated with the deficit. If a child is deaf, speech problems may have resulted from the lack or limiting of auditory input. The disorder indicates that the person has problems above and beyond those expected of a deaf (or blind) child.

Pervasive Developmental Disorders

Pervasive developmental disorders (PDD) are well named. The problems that are capsular in this group are all-encompassing. They reach in and affect every part of the individual's life. Second, they represent a major difference in functioning from their age-level companions. The deficits of many children with PDD are obvious early in the individual's development. Probably the best known of the pervasive developmental disorders is autism. It is useful to think of an autistic spectrum. We can find children at every level from the most severe forms to very mild forms that might go unnoticed.

The social interactions of the autistic individual are identified by some potential behaviors. There is often a marked impairment in the use of multiple nonverbal behaviors such as making and maintaining appropriate eye contact, appropriate facial expression, and body postures. There may also be a failure or great difficulty in developing peer relationships appropriate to the individual's age or developmental level. For example a 10-year-old child is most comfortable and chooses to play with 5-year-old children when there are other children available who would be more appropriate.

Typically, children share things that they enjoy with significant others. This might involve bringing drawings home from school or nursery school, joining with family members in fun activities, or pointing out objects of interest ("Mommy, look at the horse"). The autistic child seems to lack the motivation or skill to spontaneously share enjoyment, interests, or their achievements with other people. Finally, there is a lack of social or emotional reciprocity.

There are also qualitative impairments in communication such as a delay in, or total lack of, the development of spoken language. The child who lacks language but attempts to convey ideas, feelings, or wants through alternative modes of communication such as gesture or mime would not be considered as having the same type of communication impairment. In individuals with adequate speech, there is a marked impairment in the individual's ability or motivation to initiate or sustain a conversation with other people. Their communication often includes the stereotyped and repetitive use of words, terms, phrases, or ideas. The individual may develop an idiosyncratic language that may differ minimally or markedly from the language use of the family or of the society.

The autistic individual typically lacks the varied, spontaneous make-believe play or social imitative play appropriate to the individual's developmental level. Instead, their behavior, interests, and activities are restricted, repetitive, and stereotyped. Their interest in a subject may reflect an unusual level of preoccupation, intensity, or focus. The individual shows a behavioral pattern that seems to be inflexible, and adheres to specific, nonfunctional routines or rituals. The diagnostic sign that is most noticeable to the observer is the autistic individual's stereotyped and repetitive motor mannerisms such as hand or finger flapping or twisting, or complex whole-body movement. The clinician must be careful here, because other disorders may show somewhat similar behaviors; for example, visually challenged children often "finger-flic" by waving their fingers in front of their eyes. This causes alterations in light and shadow and is visually stimulating.

Some autistic children show incredible aptitude at a skill that is far and away above "normal." They might be able to multiply a 10-digit number by another 10-digit number at the speed of an electronic calculator. Other autistic *savants* (learned persons) can hear a piece of music and then play it from memory. These same individuals may be unable to learn to read music, but they have a "golden ear."

Finally, there may be an intense and pervasive interest with the parts of objects as opposed to the whole, such as interest in taking objects apart without the apparent curiosity of what makes the object work. They may then play with a wheel, gear, or part.

The identification of autism involves delays or abnormal functioning in at least one of the following areas, with onset prior to age 3 years: (a) social interaction, (b) language as used in social communication, or (c) symbolic or imaginative play.

Asperger's Disorder

Asperger's Disorder can be thought of as the highest functioning manifestation within the autistic spectrum. There are many of the same qualities, behaviors, and signs noted earlier. The differences may be that the individual is "almost" normal. Their awareness of social cues, attention to interactive details, or verbalizations may be close to normal, but just miss the mark. These individuals may be labeled as "eccentric," "weird," or "a little off." They may do very well in academic areas because of the high level of structure involved and required. The largest difficulty may be in their lack of attention to social cues. They seem to miss them. They might be prone to enter a conversation by interrupting and overlooking the appropriate social niceties. They may have difficulty in relationships because of their lack of attention (though not awareness) of appropriate social behavior. The disturbance causes clinically significant impairment in social, occupational, or other important areas of functioning.

Unlike the description of autism, there is no clinically significant general delay in language (e.g., single words are used by age 2 years, communicative phrases by age 3 years), and there is no clinically significant delay in cognitive development or development of age-appropriate self-help skills, adaptive behavior (other than in social interaction), and curiosity about the environment in childhood.

In many settings, these individuals may be very successful. They focus on things rather than people, so that they may be the computer geek or math nerd- who succeeds in structured, task-oriented settings, but has significant problems in interpersonal circumstances. Their nonattention or recognition of environmental or social cues may cause them difficulty.

Attention-Deficit and Disruptive Behavior

Another disorder that is commonly diagnosed in children is Attention Deficit/Hyperactivity Disorder. Once again, the pattern is maladaptive and inconsistent with the child's developmental level. There are two equally problematic components, the lack of attention and the high level of activity. These children often fail to give close attention to the details of a game, an academic requirement, or a social interaction. They often make what appear to be careless mistakes in schoolwork, work, or other activities even after they have been warned to be careful. They may be highly motivated to be careful, but their attention seems to wander. This is not related only to school activities; the child may have difficulty sustaining attention in many tasks (doing chores at home) or in play activities.

The child may not seem to listen, even when spoken to directly. The child (or adult) often does not follow through on instructions and fails to finish schoolwork, chores, or duties in the workplace. This occurs even though the individual is motivated to comply, wants to do well, and appears to understand the instructions or requirements.

Because of the attentional deficits, these children have difficulty organizing tasks and activities. They may even appear confused and disorganized and will conspire to avoid tasks that require sustained mental focus and effort. Nothing is more frustrating for AD/HD individuals and for their families than the disorganization that has the child losing things necessary for tasks or activities (e.g., toys, school assignments, pencils, books, or tools). Further, the attention problem is both caused by and typical of their ease of distraction by both external and internal stimuli.

Hyperactivity
Hyperactive children often fidget with their hands or feet or may be seen squirming in their seat. It is important to remember age-appropriate fidgeting. It is difficult for a child to always behave in every situation. When asked to stand in line and wait, the hyperactive child may be fidgeting and squirming in place. Other times, these children may leave their seat in a classroom, at the dinner table, at the movies, or in other situations in which remaining seated is the expected (or demanded) behavior. When other children are actively moving about, running, or climbing, the level of activity of the hyperactive child is excessive and may be inappropriate. When hyperactivity is seen in adolescents or adults, it may have all the previously noted actions, but also may include subjective feelings of restlessness.

When hyperactive children are expected to spend time restfully and quietly, they have great difficulty and act as if "driven by a motor." In classroom settings or at home, these children often talk excessively, impulsively, or compulsively. They have difficulty waiting their turn while other children (or siblings) are awaiting a turn. The hyperactive child often blurts out answers before the teacher's or parent's questions have been fully asked. They will interrupt or intrude on the conversations or activities of others. The frequent statement is, "but Mom . . ." A key diagnostic factor is that there must be clear evidence of clinically significant impairment in social, academic, or occupational functioning that does not occur exclusively during the course of some other disorder such as a Pervasive Developmental Disorder, Schizophrenia, or other Psychotic Disorder and are not better accounted for by another mental disorder (e.g., Mood Disorder, Anxiety Disorder, Dissociative Disorder, or a Personality Disorder).

Conduct Disorder
Conduct disorder involves a repetitive and persistent pattern of behavior in which the basic rights of others or major age-appropriate societal norms or rules are violated. These can include physical, verbal, or emotional aggression to people (children and adults) or to animals. This aggressive behavior can be cruel, bullying, threatening or intimidating behavior. These children are prone

to initiate physical fights or cause physical damage to others. They may use their hands but may also use a weapon such as a bat, brick, broken bottle, rock, knife, or gun. They may also be physically cruel to animals and injure, torture, or kill them. They may force another child into sexual activity.

They seem to have no compunction about mugging, purse snatching, and extortion, armed robbery, selling contraband, or injuring another person for profit. They may have stolen items of substantial value without confronting a victim (e.g., shoplifting, breaking and entering, forgery, auto theft).

They demonstrate a lack of respect for the property of others and seem to have little hesitation in deliberately destroying the property of others, or of public buildings (schools, churches, governmental buildings). The destructive behaviors might include fire setting with the intention of causing serious damage, vandalism, or explosives. They may be more circumspect in deceitfulness as well. They often lie to obtain goods or favors or when confronted by their actions, to avoid obligations, consequences, or punishment.

These children often come into conflict with parental, school, or legal authorities because of serious violations of rules. Beginning before age 13 years, they may violate curfew by staying out at night despite parental prohibitions, or might have run away from home overnight at least twice while living in parental or parental surrogate home. As a result of their challenges to "the system," they may be truant from school. Overall, their behavior causes clinically significant impairment in social, academic, or occupational functioning.

When the problems are mild, there are few if any conduct problems in excess of those required for the diagnosis, and the conduct problems cause only minor harm to others. A moderate disorder reflects a greater number of conduct problems and the effect on others would be between "mild" and "severe." Finally, a severe conduct disorder would involve any conduct problems in excess of those required to make the diagnosis and their conduct problems would cause considerable harm to others.

Oppositional Defiant Disorder

When a child has been diagnosed as having an Oppositional Defiant Disorder, it is often a case of parents, teachers, clergy, or coaches being unable to deal/cope/handle the child. These children display a pattern of negativistic, hostile, and defiant behavior that has been recognizable for at least 6 months, during which there are several markers including often losing his or her temper, arguing with adults over small details and issues that do not warrant the time or energy for the child to object or argue; when asked to follow rules or requests, the child shows *active* defiance or refusal to comply. The key idea is that the refusal is active as opposed to a more passive refusal. These children often seem to go out of their way to do things that deliberately annoy people. When called to task for misdeeds or mistakes, they find scapegoats or simply blame others for their mistakes or misbehavior. Hypersensitivity causes this child to be easily annoyed by others, which results in the child acting in a resentful, spiteful, or vindictive manner.

What has been described could easily describe most normal adolescents. As noted, the key to diagnosing problematic behavior is that the behavior is more frequent or more maladaptive than would be typically observed in individuals of a comparable age, gender, social setting, and developmental level. The identified behavior causes the child clinically significant impairment in social, academic, or occupational functioning.

Delirium, Dementia, Amnestic and Other Cognitive Disorders

Imagine the following: As you are reading this book the words suddenly start to run across the page, the content is confusing, you keep losing your place, and you forget the courses that you are taking and the name of your best friend. Your first response may be to self-instruct yourself to get more sleep. But what if these are not the symptoms of sleep deprivation, an occupational hazard of being a student? What if something is wrong with your brain?

The problems discussed in this section are disorders with psychological impact that are caused by temporary or permanent changes to the structure, functioning, and metabolism of the brain. The problems caused by this type of disorder range from slow deterioration of mental abilities such as judgment, memory, concentration, abstract thinking, impulse control, intellectual abilities, social functioning, and occupational functioning to a rapid and catastrophic loss. The differences between these two types of presentation are significant. Diseases such as Alzheimer's disease are well known to cause memory lapses that may range from minor (misplacing one's glasses) to potentially life-threatening (leaving a pot on the stove and forgetting it, causing a fire). These disorders come under the broad heading of *dementia*.

Part of the loss is not just to the individual who may be aware of the difficulty in remembering things, but also to their family and friends. They may, when the deterioration is serious, forget the names of their children, spouses, and friends. Hilda, married to Harry for 55 years, was placed in a care facility when Harry could no longer care for her at home. He visited her every day, and sat with her for hours, looking at pictures of their children and grandchildren. By her comments, it was clear that to her these were just nice pictures of nice children. She did not know their names, or her relationship to them. When children and grandchildren visited, it was, once again, a visit by nice people. At one point, when Harry entered her room, Hilda began screaming that a strange man was there and for someone to get him away from her. She could be calmed, but Harry was inconsolable. He had truly lost his wife. She lived and breathed, but was not available in any way for him. He grieved her loss.

When there are losses of judgment, these individuals may lose the polish and control that, over the years, characterized them. The prim and proper individual may now use coarse language, make obscene statements and gestures, make sexual advances to strangers, or make inappropriate racial, ethnic, or gender statements.

There may also be a disturbance of consciousness (reduced clarity of awareness of their environment) with reduced ability to focus, sustain, or shift attention. In addition to memory deficits, there may be disorientation, language disturbance, or the development of a perceptual disturbance that is not better accounted for by another disorder such as a preexisting psychotic process. The brain deterioration may cause fluctuation through the day, so that at one time the individual is clear and calm, and at another time, for no apparent reason, the individual's behavior is far worse.

A thorough physical examination with laboratory work is important because some of these same symptoms may be the sequelae or physiological consequences of a general medical condition, toxic reactions to drugs, food allergies, or medication overdose.

There can also be a rather rapid onset dementia that is caused by a stroke. This is caused by a reduction or loss of oxygen to the brain (which as you know, is a major consumer of oxygen). This loss of oxygen can cause the damage or even loss of language, loss of sensation, deterioration or loss of motor skills (gross and fine), and coordination problems. If the loss of oxygen is small and confined to a specific area, the loss may be minimal and the skills or abilities may return. Cognitive rehabilitation, physical therapy, and psychotherapy may all be used to assist individuals in their recovery. In other, more serious circumstances, the losses may be permanent.

Another brain-related problem is delirium. This is a state of severe mental confusion. The delirium may come on quite suddenly and may start with restlessness, a lack of coherence in thought and speech, a lack of clarity in speech (words may be mispronounced or slurred), and the individual may not be oriented to time, place, or person. There may also be perceptual disturbances and hallucinations. Many factors must be considered in treating individuals with brain-related disorders.

Substance-Related Disorders

It is Saturday night, and a group of students are setting out to have a good time. They are ready to PARTY! A likely part of that good time will involve the use of one or several intoxicants. These may be taken very quickly, or savored over a longer period. The substances may be legal (nicotine or caffeine), illegal (e.g., cocaine, marijuana, heroin, or methamphetamine), the substance may be illegal at one age but legal at an older age (e.g., alcohol). The substance may be legal for one use and then misused to achieve a "high" (e.g., inhalants, gasoline, cooking spray). The substances may be taken by choice, or ingested unknowingly as in so-called date-rape drugs.

This is not the forum for us to argue the legality, acceptability, or prevalence of substance use or the rules governing substance use and misuse. Students will have their own ideas of substance use relative to the needed quantity to have the desired effect (feeling good, getting high), availability, cost, and legality. A case might be made that despite the fact that every pack of cigarettes carries on it a warning from the Surgeon General regarding the health risks of smoking, people continue to smoke. About the only thing that these individuals stop is reading their cigarette packs.

Several terms have come to the fore, and others recede based on acceptability and political correctness of the term. Drug *abuse* has been replaced by drug *misuse*. The problems come when the choices to use or misuse various intoxicants are no longer easily made, but related to psychological or physiological factors.

Substance Dependence

Dependence is a maladaptive pattern of substance use, leading to clinically significant impairment or distress, as manifested by three (or more) of the following, occurring at any time within a 12-month period.

1. *There is tolerance as defined by either a need for markedly increased amounts of the substance to achieve intoxication or desired effect, or markedly diminished effect with continued use of the same amount of the substance.*

2. *There is withdrawal, as manifested by either the characteristic withdrawal syndrome for that particular substance inasmuch as withdrawal for some substances is far more difficult or dangerous than withdrawal from other substances, or the same (or a closely related) substance is taken to relieve or avoid withdrawal symptoms.*

3. *The substance is often taken in larger amounts or over a longer period than the individual had intended.*

4. *There is a persistent desire but unsuccessful efforts to cut down or control use of the particular substance. In this regard, the individual "means well," but has been unsuccessful at meeting personal goals of cutting back.*

5. *There is a great deal of time, energy, and effort, and possibly personal risk spent in activities necessary to obtain the substance (e.g., visiting multiple doctors or driving long distances), using the substance (e.g., chain-smoking), recover from the effects of the substance use, going into unsafe areas to obtain the substance, or risking legal problems if arrested.*

6. *The substance use supersedes social, occupational, or recreational activities. Time with family, friends, studying is given up or reduced because of substance use.*

7. *The substance use is continued despite the individual's knowledge of having a persistent or recurrent physical or psychological problem that is likely to have been caused or exacerbated by the substance (e.g., current cocaine use) despite recognition of cocaine-induced depression, or continued drinking despite recognition that an ulcer was made worse by alcohol consumption, continued smoking despite a diagnosis of respiratory distress.*

Criteria for Substance Abuse

Although abuse and dependence have many similar characteristics, there are differences in terms of the degree of severity, involvement, and maladaptive behavior in the person's life. Dependence requires three or more criteria; abuse requires only one. Substance abuse involves a maladaptive pattern of substance use leading to clinically significant impairment or distress, as manifested by *one* (or more) of the following, occurring within a 12-month period:

1. *recurrent substance use resulting in a failure (not just a limitation) to fulfill major role obligations at work, school, or home (e.g., repeated absences or poor work performance related to substance use; substance-related absences, suspen-*

sions, or expulsions from school; neglect of children, or lack of caring for one's household);

2. *recurrent substance use in situations in which it is physically hazardous (e.g., driving an automobile or operating a machine when impaired by substance use);*

3. *recurrent substance-related legal problems (e.g., arrests for substance-related possession, sales, or disorderly conduct resulting from the substance use);*

4. *continued substance use despite having persistent or recurrent social or interpersonal problems caused or exacerbated by the effects of the substance (e.g., arguments with one's spouse about consequences of intoxication, physical fights, loss of friends, expulsion from clubs or other social groups).*

Finally, the symptoms have never met the criteria for Substance Dependence for this particular class of substance (*DSM-IV-TR*, p. 191).

Criteria for Substance Intoxication

Have you ever been the designated driver at a party? It is your job to get everyone home safely because these other individuals are intoxicated. Intoxication is defined as the development of a reversible substance-specific syndrome due to recent ingestion of (or exposure to) a substance. Obviously, different substances may produce similar or identical reactions and syndromes. It may not be clear without a laboratory drug screen just what drugs are "on board" that are creating the observable behaviors.

The individual will likely manifest clinically significant maladaptive behavioral or psychological changes due to the effect of the substance on the central nervous system (e.g., belligerence, mood lability, cognitive impairment, impaired judgment, impaired social, coordination difficulty, impulse control problems, or occupational functioning) that develop during or shortly after use of the substance. It is essential to have a medical evaluation because certain neurological issues noted earlier in this chapter (e.g., stroke) can cause similar reactions and behaviors. Thus it is important to determine that the symptoms are not due to a general medical condition or are not better accounted for by another mental disorder. Some substances that are misused are prescription medications. Benzodiazepines, pain medications, sedatives, or other drugs with codeine for coughs are also drugs of abuse. These drugs may be used for a long period and may become habit forming.

A final statement relates to polysubstance abuse and dependence. Individuals involved in polysubstance abuse will ingest, smoke, drink, inhale, or inject any substance that they believe will get them high.

Schizophrenia and Other Psychotic Disorders

An old joke states, "Neurotics spend their lives building castles in the sky. The psychotic moves in." Images of homeless men and women living on the street, apparently deep in conversation with others, whom only they can see, are common. Freud called dreams the normal person's psychosis. In our dreams, we can fly, talk to people that we have never met, perform acts that we would never attempt, or go to places that we have never been. Dreams may be so real that people who have a sad dream may awaken with their face wet from tears. Your sleeping partner elbows you during the night to stop your loud laughing at what must have been a very funny joke or experience. Psychosis, however, is far more serious. Especially in schizophrenia, the patient can have positive symptoms (referring to behavioral excesses). They have observable and noticeable behaviors that are typical, pervasive, and frequent.

Psychosis may include *delusions* (ideas and beliefs that are contrary to reality). These distorted ideas are maintained despite any and all contradictory evidence—this can be summarized as "Just because I am paranoid doesn't mean people are not following me." Probably the most common delusions are those of persecution. The belief is that "people" are out to harm them. These may be from the government, outer space, or a secret society that only they know about. Often these delusions are highly detailed, use facts from the news to support their ideas, typically involve logical leaps that are hard to follow, but make sense to the individual.

There may also be hallucinations. These involve perceptions that occur without adequate sensory input. The individual will smell, see, hear, or feel things that others near them do not perceive. The most frequent type of hallucination is auditory. Visual and olfactory hallucinations are far less frequent. When the individual "hears" the voices, they often respond in conversation or respond behaviorally through action by injuring or damaging themselves or others. The source of the voice may range from George Washington to God.

They often have disorganized speech with frequent derailment or incoherence. Ideas flow at a rapid rate and while the listener may detect themes and ideas in the words, they often do not make any sense. One word/idea leads to another with alliteration or a rhyme as the only apparent connection. The Liberty Bell may, in the next sentence become the Statue of Liberty. A single idea may trigger multiple tracks for the individual.

Similarly, their dress, actions, posture may all be affected. They might fashion a hat from aluminum foil to stop damaging rays from going into their brain.

There are also negative symptoms that are behavioral deficits. These include affective flattening, wherein these individuals appear to be without emotion. No matter what the external stimuli, they evidence no external emotional reaction, although their internal emotions may be at a high pitch. With low levels of energy, they may sit and stare for hours at a time and not attend to meals, their personal hygiene, or their dress. This is termed *avolition*. They may also show *alogia*, which involves both impoverished production and content of speech. The person may show very few words, monosyllabic responses, or many words without any real content.

The schizophrenic individual typically experiences social and occupational dysfunction. Major areas of functioning such as work, interpersonal relations, or self-care are markedly below the level achieved prior to the onset of the disorder. Onset is usually late adolescence or early adulthood. When the onset is in childhood or adolescence, which is far rarer, there is more severe impairment of interpersonal, academic, or occupational achievement.

Many of the positive and negative symptoms listed could also be typical of substance use. It is essential that the disturbance is not due to the direct physiological effects of a substance (e.g., a drug of abuse, a medication) or a general medical condition.

If there is a history of Autistic Disorder or another Pervasive Developmental Disorder, the additional diagnosis of Schizophrenia is made only if prominent delusions or hallucinations are also present for at least a month (or less if successfully treated). The classification of a longitudinal course (can be applied only after at least 1 year has elapsed since the initial onset of active-phase symptoms).

To understand the complex thinking of the individual diagnosed with the Paranoid Type of schizophrenia, think of Tolkien's *The Hobbit* or *Lord of the Rings* (1986). The invention of racial groups, a genealogy, a geography, and social and political systems, displays the creativity, originality, imagination, and inspiration of a great writer. If we see the constructions of the paranoid schizophrenic as akin to this, we can start to understand why the delusions are so compelling for the individual.

The Catatonic Type of schizophrenia is characterized by alternating between episodes of extreme agitation and what has been termed "waxy flexibility." That is, patients can be placed in a particular position, or have their limbs placed in a particular way and will remain in that position. This variant is not typically seen because the use of psychotropic medication has increased.

Schizoaffective Disorder

As the name implies, this disorder is a mix of schizophrenia and an affective disorder. The individual will have hallucinations and delusions that are characteristic of a psychotic process, and symptoms of a mood disturbance during the same time.

Depressive Disorders

Depression has been called "the common cold of emotional disorders." It would be rare to find an individual who has never experienced some variant of depression from being "down," "blue," or having the "blahs." When the depressed feelings are ongoing, the individual may meet the criteria for some depressive disorder. It may be a major depressive disorder with only a single episode, and the experience may be mild, moderate, severe without psychotic features, or severe with psychotic features.

Individuals who have a number of depressed episodes may be diagnosed as having major depressive disorder, recurrent. This implies that the depression returns on some periodic basis and that there have been two or more major depressive episodes. To be considered separate episodes, there must be the presence an interval of at least 2 consecutive months in which criteria are not met for a Major Depressive Episode.

The symptoms of depression include being depressed for most of the day every day, a diminished interest or pleasure in activities nearly every day, significant weight loss or gain when not trying to lose or gain weight, problems with sleep, either difficulty sleeping or problems in waking, slowed or increased motor activity, fatigue or loss of energy, feelings of worthlessness, problems in concentration, or decision making, and suicidal thinking or recurrent thoughts of death.

Dysthymic Disorder

Many children are familiar with the characters in A. A. Milne's *Winnie-the-Pooh.* Eeyore, the donkey, is likely a dysthymic individual. For Eeyore, nothing is ever good, much less great. For Eeyore, everything is "O . . . kay." Dysthymia involves a depressed mood for "most of the day, for more days than not, as indicated either by subjective account or observation by others, for at least 2 years."

Another common variant of an affective disorder is Bipolar Disorder, formerly known as manic depression. The manifestation of Bipolar Disorder is that the individual cycles through being depressed and being manic. This includes a range of symptoms that involve a grandiose view of self, decreased need for sleep where the individual may not sleep for days, or sleep only two hours per night, speech that is pressured so that the individual speaks very quickly as if the words are being forced out under some strain, becoming easily distracted, a sensation or experience of thought racing at high speed, and the possibility of painful or impulsive behavior such as gambling, spending, or promiscuous activities.

Anxiety Disorders

Anxiety is a common and important part of human functioning. It manifests itself as an emotion, a physiological state, through behaviors, and as a set of cognitions. The basic idea underlying all anxiety is that there is danger in the world (which is true), but anxious individuals have the concomitant belief that they are unsuited or unskilled to effectively cope with the danger.

The various anxiety disorders need to be viewed as an anxiety spectrum, so that typically an individual has many pieces of the several anxiety disorders. The various types of anxiety depend on where the individual believes the danger will come from. In Generalized Anxiety Disorder, the danger is everywhere, and they must be ready to respond with their typical safety behavior of avoidance. In Phobia, the danger comes from a discrete object or situation. In Social Anxiety, the potential for danger in social situations is foremost. For Obsessive-Compulsive Disorder, the danger can be kept at a safe distance by performing specific behaviors. In Posttraumatic Stress Disorder, the danger is deeply set within a network of associations and memories that invade both waking and sleeping experience, triggering fear, avoidance, and numbing of affect.

In Simple Phobia or Social Phobia, the person may have panic attacks, but these occur only in the presence of specific phobic stimuli. The diagnosis of Panic Disorder is made only when attacks are unexpected and do not occur immediately before or during exposure to a specific situation that almost always causes anxiety. Individuals with Panic Disorder may believe that they are going to die unless they swiftly and immediately leave whatever they are doing (e.g., driving, shopping).

The distinction between Panic Disorder with and without Agoraphobia can be difficult if the agoraphobic avoidance is mild. When asked if they avoid many situations, clients with panic attacks may answer no, leading one to conclude that they have Panic Disorder without Agoraphobia. However, patterns of avoidance may be subtle or may have continued for so long that the client does not recognize the avoidance.

Social Phobia is a fear of exposure to the scrutiny of others, particularly the fear of embarrassment or humiliation due to one's actions while others are watching. Although seemingly straightforward, the diagnosis of Social Phobia can be complex. Social anxiety in and of itself is not sufficient to warrant the diagnosis of Social Phobia. There must be a persistent fear of one or more situations in which the person is exposed to possible scrutiny by others and fears that he or she may act in a way that will be humiliating or embarrassing. Social Phobias often include fear that one's anxiety will be noticed by others. Thus, a social phobic may be unwilling to write in the view of others for fear that his or her hand will tremble or may avoid social situations for fear of perspiring excessively because of nervousness.

A Simple Phobia is a persistent fear of a specific object or situation and is usually circumscribed. Fears of specific stimuli such as heights, insects, snakes, and so on are common but would be considered to be Simple Phobias if the fear and/or avoidance resulted in significant impairment or distress. Simple phobias range from the commonplace, such as fear of flying, to the idiosyncratic, such as fear of the wind.

Many clients who report a fear of germs or dirt have developed elaborate cleaning or hand-washing rituals. Clients may be so used to their extensive strategies for preventing harm that they no longer view them as rituals and may not think to mention them. Even if fears and phobias exist, a person who also has significant obsessions or compulsions would be diagnosed as having an Obsessive-Compulsive Disorder.

In Generalized Anxiety Disorder, the term *generalized* leads many to mistakenly assume that the anxiety is continuous, pervasive, and "free-floating." Careful assessment of individuals with Generalized Anxiety Disorder makes it clear that there are definite variations in the presence and intensity of anxiety, depending on the situation and cognitions of the client at the time.

Posttraumatic Stress Disorder (PTSD) has received much attention in recent years due to the high incidence of PTSD among combat veterans. However, PTSD can occur following any extraordinary traumatic event such as a natural disaster, a major accident, or victimization. Clinically, it is valuable to distinguish between PTSD resulting from a single traumatic event and PTSD resulting from recurrent trauma. Persons with PTSD stemming from recurrent trauma appear to be much more difficult to treat effectively.

For most anxiety disorders, there is some combination of the following experiences at varying levels of intensity:

- *palpitations, pounding heart, or accelerated heart rate*
- *sweating*
- *trembling or shaking*
- *sensations of shortness of breath or smothering*
- *feeling of choking*

- *chest pain or discomfort*
- *nausea or abdominal distress*
- *feeling dizzy, unsteady, lightheaded, or faint*
- *derealization (feelings of unreality) or depersonalization (being detached from oneself)*
- *fear of losing control or going crazy*
- *fear of dying*
- *paresthesias (numbness or tingling sensations)*
- *chills or hot flushes*
- *difficulty concentrating*
- *hypervigilance*
- *exaggerated startle response*

Somatoform Disorders

Somatoform disorders represent identifiable physical symptoms that are not fully explained by the individual's general medical condition or by the direct effects of some substance. The physical symptoms are not something that the individual causes or attempts to fake. Just about any bodily system can be affected by the disorder. There are several types of disorder.

In Somatization Disorder, there is a history of many physical complaints beginning before age 30 years that occur over a period of several years and result in treatment being sought or in significant impairment in social, occupational, or other important areas of functioning. Each of the following criteria must have been met, with individual symptoms occurring at any time during the course of the disturbance;

- **four pain symptoms:** *a history of pain related to at least four different sites or functions (e.g., head, abdomen, back, joints, extremities, chest, rectum, during menstruation, during sexual intercourse, or during urination)*
- **two gastrointestinal symptoms:** *a history of at least two gastrointestinal symptoms other than pain (e.g., nausea, bloating, vomiting other than during pregnancy, diarrhea, or intolerance of several different foods)*
- **one sexual symptom:** *a history of at least one sexual or reproductive symptom other than pain (e.g., sexual indifference, erectile or ejaculatory dysfunction, irregular menses, excessive menstrual bleeding, vomiting throughout pregnancy)*
- **one pseudoneurological symptom:** *a history of at least one symptom or deficit suggesting a neurological condition not limited to pain (conversion symptoms such as impaired coordination or balance, paralysis or localized weakness, difficulty swallowing or lump in throat, aphonia, urinary retention, hallucinations, loss of touch or pain sensation, double vision, blindness, deafness, seizures; dissociative symptoms such as amnesia; or loss of consciousness other than fainting)*

The symptoms are not intentionally produced or feigned (as in Factitious Disorder or Malingering; *DSM-IV-TR*, p. 449).

Conversion Disorder can occur with a motor symptom or deficit/with sensory symptom or a deficit/with seizures or convulsions.

Pain Disorders can be associated with psychological factors or associated with both psychological factors and a general medical condition. This condition might be acute or chronic.

Hypochondriasis, also termed health anxiety, involves a fear of the danger of physical illness. The hypochondriac can interpret aches, pains, bumps, and lumps as diseases and illnesses that defy medical evaluation. Despite many and frequent medical visits, hypochondriacs cannot accept that the illnesses are psychogenic rather than the result of some flaw or fault in their bodily functioning. They will spend time and money on shopping for the medical professional who can and will diagnose them as having a medical problem. Often preoccupied with their concerns about illness, hypochondriacs will have difficulty maintaining relationships and family connections. While this illness preoccupation does not reach the level of a delusion, there is a quality of reality being challenged in the constant search for elusive symptoms.

Body Dysmorphic Disorder is related to hypochondria in that these individuals believe that their body is defective and that their appearance needs to be altered. It can be the motive for numerous plastic surgeries, alterations, or enhancements. This does mean that every surgery is excessive. It is the ongoing dissatisfaction that leads to multiple surgeries.

Factitious Disorders do not involve an intentional production or feigning of physical or psychological signs or symptoms. There is an unconscious or naive motivation of the individual to assume the sick role. Individuals may even take drugs or medications to create the very symptoms for which they seek treatment. Unlike malingering, they do not do this with a goal such as economic gain or for avoiding legal responsibility. Factitious disorders can be seen with predominantly psychological signs and symptoms.

In malingering, the individual creates the disorder for some financial gain or the avoidance of responsibility. Both disorders show what appears to be a medical disorder. The malingering patient may not be as cooperative with a medical team nor comply with a prescribed medication regiment, there may be a marked discrepancy between the individual's claimed difficulty and the findings on objective medical tests, and most important, there is some outside gain or reward for maintaining the purported medical disorder.

Dissociative Disorders

The category of Dissociative Disorders includes Dissociative Amnesia, Dissociative Fugue, Dissociative Identity Disorder, and Depersonalization Disorder. The common element to these disorders is "a disruption in the usually integrated functions of consciousness, memory, identity, or perception of the environment. The disturbance may be sudden or gradual, transient or chronic." (*DSM-IV-TR*, 2000, p. 477). Dissociative Amnesia involves difficulty or even the inability to recall events or circumstances that were traumatic. Although patients may have vague and inaccurate memories, they can, over time, recover the lost data.

Dissociative Fugue is the stuff of books, stories, and movies. In a fugue state, the individual may travel at a distance from their home, be unable to remember elements of the trip, and, in the course of the trip have conversations with another person. In severe cases, the individual may assume a new identity, not remembering his or her former identity.

Dissociative Identity Disorder can also present in a dramatic manner with the individual having two or more distinct identities. Books and films such as *The Three Faces of Eve* (Thigpen & Cleckley, 1957), or *Sybil* (Schreiber, 1977) show examples of this disorder. The individual may have "alters" who are of different ages than the patient, of different gender, or a different race or ethnicity. The debate regarding the apparent increase of this disorder is whether we are becoming better able to identify such individuals or whether we are over-diagnosing the disorder.

Depersonalization Disorder involves a persistent or recurrent experience of feeling detached from, and as if one is an outside observer of, one's mental processes or body (e.g., feeling as if one is in a dream). During the depersonalization experience, reality testing remains intact while individuals may report being able to "watch themselves as if in a movie." This has also been labeled *spectatoring*.

Sexual Disorders, Paraphilias, and Gender Identity Disorders

These disorders constitute a large and troubling area for the affected individual and potentially for society.

Sexual Dysfunctions can occur in every phase of the sexual arousal cycle. This includes disturbances in desire, excitement, orgasm, or resolution. The dysfunction can be a lifelong type or acquired type, a generalized type or a situational type. Finally, the disorder might be due to psychological factors, medical/physical factors, substance use, or a combination of them.

Sexual dysfunctions include Sexual Desire Disorders such as Hypoactive Sexual Desire Disorder where there is a lack of sexual desire and an absence of sexual fantasy. The disorder may be global and include all forms of sexual expression. These individuals may engage in sexual activity with a low frequency to satisfy a partner, but would not likely initiate sexual contact or expression. If, however, this does not cause difficulty for the individual, it may not be perceived as a problem (e.g., two partners, both of whom have a hypoactive sexual desire).

In Sexual Aversion Disorder, there is a distaste, repugnance, and avoidance of sexual contact with a partner. At an extreme, it could also include aversions to kissing, touching, or fondling. To be considered a disorder, the aversion must cause significant distress and interpersonal difficulty for the individual.

Sexual Arousal Disorders for both men and women involve the inability to attain and then maintain the physiological arousal. For a woman, this includes vasocongestion in the pelvis, vaginal lubrication and expansion, and swelling of the external genitalia. For the male, it involves the ability to maintain until completion an adequate erection. (It should be noted that what is "adequate" is a debatable point. An individual male might view his erection is not adequate, yet it allows for genital-genital sex without difficulty.) Another point to consider is that the use of medications such as Viagra, Levitra, and Cialis can treat erectile dysfunction rather easily. In this case, the disorder is said to be in remission. Another consideration is that erectile dysfunction could be a sign of atherosclerosis and may signal a need for a medical evaluation.

Orgasmic Disorders are difficult to assess. They may relate to age, health, sexual experience, and sexual stimulation. The disorder may manifest as delay in, or absence of an orgasm as part of the sexual activity.

Premature Ejaculation, like other sexual disorders, is difficult to identify. How much time should elapse before the male reaches orgasm? Partner estimates often vary widely. Key ingredients involve whether the ejaculation occurs sooner than the individual or partner desires it. It may relate to factors during the excitement phase, novelty of the experience, sexual experience of the individual, and recency or frequency of sexual activity.

Sexual Pain Disorders such as Dyspareunia that is not due to a medical condition can occur in both males and females and involves pain before, during, and after intercourse.

Vaginismus that is not due to medical condition involves a persistent and recurrent involuntary contraction of the perineal muscles surrounding the outer third of the vagina. This will cause pain and difficulty in intercourse or in inserting a tampon.

Finally, sexual dysfunction can be related to the use of a substance, especially when intoxication is involved.

Paraphilias span a spectrum of behavior; Exhibitionism (the exposure of genitals), Fetishism (the sexual arousal involves nonhuman objects, e.g., shoes, underwear), Frotteurism (rubbing against or touching a nonconsenting person), and Pedophilia (a sexual focus on children). The definition of child in one state may differ in another, but the general rule is that pedophilia involves prepubertal children. Paraphilia also includes Sexual Masochism (receiving humiliation and pain), Sexual Sadism (inflicting humiliation and pain on another), Transvestic Fetishism (cross-dressing); (this is also debatable inasmuch as the wearing of the clothes of another gender may be acceptable in specific circumstances), and Voyeurism (the observation of the sexual activity of another). The common thread for the paraphilias is that the individual has recurrent and intense sexual fantasies, urges, and actions that may involve nonhuman objects, the suffering and humiliation of another person, or sexual involvement with children or nonconsenting adults. In many cases, paraphiliac actions are considered criminal acts and may result in arrest and prosecution.

Society has allowed expression for some paraphilias. Peep shows and pornography allow the individual to observe others involved in sexual activity. Transvestism may be acceptable in private or in certain places or venues in many cities. A masochistic individual may seek humiliation and pay a great deal of money for it. Pedophilia, however, is banned and severely prosecuted in every state. In most cases, excepting those sexual behaviors that hurt or impact on others, the behavior must cause distress to the individual.

Gender Identity Disorders must have two components. The first is that these individuals must evidence a strong and persistent cross-gender identification to be (or to insist that they are) of the other gender. The second component is that they are uncomfortable with their gender or believe that their gender is inappropriate. In many cases, sexual reassignment is done. This involves extensive assessment, medical evaluation, behavioral training, and social skills training to help the individuals fit into their desired gender role.

Eating Disorders

Eating disorders include Anorexia Nervosa, Bulimia, and Binge Eating Disorder. Anorexia Nervosa involves a refusal to maintain body weight at or above a minimally normal weight for one's age and height (e.g., weight loss leading to maintenance of body weight less than 85% of that expected; or failure to make expected weight gain during period of growth, leading to body weight less than 85% of that expected). There is also an intense fear of gaining weight or becoming fat, even though the individual may be medically compromised because of being underweight. There is also a disturbance in the way in which one's body weight or shape is experienced The individual uses body weight or shape to maintain a positive self-evaluation. Even when there is medical necessity to gain weight, the seriousness of the current low body weight may be vehemently denied.

In Bulimia Nervosa, the person has regularly engaged in binges of eating and purges (self-induced vomiting or the misuse of laxatives, diuretics, or enemas). First, recurrent episodes of binge eating involve eating in a discrete period of time (e.g., within any 2-hour period), an amount of food that is larger than most people would eat during a similar period and under similar circumstances. Second, the individual experiences lack of control over eating during the episode (e.g., a feeling that one cannot stop eating or control what or how much one is eating). The individual may then engage in self-induced vomiting; misuse of laxatives, diuretics, enemas, or other medications; fasting; or excessive exercise, all to avoid weight gain. As with anorexia, the individual's self-evaluation is influenced by perceived body shape and weight.

A third category of eating disorder is Binge Eating Disorder. The individual eats large amounts of food in a concentrated period of time, but without purging, enemas, or laxatives. This behavior may lead to extensive weight gain and obesity.

Primary Sleep Disorders (Dyssomnias)

These disorders include Primary Insomnia, Primary Hypersomnia, Narcolepsy, Breathing-Related Sleep Disorder, Circadian Rhythm Sleep Disorder, Nightmare Disorder, Sleep Terror Disorder, and Sleepwalking Disorder.

Dyssomnias involve a disturbance in the amount, quality, or timing of sleep. In Primary Insomnia, there is a problem initiating or maintaining sleep. There may be problems in falling asleep, middle-of-the-night waking, or waking up well before one needs to in the morning. In Primary Hypersomnia, the individual experiences excessive sleepiness, prolonged sleep episodes, or daytime sleep episodes daily. The assumption is made that the Hypersomnia is not reactive to studying late, an extreme party experience, or the use of substances.

The person with Narcolepsy experiences "irresistible attacks of refreshing sleep" (*DSM-IV-TR*, p. 567). In the middle of a conversation, the individual may show an eye flutter, a head drop, and fall asleep. While the consequences are limited when sitting in a chair at home, driving can become a lethal activity for the individual and anyone else on the road.

Breathing-related sleep disorder involves the disruption of restful sleep because of breathing difficulty, for example, sleep apnea which involves an obstruction of the airway. The most common complaints are from the individual who reports sleepiness the next day, and from sleep partners who have to deal with loud snoring, interruptions in breathing, and snorting.

Circadian Rhythm Sleep Disorder involves a disruption in the sleep-wake cycle. It could be brought on by jet lag or changing shift work. The individual experiences sleepiness until his or her body adjusts to the new sleep-wake cycle.

Nightmare Disorder creates a situation wherein the individual has episodes of waking from a deep sleep with detailed memories of frightening dreams. Sleep Terror Disorder is similar in that it involves abrupt waking from sleep, but without the detailed memory of a dream, only the autonomic arousal experienced during fear and danger.

In the midst of a Sleepwalking Disorder experience, individuals will rise from their bed, walk about, and even involve themselves in activity, for example, eating. They can be awakened with difficulty, and they do not, as the myth has it, die if you wake them.

Impulse Control Disorders

Impulse-Control Disorders include Intermittent Explosive Disorder (discrete episodes of assault or destruction of property that must be differentiated from other antisocial behavior, manic behavior, or conduct disorder), Kleptomania (failure to resist impulsive stealing or taking of property that belongs to someone else), Pyromania (setting fires to achieve gratification, pleasure, or a relief of tension), Pathological Gambling (persistent and pathological gambling that causes personal and relationship distress), and Trichotillomania (pulling out of one's own hair to achieve gratification, pleasure, or a relief of tension).

Adjustment Disorders

Adjustment Disorders involve difficulty dealing with and adapting to specific life stressors and circumstances. They require the development of emotional or behavioral symptoms in response to an identifiable stressor(s) occurring within 3 months of the onset of the stressor(s). The manifestation of the adjustment difficulty is marked by distress that exceeds what would typically be expected from exposure to the stressor, causes significant impairment in social or occupational (academic) functioning, and the stress-related disturbance does not meet the criteria for another specific Axis I disorder, nor is it merely an exacerbation of a preexisting Axis I or Axis II disorder.

Once the stressor (or its consequences) has terminated, the symptoms do not persist for more than an additional 6 months. However, some stressors are chronic or unremitting, for example, disabling physical injury.

Personality Disorders

Personality disorders, by definition, are inflexible, pervasive, stable, and enduring, and lead to clinically significant distress or impairment in functioning (American Psychiatric Association, 2000). They typically manifest in early adulthood although the prodromal symptoms may appear much earlier.

Individuals with PD are typically unaware of the extent of their problems despite the sometimes overwhelming effects of their behaviors on themselves and those around them. For many individuals, their patterns of thinking, feeling, and relating seem comfortable and familiar. It is very often the family, friends, or coworkers of the individual with a personality disorder who find the person's patterns particularly troublesome. It is estimated that approximately 1% to 3% of the general population has a diagnosable personality disorder (APA, 2000a). Many more individuals may suffer from subclinical levels of character pathology. No two patients typically present with the exact same combination of diagnostic criteria.

Some patients are superficially aware of the self-defeating nature of their personality problems (e.g., overdependence, inhibition, excessive avoidance) but are impotent in changing their behavior. Still other patients may recognize their maladaptive behavioral patterns and have the motivation to change them, but just do not have the skills to make it happen.

Axis II problems are not always diagnosed at treatment intake, though early diagnosis and treatment planning are likely to be more effective. Many Axis II patients are silent about their personality problems, or deny them, as a reflection of the disorders.

The *DSM* has divided the personality disorders into three groups or clusters. Each cluster has a unifying theme that is overarching for the component disorders.

Cluster A: Paranoid, Schizoid, and Schizotypal
The *DSM-IV-TR* describes this cluster as the *odd or eccentric cluster* (APA, 2000a). Individuals with Cluster A personality disorders are less likely than other clusters to present for treatment. The relative lack of discomfort regarding their experience may make it difficult for them to find the need or motivation to change. Because they tend to prefer solitary activities, they may have fewer familial or social contacts encouraging (or pressuring) them to seek assistance. The very nature of Paranoid Personality Disorder, is a suspicion of others, which naturally extends to any potential therapeutic relationship, thereby impeding potential assistance. The schizotypal individual is uncomfortable with others and may experience great distress in social situations. What is interesting is that this group is similar in style, though not degree to individuals with schizophrenia. Schizotypal individuals have *ideas of reference* (incorrect interpretations of casual events as having special meaning for the individual). This is differentiated from the schizophrenic individual who has delusions of reference that are far more strongly held and believed. Particular attention in the assessment phase should be made with regard to the pervasiveness of the phenomenon, especially in the absence of overt psychotic phenomena, including hallucinations.

Cluster B: Antisocial, Borderline, Histrionic, and Narcissistic
The *DSM-IV-TR* defines this cluster as the *dramatic and erratic cluster* (APA, 2000a). Individuals with Cluster B personality disorders are frequently seen in both inpatient and outpatient settings. Their manifestations are fairly easily detected and can be particularly dangerous (self-destructive or risk-taking). These clients may be erratic and impulsive, and demonstrate a high potential for harm to self or others.

Cluster C: Avoidant, Dependent, and Obsessive-Compulsive
The *DSM-IV-TR* describes Cluster C personality disorders as *anxious and avoidant* (APA, 2000a). Some of the manifestations of Cluster C disorders are socially desirable in moderation (e.g., learning to depend on others). In excess, however, they can cripple an individual.

Finally, there are problems that are common and often linked to normal stresses and tensions in living. These include Relational Problems including Relational Problem Related to a Mental Disorder or General Medical Condition, Parent-Child Relational Problems, Partner Relational Problems, and Sibling Relational Problems.

Problems related to abuse and neglect include the Physical Abuse of Child, Sexual Abuse of Child, Neglect of a Child, Physical Abuse of Adult, including partner physical abuse, and Sexual Abuse of an Adult.

Summary

As you can see by this thorough nomenclature, the classification of mental disorders is a complex and difficult process. There are no easy answers, and there are many disagreements about the current diagnostic schema. This system is, in fact, in the process of revision. The revisions will include possible new categories, revision of older diagnoses, and alteration of certain diagnostic criteria to better reflect the empirical data, respond to social changes, add new Axes, and make the diagnostic process easier for the clinician. It remains to be seen whether greater detail and complexity can be combined with a clinical "user-friendliness."

What will almost certainly stay the same is the idea that pathological behavior is determined by its being problematic, discomforting for the individual, potentially harmful to others, and inconsistent with the moderate and typical rhythms and practices of broader society.

PART 11

Basic Techniques for Clinicians— Assessment

Introduction to Assessment: The Biopsychosocial Systems Model of Human Behavior

6

Chapter

This chapter begins the focus on assessment in all aspects of clinical psychology. Different types of assessment have different goals, and these purposes are articulated. Consideration is given to differences when assessments are geared toward direct service to patients, in consultation to other professionals, and to answer specific clinical questions or monitor clinical progress. The biopsychosocial systems model is put forth as a comprehensive, integrative view of human behavior that frames assessment to be individualized, yet inclusive.

Learning Objectives

At the end of this chapter, the reader should be able to:

- Articulate at least three goals for clinical assessment.
- Describe the purpose for conducting at least three types of assessment (cognitive assessment, personality assessment, and behavioral assessment).
- Explain the biopsychosocial systems model of understanding human behavior and why this multifaceted approach is critical to understanding similarities and differences among people.
- Explain the role of biology, cognitions, behaviors, affect, social factors, cultural factors, spiritual beliefs, and physical environment, in understanding how people think and behave.
- Provide an example of how assessing the biopsychosocial systems domains of a person results in a comprehensive understanding of human behavior.

When you got dressed this morning, how did you choose your clothing? If you are like most people, you thought about the temperature outside, where you were planning to go today, whom you expected to see, and the clothes you had available from which to choose. In essence, you made an *assessment* of your clothing situation based on information you gathered from your environment; your mood, thoughts, and feelings; and your goals for the day. The sociocultural context within which you live also played a role in this decision by giving you a sense of what type of clothing is acceptable or permitted in society or in the situations you planned to encounter. In the most basic sense of the term, people make numerous *assessments* to navigate their way through day-to-day decisions, even if they are not cognizant of these decisions. Similarly, assessment is a core component of all aspects of clinical psychology.

Researchers, administrators, clinicians, professors, and other practitioners of clinical psychology use assessment as the foundation for everything they do. Psychologists must evaluate psychological phenomena before initiating further scientific investigation, before making changes in clinic or academic programs, or before initiating therapy with clients. Graduate programs in clinical psychology provide students with knowledge and skills that qualify them to conduct, administer, and interpret certain types of tests and assessments. This training often distinguishes mental health professionals with graduate training in psychology from colleagues (social workers, special education teachers, psychiatrists, nurses) who are not prepared with a graduate psychology degree. Thus, learning about assessment tools, techniques, processes, and ways to approach assessment is critical for newly developing psychology professionals.

This chapter presents a psychological assessment paradigm that is based on cognitive and behavioral principles, and behavioral assessment, broadly defined. Behavioral assessment was defined by O'Leary and Wilson (1975) as "an attempt to identify the environmental and self-imposed variables which are *currently* (original authors' emphasis) maintaining an individual's maladaptive thoughts, feelings, and behaviors . . ." (pp. 18–19). Although "behavioral assessment" has been defined in various ways (Cone, 1998), the O'Leary and Wilson definition is most widely accepted (Silva, 1993). The goals of various types of assessment, and the most common data collection strategies and techniques used by clinical psychologists are introduced in this chapter. The biopsychosocial systems model and a scientific approach to assessment (in Chapter 7) are provided as the conceptual frameworks in which to gather clinically useful information. Lastly, the clinical decision-making model (A. M. Nezu & Nezu, 1989; A. M. Nezu, Nezu, Friedman, & Haynes, 1997) is described in Chapter 8 as a structure for clinicians' to use in planning and conducting clinical assessments.

Goals of Assessment

There are many reasons for conducting a psychological assessment, and each reason requires the assessor to initiate different tasks. Likewise, selecting methods and techniques for acquiring clinical information depends on the nature and function of the assessment. Therefore, before learning how to conduct an assessment, practitioners of clinical psychology must understand why or for what purpose assessments are conducted.

In general, the major aims of assessments are to gather information about persons, systems, environments, or phenomenon (or some combination of these), and to enable *classification, description,* and *comprehension or evaluation* of current circumstances. Assessments also may be directed to *predict* future behaviors (dangerousness, suicide) or circumstances (maintaining employment). Commonly, assessments seek to respond to more than one of these goals at a time and can be tailored to address several clinical or research questions. Therefore, you will notice overlap among the strategies and techniques used for collecting information for each purpose.

Diagnostic Assessment

The purpose of diagnostic assessment is to differentiate between "normal" and "abnormal" behavior, to differentiate among various "abnormal" constellations of symptoms, and to classify individuals based on identified abnormalities or "presentation of disease" (Chaplin, 1985). Questions that diagnostic assessments can answer include the following examples. A 6-year-old child is having trouble in school, and not staying in his seat during lessons: Does the child have an attention deficit disorder, an anxiety disorder, or conduct disorder? A 68-year-old female has been increasingly forgetful, less energetic, and confused: Is she depressed or suffering from the onset of dementia? Why is the 35-year-old-male having chest pains and rapid heart rates without any biological explanation for these symptoms? Answering such questions through diagnostic assessments may lead to recommendations for treatment, establishment of the clients' eligibility (or ineligibility) for disability services (e.g., disability accommodations, reimbursement from insurance companies), or simply increased understanding of patients' symptoms, which will enable other health care practitioners to work more effectively with them.

Diagnostic assessments in a psychological setting are similar in concept to physicians' medical examinations. Medical patients arrive in physicians' offices for many reasons. Depending on the motivation for the visit, physicians either focus on a specific complaint presented by the patient, or may evaluate the entire person in the search for "what's wrong?" There is a clear mission to search for abnormality or pathology, identify the malady, and report the findings. Typically, such an examination would lead to treatment if a disease or abnormality were found. Seldom does a physician examine a patient only to identify optimal functioning; information is typically a by-product of the diagnostic or physical examination. Similarly, diagnostic psychological assessments tend to be "disease" focused and are criticized (Follette & Hayes, 1992) for following a deficit model, rather than a balanced model of strengths and deficits. Furthermore, behavioral and cognitive-behavioral psychologists (Follette, 1996, 1997) criticize diagnostic assessments for excluding contextual information about antecedents, consequences, and social, physical, and cultural environmental factors from the evaluation of persons' reported problems and symptoms. Partially, this phenomenon is a function of the classification systems that guide diagnostic evaluations.

Classification Systems

The *Diagnostic and Statistical Manual of Mental Disorders* (4th Edition; *DSM-IV-TR;* American Psychiatric Association, 2000) is the guide most commonly used by mental health professionals in the United States for diagnosing psychological, psychosocial, interpersonal and environmental problems in children, adolescents, and adults. The *International Classification of Disorders-10* (*ICD-10;* WHO, 1992) is also used worldwide, and is the preferred classification system by physicians.

Classification systems, as the basis for diagnostic assessments, are derived from enormous amounts of research on very large samples of the population. Their purpose is to provide *nomothetic* information. Nomothetic information is information that establishes general principles, norms, or laws. With regard to the *DSM-IV-TR* (American Psychiatric Association, 2000) or *ICD-10* (WHO, 1992), nomothetic information informs us how many people with certain characteristics, features, or symptoms may behave, interact with others, or reportedly feel about themselves, others, and the world around them. The information differentiates persons with such characteristics, features, or symptoms from data collected on large volumes of "normal" people, or individuals who do not have difficulty in personal, social, occupational, or academic functioning.

For example, we know that many adults with major depressive disorders often have persistent feelings of extreme hopelessness about their future, and they have felt this way for an extended period (2 weeks or more; American Psychiatric Association, 2000). Nondepressed, normal persons, while in a temporary negative mood state, may endorse intermittent feelings of hopelessness about specific situations or momentary feelings of hopelessness about their futures, but they do not typically report enduring feelings of hopelessness under ordinary circumstances. It is important to remember, however, that information in the *DSM-IV-TR* and *ICD-10* is based on average scores and commonalities in self-reports or evaluations, and that there are variations within the group and exceptions to the rules and criteria established. Therefore, not all persons who meet criteria for a Major Depressive Disorder will endorse having persistent feelings of hopelessness, but they will likely overlap with the majority group in other symptomatology.

The classification systems continue to evolve in accordance with the development in the fields of clinical and social psychology, anthropology, and epidemiology. The *DSM-IV-TR* is revised periodically to include information about populations and variables that had been underrepresented in the past. In the most recent revision, the task forces in charge of improving on the *DSM-IV-TR* have increased attention to diversity and cultural factors and strive to increase understanding and classification of patterns of symptoms that may warrant a diagnosis or specific nomenclature in future additions.

Diagnostic manuals have significant merits and have allowed for a certain degree of standardization in the field of clinical psychology. They provide a means for professionals to communicate about clients or patients, and disseminate synthesized conclusions from volumes of research. Psychologists gear diagnostic assessments, in part, to seek confirmation or disconfirmation of persons' fit with nomothetic information. The *DSM-IV-TR* provides a starting point for understanding clients' clinical presentations and for determining general directions for treatment planning. However, to solely rely on nomothetic information would be equivalent to taking a cookbook approach to identifying persons' problems and solutions to their problems. As you know from your own experience with others, and from reading Chapter 5 of this book, people are much more complex! Relying on group norms and typical or common presentations would be misleading in diagnosis and treatment. Psychologists also have an ethical obligation to consider personal characteristics of individuals assessed to ensure tests are valid for the person tested, interpretation of data is appropriate, and recommendations based on test data are culturally and individually relevant (APA, 2003, 9.0). As such, nomothetic information is balanced and integrated with *ideographic* (individual) information. Ideographic assessments are characteristic of behavioral assessments, and are defined and discussed in more detail later in this chapter.

Logistics and Details of Diagnostic Assessments

Mental health professionals who have training and experience using the *DSM-IV-TR* or *ICD-10*, and specialized measures, inventories, or structured interviews use these tools to conduct diagnostic assessments for a variety of purposes. The APA Ethical Principles and Code of Conduct (APA, 2003) specifies that only trained qualified individuals should use psychological tests, and outlines the cautions to be taken. Clients or family members of clients might request a diagnostic assessment. Clinicians routinely incorporate diagnostic assessments into their standard practices for evaluating new clients for treatment planning. Nonmental health professional colleagues (medical professionals, school administrators, teachers), or mental health professionals who desire more precise understanding of their patients' presentations of symptoms may request consultation with professionals trained to conduct diagnostic assessments. Diagnostic assessments may also be conducted to screen, classify, or assign individuals for clinical research studies according to the information obtained. Likewise, forensic psychologists may conduct diagnostic assessments to determine clients' mental competencies to stand trial or mental states related to committed crimes.

Depending on the complexity of the client's presentation of symptoms, a diagnostic assessment may be accomplished through interviewing alone, or may require interviewing in combination with other tests and measurements. A diagnostic assessment may be one component of a comprehensive evaluation of an individual, or it may be the sole purpose of an assessment. Although diagnostic assessments may be repeated over time to determine whether temporal symptoms have been alleviated, certain diagnoses are considered unremitting, lifelong conditions (antisocial personality disorder, borderline personality disorder, narcissistic personality disorders; A. T. Beck, Freeman, Davis, & Associates, 2004), and therefore, reevaluation may not occur. Unlike some forms of behavioral assessment, practitioners may conduct diagnostic assessments in almost any setting in which they work. These evaluations are not dependent on viewing clients in their naturalistic environments.

Clinical Examples

EXAMPLE 1   For a client who is self-referred to a psychologist specializing in sleep disorders, a diagnostic assessment is necessary to determine if the client indeed has a sleep disorder, and if so, what kind; or to determine if the sleep difficulties are secondary to other medical or psychological problems. Once the psychologist determines the nature of the client's difficulty, treatment interventions may be offered, or an appropriate referral made if the sleep difficulties are determined to be secondary to another psychological or medical problem.

EXAMPLE 2   Ms. Latte requested an evaluation to determine if she had an Attention Deficit Disorder. Ms. Latte saw a special program on television, and recognized that troubles she had learned to live with and work around were consistent with those of the televised woman with this reported diagnosis. Ms. Latte was functioning reasonably well, but has always felt "alone" in her problems, and "embarrassed" for being "scatterbrained" and distractible. Her goal for the assessment was simply to identify if her history and current patterns of behavior were consistent with this diagnosis. She believed that gaining this information would allow her to alleviate some of her self-deprecating thoughts and hard feelings, help her husband understand that her problems were not volitional, and possibly gain recommendations for improving her daily functioning.

EXAMPLE 3   In psychiatric emergency rooms, psychologists may conduct diagnostic assessments to determine patients' needed level of care, and to communicate this information to triage facilities (inpatient unit, partial program, or outpatient clinic) before discharging or admitting patients to other units for follow-up care.

EXAMPLE 4   If someone you know told you that her child has a reading disability, would you know how to help your friend assess the services that her child needs? Most professionals would need more specific information to develop recommendations or a treatment plan. For starters, what are the child's current learning strengths and difficulties, environmental supports, learning strategies used, individual and family expectations, and self-efficacy beliefs? Note that you can ethically help a friend consider services that might be appropriate for a particular disorder, but you cannot ethically give recommendations or treatment plans on a casual basis to personal friends and acquaintances. Assessments, just like therapy, must always be conducted within the boundaries of a formal professional relationship (see APA, 2002, 3.05, 3.06, 9.01).

Descriptive Assessments

Descriptive assessments, broadly described, are conducted to learn more about clients' cognitive functioning, psychosocial functioning, academic achievement, personality, behavior, or specific needs within an identified area of interest (e.g., caregivers' needs). Assessment questions may focus on individuals, families, groups of people (e.g., group home setting; hospital unit), or person-environment interactions (e.g., goodness of fit between a developmentally disabled adult and her social rehabilitation program setting). Mental health professionals conduct these assessments to obtain background and general information necessary for better understanding of clients' problems and factors contributing to those problems. Such assessments aid professionals in planning treatment, providing academic or occupational counseling, and designing group or individual behavior modification interventions. Researchers or program evaluators may use descriptive assessments to provide end-users of their work with information about populations or programs under study.

Descriptive assessments are often combined with diagnostic assessments, and some methods of evaluation will accomplish data collection for both purposes. Data collection techniques for descriptive assessments include a combination of interviews, observation, self-report inventories and questionnaires, reports by others, computerized assessment, and physiological assessment. Clinical psychologists with proper training can conduct most types of descriptive assessments. Psychologists also commonly specialize in assessments for specific aged populations (e.g., children/adolescents, adults, senior adults), disorders (e.g., learning disabilities, traumatic brain injury, Huntington's chorea) or psychosocial problems (e.g., court-adjudicated offenders).

Prediction Assessments

While evaluation of current functioning is critical to most types of assessment, under certain circumstances, psychologists are also asked or required to predict clients' future behaviors or the effect or impact that situations or life events will have on individuals' thoughts, feelings, behaviors, or overall functioning. Predictive assessments are often necessary in or for medical, forensic, and occupational settings, and traditional mental health in- and outpatient settings. Given the uniqueness of individuals, and the inconsistency of behaviors characteristic of persons with certain personality disorders or other problems, most predictive assessments remain tentative and qualified as "best estimations." The accuracy of any assessment, but especially of predictive assessments, relies on the availability, accuracy, and reliability of data about the *predictor* and *predicted* variables (Haynes & O'Brien, 2000). Predictor variables are those factors that are presumed to precede or co-occur with the behavior to be predicted, and to be causally related in some way.

Some behaviors are more easily predictable than others. Assuming we have comprehensive information leading to the diagnosis, it is likely that a young adult with social anxiety, without treatment, will have difficulty delivering his 30-minute presentation to the 75 students in his college course; an older adult who had little social support other than her recently deceased spouse, who also has a history of poor coping skills, may be likely to have difficulty adjusting to widowhood, and may suffer from complicated bereavement. Such predictions are fairly easy to make, given a thorough assessment of past behavior, current functioning, and other psychosocial variables, and the predictable nature of the behaviors in question.

When more difficult predictions of future behavior are requested or necessary, significant consequences may be associated with the outcome of the evaluation. For example, predictions of suicide risk, dangerousness, psychological suitability for specific medical treatments, or prediction of psychological preparedness for parenthood (adoption) require psychologists to gain as much certainty as possible, since the consequences related to poor or inadequate assessment can obviously be grave. The APA Code of Ethics (APA, 2003, 9.01) cautions that predictions or recommendations made based on assessments should specify the sources of data collected and that for mandated individuals specifically (and all others, generally), appropriate informed consent must be obtained (9.03). Some examples of prediction assessments will illustrate the complexities of this work.

Psychologists working in almost any clinical setting will be faced with the need to conduct suicide and dangerousness risk assessments. Current suicide symptoms and homicidal ideation are standard components of most psychologists' intake assessment and mental status examination. When clients endorse suicidal or homicidal ideation (thoughts), further evaluation is necessary to determine the severity of these thoughts, the clients' likelihood of acting on these thoughts and plans to do so, and their ability or access to the means by which they could execute their plans. Based on thorough assessments, clinical psychologists are expected to make predictions about a client's safety and the safety of others, before they can release the client from their presence. However, Rudd and Joiner (1998) emphasize that although the court system seems to imply that clinicians should be able to predict suicide, empirical data show that "prediction" models of suicide consistently fail (see Rudd & Joiner for references to these studies); therefore, the complexity of this task cannot be overstated. Based on research reviewed by Rudd and Joiner, clinicians' "risk" assessments (focusing on patients' current state) are more accurate and reliable than actual predictions (implying future behavior) of suicide attempts or completion. Risk assessment for suicide consists of evaluation of predisposing factors (e.g., age, sex, previous psychiatric diagnosis, history of suicidality), acute and chronic risk factors and precipitating factors (current stressors or losses, such as job, loved ones, physical or cognitive ability, chronic pain, affective disorders, poor problem-solving skills, social isolation, poor impulse control), and protective factors (active involvement in treatment, good physical health, good problem-solving ability, social support, hopefulness; see Rudd & Joiner for a complete review of references).

In medical settings, physicians constantly make decisions and predictions about patients' likely physical response to medications, medical interventions (e.g., surgery, radiation, organ transplantation), and treatments (e.g., light therapy). However, many physicians recognize that biological responses are not the only concern. Patients' compliance with medical regimens and ability to cope with necessary lifestyle and behavioral changes can be equally important. Clinical (or clinical health) psychologists aid physicians' decision making and treatment planning for patients by conducting predictive assessments relating to these issues.

For example, organ transplant recipients must comply with medication and behavioral (bone marrow transplant recipients must stay away from crowds for 6 months to 1 year, due to low immune functioning) regimens following transplants. Many recipients take as many as 5 to 10 medications following the transplant, including anti-rejection medications to prevent their bodies from rejecting the new organ. If patients do not comply with this requirement, fatal consequences could result. Physicians, therefore, want to be as certain as possible that treatment is truly in an individual's best interest. Likewise, individuals with histories of drug or alcohol abuse may be questionable candidates for some medical treatments because of the potential for them to cope poorly with the short- or long-term effects of treatment, and the lethality of mixing alcohol or drugs with the prescribed regimen they may be given. Psychologists must assess patients' past behaviors, current functioning (emotional state, desire or motivation for treatment, coping skills), psychosocial resources (strength in faith or spirituality, social support), and other factors, to evaluate the strengths and potential threats or weaknesses that can impact future behavior.

Psychologists working in forensic settings are likely to conduct predictive assessments for various reasons. For offender populations, prediction of recidivism is likely required as part of court system procedures relating to sentencing and parole, and defendant- and plaintiff-initiated evaluations. Family/marital lawyers also frequently hire clinical and forensic psychologists to evaluate clients' current functioning (descriptive assessment or diagnostic assessment), and predict future behaviors. Behaviors of interest in family/marital law might include clients' likelihood of future abusive behaviors; clients' future abilities to manage anger and aggression if rehabilitation is sought; clients' likelihood of complying with child custody mandates and abilities to maintain effective parenting skills, and children's predicted responses to custody arrangements. Numerous other examples exist.

Occupational settings provide rich opportunities for psychological assessment. Questions to be answered in occupational settings may relate to the workforce in a company as a whole, or individuals within a workforce. Prediction assessments might be sought to answer questions such as the following ones: What is the likelihood of this employee's occupational success, given the specific accommodations and training available? What variables are predictive of burnout in persons with a particular job or position (Mack, 2004; Schober & Felgoise, 2002)? What is the likely psychological impact of a specified corporate change on upper-level management? Psychologists working in employee assistance programs may conduct more traditional clinical prediction assessments.

Review

Psychological assessments generally seek to classify, describe, or predict clients' psychological functioning and behaviors. Many referral or assessment questions require evaluations structured to accomplish more than one of these goals. Clinical psychologists conduct assessments in various settings, assuming various roles (e.g., consultant, health care team, independent practitioner). Thus far, descriptions and examples of the goals and types of assessments clinical psychologists conduct have remained general. The following section describes several specific types of assessment that are conducted to answer specific questions.

Specific Types of Assessment

To differentiate among the different types of assessment, several key questions are answered within each of the following subsections to address the elements of what, when, who, where, why, and how. What are the goals of the assessment? When, relative to other life events, will the assessment take place? Who requests the evaluation or who refers clients for specific assessments? Who is (are) the person(s) to be evaluated? Where will the assessment be conducted? Why is the assessment necessary? How will the information be used? The answers to these questions vary depending on the assessment prescribed. Some overlap is also noted as the different applications of assessment are illustrated.

Although classifying an individual as mentally retarded may be useful for communicating a person's general functioning level among professionals, describing the person's strengths, weaknesses, likes and dislikes, will be equally or more important in the development of a behavior modification plan.

Cognitive Assessment

Cognitive assessment focuses on understanding brain-behavior relationships, information processing, and thinking skills. The following critical aspects of cognition may be targeted for assessment: attention, perception, memory, schemas, learning (intelligence; achievement; aptitude), cognitive development, creativity, language, problem solving, decision making, and judgment. Neuropsychological tests, intelligence tests, achievement and aptitude tests, and development tests are specific types of cognitive assessments for evaluating these areas.

Clinicians who conduct or request cognitive assessments are interested in understanding individuals' skills (strengths and deficits), abilities, and limits, and comparing these skills and abilities with clients' own displayed affect and behaviors. Individuals' functioning is usually compared with their own previous or prospective functioning, to normative standards predetermined by research, or both. Some high schools require youth football players (and other sports participants) to have cognitive assessments prior to beginning the football season. These baseline assessments provide individual norms that are later used for comparison with postinjury (concussions) cognitive assessments if football players are hurt during the season. Cognitive assessments may be conducted periodically to evaluate positive or negative change over time, such as yearly achievement testing in language development or mathematics skills. Intelligence testing exemplifies an assessment done to evaluate individuals' functioning compared with normative standards: parents may request IQ (intelligence quotient) testing to determine children's scholastic needs and readiness to begin elementary school, or later in life for psychoeducational planning.

Other reasons cognitive assessments may be indicated are numerous. Cognitive assessments may be required when persons are not reaching expected developmental milestones, such as language skills. Self-recognition or by others of nonnormative (nonaverage) behavior, either positive (superior intellectual abilities, creativity), or negative (attention problems, extreme emotional lability), often generates referrals for cognitive assessment. Significant changes in cognitive functioning are usually noticed by individuals, family, and friends, and often lead to visits to primary care physicians or emergency rooms; these health professionals may require psychologists' assistance in diagnosing or understanding the cause for the behavior change (Rozensky, Sweet, & Tovian, 1997). Such sudden or gradual behavior changes may have resulted from a known external event (accident), or a known or initially unknown biological change (tumor, medication side-effects, aging process). Thus, as these examples demonstrate, cognitive assessments are useful for individuals across the life span, for purposes of diagnosis, understanding, and treatment or future planning.

Intellectual Assessments and Intelligence Tests
Although intelligence tests are technically encompassed by discussion of cognitive assessments, their popularity warrants more detailed description. Numerous experts have defined *intelligence* in various ways, and history dating back to the 1800s reveals the development and controversy over the concept of intelligence and its measurement (see Sternberg, 1999, pp. 470–477 for a review). According to Sternberg's (1999) review of a more recent study (Sternberg & Detterman, 1986), the consensus definition of intelligence among 24 cognitive psychologists with expertise in intelligence research is as follows: "the capacity to learn from experience, using metacognitive processes to enhance learning, and the ability to adapt to the surrounding environment, which may require different adaptations within different social and cultural contexts" (p. 469). Thus, there are basic components of intelligence that are germane to all people, and also unique considerations that must be made for persons of different gender, culture, race, and advantaged or disadvantaged backgrounds.

Intellectual assessments, and the tests used to conduct them, are among the most commonly thought of psychological tests among nonpsychologists. School psychologists, counseling psychologists, and clinical psychologists all use intelligence tests for a variety of purposes, but most often for educational and vocational planning (for persons with intellectual disabilities or giftedness), and as a part of general cognitive assessment (see previous examples). At one time or another, you may have been given a version of a standardized intelligence test such as a Wechsler Preschool and Primary Scale of Intelligence—Revised (for ages 3 to 7, WPPSI-R; Wechsler, 1989), Wechsler Intelligence Scale for Children—Third Edition (for ages 6 through 16; WISC-III; Wechsler, 1991), Wechsler Adult Intelligence Scale-III (for ages 16 through 89; WAIS-III; Psychological Corporation, 1997; Wechsler, 1997), or the Stanford-Binet Intelligence Scales (Fourth Edition; Thorndike, Hagen, & Sattler, 1986). The Wechsler scales are the most popular intellectual assessment tools in use, followed by the Stanford-Binet Scales. Nonverbal intellectual tests, such as the General Ability Measure for Adults (GAMA), also exist to assess intellectual functioning in individuals with minimal to no English language ability, such as individuals with limited formal education, those who are deaf or hearing impaired, or who are from non-English speaking cultures (Bardos, 2001). The GAMA is purported to be free of bias from expressive language skills and overall academic achievement.

David Wechsler, developer of the Wechsler Scales, believed intelligence comprises cognitive, affective, and motivational factors (Ryan & Lopez, 2001). As such, he created the Wechsler Scales based on items and measures selected from existing ability tests (see Ryan & Lopez for review). The results of the WAIS-III, WISC-III, and previous versions of these tests (WAIS, WAIS-R, WISC, WISC-R) provide three separate intelligence quotient scores: Verbal IQ, Performance IQ, and the Full Scale IQ, which is an overall quotient of abilities. The raw scores for these tests are converted into standardized/scaled scores to enable comparison of individual scores with normative scores, according to age. The scaled scores are then summed and converted to IQ scores, which can be compared across age, regardless of which Wechsler IQ score was used to arrive at the IQ results. Psychologists also closely analyze comparative performance across subtests, which reveals information about cognitive strengths and weaknesses, possible neuropsychological problems, emotional problems (e.g., depression), and other important clinical material. As with all assessment, data from intelligence tests is always interpreted in the context of other information gathered from a broad-based assessment. We discuss broad-based assessment at a later point.

Users of intelligence tests are required to have training and experience, usually through graduate education, in administration of standardized psychological tests. Administration of these tests requires strict adherence to test manual guidelines and clinical judgment and knowledge pertaining to the intricacies of standardized tests. Interpretation of the test data is a complex task requiring clinical knowledge, judgment, and great care. The ability to establish and maintain rapport with test-takers is also deemed important. Lastly, clinical skill and professionalism are required to provide feedback to test-takers, their parents, and the original referral source (school, physician, guardian), since the results can significantly impact (positively or negatively) the course of the examinee's future. The APA Code of Ethics (APA, 2003, 9.10) distinctly indicates this importance by stating psychologists must be the provider of feedback, regardless of whether employees or other individuals administered the test batteries.

Personality Assessment

Definition of Personality

Various theorists have defined *personality* in many ways, over the many years that the discipline of psychology has evolved. Most definitions and theorists have agreed that personality refers to stable, enduring characteristics that uniquely define individuals' ways of being or of viewing life situations, the world, and others in it (see Chaplin, 1985, for various definitions). Furthermore, personality may be defined using the terminology of individuals' temperament and traits.

Temperament refers to a person's disposition and is often assumed to be largely biologically predetermined. Much research on temperament has been conducted on infants and children (Kamphaus & Frick, 1996). Equating temperament with personality may be appropriate according to some psychological theories, especially those rooted in the psychodynamic traditions or medical models; other theories might suggest that persons are born with a particular temperament, and stable characteristics develop in addition to this biologically predetermined disposition to result in personality.

Traits refer to individuals' relatively stable ways of thinking or behaving, or their disposition that may develop over time. The term trait implies that the environment and one's interaction with it or others may formatively develop one's personality. Traits differ from persons' behaviors—traits refer to how people *are;* behaviors describe what people *do.* If you had to describe your best friend in three sentences, what would you say? Perhaps, you might say that your friend is "fun or funny," "loyal," "kind and compassionate," "trustworthy," "sociable," "outgoing," or other similar descriptors. Most people define others in global terms, describing the most characteristic style of the individuals. They attach these global terms based on behaviors they have observed. Your friend may be described as "funny" because she tells jokes and elicits laughter. Some people are described as having "different personalities" depending on the social context (e.g., social versus business). Descriptors, such as those of your friend, are typically representative of the combination of temperament and traits, or his or her "personality."

How did you arrive at the description of your friend? If you are like most people, you have observed your friend in various situations or in interactions with you. You observed her behavior and the emotions she expressed. You also noticed her consistent ways of viewing herself and relating to others and her environment, and made inferences based on these observations. In essence, you have conducted a personality assessment, because formal assessment relies on similar processes!

Possible goals of formal personality assessment are diagnosis and understanding of persons' ways of relating to others and the environment for the purpose of description, prediction, and treatment in clinical or counseling (career or vocational) settings, employment settings, or forensic settings, among others. In your assessment of your friend, you have diagnosed (classified your friend) and attempted to understand him or her. (Don't worry; if you have chosen to pursue a career in clinical psychology, you will often be accused of or asked if you are analyzing your friends anyway!) Substantial training in psychometrics, test theory, test development, diversity variables (ethnicity, race, culture, gender, age, language, disabilities), and supervised experience are required for use of most psychological tests, including personality tests (S. M. Turner, DeMers, Fox, & Reed, 2001).

Objective and Projective Tests

Formal personality assessments use *objective* or *projective* measurement techniques rather than casual observation. Objective measurement techniques are developed based on empirical test development strategies, have established psychometric properties (reliability, validity; see later discussion), and tend to be atheoretical (Kamphaus & Frick, 1996). Interpretation of data collected from objective measurements is done by comparison of individual scores to a clinical sample of persons with the same background (e.g., age, education level) or diagnosis of interest. Examples of objective measurement techniques used in personality assessment include the Minnesota Multiphasic Personality Inventory-2 (MMPI-2; Duckworth & Anderson, 1995), the Millon Clinical Multiaxial Inventory-III (MCMI-III; Millon, 1994), and the Sixteen Personality Factor (16PF) Questionnaire (Conn & Rieke, 1994).

Projective assessment techniques and clinicians' interpretations of the data collected from them are grounded in clinicians' or test developers' choice of personality theory (Freudian theory, Jungian theory, Adlerian theory, or others). Projective tests are more ambiguous from the viewpoint of the test-taker. In other words, objective tests usually consist of direct questions requiring direct responses, usually in the form of choices provided; projective measures rely on stimuli that could elicit unlimited response possibilities from clients, without providing them with response choices. Examples of commonly used projective tests include the Rorschach Inkblots (Exner, 1993a, 1993b), the Thematic Apperception Test (Murray, 1943), sentence completion tests (Lah, 2001), and human figure drawings tests for children (Bardos & Powell, 2001).

Both objective and projective tests are prone to error in administration if test manuals are not explicit, or if administrators do not follow the directions carefully. The interpretation of results from most projective tests is also subject to variations resulting from clinicians' biases since they make more assumptions in their interpretations than in those of objective tests about patients' dynamics and behaviors across situations, persons, and time, and the etiology of such patterns.

Behavioral Assessment

Behavioral assessment aims to identify the frequency, context, and most importantly, the function of a person's behavior. The focus of behavioral assessment is on *individual, specific* behaviors and comparison of the person's behavior across situations and in different environments (home, school, work, social situations). Behavioral assessment developed from the principles of behavioral therapy, and therefore, emphasizes the importance of behavioral chains, or the relationships between stimuli and responses, and behaviors and consequences. In the truest sense, behavioral assessments focus only on operationally defined, overt, observable behavior that can be objectively measured. *Behavior* has been more broadly defined over time with the merging of the cognitive and behavioral theoretical orientations and principles. Behaviors sometimes may refer to cognitive processes such as *coping,* which has overt and covert components. Behaviorists may accept this leniency in the definition with the caveat that covert processes may be considered internal behaviors (O'Brien, Linehan, Dowd, Kohlenberg, & Nezu, 1999). For the purpose of this discussion, however, behavioral assessment will be reviewed in its truest form.

In general, psychologists might adopt a behavioral assessment paradigm as a means for evaluating clients and conceptualizing their problems (Haynes & O'Brien, 2000; A. M. Nezu et al., 1997). As a paradigm, clinicians who base all assessments on this model do so because it is usually largely consistent with their theoretical orientation to understanding human behavior, and their approach to assessment and treatment of patients. Chapter 7 in this book is based in cognitive and behavioral assessment principles.

Behavioral Assessment Questions

What types of question do you think are best suited to a behavioral assessment? Consider the following clinical applications. How frequently does Susan binge-eat? Under what conditions is Stacy likely to scream and curse at her partner—what are the antecedents or provoking stimuli to this behavior? What maintaining variables reinforce Michael's thumb sucking? What potentially useful intervention strategies could Raphael's teacher implement to increase his attention in the classroom and decrease his noncompliant behavior? Why does Lola become withdrawn and anxious in some social situations, and yet she is sociable and conversant in other situations?

Because behavioral assessment may be somewhat of a specialty or a sub-type of clinical assessment in general, it is unlikely that referral sources outside the mental health field will specifically request a "behavioral assessment." Instead, individuals will phrase their referral question in such a way that clinicians will select behavioral assessment techniques as the means to best evaluate the behaviors in question. In the most optimal situation, behavioral assessment will be conducted in the client's natural setting in which the behaviors are most likely to naturally occur. However, time, cost, and appropriateness might limit this option. If so, alternative methods are used to evaluate the behavior under simulated or somewhat artificial conditions. Or data might be collected by laypersons involved with the individual, following instruction and training by the clinician in charge of the evaluation. Lastly, clients may be instructed to self-monitor their behaviors, although this method is less reliable in most cases.

Ideographic Focus of Behavioral Assessment

Ideographic information is essentially the opposite of nomothetic information; an ideographic approach to diagnosis and assessment focuses on individual behaviors (overt or covert) and patterns of these behaviors, rather than on group norms. If an individual reports extended feelings of sadness, depressed mood, hopelessness, helplessness, and other depressive symptoms, knowing only that this person's symptoms are similar to others with the same classification, in a general sense, will not provide the detailed information necessary to fully understand this individual or effect change. The ideographic assessor must determine the severity and frequency of the specific symptoms, consistent with a nomothetic approach to assessment. In addition, much more information will be sought. What developmental factors, recent stressors, or relevant stimuli contribute to the onset of these symptoms; what thoughts, feelings, behaviors, or situations maintain the individual's depressed mood state (A. M. Nezu & Nezu, 1989; A. M. Nezu et al., 1997)? Ideally, professionals in clinical psychology will assess individuals in a manner that includes nomothetic information for understanding of normative and nonnormative behavior and symptoms, and gather ideographic information to maximize individual understanding and the potential for designing effective interventions.

Selection of Behavioral Assessment Techniques

Because behavioral assessment is largely, if not entirely, consistent with the scientific method, the principles discussed in the section on the scientific approach to assessment describe the approach psychologists take to behavioral assessment. Clinicians adhering to the principles of behavioral assessment emphasize rater/instrument-reliability (versus subject/target behavior reliability) and validity as criteria for choosing evaluation tools and methods. Observation techniques, simulated or analog experiences (e.g., role-plays), self-monitoring, and ratings by others are all techniques that are frequently used in behavioral assessment; these techniques are discussed in detail in this subsection.

You may be wondering how this differs from observations made during interviews or for mental status examinations, and if you are, this is a good question. The most obvious differences in observations and evaluations made by behavioral assessors lie in the reliance on operational definitions not only of the behavior being observed, but also of the increments of time (or frequency) in which the behavior(s) is (are) being measured, and the settings in which the behavior occurs (generalization of behaviors). If a clinician was observing and assessing the social skills of a client, in a true behavioral assessment, it would most likely not be sufficient to simply state that eye contact was or was not made if that was a target behavior. Rather, "eye contact" would be operationally defined (Does a glance count? How long does the contact have to be maintained?), *and* the period of time in which it was or was not made would be delineated. A behavioral psychologist might consider how often a person makes eye contact during a 5-minute conversation, either by counting the times the client looks at the other person, and then looks away (frequency count in a 5-minute interval), or by assessing occurrence versus nonoccurrence in specified increments of time (e.g., 1-minute intervals), in which the specific number of times eye contact is made within each minute interval is less important. Also, the behavioral assessor will be interested in knowing if this behavior changes across settings, people, or situations. This level of specificity provides more precise data from which specific recommendations for change or maintenance can be made, and thus, differentiates casual observation from behavioral observation as part of a behavioral assessment. Furthermore, the stimuli and consequences would also likely be documented, with the goal of understanding the function of the behavior within the context of the environment and others. To collect such specific data, assessors are considered to be a clinical tool and, therefore, require sufficient training to ensure that ratings are reliable, accurate, and valid.

The Biopsychosocial Systems Model of Understanding Human Behavior

The biopsychosocial systems model, in concept, if not by name, has been widely adopted by cognitive and behavioral psychologists (Belar & Deardorff, 1995; Koerner & Linehan, 1997; McDaniel, 1995; A. M. Nezu & Nezu, 1989; A. M. Nezu et al., 1997; Persons & Tompkins, 1997) and others (e.g., Caspar, 1997) as the schema for understanding individuals' presentation of problems, symptoms, and attributes. This model is presented as a logical way for clinicians to organize their approach to data collection and treatment formulation (described in Chapter 8). The biopsychosocial systems model (Schwartz, 1982) assumes that individuals are complex organisms, and the interplay of their biology, cognitions, affect, behaviors, social and physical environments, largely determine their daily functioning and general well-being. Spirituality and culture, broadly defined, are other important domains, which may permeate each of the target areas described. According to the biopsychosocial model and behavioral theory, problems may result from multiple causal factors (Haynes, 1992; Kazdin & Kagan, 1994) across these target domains, and therefore, assessments must be broad-based. Clinicians should explore individual functioning within each target area, including strengths and weaknesses, so that on completion of the assessment, a comprehensive picture of the person can be drawn to contextually understand the information originally sought.

Most variables within each of the biopsychosocial target areas are assumed to be dynamic and are expected to vary across persons and within persons across time, situations, and settings (Haynes, 1998). Clinicians should assume that people change over time, as do their problems, and similar problems in different individuals often are the result of different causal variables. A multimethod, multimodal, multiinformant, time-series assessment is described in Chapter 7 to address these issues.

The foundation for the biopsychosocial systems model as it is applied here stems from several theoretical and scientific traditions. George Engel (1977) originated the biopsychosocial model in the field of medicine. Advances in science and medicine have contributed to knowledge about organisms and biological bases of behavior, and he expanded the medical model to consider other factors pertaining to human behavior. Psychologists working in medical settings readily adopted this model (McDaniel, 1995); health psychologists—and later clinical psychologists—recognized the value of assuming a holistic approach to mental and physical health care.

Theoretically, the model makes sense to cognitive-behavioral clinical psychologists, perhaps due to the tenets of social learning theory (Bandura, 1977). Social learning theory explains that investigating reciprocal person-environment (social, physical) relationships is critical to understanding human thinking and behavior (Bandura, 1977) as opposed to studying persons in isolation. Evaluating the interactions of biological, social, and psychological variables provides critical information necessary for selection and change of target behaviors or problems. Psychologists have advocated for a multimodal approach to assessment of individuals' problems for many years (Haynes, 1998; Haynes & O'Brien, 2000; Kanfer & Schefft, 1988; A. A. Lazarus, 1989; Salovey & Turk, 1991). However, the popularity of the biopsychosocial systems model has increased over the past 20 to 30 years as research has provided more substantial evidence that the mind and body are interactive and intertwined entities, rather than separate systems (see Hergenhahn, 1992, for a review of historical perspectives), and the roles of spirituality and religion in psychology have become increasingly investigated.

Target Domains in the Biopsychosocial Systems Model

Assessment of each target area requires more than a simple checklist of items for each individual. In fact, the pertinent information will vary for each individual. Topographically, however, the examples that follow provide operational definitions for each target domain. Data within each topic comprises historical (developmental or recent past history) and current information about the individual client, and historical and current information about relevant family members or significant others, and society, if relevant. Given the enormous amount of information potentially captured by each target area, developing clinicians are reminded to consider each target area across personal, social, and occupational/vocational situations, various physical settings, and public and private domains. Information should be obtained about adaptive, maladaptive, and neutral characteristics or behaviors of each individual.

Biology

Although some health professionals might suggest that mental health problems are the result of chemical imbalances or biological predispositions, *biology* in this model refers to concrete, objective, measurable physical, biological, or physiological characteristics or data. Data collected in this target area about the patient/client include age, sex, physical health, nutrition, heart rate, medical data (results of blood tests, diabetes, hypertension, fevers), and somatic complaints (upset stomach, muscle tension, fatigue). Historical information might include an adult's report of orthopedic problems in childhood, significant illnesses or surgeries, or familial history of diabetes or cancer. Clinicians should always inquire about menstruation (onset, regularity/problems, and menopause) of adolescent girls and women, since fluctuations in hormones and changes in mood are often related. Reports of medications routinely taken provide important biological information, since chemical agents can alter other aspects of persons' biochemistry, mood, behaviors, and so on. Illicit drugs and alcohol are often classified as biological variables for similar reasons. Use of illicit drugs and alcohol as a means of coping may also be categorized as behaviors, depending on the context of the report.

Biological factors and biological assessment of neurotransmitters and brain physiology, brain tissue, genetics, brain metabolism, cerebral blood flow, and brain imaging are topic areas that are important to the understanding of human behavior. Scientists in this field have learned much about mental disorders (e.g., dementia, schizophrenia) from studying brain anatomy and neurobiology, but their work largely remains in the research domain. Since molecular biological studies do not, yet, directly impact or translate into clinical assessments (Sweeney, Dick, & Srinivasagam, 1998), the procedures and processes used are not described here. Interested readers are referred to psychiatric journals, such as *Archives of General Psychiatry* and *Journal of Cerebral Blood Flow and Metabolism,* to sample studies produced from this research area.

Affect

Affect refers to a "broad class of mental processes, including feeling, emotions, moods, and temperament" (Chaplin, 1985, p. 14). Some psychologists define *mood* as a global or general feeling state, and *affect* as a temporal feeling state, analogous to the weather-related terms *climate* and *temperature*. Others view mood as a subjective report of one's feeling state (temporal), and affect as the objective, observable mood state (also temporal) or display of emotions. Sometimes an individual's affect seems unremarkable; the person seems neither happy nor sad. Think about many people you know and the characteristics of their moods, or think about your own affective responses to romantic movies, comedy shows, or responses to being with someone close to you.

Clinicians need to assess mood and affect for several reasons. Mood and affect may provide clinicians with necessary information about clients' primary diagnoses (e.g., major depressive disorder, schizoaffective disorder), periodic changes in emotional states secondary to other related problems (e.g., medical disorders, such as Parkinson's disease or Lou Gehrig's disease), co-occurring problems (mood and medical disorders) or social appropriateness and responsiveness to others. Gaining historical information from clients or significant others about affect becomes particularly important in understanding the severity or significance of current affective information. Cognitive psychologists and cognitive-behavioral psychologists pay particular attention to clients' display of emotions and self-report of feelings, as they are viewed as cues to identify changes (or needed changes) in individuals' thoughts and actions.

Can you think of a time when you found someone close to you crying or nervous? This affective presentation cued you that something was on your friend's mind; perhaps, you asked, "What's wrong?" Your friend was likely to share some troubling experience or nervous thoughts about an anticipated event. Thus, emotions and affect provide us with useful information regularly; evaluating mood, emotions, feelings, and affect provides rich data for clinicians as well.

Behavior

In psychology today, *behavior* is often broadly defined as encompassing all human activity, whether overt or covert, objective or subjective. Behavior, in its broadest sense, includes all human experiences and is the focus of clinical psychology. This broad definition, however, is not particularly helpful in structuring data collection for assessment.

Behaviorists (John B. Watson, E. C. Tolman, C. L. Hull, B. F. Skinner) defined behavior as including only objective, observable, overt activity by organisms. In this original sense of the term, sequences of activity or movement, and patterns of movement characterized behavior. This definition is much more limiting. Contemporary clinical psychologists who identify themselves as cognitive-behaviorists, or even as behaviorists, have expanded the term behavior to somewhat of a midpoint between the original definition and the broadest one. Behavior to these groups of psychologists usually refers to overt and covert behaviors. Many behaviorists and cognitive-behaviorists will classify physiological events, and thoughts, judgment, or problem solving as covert or internal behaviors (Cone, 1995; Hayes & Follette, 1993; Linehan as cited in O'Brien et al., 1999).

For the purpose of clinical assessment, a relatively narrow definition of behavior is most useful, since cognitions will be assessed as a separate category. (For some variables, the categories may seem arbitrarily separated, but the distinction is often less important than the acquisition of all the necessary information.) Behaviors, therefore, are individuals' objective, observable actions that may or may not be purposeful or intentional. An example of behavior is the posture you are holding while reading this book; both the posture and the book reading are behaviors. Other examples are nail biting, eating, gazing off into the distance, smoking, or punching someone. Some behaviors will be observed by clinicians during the course of an assessment; others will be reported by clients or significant others. Generally speaking, a clinician assumes a client is properly describing her behavior when she reports that she swims for exercise; the clinician does not need to view this behavior. (The reliability of the data regarding frequency may be questionable, but it is likely that the client and clinician have a mutual understanding of what "swimming" behavior is and is not.) Historical reports of behaviors and reports by others are valued, as described earlier, so that clients' current behaviors can be understood in the context of their overall lives (e.g., increase or decrease of frequency, intensity, desire).

Clinicians might inquire about behaviors relating to reported emotions: What does the client do when he feels angry? Does he throw things? Hit people? Drink alcohol? Go for a run in the park to release his emotions? Call a friend? Engage in a different, less anger-provoking activity? Thus, coping behaviors are important targets of assessment. Other targeted behaviors include health behaviors (e.g., eating habits, exercise, sleeping), unhealthy behaviors (e.g., smoking), communication behaviors (e.g., verbal and nonverbal activities), interpersonal behaviors (e.g., sexual activity, social activities), recreational behaviors (e.g., movie watching), occupational behaviors (e.g., organizational habits), study behaviors (e.g., daily reviewing of materials).

Cognition

When you have recognized that a friend has made a bad decision, do you ask, "What were you thinking?" Or maybe you don't vocalize this question, but perhaps it runs through your mind! To understand behaviors, problems, and adaptive functioning, many clinical psychologists rely on the answer to this question to understand patients' behaviors and problems. Although some psychologists do not ask direct questions about specific thoughts, cognition is the core unit of information interpreted by psychologists holding many different theoretical orientations (see Eels, 1997 for a review).

Cognition, broadly defined, addresses all aspects of information processing: attention, perception, memory, knowledge representations (schemas, imagery), learning (intelligence; achievement; aptitude), cognitive development, creativity, language, problem solving, decision making, reasoning, and judgment (Sternberg, 1999). Most assessments include a *mental status exam,* which is a cursory evaluation (described in more detail later) that allows clinicians to examine clients' information-processing abilities to determine if each aspect of cognitive functioning seems to be intact (within "normal" range). Depending on which facets of cognition are not intact, clinicians may have to rely on other sources of information for treatment planning and evaluation, or conduct a more in-depth assessment that focuses on the troubled area.

In global clinical assessments, clinicians might attempt to answer some of the following questions: Is the client attentive to questions, responses, and nonverbal or verbal social cues in session? Does the client exercise good judgment when faced with social or high-risk situations? How effective are the client's problem-solving skills when faced with novel or stressful situations? Does the client engage in rational and systematic approaches to decision making, or does she make careless or impulsive decisions? What images does the person associate with his traumatic experience, and when do these images enter his consciousness (e.g., flashbacks during the day, nightmares)? How accurate or insightful do the person's observations and appraisals of self and others seem to be?

Psychologists sometimes use the narrowly defined terms *cognition* and *thought* interchangeably. Most clinical psychologists assess clients' thoughts, but the interpretations made about these thoughts vary across theoretical perspectives. Cognitive psychologists and cognitive-behavioral psychologists thoroughly examine persons' automatic thoughts and core beliefs (schemas) about themselves, others, and the world (A. T. Beck et al., 2004; Persons & Tompkins, 1997). Negative automatic thoughts and dysfunctional core beliefs are thought to be central, and causally related to interpersonal and intrapersonal problems, according to cognitive theory (J. Beck, 1995). Assessment of thoughts that occurred before, during, and after problematic situations are elicited.

Some assessment questions dictate a thorough, concentrated evaluation of specific areas of cognitive functioning. A client may be referred for an assessment of impaired memory. The clinician will need to identify if the client's memory problems are due to extreme emotional distress (depression), environmental distractions, or if processing information (making new memories, retrieving memories) is the problem; treatment recommendations will be predicated on the findings. Perception, defined by cognitive neuroscience, refers to an individual's reception of incoming sensory information. A clinician, therefore, may seek to answer questions about a child's school performance, and the role an auditory processing problem might play in this difficulty. In these situations, the other target domains become contextual rather than explanatory.

Spiritual beliefs, religious beliefs, and philosophies of life are often categorized as cognitions. Spirituality and religiosity have been defined in various ways throughout the theological, psychological, and medical literatures. *Spirituality* is concerned with "the transcendent, addressing ultimate questions about life's meaning, with the assumption that there is more to life than what we see or fully understand. Spirituality can call us beyond self to concern and compassion for others"(John E. Fetzer Institute, 1999, p. 2). Fitchett, Burton, and Sivan (1997) offers a similar definition, but suggests that spirituality can refer to activities, in addition to beliefs. Spirituality is sometimes encompassed within *religiosity* (John E. Fetzer Institute) and vice versa (Reed, 1987).

Religiosity has been defined as having "specific behavioral, social, doctrinal, and denominational characteristics because it involves a system of worship and doctrine that is shared within a group," (John E. Fetzer Institute, 1999, p. 2). Fitchett et al. (1997) further suggests that religiosity refers to the adherence to such behaviors and beliefs. Religion fosters spirituality, but people may also engage in religious behaviors without considering themselves spiritual, according to the description provided. Some professionals use these terms interchangeably (Reed, 1987; Fitchett et al., 1997), and others maintain the distinctions in research and clinical work. The Fetzer Institute working group has identified several domains of religiousness/spirituality that have stronger theoretical and empirical connection to health and mental health outcomes: daily spiritual experiences, meaning, values, beliefs, forgiveness, private religious practices, religious/spiritual coping, religious support, religious/spiritual history, commitment, organizational religiousness, and religious preference. Each of these domains continues to be investigated, refined, and objectified into assessment measures to aid research and future clinical work (John E. Fetzer Institute, 1999). *Mindfulness* has also become increasingly important in psychologists' and mental health professionals' work (J. R. Martin, 1997; Roth, 1997).

Although spirituality and religiosity had historically been less of a focus for social, cognitive, and behavioral psychologists (John E. Fetzer Institute, 1999), the past 15 years have seen a change in this orientation among psychologists as a whole (Hafen, Karren, Frandsen, & Smith, 1996; Csikszentmihalyi, 1999; D. W. Sue, Bingham, Porche-Burke, & Vasquez, 1999). The difficulty that these constructs present is that they are not quantifiable or objectively measurable, other than by the behaviors that may result from these beliefs (which obviously then shifts spirituality or religion to behavior instead of cognition). How can we quantify who is more spiritual or religious? Is someone who thinks about greater beings and higher powers more often than another person necessarily more spiritual or religious? Even if an equation could be derived to compare people on this construct, would there be any utility in doing so? Religiosity is more easily quantifiable, according to some (organizational religiosity, public religiosity, private religiosity; George, 1999; Idler, 1987, 1999; Levin, 1999), because it represents the practice of religion (behaviors). However, measurement of spirituality and religiosity is still in its infancy.

Despite the difficulty in measuring and assessing spirituality, mindfulness, and religiosity for groups of individuals and for comparison of individuals, individual qualitative assessment should be an integral part of every evaluation, since it is an integral part, or not, of everyone's life. Once an individual endorses the importance of spirituality or religion in his or her life, assessment of the impact or incorporation of religion or spirituality across target domains is most useful.

Biology may be positively affected (low blood pressure) by spiritual practices of meditation or yoga (Patel, 1993). Affect may be regulated or controlled differently for some than others, as a function of spiritual beliefs. An example may be the expression of emotions in response to the death of a loved one: Individuals who believe in an afterlife may have an easier time accepting a loss, than those who do not, and therefore, a difference in affect may be noted. Religion and spirituality may affect individual beliefs about psychological or physical illness, and health and care-seeking behaviors. Jehovah's Witnesses will not accept a blood transfusion because of their belief that four passages in the Bible instruct Witnesses not to consume blood; these passages are interpreted differently by other religious groups. In Chapter 3, we followed the case example of Doris whose religious fatalism had a notable impact on her health-related behavior. Spirituality and religion may be the focus of individual's social activities and support networks, as observed in the case of Doris. Recall how such beliefs or a person's philosophy of life influences cultural identity. Physical environment may also be determined partially as a result of a person's spiritual beliefs or religious adherence. For example, does your client live in a communal setting, such as a kibbutz or Eruv, or a monastery? Has your client taken a vow of poverty, or does he or she rely on community for living arrangements?

Spirituality and religion are important topic areas to address with all clients, regardless of the assessment goal or referral question. It is hard to imagine how these variables would *not* impact clinicians' and clients' concern, if the topics were important to them. Should spirituality and religious beliefs remain categorized as a construct within cognition (Belar & Deardorff, 1995)? Should we address spiritual practices and religious behaviors as separate constructs from cognitions? Or, does it make the most sense to consider these issues within the context of a person's social domain? We think the answers to these questions are "yes!" Classification is less important here, than broad-based assessment. As psychologists establish the empirical relevance of spirituality to clients' psychological and physical well-being, perhaps the biopsychosocial systems model will be renamed the "biopsychosocialspiritual systems model."

Social Environment

Individuals operate within the context of their environments, and among other people. Bandura's social learning theory (1977) asserts that individuals influence their environments, and environments influence people in a reciprocal fashion. Peer pressure and adolescent smoking demonstrate this relationship. If social circles dictate, "smoking is cool," adolescents may be more inclined to engage in this habit to "fit in." However, if the captain of the football team is revered by peers and decides that drinking and driving is irresponsible, he may positively influence the social climate of his classmates. Thus, understanding the social environment within which clients function on a daily basis is critical to understanding what individual variables may necessitate change (e.g., assertiveness skills), and what aspects of the social environment or which environments are related to clients' problems (e.g., the recovering alcoholic whose friends spend most of their free time in bars). Social environments can include more distal variables such as society's values and customs (laws, policies, standards) and cultural factors, or personal contexts, such as nuclear and extended family, friends and acquaintances, religious or community groups, employment coworkers, superiors and subordinates.

Strengths and weaknesses are equally important to evaluate in clients' social environments: How has the client's family responded to her interracial marriage plans? Will the client's employer permit him to work at home after his surgery, or will he have to take extended leave of absence without pay until he reaches full recovery? Also, past social factors may provide useful information about why a client is experiencing difficulty, despite functioning satisfactorily in the past: Perhaps the child's parents recently divorced, or his best friend moved away. An individual with mental retardation in a group home setting may be fearful of a new caregiver. However, a senior adult might experience improvements in mood as a result of moving to an assisted living environment where she now has competent help and a new network of social activities.

Cultural factors may be categorized with social environment (Belar & Deardorff, 1995), although a case could also be made to view cultural factors as a target domain unto itself. Culture is defined as "(a) the totality of the customs, arts, science, and religious and political behavior taken as an integrated whole that distinguishes one society from another; (b) A society or group of persons whose customs, arts, and so on, set them apart from another group; (c) The intellectual and artistic aspects of life as opposed to the purely material or technical" aspects of life (Chaplin, 1985, p. 113).

Much like spirituality and religion, culture permeates individuals' cognitions, behaviors, and social interactions, view of "appropriate" affect, living arrangements and sense of personal identity. Culture is different from the constructs of religion and spirituality, however, in that *everyone* has multiple cultural affiliations. Culture can refer to the norms and values that individuals identify with, based on their heritage (e.g., Latino culture), religion (Jewish culture), sexual orientation (gay, lesbian, or transsexual culture), mainstream society, or other factors that establish the identity of a people. Culture can be evaluated within a country (Western civilization), a geographic region ("down South"), family, or other cohort. Occupational environments, schools, and even programs within schools, have their own culture. Culture can be assessed at the individual level, molar level of society, molecular level of the person, or varying overlapping levels of each (Brofenbremmer, 1994).

Too often, beginning clinical psychology graduate students, when asked, will respond that their client has "no cultural variables to consider." How does this translate? The student perceives that "the client's culture is the same as mine," or "the client's culture is that of the majority in the local society; the client is a 35-year-old, middle-class, Caucasian male." Beginning clinicians are cautioned not to assume likeness or differences. Assessing an individual's culture at various levels is critical to completion of a comprehensive, broad-based assessment. It is also an ethical obligation (APA, 2003, 9.02b, 9.02c, 9.06). What information can be gleaned from even the basic description provided? If not answers, certainly many questions arise: What are the expectations of 35-year-old men in the client's family, religious group, or social class? Are young men expected to work 5 days a week, marry, and raise a family? Earn a certain living? How have the expectations set by cultural norms affected his view of himself, others, and the world? How have cultural norms affected his behaviors? Which of these cultural affiliations and its norms are most *salient* to the problem of interest? All these questions, and many others, are important to understanding systemic influences on your client's cognitions, behaviors, affect, and physical and social environments. Thus, clinicians are charged with the mission of understanding the cultural norms of the society in which the client lives, and the social, occupational, and familial environments within which he or she functions.

Cultural norms are defined as "a standard or set of standards in a given culture derived from the behavior of the generality of the individual members of that culture; an ordinarily expectable behavioral manifestation or pattern, against which an individual's behavior is judged" (Chaplin, 1985, p. 113). Given this definition, clinicians could have several judgments to make: How has the cultural values of this client affected (positively, negatively, or neutrally) his or her cognitions, behaviors, affect, and social or physical environments? Is the client's behavior normal within his or her own cultural norms, and how does the client's behavior compare with the cultural norms dictated by mainstream society? Is the client caught between two cultures, and experiencing difficulty with the hybrid values? Perhaps the client's functioning is not maladaptive or pathological from the viewpoint of his or her own culture, but in the mainstream culture, the person's behavior is unacceptable.

The *DSM-IV-TR* (American Psychiatric Association, 2000) has devised a special task force to look specifically at the impact of cultural variables on psychopathology. Readers are encouraged to review the *DSM-IV-TR* for further discussion of the current issues.

Physical Environment

Clinicians most often conduct assessments in inpatient or outpatient settings, and less often in clients' home or work environments. In such instances, we seldom know much about clients' living arrangements, living conditions, or neighborhood, unless we ask. Likewise, gathering information about a client's work environment, treating hospital or physician's office environment, or school setting may provide critical data necessary to understand a client's problems or to devise treatment plans to resolve them. Without this information, even the seemingly best advice may be contraindicated.

In treating a 38-year-old woman for an obsessive-compulsive disorder (OCD) that led her to check and recheck her locks on her windows, skylights, and doors, and her electric outlets constantly, the empirically supported treatment for OCD (Foa & Kozak, 1997; Kozak & Foa, 1997) requires the OCD client to be exposed to the stressor or stimuli (unlocked windows), while inhibiting the typical response (checking and locking them). The mechanism of action is that the client's anxiety peaks and then reduces as she increases her tolerance to the situation and recognizes that the anticipated negative outcome will not result. However, this woman was a recovered drug addict who had worked very hard to earn her rent for her row house in a section of the city that was known to have a high crime rate and rough inhabitants. Leaving her windows unlocked could pose an actual danger to her child and herself.

Understanding the physical environment surrounding this client's residence aided in understanding a potential contributing factor to her development and maintenance of extreme fear of losing her tangible possessions. Also, gaining a historical perspective of this client's physical environment shed light on important aspects of her presenting problem. She had a 6-year history of heroin drug use and had never kept any possessions because she had sold everything she owned for drugs, including her body (prostitution). Now that she was clean and sober, had joined a welfare-to-work program, and was pursuing her undergraduate degree, she had too much invested to have her possessions taken from her. In addition to brainstorming ways in which she might change her living arrangements, exposure and response prevention exercises were first directed at "safer" targets, such as leaving her empty car unlocked with the windows cracked, plugging a lamp into an outlet in the wall and leaving it plugged in while she left the room, and learning other techniques to reduce the frequency of her checking behaviors.

A newly married Vietnamese couple came into therapy because their sex life seemed to come to a halt after returning from their honeymoon.

Apparently, the couple had no sexual difficulties prior to marriage, and therefore, the husband was particularly disturbed by the sudden change. He made many attributions about himself and their marriage, before a thorough assessment uncovered one of the predominant problematic factors; once married, the couple moved into the wife's family's house. Prior to marriage, sex occurred most often at the husband's apartment. A thorough assessment revealed that the couple's bedroom was next door to the bedroom of the wife's parents. This was particularly problematic for the wife, because she was afraid her parents would hear their sexual activity at night. Identifying the physical environment in which the problem occurred helped to identify the wife's cognitions that were negatively impacting the couple's sexual behavior. The wife had difficulty accepting that her parents now "knew" she was having sex with her husband, and she irrationally feared that their views of her would negatively change. Additional examples in which the physical environment may contribute to, contextualize, maintain, or provide change for identified problems are many.

Summary

Understanding people, their problems, and their way of functioning requires clinicians to conduct a multifaceted assessment. The biopsychosocial systems model, based in social learning theory, acceptance of the mind-body connection, and evaluation of people and systems at various levels, provides a framework for this investigation. Clinicians are encouraged to assess individual variables (biology, affect, cognition, behavior, culture, spirituality/religion/philosophy of life), social variables (family and significant others, acquaintances, work-affiliated persons, community groups, culture, spirituality/religion adopted by significant others, etc.), and physical environment variables (living, work, and social environments). Historical, current, and potential future conditions should be explored to maximize the utility of the information gained.

A Scientific Approach to Assessment and Methods of Gathering Data

7

Chapter

Chapter 6 prepared you to think about the types of assessment clinical psychologists conduct and the biopsychosocial systems approach to assessment. A goal-oriented approach to decision making begins the process of assessment preparation. This chapter focuses on structuring the assessor's critical thinking to be the best consumer of available information. Using the scientific method to approach assessment gears the clinician toward hypothesis testing, taking an operational approach to targeted domains, and using a multimodal, multimethod, time-series assessment, as appropriate. The use and integration of the psychological assessment tools (clinical interviews, psychological testing, observation, report of significant others, report of other professionals, and self-report measures) are discussed.

Learning Objectives

At the end of this chapter, the reader should be able to:

- Explain the scientific method.
- Describe how the scientific method applies to the clinical practice of assessment.
- Define at least three heuristics and biases and explain how they impact the assessment process.
- Discuss the importance and use of multimodal, multimethod, time-series assessments.

- Describe the importance of validity and reliability of assessment tools for clinical planning.
- Explain the pros and cons, and differences, among at least 5 assessment tools for gathering data.

In the previous chapters, you learned about the historical routes of cognitive-behavioral therapies, the emphasis on empirically supported approaches to therapy, and the value of research and its contributions to clinical psychology. For the most part, these discussions focused on groups of people, according to classification systems and categorization. Focusing on individual clients poses particular challenges because of the uniqueness and variability in people's biology, affect, cognition, behaviors, social systems, and physical environments. How, then, do cognitive-behavioral clinical psychologists gather useful information about all these different factors? How do we know if this information is accurate, reliable, and valid? How does this approach differ from data collection techniques used by other noncognitive-behavioral psychologists? This chapter provides the answers to these and similar questions.

The Scientific Method

Cognitive-behavioral psychologists adopt a scientific approach to assessment and treatment. The *scientific method* dictates that inquiry begins with a research (clinical) question that leads to a hypothesis, or educated guess, regarding the answer to the question. The hypothesis is operationally defined in clear, objective, measurable constructs or terms. Data is gathered to test the hypothesis, and then it is analyzed to evaluate if the hypothesis is supported or not supported. Cognitive-behavioral psychologists would argue that the assessment process, and psychology as a whole, for that matter, operates according to these scientific principles.

Most clinical hypotheses are works-in-progress and are revised frequently to reflect acquisition of new data or changes in the client's circumstances, behaviors, or other information. Thus, according to a cognitive-behavioral assessment paradigm, hypotheses and assessments are dynamic. Likewise, psychologists' approaches to assessments must be flexible to accommodate new research, technology, and knowledge about adaptive and maladaptive human behavior.

Biases in Assessment

Hypotheses need to be flexible and dynamic, but so do the clinicians who propose them. Clinicians must be aware of their own tendencies and biases to conduct searches that only lead to support for their initial hunches. By this, we mean that it is critical for clinicians to seek information that could potentially *disconfirm* their hypotheses. Once a clinician is informed that her client, J. R., is often "impatient," according to his wife's report (or his own), the clinician may be primed to recognize all his behaviors as confirming evidence of his impatience: fidgeting in the waiting room, shifting in his chair, frequent watch checking. Without further inquiry, the clinician may make inaccurate judgments based on these behaviors and believe that her initial *assumption* about this person holds true. Clinicians' must always ask themselves, what else could explain these behaviors, or what else might these behaviors signify? Proper assessment of alternative hypotheses is required to ensure the accuracy of the clinician's hypotheses. In the case of J. R., what else could account for his behaviors—possibly an attention disorder, anxiety, or physical discomfort from arthritis? Maybe this client is attending the therapy session on his lunch hour and is afraid he will be late in returning to work. Is it possible that he really needs to find the men's room, but lacks assertiveness skills to interrupt the therapy session? "Sometimes a cigar is just a cigar," but clinicians need to thoroughly examine their data to be sure that this is the case.

Although you might like to think that you would have considered many of the possible explanations for J. R.'s behavior, early research suggests that most people would not. Herbert Simon argued that most people use *heuristics* (mental shortcuts) in decision making, and do not tend to consider all available explanations or solutions to a problem. Most people will stop searching when they find a solution that is "good enough," or generally satisfying; most people will not seek out the best solution available.

Amos Tversky and Daniel Kahnemann (1974), followed Simon's work, and furthered research in this area. Surprisingly, they found that people generally had greater tendencies to use shortcuts in decision making, than tendencies toward rational and systematic decision making based on complete information and comprehensive strategies. Don't we all always look for the easiest route to get somewhere, or the most efficient means to get something done? Of course we do. These heuristics often lead to errors in judgment. Based on knowledge gained from experimental cognitive psychology research, A. M. Nezu and Nezu (1989) point out that most clinicians are also likely to make these judgmental errors in their clinical work.

We would like to think that you strive to be better than most people, and therefore, learning about common heuristics and biases that influence clinical decision making will alert you to choose assessment strategies that minimize biases and maximize collection, use, and interpretation of truthful, verifiable clinical information. Furthermore, adopting a problem-solving approach to clinical decision making (A. M. Nezu & Nezu, 1989; A. M. Nezu et al., 1997), described later, will provide you with a framework to maintain cognizance of this process. The problem-solving model for clinical decision making discusses the assessment and treatment paradigm (theoretical orientation), biases, and heuristics as part of the clinician's *worldview* (A. M. Nezu et al., 1997), or the way clinicians understand and conceptualize patients' problems and human behavior, in general.

Common Heuristics

You take many mental shortcuts every day. How many times have you attempted to finish people's sentences for them? Perhaps, you skimmed this morning's newspaper, and thought you got the gist of the article, only to find out you overlooked the punch line. These shortcuts do not have grave consequences in your day-to-day activities, but the following heuristics might have a greater impact on your clients, and your clinical decision making about them.

The *representative* heuristic, *anchoring* heuristic, and *availability* heuristic are three shortcuts identified by Tversky and Kahnemann (1974) that people use to assess probabilities and predict outcomes to simple judgments. Often, these heuristics work when we use past experiences and patterns to make judgments about current events and situations, but there are also many opportunities for these shortcuts to be inaccurate. These judgments may be inaccurate when people only rely on their own experiences or stories they have learned, and disregard or do not consider the prevalence of situations or events as they occur in the general population. We tend to do this when it fits our needs, even though we may not realize it. A 38-year-old man who is told repeatedly to quit smoking may retort by exclaiming that his 90-year-old grandmother has smoked two packs of cigarettes a day for the past 60 years. Why should he believe his health is at risk by this behavior?

The representative heuristic suggests that people attempt to assess probabilities based on the degree of likeness between the current object or stimuli and a previously developed concept or established stimuli. Essentially, decisions are made based on how much "A" resembles "B." If asked to guess the profession of an older woman who wears conservative clothes, her hair in a bun, and square reading glasses hung on a metal chain, you are more likely to classify her as a librarian than as a volleyball coach. How often have you seen a muscular, thin, and fit person and assumed he or she must exercise a lot or be athletic? Others make the judgment that "women who are very thin must not eat." We can all think of people who fit these descriptions accurately, and many people who do not if we push ourselves to consider fitting examples, and ones to the contrary. You might be thinking, "How is this different from stereotyping?" If you are, then you are thinking along the right track. Stereotypes are built on heuristics; fitting someone into that stereotype, then might be an example of the representative bias.

The representative heuristic is related to the concept of *schemas*, which should be familiar to you based on your undergraduate course in cognition, and our discussions in this book. Applied here, people have an associated framework or mental set (schema) within which to consider incoming information. Thinking about a visit to a psychologist's office should activate the schema that represents this notion: an academic office, or perhaps, a clinical outpatient setting. In assessment, errors in thinking occur when a schema is accessed to the exclusion of other schemas. A clinician may inappropriately only think of anorexia as a diagnosis when assessing an underweight adolescent female, and therefore, does not conduct a thorough evaluation of other target areas of the patient's life. Or a clinician may assume that a 75-year-old female patient who is obstinate with interpersonal difficulties is experiencing cognitive decline or dementia, when in fact, the patient may have a history of behavior consistent with borderline personality disorder (Nutkowitz, unpublished manuscript). One way to correct this error in judgment is to remember the importance of always going outside and beyond what you "intuitively know" or what you think is occurring, and look for disconfirming evidence or alternative hypotheses.

The *anchoring heuristic* (Tversky & Kahnemann, 1974) is a shortcut method of estimation or prediction, involving situations in which final decisions are based more on initial impressions than on subsequent information.

Yes, your mother was right. You had better make a good first impression, because research shows that these impressions are lasting. Although therapists would like to think their clinical decisions are solely based on facts gained from their skilled inquisition or observations, we are all at risk for biasing our judgments with first impressions unless we guard against these tendencies.

Consider the following scenario in which a seemingly timid, polite and proper, well-dressed female client, Wilma, describes her husband in the context of her distress over their marital problems. She tells you that her husband Roger is insensitive, does not listen to her, and is disrespectful. With further prompting, Wilma describes several situations in which Roger tells Wilma her work-related problems are her fault, walks out of the room in the midst of conversations, and embarrasses her in public by apologizing for comments she makes. Given that Wilma seems quite accommodating and pleasant, how do you feel about Roger and his treatment of Wilma? The clinician who is aware of biases and judgmental errors wants to gather additional information, and consider alternative hypotheses so Roger is invited to attend the next session.

When Roger accompanies Wilma, you suddenly learn new information. This "timid, polite and proper" woman hollers and curses at Roger constantly, seemingly without provocation. He reports that she is critical and insulting to him, and does not allow any flaw to go unnoticed. What you now learn is that Roger's tendency to walk out of a room, or quiet her in public places are his coping strategies to deal with her maltreatment. *Now* what are you thinking? The anchoring heuristic might have allowed the clinician to continue to think of Roger as an insensitive, nasty husband, instead of considering his behaviors as coping strategies. Wilma's therapy would have taken a very different path if the new information was not obtained or considered in the formulation or analysis of the couple's relationship.

To minimize the potential for the anchoring heuristic to cause judgmental errors in assessment and therapy, therapists must systematically consider all data gathered over the course of time, not just in the initial intake. Thus, the scientific approach to clinical assessment requires *time-series* or ongoing assessment (Haynes, 1998). Gaining information from multiple sources also helps contain the tendency to jump to conclusions. Other stimuli that might be red flags for new clinicians include first impressions of clients with diverse backgrounds or differences from the clinician. As stated, most people make initial judgments about everyone they encounter; consider how these heuristics may bias your evaluation of persons with various ethnic, gender, age, sexual orientation, or other cultural features that are different from your own. Or even more likely, consider how the representative or anchoring heuristics might bias your evaluation of persons you assume are similar to you!

The *availability heuristic,* another judgmental error identified by Tversky and Kahnemann (1974), describes people's tendency to use readily recalled information, examples, or instances as the basis for estimating the frequency or probability of an event. The salience and recentness of events tend to affect availability estimates and the likelihood of making a judgmental error of this type.

A classic example of the availability heuristic is the "medical school syndrome." One day in class, students learn about a rare medical phenomenon that presents with a multitude of symptoms. Alone, these symptoms are common, but in combination they are potentially fatal. Later that evening, a student experiences a symptom similar to what was discussed in class earlier that day. He then becomes 100% certain that he *has* the disease under study because the first explanation that comes to mind is what was discussed in class. Learning about illnesses puts this information in the forefront of students' minds. Psychology students are also prone to this syndrome. During your psychopathology class, be sure to count how many behaviors you have displayed that are consistent with various diagnoses. Chances are, for most of the criteria, you can think about information that is inconsistent with your current line of thinking, and you will be disregarding information that does not fit the criteria you are examining.

The availability heuristic may influence clinicians' thinking in various stages of assessment and treatment. Suppose a new psychology student, Mary, has three sessions to test and diagnose a woman who claims she is having trouble concentrating due to racing thoughts. In the first meeting with her, the client spends the first 15 minutes crying about the recent loss of her pet and the student has trouble comforting her. Since Mary was not expecting this interaction to be filled with intense emotions, it will likely leave a lasting impression on her, even if the rest of the two-hour session is particularly uneventful. Mary's day became very busy, and she forgot to write her progress note. When she remembers to do so on the next day, she emphasizes how emotional this client was *throughout the session*. This inaccuracy in recall would likely be due to the availability heuristic. The saliency of Mary's own discomfort in this experience led her to make an error in her judgment and recall.

Other Biases

A. M. Nezu and Nezu (1989) discuss several other judgmental errors that can occur in clinical work if proper measures are not taken to prevent them. Such errors can result from *biased search strategies, overconfidence,* and *causal attributions.* None of these terms are likely to be unfamiliar to you but discussion of the application of these concepts to clinical decision making is critical for new and even senior clinicians.

Each assessment you conduct and every therapy session you provide will require you to evaluate many aspects of your client, the session, and your work. You need to determine the status of your client's improvement in chief complaints and responsiveness to treatment in each session. *Biased search strategies* lead clinicians to falsely confirm their hypotheses about their clients' diagnoses, case formulations, progress, receptiveness to treatment, or other hypotheses as a result of *only* gathering or searching for information or *only* using search strategies, instruments, or tools, that are consistent with one's way of thinking, and excluding or disregarding search tools or information that could potentially disconfirm hypotheses. Selective attention, or only paying attention to cues or information consistent with one's way of thinking, may be considered a part of biased search strategy errors.

Consider, for a moment, the last courtroom drama you saw. The attorneys inevitably have a position to defend, and the questions asked of the witnesses they bring forward are directive and closed-ended; "Mrs. Xavier, isn't it true that you placed your brother in a psychiatric institute so that you could take all of his money?" Now, this example may be a bit extreme in clinical psychology, but not by far. Closed-ended and leading questions do not allow disconfirming evidence to surface easily. "Mr. Marcos, you look a lot better than the last time I saw you. The relaxation techniques must be working, aren't they?" By asking this question, the clinician may not come to know that Mr. Marcos just returned from a week's vacation in Puerto Rico, where he had no work or family responsibilities, and slept more hours than usual—without practicing his techniques at all. However, is he likely to admit this when he is receiving such praise? Possibly, but possibly not! Biased search strategies can be avoided by conducting broad-based assessments, covering areas that seem particularly relevant, and others that may not initially seem important from the clinician's point of view. Seeking alternative explanations for targets of interest is also critical.

Errors in clinical decision making about any aspect of assessment, case conceptualization, treatment, or discharge can also result from clinicians' *overconfidence*. Even the most seasoned clinician should adhere to the systematic and scientific techniques proposed in this chapter, because senior clinicians just like newly trained clinicians are liable to make errors in clinical work if they are not careful. Specifically, A. M. Nezu and Nezu (1989) suggest that being overconfident about one's knowledge can lead to sloppiness or errors in clinical reasoning. Clinicians who think their expertise is superior may engage in biased search strategies (looking for reinforcements or supporting evidence that they are great clinicians or researchers), or engage in other judgmental errors, such as overlooking the need for peer consultation due to inaccurately perceiving their ability to work with certain complex or difficult patients. An overconfident clinician may be subject to the representative heuristic by misattributing his competence; "I treated the last patient with anger management problems successfully so I think this patient will be similarly easy."

Everyone is susceptible to engaging in errors in reasoning, or biases in thinking for many reasons. An overarching bias that all clinicians maintain is that of their own theoretical orientation. The belief systems adopted by clinicians are based on some empirical research, theories, and assumptions (our biases are showing), that are not based entirely in verifiable truth. Belief systems, or "worldviews" (A. M. Nezu & Nezu, 1989; A. M. Nezu et al., 1997), lead clinicians to make *causal attributions* about patients' behaviors according to their theoretical perspective, which may neglect other important contributing factors. A cognitive psychologist may only examine cognitions to explain why a client is depressed. If the clinician neglects to send the client for a medical examination to rule out biological factors, and this client's problem stems from a thyroid condition, he may be wrongly treated.

As you have been reading this section on heuristics and biases, some of the examples and scenarios may seem obvious or extreme. In daily practice, when clinicians do not have the luxury of metacognition (thinking about the way they think), such errors in judgment may occur more frequently than any of us would like to believe. Perhaps this itself is a self-protecting bias. The next section expands on the methods, strategies, and scientific techniques provided to minimize use of faulty heuristics and biases, and an overall assessment paradigm that will improve the accuracy of our clinical evaluations, judgments, and decisions.

A Closer Look at a Scientific Approach to Assessment

A scientific approach to assessment, largely based in the behavioral assessment paradigm (Haynes, 1998), emphasizes, "Empirically based, multimethod, multimodal, and multiinformant measurement of lower-level, precisely specified, observable behavior and contemporaneous causal variables. The paradigm emphasizes the application of well-validated minimally inferential assessment instruments, applied in a time-series format" (p. 2). That is one quote you would do well to memorize (once you understand the terminology, of course). The remainder of this section explains what Haynes, and other colleagues who contributed to the development of this paradigm (see Haynes, 1998, for additional references), meant by this statement, and why we advocate for following this model.

Following the biopsychosocial systems model, clinicians should use multiple methods (*multimethod*) to assess clients' strengths and weaknesses, problems, and supports. Examples of methods that might be used include interviews, observations, computerized assessments, physiological measurements, self-report inventories, and other techniques. The key is that one method alone may not capture the full picture of what you are trying to assess. Someone who does not appear anxious may still have an accelerated heart rate that is detected by physiological measurement, when led to think about perceived threatening situations. Thus, relying on observation alone would not provide sufficient information about the client's reduction of anxiety during treatment.

A *multimodal* assessment requires assessment of motor behaviors; verbal behaviors, expressions, or statements; biological factors; affective responses; and cognitive processes. In Chapter 6, the biopsychosocial systems model was discussed. You should already be prepared to understand this concept.

In an ideal world, clients come to therapy fully knowing and understanding their problems and how these problems manifest themselves (behaviors, affect, etc.), and therefore, their report about their problems provides accurate and complete information. In the *real* world, many clients lack insight about their problems and have altered perceptions of their own contributions to the problems, or how others are affected. Information from the perspectives of the client's peers, parents, significant others, bosses, and teachers, contributes enormously to a truly comprehensive picture of the client's life problems, strengths and weaknesses, and interpersonal relationships. Data from multiple informants (*multiinformant assessment*) provides a context for information gained directly from clients. Of course, clients' informed consent is always required prior to contacting these additional persons.

Lower-level variables require clinicians to go beyond diagnoses or theoretical constructs that are general in many ways, to *exactly* specify the target of assessment or change. If someone is "depressed," your overall goal might be to decrease depression. However, just knowing someone is depressed does not help you to know what you are evaluating. Does the person have thoughts that she will "never meet a partner?" Is she able to go to work or enjoy activities she previously enjoyed? Does she have poor problem-solving skills? Identifying lower-level variables requires clinicians to become more specific in their assessment so that they can understand the client's problems. The goal is to find out what the manifestations of depression are for this particular person, and what the contributing and maintaining variables of these depressed features might be. Identifying the lower levels of the problem also will allow treatment planning to be more focused.

In accomplishing the identification of lower-level variables, cognitive, behavioral, and cognitive-behavioral clinicians focus on behaviors (overt or covert) rather than on traits. That is, they focus on what people *do,* versus who they *are.* To help you recognize the difference, take a moment to recall your three-sentence description of your best friend. Most people offer descriptions such as, "My friend is fun to be around. S/he is loyal. My best friend is dependable." These statements represent *characteristics* or *traits* of your friend; they are general statements. Now think about how you came to these conclusions. Chances are, you arrived at these characteristics by engaging in three steps: you observed or experienced your friend's behaviors; summarized and labeled these behaviors; and *inferred* that what he or she does because of these traits. Relying on inferences in clinical assessment and therapy can result in problems we have already discussed—heuristics and judgmental biases. Therefore, clinicians are encouraged to assess measurable constructs or variables whenever possible. When traits and characteristics are discovered through personality testing, clinicians would do well to explore these findings further to arrive at the lower-level variables related to these features. Identifying what people *do,* broadly defined, rather than who they *are,* will enable determination of specific assessment and treatment goals.

Precisely specified variables are concrete and, according to behaviorists, objective. Although objectivity is not always possible in clinical assessment (e.g., pain cannot be objectively measured), minimizing ambiguity about persons' problems and behaviors usually is possible. *Operational definitions* aid in minimizing ambiguity as information is shared among professionals and between professionals and clients. Operational definitions are discussed in detail later in this chapter.

True behavioral assessment focuses only on what a human objectively sees; thus, the paradigm calls for *observable behaviors.* Cognitive and cognitive-behavioral therapists have often expanded their assessment to cognitions as well. Our earlier discussion of the biopsychosocial systems model elaborated this point. Our bias is that assessment and treatment should not be focused on hypothesized intrapsychic factors, but on operational, precisely specified overt or covert (cognitions) behaviors. Recall our behavioral example of someone doing something; a person (you) sitting in a chair (behavior), reading this book (behavior). Now add to that observation, the cognitive behavior of learning (concentrating, recalling, abstracting) and evaluating (this textbook is really interesting!). These are all potentially observable behaviors, if you know the proper methods of observation.

Furthermore, focusing on *contemporaneous events*—current events, thoughts, behaviors, and feelings that are happening in the relative moment—yields more useful targets in assessment and therapy than historical events. Historical information may provide understanding about the etiology of patients' problems, distal contributing factors to the presenting problem, and a context for understanding patterns of behaviors. All this information is deemed important to case conceptualization; history, however, cannot be changed, but how one thinks and feels about it can be. Historical information may be pertinent or even critical, but how someone is thinking, feeling, and behaving currently as a result of a historical occurrence or about a historical event should be the foci of attention and the targets for change.

Because this model of assessment supposes that (a) behaviors, thoughts, and feelings are ever-changing, (b) contemporaneous variables should be targeted, and (c) assessment is dynamic, clinicians ascribing to this model should conduct *time-series assessments.* Basically, what you know about a client today may not be true next week, and therefore, one assessment does not provide a lifetime of answers, but rather a peek through a keyhole revealing what is going on at the moment. The adolescent girl, who "hated" her mom last week, may have been over it a few days later. You might be misguided to assume that you should pick up where you left off, without a review of the past week's session and a request for an update.

Most clinicians begin their sessions asking how the client is currently feeling (more specifically, how depressed are they? How anxious have they been in the past day/week? etc.). The behavioral assessment paradigm suggests an even more systematic approach to monitoring patients' symptoms and behaviors. Information gathered only at one point in time may lead to erroneous practices and judgments for many reasons. Consider our earlier example of the client who was distraught over her dog's death. She is not necessarily always tearful and weepy, but the clinician will only know this if assessment occurs repeatedly over time. Repeated measurement ensures that the behaviors (thoughts/cognitions, feelings, etc.) assessed in the first meeting are consistent and representative of the person, rather than a rare occurrence. Time-series assessments may be accomplished through self-report diaries between sessions, brief assessments at the beginning of each assessment session, and so on. Once therapy has begun, ongoing assessment must continue to monitor changes resulting from the intervention or other factors. Without ongoing assessment, clinicians are unlikely to know if clients are compliant, if treatment is effective, or if other major concerns arise.

Now you have a better idea of what it means to build an assessment on "empirically based, multimethod, multimodal, and multiinformant measurement of lower-level, precisely specified, observable behavior and contemporaneous causal variables" (Haynes, 1998, p. 2), with assessment occurring over time. The next section describes what is meant by, "the application of well-validated minimally inferential assessment instruments" (Haynes, 1998, p. 2). Reliability and validity are critical issues to assessment, and other aspects of clinical psychology, such as research, test construction, and program evaluation. These core concepts, therefore, warrant in-depth discussion.

Reliability, and Validity

Clinicians who maintain a scientific approach to assessment and treatment gather data by using tools and techniques that are strategically selected for their psychometric properties. Specifically, cognitive-behavioral psychologists strive to obtain information with *reliable* and *valid* tools and techniques. This is not to suggest that noncognitive-behavioral psychologists prefer to use unreliable and invalid methods; however, the degree of emphasis on developing and using techniques with known psychometric properties varies across theoretical orientations (see Eels, 1997, for comparisons). Clinicians ideally determine the reliability and validity of psychological instruments and measures prior to using them to maximize the likelihood that the data they gather are meaningful. Some instruments require periodic checks to ensure these qualities are maintained over time.

Operational Definitions

An "operational definition" is defined as "(a) the procedures or measures that are used to define a construct; (b) a definition of a construct in terms of the operations used to produce and measure it" (Johnston & Pennypacker, 1993). Use of operational definitions minimizes inferences made by clinicians or by others using information obtained from an assessment. They are important for various aspects of assessment: understanding the variables being evaluated, understanding the intended use of particular psychological instruments, defining "target behaviors," interpreting results or collected information, and communicating results to others.

If you provided a clinical assessment report to another therapist and simply stated that the client, Molly, has "difficulty relating to others, specifically people who remind her of her mother," will the other therapist know what you mean? What does "relating," mean? Is the client incapable of making friendships, holding conversations, cognitively understanding and interpreting verbal and nonverbal information? And which characteristics of her mother are important in differentiating between people who are "like her mother" and "unlike her mother?" Operational definitions of the terms *difficulty,* and *relating,* and descriptions of the characteristics about "mother," would allow you to perform more precise and accurate data collection and provide a more useful report of the information you obtain.

As a guiding rule, an operational definition needs to be specific enough to allow two skilled or trained people to observe the same behavior or construct and obtain the same results. "Difficulty," for Molly, therefore, may be defined as her "uncontrolled thoughts about others' perception of her, increased sweating and flushing in interactions involving only her and one other person in direct conversation, and induced stuttering when asked direct personal questions." More precision in definitions of "relating," and "remind her of her mother" would also be required.

Understanding what a client means when he reports feelings of "sadness" may also require an operational definition to foster clearer understanding between the clinician and the client. A clinician's definition of "sadness" may be different from that of the client. To monitor the increase or decrease of sadness in a client, an operational definition must be created. The client might operationally define sadness as exhibiting tearfulness or absence of smiles, feeling "alone," and "empty." If the clinician does not satisfactorily understand this definition, he might ask for an objective definition, "If you are feeling sad, what would an observer see?" Also, a clinician may ask a client to quantify the severity or intensity of his sadness by rating his feeling on a scale of 1 (absence of sadness) through 10 (most intense sadness). Using this subjective rating scale will allow the clinician to assess whether the client's sadness improves or worsens over time, according to his own report. These are just a few ways that cognitive-behavioral psychologists attempt to increase precision in their own understanding of clients' problems using scientific, concrete, objective methods. Operational definitions are critical to ensuring accuracy in assessing and reporting human behavior; they also are essential to establishing reliability and validity of assessment tools and data.

Reliability

Reliability is another criterion for selecting useful assessment measures and techniques. The APA Ethics Code (APA, 2002, 9.02a, 9.02b) states that psychologists use assessments in the manner supporting research deems appropriate, valid, and reliable for the population being tested. The concept of reliability is often referred to in discussions of measurement in general, and specifically in clinical assessment and research. *Reliability* of tests and instruments refers to how accurate or free from error a tool is with regard to measurement. A reliable assessment technique or measurement will almost always produce the same data according to a gold standard. Every time a 5-pound weight is put on a scale, the scale should read "5 pounds."

Precision and exactness is necessary to have reliability, but unique to reliability is the idea that data gained from a particular technique or instrument will be consistent *over time* or *across observations* or *people*. A measurement tool or instrument can be *reliable* but not valid. Your bathroom scale can reliably over- or underestimate your weight, meaning that if your scale tells you that you weigh 150 pounds, and you measure 150 pounds each time you stand on it (assuming you have not gained or lost any weight), your scale is said to be reliable. However, your scale could overvalue your weight by 20 pounds, according to your physician's scale, which was calibrated by standardized weights and measures. If this were the case, your bathroom scale would be reliable but not accurate. Note, however, that measures cannot be consistently accurate and not reliable—give that some thought!

It is important for you to know if a test is reliable. Otherwise, any changes detected over time will be difficult to interpret. Are changes in scores due to change in the behavior or trait of the person, or due to the inconsistency of the measure? Are changes due to measurement error such as instrument calibration? Or are changes due to error in the measurement technique? Clinicians and researchers need to predict the answer to these questions based on their measurement selection.

Several common types of reliability are considered in test construction and selection of assessment measures (Kazdin, 2003). *Test-retest reliability* describes tests with *temporal stability;* tests with high test-retest reliability show little interference by influence of everyday life, and reveal consistent scores over a specified elapsed time frame. We would expect that one's IQ (intelligence quotient) or GRE scores would have high test-retest reliability over a one-month time frame, assuming no formal instruction was provided in the interim. In contrast, we would not expect, nor want an anxiety measure to have temporal stability. Thus, test-retest reliability, in part, refers to the measure's ability to detect differences over time, and also depends on the construct's stability over time (i.e., humor trait versus anger state). *Alternate-form reliability* describes the consistency between two forms of a test measuring the same construct by use of a similar set of items. Standardized tests should possess this psychometric property since the different versions of the test, administered at different times across students or within one administration, usually contain different questions. (Perhaps you remember getting either pink or yellow test booklets, depending on which row you sat in during one of your undergraduate class exams.)

Internal consistency represents a similar concept to alternate-form reliability. However, this form of reliability refers to the consistency within one test. So, if an exam had 100 questions, these 100 items should statistically show positive relationships among them. *Interrater reliability* refers to the consistency between two or more persons scoring a test, interview, or other stimuli, or recording or classifying observations, where some subjectivity could conceivably interfere with the results. If you and your classmate both interviewed 10 clients today, interrater reliability would tell you how consistent you are in diagnosing clients using the *DSM-IV-TR*. Interrater reliability is often achieved by training, practice, and reevaluation of raters' performance. Interrater reliability is especially important in behavioral assessment and evaluations of research treatment protocols, and in establishing clinicians' ability to use certain semistructured interviews and clinician-rated or report-by-other measures.

Special types of correlation coefficients are used to evaluate reliability statistically, and most psychometrically sound tests will report these *reliability coefficients* to allow consumers to determine if the test is reliable for their intended use. Some tests that are used include the Kuder-Richardson test and coefficient alpha (internal consistency), kappa (interrater reliability), and Pearson product-moment correlations (test-retest reliability, interrater reliability). Further discussion of reliability coefficients is beyond the scope of this chapter; we defer to your statistics professor for this explanation.

Validity

In the test construction lingo, when psychologists refer to validity, we are addressing whether a test *adequately* rather than just *accurately* measures what it is supposed to measure (based in part by Anastasi's, 1988 definition). Two general questions need to be answered: Does the instrument adequately measure or represent the subject matter intended? Will the data gained from the measure really mean anything? More specifically, will the data be useful to learn what this measure will tell us for the purpose of *this* particular assessment of *this* particular person, in a particular situation (adapted from Paul, 1969). As described here, validity is referring to the *function* of the assessment tool or protocol, rather than just the structure. This description would also fit a discussion of the *validity* of a therapy intervention, a client's self-report, or a significant others' report. Several types of validities are specific to test construction/assessment measures, but only a few will be discussed here: construct validity, content validity, concurrent validity, divergent or discrimination validity, and predictive validity. You should become familiar with these validities, as you will want to evaluate these psychometric properties for each assessment tool you consider in your work. Your assessment and research courses will cover these topics in more depth.

Construct and Content Validity

Many psychological tools have names that represent what they measure, specifically, the underlying concept or *construct* that is being addressed. The Beck Depression Inventory-II (A. T. Beck, Steer, & Brown, 1996), is one of the most popular measures of depression. The content of the questionnaire is consistent with the diagnostic criteria of depression, and experts would agree that this measure inquires about symptoms most commonly associated with depression. The measure has established *construct validity,* or is said to represent and cover information assessing the construct of depression.

It is important for measures to have established construct validity, and for users of assessment instruments to ensure this of the measures they choose. Caution is warranted because a measure's name may *suggest* it covers a certain topic area, or addresses a particular underlying psychological phenomenon, but this may not be an accurate label. Quality of life measures vary greatly in how "quality of life" is operationally defined. Some measures are geared toward assessment of medical patients, and therefore, focus largely on strength and physical function. Other measures of quality of life include more items relating to spirituality, social and physical relations, and psychological constructs (Simmons et al., 2006). Researchers and clinicians are still trying to operationally define "quality-of-life" in a meaningful way that allows measures to be developed to represent this concept. Similar difficulties arise in defining the construct of spirituality, transcendentalism, and other nonobservable psychological constructs (self-esteem, cognitive dissonance).

Once a construct is established, test developers are challenged to ensure that measures of the construct are *content valid.* Do the items in the test or measure accurately reflect the construct or domain of interest? How well does the measure represent the theoretical or scientific construct that has been advanced? When a construct is defined by a particular measure, it is difficult to separate construct and content validity. The Burnout Inventory (Maslach & Jackson, 1981) was developed to measure burnout. This instrument includes scales of exhaustion, skepticism, and personal self-efficacy; these terms are precisely what have been offered to define and explain burnout, and essentially no other measures of burnout exist. Users are left to assume that the items in the inventory assess "exhaustion," "skepticism," and "personal self-efficacy," (suggesting content validity) and that these scales represent the greater construct of burnout. Without other measures of comparison, it is difficult to conduct further studies of validity (i.e., convergent validity, to be discussed).

Users of psychological assessment tools need to evaluate tests' psychometric properties to verify how the authors assure users that the test measures the topic area it intends to measure, and for what populations (for persons of what ethnicity, age group, or other personal characteristics), the content is valid. Construct and content validity are particularly important because without knowing the validity of the measure chosen to evaluate individual characteristics, how can researchers or clinicians know how to interpret the findings they achieve? Other forms of validity such as convergent and discriminant validity aid in this evaluation. These types of validity are also common and important for selecting and determining the utility of a particular test or measurement for a specific purpose.

Concurrent Validity, Convergent Validity, and Discriminant Validity

Choosing among the numerous assessment instruments that may be available for a given construct or topic area is typically based on a variety of factors. If the psychometric properties are sound, the clinician will then consider the cost of the instrument, the time it takes to administer or complete it, the time to score and interpret the results, credentials required to use the test, reading and writing ability required, appropriateness for intended age group, cultural background, client's language, and other related reasons. Clinicians and researchers need to know how the measures they may select compare with other measures they have available to them. Reported data on a measure's concurrent validity provides this information for users.

Concurrent validity refers to how closely the data gleaned from an assessment tool correlates to performance on a different measure at the same point in time. If childhood anger and childhood aggression are expected to be highly related in boys with oppositional defiant disorder, it would be expected that measures of each of these constructs (anger, aggression) will be highly related when given to a group of boys with these characteristics. As another example, a test of fine motor skills and a test of speed in copying symbols are likely to be correlated in senior adults.

Convergent validity is a form of concurrent validity (Kazdin, 2003), and is related to *discriminant validity,* which is described later. Convergent validity refers to the overlap or similarity of two measures' abilities to assess the same construct, trait, or behavior. If one measure is compared with another measure that has predetermined reliability and construct validity, and they are intended to evaluate the same construct, a high correlation between the measures suggests the comparative measure has convergent validity. If you created a new depression inventory that was going to be free for public use, took two minutes to complete, and could be self-administered and scored, potential users would want to know how your measure correlates with the Beck Depression Inventory-II (A. T. Beck et al., 1996) or the Hamilton Rating Scale for Depression (Hamilton, 1960) since these two measures are well-known to have good psychometric properties and much research to support their use.

When evaluating a measure's convergent validity, ideally the correlation between the measure in question and measures of comparison will be strong enough to suggest that the two measures are evaluating the same construct and gaining relatively the same information if the measure being evaluated improves on or has some advantage over the existing measure. If the goal is to identify a secondary measure of a particular construct (depression), then finding a measure that is strongly but not entirely correlated with the second measure is ideal. This suggests that the combination of the two measures provides a more comprehensive picture of clients' depression than use of only one of the measures.

Discriminant validity, in essence, is the opposite of convergent validity. Discriminant validity refers to the ability for the measure in question to reveal different information than another measure that is expected to measure a theoretically different or unrelated construct. "Stress" is a different construct than optimism. Stress has been defined as an imbalance between the actual or perceived demands on someone, and the person's perceived ability to cope or respond to such demands (R. Lazarus, 1999). Optimism is defined as "an inclination to put the most favorable construction upon actions and events or to anticipate the best possible outcome" (*Merriam-Webster Online Dictionary*). These two constructs are obviously different in theory and presentation. A measure of depression and a measure of stress may show some relationship when compared in large numbers, but the correlation between these measures is expected to show little or no correlation, since they are measuring separate and distinct constructs (Kazdin, 2003).

Predictive Validity

Whereas concurrent validity refers to how closely the data gleaned from an assessment tool correlates to performance at *the same point in time* on a different measure, *predictive validity* is established by examining the relationship between a measure under question and performance on another measure *at some point in the future*. To enter graduate school, you most likely had to take the Graduate Record Examinations (GREs), and the Miller's Analogy Test (MAT's). These tests are intended to *predict* performance in graduate education. If the results of these examinations correlate with graduate students' grade point averages (or some other measure of academic performance), then these tests would be said to have predictive validity. Predictive validity is not essential to all tests or measurements, unless the intended use of the measure is to serve a predictive function. Some instruments are designed for use as point-in-time assessments only, and therefore, their ability to predict future behavior or performance on another measure is not deemed essential.

Methods of Gathering Data

Some assessments are more systematic (scanning the refrigerator and pantry before going to the supermarket; evaluating budgets in consideration of purchasing large-ticket items), and others are less so (comparison of lines to stand in at the grocery store). Similarly, assessment techniques in clinical psychology vary greatly in their purposes and goals, and the methods by which data collection is accomplished. This section discusses methods of data collection, rather than data instruments directly. Emphasis is placed on structured, formal assessment techniques, rather than on informal methods. Brief explanations of the following tools are provided: interviews, tests, inventories and checklists, observation, logs and diaries, projective measures, physiological assessment, analog assessment, and instrument-assisted and computer-assisted data collection. Further reviews of these methods of data collection are likely to be covered in full assessment courses.

Interviews

The clinician's most basic tool is an interview. Whether the purpose of a client-therapist interaction is for assessment only, therapy, forensic evaluation, job counseling, or some other purpose, most interactions do or should begin with an interview of some sort. In actuality, most first human encounters take the form of an interview in some sense of the term. One person initiates a series of questions of the other person to gain more information about the other's background, expectations, goals, and needs. Think about your last encounter in a retail store. The salesperson probably asked you the following questions: "Can I be of help to you? Are you looking for anything in particular? Do you have a specific price range within which you aim to stay?" The goal of this line of inquiry is to gain information about you. This is the same goal of clinical interviewing.

Like effective sales techniques, clinical interviewing goes beyond these basic questions. Clinical interviewing is goal-directed, requires active purposeful questioning, effective listening and requesting of clarification, observation, and the "nonspecific factors" (Beutler & Clarkin, 1990; Castonguay, Goldfried, Wiser, Raue, & Hayes, 1996; Lambert, 1986) of good rapport (warmth, empathy, and unconditional positive regard). More details about how to structure an interview (even unstructured interviews) and incorporate these components are discussed in Chapter 8.

The most common types of interviews include initial intake interviews (first meeting overview), exit interviews (closure to a clinical relationship), mental status interviews, crisis interviews, and diagnostic interviews. The goals and purposes of these interviews are the same as the overall goals of assessment. Among these types of interview, there are three major formats: structured, semistructured, and unstructured.

Interview Formats

Structured Interviews
Structured interviews are usually published or preestablished and standardized lists of questions with specific directions or flowcharts of questions to ask following certain responses. These interview outlines (similar to scripts or questionnaires) are used for predetermined purposes (diagnosis, symptom, or behavior description) and allow for comparison of responses across individuals or therapists. Since the interviews require little clinical judgment or inference, persons without graduate training in psychology can be trained to use structured interviews under supervision. The Diagnostic Interview for Children and Adolescents (DICA-R; Reich, Jesph, & Shayk, 1991) and the Structured Clinical Interview for *DSM-IV* (SCID-I; First, Spitzer, Gibbon, & Williams, 1997) are two examples of such interviews.

Semistructured Interviews
Semistructured interviews require more clinical skill and judgment. These interviews, such as the Hamilton Rating Scale for Depression (Hamilton, 1960), provide a list of questions or content areas that need to be covered. The exact wordings of the questions or order in which they are asked are determined by the clinicians. Often, the flow of a semistructured interview seems like a more natural dialogue between the clinician and client compared with a structured interview, which provides little opportunity for tangential patient self-disclosure or input into the direction of the interview. Much like structured interviews,

many semistructured interviews are published in manuals and provide scoring instructions and normative or comparison scores. Semistructured interviews are commonly used in qualitative research and in clinical assessments.

Unstructured Interviews

Unstructured interviews are clinician driven, and are usually individualized to the purpose of the assessment. Since they are not manualized and are not accompanied by administration or scoring instructions, unstructured interviews are rarely, if ever, used in research settings. The quality of data gathered by clinicians using unstructured interviews is entirely dependent on the clinicians' interviewing skills, clinical judgment, and insight. This type of interview structure is most susceptible to individual biases and requires the greatest amount of training and skill for maximum results.

Uses of Interviews

Initial Intake Assessment

Initial intake interviews are designed to gain an overview of a patient's problems, strengths, and resources, and reasons for seeking assessment, treatment, or hospital admission. In some ways, it can be viewed as a needs assessment of the patient, and an opportunity for the clinician's observation, diagnosis, and short-term and/or long-term clinical pathway goal planning. Intake interviews often include a combination of mental status interviews and diagnostic interviews.

Mental Status Assessment

Mental status interviews focus on a client's current psychological functioning. The goal of a mental status interview is to gain an overview of client mental health, and identify normal versus abnormal or unusual thinking, thought processing, behaviors, or other characteristics. This type of interview has specific components and is mostly factual and data-based. Clinicians make little to no interpretations of data collected in this type of interview, with the exception of some estimation of judgment, insight, and intellectual functioning, which may be largely based on clinical impression.

The mental status interview goes beyond the exchange of questions and answers, and incorporates many behavioral observations. Behavioral observations include evaluation of the client's hygiene based on presentation, gait, speech (normal, pressured, slowed, slurred), eye contact, posture, behavioral manifestations of mood disorder (e.g., anxiety as represented by excessive fidgetiness or handwringing), and other observations. Traditional questioning is used to inquire about a client's orientation to persons (Who are you? Who brought you here? Who am I? Who is the President of the United States?), places (Where are you now? What city and state do you live in? Where were you born?), and time (What time of day is it? What day of the week is it? What year are we in? What holiday is coming up next?), thoughts, mood, affect, behaviors, short-term memory (e.g., remember this list of three objects, and I will ask you about them again later) and cognitive functioning (attention, concentration), medical status (e.g., use of medications), illicit and legal substance use, estimate of intellectual functioning, suicidal and homicidal history or current thoughts or plans, insight, and judgment. Assessment of delusions and hallucinations is typically included in this evaluation.

As mentioned, most mental status interviews are conducted as part of an intake or subsequent evaluation. Because this interview is a standard clinical method of assessment and not typically used for comparative purposes, formalized rating scales are rarely if ever used. Shea (1988) and Morrison (1995), among many others, provide a more extensive discussion and guidelines for mental status interviews.

Crisis Interviews

Psychologists who work in acute psychiatric services, emergency rooms, or outpatient mental health clinics are most likely to conduct crisis interviews. However, most clinical psychologists need to conduct crisis interviews periodically, regardless of their setting of employment. Crisis interviews are directed toward clients who are in acute distress due to an exacerbation or increase in psychological disturbance, or who have suffered a traumatic or life-threatening incident. Because these situations can arise in any setting (psychiatric, medical, school, research, etc.), all therapists must be prepared for the responsibility of determining clients' imminent risk for harming themselves or someone else, or inability to care for themselves, given a heightened state of psychological arousal or psychotic episode.

Crisis interviews are more focused than intake interviews, and diagnostic interviews. Often, portions of a mental status exam, if not an entire exam, will be incorporated into this type of interview. Crisis interviews have the specific purpose of informing therapists' decisions about patients' safety, placement (psychiatric or medical hospital admission), or immediate intervention (crisis hotline leading to police outreach). Questions are typically focused on gaining information about crisis situations, chief symptom complaints, symptom duration and severity, clients' safety, resources and supports, risks, and overall client functioning. Rational and systematic clinical decision making, and knowledge and facility with procedures for individual settings (e.g., emergency help contacts, involuntary commitment procedures, steps for assisting women to leave homes of domestic violence) are two of the most important therapist attributes necessary for management of crisis situations and crisis interviews.

Exit Interviews

Exit interviews are conducted at the end of an inpatient or outpatient treatment, medical inpatient visit, or occupational tenure. These interviews provide therapists or another designated professional or paraprofessional with an opportunity to review assessment or therapy content with clients; provide feedback on progress; help clients engage in future thinking about maintenance of treatment gains or managing future problems; create plans for future crises, relapses, or booster sessions; and gain clients' feedback on the usefulness of various aspects of the treatment. When exit interviews are conducted by the therapist at the end of treatment, these interviews are often called "termination sessions," although one could argue that ending treatment marks a new beginning for clients, rather than an ending. A termination interview provides a forum for clients to appropriately express their feelings and emotions about ending therapy. Effective termination is explored more fully in Chapter 14.

Test Instruments

Tests used in clinical psychology are similar in structure and function to tests you have been exposed to throughout your education and training. Standardized psychological tests are tools that assess clients' functioning in terms of personality, educational or cognitive content areas, adaptive skills, or abilities. Typically, the word *test* implies that these tools ask questions or use tasks that have "right" and "wrong" answers to which clients' responses are compared. Usually, tests are accompanied by manuals that provide scoring information, decision rules, and instruction for administration, and standardized results or scores on the test based on large groups of individuals with specific characteristics (e.g., age groups, culture, gender, "normal" versus "clinical" population). The results of standardized tests are usually provided in terms of scores on subscales and overall test performance.

Cognitive Function Tests
Tests that are commonly used in clinical psychology include tests of cognitive functioning: attention, perception, memory, intellectual abilities (e.g., intelligence or IQ testing, such as the Wechsler Scale of Adult Intelligence-III revision; WAIS-III; Wechsler, 1997; Psychological Corporation, 1997), speed in information processing or dexterity in fine motor skills, and other areas of neuropsychological or cognitive abilities. Consistent with the assessment goal of prediction, psychologists might administer *aptitude tests* to determine clients' potential abilities. Aptitude tests are defined as "designed to give a quantitative estimate of a subject's ability to profit by training" or measure "future achievement" (Chaplin, 1985, p. 34). *Achievement tests* are similar to aptitude tests, except that *current,* rather than future, abilities are evaluated. Achievement tests may be subject-specific, or more global in content. The Wide Range Achievement Test (WRAT; Wilkenson, 1993) is a commonly used achievement test.

Personality and Symptom Checklists, Inventories, and Scales
If you have ever been surveyed at your local shopping mall, or have completed a physical history form at your physician's office, chances are that you have completed a checklist or inventory. Unlike standardized tests, checklists and inventories generally do not have right or wrong answers, although they should have psychometric evaluations of reliabilities and validities provided in their manuals, and typically have comparison scores for various populations. Their purpose is to assess the presence or absence, or occurrence or nonoccurrence of particular thoughts, feelings, behaviors, characteristics or traits, over a designated period (e.g., today, past week, past month). The Fear Inventory (Cautela, Cautela, & Esonis, 1983) is an example of an inventory that offers a list of items that children commonly fear. An assessor might read this list to a small child and ask him to endorse items or objects that make him scared: "Are you afraid of . . . a vacuum cleaner? A barking dog? The dark?" Alternatively, the child's parent might respond to the written questions. The Minnesota Multiphasic Inventory-2 (MMPI-2; Duckworth & Anderson, 1995) is a very common personality inventory used in clinical psychology. Clients are asked to read 567

adjectives and respond whether each adjective does or does not describe them by responding to a true-false format.

While checklists are almost always in the form of "check all that apply," or "check the top three that apply," and inventories may take the form of questions or statements to be endorsed, *scales* assess the *frequency* (how often?) or *quantity* (how much?) of occurrence or nonoccurrence of the characteristics in question, or the degree to which the individual agrees or disagrees with particular statements. *Likert-type scales* versus *Thurstone scales* (to be described) are used to measure the attitudes, frequencies, or quantities according to ranges expressed in words representing incremental increases (always, sometimes, never; strongly disagree, moderately disagree, disagree, neutral, agree, moderately agree, strongly agree), or numeric values that have anchors specified on the instrument (on a scale of 1 to 5, 1 = never, 5 = always). A true Likert scale is an attitude scale focusing on agreement or disagreement with three or five incremental values (Chaplin, 1985). This commonly used rating scale method has been adopted by many and adapted to use ranges from 3 to 10 ascending or descending values; thus, the format is often referred to as a "Likert-type scale" versus "Likert scale."

A Thurstone scale is similar to a Likert scale in that clients' attitudes are being assessed about standardized questions, situations, or characteristics. However, rather than assessing degree of agreement or disagreement, clients select a statement from a range of statements that is most consistent with their views. The Beck Depression Inventory (BDI-II; A. T. Beck et al., 1996) uses a Thurstone scale. An example item similar to those on the Beck Depression Inventory is as follows: Please endorse the statement that best describes how you feel: (a) I do not feel stressed; (b) I feel stressed; (c) I feel stressed all the time that I can't control it; (d) I feel so stressed all the time that I can't stand it. The method for deriving the pool of statements is beyond the scope of this chapter; however, as with other clinical instruments, psychometric properties of any tests, inventories, checklists, and scales should be evaluated prior to selection.

Checklists, inventories, and scales can either be designed for the client to complete or for someone else to complete about the client. Given that most assessments should take a multimodal, multimethod, multiinformant approach, rating-by-others instruments provide a time-efficient means of collecting such data. Child and adolescent assessments especially rely on ratings by others, such as ratings by parents, teachers, peers, or significant others. The Conners Rating Scales for assessment of attention deficit disorders exemplify three versions of a similar scale: self-report, parent or significant other report, and teacher report.

Observation

Observation is an important part of various types of data collection, such as interviews, role-plays, or analog assessments. However, observation is a data collection method in its own right. It is one of the key tools used in behavioral assessments, and various strategies are used in this method. Observations may be conducted in a *naturalistic setting* (the client's own home, work, school, or social environment), or in a *controlled environment* or *situation* (a simulated environment that the psychologist creates in which the behavior of interest is likely to occur). Cost, time, frequency of the behavior, and public or private nature of the behavior will dictate which setting is likely to be used.

Psychologists and training laboratories often have two-way mirrors in their offices designed so the client(s) can be in one office where the situation is set up to encourage the behavior in question, and the psychologist can discretely observe the behaviors in the adjacent office on the other side of the two-way mirror. This setup is an example of a controlled situation. A couple who is having marital trouble and difficulty communicating may be told to sit in a room and discuss their finances for 20 minutes, during which time the psychologist observes behaviors such as use of "I" statements ("I feel," "I think" versus "you make me feel" . . .), effective listening, interruptions, summarizing statements, raising of voices, cursing, hostility, validation of feelings, and possibly other behaviors.

In the absence of two-way mirrors, other controlled situations such as *role-plays* may be used. Sometimes also called *analog assessments,* role-plays are brief interactions between the patient and therapist (posing as someone else significant to the contrived situation), between two clients, or a client and psychological assistant (a confederate), that involves the simulation of a scenario in which the client would likely engage (or not) in the behavior under review.

A 32-year-old male, Jon, who has social anxiety, may be learning techniques to assert himself. During the course of treatment, he decides he wishes to ask a woman to go on a date, but he feels nervous about doing so. The therapist may ask the client to imagine having the opportunity to speak with the woman privately, and engage in the dialogue he might have with his potential date as the therapist role-plays the woman. The importance of role-plays is that clients actually engage in the behavior, rather than tell the therapist what they *would* do. So, instead of Jon saying, "Well, I would walk up to her and maybe I would say 'hi.' I would then probably ask her how her weekend was," Jon would actually stand up, cross the room, and approach the therapist as if he was in the room with the woman he is speaking about. He would initiate conversation as if it were a real-life situation; "Hi Maria. How are you? How was your weekend? . . ." This interaction is similar to acting in a play. Role-play is a valuable technique for ongoing assessment, but is also useful for rehearsal to acquire new skills. Several standardized role-play tests exist (e.g., C. M. Nezu, Nezu, & Gill-Weiss, 1992), although the majority of these exercises are developed in the moment by clinicians.

Observation as a strategy minimizes the biases that could be introduced into self-report measures or report-by-others measures (interviews, checklists, inventories, scales), such as clients intentionally presenting themselves in a certain way (e.g., good, bad, innocent, passive) by providing inaccurate information. However, the presence of the observer may introduce a new bias. In naturalistic or controlled settings, the presence of the observer may impact the frequency or natural occurrence of the client's behavior in question. A client may want to put his best foot forward, and therefore, may demonstrate his "best" behavior, more than he would if he was not aware that he was being observed. Likewise, another client may become shy or inhibited and reluctant to engage in certain behaviors if she knows she is being watched. Observers, therefore, usually situate themselves in inconspicuous places where their presence can eventually be disregarded to some extent. Observations of clients and their target behaviors take place for a long enough period to acquire a reasonable "sample" of behavior, and allow the client(s) to *habituate* to (get used to and tune out) the presence of the observer.

Clinical Example

A psychologist was conducting a behavioral observation of a 9-year-old Hispanic female, Gia, who reportedly had behavioral problems in the classroom. On the first visit to the classroom, the psychologist sat in the back of the room, so that the other students would not be constantly watching the "stranger." However, the first hour of observation resulted in little unbiased data because several of the student's classmates turned around frequently to ask questions such as, "Doctor, do you speak Spanish?" "Doctor, are you here because Gia is crazy?" "Doctor, look at my cool pencil bag!!" and Gia was initially seeking the psychologist's attention. However, with proper redirection and nonattendance ("extinction") of the children's behaviors, eventually, they found other activities to entertain them, and they lost interest in the stranger!

For the purpose of data collection, observations usually rely on a therapist-created systematic data collection system, and are based on operational definitions of behaviors to be monitored, called *target behaviors*. Systematic data collection systems include measuring the frequency of the occurrence or nonoccurrence of a particular behavior, descriptions of the behaviors that occurred (perhaps according to a checklist of adjectives), and record keeping of events of *antecedents* and *consequences* to the target behavior. Antecedents are behaviors, events, or stimuli that are observed to precede the target behavior. Consequences are those behaviors or events that are sequelae to the target behaviors.

Recording observations of antecedents, target behaviors, and consequences allows data collectors to look for patterns in situations that increase, decrease, or maintain the behaviors in question. Skinner (1953) referred to this type of data interpretation as a *functional analysis.* Such analyses allow clinicians to understand, for example, why a mother "loses her control" with her 3-year-old daughter. After making observations either during home visits or discrete office interactions in the waiting room, the clinician realizes that the child begins yanking on her mother's sleeve and tapping her relentlessly when the mother is talking to others or engaging in an activity that does not involve the child. The mother, in response to this behavior, swats the child from her sleeve and tells her to "wait a minute." However, the minute comes and goes, and the child continues this behavior, until finally, the mother turns and yells at the child. Once she yells, the little girl cries and the mother ultimately picks her up to soothe her. Based on that brief description, supposing that the child's nagging behavior is the target, what do you think are the antecedents and the consequences? Why does the child continue to engage in this behavior time after time?

Psychologists, clinicians, or laypersons trained by professionals can make observations and collect data systematically. It is common for clinicians to provide clients or significant others with a data collection system (or record sheets) and ask them to record their own observations of their behaviors in between sessions. This introduces the biases mentioned about self-reports, but useful data may still be obtained. Such observations or rating forms are sometimes referred to as diaries or self-monitoring logs. Data collected by diaries or self-monitoring logs include food diaries (recordings of dietary intake); individual's thoughts, feelings, and behaviors relating to specific problem situations (A. M. Nezu, Nezu, Friedman, Faddis, & Houts, 1998); record of daily activities; data logs of daily time spent for relaxation; and mood record forms detailing individual's maximum anxiety, depression, and pleasantness experienced each day.

Projective Measures

Tests and stimuli such as the well-known Rorschach inkblots, Sentence Completion Tests, and Thematic Apperception Test (see Groth-Marnat, 1990, for a comprehensive review) are called projective measures because they require examinees to *project* their unconscious thoughts, feelings, beliefs, wishes, and understanding of the world onto the ambiguous or semistructured stimuli. To understand the concept of projection, you must consider Sigmund Freud's theory that persons are born with an *id, ego,* and *superego.*

Id, Ego, and Superego
According to Freud, the id represents basic instincts that are uninhibited and focused on libido, immediate gratification, and excitement; the id is the deepest level of a person's unconscious. The ego represents the conscious self, and is the part of a person's mind that is aware of others' needs in addition to one's own. The ego is the part of the mind that is responsible for thinking, perception, memory, and other cognitive processes. It is also responsive to the need for gratification and may often be conflicted between what the person wants versus what is appropriate in reality. Lastly, the superego is one's conscience that leads individuals to distinguish and act according to what is socially right versus wrong. The superego operates without individuals being aware of it acting; the superego keeps the ego and id in check!

Projection as a Defense Mechanism
Freud theorized that projection is one of several defense mechanisms a person's ego (conscious self) uses to protects itself from trauma.

Projective measures go hand-in-hand with personality assessment and psychodynamic approaches to assessment and case conceptualization. Projective measures are also used to aid in diagnosis although results from these tests alone are not sufficient to make a definitive diagnosis, since this was not their intended use. Projective measures enable clinicians to obtain more data than direct questioning or objective tests and measures for clients who are resistant to share information or simply for individuals whose defense mechanisms (psychodynamic explanation of persons' ways of psychologically protecting themselves) prevent conscious recognition of their own dynamics and characteristics. This rationale is more consistent with psychodynamic theories than with cognitive-behavioral theories. The advantage of uncovering information from clients' sub-conscious, which may be unavailable to clients' consciousness, is balanced by the fact that the conclusions drawn from data obtained are based on evaluator's interpretations and theoretical assumptions about personality. For instance, a client is asked to describe a picture that objectively shows two males on a park bench looking at the same focal point. The client explains that the picture is of two orphans who are sadly watching a family enjoy a Sunday afternoon at the park. There is nothing in the picture that objectively indicates that this is fact. However, the response may reflect background information about the client's personal life, occupational experience, or sense of social awareness. The expla-nation of the picture goes beyond the objective facts. The interpretation of the response goes beyond the facts about the client. The client's description of the picture is thought to project his or her own thoughts, feelings, beliefs, or experi-ences. The interpretation of the client's response may also reflect biases and be-liefs the assessor holds about the client.

Physiological Measures

Direct assessment of individuals' bodily responses to internal and external events is accomplished through physiological assessments. Such assessments are common in relation to bodily responses to stress and relaxation, pain (e.g., headaches), sexual functioning or dysfunction, and sleep. Examples of physio-logical assessment devices include biofeedback instruments measuring galvanic skin response (skin temperature changes), blood pressure, heart rate, and res-piratory sinus arrhythmia (relating to depth of inhales and exhales). Special training in the use of physiological assessments is required and can usually be offered through graduate courses, practicum or supervised learning place-ments, or on-the-job training for technicians.

Taking a closer look at possible uses of physiological assessment, consider the last time you had an argument or were unexpectedly confronted by some-one who was angry with you, do you recall the physical sensations that accom-panied your rise in stress? If you are like most people, your heart rate increased, perhaps your face flushed and your hands became warm, and you may have en-gaged in rapid breathing patterns (shorter breaths). These sensations might have also resulted from an internal cue, such as the moment you remembered that you had forgotten your coat at the restaurant you left 30 minutes prior, or the recognition that you had forgotten to bring your wallet when you were ready to pay for your groceries! Physiological assessments allow professionals to evaluate such responses in individuals to determine the extent of the impact of internal and external stressors or relaxation practices on their physiology.

An example of physiological assessment in the evaluation of sexual func-tioning (normal and deviant response patterns) is provided by discussion of the penile plethysmograph. This instrument is used to measure penile tumescence or physiological arousal in males in response to provided stimuli (e.g., audio-tapes of potentially arousing scenarios, sexually arousing visual images). The penile plethysmograph has been used frequently in the assessment and treat-ment of sexual offenders.

Technology-Assisted Data Collection

With the advancement of technology, test developers have sought to ease the cost and time associated with psychological test administration and interpretation. Computer-assisted interviews are sometimes used to collect initial client contact information and even diagnoses-related data. Some clients may prefer to disclose personal information in this seemingly more private fashion; others may be less likely to share details of their past or current circumstances without human contact and gentle prompting or questioning. As an initial screening tool, this method may allow for information to be gathered in a time- and cost-efficient manner.

Many self-report inventories are also available in computer program format (e.g., MMPI-2). Clients respond to questions on a computer screen, rather than in the traditional pencil-and-paper format. Responses to such inventories are computer-scored, and computer-generated interpretative reports can often be furnished. The benefits of this format over pencil-and-paper formats are obvious—patients are less likely to miss items, legibility is not an issue, and computer scoring saves time. Furthermore, test administration is sure to be standardized when administered by computers, and decision rules required by administration of many tests will surely be followed.

There are certain risks or limitations that should be considered. Clients unused to computers might be computerphobic (older adults, persons who do not use computers in their daily work or personal life), and therefore, technical aspects of the computer may distract them from the task. Persons with visual impairment or mobility/dexterity problems may have difficulty using computers. Another possible limitation is that test administrators may rely too heavily on computer-generated reports and overlook supplementary or complementary material gathered from other sources, even though the APA Ethics Code advises caution on this matter (APA, 2002, 9.06). The initial cost of many of the administration, scoring, and interpretation programs can be exorbitant, and many programs can only be loaded onto one computer, limiting the portability of the tests, or accessibility of tests to group practice professionals. Computer-assisted tests are becoming more popular, as the pros seem to outweigh the cons, and the pencil-and-paper tests remain available as alternatives. The Conners' Continuous Performance Test is an example of a useful computer-assisted assessment for Attention-Deficit/Hyperactivity Disorder.

Psychologists and other mental health professionals often use other technology to assist in data collection. Tape recorders, video recorders, pedometers, telephones, and personal handheld computing devices (PDAs), can assist in data collection and ongoing monitoring of target symptoms, thoughts, feelings, or behaviors. As a homework assignment, couples may be required, to tape-record their efforts to discuss difficult topics using newly learned communication skills. The clients or clinician can review tape recordings in session, or privately for reevaluation or provision of feedback. Video recorders might be used during implementation of behavior modification plans or for parent training. Clinicians might instruct clients to leave voice-mail messages about completion of daily homework assignments or mood-scale reporting. Handheld devices may be the ideal place for patients to record their coping attempts or food diary since PDAs are usually carried with avid users at all times, allowing for immediate recording of pertinent information. These suggestions represent only a small sample of possible data collection enhancement via computer and other electronic devices.

Summary

The scientific method provides a paradigm to guide clinicians in conducting assessments. A hypothesis-testing approach to answering assessment questions leads to a broad-based evaluation of individual strengths, weaknesses, and targeted areas that is open to correction and validation, regardless of the type of assessment being conducted. Operational definitions are critical to specify exactly what is being examined and for what purpose. Clinicians' own biases and heuristics are potential confounds to the assessment process, and mindfulness of one's viewpoints is deemed critical. Assessment tools must have reliability and validity, as emphasized in details about these psychometric concepts. Lastly, several data collection methods, including interviews, tests, checklists, scales, observation, physiological measures, and technology-assisted data-gathering techniques were discussed highlighting the uses for each of these techniques, and preferably a combination of several.

The Logistics of the Assessment and a Closer Look at Interviewing

$\mathcal{8}$

Chapter

In this chapter, we take a closer look at how to build an assessment protocol, how to decide what needs to be assessed, and how to integrate clinical assessment into clinical practice. We discuss the use and integration of psychological assessment tools including clinical interviews, psychological testing, observation, reports of significant others, reports of other professionals, and self-reports. A problem-solving approach to clinical decision making and assessment, in particular, is emphasized to assist clinicians in the assessment and treatment process.

Learning Objectives

At the end of this chapter, the reader should be able to:

- Explain what a problem-solving approach to clinical decision making is, and why it is helpful to the process of assessment.
- Describe the steps in problem solving, as applied to clinical decision making.
- Discuss the process of obtaining informed consent and its importance to establishing rapport.
- Compare and contrast at least two different types of interview questions.
- Provide at least two prompts that can be used to keep an assessment interview flowing.
- Understand and explain the impact of feedback communicated to patients and referring parties.
- Recite at least three tips for successful report writing.

195

Thus far, we have discussed the goals and various types of psychological assessment and the biopsychosocial paradigm as a model to guide assessment. We have also applied scientific principles to data collection and outlined methods and tools to conduct assessments; qualifications for responsible test use; and ethical principles for assessments. You may still have many questions about assessment procedures. You might be wondering, (a) How do psychologists decide whether to accept a referral for assessment? (b) How do they choose the type of assessment to conduct? (c) What role does the clinical interview play when so many standardized tests are available to gather information, and what does it really entail? (d) How are assessment tools, such as particular tests, selected for specific assessments, beyond looking at the psychometric properties (reliability and validity) of the instruments? (e) What do psychologists do with all the information they gather—how is information communicated?

The goal of this chapter is to answer these questions, which all relate to decisions that the clinician must learn to make involving the *logistics* of assessment. The clinician must learn these logistics in terms of strategies as well as procedures. We begin with a discussion of the problem-solving model of clinical decision making (A. M. Nezu & Nezu, 1989; A. M. Nezu et al., 1997) as a model for assessment strategy. This model provides a useful framework to guide the assessment (and treatment) process. It will orient you toward thinking critically about each decision that needs to be made throughout the assessment and therapy process, regardless of theoretical perspective. This chapter is intended to help you "put it all together," which is probably one of the biggest challenges graduate students face in applying didactics to clinical settings!

Strategic Logistics and a Problem-Solving Approach

One of the most fascinating and stimulating aspects of clinical work is that no two clients are the same, and each person is uniquely complex and challenging. This reality is also what makes clinical decision making and critical thinking difficult to teach to new clinicians—no "cookbook" exists to guide clinicians through decision making for assessment and treatment. A. M. Nezu and Nezu (1989) developed a problem-solving approach to clinical decision making based on a social problem-solving model that has been applied for treating a variety of clinical disorders and for increasing social competence (see D'Zurilla & Nezu, 1999, for a review).

Social Problem Solving

According to the problem-solving model, *social problem solving* is the cognitive-behavioral process by which individuals understand problems in living and directing their efforts at finding solutions to them (D'Zurilla & Nezu, 1999; A. M. Nezu, 1987). According to the clinical decision-making model, the clinician is the problem solver, faced with the many challenges that accompany each stage of the therapeutic process. We discuss the therapeutic process according to the following stages: (a) screening and understanding the reason for referral; (b) broad-based assessment, including in-depth consideration of the chief complaint, (c) treatment design, and (d) evaluation of treatment effects.

Understanding the social problem-solving model requires familiarity with the operational definitions provided for *problems, solutions,* and *effective solutions.* After establishing that foundation, we discuss the core components of the social problem-solving model: problem orientation, problem definition and formulation, generation of alternatives, decision making, solution implementation and verification (D'Zurilla & Nezu, 1999; A. M. Nezu et al., 1998).

A *problem,* according to the social problem-solving model, is a discrepancy between one's current state of affairs or situation and one's goal (A. M. Nezu, 1987). In daily life, persons are constantly presented with situations or tasks (demands) that require responses or action to achieve desired goals. These demands may be placed on oneself, or come from others, or the environment. Discrepancies occur between "what is" and "what one would like a situation to be" when *obstacles* interfere with one's ability to affect the situation or demand. Obstacles to goal attainment might include intrapersonal variables (maladaptive thinking, biases, actual or perceived skill deficits), extrapersonal variables (unrealistic demands of others, competing demands or responsibilities, differing goals between self and others), situation-specific variables (uncertainty, unpredictability, novelty), inadequate psychosocial or tangible resources, or other conflicts or challenges. Problems may be isolated events (e.g., dealing with a client in crisis), a series of similar or related events (e.g., classes that run past the designated ending time, unreliable hired child-care providers leading to work absenteeism for parents, anger outbursts during interpersonal disagreements), or a pervasive difficulty that occurs for a short or long duration (e.g., procrastination, stuttering, poor time management, inability to say "no"). Situations may result in problems for one person, and yet the same situations may be manageable by another person. Problems are individualistic, and therefore, definable only by the person(s) who is (are) experiencing them.

Using the preceding definition, the problems clinicians confront in the therapeutic process are still many. Clinicians begin a first session with minimal information about a client and must eventually understand why each client is presenting for testing, treatment, or other clinical services. Just because clients request services of a mental health professional does not mean that the clinician must agree to work with them; deciding whether one is qualified to provide the requested services for each individual is a critical problem that requires an important decision. This problem may resurface at various time points in the therapeutic process. Selecting appropriate approaches to assessment from all the available techniques, tests, and formats represents another clinical problem. Likewise, the intervention stage presents numerous problems to be solved: selecting and designing, implementing, and evaluating treatments appropriate for each client, given the individuality of each person's circumstances, strengths, resources, deficits, needs, and other factors consistent with the biopsychosocial assessment conducted.

Solutions are defined as *any* coping response designed to change a problem situation, one's emotional reaction to it, or both (A. M. Nezu, 1987; A. M. Nezu, Nezu, & Perri, 1989). Solutions are also individualistic (one person's choice to create a month-long study schedule to prepare for an upcoming exam versus another's plan to cram the night before an exam). The same solution for one person may be adaptive (spending extensive time alone), whereas it is maladaptive for another, or may be adaptive in one situation, but maladaptive in another for the same person. Solutions may be effective (assertiveness to prevent disrespect) or ineffective (i.e., aggression in response to disrespect).

The goal of social problem solving is to devise and implement *effective solutions*. Three specific criteria define effective solutions. Effective solutions, evaluated according to the problem solver's judgment (a) solve the targeted problem (meet the desired goal state), (b) maximize the positive consequences, and (c) minimize the negative consequences. Systematic evaluation of solutions warrants consideration of individual variables, one's environment, and the person-environment relationship (D'Zurilla & Nezu, 1999). Thus, the goal of each clinical task in the therapeutic process is to achieve the preestablished short-term or long-term goals by identifying, selecting, and implementing effective clinical solutions (identify and operationally define the patient's problems; prescribe and teach relaxation training to an anxious person in need of behavioral controls for pain resulting from muscle tension; overcome obstacles to treatment, such as poor attendance or noncompliance with homework assignments).

Components of Social Problem Solving

Effective solutions and optimal outcomes are achieved through adaptive social problem solving, according to the clinical decision-making model (A. M. Nezu & Nezu, 1989). Nezu and Nezu assert that using systematic, rational problem-solving skills aids clinicians in minimizing judgmental errors, and maximizing the likelihood of selecting and implementing optimal treatments for individual clients.

Social problem solving consists of five main interactive, reciprocal component processes that are further broken down into specific skills and tactics. The component processes are *problem orientation, problem definition and formulation, generation of alternatives, decision making,* and *solution implementation and verification.* The following explanations are not as detailed as the original model because a comprehensive discussion of the problem-solving model and its applications is beyond the scope of this chapter. The interested reader is referred to several problem-solving therapy manuals (D'Zurilla & Nezu, 1999; A. M. Nezu et al., 1998), and the most relevant clinical decision-making book (A. M. Nezu & Nezu, 1989) for in-depth discussion.

Problem Orientation

Problem orientation is a motivational set or *worldview*—how a person tends to *think* about problems, based on his ideas, beliefs, and assumptions. Does he view problems as challenges or barriers? Does the problem-solver believe in her ability to solve problems effectively, or does hopelessness or helplessness override her feelings of self-efficacy? Problem orientation can either facilitate or hinder effective problem solving, and the use of the other problem-solving skills.

For clinical decision making, worldview incorporates one's theoretical orientation, or the set of ideas, beliefs, and assumptions about human behavior, personality, and change, that the clinician uses. Adhering to the biopsychosocial model as a paradigm for understanding behavior, subscribing to multimodal, multimethod, multiinformant, time-series approaches to assessment, or adhering to specific ethical guidelines represent components of one's worldview. Clinicians' worldview is believed to guide problem-solving efforts relating to clinical decisions (A. M. Nezu & Nezu, & Lombardo, 2004). The common use of heuristics (discussed in Chapter 7) and biases that are likely to positively or negatively influence clinicians' decisions are also encompassed in their worldview.

Problem Definition and Formulation

If you went to your physician's office today and told him or her that you "don't feel well," how will he attempt to rectify this problem? Will he provide you with aspirin? How about an ice pack? Will she offer an ointment of some kind? Will he recommend bed rest *or* more exercise? Unless you are truly not feeling well at this moment (in which case your mind immediately gravitated to your specific symptoms), neither you nor your doctor could predict how you would be treated. Why? Because not feeling "well" could mean many different things. Your doctor would not know whether (s)he should concentrate on your eyes or your ankles! Most likely, your doctor would ask you specific questions about your current state of well-being, or lack of well-being. The physician needs to *identify* the specific problem(s), *clarify* his or her understanding of the problem, and *establish goals* for treatment outcome.

This is the essence of the problem definition and formulation component of problem solving, and the importance of this step in the process cannot be sufficiently emphasized. Identifying and defining problems and establishing goals for each stage of therapy are essential to progress efficiently and effectively toward needed results. The following questions highlight some of the problems to be defined throughout the therapeutic process: Why is the patient seeking treatment? What are the components of the person's problem, such as cognitive distortions, dysfunctional family patterns, newly acquired physical disability? What unique client or therapist variables limit the clinician's ability to implement a particular empirically based therapeutic intervention? Why hasn't a treatment regimen led to the gains expected?

Effective problem definition and formulation relies on several skills and tasks. Problem solvers (clinicians, in this case) engage in the following practices. They (a) seek all available facts and information about the problem; (b) describe these facts in clear and unambiguous terms; (c) differentiate relevant from irrelevant information, and facts from assumptions; (d) identify the specific factors that make the situation a problem for the particular therapist, client, or both; (e) set realistic and attainable problem-solving goals (D'Zurilla & Nezu, 1982, 1999; A. M. Nezu & Nezu, 1989; A. M. Nezu et al., 1989, 1998).

Generation of Alternatives

Once a problem is defined and realistic goals are set, problem solvers need to find ways to reach these goals. To attain goals, effective solutions, as earlier defined, must be identified. This is not an easy or immediate task for many people. If it was, a problem might not have occurred in the first place! The goal of the generation of alternatives component of problem solving is to use creativity and broadened thinking to conjure up as many potential solutions as possible; evaluation of the alternatives comes later.

Brainstorming skills are prescribed to identify effective solutions, according to the problem-solving model (D'Zurilla & Nezu, 1982, 1999; A. M. Nezu & Nezu, 1989; A. M. Nezu et al., 1989, 1998). Two rules govern brainstorming efforts: (1) the quantity principle, and (2) deferment-of-judgment principle. The quantity principle simply suggests that generating as many ideas as possible will increase the likelihood that an optimal solution will result—quantity *leads to* quality. Since people are often used to relying on previously developed skills, ideas, or techniques, it is sometimes difficult to "think outside the box," and as a result, a person's usual ideas surface and may be quickly rejected. The deferment-of-judgment principle dictates that ideas are not evaluated during brainstorming, since "nay-saying," or "yes-butting" (yes, but, this won't work because . . .), closes off the creative process, and stifles efforts to think of novel alternatives or use ordinary solutions in novel ways. Thus, more high-quality ideas are likely to result if judgment of alternatives is suspended during this process.

Generating alternative solutions to clinical problems becomes necessary in a variety of circumstances. Consider how the complexity of individual client variables might affect assessment or treatment planning. Cognitive or physical disabilities might limit the type of standardized tests you could administer, either because the client cannot understand the tasks presented, is incapable of carrying out the required tasks because of physical limitations (visual impairment, loss of limbs or mobility), or the test manuals do not provide normative data to compare results you might acquire by alternative means. Language barriers between clinicians and clients also pose a problem to be solved to effectively assess and treat individuals from differing backgrounds.

Another challenge frequently faced by clinicians is how to comprehensively assess and treat individuals who present with multiple symptoms and diagnoses. Although the repertoire of empirically validated and empirically supported treatment options is growing, many of these preferred treatments provide limited guidance for working with patients who are concurrently taking psychiatric medications or have multiple diagnoses. Lack of available prescribed treatment options for certain patient populations (e.g., individuals with mental retardation or comorbid psychosis), therapists' or clients' constraints on time, and inadequate money, resources, or availability to provide or receive the optimal treatment needed suggest additional problems where brainstorming for solutions will be particularly necessary.

Decision Making

If the rational problem-solving process was followed sequentially up to this point, the clinician has identified the problem to be solved, goals, and possible alternative solutions. Decision making comprises a set of skills to facilitate the selection of the potentially most effective alternative solution and the construction of a decision plan. Solution alternatives are evaluated based on the anticipated or predicted consequences that might result if particular alternatives were implemented. The selection process is based on consideration of the utility of each alternative (C M. Nezu & Nezu, 1995). The utility of an alternative is judged by two factors: the likelihood of obtaining the identified goal, and the value of the alternative, which is evaluated by considering the effects on oneself (personal effects; e.g., as a therapist) and others (social effects; the client and those affected by the client's treatment), and the effects likely to result in a short-term and long-term time frame. Such anticipated consequences are evaluated in terms of a cost-benefit analysis. A rating system (positive [+], negative [−], neutral [0]) allows the costs and benefits of each alternative to be compared when the analysis of all solution options is completed.

Applied to clinical decisions in assessment, the therapist must consider the utility of each possible means of assessing a client. If a client's characteristics seem to suggest a personality disorder, brainstorming would promote exploration of means to assess personality to identify the type and nature of the client's personality disorder. Review of assessment literature reveals numerous assessment options: objective personality tests (e.g., the Minnesota Multiphasic Personality Inventory, the Millon Clinical Multiaxial Inventory), projective tests (Rorschach inkblot test), clinical diagnostic interviewing, and so on. The assessor then needs to consider (a) the likelihood that a specific assessment tool or a combination of specific assessment tools would confirm or disconfirm the personality disorder suspected; (b) the personal effects the use of each test would have on the therapist (what does the therapist need to do to ensure ethical, competent use of the test, how much time and effort would administration take, and is this reasonable within the constraints of his or her practice?); (c) the effects on others (the client and those affected by the client's assessment; e.g., what will the emotional or financial cost of the assessment be for the client, and how will the assessment help the client in treatment planning? Is the client dependent on someone else for transportation, and if so, how will the time requirements of the assessment affect this person?); (d) the immediate short-term effects of assessing a personality disorder in a particular client, such as increasing the likelihood of selecting an optimal treatment approach for the individual; and (e) the long-term effects (e.g., what ramifications will result from labeling the individual as having a borderline personality disorder?).

Examples provided here only represent one or two possible consequences under each heading. During the decision-making phase, problem solvers are encouraged to think about as many predicted consequences as possible under each of these headings, and to evaluate each alternative by comparing the overall positive, negative, and neutral consequences that exist for each possibility. The goal of the decision-making step is to select the optimal or most effective solution by finding the alternative that reaches the predetermined problem-solving goal, maximizes the positive consequences and minimizes the negative consequences.

Once an alternative is selected, the problem-solving model (Felgoise, Nezu, & Nezu, 2002; A. M. Nezu et al., 1997) recommends making a *decision plan*. A decision plan requires the problem solver to consider the best means (e.g., under what conditions or circumstance?) for implementing the solution selected, and to develop a method to monitor and evaluate the actual consequences that result from implementing the solution plan. If home visits were required for assessment of a child with behavior problems, when would be the best time of day or week to increase the likelihood of observing the problematic behaviors or troubling interactions? What equipment or observation recording tools should the assessor bring along? These are just two of many points to consider in developing a solution plan for this problem.

Solution Implementation and Verification
The first three components (problem definition and formulation, generation of alternatives, and decision making) of the problem-solving process are intended to collectively result in the selection of a solution. In the solution implementation and verification stage, the solution is actually carried out, and

the resulting consequences are observed and evaluated in comparison with the consequences that were previously predicted or anticipated (D'Zurilla & Nezu, 1999). The effectiveness of the solution is determined based on this evaluation, and the problem solver is encouraged to either self-reinforce ("give yourself a pat on the back") if the problem is solved, or troubleshoot if the problem is not resolved. Details of these steps are incorporated into the following vignette.

Suppose you have decided that a cognitive-behavioral treatment for social anxiety would be most appropriate for your 22-year-old male client named Gerry. This decision was made based on a thorough multimodal, multimethod time-series assessment, and Gerry agreed with your proposed intervention. When you selected this option, you considered the personal, social, short-term and long-term consequences for yourself as the therapist, and Gerry—the client. The predicted consequences of this alternative (in comparison to no treatment, drug treatment, other therapies, or a combination of various options) appear to be largely positive across all domains for all individuals involved. The expectation is that Gerry's anxiety will decrease in social situations as evidenced by an increase in his ability to attend social gatherings, hold conversations with peers, and eventually ask others to join him for a social outing (either a date or a group gathering). You also anticipate that Gerry will have a decrease in negative intrusive thoughts about himself and others' perception of him, and that he will decrease his avoidance of interacting with others. As part of the decision plan, you and Gerry created several self-monitoring forms for him to use to monitor his thoughts, feelings, and behaviors.

Once treatment begins, these forms become the basis for evaluating the magnitude of the intervention's success. If the frequency of negative thoughts and feelings decrease, and positive behaviors increase within a reasonable time frame, and therefore, the anticipated outcomes and the actual outcomes match, reinforcement of Gerry's efforts and success is warranted. If Gerry does not improve as expected, and a discrepancy between anticipated and actual consequences occurs, reevaluation of the intervention (type chosen, manner of implementation, etc.), and perhaps, the specifics of the assessment (circumstances in which change is required, or targets for change), is necessary to determine the interfering obstacles. Even if treatment is not successful at this stage, clinicians are encouraged to independently reinforce clients' attempts to work toward their goals.

With problem solving and decision-making strategies in mind, let's look at the step-by-step procedural logistics of conducting a clinical assessment.

Procedural Logistics and Clinical Skills

How does one go about conducting a psychological assessment? The process requires two primary sets of clinical skills; gathering relevant data and integrating information into an explanatory case report. We are going to work backward in our illustration, beginning with an example of the case report and then detail how data were gathered and information integrated and used toward the initial purpose.

In keeping with the problem-solving model, the following case report illustrates the goal for an intake assessment. The ultimate goal of an assessment is to gain enough information about the individual (couple, family) to develop an understanding of the person's identified problem and what is maintaining the problem, and to offer recommendations commensurate with the collected and interpreted data to answer the referral question. This information is integrated in some written fashion in the client's formal record of clinical service. Particularly when the information needs to be communicated to a third party, the clinician may prepare a comprehensive integrative report, similar to this case illustration.

The following case report is presented in its entirety and then dissected to show how information is obtained and then integrated for a specified purpose. Readers should note that the format of this report represents only one model of a psychological report, although it is a fairly prototypic example. Many other excellent styles and useful formats exist. The description of Mrs. Giunardini represents a composite case example to protect individual identities.

Psychological Assessment Report

Patient's name: Gina Giunardini

Date of Evaluation: Wednesday, June 19, Some Year

Date of Report: Friday, June 21, Some Year

Identifying Information: Mrs. Giunardini is a tall, 32-year-old, first-generation Italian female, with dark hair and slim build. She presented in casual and neat dress, slouched posture, and anxiety manifested by handwringing, fidgeting in her chair, and pressed speech.

Reason for Referral: Mrs. Gina Giunardini is a 32-year-old mother of two male children (9 and 11 years old), who separated from her husband 2 weeks ago as a result of his extramarital relationship. Three days prior to her clinical intake, Mrs. Giunardini learned she is 2.5 months pregnant with her husband's child. Her gynecologist referred her to the mental health clinic as a result of her extreme emotional distress in response to this news, and her self-reported confusion and perceived inability to cope with the decision that needed to be made regarding her pregnancy. The physician

stated that in addition to being "shocked and scared," Mrs. Giuanardini made several references to "not being able to handle things," and "needing a way out."

Background/History

Social/Family/Religious History

Mrs. Giunardini lived with her parents until she married her husband, Anthony, at the age of 20. She had one prior relationship with another male for 6 months. Initially, she and her husband moved into an apartment, but returned to live with her parents within a few months because they could not afford the rent. Mrs. Giunardini became pregnant with their first child within a year of their marriage, and their second child, 2 years later, at which time they moved into the three-bedroom row house where she and her children currently reside. She describes herself as someone who "went right from being a kid to being a wife and mother." Her mother helped her raise her children in their early years. Mrs. Giunardini reports having had little social contact

(continued)

Psychological Assessment Report (Continued)

with other women her age, other than through playgroups, parenting responsibilities, and occasional get-togethers with her husband's friends and their wives. She reports having no close friends, other than her mother, her three brothers, and her husband. Her primary daily activities, in addition to childrearing responsibilities, include jogging, spending time with her parents, and watching late-night television.

Mrs. Giunardini's family of origin consists of her mother and father, both immigrants from Italy, and three brothers, ages 39, 41, and 42. She reports good relations with all family members. Her mother was described as "caring, but she holds her emotions in; she keeps the family in line. She can be stubborn and touchy, but she's had a hard life." Her mother has a progressively worsening case of emphysema, and has seemed "depressed" for the past several months. Mrs. Giunardini assists her father in caring for her mother, in addition to routinely cooking for her parents. Mrs. Giunardini described her father as "a good guy who doesn't say too much. He is stern, but loving and protective." Her parents have emphasized the importance of family and church, and, according to Mrs. Giunardini, have sacrificed a lot on behalf of their children. Her brothers are all married with children, and reportedly protective and watchful of Mrs. Giunardini; she sees them approximately one time per month. According to Mrs. Giunardini's report, the family embraced her husband Anthony as if he were their "own blood."

Mrs. Giunardini reports having a strong religious belief system rooted in her Roman Catholic upbringing. She had always attended church weekly with her family, until her separation.

She has not attended church since the separation because her husband attends the same church. Although her faith is a source of strength for her, she stated that she has not been able to "figure out the lesson" in Anthony leaving her.

Educational/Vocational/Occupational History

Mrs. Giunardini completed high school at a private Catholic high school. She states that she did not go to college because she did not have a direction for a particular career. She worked for her father's construction company by answering phones, until she married. Once she married, Mrs. Giunardini states she focused on being a homemaker, but occasionally helped her husband in his deli. Currently, out of perceived necessity, she is considering career and educational options, and contemplates pursuing a nursing degree.

Medical History

Mrs. Giunardini reports no significant past medical problems. Her two prior pregnancies were unremarkable. A history of positive health behaviors regarding diet, exercise, minimal use of alcohol (1 glass of wine daily) and tobacco (none) were reported. However, Mrs. Giunardini believes she may have gained some weight (5 to 7 pounds) in the past few weeks. Mrs. Giunardini reportedly drinks two to three cups of coffee daily.

Mental Health History

Mrs. Giunardini reportedly participated in brief therapy (1 month; 4 sessions) with a social worker after the birth of her second child, in response to a recommendation from her obstetrician/gynecologist. She reported feeling overwhelmed, "a little down," and "sort of

Psychological Assessment Report (Continued)

trapped." Her ability to cope with the adjustment of her growing family increased during this supportive psychotherapy according to her report. She could not recall specific skills gained during treatment. No other treatment or need for treatment was reported.

Mental Status Examination

Mrs. Giunardini, a 32-year-old Italian-American female of tall and slender build appeared her age, was oriented to person, place, and time, and was cooperative with the evaluator. Dressed casually and neatly with her long hair tied back, Mrs. Giunardini maintained a slouched posture and intermittent eye contact throughout the interview. Her speech tone was quiet and her speech rate was pressed. She manifested anxiety as evidenced by her worried thoughts, "I can't stop thinking about what has happened. . . . I am so worried about what will happen to us (herself and children). . . . My thoughts keep racing about what to do"; and behaviors, including fidgeting in her chair and handwringing.

Her mood was sad, anxious, and angry; her affect was appropriate to topic, and she reported feeling "desperate" and alone; she was tearful at times. Additional content of Mrs. Giunardini's thoughts revolved around her role as a wife, mother, and daughter. She thinks of herself as a "good mom and daughter," and now questions whether she has been a "good" or "bad" wife, due to the circumstances with her husband. She focused on her need to make a decision regarding her pregnancy (to maintain it or not), how she would manage to raise three children as a single parent, and what was "fair" to her sons. Although Mrs. Giunardini stated

that she sometimes wishes she would "go to sleep and not wake up," she denied active suicidal ideation, past or present. She dismisses thoughts of suicide due to her strong religious beliefs and her responsibility to her children and parents. No evidence of a thought disorder was observed; short- and long-term memory is intact; hallucinations and delusions were denied.

Mrs. Giunardini reportedly drank one glass of wine per day, prior to learning of her pregnancy; she denies current or past tobacco or other substance use. Mrs. Giunardini is estimated to have average intelligence, good insight and judgment. Prognosis is estimated to be good based on past coping history, positive response to therapist, statements of feeling more "hopeful" by the end of the session, and willingness to pursue intense therapy (crisis counseling) for the next 2 weeks, and as needed thereafter.

DSM-IV *Diagnosis*

Axis I: Adjustment Disorder with Mixed Anxiety and Depression

Axis II: Deferred. R/O Dependent Personality Disorder

Axis III: Pregnancy

Axis IV: Psychosocial stressors: Family (caring for her mom); marital relationship; occupational problems

Axis V: Current Functioning: GAF: 65; Highest GAF in past year: 90.

Clinical Impressions

Mrs. Giunardini is a young Italian-American female who has been raised with traditional cultural beliefs emphasizing the woman's place in the home

(continued)

Psychological Assessment Report (Continued)

and family as a primary responsibility and role. She has enjoyed and relied on the support of her family of-origin, husband, and children for social contact and development of her identity as a daughter, mother, and wife. She identifies herself through these roles, as does her mother and sisters-in-law. She is, therefore, experiencing extreme distress in reaction to the disruption of her primary role as a wife, her "failed relationship" with her husband, in addition to the reality that she is pregnant and faces the possibility of being a single, divorced mother who has not held steady employment since her teenage years. These major life changes present the possibility of embarrassment to her and her family, and the necessity for her to reevaluate her strengths, weaknesses, and capabilities, although she has not begun to do so. Mrs. Giunardini has not contemplated or explored the possibility that her marriage might be reparable or that her husband might wish to return to his family.

As a result, of these life changes, Mrs. Giunardini has had many negative automatic thoughts relating to poor self-confidence ("I don't think I can handle life on my own."), poor coping ("I have no way of handling things. I'm going to lose it. I'm going to fall apart."), poor self-efficacy for independence ("I couldn't make it on my own. I have no job, no skills, no money of my own, and no way of getting these things while I am taking care of two or possibly three children."), and catastrophic thoughts pertaining to others' possible perception of her ("Gina must have been a horrible wife. Gina couldn't satisfy her husband or keep her family together. What did Gina do to drive her husband away?"). Her feelings of despair, fear, and anxiety

are related to the novel situation she never anticipated experiencing, her perceived lack of ability to cope with the situation, and her self-imposed isolation from persons other than her parents, since the separation. Her predominant coping behaviors have included eating more than usual, crying frequently, avoidance of others, and seeking therapy. It seems likely that Mrs. Giunardini's avoidance of others, her mother's poor health, which has rendered her unable to comfort Mrs. Giunardini in her usual manner, and her pattern of panicked, anxious, and depressed negative thoughts, feelings, and behaviors are maintaining her current feelings of helplessness and inability to effect positive action.

Mrs. Giunardini's initiation of therapy and her response to the first consultation/intake session suggests that Mrs. Giunardini is open to gaining guidance in adopting more rational and systematic thinking and learning new coping skills, such as problem solving, relaxation techniques, communication skills, and other independent skills that will aid her in accomplishing the new life challenges at hand. With regard to her decision making about the pregnancy, it is expected that Ms. Giunardini will be able to arrive at an acceptable decision within the next week by attending biweekly therapy sessions and following agreed-on homework to facilitate her problem-solving process. She does not appear to be in imminent danger of hurting herself or others (children, husband), seems stable to continue to reside and care for her children (although she was encouraged to seek familial support for the next 2 weeks), and seems reliable and trustworthy regarding her commitment to return to therapy.

Psychological Assessment Report (Continued)

Recommendations

Mrs. Giunardini was encouraged not to make an immediate decision about the pregnancy (within the first few days of gaining this news), due to the tendency for her emotions to interfere with rational decision making, and the potential for regret if she makes an impulsive decision. As a result of cooperative problem solving in session, Mrs. Giunardini was prompted to consider all persons who could be supportive and helpful to her during her decision-making process (older brother's wife, mother, priest, gynecologist), and evaluate the probable positive and negative consequences that might arise from her seeking their support in this decision. Likewise, in-session discussion aided Mrs. Giunardini to begin evaluating both positive and negative consequences to maintaining the pregnancy and giving birth, rather than only the negative consequences that seemed readily apparent. She was directed to begin considering consequences for herself, her sons, her family, and other important persons in session, and complete this effort prior to the next session.

Mrs. Giunardini agreed to record her thoughts, feelings, and behaviors relating to her pregnancy, separation, and future to help her to gain a better understanding of her responses to these major life stressors, and to aid the therapeutic process in identifying areas for change. Education regarding the connection between thoughts, feelings, and behaviors, and the impact of her role models' and her own past coping efforts on her current functioning were explained. Due to the complexity and critical time frame within which Mrs. Giunardini must decide to keep or terminate the pregnancy, she was encouraged to consider what areas of her life would need to change if she chose either of the two options, and to consider *if* these changes seemed at all possible (e.g., obtaining a job or financial assistance, or seeking forgiveness from the church and herself if she chose to terminate the pregnancy), but was directed to postpone thinking of *how* she would make these changes until later. These recommendations were made in attempt to focus Mrs. Giunardini, reduce her overwhelming feelings, and break down her problems into a more manageable framework. It was recommended to Mrs. Giunardini that she consider others' opinions within the context of her own situation, morals, and ideals, and that therapy would be led in an objective manner, without influencing her toward either decision based on anything other than her own rational and systematic decision-making process

Reflective Questions

Now that you have read the comprehensive intake evaluation of Mrs. Giunardini, take a moment to reevaluate the report in the context of what you have learned from Chapter 7. What was (were) the apparent goal(s) of the assessment? In reviewing the biopsychosocial model of assessment, were all aspects of this model considered and represented in this summary report? What additional information would you want to obtain in a second session with Mrs. Giunardini, if you had one?

Because the report represents only one meeting with the client, the information is entirely based on self-report. What additional strategies or methods would you choose to further the evaluation and take a multimodal, multimethod, multinformant, time-series approach to assessment? Based on Mrs. Giunardini's primary problem, would you have the luxury of conducting such an evaluation in the necessarily limited time frame? If not, how would you decide what to include or not to include? Consider the problem-solving model of clinical decision making in your exploration of these questions.

Once you have given these questions some thought, you are ready to proceed to the following sections on clinical interviewing and the procedural logistics of conducting an assessment.

Methods of Data Collection

Our discussion of the procedural logistics of assessment follows the framework of the report previously generated. In this section, we address where information comes from and how we collect it. The strategies and skills described will help you arrive at the information necessary to include in an intake evaluation such as that of Mrs. Giunardini. Our discussion of assessment procedures looks carefully at the clinical interview as a primary tool, and how the clinician integrates various methods of data collection into the clinical interview.

Identifying Information

A brief description of the client is usually provided in the beginning of each report to help orient the recipient of the report (other than the client) to recall the patient. Likewise, if another professional receives a report prior to meeting the client, it will help the professional identify the client on arrival. Identifying information is usually gathered from the referral source and directly from the client.

Reason for Referral or the Referral Question

Each client-professional relationship begins because someone (the client, a client's family member, another professional) has requested consultation, assessment, or therapy for the identified patient. The specifics of this initiation are critical to planning what should happen in the first meeting and subsequent meetings, or even the appropriateness of a meeting at all! Using the problem-solving approach to clinical decision making (A. M. Nezu & Nezu, 1989), the first "problem" presented here is to concretely and objectively define the reason for referral. Answering the questions "Who?" "What?" "When?" "Where?" "Why?" and "How?" will help clarify the reason for referral.

Who?
It is not always clear who the identified client will be. If a husband and wife appear in the office together, is it because they are both seeking treatment, or is one spouse attending to be supportive of the other? If a child is having problems in school, is the child the focus of the evaluation or is the family unit the in-

tended client? So the question, "Who is to be evaluated?" although seemingly basic at first glance, may not be. There are other important "who" questions: Who is requesting the evaluation (referral source)? Who is paying for the evaluation (the school, courts, self, other)? Who will receive copies of the final report? Who will provide the feedback to the client (the referring physician or you, the clinician)? Who, if anyone, has explained to the client the purpose of the evaluation?

In the case of Mrs. Giunardini, most of the answers to these questions are evident. Some, however, are known to the clinician, but were not relevant to include in the report. Knowing who will receive the report is important to direct the language used in the report and the amount of detail provided. Knowing who will pay for the evaluation is important for billing purposes, and if it is not known ahead of time, reviewing these questions will cue the clinician to handle financial matters before beginning the professional relationship.

What?

Probably the most important "what" question is, What is the *goal* of the assessment? The answer to this key question will ultimately guide the rest of the evaluation. Remembering back to Chapter 7, is the goal to diagnose/classify or describe the person's problems or predict future behavior? More specific "what" questions pertaining to the client's problems and goals will further define the structure and content of your assessment: What are the reasons that led to the referral? What is the client's chief complaint? What is the referral source's impression of the client (if the client is not self-referred), including his or her perception of the problem? What is the expectation of the referral source for the visit (consultation, assessment and treatment, evaluation only, specific testing), and can you meet this expectation? What is the client's goal for seeking your services? What information can the referral source or others provide you with to help you better understand the purpose of your assessment (previous records, recent evaluations, medical information)?

If you cannot gain answers to the "what" questions presented here (and often you may not be able to), you must prepare yourself to obtain this information directly from the client. If a potential client speaks with you to schedule the first appointment, perhaps you will ask some of these questions over the phone. If you have someone who schedules your appointments for you or you see walk-ins, you may have to begin an initial evaluation with very limited information, and ask questions to obtain answers on meeting the client. In the case of Mrs. Giunardini, the gynecologist called the clinician directly, and therefore, some dialogue allowed the clinician to gain the physician's perspective prior to meeting Mrs. Giunardini. This was particularly helpful for the clinician because she could consider the parameters of her assessment prior to sitting down with the patient.

When?

Many "when" questions can be asked. When did the problem begin, and when (under what circumstances) is the situation most problematic? When was the referral made, and how long did it take for the client to follow through with scheduling an appointment? When does the assessment need to be completed to answer the referral question or aid the referring person? If surgical treatment is dependent on clearance from a psychology professional, it is likely that the evaluation must be completed immediately to be of any value. If the referral person's time frame is not reasonable given your practice schedule, the client's schedule, or the length of time needed to conduct a thorough assessment, the clinician must engage in problem solving to consider how this problem will be resolved.

Where?

At this stage of the evaluation, regarding the reason for referral, *where* relates to both the chief complaint or problem and the setting in which the evaluation will take place. Where does the problem occur (workplace, home, social situations)? Will the patient be seen in an inpatient or outpatient clinic, a medical hospital, or physician's office for the psychological evaluation? In the later sections of Mrs. Giunardini's report, many "where" questions are answered: Where does she live, or where does she participate in social activities? The basic "investigative reporter" questions (e.g., Who? What? Where?) leading to a clear definition of the reason for referral will be used throughout the evaluation process.

Why?

Why is the client seeking a consultation, evaluation, or treatment *now* (at this particular time in his or her life)? This question addresses the motivations of the client and the precipitating factors that led to the need for the clinician's services. One might also ask, why is the client seeking the services of a mental health professional (versus another health professional or other care provider)? This is an important question to consider when a referral is made or when an initial meeting is held. Perhaps, the client has little understanding of what psychologists or therapists do. Is there an expectation for treatment with medication or spiritual guidance? Has the person exhausted all other options and is meeting with the psychologist as a last resort? Gaining the answer to this important "why" question serves as an impetus for conversation to ensure that the client's expectations are reasonable and the clinician's understanding and expectations placed on him or her are also accurate and realistic.

Mrs. Giunardini was referred to the psychologist because she was "confused," perceived herself as unable to cope, and needed to make a decision that was beyond the realm of the medical information her gynecologist provided to her. Although the clinician agreed to meet with Mrs. Giunardini and believed the referral was appropriate to her expertise, she also recognized that Mrs. Giunardini had strong spiritual and religious convictions that would influence her decision making, and might require discussion beyond what the psychologist could provide to her. Her recommendations included advice that Mrs. Giunardini consult with her trusted priest about matters that would influence her decision-making process.

How?

How questions pertaining to the reason for referral might overlap somewhat with the why questions already presented. How can you help the client? How much interaction will you have with the referral source prior to and following the evaluation? How much information does the client expect you to have about him or her? How much information does the referral source want back from you? How much information, if any, will be shared with other persons involved in the identified client's problem? Considering these questions will remind clinicians of their legal and ethical responsibility to obtain *informed consent* forms and *release forms* for any information from the client and all other relevant parties. These important documents are reviewed later on in this chapter.

By answering the preceding questions, and certainly any additional ones that fit within this context, you should have gained a solid basis for your meeting with your client, and have established that you are an appropriate person to conduct the intake or assessment. Having a clearer understanding of the specific goal of your meeting will enable you to tailor your first interview to address the relevant topics that will allow you to answer the referral question, or to identify what further meetings will be needed to accomplish this. Use of the brainstorming technique followed by decision making will allow you to formulate your plan. Solution implementation is illustrated in the following sections, which describe data collection and interviewing.

Background or History, Mental Status, and Information for Clinical Impressions

In most reports that are generated from initial interviews, intakes, or comprehensive assessments, psychologists include the same basic components: background history, current mental status, summaries of objective and subjective testing, *DSM-IV* diagnosis, clinical impressions, and recommendations. As you can see from Mrs. Giunardini's report, a lot of information must be obtained in usually a relatively short period (anywhere from 30 minutes to 90 minutes, depending on the circumstances). Information for the overall evaluation may come from a variety of assessment techniques (interviews, tests, questionnaires, inventories, etc.). However, all psychological evaluations require an interview, at minimum. Hence, the clinical interview is emphasized.

Begin with an Interview
Once the referral source has been contacted and you have clarity about the purpose and goal of the assessment, the actual evaluation or intake begins. Regardless of whether you are conducting an intellectual assessment, personality assessment, diagnostic assessment, or evaluation for some other purpose, the interview should always precede any other formal testing procedure.

It is not recommended practice to initiate IQ testing on first meeting a client, without first conducting an interview. Likewise, ambitiously presenting Thematic Apperception Test cards prior to establishing rapport and gathering basic knowledge of a client through an interview would also be inadvisable. However, it is not uncommon for some clinics or clinicians to have patients complete pencil-and-paper questionnaires or inventories prior to their first visit or while they are in the waiting room. Such standard practices allow clinicians to obtain certain information without spending time in session to do so, or provide a baseline of the client's functioning or symptoms (e.g., depressive symptoms), prior to the first meeting, which may impact the client's mood. The clinician will likely review these responses prior to the first interview and then at least briefly acknowledge their completion and content in the first meeting.

Conducting a clinical interview prior to formal testing serves many important functions. This first face-to-face contact between the client and professional allows the basic elements of structuring a session to take place (see following discussion), and allows the development of a positive rapport. Interviews also often reveal new information that was not obtained by the referral source or phone intake, prior to meeting the client. The course of the evaluation and your approach may change when new information is presented. Perhaps the client was too embarrassed to tell the secretary the true nature of her complaints, and therefore, what you expect to discuss and what she actually shares with you in your interview may be quite different. Or, the first interview may reveal that the client is not forthcoming with information, and therefore, standardized or projective testing might be necessary to gather information that you otherwise would have gleaned from your interview. This occurrence exemplifies when the clinician as problem solver recognizes the change (solution verification) and troubleshoots, as necessary.

Interviewing prior to testing is also important to have some understanding of the client's way of thinking, feeling, behaving, coping, and responding to different circumstances to help conceptualize responses provided during formal testing. Having such information will minimize guesswork and assumptions. So, for many reasons stated, and many more that are probably not stated, it is recommended that a standard, semistructured, or clinician-structured interview is the first technique used in the assessment process.

During or following the first interview, the clinician is advised to engage in the problem-solving process again to determine the specifics of the remainder of the assessment. Decisions need to be made about the techniques, tests, or tools to be used in the assessment, the length of time for the entire evaluation (number of sessions, time permitted in each session), and who else, if anyone, will be included or invited to each session besides the client. Even if the assessment is done in a stepwise fashion, meaning that the need for subsequent testing is determined based on results from initial testing, informing the client of this projection will provide some general idea about the direction the process will take. Outlining the assessment framework ahead of time allows the clinician to set realistic expectations for the client, the referral source, and him- or herself, so that everyone can plan accordingly.

Often, new clinicians who have their assessment plans well designed in their mind innocently forget to do anything other than forage ahead toward their goal of collecting data! These clinicians forget to check in with their clients and ask them how comfortable they are with the assessment process. Clients may have concerns they will not volunteer without being asked, or they could become fatigued and less present in the session. It is important to remember to offer breaks during the evaluation process, if you continue beyond a 60- to 90-minute session, and to check in with the client periodically. Also, remaining too focused on one's own plans, procedures, and questions to be asked can result in missing nonverbal behavioral information that could otherwise be easily obtained through observation.

Neglecting to request client feedback and missing observational data are even more likely to happen if the clinician's note-taking process becomes too involved or distracting. Note-taking helps to maintain accuracy in recording details, but one must be cautious not to allow note-taking to become a barrier or obstacle between you and the client. In fact, clients often appreciate and feel more relaxed when clinicians inform them that the notes taken are merely recordings of information they are providing, rather than the clinician's analysis and opinions of what is occurring. Of course, this should only be stated if true.

Goals for the First Interview

In addition to gathering information, clinicians are advised to attend to several concurrent goals focusing on the clinician-patient relationship.

Establishing trust and a good rapport, socializing the patient to the assessment and therapy process, establishing professional boundaries and a confidential relationship, and a collaborative approach to assessment and treatment are all critical goals worthy of immediate attention. Meeting these goals begins with establishing the interview structure and keeping sessions focused; setting an agenda; discussing confidentiality and gaining informed consent; and using good therapy skills, such as asking effective questions, periodically soliciting feedback, demonstrating warmth and genuineness, and being mindful of nonverbal behavior. Each of these topics warrants further discussion.

THE INTERVIEW STRUCTURE   Once the general goal (diagnose, describe, predict, etc.) of the intake evaluation has been determined, the format of the interview is decided. Interviews may be highly structured or standardized, such as interviews guided by the Structured Clinical Interview for the *DSM-IV* (SCID-DSM-IV; First, Gibbon, Spitzer, Williams, & Benjamin, 1997), the Diagnostic Interview for Children and Adolescents (DICA; Reich, Shayka, & Taibleson, 1991), or an intake form according to the designated practices of an individual clinic. Semistructured interviews allow clinicians some flexibility in determining the order of questions to be asked, the manner or phraseology to be used in questioning, and in determining when more in-depth questioning pertaining to specific topics seems relevant. Unstructured interviews refer to interviews that are not predetermined in style, length, or specific content. However, interviews should not truly lack structure in the more general sense of the term. All interviews should have a clear beginning, middle, and end that are evident to the client and clinician and discussed in the process of setting an agenda.

To begin an initial interview, which is typically the first contact the clinician is having with the patient, proper introductions are important. First, the clinician briefly states her preferred way to be addressed, and briefly describes her credentials. Clinicians should also ensure that they are addressing their patients properly by pronouncing their name correctly, and using preferred nicknames or titles. Also, within an introduction, the clinician has the opportunity to address issues such as time factors and note taking. Stating the allotted time for the intake evaluation and future sessions, if relevant, begins the process of establishing the client's expectations for your work together, aids in structuring sessions, and maximizes the efficiency of time-use. Informing clients about the purpose and content of note taking, as stated earlier, demystifies the interview process and portrays the clinician's intention to be collaborative. An introduction might proceed in the following way,

> *Good morning Mrs. Giunardini. I'm Dr. Smith. I'm a licensed clinical psychologist and work at the Feeling Good Clinic full-time. Dr. Shilpa, your gynecologist, told me she met with you, and that the past week has been particularly difficult for you since you were told that you are pregnant. I am hoping that you are willing to speak with me for the next 45 minutes to talk about your visit with Dr. Shilpa, and any difficulties you might be experiencing as a result? . . . My hope is that by the end of our conversation, I'll have some ideas about how I might be able to help you, or offer some suggestions about what services or supports might be available to make things a bit easier for you. Would that be okay? . . . If you don't mind, I will be jotting a few notes down while we speak, just to make sure I don't forget important information or details you might share.*

In review of this monologue, you might notice that the therapist stated her general intentions for the assessment session, but was vague in describing how these goals would be accomplished. Also, the client has not yet had an opportunity to state her goals or expectations for the meeting. If this session continued without attention to these factors, Mrs. Giunardini is likely to be unclear about the assessment process, may not have an opportunity to express her needs, and the session may not produce the results necessary for Dr. Smith to fully develop useful clinical impressions or recommendations, as needed by Dr. Shilpa. Collaboratively setting an agenda, after briefly exchanging introductions will help to ensure these problems will not arise.

SETTING THE AGENDA   Agenda setting is common practice in many types of therapies, especially cognitive, behavioral, and cognitive-behavioral therapy. Much like your instructors provide you with syllabi at the beginning of each course, and perhaps, an outline at the beginning of each lecture, agenda setting in assessment and therapy sessions provides a road map for patients and clients alike. The difference between your class agenda and agenda-setting in the context of a patient-professional relationship is that the patient helps to create the agenda for each session. Clients may have somewhat less influence on the course of formal assessments compared with therapy sessions, but intake sessions and interviews, usually benefit from collaboratively set agendas. The agenda is a mutually agreed on schedule, established within the first few minutes of a session, that delineates how time will be spent and what specific topics will be discussed.

The process of setting an agenda should be brief. In the first contact with a client, the clinician should provide a rationale for setting an agenda, explain that agendas will be set in every encounter, and that sticking to the agenda is the joint responsibility of the client and professional. Taking this approach to each session ensures that the client will be an active participant, and that important aspects of assessment or treatment are reinforced, such as assigning, completing, and reviewing homework. Providing clients with a rationale for using agendas in each session is imperative, so that the high degree of structure and task-focused approach does not have an antithetical impact, such that the client feels dictated, imposed on, or rushed.

PROVIDING A RATIONALE FOR THE AGENDA   In clinicians' explanations for agenda setting, several points of information might be conveyed. First, explaining that setting agendas will provide both the client and the therapist with an understanding of "what to expect" increases the likelihood that proper time is allocated to topics that are deemed most important, while minimizing waste of time. If the client needs the clinician to complete medical forms for the client's insurance, a request made in the last 5 minutes of a session may have little chance of being fulfilled on that day. From the clinician's perspective, agendas minimize the likelihood that "surprises" will occur at the end of a session. Likewise, a therapist may intend to spend the majority of an assessment session learning about the patient's biopsychosocial history, without realizing the client is pressed to make a time-sensitive decision due to an imminent concern, as in Mrs. Giunardini's situation. Setting an agenda allows the clinician and client to state their intentions or goals and negotiate which goals are priorities. In testing sessions during the course of an assessment, and in early therapy sessions, the clinician generally takes more responsibility for establishing the agenda.

WHAT TO INCLUDE IN THE AGENDA   When the professional-patient relationship is strictly focused on evaluation, rather than therapy, the agenda is somewhat more straightforward for each meeting. The clinician would first state the amount of time allotted for the day's meeting, and then proceed by outlining the proposed structure for the beginning or continuation of the evaluation process. The clinician might first plan to have the client complete brief pencil-and-paper questionnaires to assess mood, frequency of symptoms experienced in the past week, or other similar behaviors, followed by a 30-minute interview. The clinician might then explain that he or she will be doing a series of short tests with the client (Wechsler Memory Scales), and then plan to have the client complete some computerized testing prior to ending the testing session. Toward the end of the session, the clinician might plan to discuss questionnaires, self-monitoring, report-by-other inventories, or other assessment measures that he or she requests for the patient to complete prior to the next session, or have a family complete by that time. The last 5 minutes or so might then be reserved to allow the client or clinician to ask any outstanding questions that were not addressed earlier. In subsequent sessions, the first agenda item might consist of reviewing homework previously assigned, asking followup questions to the preceding session's evaluation, or responding to new concerns raised by the patient, the referral source, or a third-party contributor to the data collection. Ideally, the client would have an opportunity to affirm this plan and add or negotiate any additional requests for time use for that day. Take a moment and imagine the script that might have transpired between Dr. Smith and Mrs. Giunardini in setting the agenda for the intake evaluation.

OBTAINING CONSENT AND DISCUSSING CONFIDENTIALITY   Clinicians old and new often underestimate the importance and value of obtaining consent, discussing confidentiality, and clarifying the goal and use for a comprehensive assessment. We hope that the following discussion will be persuasive enough that you will not become one of "those" clinicians!

Although these three components of an introductory session seem routine and standard to the clinician, they may not be familiar to the patient. So, aside from the ethical and legal responsibilities, if attended to sufficiently, these three core components of an intake session can help develop good rapport and open communication between professionals and their patients.

OBTAINING CONSENT Gaining consent for assessment or treatment implies that clinicians have thoroughly explained the purpose, goals, and objectives of the assessment or treatment, potential client risks and benefits for participation, who will have access to information obtained or produced from the assessment (limits of confidentiality), consequences to discontinuation or nonparticipation in the assessment or treatment process, and alternative options to those recommended by the clinician. Depending on the setting of the assessment (school, private practice, community mental health center, other), whether the assessment is self-requested, initiated by the treating therapist, or a third party, and the purpose of the assessment, the informed consent process may be more or less formal. Formal informed consent is obtained through discussion and signing of informed consent forms that are often kept in the patient's file, copied for the client, and possibly sent to the referral source or intended recipient of the evaluation report. If other parties are not involved, some clinicians may opt to discuss the issues relating to informed consent verbally and accept the patient's verbal consent to pursue the evaluation, treatment, or both. When informal consent is obtained, clinicians should always document that verbal consent was obtained for the recommended course of the assessment or treatment. For clinicians in training, it is more likely that formal consent will be used.

When done properly, meaning that the clinician discusses each aspect relevant to informed consent, the client gains an increased understanding of what to expect from the evaluator and the evaluation, and can ask questions that might otherwise not be realized or addressed. Clinicians who routinely place informed consent on the top of their agenda may also reduce the risk of forgetting to address issues of confidentiality or having a client become frustrated with an assessment process that might differ from their self-created expectations.

To obtain informed consent, clinicians must describe the purpose and nature of the assessment. This introduction to the assessment often provides a perfect opportunity to first have clients explain their understanding of why an assessment is needed, and to give corrective feedback, if necessary. The clinician might ask, "What is your understanding of why Dr. Shilpa recommended for you to visit me today?" In response, clinicians can correct misconceptions, and then begin discussion by communicating their general goals for clients, such as to understand their strengths and difficulties, which will allow them (or the referral source) to provide recommendations to help the client improve day-to-day functioning (coping with problems, reducing anxiety, "feeling better," or whatever relates to the purpose of the assessment). More specific goals should then be addressed, such as stating that the focus will be on trying to identify the client's confusion and memory problems.

In Mrs. Giunardini's case, the clinician's goals were to understand why Mrs. Giunardini was experiencing extreme distress relating to the pregnancy, evaluate whether she had the resources to cope with this distress and make necessary effective decisions, and provide recommendations to help her through her perceived crisis. Dr. Smith was likely to modify her description of these goals when stating them to Mrs. Giunardini, so that they would be appropriate to her understanding and sensitive to her situation. As illustrated, providing general, and then a more specific rationale helps the client to recognize that an assessment is something that is done *for* clients, and *with* clients, rather than *to* them.

Discussion of the purpose and procedures for the assessment also provides the opportunity for the clinician to highlight the collaborative nature of the assessment, such that the patient is the expert in his or her experiences, and the clinician is the expert in assessment or _____ (insert the focus of your work relating to the client's difficulties, memory, anger management, anxiety, helping people cope with losses or life changes). By addressing the purpose, goals, and objectives of the assessment, the procedures to be used (testing, biofeedback, interview), and the teamwork approach to be taken, clients may already begin to develop appropriate expectations for the assessment process and feel more at ease.

Mrs. Giunardini immediately expressed relief when the assessment process was described, and attention to the uniqueness of her situation was acknowledged. Her initial misconception was that Dr. Shilpa thought she was "out of control" and "losing it," because she had cried in the doctor's office. Although she endorsed feeling this way at times, she was concerned about having these fears validated by a professional.

In discussion of the purpose and goals of an assessment, the clinician explains how the information will be used, and possible associated risks or benefits. In a forensic evaluation, the results may not necessarily be helpful to the client, depending on the outcome. The client should know exactly what the possible consequences are that could result from the data revealed in an evaluation requested by the opposing attorney. If the evaluation is related to a child custody suit, and a Rorschach inkblot test reveals psychiatric instability, poor judgment and impulse control in a parent, this information must still be conveyed to the referral source. To allow the evaluation, the client must be aware of the risks associated with it prior to giving consent, and agree to the testing under those known circumstances. Another potential risk of a clinical assessment might include the tendency for some people to become upset when questioned about sensitive or emotionally painful topics. In these circumstances, the discussion of risks and benefits at the outset will help to foster rapport between the professional and the patient, rather than allowing the consequences to ensue without prior warning. It also becomes more apparent that the relationship between the professional and patient in the context of an evaluation or assessment can differ significantly from that of the professional-patient relationship in the context of therapy. The clinician who is only providing an evaluation is not designated as the person who will ultimately guide the patient through the process of managing or alleviating his problems.

LIMITS OF CONFIDENTIALITY   Patients may automatically assume that confidentiality laws bind a professional-patient relationship. In many cases, however, there are limits to these boundaries. In hospital settings, patient evaluations often become part of the patient's medical record—a document viewed by many health care professionals. Evaluations conducted at the request of school counselors might become a part of the student's academic record, and surely parents may gain access to students' evaluations as their legal guardians. Forensic evaluations have specific purposes and requirements for sharing such documents between plaintiffs and defendants as well. Given these limitations to confidentiality, and many other circumstances where boundaries are less clear, such as with insurance companies, clinicians are obligated to inform clients of the scope and limits of the confidentiality they can offer.

Contrary to the expectation that *all* information is confidential, some clients fear or expect that their evaluation will be available to inquiring spouses, family members, collaborative medical practitioners, or other parties. Assuring clients of their rights and protections within the professional relationship may build trust and give permission to the client to be honest and forthcoming with pertinent information he might otherwise have withheld for fear of repercussions. Clinicians who discuss the bounds of confidentiality and the clients' related concerns or questions can clarify misconceptions, set realistic expectations, and establish the parameters of the relationship immediately, so that client assumptions do not negatively impact the assessment.

RELEASE OF INFORMATION   At some point during the assessment process, the clinician may wish to speak with the client's family, spouse, friends, teachers, coworkers, or other health practitioners to gather additional information or medical or mental health records. Likewise, the clinician will want to exchange new information with medical or mental health professionals involved in the patient's care. Given the bounds of confidentiality, and supposing that the client was originally ensured that information would not be shared with anyone other than the referral source, simply calling any persons in reference to the client would breach confidentiality because they would automatically know the client was being seen by a mental health professional. Clinicians must present another consent form to the client to gain permission to have any interaction or dialogue with other persons. This consent form, often called a "release of information" form, specifies who will be contacted, what information will be requested, what information will be shared, the purpose of the information exchange, and the time frame for which the release form is viable. If clinicians carefully review with clients the information they want to disclose to the persons they contact, the clinicians can then honor any restrictions that their clients impose. Enlisting feedback from clients in this process is both required and critical to maintaining a good working alliance.

In the case of Mrs. Giunardini, Dr. Smith obtained her informed consent for the evaluation, a written consent form to release information to Dr. Shilpa, even though she was the referral source, and a written consent form permitting Dr. Shilpa to release information to Dr. Smith. A thorough rationale for requesting this permission accompanied the discussion of the forms presented. Mrs. Giunardini had the opportunity to ask questions and feel comfortable with the psychologist's responses prior to signing these forms.

Data Gathering in the Interview: Asking Questions

A well-formed and strategically placed question is the clinician's primary tool for gathering information in the interview. Competence as an interviewer depends on one's mastery of the use of questions. Using open-ended versus closed-ended questioning while maintaining focus and control of the interview, knowing how to prompt clients to provide more depth in their responses, and being able to ask difficult questions requires much practice. Considering the sensitive nature of Mrs. Giunardini's problems, one can understand why a delicate style is needed, at times, and directive questioning and feedback is necessary at others. The following tips introduce you to these important skills. You can practice these skills with anyone you know in the context of daily conversation—assuming you will not be asking clinical questions, or engaging in therapeutic conversation that could be construed as leading to a dual relationship!

CLOSED-ENDED, MULTIPLE-CHOICE, AND OPEN-ENDED QUESTIONS   Before proceeding, answer the following sets of questions for yourself; preferably, write your answers on a piece of scrap paper. Set 1: Did you have a good day? Have you had at least eight hours of sleep each night, for the past week? Do you like classical music? Are you feeling sad? Set 2: Do you have difficulty getting along with others or do you have a lot of friends? Are you happy with your graduate program or do you wish you had chosen another field of study? Do these questions seem simple, pointless, or curious to you? Set 3: How do you describe your energy level in the past week? What activities do you enjoy for recreation? What is your approach to writing term papers?

Review your responses and give some thought to any patterns you might notice within each set. The first set of questions represents closed-ended questions, or questions that require responses of only one or a few words. "*Yes*, I've had a good day." "*No*, I have not had eight hours of sleep each night in the past seven days." "*Yes*, I like classical music." "*No*, I do not feel sad." Imagine having a conversation in which the dialogue consisted of such exchanges. If you were asking the questions, how much information would you have acquired about each topic area? Most likely, you have not learned much more than specific responses to what you have asked.

Closed-ended questions are restrictive in the information requested and obtained. Also, the questioner or clinician has to work hard to continue this line of questioning when the responses are brief and not particularly informative. Each question could be followed up with another question, and if the subsequent question is also closed-ended, similar responses will be elicited. For example, "*No*, I have not had eight hours of sleep each day for the past week"; might be followed by asking if the individual has had more or less than that amount. Again, a one-word response would suffice to answer the question, but little would be known about the individual's sleep habits or patterns. One can almost imagine the volley of questions and answers that would be exchanged, using this inquisitive style. Such questions are typically asked in gaining a patient's medical history: "Have you ever had surgery? Have you ever tested positively for Hepatitis C?"

The second set of questions represents what we call, "multiple-choice questioning." The questioner has intentionally or unintentionally designated the appropriate responses available to the person being asked. For example, the question, "Do you have difficulty getting along with others or do you have a lot of friends?" almost forces the respondent to fit into one of the two predetermined categories of *either* having difficulty getting along with others, *or* having a lot of friends. This question presupposes that the person being asked has not just moved into a new area where he has not yet met many people although he believes he can make friends easily and get along well with others. Likewise, the following question presupposes that individuals could not be happy they selected their chosen field of study and not be happy with their program, "Are you happy with your graduate program or do you wish you had chosen another field of study?" To give a different answer, the respondent needs to contradict the questioner's question: "Actually, these questions do not seem simple, pointless, or curious to me. Rather, these questions seem to be unrelated to one another." From our experience as clinical supervisors, clinicians who ask many multiple-choice questions do so for several possible reasons: They have a specific hypothesis about what is going on with the client, and they wish to inquire about this hypothesis; they are concerned they are not communicating their thoughts or questions clearly to the client; or they lack confidence in the questions they are asking, and therefore, they might believe that providing possible responses will help the client understand them better. They have not learned and practiced the skill of asking questions that provide more comprehensive responses; or perhaps there is another reason for this behavior. Asking an open-ended question, such as, "Why do you ask so many closed-ended questions?" might provide a few additional reasons!

The third set of questions exemplifies open-ended questions. To respond to any of these questions requires information derived strictly from the person asked the question, without influence from the questioner about possible responses that could be given. Furthermore, it is likely that more in-depth responses will be solicited by open-ended questions because the respondent will not have been given inadvertent guidelines regarding the amount of detail sought. Answering the question, "How do you describe your energy level in the past week?" could result in the following responses, or a variety of others, "I have had a lot of energy this week because I finally was able to catch up on sleep after two weeks of sight-seeing"; or "I have had very little energy due to the heat outside and my recent decision to give up caffeine." These sample responses illustrate how open-ended questions elicit unbiased or uninfluenced responses to questions, while also providing additional, possibly useful, information. Asking, "what activities do you enjoy for recreation?" instead of "Do you like to play baseball?" will achieve the goal of gathering more information from the respondent. Likewise, asking, "What is your approach to writing term papers?" versus, "Do you make outlines before writing term papers?" will result in a more comprehensive reply. Many clinicians begin their intake interviews by asking patients, "What brought you in to see me today?" or

"Why have you decided to seek therapy *now* (versus 3 months ago, one year ago, etc.)?"

COMPARING OPEN-ENDED, CLOSED-ENDED, AND MULTIPLE-CHOICE QUESTIONS   The three styles of questioning—closed-ended, multiple-choice, and open-ended—each have pros and cons. Which type of question would most likely be incorporated into a structured interview? Unstructured interview? Semistructured interview? After reading on, you should be able to answer these questions.

Asking open-ended questions helps clinicians gain more information from clients by "giving them the floor" to speak freely about topics raised. Open-ended questions tend to direct the focus of an interview on clients' stories and personal information, rather than the clinician's checklist of information sought. The result is a more conversational style of interviewing and responding, and possibly more voluntary information and self-disclosures that inform clinicians about subjects not previously considered. The drawback to asking only open-ended questions is the risk that an interview can lose focus by allowing loquacious clients to speak endlessly about seemingly irrelevant topics, or that only a few questions are answered within a predetermined time.

Closed-ended questions increase the likelihood that many questions can be answered in a short time, but more limited information is likely to result. Asking only closed-ended questions is likely to tax clinicians, unless the questions are gleaned from a structured interview. Likewise, interrogating patients with mostly close-ended questions makes some patients feel rushed, not understood, or surveyed, rather than interviewed. Multiple-choice questions are least desirable as part of most interviews, unless responses need to be standardized for the purpose of comparing answers to the same questions across individuals. Such questions tend to influence respondents' answers because automatic responses are seemingly stifled by the options presented.

Ideally, semistructured or unstructured interviews consist of a reasonable combination of both open-ended and closed-ended questions. Beginning with open-ended questions provides the greatest amount of unbiased information, and then responses can be followed up with more specific closed-ended questions. Closed-ended questions typically dominate written questionnaires and are less likely to be exclusively useful in semistructured or unstructured interviews. Multiple-choice questioning is only advisable when the questions are derived with some basis for restricting the response options, such as in structured interviews.

Now that you have considered the differences among the three styles of questioning, for practice, try to create open-ended questions in place of the closed-ended questions to solicit more comprehensive responses. Next, create closed-ended questions to focus an open-ended question for which you would like to obtain a specific answer. Lastly, think about how your answers to the multiple-choice questions might have differed, if restrictions were not imposed on your responses. Throughout the rest of the day, focus on asking open-ended questions in your daily conversations, since this type of question is typically the most difficult for new clinicians to incorporate into their semistructured or unstructured interviews.

The questions that follow illustrate some of the questions Dr. Smith used to obtain information reported in the background/history section of Mrs. Giunardini's clinical report. The excerpts follow the introductory portion of the initial assessment, where consents were obtained and the client's initial questions were answered. It is also important to note that these are just samples of questions, not the interview in its entirety. Questions were not asked in this order. Some responses are provided to exemplify the types of answers given to open-ended or closed-ended questions.

Dr. Smith (Dr. S.):   Mrs. Giunardini, although I have some information from Dr. Shilpa, it would be helpful if you could tell me in your own words what brought you in to see me today, and how you are hoping I can help you?

Mrs. Giunardini (Mrs. G.):   My life fell apart in the last few weeks. I'm so confused; I don't know where to start. I need help figuring out how to put my life back together, if I even can. My husband left me. If that's not bad enough, I'm 2.5 months pregnant and he doesn't even know. I have two kids, no job, and no husband. I don't have anywhere to turn. I don't know what to do.

Dr. S.:   It sounds like a lot has changed for you recently, and very quickly. Since there is so much going on for you, we obviously won't be able to talk about everything today, so I think it is important for us to agree on what is most important to talk about. Where would you like to start today?

Mrs. G.:   Well, the job, my husband—those things happened—I have to deal with that, but I don't expect anything's going to change about over night. I'm really most scared about this pregnancy. I don't know what to do. . . . I only have about 1 week to figure out if I am going to keep this baby or not. I can't imagine having this baby on my own, but then again, how could I *not* have this baby?

Dr. S.:   You can't imagine having the baby, but you can't imagine *not* having this baby. (*Reflective Statement.*) Tell me more about the thoughts you are having regarding this dilemma. (*Prompt.*)

Later in the session . . .

Dr. S.:   You said that your husband just left you a few weeks ago. (*Prompt: Reflective Statement.*)

Mrs. G.:   Yes, it came out of left field—he totally took me by surprise.

Dr. S.:   Mrs. Giunardini, please you tell me about your marriage, beginning with when and how you met Anthony, and what life has been like for you since then? *Here you will note that Dr. Smith asked a combination of questions to get Mrs. Giunardini started in providing some background information about her relationships. Dr. Smith needed some specific information regarding the time-length of the relationship, and the remaining questions were open-ended, but with some direction to keep her focused. This question resulted in much of the information contained in the social/family/religious history section of the report.*

Dr. S.:   Have you had any other intimate or committed relationships, with someone other than your husband?

Mrs. G.:   Yes, just one man before I married Anthony. *As evident here, the closed-ended question only resulted in the specific information requested. As such, a prompt (i.e., "If you don't mind, tell me more about this relationship") was needed to gain more details.*

Dr. S.:   We've spent some time talking about your relationship with Anthony, the birth of your children, and how you have been spending most of your days in the past few years. (*Summary Statement.*) Let's take a step a little further backward. How would you describe your family members (parents, brothers) and what it was like growing up in your household?

When we first began today, you told me that one of your concerns is that you have no job, and now, no husband to provide for you. It would be helpful to switch gears and focus on this for a few minutes so that I can better understand your situation, is that okay with you? (*Rationale provided, and feedback solicited from client.*) How far did you go in school? (*Closed-ended question.*) Have you ever had any jobs outside your home? (*Closed-ended.*) Tell me about them. (*Prompt.*) Have you given any thought to what type of a job you might like to have, if you decided to pursue work outside your home?

Keeping the Interview Going: Prompts, Reflective Statements, Summary Statements, and Transitions

Questions obviously provide excellent means to getting patients to talk about their problems, strengths, weaknesses, background, or most topics suggested by the clinician. However, firing a straight line of questions at a client for 45 minutes or longer would get very tiresome and even grueling for most patients and clinicians.

Prompts, reflective statements, and summary statements help to keep the dialogue in a session moving along, without the patient feeling interrogated. Using such techniques also reduces multiple-choice questioning and therapists' tendencies to assume too much about what clients are thinking. Also, these techniques help clinicians keep clients focused on important topics by emphasizing the portions of client responses that are most pertinent to the clinical issues at hand.

Prompts are brief, gentle suggestive comments made by therapists to encourage clients to provide more detail about topics already initiated, to (re)direct clients to focus on particular aspects of their stories, or to elicit more complete responses. A client responding to the question, "What types of physical activity do you enjoy?" with the answer, "All types," might be prompted for more detail by the therapist's incomplete remark, "Such as . . . ?" Other statements commonly used as prompts include, "tell me more . . ."; and "go on . . ." Consider the excerpts from the preceding interview; can you identify the prompts made by Dr. Smith? In addition to these generic statements, reflective statements also serve as useful prompts during assessment and therapy sessions.

Reflective statements are statements made by clinicians that are essentially verbatim remarks initially made by the client moments earlier. These words are repeated to ensure the client that the therapist heard what was said, to prompt the client to expand or clarify what was meant, or to magnify the importance of the comment. In the preceding dialogue, Dr. Smith reiterated what Mrs. Giunardini stated regarding her dilemma about having or not having her baby. This signifies the importance of her comment, as Dr. Smith directs her to talk more about this subject.

Summary statements are offered periodically by clinicians to make sure they understand their clients' reports accurately, to verbally affirm they are listening, or to gently interrupt clients' speech to ask for clarification, change subjects, or redirect the focus of the discussion. The following script is Mrs. Giunardini's response to Dr. Smith's question, "Tell me about yourself, and what your life has been like since you met Anthony."

I am a 32-year-old mom with 2 kids. I lived with my parents until I got married at 20. My husband and I moved into a little apartment, but then we couldn't pay the rent. We moved back in with my parents for a few years. We had kids pretty quickly and my mom helped out a lot. Anyway, I guess I went right from being a kid to being a mom. My kids are now 11 and 9, both boys. My mom is really sick now and I am helping my dad out with taking care of her. She has emphysema. Between my kids and my parents, I really haven't had much time for myself. I go running every morning, but that's about it. Usually, I'm just rushing from soccer games to baseball practices for the boys, and then to my parents' house to cook for them. I guess I think of myself as a good mom and a good daughter, but I guess I haven't been a very good wife. I mean, I didn't used to think I was a bad wife, but I guess my husband thinks I am.

Dr. S.:   From what I'm hearing Mrs. Giunardini, your life for the past 12 years has focused on taking care of your husband, your children, and your parents, and those responsibilities have pretty much defined who you are. You've managed to take a little time to exercise each day, but otherwise, it doesn't sound like you have had much time to dedicate to yourself. Now that your husband has left you, it sounds like you're beginning to question your identity a bit?

Dr. Smith's summarized what Mrs. Giunardini had told her by using her own words, and adding a slight interpretation of what she thought Mrs. Giunardini was thinking. The statement added to the end of the summary provides a prompt for Mrs. Giunardini to express her thoughts regarding her current situation and her need for help in therapy. Of course, Dr. Smith's decision to focus on this aspect of Mrs. Giunardini was made in the context of the rest of the interview. Other clinicians might have chosen to inquire about other aspects of her self-report, depending on what their clinical hypothesis was or the information they deemed necessary to obtain.

Topic transitions present a common difficulty for practitioners-in-training. Students are usually concerned that switching subjects might be perceived as abrupt, rude, or unnatural. They have difficulty interrupting clients because they do not want their clients to infer that they are disinterested in what they have to say, or that what they have to say is unimportant. This common concern leads new clinicians to wait for an opportunity or segue that may or may not come. To accomplish all that is necessary in an assessment interview, clinicians need to maintain some control of the session and guide the interview according to the agenda set. We have several suggestions for making transitions in session.

First, in the process of setting an agenda for the interview and shaping expectations for the session, the clinician might inform the client that many topics will need to be covered. A statement such as, "During the interview, I will be asking you a variety of questions. Some will be specific to your reason for being here today, and some may be more general questions that I typically ask of people when I first meet them. So I need you to bear with me if my questions jump around a bit." Second, if a client is very talkative and seems to be providing much irrelevant detail in response to questions after the key information was provided, the clinician might gently interrupt and state the following, "Mr. Jones, it sounds like discussing this topic has brought back a lot of memories for you that are very interesting. I would like to hear more about this, but I am hoping it is okay with you if we discuss this again at a later time, to make sure that we can cover all the things we need to discuss today. Would that be okay with you? Is there anything else about this topic that you think I should know right now?"

Many times a loquacious client is not the cause of difficulty in transitioning from one topic to another. In fact, clients who tend to give short answers, or those answering mostly closed-ended questions, might present a bigger difficulty to new practitioners. If questions are answered concisely and without more information than requested, little is offered for the clinician to reflect or transition to the next topic. The third suggestion to aid in this transition is for clinicians to acknowledge the switch in subject matter. In assessment of depression, a clinician might change subjects as follows:

I've asked you about your sleeping, eating, energy level, and physical feelings of tension. I'm going to switch gears for a moment, if that's okay with you. (Client nods.) Besides having a lot of worries, oftentimes people who are feeling down about themselves or their situations also report feelings of worthlessness or helplessness. Do you find yourself feeling this way at times?

In this transitional statement, the clinician summarized the recent portion of the interview, informed the client of the direction the interviewing was going, and asked permission to make this change. Likewise, if a client had provided a lot of detail within one uninterrupted response, the clinician might be concerned that the opportunity to ask for more information about the beginning portion of the response was lost. Simply summarizing what the client reported will validate the information obtained, will then allow the clinician to return to an earlier topic. Dr. Smith might have replied to Mrs. Giunardini's description about herself and her life by making the same summary statement provided earlier, and then continuing as follows:

From what I'm hearing, Mrs. Giunardini, your life for the past 12 years has focused on taking care of your husband, your children, and your parents, and those responsibilities have pretty much defined who you are. Is that right? (Intentionally asking a closed-ended question simply to seek confirmation.) You mentioned earlier that your mom has severe emphysema, and you are caring for her as well. Can we go back to that for a moment? Tell me more about what that has been like for you and your marriage.

The two preceding examples demonstrate that noting the abrupt change makes it less awkward, and relieves the clinician of having to find the perfect moment or easy way to slide in the questions that do not otherwise fit into normal conversation.

Difficult Questions
Even more challenging for new clinicians is the task of asking questions about difficult or seemingly taboo topics such as suicide, homicide, sexual orientation, sexual functioning and sexual practices, drugs and alcohol, and hallucinations and delusions.

Many practitioners-in-training neglect to raise these topics in initial interviews; anecdotally, the most common reasons for this include "It didn't come up"; "It didn't seem relevant to the reason the client was referred"; "The patient didn't give me any reason to believe that suicide (homicide, drugs/alcohol, hallucinations, delusions, etc.) is something to be concerned about with him"; "I didn't get a chance to ask." The fact is, clinicians most likely will not be *given* a chance to ask these questions, but rather, need to create the opportunity to ask these questions. In keeping with the principle of forming clients' expectations for the interview, as described earlier, simply telling clients that some questions to be asked are routinely asked of all patients will decrease personalization of the questions.

Another technique that facilitates inquiry about difficult questions is that of prefacing questions with statements that suggest others sometimes have thoughts, feelings, or behaviors consistent with what will be asked. Doing so normalizes the individual's experiences, rather than creating suspicion or embarrassment for the client, as to why the clinician asked. Dr. Smith addressed the question of suicide with Mrs. Giunardini as follows, "Sometimes when people are feeling hopeless or helpless about their circumstances, they can feel trapped and at a loss for what to do. When feeling this way, some people have thoughts about hurting or killing themselves; have you ever had any similar thoughts?" This closed-ended question will likely result in a "yes" or "no" answer. Dr. Smith would then respond with more specific questions, if necessary. Suggesting that others have experienced suicidal thoughts gives permission to clients to reveal they have also had these thoughts, without feeling unique or deviant.

Questions of sexual orientation, sexual functioning (interest in sexual activity; pleasure gained or difficulty with sexual functioning; menopause), frequency and carefulness of sexual activity, and other sexual practices are often more difficult for new clinicians or practitioners-in-training to ask than they are difficult for clients to answer. Surprisingly, many physicians and other health care professionals do not inquire about this facet of patients' quality of life either, unless it directly relates to patients' chief complaints. Assuming that reasonably good rapport has been established and clinicians are sensitive to the background, history, and reason for the assessment, asking questions about sexual functioning does not need to be threatening to either party. In fact, some patients are thrilled that someone has asked them about this aspect of their life.

Clients may have had concerns or questions they were not sure were appropriate to address, or may positively receive such questions simply because they appreciate their clinicians' sensitivity to personal preferences and individual differences. As such, the best way to approach such topics is to do so in a straightforward manner, with the same tone, intonation, and comfort level used to inquire about less seemingly taboo subjects, such as sleeping habits. Here, some cognitive restructuring might be necessary for clinicians to recognize that asking persons about depressed thoughts or worst fears is equally as personal as asking about sexual behavior!

The same principles and techniques recommended for inquiry about sexual functioning and suicidal thoughts are also useful for asking about drug and alcohol use, deviant behavior, arrest histories, and hallucinations and delusions. Sensitive, yet direct questioning about these topics decreases the awkwardness that could otherwise result from trying to slip these questions in or indirectly assessing these aspects of clients' past or present behaviors. A common barrier to initiating these questions, besides feeling uncomfortable with the practice, is making the assumption that the behavior or topic is not relevant for a particular client. Therefore, asking questions directly minimizes the chance that the clinician will be corrected for misattributions or assumptions that could lead the client to distrust the therapist. The moral of this discussion also serves as a word of caution: *Do Not Assume Anything About Anyone!!!* Aside from the professional and ethical responsibility to be culturally sensitive to clients, and to minimize biases and stereotype-based judgments, clinicians are often surprised by the unassuming middle-aged professional who reveals a long-standing habit of marijuana use, or the young law student who reveals delusional thinking or non-drug-related hallucinations.

Ending the Interview

As the time draws near the end of interview sessions, clinicians are encouraged to provide at least a 10- to 15-minute notification to clients to ensure that time is allotted for proper closure. Clinicians may want to ask if any pertinent topics have not been addressed, so that clients have the opportunity to fill in any blanks they perceive, or initiate discussion they had not approached earlier. Clinicians might find it beneficial to ask the question, "Is there anything that I haven't asked you that perhaps I should have?"

Within this closing time frame, clinicians should also review data they gathered to ensure they covered all aspects of their client's life, relevant to the chief complaint. Clinicians are encouraged to ask themselves if they inquired about all domains of the biopsychosocial model, including current and developmental perspectives; the topography (stimuli, responses, consequences) of the problematic behavior and adaptive or maladaptive coping efforts, and information across situations and settings. Permission should be verbally requested for clinicians to contact their clients, if further questions arise in reviewing interview and assessment materials. Finally, clients should be given an additional opportunity to ask questions, after clinicians review the assessment process and the remaining steps of the assessment process to follow.

Collecting Additional Information

Once the assessment interview is completed, clinicians must review data gained from the session(s) to ensure completion of material and to evaluate hypotheses originally generated. At this point, clinicians continue with the problem-solving process to evaluate what hypotheses about their clients were supported or unsupported, and to reevaluate their goals and possible obstacles. Using the brainstorming techniques in the generation-of-alternatives phase of problem solving, clinicians should consider what additional information or from what additional sources should confirming or disconfirming information be sought. Clinicians need to consider the possible utility of incorporating other assessment techniques, informants, methods of evaluation, or time points to complete the assessment to answer the overall referral question. Review of the methods and practices of assessment techniques described in Chapter 7, such as observation, projective and objective testing, will remind readers of some options that are available.

Drawing Conclusions and Giving Feedback

The assessment concludes with development of conclusions or recommendations based on the information that has been gathered. The next procedural step is to use that information for feedback to relevant parties. Providing feedback is essential to completing an assessment. The information derived from an evaluation is only as good as the evaluator's ability to convey the essence of the individual's functioning to those who requested the evaluation, and to the patient, if relevant. The results and impressions from a formal assessment are usually communicated in the form of a written report or a summary report, and verbal feedback.

The Written Report

Where and to whom a report goes depends largely on who requested the evaluation in the first place. The main three scenarios for report delivery include providing written feedback to (a) another treating nonpsychologist professional who requested the assessment to aid in the care of the patient (physician, school, courts or legal representative), (b) the client or the client's parents (in the case of minors), (c) the clinician's own records, if the evaluation was intended to aid the clinician in the patient's treatment planning, and (d) to another psychologist or mental health professional who does not conduct the type of assessment required for this client.

Referrals requested by other professionals to aid in their treatments or care of patients, obviously require formal reports with details about the assessment conducted, tests, inventories and questionnaires administered, diagnoses, clinical impressions, and recommendations, if relevant. To release such a report, clients must provide informed consent and appropriate releases of information forms, as discussed earlier. These forms are required even if the referral source is the reason the client ended up in your office.

When providing an evaluation for another service provider, it is wise to clarify with the referral source which of you will provide the patient with direct feedback. This should be determined prior to evaluating the client, so that this information can be incorporated in the informed consent and subsequent patient-evaluator discussions. In many cases, nonpsychology professionals appreciate their psychology colleagues conducting the feedback session and answering necessary questions, since such questions are likely to be beyond their expertise. In other cases, the psychological evaluation was conducted as part of a greater multidisciplinary assessment, and therefore, it might not be in the patient's best interest to receive partial information separate from other clinical feedback. Because feedback is critical, everyone's roles and functions must be clearly determined. Most importantly, psychologists have an ethical obligation to ensure proper use of clinical assessment outcome data, and responsible care for their clients.

Some referral sources recommend that clients seek evaluations to aid in their own search for care. A physician might suggest to a client that the difficulties she is reporting about doing the schoolwork in her adult learning program might signify learning problems. The physician might then suggest that a psychologist could evaluate her for a possible learning disorder; in which case, recommendations may be available to facilitate her success in school. The patient is technically the end-user or end-recipient of the assessment in this case, not the referral person. It is most likely not appropriate to provide the client with a detailed report because technical information could easily be misinterpreted or misused, and possibly be harmful. In this scenario, it is likely that clinicians would provide the client with a brief version, or summary, of the findings with specific recommendations. The evaluator would maintain the formal report in the client's record. A summary might include a list of the tests conducted and what their general purposes are, a diagnosis, a summary of clinical impressions, and a detailed list of recommendations. Clients can always choose to have a complete formal report sent to another professional at a later date. Formal reports, accompanied by appropriate releases of information forms, are sent directly from one professional to another. In the case previously mentioned, the client may decide to have a report sent to her primary caregiver (referral source), adult learning program, or guidance counselor, or not to send anyone a report and independently follow up on the evaluator's recommendations.

In any case, it is never good practice, nor ethical to provide clients or untrained (nonpsychological) professionals with raw data from evaluations, or in many cases, numbers (test results) that are not easily understandable without some sophistication and written and verbal explanation. Likewise, testing and assessment reports should not be given to patients without providing proper verbal feedback and giving the client the opportunity to ask questions, clarify understanding, and discuss the findings with the qualified mental health professional. Verbal feedback will be discussed in more detail later.

Tips for Successful Report Writing
To be most useful to professionals and laypersons, reports should be clearly written, logical, well organized, and user friendly. An assessment course, supervisors, and practice will provide you with various report models and development of your own report structure. The following tips are based on years of review of helpful and unhelpful reports, reports by seasoned professionals, and reports by clinicians-in-training. These tips apply to most types of written

report, regardless of the report recipient, referral question, format, or template used.

Some recommendations might seem to be incredibly obvious statements, but we mention them here because we have come across more than a few reports that led us to believe that even what we consider obvious should not be taken for granted. Reports should always be *proofread and checked for spelling and grammar* errors. Yes, we have received professional reports that did not met these basic criteria. Reports that *minimize professional jargon,* or psychology vocabulary that can be replaced by simple layperson terms, are easier to read and understand and will be more helpful to most audiences. Overall, the *language* in reports should be intelligently simple and not reflect heavy use of a thesaurus.

The structure of the report can be more easily followed when evaluators *use headings* to guide readers through the report, or allow them to skip to specific sections of interest easily. Mrs. Giunardini's report provides an example of headings that might be appropriate for a clinical intake assessment. Other headings were discussed earlier in this chapter. While headings help organize a report, keeping report lengths within reasonable limits is also important. We cannot provide an ideal length of report because this will vary depending on the referral question, the depth of the assessment, the comprehensiveness of the evaluation conducted, and the complexity of the client. Yet, while writing, it is prudent to try to *get to the point* quickly and include *only relevant information.*

Consistent with the advice provided in the problem-solving model of clinical decision making, the content of reports should *focus on facts and data,* rather than assumptions. A written report should provide the reader with knowledge about how the results (what tests were given) and clinical impressions were obtained; readers should be able to *clearly differentiate data from interpretations and impressions.* Clinicians are cautioned to *be very selective about raw data* that they incorporate into a written report. Often, the raw data (numbers, test scores) are of limited value to nonpsychologists or mental health professionals and can lead to confusion, misinterpretation, or misuse instead of looking impressive, as some might intend. *Incorporating a few examples of relevant client comments and description of behaviors* can aid readers in concretely recognizing what the evaluator is referring to, and can almost bring the report alive—again making the report more user friendly. When standardized tests or inventories are used, *providing references and comparative scores* (normative scores, population to whom data was compared) helps professionals form their own impressions about the findings. Similarly, reports on obscure problems might benefit from being supplemented with literature references to substantiate claims made and provide the referral source with additional information to facilitate understanding. *Discussing strengths* rather than just weaknesses or limits is also important to ensure that the report is balanced, does not present or create biases, and that the referral source can identify clients' resources that may aid in treatment delivery. Most importantly, the report must *address and hopefully answer the referral question* (the goal of the assessment)!

Many referral sources are most interested in the answer to their question: "What is the problem and what can be done about it?" It is common for non-mental health professionals and laypersons to immediately skip to the clinical impressions, diagnosis, summary, and recommendations sections. So be sure that if someone only reads these sections, the information presented there is completely consistent with the rest of the report. Since recommendations are typically most sought after, more extensive advice is proposed here.

Clinicians should always *include a comprehensive list of recommendations* for the client across all relevant biopsychosocial aspects assessed (if faulty cognitions are noted, give recommendations to change them; if behaviors are problematic, interventions to target behavior change should be provided), referral source (if relevant), and family or school system or environment (if appropriate). Recommendations that *focus on what clients can learn to change or control* are most helpful, rather than recommendations that suggest changes in environment or significant others who are not contracted for treatment (spouse should be less accepting of patient's drinking and erratic behaviors; coworkers should be advised to ignore hostile outbursts). In some cases, environmental changes might be appropriate, especially for helping to change child and adolescent behaviors, or to assist in modifying behaviors of elder adults under residential nursing care or home care by others. In these cases, evaluators might recommend interventions that require cooperation of patients' social systems, if individual change is less likely to be successful through individual intervention.

Overall, *recommendations, conclusions, and data must be consistent.* No recommendations should be made that do not have some justification in the data provided. In other words, the recommendation to "increase social interactions with peers" should not be made, unless the clinician has inquired about the client's social interactions, has data or self-report information to suggest that current social interactions are insufficient, and that the current social limits are impacting on the reason for the referral. Prior to any and every release of a report, clinicians ought to review the whole report and then reread the recommendations to verify that the claims made are justified.

Comprehensive recommendations are critical to ensuring the utility of the report provided to the referral source. If clinicians simply elaborate on history, background, and the details of the already evident problem, what to do about the problem remains unknown. This is also why *clinicians should not recommend further testing* if their role was to evaluate the client as needed. If further testing is needed, evaluators should either do it or refer the client within the assessment process. In many cases by using the clinical decision-making model, evaluators can recognize early in the assessment process that they are not the best person to accept the referral. In some cases, evaluators may later learn more about a client and decide they cannot conduct necessary portions of the evaluation. These evaluators should make necessary provisions for the clients to gain the additional testing or assessment, and then incorporate the additional information into their report.

Verbal Feedback

Patients require a thorough explanation of how diagnostic and clinical impressions were formed, what recommendations were made, and why. The utmost care is needed to communicate sensitive results and troublesome findings. Many of the same suggestions made for written reports are offered for the verbal feedback session: clarity, concrete and simple language, minimal to no jargon, logical presentation, and provision of a balance between clients' strengths and weaknesses or deficits.

Clients are likely to have questions following the feedback session, and clinicians should be available for these questions to ensure proper debriefing and understanding of assessments. However, clinicians need to reinforce the professional-patient roles; the professional should maintain the role of evaluator, not therapist, and not primary care provider. Clients at times may need direction following assessments. Similarly, clinicians must also be aware that clients have various motives for assessment and depending on the outcomes, may or may not agree with the findings. Clients who do not agree with assessment findings may attempt to persuade evaluators to change reports in some ways, or may try to persuade evaluators that their impressions were incorrect for one reason or another. If either of these scenarios arise, evaluators are reminded to rely on effective clinical skills to manage such sessions, and to use the problem-solving model to identify problems, obstacles, goals, and solutions to these problems. It is wise risk management to make note in the client's clinical record of any points of disagreement that were discussed during the verbal feedback session.

Verbal communication to professionals often precedes their receipt of the formal written report. It is imperative that clinicians are prepared to provide diagnoses, brief clinical impressions, and recommendations when phone calls to referral sources are placed. In other words, be prepared to answer questions and provide substantiated claims, not first impressions or hypotheses regarding patients' problems. This advice is predicated on the fact that most professionals are very busy, and while the formal written report will be useful to have in patients' charts for future reference, they are more interested in getting their questions answered immediately than reviewing 5 to 10 pages of psychological prose. Also, time constraints might require their immediate action, rather than afford them the luxury of waiting for reports to be completed and sent. As such, important decisions are often made based on clinicians' follow-up phone calls, prior to receiving the entire clinical report.

Several years ago a graduate student returned a phone call to a physician about the status of her evaluation with a patient being considered for a bone marrow transplant. The patient had been ornery and noncompliant with nursing staff, and therefore, the physician was not optimistic that she would follow detailed instructions pre-, post- and during the procedure. The psychology extern was consulted and asked to provide an opinion on this person's candidacy for the transplant, given what is known to be involved. The student called the physician after an unsuccessful attempt to meet with the patient. She told him, "I went to her room twice to try to meet with her and she turned me away both times after very brief encounters. So far, I haven't been able to evaluate her as I normally have evaluated your other patients." Before the student could finish her commentary, the physician responded, "Thank you. That's all I needed to know!" The student nearly panicked because the physician was making life-affecting decisions based on her verbal feedback, without her intending for it to be taken as such. Fortunately, she was being supervised in a teaching hospital and the supervisor (SHF) could contact the physician to further explain and evaluate the situation.

Summary

Assessment and evaluation is a complex process that goes beyond knowing what tests to give, how to administer and score them, and giving a diagnosis. This chapter focused on the logistics of how to "put it all together." The problem-solving model of clinical decision making (A. M. Nezu & Nezu, 1989; A. M. Nezu et al., 1997) was offered as a logistical strategy to structure and organize clinical thinking, and to guide clinicians in integrating complex information. The case of Mrs. Giunardini, a 32-year-old female faced with a time-sensitive life-altering decision, was presented to illustrate the procedural logistics of actually conducting a clinical assessment and creating a clinical intake report.

Procedural logistics of an assessment include socializing patients to the clinical process and procedures, obtaining informed consent and releases of and for information, discussing limits and parameters of confidentiality, and creating a decision plan for the approach to the assessment. Once these issues have been covered, most assessments begin with some form of an interview. The goal of the assessment, determined by the reason for the referral, will dictate the type and format of interview that is most appropriate: diagnostic, mental status or general clinical interview; structured, semistructured, or unstructured interview.

Interviewing is a complex skill that requires much rehearsal and role-playing, clinical practice, supervision, and critical thinking. Interviews are most often the basis for all subsequent assessments, or serve alone as the comprehensive method of assessment. Clinicians, therefore, must learn to make clinical decisions within the interview that allow them to keep the session focused, inquire about all aspects of the biopsychosocial systems model, maintain good rapport and trust, and develop collaboration with the client. Throughout the interview, clinicians are encouraged to be observant of verbal and nonverbal behavior, and clients' reactions to questions, tests, or other interactions within each session.

Discussion of Mrs. Giunardini's case illustrated what we consider to be the essence of clinicians' interview tools—questions, prompts, and transitions. Attention to asking difficult questions was given, due to our witnessing the difficulty that many practitioners-in-training experience surrounding sensitive topics. Interviewers were reminded to consciously review the data gained in an interview session prior to dismissing the client to identify and fill gaps in the data. Lastly, the topic of feedback was addressed, with suggestions for preparing user-friendly written reports and for providing verbal feedback.

PART 111

BASIC TECHNIQUES FOR CLINICIANS— INTERVENTION

Developing a
Case Conceptualization

9
Chapter

The basis of any psychotherapeutic intervention is the case conceptualization. In a useful conceptualization, the clinician takes the accumulated data and forms a model for understanding and explaining the patient's difficulties, as well as selecting and timing strategies that will be relevant and effective. A useful conceptualization is developed and revised in a step-by-step fashion as information is gathered and hypotheses are tested. The clinician shares this conceptualization with the patient, typically using common language or illustrations rather than professional technical terms. In this way, the clinician engages the patient in self-examination and planning for change.

Learning Objectives

At the end of this chapter, the reader should be able to:

- Understand what is meant by "case conceptualization."
- Discuss how the case conceptualization relates to the biopsychosocial model.
- Describe the functional purpose of a case conceptualization.
- Identify five conceptual approaches or styles among therapists.
- Understand case conceptualization as an active process.

It is Friday evening at the Albert Ellis Institute in New York. Dr. Ellis is sitting on the platform with a volunteer "patient" from the audience. The volunteer is talking about how she has difficulty getting her schoolwork finished. Ellis listens briefly and then responds:

> *"You are being a perfectionist. You are telling yourself that you MUST do perfectly well or there is something terribly wrong with you."*
>
> *"But" the volunteer patient starts to explain, "I need to do the very best that I can. This is what my professors expect, this is what my parents have always expected, and I believe that I should not be satisfied with being mediocre."*
>
> *"Your problem is that you say that you MUST be perfect rather than accepting that you are a fallible human being and that if there are times that your work is less than perfect, you will survive. If you said that you would prefer to do well, but you didn't always have to be perfect, what difference would that make in your life?"*
>
> *"I guess I wouldn't always be beating myself up."*
>
> *"Yes. You believe that if you did something less than perfectly, it would be awful and that it would prove that there was something terribly wrong with you."*
>
> *"But that is what I was always told."*
>
> *"Just because someone told you some nutty thing about always having to be perfect, you don't have to believe it."*

The preceding interchange could be viewed in many different ways. On one hand, a fan or believer in Ellis's approach to therapy might view this as an elegant and parsimonious intervention. A critic, on the other hand, might decry the lack of information gathering, the lack of rapport building, the lack of a therapeutic contract, and the very directive and forceful nature of the intervention. The critics would find fault and perhaps even resent Ellis's apparent "shooting from the hip" without establishing a solid database. If you can imagine being the volunteer patient described in this vignette, or perhaps imagine your best friend as the volunteer patient, how do you think you would react? Would you appreciate the direct and incisive feedback, or would you want to run screaming from the room to warn others to stay away? If you think the approach might be useful for some people but not others, who do you think would be most likely to benefit?

We can also view the interchange as a superb example of case conceptualization. It would be incorrect to view what Ellis did as "shooting from the hip." Ellis's conceptualization is based on two psychological elements (Ellis, 1962). The first element is his basic A→ B→ C model of the relationship between cognition, affect, and behavior. The patient's response to the situation (A) of work requirements is influenced by her beliefs (B) about the need for perfection, and results in her work-related emotional and behavioral paralysis (C). So the sequence is A = I have an assignment for school. B = I must do it perfectly well or something awful would happen to me, and C = I ruminate and procrastinate about it or spend inordinate amounts of time on the assignment, no matter how minimal the assignment.

A second psychological element of Ellis's conceptualization is the assumption that all problems can be broken down into three types of beliefs: (1) demands on self (I must be perfect), (2) demands from the others (They should not make demands on me), and (3) the view that the world should be fair (The world should be fair and equitable and not burden me as it does). With these two elements as a base, we can see that Ellis's psychological interventions come quickly and clearly as a result of his conceptualization of the patient's problem. This is, of course, coupled with his 50 years of clinical experience.

Contemporary psychotherapy has taken a decidedly scientific turn as we enter the twenty-first century. The definition of the therapist as simply a good listener whose job is to help the patient *feel better* has changed to the definition of the therapist as an active and directive participant-observer whose job is to help the patient to use empirically supported techniques to change and to *get better*. Indeed, long before the advent of managed care, many therapists approached therapy by developing an overall conceptualization that integrated multiple systems or levels of functioning of each individual.

What Is Case Conceptualization?

Case conceptualization refers to a systematic and comprehensive process of organizing and explaining the information pertinent to each patient. Conceptualization generally involves building a model that can be viewed and examined in three dimensions and in multiple layers of detail. Whenever architects design a building or sculptors plan a large work, they build a model in clay, wood, plaster or, more recently, as a three-dimensional computer model.

The model helps the artist visualize the various elements of the sculpture. The architect can examine the size, shape, proportion, fit, and position of the structure relative to other structures in the environment. Blueprints of the plumbing, electrical, ventilation, and structural systems, as well as a layout for finishing details such as paint colors and landscaping may be part of the model, showing how all the systems will work together in one structure. Changes can be made when the model comes out of the ether, off the page or drafting board, and into the real world. The clinical case conceptualization does the same thing for the therapist. The development of a treatment conceptualization is a matter of psychological model-building. Without this model, the therapist is forced to fly blind and to randomly attempt interventions without an order, focus, or goal.

Historically, psychological model-building has been based primarily on theory. The therapist's approach to case conceptualization reflected his or her affiliation with a particular theory or school of therapy. The quality of the psychological model depended on the therapist's skill and flair for applying the concepts of a specific system. Contemporary conceptualization, however, has gradually shifted away from a relatively narrow theoretical orientation toward a broader, more comprehensive biopsychosocial model of human behavior. The biopsychosocial model emphasizes scientifically grounded concepts and multiple layers or interacting systems to explain human behavior and psychopathology. Psychological factors do not exist in isolation from biological and social elements of the patient's life, but rather interact in ways that affect the whole system. In the psychological realm, affect, cognition, and behavior are all dynamic and interacting subsystems that can be detailed as parts of the overall conceptual model. All assumptions of the model either have a clear scientific basis, or are posited as hypotheses to be tested for accuracy and validity.

This scientific approach to conceptualization is, of necessity, based on the assessment data from family and developmental histories, test data, interview material, reports of previous therapists or other professionals, and information gleaned from the patient's experiences with educational, legal, military and other cultural systems. It takes into account the patient's life context, stated problems, strengths, and deficits. It is also revised as needed throughout the treatment.

The conceptualization must meet several criteria. It must be specific, concrete, coherent, consistent, and reasonable. Conceptualizations that are vague, global, and abstract are far less useful. The conceptualization must be simple and parsimonious. The more complex, the less valuable it is. The conceptualization must have an internal consistency. When there are large gaps in the conceptualization, the clinician must account for these gaps. To fill in the gaps with theoretical constructs such as "unconscious" is highly questionable. To concretize the conceptualization, it can be illustrated or diagrammed. This picture or image can then be shared with the patient.

Even though case conceptualization is essential to effective therapy, it is rarely taught in graduate programs. Instead, students learn about different systems and schools of therapy without necessarily learning conceptualization skills. Then, as novice therapists, they learn a list of techniques for "doing" therapy in a cookbook fashion, as if all problems could be addressed with the same techniques applied in a formulaic fashion. To get some sort of result, the therapist may resort to the "shovel" approach in applying techniques. The basic notion of the shovel approach to therapy is that if enough techniques are thrown at a patient, something may stick or work. A case conceptualization, instead, provides direction and logic to the interventions selected for the particular problems of a particular patient.

Functional Purpose of a Case Conceptualization

The functional purpose of a case conceptualization is to promote effective and efficient use of therapeutic resources. If the therapist has a treatment conceptualization, the therapy will be proactive and not simply reactive. In fact, a conceptualization-based approach makes treatment easier. It provides the therapist and the patient with a road map for their meetings and interactions. The plans for therapy, the types of changes that patients can reasonably expect, and the path to reach the goals all derive from the therapist's formulation or the case conceptualization. Rather than simply restating the patient's words, or reflecting the patient's mood, the active therapist will share hypotheses, use guided discovery, encourage the patient, serve as a resource person, be a case manager, and, in certain limited cases, be an advocate for the patient. Only with a clear case conceptualization can the therapist confidently choose when and how to apply these various intervention strategies.

We cannot assume that a single size (intervention) fits all and that just because a model works with one disorder (e.g., depression) that it will work equally well without modification on another (e.g., anxiety). The treatment chosen in one case may be contraindicated in another. Even if the disorder is the same, the treatment plan for one person may not look at all like the plan for another. Each treatment conceptualization is unique, reflecting the particular details and specific issues of the individual patient and his or her circumstances.

If the conceptualization is accurate, it will do three things. First, it will account for the patient's past behavior. Second, it will make sense of the patient's present behavior. And, finally, it will allow prediction of the patient's future behavior. Case conceptualization is essential to developing an understanding of patients, their life, their home and work situations, their interpersonal style, their problems and the strategies that may be most appropriate for facilitating change.

The demands of contemporary psychotherapy often call for a time-limited approach to therapy. This is not because of the forced limits of managed care but because empirical data suggest that time-limited therapy is effective. Efficacy research protocols generally involve around 12 to 20 sessions, over a period of no more than 20 weeks. In clinical practice, however, the course of treatment is not limited to 20 weeks. For certain patients, the length of therapy may be 6 sessions; for other patients, 50 sessions. The length of the therapy, the frequency of the sessions, and the session length are all negotiable and based on the conceptualization of the patient's functioning. The problems being worked on, the skills of the patient and of the therapist, the time available for therapy, and the financial resources must be factored into the conceptualization, and all have the potential to dictate the parameters of treatment.

Conceptual Approaches

The novice therapist can learn a great deal by observing an experienced therapist at work. The experienced therapist often makes therapy look deceptively easy. Supervisees frequently ask, "How do you know what interventions have the greatest utility with a specific patient? How do you recognize the best time to use a particular strategy or specific intervention? How far do you press a particular strategy or intervention until you either revise it or abandon it?" The simplest response would be the old cliché, "Therapy is an art form, not a science." Students just have to study the art and, if talented, one day will magically "understand" how to emulate the master therapist. Alternatively, if they believe that the therapeutic process needs to be scientific, they will examine the process, identify the elements that combine for successful therapy, and evaluate their efforts in a systematic way.

The conceptual approach can be related to the therapist's style or philosophy of therapy. We can identify five types of therapist based on their conceptual style, which transcends any particular theoretical background, training, or practice. They are the theoretician, the technician, the magician, the politician, and the clinician.

The theoretician is well grounded in the theory and research of therapy, but does not believe that one has to gain skills in therapy to do therapy. They operate on the assumption that if the theory is correct then the implementation is a mere technical maneuver that anyone of normal intelligence can implement. These individuals spend their time teaching about therapy, discoursing about therapy, theorizing about therapy, and researching therapy, but not much time doing therapy. Instead, they focus on developing and elaborating a particular theory.

The technician is the therapist who acquires specific skills, regardless of the model. They can do therapy "by the book." That is, they do a little bit of this and a little bit of that, emulating the teachers whom they regard as masters of a particular skill. They go to conferences and attend numerous skills workshops so that they can enhance their bag of technical tricks. They do Gestalt work, behavioral work, and analytic work, and so on. These individuals often term what they do as "eclectic." What they lack, however, is a unifying conceptualization of development, behavior, and approach to therapy. They try to do what they believe works, without a healthy skepticism about the potential limits of their methods. They view philosophical or theoretical discussions as distracting and boring and avoid them.

The magician doesn't need skills. They are charismatic, so that an hour a week in their aura is, by itself therapeutic. Like the theoretician, they would not think of lowering themselves by learning mundane technique. They don't try to emulate the experts because they believe themselves to be experts with the therapeutic relationship. When pressed, they may label their work as "supportive." They often pride themselves on having avoided extensive therapeutic training, and focus on their ability to discuss esoteric therapeutic issues in obscure journals. In the view of the magician, the mental "laying on of hands" is enough to effect a therapeutic change. They believe that therapy will just happen by force of their emotionally provocative presence.

The politician is technique and brand-oriented, and practices what is most popular at the moment. Whether Primal Scream, marathon encounter groups, or cognitive-guided disco-behavior therapy is used, the politician is on the cutting edge of political correctness and popularity. They are presently waiting to see what is next on the horizon and will be first in line with the latest movement. They don't wait for scientific results to accumulate; they embrace the latest and just move on when public interest wanes.

The fifth type of therapist, the clinician, combines some elements of all five types in his or her philosophy of therapy and approach to conceptualization. The clinician has a theoretical understanding of development and behavior, therapeutic skills, an understanding of the therapeutic techniques that work within that framework, and can develop and maintain a strong working relationship with the patient. This type of therapist is far more likely to attend both theoretical meetings and skills sessions at a conference. These therapists are willing to combine modalities such as behavioral-marital therapy, and try to develop models that are broader in depth and scope. The clinician learns about what is popular and cutting edge, but evaluates the evidence before adopting new techniques or methods.

The Conceptualization Process

The conceptualization is an ongoing process of formulating and testing hypotheses. The process begins with the first contact with the patient either directly, through significant others, or through a referral from a colleague. The process will, of necessity, go through several incarnations. There will be the initial conceptualization, followed by all the requisite revisions and emendations made as additional data is collected. This data may come through patient report, or through the in vivo experience of the therapeutic collaboration. If the conceptualization is cast in granite, the therapy will be limited and rigid. The static conceptualization will limit the therapist's ability to account for actions, thoughts, and behavior that emerge in the therapy. With a rigid conceptualization as the primary tool for guiding therapy, the therapist is like the carpenter whose only tool is a hammer, and every new development becomes a nail to be hit with that hammer.

One difficulty in the conceptualization process for many clinicians is that they accept patient complaints as problem statements. If a patient comes in with the complaint of depression, the therapist has to help the patient identify the problems that come together to cause the state that we have learned to label as depression. The patient's low self-esteem, pessimism, hopelessness, decision-making difficulty, decreased libido, or sleep difficulties are the problems. By delineating the problems and not focusing on the complaints, the therapist can examine and evaluate causal or maintenance factors in the patient's life for each problem. Similarly, the patient who reports having panic attacks needs to have the broad term of panic broken up into the component problems.

Effective conceptualization starts with the premise that behavior has reason, meaning, and purpose. Behavior is not random, but is guided by what has been learned, or what has been acquired through conditioning. Behavior is affected by biological, social, and psychological systems and serves a function within these systems. The comprehensive conceptualization will consider psychological factors in the context of other biological and social information. In the next step of the conceptualization process, the therapist develops hypotheses about the reasons for a particular patient's behavior in a particular context and what maintains the patient's thoughts, actions, and emotions. If on target, the conceptualization can also suggest the course of therapy, the strategies for intervention, and the most promising interventions. For maximum impact and effectiveness, the therapist will build a treatment plan and then use a range of skills and techniques to implement the treatment. Specific techniques or combinations of techniques are selected to suit the purpose and goals of therapy, the therapist's conceptualization of the problem(s), the patient's readiness and motivation for change, the resources available in the patient's environment, and the therapist's skill and style.

Understanding Schemas

At the core of the psychological component of conceptualization is a grasp of the patient's schema, or cognitive templates for perceiving, organizing, and responding to experience. Some schemas are broad and include a variety of more specific schemas (e.g., the schema for pets is very broad and might include a large variety of creatures, from parakeets to tarantulas). Some schemas are organized around polar opposites, particularly schema for emotionally relevant concepts. The schema for safety is highly related to the schema for danger. If you happen to be vision-impaired and rely on your trained seeing-eye dog for your mobility, then your schema for pet is highly active and your sense of safety is associated with being near your dog. If your dog goes missing, this would activate your schema for danger. But, if you grew up in a family that disliked pets and feared dogs, your schema for dogs might include beliefs such as "stay away from that animal or he will bite you!" Any dog, even a fluffy miniature poodle peeking out from a woman's purse might trigger your schema for danger. In the latter example, the schema for pets does not include an association to a schema for safety.

Operative or Salient Schemas

It is essential to understand the patient's operative schemas. Particular schemas may engender a great deal of affect and be emotionally bound by both the individual's past experience and by the sheer weight of the time in which that belief has been held. In addition, the perceived importance and credibility of the source from whom the schemas were acquired plays a part in their strength and durability. There is a cognitive element to the schemas that pervades the individual's thoughts and images. With the proper training, individuals can be helped to describe schemas in great detail or to deduce them from behavior or automatic thoughts. Finally, there is a behavioral component that involves the way the belief system governs the individual's responses to a particular stimulus or set of stimuli. For some patients, the sequence may be cognitive-affective-behavioral; for another patient, the therapeutic sequence would be behavioral-cognitive-affective.

Inasmuch as the schemas become, in effect, how people define themselves, both individually, and as part of a group, they are important to understand and factor into the treatment conceptualization. They may be said to be unconscious, using a definition of the unconscious as "ideas we are unaware of," or "ideas that we are not aware of simply because they are not in the focus of attention but in the fringe of consciousness" (Campbell, 2003).

Inactive schemas are called into play to control behavior in times of stress. Stressors will evoke the inactive schemas, which become active and govern behavior. When the stressor is removed, the schemas will return to their previously dormant state. Conceptually, understanding the activity-inactivity continuum explains two related clinical phenomena. The first involves the rapid, though transient, positive changes often evidenced in therapy, the so-called transference cure or flight into health. The result of this phenomenon is that a patient with clinical symptoms seems to have a partial or full recovery in a surprisingly brief period and will then seek to terminate therapy as no longer needed. What we may be seeing is the patient, under stress, responding to the activation of several dormant schemas. They may direct the patient's behavior in dysfunctional and self-destructive ways. On entering therapy and experiencing the acceptance and support of the therapist, stress is lowered, and the problematic schemas are deactivated. If, however, the patient leaves therapy without gaining the skills for coping with stress, the problem may reemerge when, and if, the stressor returns. Individuals who develop effective coping strategies may be able to deal with stress throughout their lives and rarely have dormant schemas activated.

Dormant Schemas

The second clinical phenomenon is the arousal of dormant schemas that cause the patient to appear, on intake or admission to the hospital, to be extremely disturbed. After brief psychotherapy, pharmacotherapy, or combination, the patient appears far better integrated, far more attentive, and far "healthier." In fact, after the stress is removed, the therapist may question the existence of the psychopathology.

The particular extent of effect that a schema has on an individual's life depends on several factors. The first issue is to evaluate how strongly the schema is held. Schemas that are seen as part of the patient's view of self are likely to be more strongly held. These schemas are difficult to change as they are how individuals define themselves and see themselves in the context of their world. These compelling schemas are often easily seen by the therapist but may be the hardest to address and change. After all, individuals who hold onto their beliefs even after being threatened with death are labeled *hero* or *martyr*.

A related issue is how essential the individual sees particular schema to be to their safety, well-being, or existence. Does the patient engage in any disputation of one's thoughts, actions, or feelings when a particular schema is activated? This is related to the individual's previous learning vis-à-vis the importance and essential nature of a particular schema. Probably the most important issue is related to how early a particular schema was internalized. The earlier the schema was acquired, the more powerful it will be, and the greater effect it will have on the individual's behavior. Layden, Newman, Freeman, and Byers-Morse (1993) speak of the impact of an early internalized schema as being in a cloud. This schema will influence behavior, but the patient may not be aware of where the direction and power come from.

Case Illustration of Conceptualization Process

The following examples illustrate the building of a case conceptualization as data about biological, psychological, and social functioning are gathered. In the cases that follow, note the interactions between physical functioning, psychological perspectives, and role functioning and interpersonal relationships.

Example 1

Case Conceptualization Following a Suicide Attempt

Alex, a 44-year-old married male was referred for therapy by his family physician following a severe suicide attempt. He had been hospitalized for a week. The early part of the in-patient time, Alex was in a coma. It appeared that a number of psychosocial issues combined to push him over the edge. He was hopeless about his perceived business failures, his marriage, his health, and his finances, in that order. He came for his initial therapy appointment directly from the inpatient medical unit. He had refused any psychiatric consultation while in the hospital, and agreed to the therapy appointment as a condition and promise to the family physician. He came to the appointment accompanied by his mother.

First Data Point

His appointment time was 2:00 P.M. He arrived at 1:45 P.M. with his mother. Given these data, the clinician can begin

(continued)

Example 1 (Continued)

to develop conceptual hypotheses. We cannot be sure of the accuracy of the initial conceptualization. This will be confirmed as the data collection and the consultation unfold.

Working Hypotheses

- Alex follows rules (he shows up on time).
- He is a people pleaser (he does what the doctor asks).
- He is dependent (he does what he is told).
- He is unable to do things independently (he comes with his mother).
- He is overwhelmed by life (he made the suicide attempt).
- He is emotionally estranged from his wife (he is with his mother).

Can you think of any other hypotheses to propose?

Second Data Point

Alex was asked by the receptionist to complete basic demographic information forms. After these were completed, the therapist was informed and came into the waiting room to greet Alex. The therapist approached Alex, shook hands. Alex stands up in response to the greeting.

Working Hypotheses

- Alex understands social conventions (he responds to the therapist's greeting in a socially appropriate manner).
- Alex fears being scolded by his mother if he does not comply.
- Alex does not want to be embarrassed in front of the receptionist.

Can you think of any other potential hypotheses?

Third Data Point

Alex is invited into the therapist's office. At this point, his mother stands up and starts to follow Alex into the therapist's office. The therapist asks, "Can I help you?" She responds, "I'm his mother."

Working Hypotheses

- She views him as unable to care for himself (she comes with him because she thinks he needs her).
- She is a caring concerned mother (she comes with him because she does not want him to be alone with a stranger).
- She assumes that she has license to do what she wishes without asking (she comes with him, and starts into the office without an invitation).
- She blames herself for his failures and suicide attempt (she comes with him because she must now learn how to fix her mistakes).

Can you think of any other working hypotheses?

Fourth Data Point

The therapist acknowledges her and states that he would like to meet with her after meeting with her son. She turns to Alex and says, "Alex is there a problem in my coming in?" He says, "No mom. It's alright."

Working Hypotheses

- They are enmeshed (he accepts her presence because he does not see her as separate from him).
- He is afraid of her (he accepts her presence because he does not want to provoke her anger).

Example 1 (Continued)

- He is afraid of the therapist (he accepts her presence to feel safe).
- He needs her support to survive (he accepts her presence because he depends on her).
- He sees the session as potentially dangerous (he accepts her presence to avoid something bad happening to him).
- He is passive (he accepts her presence because he has no energy to resist).
- They both want to make sure that no family "secrets" are divulged. (He accepts her presence because they both must abide by this family rule.)

Do you have any other working hypotheses?

Fifth Data Point

Upon entering the office, the therapist says to both, "Please, be seated." Mother sits in the chair next to the therapist and Alex sits in a chair at a distance from the other seats.

Working Hypotheses

- He wants her to do most of the work (he lets her sit first).
- She will protect him (she sits closer, allowing Alex to be at a distance).
- She sees herself as more central (she sits closer, allowing Alex to be at a distance).
- He is willing to be in the session but does not want to be involved (Alex sits at a distance).
- She will be the main worker in the session (she sits closer, allowing Alex to be at a distance).
- Few secrets will be divulged (she is in the room).

- More will be accomplished by her being there (she wants to make sure that Alex gets help).
- Alex is gender-socialized to give the best seat to his mother (he allows her to sit first).
- She does not trust the competence of the therapist (she sits closer to ensure that he does his job).

Are there any other reasonable hypotheses?

The reader might wonder why the therapist allowed mother into this first session. The answer is an important part of the conceptualization. By allowing Alex and his mother to make this determination, the therapist gained important information regarding the degree of power that mother had in Alex's current situation. To exclude her would have spelled the end of therapy at the outset. For therapy to continue beyond Session 1, mother would need to be "cultivated" as a therapy assistant. To begin altering their system of interpersonal interaction this soon would likely result in her sabotage of therapy, either directly or indirectly, or Alex's failure to engage in therapy at all.

Sixth Data Point

When questions were addressed to Alex, his mother provided the answers.

Working Hypotheses

- He is too depressed to speak.
- He is too afraid to speak.
- He has been told by his mother that she will answer all questions so he can conserve his energy.
- He is psychotic.
- He is passive aggressive.
- He thinks the meeting is a joke.

(continued)

Example 1 (Continued)

Seventh Data Point

When the therapist addresses questions directly to Alex, his mother gets very angry stating, "Stop putting so much pressure on him. Don't you know how fragile he is?"

Working Hypotheses

- He is too weak to respond.
- She is terrified that he will die.
- She was traumatized by his suicide attempt.
- He is reluctant to assert himself with his mother present.

Eighth Data Point

Toward the end of the session, the therapist asked Alex to have a seat in the waiting room and he spoke with the mother. Although wary, she responded well when the therapist asked if she would be willing to help the therapist in working with her son. She agreed and asked what she could do. When told by the therapist that it was not clear that Alex would return for a sec-

ond session, his mother assured the therapist (her new working partner), "He'll be here."

The treatment for Alex would have to focus on any, or all, of the following with the agreement of the patient: reducing hopelessness, developing motivation for treatment, marital therapy, assertive training, building self-esteem and personal efficacy, and separating from his mother. He is still physically weak from the suicide attempt and coma, and could benefit from time off from work on a medical leave to fully recuperate. Although he has had some difficulty with his work and is sensitive to perceived failures, he is still in good standing with his employer. Both his "failure" and his "alone" schemas have been highly activated, even though his perceptions in these realms are not entirely accurate. He has the family support of his mother who will be attentive in looking after his best interests, and his children are highly concerned about his recovery. This initial model is open to revision as additional data is collected and processed.

Example 2

Case Conceptualization with a Busy Outpatient

In the next example, the same biopsychosocial strategy is used to build the case conceptualization.

First Data Point

Case conceptualization begins with an initial telephone call to the therapist's office at 3:00 P.M. on a Thursday from a prospective patient requesting an appointment.

Patient: Hello, Dr. Black?
Therapist: Yes.
Patient: You don't know me, but I was referred by Dr. Smith here in Smalltown. He is a former classmate of my primary care physician, Dr. White. Dr. Smith said that I need to see you and I would like to set up an appointment as soon as possible. What would be the earliest you could see me?
Therapist: I have two openings. How about Monday at 1:00 P.M., or Wednesday at 11:00 A.M.?

Example 2 (Continued)

Patient: Is that the earliest appointments that you have? How about Saturday? I could come in on Saturday.

Therapist: I'm sorry, but I'm not in the office on Saturday.

Patient: Well let me see. Monday at 1:00 P.M. or Wednesday at 11:00 A.M. Could you make it Monday at 11:00 A.M.?

Therapist: I'm sorry, but that time is filled.

Patient: The 1:00 P.M. is late. I'll take the Wednesday at 11:00 A.M. Wait, wait, could you make it Wednesday at 11:30 A.M.?

Therapist: No, 11:00 A.M. is the available time. I could make it Friday at 11:30 A.M.

Patient: That's too far away. I'll take the Wednesday. . . . No, make it the Monday. Yes, the Monday. I have to get my hair cut. Besides, Friday I play tennis. Wait, do you think that the later, I mean earlier, time will open up? Oh never mind.

Second Data Point

One hour later, the patient calls back.

Patient: Dr. Black, is the Wednesday still open?

Working Hypotheses

- The patient has difficulty making decisions.
- The patient expects the therapist to change to accommodate her wishes and needs.
- Her needs and wishes supersede the needs of all others.
- Therapy may be difficult in terms of setting and keeping appointments.
- The patient views the therapist as an employee.

Based on this sample of the patient's psychosocial functioning, it is likely that therapy would need to include limit setting for the protection of the therapist and to offer structure to the therapy.

The patient's social skills, fear of abandonment, dependence, obsessive-compulsive characteristics, and demanding behavior may all be part of the picture that can be used to develop the conceptualization and then become part of the problem list that can be offered as grist for the therapeutic mill.

Sharing the Conceptualization with the Patient

Because the conceptualization guides the process of therapy, the working hypotheses can be shared with the patient using a Socratic dialogue. Rather than interpreting the patient's thoughts or actions, the therapist can raise questions about the thoughts, actions, and feelings. In fact, the therapist who verbally communicates evolving hypotheses as interpretations runs the risk of appearing to be mind reading the patient's thoughts and intentions. Further, offering an interpretation such as "you seem angry" may evoke agreement from patients when they really are more annoyed than angry. It may seem simpler to accept the therapist's statement than try to disagree and seem ungrateful or contrary. The questioning format allows the patient to maintain integrity and allows the therapist to gather the most accurate data. The overall case conceptualization is thus shaped by developing and testing various hypotheses through therapeutic dialogue.

Sharing working hypotheses can sometimes be problematic for the therapist. If a depressed patient asks, "Doctor, what's wrong with me?" we may have no difficulty in offering an explanation of the diagnosis. After all, one can read about depression in any number of popular books and magazines as a widespread problem that could happen to anyone. We may have no trouble discussing or describing diagnoses of anxiety, panic, or phobia. The difficulty occurs when the diagnosis is more serious (e.g., an Axis II problem). What can the clinician say when the working diagnosis and conceptualization is Borderline Personality Disorder? Any reference to a disorder of personality is a potentially volatile statement and easily misconstrued. These categories are less well known to the general public and are filled with many pitfalls. Is the problem easily solved? Can it be treated with medication? Will it last forever? Can therapy cure this disorder? What motivation is necessary to cure or help this problem? How long will it take? Where does it come from and whose fault is it? Why is this necessarily true about me? These are all reasonable questions.

We can be evasive and take the position that these questions can only be answered over the long term of the therapy. If we are conceptualizing the patient's problems as Axis II, we know that the problem is generally more difficult to work with, motivation is low, medication is not generally useful, and so on (A. T. Beck et al., 2004). Because of problems in defining the Axis II categories, the sharing of a diagnostic label is probably less helpful to the patient than a descriptive explanation of specific problems. However, it is essential to share the conceptualization so that the patient can know what the therapist is seeing and direction of the therapy.

Using reframing, the therapist can share the conceptualization that provides a basis for understanding and organizing the symptoms and struggles of the patient, while still showing respect and regard for the patient's autonomy. In working with the schizoid patient, the therapist can highlight the patient's independence: "You tend to like doing things on your own." For the dependent patient, the therapist can say, "You prefer to have lots of others around you," or "You generally try to arrange your life to have consultants or people you can call on to help you make decisions." The patient can then be asked whether this is congruent with their personal view.

The working hypotheses are shared with the patient to foster understanding and collaboration on the most useful approach to change. One technique for sharing hypotheses is for therapists to make sketches of how they "see" the patient. These sketches force the therapist to graphically and concretely look at their conceptualization, to simplify it, and to share that model with the patient. Consider the following illustrations of sharing the working hypotheses.

Sharing a Working Hypothesis: Don (Vignette 1)

Don, a 52-year-old attorney came for therapy with diagnoses of avoidant personality disorder, obsessive compulsive personality disorder, and generalized anxiety disorder. He spent great blocks of time in activities that he recognized as wasted effort, yet necessary in his view. The therapist drew the following sketch with an explanation (Figure 9.1).

Sharing a Working Hypothesis: Don (Vignette 1) (Continued)

Figure 9.1

Search for Safe Crossing

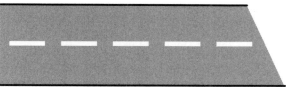

Therapist: What you describe is a life where you want to cross the road. But you're afraid that a car will race down and run you over. So to avoid that situation, you run a mile to your left to see if there are any cars coming. If there are none, you return to your starting point. But you cannot cross yet, because there may be danger. You still cannot cross the road because while you were off to the left, a car may be coming from the right. So you spend your life running miles, but never crossing the 20 feet of road. The goal of therapy will be to help you find a safe crossing without so much wasted effort.

Sharing a Working Hypothesis: Alicia (Vignette 2)

Alicia, a 29-year-old woman was diagnosed with borderline personality disorder. She reported that any stressor would cause her to "explode." She had great difficulty in interpersonal relationships. She appeared to have a very tenuous balance that was easily shaken.

The therapist drew the following Figure 9.2).

Figure 9.2

A Tenuous Balance

Therapist: From what you describe, your life is very difficult. You end up balanced on the pinnacle of the mountain. Most of your energy is spent on maintaining your balance so as to avoid falling off the mountain and being injured or killed.

The patient looked at the drawing and stated, "That's exactly how I feel."

The therapeutic goal is to help Alicia to have a firmer, more solid base.

Sharing a Working Hypothesis: Marion (Vignette 3)

Marion was the identified patient. She was 10 years old and was referred by the school because she had developed a pattern of intimidating others. She tried to intimidate the teachers and all the children in her class. She would take or break another child's things if she did not get her way. She would throw tantrums in the classroom if the teacher frustrated her wishes.

On interviewing the parents, it was clear that Marion did the same thing at home. She intimidated her mother and frightened her younger brother. Her father's response was to leave for work early in the morning and return late at night. He chose to leave the management of Marion to his wife. This was a task that was difficult for two people, impossible for one.

The therapist drew the following picture (Figure 9.3).

Figure 9.3
Family Power Structure

Therapist: Mother and brother are under the child's control. The child is the biggest figure by virtue of having so much power. Father is out of the picture. The goals of therapy, in sequence, would be, first, bring father into the family. Second, bring mother out from underfoot and have her team up with father to increase their power. This would involve helping them develop more collaborative and effective parenting skills. The third step would be to try to help Marion attain power from less dysfunctional behaviors. If, instead, the therapist tried to "shrink" Marion by taking away some of her power, a struggle would ensue. If the goal was to empower mother to remove herself from underfoot without father there to support her, she would likely be pushed down again by the child. However, if father were not available, the therapist would need to seek resources to support mother. These might include involving family, friends, or a support group as supporters. The therapist could be an important support for mother, were father not available.

Impact of Sharing the Conceptualization

As the therapist begins to share the working hypotheses and further develop the case conceptualization in partnership with the patient, we can expect that there will be an impact on the patient. Sharing a conceptualization is a powerful action that can and likely will destabilize the patient's familiar patterns. The hope is that this will promote psychological growth and change.

According to dynamic systems theorists (Caspar, Rothenfluh, & Segal, 1992; L. S. Greenberg, Rice, & Elliott, 1993; Mahoney, 1991; Schiepek, Fricke, & Kaimer, 1992), psychological growth is a lifelong process that is characterized by periods of stability and instability. Psychopathology, like any state of being, is viewed as a state of dynamic equilibrium, where the predominant state consists of well organized patterns of cognitive/affective/behavioral and somatic functioning that interfere with the individual's well-being and everyday adaptive functioning (Mahoney, 1991). Destabilization is viewed as a necessary and natural process that allows for growth and change. It is through this "shaking up" process that change can occur. Mahoney (1991) described destabilization as a period of systemwide disorder marked by increased variability in such domains as thought patterns, affect, behavior, intimacy, sleep, appetite, and somatic functioning. Given the organism's natural movement toward stability and balance, the system in disorder will attempt to move toward order.

In Mahoney's (1991) dynamic systems perspective, it is natural and healthy for an individual to resist moving too far and too quickly beyond familiar patterns, even if those patterns interfere with functioning and cause distress. Freeman and Leaf (1989) use the metaphor of a safety zone in explaining the change-related discomfort or avoidance phenomenon. Normally, each individual lives in a safety zone. The boundaries of the safety zone are often fairly well defined. For some individuals, the limits of the safety zone may be the walls of their house or the fence in the front yard. For others, the safety zone may be defined by certain people or limited emotional states. Anything outside the safety zone is labeled by the individual as "dangerous" or "threatening." Approaching the boundaries of the safety zone will elicit a withdrawal, avoidance, or safety-seeking response. If the individual stays well within the safety zone, there will be minimum anxiety.

Movement toward reestablishing order in light of the new conceptualization will occur first by using old, well-established patterns (assimilation), and if these more practiced behaviors do not work, small incremental changes will follow (accommodation). Ideally, the therapist can guide and shape the accommodations by providing the setting (a safe one), the skills (increased repertoire of techniques), and the support (encouragement of risk taking) needed for this difficult task. Providing a secure, supportive therapeutic environment and strengthening internal and external resources can prepare the patient to undergo the destabilization that accompanies reexamining and reorganizing one's concepts about oneself, other people, and one's future.

Summary

The highest order cognitive skill in psychotherapy is the ability to develop treatment conceptualizations. Too often, therapy is a reactive process; the therapist responds to what the patient brings into the therapy or the specific session. Proactive therapy involves a careful evaluation of the patient's problems based on a synthesis of the relevant data. Different therapists have different styles or approaches to building a case conceptualization. The clinician is the most thorough, incorporating some modified elements of the more limited styles of the theoretician, the magician, the politician, or the technician into a more comprehensive and systematic, scientifically grounded approach.

Case conceptualization is a process of organizing and comprehending information about each patient. It is based on data and considers the interacting biological, psychological, and social systems of the individual. The functional purpose of the case conceptualization is to promote the effective and efficient use of therapeutic resources. The conceptualization begins with the first bits of information, and as information accumulates, the therapist develops working hypotheses about why the patients respond the way they do, what were probable formative elements in the style, what are the operative schemas, and what are the best possible points of entry into the system. The therapist then shares these working hypotheses with the patient to gather more information and shape the overall conceptualization. The evolving conceptualization is a guide for determining direction and targets for therapy.

The core psychological construct in the conceptualization is the patient's schemas. The schemas are the organizing templates through which perception is built. Many schemas occur in complex combinations and permutations. The schemas may be personal, family, religious, cultural, age-related, or gender related, or any combination of these factors. The schemas become, in effect, how one defines oneself, both individually, and as part of a group. Schemas are in a constant state of change, evolution, and activation or deactivation. From the child's earliest years, there is a need to alter old schemas and develop new ones to meet the different and increasingly complex demands of the world. Schemas are not maladaptive per se, no matter how they are stated. The expression of the schemas in the person's life, and the goodness of fit with personal goals and skills, and with societal expectations are primary concerns in schema activation and modification.

Working hypotheses provide a concrete way to share the schema conceptualizations with the patient. This allows the patient to understand what the therapist understands of their problem and fosters their collaboration on building the most useful conceptualization and approach to change. A technique for sharing working hypotheses is for therapists to sketch how they perceive their patients' problems with some form of metaphor or graphic example.

When patients are engaged in conceptualizing their own functioning in new ways, some degree of destabilization can be anticipated. The therapist needs to provide structure and support during this process, and understand that disturbance in the system will produce predictable efforts to reestablish order. Guiding these efforts within a safe environment is a crucial therapeutic task.

Conceptualization is the backbone of effective and efficient therapy. With an accurate initial conceptualization, the clinician will be well prepared to implement the subsequent steps of establishing and maintaining a working relationship, selecting intervention techniques, and guiding the overall process of change.

Developing a Treatment Plan: Therapeutic Alliance and Collaborative Goals

10
Chapter

Once the clinician has a basic conceptualization of the patient's difficulties, the next question is, "Where do we go from here?" Two essential elements are needed to establish this direction: A directed plan for treatment and a collaborating relationship between or among the participants.

Learning Objectives

At the end of this chapter, the reader should be able to:
- Understand the collaborative roles of patient and therapist in a working alliance.
- Identify three core collaboration skills, why they are important, and how they are acquired.
- Translate chief complaints into measurable goals.
- Develop a problem list and a comprehensive treatment plan.
- List five techniques for building and maintaining the therapeutic relationship.
- Identify relationship beliefs that interfere with collaboration.
- Identify five indications of a good working relationship.

As we move from the abstract task of conceptualization into a practical application of treatment methods, it is important to recognize that several participants may have a stake in this transaction. All parties involved in a psychotherapeutic endeavor want the effort to be successful and worthwhile.

Patients want to relieve symptoms and find ways to improve their emotional and behavioral health. Clinicians want to help others by sharing the knowledge and technology of psychotherapy. Insurers and third-party payers want a quality service provided at lowest possible cost. Employers want their benefit programs to enhance the stability and productivity of their employees. Significant others of the patient want relief from their worries and concerns as well as improvement in the patient's personal functioning. To satisfy these many vested interests, clinicians must translate the conceptualization into a treatment plan that will focus on relevant, measurable goals and objectives.

A detailed conceptualization is an important foundation of the treatment plan, but there are also other components. Clinicians must develop an effective working relationship with their patients that engages them in their own internal process of psychological change. Rather than simply deciding what must be done *to* the patient, psychotherapy clinicians must work *with* the patient to forge an agreement concerning the goals and tasks of treatment (Bordin, 1979). Sufficient intellectual skill and cognitive effort are necessary parts of a treatment process, but interpersonal, emotional, and behavioral skills also are essential to shape those goals into an experience that is deemed worthwhile to all relevant parties.

Roles of Patient and Therapist

Because the traditional framework of psychotherapy was built on a medical model, the role of the therapist began as one of a prescriptive expert who selected interventions and applied them to a receptive patient. The patient's role within this medical formulary was to be compliant with procedures and dutiful in following recommendations. The typical clinician was an educated white male, further reinforcing the broader gender and social stereotype of a dominant authority figure. Only recently has this profile of the provider population begun to include a representative diversity. Although vestiges of this paternalistic prototype remain, therapeutic roles have shifted toward an egalitarian and collaborative relationship (e.g., A. T. Beck et al., 2004; A. T. Beck, Rush, Shaw, & Emery, 1979). In a collaborative partnership, both parties have an active role in sharing information and developing an overall plan. Collaborative treatment planning is based on direct and explicit communication about specific problems, goals, techniques, expectations, and informed consent. The therapist's role is to guide the process and protect the patient's best interests. Part of the therapist's responsibility is to create and maintain a formal record that is accessible to the patient and available at the patient's request to inform other providers who might be involved in the patient's care.

Many factors that have helped shape this paradigm shift away from an authoritarian power structure toward a more communicating partnership. One factor is that the general public is more informed about biopsychosocial processes and treatments, and thus expects a more informed discussion as part of their experience. Another factor is that consumers have been empowered by laws that stipulate their rights for accessing and controlling private health care information. In addition, the increasing demand for accessible and cost-effective treatment has vastly influenced the need to actively engage the patient as rapidly as possible. Can you think of any other reasons the roles of patient and therapist have shifted? In what ways do you think that the provider-patient relationship has retained a hierarchical power structure?

Importance of Collaboration Skills

Being able to engage patients in working together productively (the "working alliance") and maintaining a collaborative focus throughout treatment are fundamental to successful therapy. Evidence from the past several decades of psychotherapy research consistently supports the importance of these basic ingredients. Approximately 30% of the variance in patient outcome in psychotherapy can be accounted for by relationship factors that are common across different types or techniques of therapy (Lambert & Barley, 2002; Wampold, 2001). The common factors in psychotherapy, as defined by Frank and Frank (1991, p. 30), are (a) an emotionally charged, confiding relationship with a helping person; (b) a healing setting; (c) a conceptualization; and (d) a set of procedures based on the conceptualization that requires active participation of patient and therapist.

As this definition of common factors shows, the theoretical conceptualization and associated procedures are fundamental aspects of therapy, yet there is also a context of active participation in a healing enterprise. The interactions between patient and therapist, and their respective cognitive and emotional reactions to these exchanges are typically referred to as the *process* component of therapy. In a review of over 2,300 empirical studies, Orlinsky, Grawe, and Parks (1994) concluded that patient participation is the single most important element of therapy process and has the greatest single impact on the eventual outcome. Patients will participate more effectively when therapists fully set the stage with specific techniques in the context of an encouraging, positive relationship. Intervention techniques such as exposure or cognitive restructuring are important, but their impact can be enhanced, diminished, neutralized, or otherwise altered by the interpersonal and emotional relationship between patient and therapist. Similarly, the results that may be achieved through strategic use of specific techniques can reinforce a basically positive therapeutic alliance with confidence, hope, and mastery. Thus, technical strategies and relationship factors are interdependent parts in a single psychotherapy process (Safran, McMain, Crocker, & Murray, 1990; Safran & Segal, 1990).

The ability to establish and maintain collaboration with the patient is perhaps best considered as a set of skills that therapists develop and refine through training and experience. Although therapy interactions are complex and multifaceted, research has spotlighted key features and skills of effective therapists. As we might expect, therapists who are viewed by their patients as helpful interact in a positive manner, show interest, attempt to make patients feel comfortable, offer encouragement and reassurance, instill hope, show sensitivity to patient feelings, and focus on practical assistance in problem solving and coping

(Maluccio, 1979; McLeod, 1990). Cognitive-behavioral therapists tend to be more active and directive than therapists of other orientations, but they also communicate more support via encouragement, recognition of patient effort and progress, and reinforcing statements (Keijers, Schaap, & Hoogduin, 2000).

Empathy, warmth, and genuineness, some of the earliest factors identified as key to an effective therapeutic encounter, are just as relevant in cognitive-behavioral treatments (Beutler, Machado, & Allstetter Neufeldt, 1994; Keijers et al., 2000). Empathy may be communicated by acknowledgment or inquiry about the patient's emotions, along with statements that reflect acceptance or understanding of those emotions, without criticism or judgment. Behaviors that communicate genuineness include being consistent, nondefensive, re-laxed, honest, and interested (Egan, 1998). Warmth may be conveyed through respectful actions and statements, encouragement, and recognition of client effort and progress (Serran, Fernandez, Marshall, & Mann, 2003).

Acquiring Core Skills of Collaboration

It is relatively easy to identify positive interpersonal qualities that characterize an effective therapist. But ask yourself these questions: Do you think that these qualities can be taught or acquired? Why does the therapist care about his or her patients? How was this capacity acquired or learned? What does it take to become confident as a therapist? Can this be learned? What about being coher-ent in one's approach to therapy? Is there a manual that discriminates therapist coherence from incoherence?

Typically, the developmental trajectory of a psychotherapist is long and de-manding emotionally, physically, and financially. Therapists accumulate hun-dreds of hours of supervised experience over several years prior to independent work. To attain the privilege of offering services to the general public, clinicians must acquire sufficient knowledge and self-control and become acculturated to professional standards. During the course of training, one learns to recognize and productively direct the dynamic emotional components of psychotherapy, including the thread of his or her own affective contributions. Emotional expe-riences of novice therapists often include anxious arousal (feeling tense or guarded; freezing), uncertainty ("I'm not sure what to do,"), self-doubt ("I'm probably doing this wrong,"), and a search for a sense of competence ("I wonder what my strengths really are").

The tasks of collaboration can loom large for novice clinicians. First, they have to elicit trust and confidence from a virtual stranger. Then they have to decide which interventions might be relevant for a particular patient, and skill-fully apply them in a context of emotional arousal. If that isn't difficult enough, these unpolished efforts then have to be presented to an authority, the supervisor, who will observe and formally evaluate the quality and effective-ness of the interaction and plan. Often apprenticing therapists receive a formal academic grade for their performance of this challenging work. The demands of this learning process can directly conflict with the expression of empathy, warmth, genuineness, and the productive emotional connection that maxi-mizes patient participation.

Over the course of embracing this challenge, core collaboration skills are forged, and together with core technical skills, are woven into an overall competence and effectiveness. These skills are conceptualized as caring, coherence, and confidence.

Caring

Literally hundreds of empirical studies support the conclusion that emotional involvement and caring on the part of the therapist is a crucial ingredient to successful therapy (Horvath & Symonds, 1991; D. J. Martin, Garske, & Davis, 2000; Orlinsky et al., 1994; Safran & Muran, 1995). Even in structured treatments (e.g., in vivo exposure, behavioral marital therapy), or those applied to specific problems (problem drinking; sex offenses), patients who view their therapist as warm and empathetic are more involved in their treatment and ultimately have a better outcome (e.g., Holtzworth-Munroe, Jacobson, DeKlyen, & Whisman, 1989; Miller, Taylor, & West, 1980; Serran et al., 2003).

A great deal of the emotional charge to the therapy relationship is activated or deactivated, by the patient's belief that the therapist cares. The therapist must find effective ways to establish this vital link in the working alliance. There is no universal operational definition of caring, so we must rely on basic strategies and be mindful whether our patients have received the intended message. Further, we must attend to our own emotional state, and be alert to any factors that diminish the care that is intended, felt, and communicated to the patient.

Some basic strategies for establishing and communicating a sense of caring include treating the patient with respect as a person, responding directly and promptly to patient inquiries and requests, asking for feedback, anticipating possible difficulties or inconveniences, and allocating sufficient attention and energy toward the patient (Wright & Davis, 1994). Therapists who show interest, offer encouragement and reassurance, instill hope, and offer practical assistance for increasing problem solving and coping are seen by their patients as being most helpful (McLeod, 1990).

The notion of treating the patient with respect as a person is a broad concept, and readers are encouraged to explore varied contexts for interpreting what this means to people from different cultures and walks of life. Greeting the patient at the appointed time with a friendly remark and including a formal address at the first meeting can establish basic respect and caring for the person's dignity (e.g., "Good morning, Mr. Jones. Are you ready to come into my office now?"). Providing a comfortable environment for meeting that is both private and free from distractions also demonstrates respect. Unexpected intrusions, distractions, or delays should be discussed in such a way as to apologize for any inconvenience to the patient, and an attempt should be made to protect the planned meeting. Similarly, presenting oneself as attentive, well rested, and focused on the patient's concerns demonstrates caring and respect for the trust given to you. In more traditional or psychodynamic orientations, this might be referred to as the therapeutic "frame" and is attended to quite scrupulously.

Clinical Example 1

At the end of his third session, Frank and his therapist were reviewing the treatment plan and Frank shared the following impressions about his experience thus far. "I would very much like to continue with this plan because it makes sense (coherence), it sounds promising (confidence), but most importantly, I really get the feeling that you care. You've been very up front, explained things, answered my phone calls and my questions, and the way that you seem to approach things says that you are on my side. Someone might be really smart or well known in their field, but if you can't get the feeling that they care about *you*, then there isn't much point in continuing because it just isn't going to work."

Clinical Example 2

Chet and his therapist were working on a list of stress triggers when he described a series of hassles with other service providers. "First, I find out my hair-stylist is going to be working part-time at a distant location, and I think, Oh great, now he won't have time to see me. Then, my massage therapist moved and they called me and now her schedule is all messed up, and I can't have my regular time. And my favorite exercise class was suddenly canceled." Having just relocated her office as well, the therapist inquired whether Chet had also felt stressed out about the change in therapy venue. He replied, "No, I really didn't worry about this. You were very clear and reassuring about this change. You told me just when the move was happening, where to come, how to get here and where to park, and that my appointment time would stay the same. I didn't feel I was left hanging in any way."

Behaviors that may deactivate the patient's belief that the therapist cares include overstructuring therapy, inappropriate self-disclosures, rigid use of transference interpretation, inappropriate use of silence, criticism, hostile tone or content, personal tension or distraction (Ackerman & Hilsenroth, 2001), or confrontational approaches (Marshall et al., 2002). Confrontational approaches that include aggressive criticism and sarcasm are thought to be especially harmful to clients who have low self-esteem or are at the precontemplation stage of change (Serran et al., 2003). The patient who experiences the therapist as confrontational is likely to discredit or challenge the therapist, dismiss or devalue the issues, or agree on the surface but actually fail to participate (Cormier & Cormier, 1991).

How therapists personally develop internal feelings of caring for the patient, or fail to experience caring, is certainly a complex question. From a therapist's developmental perspective, we might predict that nascent skills require a degree of self-preoccupation that could interfere with the experience and expression of caring. In general, therapists are most likely to be helpful when happy and unhurried (Myers, 1996). However, the demands of clinical training do not typically create a leisurely, feel-good experience.

It is difficult to be genuine or fully empathic with the experiences of another when mental tensions or personal concerns are intruding on the therapist's awareness. Questions of what to do next, how to implement a technique, whether one is measuring up to the model of the manual, concern for the performance demands of supervision and evaluation, as well as general personal concerns about career opportunities or stability (e.g., "Are there any decent jobs left in applied practice?" or "Maybe I should just concentrate on research or teaching") are typical among novice clinicians. These concerns become part of the context in which the therapist perceives and thinks about the patient. Novice therapists may care passionately about their patients, but they also need to feel some internal stability in their self-confidence and self-direction. They are most likely to feel a sense of caring for patients whom they can understand and help. Patients who are quite different from themselves are likely to be the most challenging. Patients with multiple problems, or those who are slow to change will not offer the same level of self-satisfaction that the therapist might hope for as reinforcement for the effort of caring. If other system challenges such as paperwork overload or low pay provoke the therapist to question his or her commitment to this professional role ("Is law school still an option?"), this relative detachment might lead to a decrease in the emotional intensity of caring.

Therapists who receive their clinical training in a program with strong research emphasis may be especially vulnerable to a double bind in caring about their patients. Their emotional involvement with applied clinical practice may be treated, overtly or covertly, as an impediment to the priority of research productivity. They may feel guilty for the time involved in clinical work, disloyal to their advisors or faculty when gaining satisfaction from working with patients, and perhaps fearful that clinical involvement will significantly compromise their research progress. Moreover, there may be internal personal conflict about their professional identity as they consider career plans and options. They may be gratified by the emotional experience of caring, yet reluctant to openly admit these feelings. They may fear the disapproval of academic mentors or feel alienated from their own internalized ideals of becoming an academic psychologist. Anticipating this potential bind, the training program can endeavor to validate the emotional experience of the trainees, support the importance of caring and role of the clinical therapist, and encourage opportunities for integrating research and practice throughout the training program.

Taken together, these factors illustrate why burnout is a notable risk for novice psychologists. Such therapists have less experience, fewer well-established skills but high demand work roles, and are more apt to have role conflict and role ambiguity. Caregiver burnout can occur at any career stage, and may also be a notable risk in middle to late career if skills have eroded, or personal stressors significantly interfere with work focus. The issue of burnout across the career is discussed further in Chapter 15.

Coherence

The treatment plan must be presented in a way that is coherent to the patient, and consistent with the problem conceptualization. Patients are apt to lose trust in the therapy or in the therapist if the rationale for intervention is unclear or if the proposed techniques do not make sense, based on the patient's personal theory of problem origin.

If a therapist offers vague, stereotyped, or overly intellectualized recommendations, if they switch techniques abruptly or fail to provide a rationale, or if they are insensitive to the patient's cultural worldview, patients can lose hope and think of their therapist as incompetent or uncaring. Both underexplaining and overexplaining are risks to treatment coherence. Patients who switch from one therapist to another, perhaps seeking a different "brand" of therapy, may do this because there is no coherent plan to the therapy.

Clinical Example 3

Ellen, a 38-year-old mother and health care professional sought therapy for anxiety, panic attacks, and phobias. She explained that she had been in supportive therapy for over 2 years, and although her therapist was very pleasant and sensitive as a listener, the therapy seemed to lack direction or purpose. Ellen wanted to learn ways to overcome her phobias and panic attacks, but did not see how her current therapy, which consisted of repetitive discussions of her childhood and her relationships with her parents, was helping her to accomplish these objectives. The connection between these discussions about her past relationships and her current symptoms was fuzzy and inconsistent with her worries about having a chemical imbalance or physical disease.

Ellen's therapist acknowledged the previous therapist's efforts as a relationship-focused approach that is helpful in some instances of anxiety disorder. She then offered a brief rationale for an alternative approach focusing on thoughts, feelings, and beliefs associated with different body sensations, particularly unexpected sensations. By not directly criticizing or discrediting the previous therapy, Ellen's new therapist fostered continuing confidence in treatment in general and provided an acceptable rationale for Ellen to discriminate past from current experience. Further, the therapist engendered a coping model by acknowledging that it made sense to try the former approach, but given Ellen's view of her problems, it also made sense to try different tactics.

Confidence

Confidence is important for both therapist and patient, but it is not very effective to simply demand or expect confidence in yourself, or from your patients. Rather than coaxing with a directive to "have confidence," it may be more productive to review the ways that you can increase (or decrease) confidence in the therapy process, in your therapy skills, and in the application of specific skills with specific people.

First, therapists who hold positive beliefs about the value of therapy in general, and about the potential usefulness of specific techniques will be more likely to communicate this confidence to the patient. For general confidence, it may be helpful to recall that a substantial body of empirical research across different forms of psychotherapy has shown that approximately 80% of those treated will realize positive effects (Wampold, 2001). For specific techniques, the number of studies demonstrating positive effects with different disorders grows every year, and can quickly be accessed with a directed literature search. Continuing education in its various forms can help therapists stay up to date on the latest empirical findings that support specific techniques and interventions, and thus boost their confidence in making recommendations and encouraging the patient to look for potential benefit in the treatment.

Confidence in individual therapy skills and specific technical skills with different disorders is typically acquired through accumulated experience, evidence from the outcomes of that experience, formal evaluations, informal feedback and observing the work of others. For beginning therapists, or those unfamiliar with a particular disorder, this discovery process begins with the first patient, where feedback from the patient and his or her clinical response, as well as self-observation and supervision guide the systematic building of assurance and belief in both technique and ability. Errors are recognized and corrective actions taken. Some degree of confidence is built on learning the hard way what *not* to do.

With further experience comes the ability to recognize limits and to communicate appropriate reservations and consideration of alternatives without undue doubt or hesitation. Therapists who communicate a "coping" perspective (e.g., "We can work together systematically to see what works and what doesn't") engender a stronger bond and more effective results than those who project a "mastery" perspective (e.g., "I have to come up with the answers to fix your problems"; Kassinove & Tafrate, 2002; Mahoney & Norcross, 1993). Thus, the confident therapist is apt to hold the following beliefs: "Therapy is generally worthwhile and useful if conducted in a professional manner"; "Specific techniques tested with similar patients may be beneficial to this patient"; and most importantly, "I am capable of working with this patient to apply these techniques in the interest of his or her personal goals; the evidence will help us decide what works best for this individual."

These beliefs, or similar ones, will help the therapist achieve a paramount objective, which is to help the patient comprehend and test the conceptualization as an authentic explanation for their problems, or means for achieving their goals. This builds the patient's confidence in both the therapist and the activities that the two will undertake in service of the patient's objectives. Patient confidence is apt to have a reinforcing effect on the therapist, who will then more confidently encourage the patient to undertake the specific tasks of therapy.

It is not unusual for patients to have doubts about therapy, particularly as it may apply to their particular problems. Gentle suggestion is often sufficient to encourage the patient to "give this approach a fair try." The structured cognitive-behavioral approach is helpful in this regard, as there are typically points of evaluation and feedback both during sessions, and across the course of treatment. Some patients will be much more skeptical, however, and may repeatedly demand to know what the therapy is going to do for them. At the points of pressure, it is crucial that therapists not allow this challenge and the subsequent arousal it may provoke to puncture their confidence. The confident therapist will most likely encourage persistence and focus on the treatment strategies.

This persistence under pressure of doubt and demand from the patient both emanates from and reinforces a more general confidence in structured treatment, and one's ability to conduct that treatment. At times of challenge, the therapist can also amplify efforts to demonstrate caring, and to maintain a clear and coherent rationale for treatment. A confident therapist will reflect on the clinical implications of the patient's doubts and demands for certainty and use this information to sharpen the problem conceptualization.

Clinical Example 4

Melody, a psychology intern, reported to her supervisor that she was feeling increasingly anxious and depressed about her rotation in the mental health center family services. She had even experienced a few panic attacks, although these occurred on weekends, times when she hoped to be relaxing but instead worried about her clinical caseload and client progress, or lack thereof.

Melody's graduate training had emphasized critical thinking skills and she was well versed in pinpointing empirical weaknesses or flaws in the existing literature. On her internship, however, she felt overwhelmed by the demands of conceptualizing cases and developing treatment plans. She was often flooded with negative thoughts about the limitations of various forms of therapy. Before and after sessions, she might think, "There's no way I can make a difference with this family." During staff meetings when cases were assigned, she would try to avoid accepting new clients because most of them had problems for which there is no tested protocol. Her clients typically had numerous problems, only some of which could be addressed with standard manualized therapy. Melody had very little confidence in the potential benefit of her efforts, in part because her attention was highly focused on treatment limitations, and she was easily discouraged by complicating variables.

Melody agreed to develop more of a coping perspective in her work, and with her supervisor's guidance, focus on increasing her basic collaborative skills. Rather than trying to fit patients into a prototype, she planned to work with each client on targeting a specific list of problems, and then to apply different treatment strategies with those problems one at a time. Together she and her supervisor worked out a plan for Melody to respond to her "empirical critic" thoughts with encouraging alternatives (e.g., "I have some ideas to try in this session and can test how they work"; "I'm sure I can find one idea that may be helpful to offer to this client today"; "There is no definite reason to believe that therapy *can't* help this person, especially if it is based on empirically supported models and makes good use of the common ingredients").

Sometimes therapists undermine their own confidence through the distortion of "idealizing the masters." This occurs when the therapist comes to believe that others, perhaps those who have lectured or shared positive clinical examples in a public forum, are especially gifted in ways that they are not. When confronted with a difficult clinical situation, therapists may attribute fault to some internal inadequacy and harbor the belief that the clinical master would have no difficulty in such a predicament. Thus, therapists may systematically engage in a judgment of their personal efforts as inferior compared with the imagined efforts of a master, slowing down their own effective problem solving and weakening their self-confidence. Like doubts about the therapy process, a coping perspective is needed for confidence to build. It may also be important to consider the alternative notion that clinical challenges are difficult for everyone, even highly experienced clinicians. Therapists must allow themselves to have confidence of effort, even though they may not feel like an expert.

Goals and Tasks of Treatment

The cornerstones of a treatment plan are the goals and tasks that patient and therapist select. Treatment goals, quite simply, are the changes that the patient hopes to realize. Through the processes of assessment and conceptualization, the therapist helps the patient shape an operational definition of the goals in terms of something that is observable, measurable, and can be increased or decreased. Therapists may propose additional goals for the patient's consideration, based on their professional judgment of what may be in the patient's best interest, with an emphasis on supporting the greatest degree of patient autonomy.

The tasks of treatment are the strategies that will be used to achieve the goals. These are the strategies and techniques that the therapist will offer and explain, and that the patient will either accept or decline. From the list of changes desired by the patient, the therapist will outline a corresponding list of tools and strategies, and will help the patient apply these interventions and evaluate the impact. Agreement between patient and therapist on these goals and tasks is crucial to the success of treatment, and as noted, lack of agreement will decrease the patient's participation and undermine the positive emotional charge of the therapy.

Translating Chief Complaints into Measurable Goals

Beginning at intake interview, the patient cites problems, symptoms, and reasons for seeking therapy. The provider then attempts to discover what the client hopes to gain from therapy, and what results are desired. Often, the patient's response is framed in terms of cessation of the symptom or complaint (e.g., to "stop procrastinating"). Sometimes the patient's stated objective is vague and global, as in "get my old self back," or "get my head together," or "to be a happier person."

Occasionally, the patient may have no goal for therapy other than to show up. Someone else may think that the patient should be in therapy, so the goal is to make that other person happy or to get out of trouble by going to therapy. The patient may show up with the mistaken belief that going to therapy and complaining about others will somehow change those people. Sometimes, therapy is sought for self-enhancement, motivated by curiosity about one's psychological functioning, or perhaps motivated by an attempt to cultivate social status through an accumulation of relationships with supposedly stylish service providers.

In every instance, it is important to specify treatment goals in operational terms. This will focus the treatment on a purpose and ensure agreement between patient and therapist for the intended aims. One type of operational goal might be the reduction of a specific symptom or set of symptoms (e.g., panic attacks less than once per month; depressed mood reduced to mild range or less on symptom index). Another type of operational goal might be achievement of a specific task or set of tasks (e.g., fly cross-country on a commercial flight; attend family functions, become more socially active with friends).

Operational goals can also incorporate broader emotional experiences such as achieving more satisfaction in marriage or living a more peaceful, joyful, and less worried day-to-day life, or functioning better in a particular role (e.g., being an effective parent). The details of an operational definition for a broader goal would typically have specific behavioral reference points with meaning and relevance to the patient. These reference points may not be known at the beginning of therapy, for the task of therapy is to explore and define the behavioral targets. For one patient, a joyful life might be having time to exercise and plant flowers. For another, a joyful life might be found in more challenging work and greater self-discipline. For yet another patient, joy might be discovered by learning how to defuse the mental process of worry and accept a range of emotions in daily living. Similarly, the goal of being a better parent is anchored in meaning and relevance to the patient, in the context of the particular challenges being addressed. For one parent, this might mean increasing the number of positive and nondisciplinary interactions. For another, it might mean tolerating some conflict in the interest of applying more consistent limits and age-appropriate demands.

Agreements and Contracts

It is important to begin formulating a direction and plan for therapy from the initial contact. A preliminary formulation might be offered in the first meeting, with the provision that this plan will be updated as more information is gathered and progress is made. It is also useful to establish a written summary of the initial treatment plan, both to facilitate the agreement of both (or all) parties, and to keep a record of the intended aims of the work.

Therapists may differ in whether they have the patient sign a written treatment plan, or rely primarily on verbal collaboration and keep a written record for their own purposes. Some believe that formal contracting enhances motivation and adherence with treatment procedures, as well as provides a reminder to the patient about treatment options and contingencies that may be forgotten over time or under stress (Otto, Reilly-Harrington, Kogan, & Winett, 2003). Others find that the verbal agreement is sufficient and appropriate, especially with patients who present in the early stages of change (see Chapter 12). The patient's state of readiness for change has a big impact on how the treatment plan is perceived. Reluctant or uncertain patients who are tentative about therapy and just beginning to think about change may react negatively to contracts and consent forms. Asking them to sign a written treatment plan could strain the working alliance beyond a critical tipping point and cause a retreat from therapy. Verbal agreement to try a limited treatment plan may offer a better way to engage the uncertain patient. If the patient is fully committed to change and ready to begin planning action, the patient's homework might include writing parts of a treatment plan. This encourages patients to function as their own therapist, with the professional providing consultation. We prefer to keep in mind the heuristic of treating patients, not pieces of paper, and remain flexible in how we formally organize the plan for treatment.

An example of a comprehensive treatment plan is illustrated in Box 10.1. Client assets and potential obstacles to motivation are included, along with a list of problems and general strategies to use in addressing those problems. The addition of a specified time frame is helpful for sketching a target for completion, although this may not be clear in every instance.

As noted, having the patient review and sign the document is optional. The therapist may still use the same or similar written format for record-keeping purposes, but present the ideas verbally to confirm the patient's agreement and collaboration. In either case, the treatment plan is discussed, and the patient's informed consent obtained. This discussion is noted in the progress record, including reference to a review of the risks, potential benefits, alternatives, and any pertinent concerns of the patient. It may be appropriate to expand, or update this plan as more information is gathered, the patient progresses in readiness for change, or as initial problems recede and new problems emerge.

Clinical Example 5

David, a 33-year-old business professional came to therapy because of long-standing mild to moderate depression. His problem list included loneliness, procrastination, and anxiety about his work performance. In his initial interviews, it was also noted that he often coped with stress by drinking alcohol, sometimes more than 5 drinks in one episode. However, he was conscious of his health, was of normal weight, maintained an exercise program of running and biking, and had always been a nonsmoker. His most recent physical checkup was 4 months prior, and he was evaluated as free from any major health problems other than depression. When asked about his goals for therapy, he stated that he wanted to "be in control of my life and get over this depression."

David's therapist summarized the assets that might facilitate his progress as his good physical health, stable employment with adequate health care benefits, and his motivation to engage in a process of self-change. The challenges that might interfere with progress or prolong treatment included his long-standing social isolation (no family nearby, few social contacts, no friends in the area), his tendency to cope with stress by drinking, often alone, his prolonged work hours, and the persistent duration of his depression. They agreed to the general goals of increasing his sense of control over his work life, his social life, and his mood. The provider explained that they would focus on understanding and altering the learned response patterns, that is the thoughts, beliefs, actions, and feelings that were associated with each of these problem areas.

Box 10.1
Comprehensive Treatment Plan

Name _____

Date of First Visit _____

Assets facilitating treatment:

Barriers or challenges potentially interfering with treatment:

Problem List:

Goals: Methods: Initial Time Frame:

Patient Informed Consent and Participation

I have discussed this plan with Dr. _____, understand it, and
with my full and informed consent agree to the course of action outlined above.

_____   _____
          Patient Signature   Date

Selecting the Initial Problem for Intervention

After setting out the general direction of therapy, the next logical question is "What is the best place to begin with the list of problems?" Several considerations will help focus this important step. The first consideration is the relative level of the patient's overall functional impairment and degree of activation. For those who are more severely impaired and functioning poorly in basic role expectations, it is important to initially focus on remediation of functional deficits in activity level. First, patients often find it easier to grasp the idea of taking a specific action as a place to start, in favor of the more abstract task of working with thoughts and beliefs. Second, it may relieve the patient's anxiety somewhat to have a concrete plan to do something, as this supports feelings of control, empowerment, and hope. Third, changes in behavior, even small ones, often precipitate a ripple effect on functioning overall, bringing a large measure of relief relative to the effort expended.

There are two other significant considerations in picking initial target problems. One is the importance of the problem for the patient's self-esteem and personal responsibility, and the other is the urgency or potential risk of the problem. Any problem that is potentially life-threatening should be addressed immediately and sufficiently. Beyond life threat, any problem that is apt to develop into a crisis and could put someone else at risk, or significantly harm the patient's stability would be a definite priority. If a depressed mother reports spending her day in bed while her children "sleep," watch television, or "play on their own," her level of interaction with the children and childcare support need to be addressed immediately.

With this in mind, it is also important to rapidly address the primary issues that the patient wants to address in therapy, the chief concerns that precipitated the decision to seek service. Many times, the area of crisis is the problem of greatest risk, and both patient and therapist agree on the priority of treatment. If there is disagreement, there may be a way to acknowledge the patient's priorities while focusing on a key neglected issue. If the depressed mother presents her biggest concern as her weight and she acknowledges the parenting issue only peripherally, it may be possible to link the two problems to a similar initial intervention. She could be offered the option of working on both problems at the same time through behavioral activation, perhaps by taking the children to an indoor or outdoor playground. Without criticism, the therapist must bring the patient's attention to the neglected problem and activate a process of considering change. Therapists must also know the boundaries of neglect or endangerment that would precipitate some further directive action such as involving child protective services.

Clinical Example 6

Let's return to the discussion of David, the depressed businessman. Once the general goals of therapy were agreed on, David's therapist asked him to describe the elements of each problem area that he wished to better control, to develop a clearer, more operational view of the nondepressed life he wished

(continued)

Clinical Example 6 (Continued)

to achieve. At first, he responded with more global answers to the therapist's inquiries. For example, when asked what he wanted to better control at work, he stated that he wanted to "get things done when they should be done." From this, the therapist gently persisted in obtaining further detail that would pinpoint a more specific and measurable target by asking what particular things David needed to be getting done now that had been put off.

With this directed questioning, David listed some specific tasks at work such as his quarterly budget reports, his purchasing requests, some written correspondence, and meetings he needed to schedule. The therapist then introduced the techniques of graded tasks to help him initiate changes in his behavior, and guided discovery to explore poten-

tial thoughts or circumstances interfering with execution of these desired tasks. Feedback from David was requested, to check his understanding, motivation, and involvement in the agreed tasks, as well as to elicit any further interfering thoughts or possible negative reactions to the therapist or the therapeutic exchange.

David felt a large measure of relief from scheduling a few specific tasks that he had avoided and neglected, thus improving his work performance. Work problems were addressed first as this was central to his self-esteem, identity, and overall stability. Poor work performance, missed deadlines, or a bad work review would likely have a serious destabilizing impact overall, and thus presented a greater risk relative to his other ongoing problems.

Building and Maintaining the Therapeutic Relationship

The therapist's opportunity to build and maintain a relationship with the patient begins with the very first contact, often over the telephone, and continues throughout the duration of active contact. Each interaction represents another chance to construct and extend a positive relationship by attending carefully to the interaction. Even the best plans for treatment are worth little if there is not a sufficiently positive therapeutic relationship to support the patient's involvement in the treatment. As noted by Carkhuff (2000), the tools of observing and listening are essential to the relationship process. It is difficult if not impossible to build a positive therapeutic relationship without a strong foundation of basic active listening skills.

A collaborative relationship is built not only through keen observation, but also by providing a caring and thoughtful response to what has been seen and heard. The therapist does not just passively absorb all the patient's complaints, as nontherapists sometimes imagine when they wonder how someone can sit and listen to problems all day long. Instead, the therapist is actively focusing attention and processing information at multiple levels to both synthesize information and foster a positive, friendly interpersonal exchange. The following techniques can be used as a framework for general relationship building within therapy. Not surprisingly, these techniques also work well in developing relationships across many other contexts.

Softly Focus Attention on the Patient

Deliberately and mindfully focusing on the patient directs energy toward the therapeutic relationship. For most people, this is a pleasant and perhaps rare experience. This focused attention should be soft and friendly, not harsh or judgmental. Kindly and patiently taking in as many details of the patient's presentation as possible, both verbal and nonverbal, communicates a message of accepting and valuing the patient as an individual. However, the therapist's pace, tone, and nonverbal body language should avoid extremes of intensity and be responsive to the patient's nonverbal cues. Staring at the patient, scowling, or gathering information in an interrogating manner can foil the positive relationship, as can being too soft or diminutive. Keen observations of the patient's posture, facial expressions, tone of voice, dress and grooming, and flow of conversation can provide important clues to the emotional content of communications. These observations support the accuracy of the conceptualization, which is vital to validating the patient's feelings and allowing them to feel understood.

Resist Distractions

It is difficult to build a relationship when you are only partially present in the interaction. Although distractions are inevitable, you can make efforts to reduce, prevent, and resist the division of your attention while in the presence of your patient. All conversations with others besides the patient should stop, including covert conversations with yourself or others about unrelated matters.

It is important to note your internal reactions and hypotheses while talking with the patient, but the focus of the provider's attention is still with the patient. Problems in being distracted by nonpatient concerns may be a function of a temporary state (e.g., fatigue or illness), and may be dealt with coping tools appropriate to the distraction. For example, you might take medication to alleviate symptoms of an illness or make it a point to be sufficiently rested before work. For most distractions, an appropriate coping remedy can be tried. If the distraction cannot be delayed for the duration of the session, that is a good indication of a need to cancel or reschedule the meeting.

If the distraction seems to be triggered by contact with the patient, a conceptual review of the interaction and emotional reactions is warranted, perhaps with clinical consultation. The distraction is not due to a circumstance of the therapist (e.g., "I need to be home with my sick child"), but rather is a function of something happening in the therapy (e.g., "the client is being tangential again and I'm getting bored and irritated"). If the therapist ignores or indulges the distraction by letting attention wander away from the patient for extended segments of time, the patient may detect this break in connection and respond with corresponding emotional detachment.

Recall Information about the Patient

The more that the therapist can remember about the details of the patient's world and life experience, the more the patient will feel known, understood, and hopefully accepted by the therapist. The feeling of closeness and trust begins when the patient first shares details of self. This bond of trust grows much stronger when the therapist demonstrates having retained an actual memory of this information. Recall of family members' names, critical events, or important relationships all suggest a degree of attention and emotional involvement associated with a personal relationship with the inference that the therapist cares about the patient.

Disclosure of information about oneself can enhance a therapeutic bond, but this must be done carefully in the service of the therapeutic objectives. Judicious sharing of selected personal information can contribute to identification and feelings of trust in the best circumstances. However, significant clinical and ethical implications must be considered to ensure that the patient's best interests remain the focus and harm does not occur (Barnett, 1998).

A therapist might disclose to Mrs. Green that like her, she also has two sisters, and this enhances their bond because of a sense of shared experience. Mrs. Green now believes that she and her therapist share something in common, and her therapist understands her unique experiences. However, if Mrs. Green was always the caretaker of her two younger siblings, it may not be useful for her to know that the therapist was the youngest in her sibling group. Now Mrs. Green begins to project the image of "little sister" onto her therapist, and directs her attention to unnecessary and unhelpful caretaking actions. She worries if the therapist is comfortable, happy, or eating enough. If not watchful, the therapist may progress down the slippery slope and allow valuable therapy time to be diverted toward the therapist's personal needs and concerns. Mrs. Green's therapist might be more effective in building a strong relationship bond through her efforts to remember details about the adventures and travails of Mrs. Green and her sisters.

Because of the potential implications of self-disclosure that can be difficult for even the most experienced, beginning therapists are well-advised to use extreme caution. Although stiff attempts to maintain a shroud of secrecy around one's personal life are a misguided effort (Barnett, 1998), venting or proffering too much information can impair rather than facilitate the therapy relationship.

Recognize and Control Judgmental Tendencies

An objective perspective is a crucial component of relationship building in therapy. We maintain this for both ethical and technical reasons. First, patients have a right to expect the therapist to be a compassionate listener who will address their concerns in a responsible and nonbiased manner. The professional role of therapist implies reserving personal judgment and focusing on the patient's needs. Second, the patient will typically be more open and less resistant if the therapist models the ability to weigh the problem without judging the person. The therapist's emotional reactions to the problem can be viewed as a cue for how others in the patient's world might react, and perhaps how the patient feels about him- or herself. For the sake of the relationship, the therapist exercises reserve and caution in sharing those feelings, and is alert to his or her own personal biases.

A therapist would *not* say to the patient, "Wow, you are extremely irritating to me. You seem to be an incredibly self-centered person." Instead, the therapist would use an emotional response as a guide for clinical exploration, in the interest of therapeutic contemplation of the problem. So the therapist might ask, "Do your friends or family ever seem to be exasperated or short-tempered with you? Let's talk about some of the possible triggers for that."

In situations where the patient "pushes the therapist's buttons," the therapist's personal emotional reactions threaten to distort the clinical relationship. From an objective perspective, the patient is not doing anything that others would find particularly irritating. Rather, it is the therapist's sensitivity and judgment of the patient or the patient's problem that is triggering the feelings of irritation, perhaps because of a personal bias or a stereotype. A therapist who has difficulty managing judgmental tendencies has a range of options, including supervision, consultation, or transfer of the patient. Ask yourself which types of patients or problems might challenge your own emotional and judgmental reserve? How could you address these challenges?

Elicit Input and Feedback

A contemporary collaboration includes an active exchange of information and shared decision making. Although the therapist is responsible for structuring both individual sessions and the therapy as a whole, this objective can only be achieved with active input and feedback from the patient. Patients are empowered to select problems and priorities and to set the pace of change. Patient feedback is directly solicited so that the provider can discern the most personally meaningful elements of the intervention. This important process of *negotiation* between patient and therapist (Safran & Muran, 2000) is more than superficial consensus; it is both a necessary condition and an intrinsic part of a change process. In this atmosphere of ongoing negotiation, it is more likely that misunderstandings or negative reactions can be pinpointed early and resolved, rather than allowed to fester and possibly derail a potentially productive venture.

Sensitivity to the patient's personal need for structure is particularly important to successful collaboration. A single type of session structure does not fit all individuals and personalities. Some patients respond well to highly active therapists who ensure that each session has a discrete beginning, middle, and end. Others find it more productive when the session follows a more conversational flow that pinpoints key issues. Some patients are comfortable in setting their own agenda; others need more socialization to their options within therapy. When the need for structure is a component of a broader clinical issue, as in the case of someone with a dependent personality, the behavioral aspects of structuring the session can be broken down systematically and approached as important skills to be developed.

Problems in Collaboration

Some therapy relationships are relatively uncomplicated as patient and therapist take readily to their respective roles and a productive working alliance follows. Both parties have functional expectations that need little if any explicit discussion. With other patients, more specific effort is needed because there are particular problems in therapeutic collaboration. Passive noncollaboration and avoidance are two types of problematic collaboration. Passive noncollaboration may be distinguished from active avoidance by the underlying antecedents or triggers for the response (Davis & Hollon, 1999). Passive noncollaboration may stem from low expectations for success, but active avoidance suggests negative, personalized meanings such as distrust of therapy or externalized blame.

There are many possible reasons for noncollaborative responses, although very few will actually reflect an internal motivation toward illness. These reasons can appear in any combination, and may vary according to changes in the patient's life circumstance as well as progress in therapy and response to the therapist's skill. Among the causes of patient noncollaboration are beliefs that interfere with a good working relationship, such as the following commonly encountered ideas:

- Being in therapy means I am a weak person.
- I don't really trust therapists; my therapist has to prove he or she cares and is an expert.
- If I make the changes the therapist suggests, I will become a selfish, uncaring person.
- If I make the changes the therapist suggests, I will be letting others down.
- If I make the changes the therapist suggests, I will be forced to do things I cannot do.
- My therapist needs to know everything about me before I can change.
- My therapist should be able to know what is bothering me.
- My therapist should be able to fix me; feeling better should just happen.
- My therapist should force me to do things to make me better.
- I want to be my therapist's favorite patient.

There are several ways that the therapist might assess the salience or influence of any or all these beliefs. One is to raise a discussion about the patient's expectations and experience of therapy progress. Sometimes the patient will directly disclose the belief, or express a feeling that with some gentle probing will allow access to the belief. The following dialogue illustrates how this might occur:

T: How do you feel about your progress so far in overcoming your anxiety and doing things that are difficult for you to do?
P: Frustrated. I want to be a lot further along.
T: What do you think has gotten in your way, or held you back?
P: Nothing really, but I think I need someone to force me to do what is difficult. I'm not very good at disciplining myself, and I need a demanding taskmaster to make me do what I don't want to do.

Obviously, further discussion of this belief and its implications, including the long-term effects of depending on someone else for self-discipline, and possibly experimenting with graded tasks will be an important part of the overall therapy, and therapy collaboration.

Another avenue for detecting therapy-interfering beliefs is in reviewing homework assignments, especially the perceived benefit and perceived difficulty of doing the homework:

T: I'd like to hear about your homework, which if I remember correctly, was to schedule an hour for doing something just for yourself that you might enjoy. We discussed some ideas, as I recall. Were you able to try out any of the things we considered, or did you try something completely different?

P: Well, I thought about the assignment a lot, but didn't actually do anything.

T: That sounds like some important cognitive work. Can we talk further about that?

P: Okay, but I don't know what there is to talk about. I didn't do anything.

T: That's okay; what is important is to understand your thought process. Can you tell me about your internal conversation about this idea? Was there sort of a back-and-forth deliberation?

P: Yeah, there was. I really sort of wanted to do something just for me. The idea sounded good, like something I never do. I even called and scheduled an appointment at a nail salon to get a pedicure and was looking forward to a nice treat. There is a coffee shop next to the salon, and I was going to get one of those delicious caramel frappachinos and just relax and enjoy being pampered for a little bit. But then I realized that I would be taking time away from my family and spending money on myself, and I just didn't feel right about it. I guess I felt that taking time for me was going to turn me into one of those selfish, uncaring, "high maintenance" types and I just couldn't do it. If I took that time for myself, I felt like I would be letting my family down. So I spent the afternoon ironing clothes instead.

When the belief is revealed in the process of discussion, there is an immediate opportunity for further exploration and possible modification. Working with the patient's beliefs that her behavioral change will produce selfishness, uncaring behavior, and negligence of responsibility to others is a prerequisite to any sustained shift in her behavior. If the therapist had simply focused on trying to prompt the behavior of scheduling pleasant activities and not explored the therapy-interfering beliefs, some strain and tension probably would have been introduced into the working alliance, and progress could stall or deteriorate.

Another useful way to detect therapy-interfering beliefs is by noting and gently exploring behavior or affect within the context of therapy interaction. When the patient shows an affective shift during a session, it is often useful not only to inquire "what went through your mind just then," but also to inquire, "is there anything about what I have been doing or saying that might provoke that feeling?" For example:

T: I noticed you winced just then, and seemed a bit agitated. Was there something that crossed your mind just then?

P: Actually, I was feeling irritated.

T: Was the irritation related to the topic we are discussing, or possibly something in my manner?

P: Well, I don't like answering questions. I feel uncomfortable trying to put my feelings into words. I wish you would just already know what is bothering me.

Yet another way to consider possible interfering beliefs is to make an observation and present the belief as a hypothesis. If the patient talks a great deal and has a difficult time setting an agenda, and seems to work hard to "get everything out" by filling the therapist in on all the details of their life, the therapist might offer the following capsule summary.

T: I really appreciate your effort to be thorough in telling me how you are doing. I want to ensure that we stay productively focused, but it's a little hard to do that and take everything in. I'd like to check out a possibility with you that might help us be more efficient. Do you think that it is necessary for me to know everything that has happened to fully understand and help you? Is that maybe one reason why you work so hard to tell me everything?

P: Well, yes. I don't really know what is important. So I need to get all the information to you so that you can figure out how to solve my problems.

T: So your assumption is that I need to know everything so that I can figure out the solution to your problems.

P: Yes.

T: Is that strategy working very well so far?

P: Not really. I'm working really hard and I haven't really gotten to hear what you think I should do yet.

T: How about if we consider some different ideas about how to make our work more productive?

This strategy of summarizing data from the patient in terms of observed behaviors and reactions, and proposing an inferred belief can be a rapid way to address collaborative problems. This method may be especially useful with beliefs that are difficult to elicit through a series of Socratic questions. However, it may be wise to use this tool judiciously, as it can come across as heavy-handed, or may imply that the therapist knows what patients are thinking, and in a sense, can "read their mind."

Five Indications of a Good Working Relationship

How do you know if you have a good working relationship with your patient? The provider's personal perspective on this might suffer a self-serving bias. We have a good working relationship, we think, because we *intend* to have a good working relationship. Our patients might deem the working relationship good for the very same reason. Virtuous intentions aside, what does a good working relationship look like? Extensive and detailed empirical study of this issue (see Horvath & Greenberg, 1994; Safran & Muran, 2000) has consistently identified a good working relationship as one that is characterized by friendliness and a moderate, reciprocal degree of interpersonal control between patient and therapist.

Because the therapeutic relationship is an ongoing process, it is useful to consider ways to self-monitor the current state of this working relationship. In addition to assessment of the patient's clinical progress (reduction in anxious symptoms, progress toward specific goals), we can assess the following five indicators of overall friendliness and a balance of control:

1. *There is a desire to have contact.* A simple indication of the positive quality of the working relationship is the overall motivation to have contact with this

specific person. Even if progress is difficult, those in a friendly relationship will want to meet, as the contact is perceived as pleasant and therefore interpersonally reinforcing. Understandably, the patient's ambivalence about contact, observed perhaps by lateness, cancellations, long lags between meetings, general lack of anticipation of the meeting, or even anxious apprehension may be a function of hopelessness or low self-esteem.

The friendliness of the interaction may be just the single thin thread that helps motivate the patient to reconnect even through these difficulties. If the therapist has difficulties in finding the motivation for contact with a patient, perhaps observed by avoiding phone calls, negative anticipation of the scheduled meeting, a wish for the patient to cancel, or desire for transfer or termination, this also indicates a threat to the quality of the relationship. Conceptualization of the pertinent triggers for the contact avoidance is needed, as well as possible consultation or supervision.

2. *Information is shared.* A good working relationship is a confiding experience, where the patient discloses personal thoughts and feelings. The patient has things to talk about, and is able to discuss emotionally laden topics, hopefully in depth. It is usually a good sign when the patient says "I've never told anyone that before," or "Only very few people know about this." In a productive relationship, the patient might also discover new thoughts and formulations during the process of confiding in you. The patient may spontaneously remark, "I've never thought about this in quite this way until I started talking about it out loud to you." When there is a dearth of information, either clients have successfully resolved their problems and no longer have pressing concerns, or specific beliefs may be inhibiting the collaboration.

3. *Positive affect is expressed.* A backdrop of friendliness in the relationship can be noted by each individual expressing some positive affect, ideally as a result of the interpersonal exchange. Usually this occurs in a spontaneous fashion, perhaps as a shared smile or laugh in the course of the therapy dialogue, or by a sigh of relief and a release of physical tension.

Although humor is typically used judiciously in therapy, the skillful accomplishment of a positive affective exchange marks a good working relationship. Deeply depressed patients may express only a fleeting smile, but report an increase in their sense of hope. Anxious patients may relax a bit, and report feeling more encouraged. The expression of positive affect can also include some forms of physical contact that fall within professional and clinically appropriate limits. The therapist might offer a handshake or the patient might reach out for a hug. Positive affect that crosses physical boundaries of intimacy is never appropriate, however. The patient and therapist do not kiss or hold one another in intimate positions or engage in any questionable physical contact to express positive feelings.

4. *Sense of teamwork.* Closely related to the expression of positive affect and the desire for contact is a mutual perception that the patient and therapist are working effectively as a team. This perception can be checked on a regular basis by directly asking the patient. The therapist can monitor the degree of control exhibited during the session and strive for balance and reciprocity. Therapists must avoid responding to passive behavior in patients by taking over too much control. Allowing the patient to dominate

the session with unproductive ruminations, complaints, tangential story-telling or analysis of the problems of other people is just as unproductive. When there is teamwork, all the participants will feel as though they are getting somewhere, even if the progress is slow.

5. *Negative sentiment is productive.* As Safran and Muran (2000) note, there is general consensus for the notion that strains in the therapeutic relationship are inevitable. The ability to deal therapeutically with negative process is among the most important aspects of a good working relationship.

Do both parties believe that they can confront and effectively use negative feelings or disagreements? If the patient is confused or upset by something the therapist says or suggests, does he or she feel able to speak up? Can the patient ask questions? Does the therapist detect possible negative reactions in the session and check them out? Does the therapist pick up on disagreement from the patient or is it deflected and ignored? Can the therapist take criticism without becoming defensive? Does the therapist explore other possible indicators of negative process as a source of useful information such as discussing the patient's ambivalence about continuing in therapy?

In a good working relationship, useful results are drawn from negative events. We are concerned about the working relationship where everything is "perfect," but not much affect, either positive or negative, is being exchanged. We are most concerned about the working relationship marked by tension and negative exchange only, with little resolution or sense of productivity attached to the contact.

Summary

Over a relatively long period of training and development, therapists acquire the core collaboration skills needed to fulfill the role of being a professional therapist. They also learn specific skills for structuring and directing therapy with comprehensive treatment plans. Developing and implementing a treatment plan is as much a matter of caring and confidently engaging the patient in a coherent approach to problem solving as it is selecting effective techniques and strategies. Some techniques for effectively engaging patients include focusing attention, resisting distractions, recalling personal information, reserving judgment, and calibrating the structure based on individual responses and feedback.

In addition to collaboration and relationship skills, specific techniques for structuring treatment are needed to create a sufficient support for the patient's efforts to change. Chief complaints need to be translated into measurable goals, and an agreement as to the direction and tasks of therapy needs to be negotiated. It is useful to keep in mind a plan for self-monitoring the quality of the collaboration, and not to rely on good intentions as the only measure. Important indicators of a good working relationship include a motivation to have contact, sharing of emotional information, expression of positive affect, a sense of teamwork, and the ability to draw productive conclusions from negative sentiments. For all parties with a stake in the usefulness of therapy, success lies not only in the sophistication of the treatment plan, but also in a skillfully tended therapeutic relationship.

Therapeutic Methods: Building Psychotherapy Skills

11
Chapter

Psychotherapy is a complex endeavor that requires extensive knowledge and skill. To become competent as a psychotherapist, you must build a strong repertoire of conceptual skills, relationship skills, and procedural skills. Having addressed conceptual and relationship skills in the previous two chapters, we now turn to specific procedures used in psychotherapy.

Learning Objectives

At the end of this chapter, the reader should be able to:

- Discuss the importance of having a range of procedural skills.
- Describe eight interpersonal and systems interventions.
- Describe eight affective interventions.
- Describe eight behavioral interventions.
- Describe eight cognitive interventions.

If you ask 10 laypersons what specific things a psychotherapist does, you might be very surprised by what you hear. Try this, and see what you discover. To some, there are few obvious differences between the actions of therapists and the actions of good friends. Therapists listen, care, and offer supportive comments as you need them. Others think of therapist actions as similar to a scolding parent, complete with a wagging index finger, cajoling tone, and unfaltering advice. Still others magnify the therapist's intellectual powers and infuse the clinical action with a mystical or psychic quality. The therapist absorbs every detail and applies an elaborate understanding of deep motivations. Yet another view expects the therapist to assist in emotional catharsis and the release of pent-up feelings. Such therapists would elicit intense affect, and assist clients in expressive actions such as weeping, shouting, or thumping pillows. Finally, and perhaps most popular, is the vision of the therapist as being gifted with perfectly calm insight, quickly ascertaining the sources of emotional distress, and dispensing concrete, direct, and effective solutions. This therapist, like the scolding parent, seems to have all the answers and can tell you how to fix yourself in a few simple steps, without the authoritarian tone. In reality, all these impressions are based on some kernel of truth about the specific interventions that therapists use.

Each of these descriptions is based on a different snapshot of the relevant content of therapy, and the associated procedures or methods. Therapists have traditionally identified themselves in one or another of these snapshots on the basis of their chosen school or system of approach to psychotherapy. Client-centered therapists are warm facilitators; psychodynamic therapists are intrapsychic interpreters; humanistic therapists are guides for personal discovery and expression; and cognitive-behavioral therapists are coping skill dispensers.

Decades of accumulated research on the effectiveness of different systems of psychotherapy have gradually induced a paradigm shift toward understanding the foundations of psychotherapy as a flexible set of procedures applied in the context of a clinical relationship. Whether clinicians conceptualize psychotherapy as a set of *empirically supported treatments* designed to ameliorate specific clinical syndromes (e.g., Chambless & Hollon, 1998) or as *empirically supported relationships* that are designed to meet the needs of specific persons (e.g., Norcross, 2002; Wampold, 2001), adherence to a single school of therapy and one-size-fits-all methods is increasingly outdated. As Norcross notes, "The research shows an effective psychotherapist is one who employs specific methods, who offers strong relationships, and who customizes both discrete methods and relationship stances to the individual person and condition."(2002, p. 13). In essence, we are moving *away* from an "allegiance" model of practice where the psychologist makes a categorical decision to adopt a single theoretical orientation and *toward* a broader scientific model where the psychologist integrates empirical information into a biopsychosocial model of human behavior. The core units of competence with the biopsychosocial model are the ability to think critically and to approach clinical phenomena in a systematic and unbiased manner.

Applying Specific Procedures

As you read about specific procedures, keep in mind that the success of any intervention depends in part on the context in which it is applied. In practice, both instrumental and interpersonal dimensions are part of the same context, and have a reciprocal interaction (Safran & Muran, 2000). The usefulness and potency, for good or ill, of any procedure is highly affected by when and how the therapist applies it, for what purpose, and how the patient feels about it.

The procedure may be well tested and useful in a general sense, but not workable in a given clinical situation for any number of reasons. The explanation of the procedure may be insufficient, it may not suit the learning style of the particular patient, it may be awkward or uncomfortable to either party, or it may be peripheral to the patient's current problems, just to name a few possibilities. Thus, you may find that these potentially effective procedures do not always work in the straightforward way that our examples suggest.

Effectively using a broad range of procedures requires conceptual and technical skill, timing, and interpersonal rapport. Stuffing a large number of techniques into a given client's therapy will not necessarily lead to better outcome. Overreliance on techniques or over-using a few techniques can make therapy shallow and gimmicky. Forcing a particular procedure on a reluctant client is perhaps the riskiest venture because the therapist might be confusing the procedure with conceptualization, thinking that the essence of therapy is defined by some prototypic action. The therapist may be caught in a "should" and "must" trap about techniques of therapy. For example, the therapist might think that every cognitive therapy session must include an automatic thought record. There are many risks in this sort of rigidity, including the risk of alienating the client from the opportunity of therapy.

Readers should keep in mind both the interpersonal and clinical context for any procedure. The following sections describe some of the basic tools with which the provider can craft a more comprehensive intervention. These are not intended to be exhaustive summaries, but rather a foundation of procedures for building basic practice. For the sake of discussion, these procedures are divided into interpersonal and systems, affective, behavioral, and cognitive categories, reflecting the primary mode of the intervention. Each category includes descriptions of eight useful intervention procedures. In practice, these interventions are often combined and applied in the context of a collaborative relationship. Other relevant factors including the principles, stages, and levels of change are also part of the conceptualization that guides selection of procedures such as those described here.

Interpersonal and Systems Interventions

Interpersonal and systems interventions are geared toward functional changes in patterns of communication and processes of social and group interactions. Depending on how the client presents for therapy, interventions of this type may be appropriate early, in the middle, later, or instead of individually focused work. Clients with a chaotic, neglectful, controlling, or otherwise unstable family history may especially need to address the interpersonal components of their problems. Interpersonal interventions develop skills and interactions needed for effective functioning within relationships and groups. For a given client, there may be internal barriers to more effective functioning such as faulty beliefs or pent-up feelings that need to be addressed with affective and cognitive interventions either before or concomitant with interpersonal changes.

Family and Cultural History

Family processes play a pivotal role in the psychosocial development of individual members. This is especially true for the impact of a family of origin on its children, as some degree of connection to these family processes is present throughout an individual's life span. Family patterns are also embedded within a cultural context of values, beliefs, and affiliations that shape the norms within a family for acceptable behavior and expected family functioning (Teyber, 2006).

All approaches to therapy include at least an overview of family and cultural experiences that affected an individual's child and adolescent development. Most core beliefs and associated behaviors have their origins in these early experiences. The task of reviewing a family history can take an oral narrative form in therapy sessions or it can be written as a homework assignment and discussed in the sessions. Yet another option is to illustrate a complete, cross-generational family history with a formal genogram (McGoldrick, Gerson, & Shellenberger, 1999). The objective in such explorations is to better understand the client's behavioral and emotional learning history. Hypotheses can be drawn about the beliefs and conclusions the client formulated concerning the self and other people on the basis of these experiences with significant others.

Interactions with family may have shaped the personal beliefs "I am unimportant," and "other people will reject my needs." When activated, these beliefs will likely show up in current interactions discussed in therapy, and in relating to the therapist. Connecting beliefs to the family history spotlights the implicit, inflexible and durable nature of these ideas as the basis for a pattern of relating to the self and the world.

When these beliefs arise during the therapy interaction (e.g., if the client is overly apologetic about rescheduling an appointment), the therapist can spot the activation of the core belief and help the client recognize the pattern and learn to discriminate the past from the present. In addition, the healing process includes helping the client to realistically understand family events and coalitions and to come to terms with both the good news and the bad news in their families (Teyber, 2006). Important areas to explore include family economic and health history, major events, cultural affiliations, affective and behavioral rules, and the impact of any family secrets.

Case Example

Donna came to therapy because of acute anxiety problems. Her mother had died suddenly a few years ago, and ever since then, Donna has suffered recurrent panic attacks and depression. Her childhood had been economically, socially, and geographically unstable, with her mother as the source of reassurance during tough times. Her father was a minister who moved from church to church, eventually alienating each successive congregation with his stern, judgmental, and self-centered attitudes. He made favorable first impressions

Case Example (Continued)

with his impassioned approach to religious leadership, but inevitably he would cross the wrong person and have to move on to another locale. He was emotionally distant and punitive with his children, and he expected most of all that they should make him look good in public. The children were strongly admonished not to discuss their father's methods of corporal punishment outside their home, and they were not allowed to talk back to him. Donna learned "I must seek the approval of others," and "other people are threats to my safety."

At her mother's funeral, Donna had the opportunity to have contact with her mother's family, with whom they had very little communication over the years. She even met several cousins and their families for the first time and found them to be warm and charming. This did not fit at all with the negative image of heathen, immoral alcohol-abusers that had been offered by her parents as the reason for the family distance. In talking with her maternal aunt, Donna discovered the true reason

for their distance had been her own mother's shame over her father's instability and abusive behavior toward the children and her father's controlling attitudes about family associations. There was a history of alcoholism in her mother's family, which was the main reason that her father had discouraged and even forbidden their contact.

Donna was now redefining her family relationships, including her family of origin and her extended family of in-laws. She wanted to be more assertive and increase her contact with her mother's family and decrease her contact with her father, and limit her interactions with certain in-laws who seemed to be highly status oriented, but she found this triggered her global fears of disapproval. In discussing her choices with her therapist, it became evident in their interaction that she was also seeking the therapist's endorsement as part of the interpersonal pattern of her core belief about the need for approval of her actions.

Trace an Interpersonal Developmental Time Line

An overview of the client's personal developmental time line in terms of interpersonal skills, challenges and resources can refine global self-perceptions and activate a hopeful perspective. Being in a state of distress often produces memory distortions such that current difficulties are recalled as being continuously present, and are then projected to either stay just as bad or worsen indefinitely into the future. The client says, "It's always been this bad, I've been a misfit my whole life. If I am not any better with my relationships now, how am I ever going to face the challenges of my future? I'll certainly fail and be alone forever." If encouraged to test the accuracy of this thought directly, the client is most likely to defend the perception as true.

Another way to test the accuracy of this generalization is to go back in time. For many clients, it may be useful to begin the time line in childhood, perhaps

Clinical Example

When Jan lamented that she had been a "reject" her whole life, her therapist remarked that this was indeed an exceptionally rare problem. Because success and failure are typically coexisting processes that come and go in everyone's life, it might be important to understand how Jan could have only continuous failure. Usually the feelings of success or failure wax and wane over time as life tasks are alternately easier or more difficult.

So to really get a sense of this in any one particular life, it is useful to trace a time line with notation of any recognizable successes or failures. They began, in a systematic way, to trace Jan's life experiences in segments of 5 years, beginning from birth to age five, when Jan succeeded in many interpersonal tasks (forming a place in her family, learning basic verbal manners such as "please" and "thank-you," attended mother's day out), but perhaps failed in others (too afraid of the other children to ride the bus to school). The time line continued in this way, traced out on successive sheets of paper, bringing interpersonal experiences and skills into the present day. In the end, many forgotten or unacknowledged successes were brought to light, and failures were put into perspective, so Jan's overall conclusions about her interpersonal skills and value were less globally negative and failure oriented.

their preschool years, and inquire about interpersonal functioning in segments of time proceeding through their development. The perspective gained by this exercise, in addition to a vast wealth of information about their life history, is often one of ups and downs. At a broad level, the global conclusion that "I've always been a misfit," is disconfirmed by the historical review. Important information about functional relationships can be used in planning current options and alternatives (see cognitive interventions).

Take a Current Interpersonal Inventory

People interact within interpersonal circles and social networks. Taking an inventory of current interpersonal relationships provides a systematic way to focus on these relationships. Important dimensions of these relationships can then be discussed, such as degree of intimacy, frequency of communication, power and influence, and connections with specific group affiliations. An adequately populated and functioning social network is needed to satisfy individual emotional needs for companionship and enjoyment. Affiliations with others also create a social reference group and a means of constructing and maintaining a social identity. A current inventory can pinpoint gaps and possible deficits as well as areas of tension or conflict. This inventory can begin with a list of important current relationships as well as more casual contacts or acquaintances, followed by an exploration of potential areas of discomfort, difficulty, and potential change.

Clinical Example

Ray was depressed and lonely. He was estranged from his extended family, his father was deceased, his mother was in a nursing home due to severe and progressive dementia, and his only sibling lived in a distant state and was disabled by years of alcohol and drug abuse. He and his wife were separated but not divorced due to religious reasons, and they rarely spoke. His work as a consultant required regular travel throughout the country for short-term assignments, and as a result, he had no work colleagues to speak of. His office was in his home, where he lived alone. Because of his work travel, he kept no pets. He no longer attended church and he belonged to no groups or associations.

Ray's interpersonal network had such a deficit in the number of people that he was basically interpersonally impoverished. His social skills for casual interactions were strong, as he had no problem traveling about and interacting with new people in different work settings all the time. However, his skills in making and establishing more intimate friendships and relationships that would continue past a fleeting contact were much more limited. In addition, conflicts and tensions from his family of origin affected not only the number of people participating in his life, but his willingness to risk trust and intimacy with others.

Explore Roles and Role Transitions

Most people will assume different social roles over the course of a lifetime. From student to apprentice to friend, relative, coworker, adult, boss, teacher, parent, spouse, neighbor, classmate, professional or many others, our social roles have a fundamental impact on our psychological sense of self and worth. Some of our roles are deeply invested with meaning whereas others may be considered peripheral or relatively unimportant. Being a parent may be central for some while roles held for employment are simply jobs that are necessary to pay the bills. For others, career roles have high priority, but family roles are incidental. Most people strive for some balance of family and career roles as both are important to their sense of self.

Difficulties with role adjustment are possible targets for therapeutic intervention when psychosocial roles are ambiguous, overloaded, or ill-fitted to the skills or expectations of the individual. Many role difficulties will emerge during a time of transition, when any discrepancy between the skills and abilities of the individual and the role demands becomes apparent. This may occur because the person does not fully understand the tasks and demands, does not have the skills for fulfilling the demands or has become incapacitated by the increasing demands of multiple roles or significantly more complex roles. Discussion of the specific expectations and requirements of the role and the process of change can help mobilize a more effective coping perspective. When needed,

Clinical Example

Mark came to therapy at the insistence of his wife, Renee, who was at her wit's end with role overload. She was working full time, taking care of their infant daughter, and helping Mark's mother deal with breast cancer and a failing business. Mark had completed a college degree in music education and a master's degree in educational administration, but he had yet to apply for any jobs. Instead, he spent his days at home, smoking pot and playing video games. Renee took the baby to day-care, worked all day at an administrative job she disliked, picked up the baby, and returned home, only to be greeted by Mark, sitting on the sofa surrounded by mess, asking "what do you want to do about dinner?" Mark would then go to the supermarket, if Renee gave him a list, although he might get sidetracked by stopping off to visit with friends along the way. Mark was comfortable in his role of extended adolescence, but was on the verge of failure in fulfilling the new roles of spouse and father. Part of Mark's difficulty was role ambiguity. He had not given much thought to the actual changes that were taking place in his life and thus did not become oriented toward the new roles. He was still in his mid-20s and he viewed adult responsibilities as something for his 30s. This was still the time for having fun, and as long as Renee was working and they could pay their bills, he did not see the need to make any changes.

Sometimes role transitions can be eased by obtaining practical help from other people, at least until the skills needed for the new role can be fully developed. Some roles are demanding precisely because there added or more complex responsibilities. Sometimes delegation to others is unavoidable. The client may not have attempted to obtain help because of the effort or expense, because of being unfamiliar or uncomfortable with doing so, or because assistance was not readily available. Many people either are in a practical situation where they do not have ready access to people as resources, or are in a psychological situation where they avoid this option. There may be internal cognitive or emotional barriers to this process (e.g., "I should be able to handle all this myself; I am failing if I do not."). However, at a fundamental practical level, it is important to ask whether the role strain could be eased by obtaining assistance.

specific skill development may help with role adjustment. For example, retirement planning classes may help with the shift from full-time professional to part-time volunteer.

Provide Instruction in Assertive Communication Skills

This intervention involves assisting clients in recognizing and choosing to express their thoughts and feelings in a manner that is conducive to effective social interactions. The focus of the intervention is the behavioral expression of clients' underlying feelings in ways that show respect for both self and others.

This intervention has several components. First, the client learns to recognize signs of unassertiveness, such as being too passive and feeling victimized or disappointed, or signs of being too aggressive, demanding, or inattentive to

Clinical Example

Thirteen-year-old Ian was embarrassed and angry with his math teacher for habitually mispronouncing his name with a long vowel sound like "eye," and teasingly referring to him as the "eye-man." Thus far, Ian had said nothing to the teacher, but he had gotten a detention for talking in his class and not paying attention. Ian and his therapist noted that he was feeling distressed and angry, but his behavior was passive and indirect, possible signs of unassertiveness. His therapist pointed out that although it might not be easy, Ian did have the option of sharing his feelings more directly with the teacher, and making a request. They considered the best time to initiate this communication and practiced the specific actions with a role-play. Ian decided to stay after school and approach his teacher when there was less likelihood of anyone else being around. He practiced acknowledging possible thoughts and feelings of the teacher, acknowledging his own feelings, and making a request. His intended communication was to sound something like this: "Mr. Green, I know you like to make things funny in class, but I get embarrassed being called *eye-man*. I would like it better if you would use the pronunciation of my name that my parents use, which is *ee-an*. Thanks."

the rights of others. Second, the client practices consideration of the possible choices for expressing thoughts and feelings in the context of specific situations. Therapists can discuss with the client different ways to assert feelings, such as refusing an offer, expressing an opinion, or making a request, and practice some actual words or statements to use.

These actions need to be placed in an overall context for effectiveness in a social situation. For example, refusing an offer from a nervous second-grader who is trying to sell gift wrap for her school is very different from refusing a sales pitch from a professional salesperson offering timeshare vacation condominiums. The benefits of assertive communication will likely be greatest when sufficient consideration of mutual respect (respecting both the rights of self and the rights of others) and social context is given. Thus, this technique involves developing skills in recognizing one's feelings, sizing up the situation, and choosing a response, as well as finding some effective words and using them in a respectful way. The essence of assertiveness may rest in the recognition of the choices available in social situations, and the specific exercise of a choice.

Routines and Rituals

Routines and rituals help to stabilize individual and group systems by ensuring that crucial tasks are completed. Informal routines of daily habits provide a structure that gives continuity and a sense of security to ambiguous and repetitive situations.

Encourage the client's use of routine to stabilize behavior or improve the efficiency of important tasks. Having a particular sequence of behavior at bedtime can help ensure a restful night of sleep. Getting back to the routines of

Clinical Example

Molly felt enduring guilt about having had an affair with a married man when she was in college, even after extensive work with cognitive reframing. Although it had been a long while since she had participated in religious services, she was receptive to the idea of attending services designed for atonement. She decided to attend services with an attitude of simply participating in the ritual and being open to whatever might occur. In reporting back to her therapist, she described a wonderful and liberating experience that crystallized when she read a particular scriptural passage that she had not fully noticed in the past. The passage instructed the reader to turn away from sin and to live; in reading this, she saw the intended message as letting go of her guilt and moving forward with her life.

everyday living with designated times for regular tasks can be stabilizing in the wake of a traumatic event, or in recovering from a significant loss. From reading the newspaper every morning to exercise on Monday-Wednesday-Friday to grocery shopping and laundry on Saturday to eating waffles on Sunday, the regular routine provides consistency and direction. Key to an effectively functioning system, is the ability to adjust routines as needed to meet temporary demands for flexibility.

Formal rituals also serve important emotional functions. Cultural rituals such as weddings, funerals, graduations, and holiday gatherings create a sanctioned way to acknowledge membership within the group. Participating in such rituals gives the individual an impetus to focus on the emotional component of the relationships, to express emotions in a social context, to acknowledge both change and continuity in relationships and groups and to attach meaning to specific social commitment.

Attending a funeral of someone who has died usually helps us process our own feelings of grief, loss, and separation by sharing those feelings with other loved ones, recognizing the social changes precipitated by the death, and gaining perspective on the importance of friends, family members, or even fond acquaintances. Other more joyful rituals help us and those around us recognize our movement through life (e.g., graduations, weddings, christenings, birthday parties) and attach certain emotions and meaning to that movement. The obvious exception to this strategy is the problem of obsessive-compulsive behavior that involves excessive and senseless rituals that interfere with normal living.

Family and Collateral Meetings

Consultation with family members or significant others can be useful in many therapeutic contexts. Sometimes the family unit is the focus of treatment and all sessions involve some combination of family members. Usually one person is the identified patient and any others present are identified as "collateral" participants. Family consultations are usually actively structured and directed by the therapist in pursuit of specific goals. Typical goals for collateral consulta-

Clinical Example

Eloise's severe arthritis at age 75 had advanced to where she required a full-time caregiver in her home. She was delighted to have Robin with her each day to help with dressing, bathing, eating, light correspondence, and outings such as trips to the doctor and hairstylist. Each night, either Eloise's husband or his sister stayed with her in case she needed any assistance during the night.

Eloise had been in intermittent therapy for approximately 25 years for recurrent depression and severe obsessive anxiety. Recently, she was devastated to find out that her husband had a long-standing intimate relationship with a younger woman that he was unwilling to end. When Eloise returned for individual therapy, her therapist included some collateral visits with Robin and Eloise as part of the treatment plan. Robin provided information on Eloise's mood, revealing clear shifts related to the husband's comings and goings, particularly if he was gone all night. Eloise was able to express her appreciation to Robin for her emotional support, and the therapist was able to provide Robin with guidance and encouragement on managing the emotional and interpersonal challenges of this situation.

tions include one or more of the following: gathering information, sharing information among participants, providing psychoeducation, identifying primary concerns, expressing feelings, improving communication patterns and skills, communicating about progress and change, facilitating stress management, conflict resolution or problem solving, and evaluating and stabilizing roles and emotional involvement.

Balance Autonomy and Relationship/Group Affiliation

Our culture is very heterogeneous with respect to an emphasis on individual pursuits over social and familial commitments (see Chapter 3). We tend to endorse the freedom to pursue one's true inner self, yet we still define one another and ourselves through various relationships and memberships. This freedom can bring confusion or tension regarding a functional balance between personal fulfillment and social connection. Clients may come to therapy as a result of the stress of such conflicts and need help reconciling their beliefs, overcoming barriers that stand in the way of their choices, and recognizing behavioral options for personal and interpersonal involvements.

Signs of this imbalance might include feeling controlled by a relationship or group membership, feeling stretched too thin and having no personal time at all, not being able to say no to demands or expectations out of a fear of the social consequences, feeling compelled to do things that are personally harmful or inconsistent with one's values, becoming alienated from one's priorities and personal goals, or feeling alone and disconnected from any sense of belonging to a community or dissatisfied and searching for something missing. The focus of this intervention is to help the client see available choices for both making and limiting interpersonal involvements with the goal of striking a personal

Clinical Example

Ryan enjoyed his sales manager position, but the job required a great deal of entertaining and socializing on the nights and weekends. These work events always included alcohol and there was much heavy drinking by the sales staff and the customers. Now that he was married and had a young child, Ryan wanted to spend more of his evenings and weekends with his family. He also wanted to pursue his hobby of cycling for sport and fitness, but this was an interest that few of his customers or coworkers shared. He felt as though he had more bases than he could reasonably cover and began to think that his life was not going in the direction he most desired. The signifi-

cant financial rewards of his sales job made Ryan feel successful, and he felt strong bonds with several of his coworkers, including the regional manager who was his mentor and "like a father figure." When he tried to reduce his contact with the socializing and drinking, Ryan received much direct and indirect pressure from his colleagues to maintain the status quo. Ryan eventually decided that it was in his best interest to make a career change altogether. He resigned from his position, began attending AA (Alcoholics Anonymous) to stop drinking, and enrolled in a master's degree program to earn his teaching certificate.

balance that is healthy and functional. Using or developing assertive communication skills may be a part of implementing the choices in this intervention.

The behavioral implications of the client's choices are to increase, decrease, or redirect selected interpersonal contacts. A client who does not want to date a drinker would do well to steer clear of bars, nightclubs, and drinking parties, and seek friendships through nondrinking venues. If a client thinks he would enjoy more intellectual stimulation from others, enrolling in a class might make this accessible. If a client would like to meet others with similar political interests, it might be useful to volunteer for a political campaign.

Affective Interventions

Affective interventions are focused primarily on the experience of emotions and bodily sensations. Objectives of affective interventions are to increase conscious awareness of the emotional components of an experience or situation, to reduce avoidance of an affective reaction, to increase the client's tolerance of emotional experience, and to assist in the functional use of emotion. The overall goal is to shape the recognition of a range of affective states as a source of vital information in adaptive living.

Intensity and authenticity are elements of the client's subjective emotional experience that represent individual differences, and should be respected as such. The clinician wants to avoid any implication that there is a "right" or "proper" type or degree of emotion for any given situation. The expression of emotion (e.g., anger) may have functional and dysfunctional parameters that can be addressed with other behavioral, cognitive, or systems interventions.

Mindfulness Practice

There are many strategies of mindfulness practice (see Hanh, 1987; Hayes, Strosahl, & Wilson, 1999; Linehan, 1993; Segal, Williams, & Teasdale, 2002). The common thread among these approaches is the focusing of awareness on internal components of experience and increasing one's skill in observing perceptions, sensations, and thoughts without attempting to change them. Mindfulness can be done in a quiet, eyes-closed state, or it can be practiced during an activity such as walking, folding laundry, or eating. This practice often has a calming effect, although that is not a direct objective. Regular mindfulness practice is intended to decrease the fusion between problematic thoughts or emotions and actions, and promote greater awareness of the different dimensions of experience as contents of the mind.

Clinical Example

Betty kept worrying about a family situation that was beyond her control. It was getting to the point that she barely noticed what she was doing during the day as her mind focused on the family circumstance. She was instructed in mindfulness practice as a way to help herself live fully with her experience of worry and concern. Each day, for 10 minutes, she would sit in a quiet place and focus her attention on feeling herself breathing, noticing any bodily sensations as they occurred, without struggling with those sensations or trying to get rid of them. She practiced noticing the content of her mind, without judging or evaluating it, or pursuing the content in any directed way. She would notice that worries about her family were popping into her mind, but she did not attempt either to get rid of them, or to try to search for possible solutions. She simply refocused her attention on breathing again and again, and would always conclude the exercise with attention to her breathing.

Emotional Deepening and Validation

Helping clients identify, deepen, or extend their understanding of the emotion, and accept rather than deny or reject the experience is a fundamental affective technique. This begins with listening actively for indications of emotional content, and providing reflective feedback to the client. Bringing explicit attention to the emotional domain, and helping to provide labels for the emotions gives importance to this dimension of the client's personal experience, and can help articulate the experience (see L. S. Greenberg et al., 1993; Linehan, 1993).

Beginning therapists are often prone to underestimate the importance of this technique and become frustrated with "just listening and not doing anything." To overcome this error, it is helpful to realize the potential benefit in skillfully attending to emotional content, appropriately drawing this into the discussion, encouraging the client to attend to the thoughts and sensations that are aroused, and providing crucial social support in the form of validating the understandable triggers of the emotional response.

Clients may have in the past or present encountered those who *invalidate* their emotions ("You shouldn't be depressed; cheer up!"), and they may have acquired the habit of invalidating their own emotions. Effective listening and validation by the therapist will often, but not always, help clients reduce their level of distress, and begin to induce some positive affect as well as a greater receptiveness to problem-solving or suggestion.

Clinical Example

Kay was troubled by family interactions with her parents. In the following dialogue, the therapist draws emotional content explicitly into the discussion and validates Kay's experience.

Kay: It's weird when my parents visit. They're really a big help with the kids and all, but they're so messy, and they're always giving me advice about what my husband should be doing better.

Therapist: So some conflicting feelings come up when they visit. It sounds like you feel happy and grateful for their help with the kids, but uncomfortable with the unwanted help with your husband, and the added stress of more mess in your house.

Kay: (Nods) Uh huh. I don't want to be ungrateful, or take advantage of them, and I do want them to visit, and have a relationship with the kids. Oh, I don't know. I should just count my blessings and stop griping.

Therapist: Well, we can certainly take some time to talk about ways to deal with these feelings that make you want to gripe. But first, let's take time for you to understand those feelings and have room to have them.

It makes sense to me that you would feel pulled in two directions given these circumstances, feeling both grateful and annoyed at the same time. Does that describe some of your experience?

Kay: Yes. I think I'm mainly annoyed with myself that I can't just ignore what they say about Bob and go on.

Therapist: Do you feel that tension inside yourself right now?

Kay: (tearing up) Yes. My throat and stomach are tight. I just don't know how to respond to what they say, so I just try to blow it off.

Therapist: Well, it seems logical that a person would feel some tension and distress when two feelings are conflicting like this, especially when those feelings are related to such important relationships.

This dialogue would continue with exploring the client's feelings and eventually move toward problem solving, encouraging the client to recognize how she tends to invalidate and dismiss her own feelings and modeling an alternative of acceptance via the therapeutic interaction.

Interoceptive Exposure

The experience of an affective state may trigger a reaction of fear and avoidance, perhaps because of beliefs related to the unacceptability of certain feelings or their outward expressions, or possible dangerousness of the internal sensations. Avoiding these internal sensations can lead to broad and elaborate networks of avoidance and safety behavior.

For lasting change to occur, it may be necessary to work directly on exposure to the actual sensations, to increase tolerance and decrease the sense of associated threat, and to detect any especially problematic thoughts connected to the sensation. The particular internal sensations feared by the client will be unique, but are typically associated with an uncomfortable or undesirable outcome, such as choking, collapsing, or dying. Interoceptive exposure involves activating those sensations, typically in low to medium intensity, to allow for deconstruction of the sensation in physical terms (e.g., just tension in the muscles) and greater tolerance for the physical experience as well as recognition of its passing nature, thus decreasing the perceived threat and concomitant fear of the sensation.

Clinical Example

When Bob felt panicky, he was especially troubled by tension in his throat, difficulty in swallowing, and a choking sensation. These symptoms were explained as due to muscle tension activated by a fear response and not indicative of any state of medical compromise. Bob had recently been evaluated medically and was deemed to be in good health. With his therapist's prompting, Bob practiced bringing on the sensations of tension in his throat and chest. He was instructed to tighten the muscles in his throat, and then to stop a swallow half-way through and hold it for 30 seconds. Then he tightened his chest and held his breath for 45 seconds. This was repeated several times, each time discussing the degree of distress Bob felt with the sensations, noting that his distress went down with repeated exposures.

Willingness Exercises

Willingness interventions are exercises of the client's choice to pursue a desired activity with the understanding that certain *undesired* emotions may occur. The exercise is one of being willing to have the emotion if it occurs, and still carry on with the plan. So the client might choose to be willing to go to work, even though depression or a sad mood might occur. Or the client might choose to give a presentation, even though anxiety might be part of the experience. The objective of these exercises is to pursue behaviors or activities that are important to the client and give meaning to their life, without trying to control all emotional components of the experience. The client is practicing the willingness to have emotions.

Clinical Example

Shirley prepared a special healthy snack for her daughter's first-grade class and then felt humiliated when the children did not like it. She was so upset by this personal failure that she was not willing to have any further contact with her child's school or class activities. For a time, she had required her husband leave work early to pick up their daughter because she "couldn't show her face" at the school.

Being an involved mother was important to her, so she agreed to challenge herself to experience some undesired emotions to care for her daughter. First, she returned to school pickup, and when she did so, she felt an "anxious rush" while waiting in the car line. She was instructed to simply ask herself whether she was willing to have that feeling, and to encourage willingness. She found the anxious feelings subsided rather quickly as soon as her child got in the car. After 2 weeks of regular pickup, a day of late activity required her to go to the classroom. Again, she made note of the physical sensations, including blushing and feeling fearful and slightly nauseous, and focused on her willingness to have these feelings in the service of being the mother she wanted to be. She continued this same exercise of willingness over and over, until Shirley felt that she had resumed all her previous activities. By this time, Shirley was even ready to try again with a snack for the class Valentine's Day party, and was willing to experience whatever came up in this endeavor.

Values Assessment

Values exercises bring out the client's emotional investment in various life activities. Values are pursuits or roles that have an importance for the client that will typically endure across time and situations. Some values may be more salient at different times in life, and thus matter more because of developmental demands. Being a good parent may take priority over other important values when the client is raising young children. An unmarried, childless client may highly value being a good parent, but other values such as career or friendships have more immediate salience. We can help clients detect the strength of their attachment to various values, and connect this to the direction of their energy.

Clinical Example

Phillip was in therapy for motivational problems at work. In exploring his overall values, Phillip was asked to close his eyes and imagine his funeral. In this fantasy exercise, anything was possible, so he was to select all the peo- ple he wanted to attend his funeral, not just those he thought *would* attend. He then imagined selecting someone to speak about him, and what that person would say. He then imagined two or three more people speaking about him,

Clinical Example (Continued)

and what they would say about his actions, his intentions, and his impact on others. After the fantasy concluded with some final words about how he would be missed and remembered, Phillip and his therapist reviewed his reactions.

Phillip discovered that he wanted people to recognize him as a devoted member of his church and a willing participant in charitable activities. He imagined the church filled with dozens of people who had known him for a long time, many of whom attested to

his extensive contributions to the community. He also felt that, in the end, his work success was relatively unimportant, and that his current motivation issues were probably related to the greater sense of priority he gave to charitable activities. This helped him also recognize that his primary motivation for work was to create stability and social standing for his family, and not to produce greater profits for the business. With a clearer sense of why he was pursuing his work, he overcame some of his avoidance and frustration.

Metaphors

Metaphors offer the opportunity of both a memorable way to present a concept of change, and an indirect mode of suggestion that may minimize reactance or resistance. A visually vivid metaphor can create an image that crystallizes an abstract concept that might be difficult to remember in verbal form. Many clinical metaphors have been developed and tested for use in the clinical approach of acceptance and commitment therapy (ACT; Hayes et al., 1999). In addition to using common metaphors, selecting metaphors for change principles can be guided by the client's own life experiences and interests.

Clinical Example

Cathy felt overwhelmed when faced with important decisions. She struggled with several dimensions of decision making, including the fear of making a mistake, failing to make the right choice, and feeling uncertain about her own preferences. She identified a metaphor that explained how she went about making decisions, whenever possible, and the degree of certainty that she perceived was necessary in making a good decision. When she was small,

she had a favorite book that was entitled, *Patty Likes Pink*. The story depicted a child who always knew what she wanted, confidently choosing pink. Patty was untroubled by doubt and seldom, if ever, experienced disappointment, because she lived entirely in a world of pink. For Cathy, the story was a metaphor for the desire to remove all doubt, uncertainty, and risk of disappointment, but at the cost of a limited scope of experience.

Imagery Replacement

Images can be brought under conscious cognitive influence, much the same as other verbal constructions. In instances where a client lacks positive images, or tends to recall only negative images, a direct activation of positive or coping images may induce a more positive association or greater willingness to approach a difficult situation. Positive images can also be used as a distraction technique for disrupting ruminative thoughts, dwelling on intrusive or negative images, or coping with a difficult or painful experience. The objective should not be to suppress or avoid the occurrence of any particular thought, but rather to prompt the access to positive, enjoyable, or coping images. Creating a picture in the mind activates the positive affect associated with the image.

Clinical Example

Marge, an elder client who was depressed since the death of her spouse, had frequent visual images and memories of her husband in his sickbed, and deceased at his funeral. She understood these images were naturally going to come into her mind. She did not try to suppress them as they were part of a grieving process. However, she was also encouraged to activate additional images drawn from her memories of the couple's happy times together. She recalled the image of them on their wedding day, and some images from their honeymoon. She remembered images of the two of them on a camping trip, holding hands and being close. Marge found it very pleasant to linger on these images, and to enjoy in her mind the sense of being with her spouse and enjoying the soothing warmth of a campfire together.

Expressive Monologue

An expressive monologue is an exercise to help clients articulate feelings that have been suppressed or unresolved for various reasons. The key element is that the monologue is directed toward a specific person or group, approximating the experience of clients actually telling the person how they feel.

Sometimes this is referred to as the "empty chair" exercise, because it is useful to imagine the person present, and to talk as if he or she is listening. There may be a dialogue component to the exercise as well, where the recipient's responses are included and a conversation enacted. Expressive monologue can also be carried out in written form, perhaps as a letter to the designated person. The letter is primarily for expressive purposes and is not necessarily going to be sent. The client will choose that after completing the exercise. The therapist can provide support and encouragement throughout the expression of feelings.

Clinical Example

Ben's best friend was killed in a hit-and-run car accident while attending graduate school. Given the demands of their respective busy schedules and living in different cities, Ben had not been in contact with Matt in a few months. He felt devastated by the news of Matt's death and extremely remorseful over having been out of touch. Ben's therapist asked him to participate in an exercise of expressing his feelings in a conversation with Matt in the empty chair.

Therapist: Let's bring Matt into the room, and allow him to be here to listen to what you most want to tell him. Imagine he's here in this chair (points), and wants to hear what you have to say. Go ahead and let him know what's in your heart.

Ben: "Matt, you were the best friend I ever had, and you can only imagine how much it hurts to lose you. I hate it that your life ended this way, and if you have any awareness in the afterlife, I bet you hate it, too. There's a great big hole in the place you used to be . . . especially when I think about having someone to share things with, or just help me keep my head on straight. I know I have other friends, its true, but none of them will ever be the friend I grew up with, went to college with, chased all those girls with, and had all the good times with. And had a few rough spots, too. It's sad to think there will be no more good times, no more rough spots, just memories. Somebody else will have to be the best man in my wedding, when it should have been you. But when the time comes, I'll be thinking of you, so you'll be there. You'll always be there."

Behavioral Interventions

Behavioral interventions focus on concrete actions and responses of the client with the goal of establishing functional and adaptive patterns of behavior. Adaptive behavior may be very circumscribed (e.g., to be near dogs) or it may be very broad (to be a better parent). Behavioral interventions address what the client does, not just in isolated instances, but repeatedly over time. Often behavioral interventions help the client acquire new responses and build skills. Or they may prompt or trigger previously learned responses, generalize those responses to new situations, or better match the client's behavior to appropriate situations.

Adaptive behavior can be acquired through observation, practice and positive reinforcement. Maladaptive behavior can be weakened by developing incompatible alternative behavior. The unit of interest may be fairly small, but is important in activating or disrupting a chain of other behaviors. When complex skills are involved, the unit of interest might include several elements, including cognitive elements. Cognitive and behavioral interventions are often intertwined, but are presented separately here for descriptive purposes.

Define Target Behavior and Monitor Baseline

Clients often come to therapy with vague goals that have no specific behavioral reference points. If they state that they wish to be able to drive on freeways, or to get their home in order, these goals imply behavioral objectives, even if more specification is needed (e.g., which aspects of the home need to be gotten into order, and what would the desired order look like?). When a client's stated goal is "to be less fearful," or "to find self-confidence," it is important to explore actions that could be associated with such a state, to provide anchor points and to begin to translate diffuse objectives into something manageable and specific.

This is the process of creating an operational definition of the goal in terms of target behaviors. The client can be asked, "What would self-confidence allow you to do that you are not doing now?" Or perhaps, "What are some of the things that self-confident people can do?" Or, "If fear didn't stand in your way, what would you be doing?" The operational definition needs to be relevant and meaningful to the client. Using some generic idea of

Clinical Example

Marge, described earlier, came to therapy because she was depressed about the death of her husband some months ago, and she had a long history of anxiety and worry. Her stated goal was to "not be so sad all the time." The therapist asked Marge to describe what her life was like before all the sadness. Marge had always been quite active and happy, even if she tended to worry and fret. In recent years, most of her daily structure had revolved around spending time with her husband who was in a nursing care facility adjacent to her assisted-living residence. Since his passing, she was at a loss for what to do with each day other than to sit around and be sad all the time.

Marge's therapist suggested that being sad following the death of a spouse was understandable and that some degree of sadness would likely remain with her, but it could possibly ebb and flow over time. The therapist then suggested that they discuss some activities that she used to do, with the broad behavioral target

of increasing her overall activity level. They explored which activities helped reduce sadness, and which did not. This helped them set more specific targets for activities that were valuable to Marge and extracted her from the inactivity of sadness. Thus, the operational definition of her goal was to engage in more activities that brought her positive feelings instead of sadness.

For 2 weeks, Marge kept track of how many times she ate a meal in the company of others, either going to the facility cafeteria, joining in on scheduled outings, making specific plans with someone, or when a family member came to visit. She noted that she was happier when she had meals with others, and tended to be more sad and "mopey" when she ate alone. In fact, she tended to skip meals when she had no companionship. Just keeping track of this behavior encouraged her to sign up for a facility-sponsored activity where a group of residents went out together to a local restaurant.

what a self-confident or less fearful person "should" do would be unlikely to help the client.

The next step in beginning to change a behavior or class of behavior is to monitor its frequency and circumstances of occurrence, without any specific attempts to change the behavior yet. Baseline monitoring is extremely helpful for increasing clients' awareness of their actions, as well as connections with triggers, associated thoughts, and emotional and social consequences. Baseline monitoring is usually nonthreatening and a good way to increase the client's involvement in therapy and movement toward active change.

Greater compliance is likely to be achieved with simple methods of monitoring, such as making a check mark on an index card, or making a note in a calendar when and if an action occurred. The frequency of a specific thought or class of thoughts, such as dwelling on a bad test grade, or thinking about a spouse's limitations can also be monitored. Infrequent behaviors that the client wants to increase should be monitored to determine if there is indeed a low frequency. This may be the case, or it may be that the client has a problem with distorted perceptions or judgment, perhaps the result of a mood disorder. If the client says that he never or hardly ever gets to exercise, it might be helpful to use a calendar monitoring exercise activities and to count up the current frequency of occurrence in a week's time. The process of observation alone may produce some change, often referred to as "reactivity." If this occurs, it can be regarded positively as a sign of the client's readiness to change as well as ability to self-regulate behavior through awareness and intention.

Scheduled Activities for Pleasure and Mastery

This intervention involves prompting or scheduling behaviors that are likely to elicit positive internal experiences. Positive activities might be something commonly regarded as enjoyable (e.g., watching a movie, sitting in the sunshine), specifically pleasurable to the client (e.g., getting a manicure, hitting golf balls), or related to a sense of mastery or accomplishment for the client, given his or her current mood, strengths, and responsibilities (e.g., doing the taxes, scheduling an appointment, cooking a meal; A. T. Beck et al., 1979). This strategy may be most useful for clients who have clear deficits in positive affect and a low or insufficient rate of behavior related to either pleasure or mastery.

Options for pleasure and mastery are selected by first generating a list of possible activities that the client associates with the potential for positive emotions such as joy, connection, pleasure, accomplishment, achievement, or the like. It is important that the possible activities are ones that the client finds acceptable and potentially worthwhile, and does not find demeaning or immoral.

Generating such a list of options can be a significant task, particularly if the client has a significant pattern of withdrawal, avoidance, or low emotional engagement. In their self-help book on self-esteem, C. M. Nezu and Nezu (2003) describe this task as developing a "joy profile," and they draw from three categories of activity—social, productive, and sensory pleasure. Generic lists such as those offered by Nezu & Nezu can prompt ideas that might be appealing or suitable for a particular individual. Exploring the client's past for

Clinical Example

Lorrie, a divorced mom with two teenage boys at home, complained that she felt completely overwhelmed by the clutter and disorganization in her home. She worked part-time and had "plenty" of time to keep up her home. When she tried to tackle the housework, she felt pangs of anxiety and guilt about how much there was to do and how badly she had let things slide. These feelings would propel her into her favorite easy chair to "relax" a bit before getting started. Often, she either fell asleep, or became caught up in watching a sequence of television programs. A crisis developed when her air conditioner failed during an extremely hot spell of weather. Because her living room was such a mess, she would not call a repair person until she at least cleared a path between the door and the air-conditioning unit.

Accomplishing this small goal made Lorrie more determined to work on or-ganizing and cleaning her home, room by room. Her social constrictions had become extreme, to the point that she would not allow her boys to have friends over because the house was in such bad shape. Motivated by her sense of parental responsibility and her own de-sire to have a more presentable home, she decided to schedule a weekend blitz to start the cleanup. She called in a very close friend to spend the weekend help-ing with the decluttering project. To-gether, they cleared out the major spaces and organized the things that she needed to keep. Lorrie found the impact of these changes so pleasant and encour-aging that she decided to schedule daily housekeeping tasks to keep things in or-der. She also decided to schedule time for exercise as a way to increase another desired but difficult activity.

ideas about activities he or she used to enjoy is another method to detect possible options. Discussion about things the client finds intriguing or views as "looking like fun" might be another avenue for new but untested options.

The behavioral component of the intervention is to then schedule a time and place to try something new or to increase the frequency of activities on the list. A client might designate the weekend as a time for one new pleasant activity such as attending a play or live music performance. The client might also plan to use her break at work every day rather than skipping it and continuously working. By taking her break, she can increase her contact with pleasant activities such as walking in the sunshine or visiting the cafeteria to chat with coworkers.

From a behavioral standpoint, the effort made to engage in some activity is the most important outcome to monitor. Some activities, such as regular exercise, require persistence through times of "not so much fun" to gain a tangible sense of accomplishment. Other activities, such as browsing the bookstore, may be more reliably pleasant. Old pleasures may be outgrown, but first clients must make the effort to find this out. Thus, the emphasis is placed on shaping a pattern of behavior rather than producing immediate, specific results.

Graduated Tasks

This intervention involves breaking a more complex activity into its component parts, and encouraging the client to undertake a challenging action by starting with the easier components. A metaphor that is sometimes helpful in explaining this strategy is to imagine picking fruit from a tree or bush, and to think of picking the ripest fruit within reach. One might think of picking the "lowest apples first," or the "ripest berries off the top." This often goes hand in hand with scheduling activities for pleasure and mastery because clients frequently view a desired activity as too difficult or formidable to undertake as a whole, especially if it is something new or previously untried. It is typically much easier to make small changes in a graduated manner, than to make large changes and try to "leap tall buildings in a single bound."

The following questions are helpful in establishing the graduated tasks: "What is the first thing that you would want to do to get started?" Or, "What needs to happen to make it possible to (engage in X)?" From this, a sequential outline of each action can be developed, breaking things down into greater detail when the client needs greater assistance because of roadblocks or lack of clarity.

Clinical Example

Sandra wanted to invite her family over for a birthday dinner for her husband, but she felt overwhelmed and anxious about "throwing a party." So she and her therapist outlined a list of graduated tasks that broke down this complex idea of "throwing a party" into specific behavioral components. First, she identified a possible date and time (Sunday evening, the week of his birthday). Then she planned the components of the meal and how she would get them prepared (purchase prepared lasagna, make a fresh salad and a cake, ask family members to bring appetizers).

Next, she phoned family members to invite them and see if they could come. After that, she purchased the needed ingredients for the meal. She also purchased a special gift and wrappings as well as a birthday banner and some flowers for decorations. The day before the dinner, she planned to clean up the house by vacuuming the floor, dusting, and cleaning the bathroom. On the cleaning task, it was important to be specific about what was really feasible and necessary. Sandra recognized that she could easily become overwhelmed if she was not specific about what it meant to "make the house presentable." This did not have to include polishing the silver and cleaning the gutters. On the day of the dinner, she planned to bake the cake, make the salad, and put on her favorite dress and jewelry. The last items on the graduated list of tasks were to remind herself to use her hostess social skills (when guests arrive, open the door, smile and greet them warmly, invite them in), and to focus her attention on her family rather than any worries or concerns that might pop into her head.

Systematic Exposure

This intervention involves assisting the client to confront a difficult, anxiety-provoking situation through repeated or extended contact. Exposure can be broken down into component parts of maximally tolerable contact, much like the strategy of graduated tasks. However, the focus in systematic exposure is the experience and toleration of arousal, and testing specific cognitions related to that arousal or the stimulus itself. Exposure to one component or level of arousal may need to be repeated a few or many times before the client is ready or willing to undertake the next component. In graduated tasks, the components of the overall task tend to flow more readily, one to the next, without much, if any, repetition.

Clinical Example

Craig, an expectant father, had a fear of changing a baby's diaper. He was afraid that the baby would be uncooperative and cry, urinate on him, or that he would become nauseated by stool-filled diapers, or be unable to wipe the baby's bottom and secure the clean diaper effectively. He was quite panicked by this fear, thinking that it made him a "wimp" and a baby himself. Both he and his wife expected him to "suck it up" and be ready to change diapers for his expected son. Craig's therapist started by reassuring him that his reactions were completely understandable, and that these should get less intense with repeated exposure and familiarity with his baby, but more difficult with continued avoidance. They began a plan of systematic exposure using a doll to practice changing and wiping, and increasing the arousal by having his wife place brown mustard in the doll's diaper for him to change. Next, they arranged a visit to the newborn nursery where Craig watched through a window as a nurse changed an infant's diaper.

In each of these exposure exercises, Craig noted his level of arousal on a scale of 0 to 10, how well he tolerated that arousal, and whether any of his fears were confirmed or disconfirmed. Exposure continued after the arrival of their son, as Craig first watched the nurse change the baby, and then his wife change the baby; finally he tried changing the baby. At first, he changed the baby with a dry diaper, then a wet diaper, then a diaper with stool. He noted that one of his fears was confirmed (the baby might urinate during changing), but that it was tolerable and did not create much arousal. He also realized that the baby sometimes became fussy during changes, but usually diaper changing helped the baby calm down, disconfirming another of his fears. Finally, he found that although he was uncomfortable with dirty diapers, the discomfort was tolerable and became less noticeable over time.

Behavioral Rehearsal and Time Management

Behavioral rehearsal involves practicing or role-playing a behavior or sequence of behavior to improve the client's confidence and chances of successfully carrying out the behavior in its normal context. Behavioral rehearsal might include practicing a difficult conversation by role-playing with the therapist. Or it might involve an imagined practice where the client and therapist verbally describe a sequence of actions, as if they were describing an action scene from a movie or play.

Sandra, in the clinical example of graduated tasks, behaviorally practiced her hostess skills by imagining and describing specifically what she would do during her party. Behavioral rehearsal is a particularly useful tool for building time management skills, and dealing with the complexity of organizing one's behavior in the context of real time.

To begin behavioral rehearsal of time management, discussion can start with either a designated time to be structured (e.g., weekends), or the activities that need to be planned (e.g., find time to exercise). The first step is to *allocate time* for specific actions. It is important to be specific, denoting real times and clear, observable behaviors (e.g., walk or cycle from 4:00 to 5:00 P.M. on Tuesday, Thursday, Saturday, and Sunday). Even if the planned action actually takes place at a different time or in a different form (went to the gym at noon because it was raining and I had a break), the listing of specific times increases behavioral orientation toward action and helps the client move out of wishful thinking and vague imagining. The client's own personal calendar can be used to sketch out a plan and monitor its implementation, or the therapist can provide a simple list of times of the day, with space to fill in the actions.

The next step in rehearsing time management is to establish a realistic transition time between activities. Allocating time between activities for a transition is much like leaving a margin on a written page, or creating a frame around a picture. There is a need for some blank space, to allow our senses to have a stopping point and some brief rest, to demarcate the lines between when one thing stops, and another begins. All too often, our time margins are either quickly gobbled up, or entirely neglected in the interest of heightened productivity or an ambitious agenda. Without a time margin, there is no room for dealing with unexpected delays, enjoying a lingering moment, or taking advantage of a spontaneous idea. A situation may be experienced in very different ways, and perhaps have a different impact or outcome, when there is sufficient ease in time versus pushing the effort right up to the limits in time. Clients are much more likely to report a sense of mastery when they can complete things in the time available, instead of not even coming close to completing a particular agenda or list of activities. This simple situational change can precipitate fairly significant changes in the qualitative experience of an activity.

The final step is to rehearse ways to revise the plan of action should that be needed along the way. Because so often our estimates of needed time are just that—estimates—it is not uncommon to find ourselves in the midst of an unworkable agenda. Even with good planning and reasonable margins, something

Clinical Example

Corey, a 35-year-old sales manager, entered therapy with complaints of chronic stress, the feeling of being overwhelmed, and difficulty in achieving personal goals. Although he functioned reasonably well in the context of his work, he felt that his greater difficulties were in the domain of his personal life. On the weekends in particular, he was frustrated with his "inability to ever get anything done." He had aspirations to exercise more and get together with friends for a pickup game of basketball, and he wanted to enjoy time with his family, have time to check in on his elderly mother, take care of home maintenance tasks, and occasionally get away to the lake for some fishing.

Instead, his weekends were consumed by a slew of what seemed to be unending errands and "who knows what." On a recent weekend, as he was on a trip to the drugstore with his child, he experienced a panic attack. This terrified him, as it appeared that his health was now declining as a result of his ongoing stress, and he sought both therapy and medical evaluation. The medical evaluation revealed no abnormalities, and he was encouraged to begin a regular program of exercise.

Corey's therapist suggested that they take his list of desired activities for the weekend, and discuss some possible times to designate for specific endeavors. The pickup basketball game was the easiest place to start, because there already was a group meeting at a nearby gym at 2 P.M. on Saturdays. Corey could either just show up with that group, or arrange to meet friends for a scrimmage. To effectively make this commitment, however, Corey also had to pick a designated time for his other important activities, to insert some margin into his plan, and practice making revisions while in action when delays or interruptions occurred. He worked up a short list of home maintenance and family activities to take place prior to the basketball game, with a specific time to stop and shift his attention toward getting to the gym. He then designated Sunday as a flexday, to include time for visiting his mother and enjoying recreation such as fishing. His therapist encouraged him to practice working out a plan on paper, so that he could best create a situation that allowed time for each thing. His plan looked like this:

Saturday: Breakfast with family
7:00 A.M. to 8:00 A.M.

Mow grass or wash car
8:00 A.M. to 9:30 A.M.

Daughter's soccer & lunch
10:00 A.M. to 12:00 P.M.

Stop at Home Depot after soccer
Fix toilet
12:30 P.M. to 1:30 P.M.

Leave for gym
1:30 P.M.

Basketball
2:00 P.M. to 4:00 P.M.

Rehearsing the sequence of actions and writing it down helped Corey practice organizing his behavior in the context of real time. He became more successful in getting around to what he wanted and needed to do. He realized that thinking about everything without a plan for designated times was immobilizing him from getting much of anything done.

may significantly alter the original plan. Recognizing this has happened and revising the agenda in the midst of action is all part of effective time management.

Stimulus Control

Specific behaviors become more likely to occur in the presence of certain cues or prompts. Conversely, they can be weakened or made less likely be altering or removing the cues. Complex patterns of behaviors typically have a recurring sequence, or chain of action. Each behavior acts as a cue or trigger for the next action in the sequence. When change is desired, it can be useful to map out the currently occurring chain, and plan ways to alter this chain to achieve a different outcome. This can be graphically drawn out on a piece of paper or chalkboard, illustrating the typical chain from a logical starting point, noting possible and likely points to alter the sequential cues. The net result is response prevention, as a highly likely response is prevented from occurring by altering the chain of action.

Clinical Example

Brock, a 40-year-old business owner wanted to decrease the frequency and amount of his alcohol use and unproductive "screen time" at home in the evening. After monitoring the baseline amount of alcohol typically consumed and time spent on his computer or watching television, he and his therapist mapped out the typical chain of behaviors that occurred each evening, beginning when he walked in the door. First thing, he greeted his dog. Then he thought about how stressed he felt, turned on the television, and mixed a drink. He sat on his sofa, drank the cocktail and watched the news. When his glass was empty, he got up and mixed another drink and returned to the sofa to watch more TV. After the second drink was finished, he got up and microwaved a frozen dinner, ate it, fed the dog, and then mixed another drink and went to his computer. He sat down and read e-mail, sent instant messages, and surfed chat rooms.

Sometimes he would continue mixing drinks or pouring glasses of wine and returning to the computer to chat for several hours, losing count of the number of drinks or amount of alcohol consumed. However, the most frequent behavior chain followed the pattern of two to four drinks of alcohol, and several hours of screen time. He and his therapist drew this chain of actions out on a piece of paper, describing each action in connecting, sequential circles. With this graphic example to support their discussion, they reviewed possible places that he might alter the chain, to prevent the typical sequence of drinking so much or spending so many hours in front of a screen.

As part of this plan, Brock specified measurable behavioral goals: to have no more than 3 drinks in any one day and no more than 10 drinks per week overall, with a target of 0 to 2 drinks per day and a screen time of no more than 3 hours of combined computer

(continued)

Clinical Example (Continued)

and television time. His alternative plan was to use his evenings more productively for reading, working on his house, entertaining, or just playing with his dog.

Brock used behavior monitoring to keep track of the number of drinks he consumed each evening, and he rehearsed behavioral changes at very specific points in the sequence. He decided to greet the dog, and then instead of mixing the first drink, to take his dog for a walk and play with him in the backyard. He also decided to skip watching the news on a regular basis before dinner, and to spend more time actually cooking dinner, something that he enjoyed. He might choose to have a glass of wine with his dinner, or not, but he would postpone having a mixed drink until after dinner, if he had one at all.

Over the course of several weeks, he discussed the challenges and successes in making these changes in his habitual evening pattern. This discussion helped him to rehearse specific, discrete behavior changes as a form of altering his responses to cues and situations encountered on a daily basis. Although the changes may sound relatively straightforward, considerable effort and persistence were involved in executing this intervention. However, Brock significantly reduced his alcohol consumption, avoided binges of drinking an uncertain quantity of alcohol, maintained his targeted objective of moderate alcohol consumption, and increased the quality of his leisure time.

Behavioral Relaxation

This technique specifically refers to tension reduction in terms of both cognitive activity and muscle tension. Many techniques are available for assisting clients to reduce muscular tension, and adjust cognitive tension.

The general procedure is to start with adjusting external sensory stimulation by dimming lights, providing a comfortable chair or recliner, adjusting the temperature, and reducing intrusive noise (and perhaps including a soothing sound). The client then focuses on physical sensations, particularly breathing, and is instructed either to simply release tension throughout different parts of the body (e.g., let the arms relax, let the shoulders relax, let the face relax), or to tense and then release different muscle groups (see D. Bernstein & Borkovec, 1973; Otto, Jones, Craske, & Barlow, 1996). Instructions for cognitive tension release typically include allowing thoughts to occur, but refocusing attention on physical sensations, or simply relaxing and letting thoughts happen without responding or otherwise attending to them. Relaxing or calming imagery may be included as part of the exercise, creating visualized places that the client associates with pleasant, relaxed states, such as floating in a pool, sitting by a fountain, lying on a sofa, or swinging in a hammock. This intervention is useful as a general method for improving well-being, as well as for disrupting dysfunctional states of overall tension.

Clinical Example

Beth was prone to extreme states of tension and worry. She had obsessive worries about her health and her medications, side effects, allergies, and interactions among the drugs. She worried about what people thought of her, and about their reactions to her health problems. In particular, she worried about her interactions with health care professionals, which were numerous and frequent. In her chronic and sometimes extreme state of worry and tension, she would experience increases in various side effects and allergies, such as unusual sensations, itching, rashes, and sensitivity to foods. Her inclination was then to worry more in an attempt to figure out what to do about her reactions. Behavioral relaxation helped her disrupt this spiraling chain of tension and worry. She experienced a decrease in her overall rating of experienced tension in the moment by taking 10 to 20 minutes to systematically tense and release her muscles, focus her attention on breathing, and imagining napping in a hammock.

Generalization of Behavior

This intervention involves either prompting or identifying established behaviors that can be used in new ways, or in new situations for better adaptations. The focus of the discussion between client and therapist may be on skills, where they take inventory of the skills used in one situation that may apply to a new or more challenging situation. This intervention can be particularly useful for clients who are having some difficulty with a role transition or adjustment.

Clinical Example

Mary Jo was thinking of dropping out of nursing school for fear of being unable to complete her required clinical practice placement some distance from her home. She was anxious about driving a stretch of road that included interstate travel over a mountainous region. The time of year increased her chances of having to drive in rainy weather, perhaps in the dark if she had to stay late. She was also worried about being able to relate to the patients, many of whom would be elderly. Her therapist asked her to think about the specific skills involved in each of these situations, and whether she had any previous experience to build on. She had driven extensively on the interstates, once even traveling halfway across the country. However, the situation of driving regularly over a mountain, sometimes in inclement weather or conditions of darkness was new to her.

So Mary Jo and her therapist discussed in some detail what skills of interstate driving might generalize to this

(continued)

Clinical Example (Continued)

new situation, and what additional skills she might need. She also recognized that darkness and wet weather were not new conditions, and that she already had specific skills that could generalize to a new situation of driving over a mountain, such as slowing down in the rain, looking for the outer white line to follow the road in reduced visibility, not braking suddenly if possible, and staying in her lane except to pass.

As for relating to her elderly patients, they discussed what experience she had in relating to elderly people that she could apply to this new clinical context. Mary Jo recalled spending summers with her grandmother, enjoying her interactions with grandmother's card-playing group, all of whom were older people, and family gatherings with her mother's family, where six or more older persons often were present. This helped her realize that she had some skills in making small talk or conversation with older persons, and that she knew how to take an interest in people, both skills that could generalize to her placement experience.

Cognitive Interventions

With cognitive interventions, the therapist and client are delving into the content of specific thoughts to alter the functional impact of those thoughts. Cognitions are frequently altered indirectly through the other interpersonal, affective, and behavioral forms of intervention. The unique element of a specific cognitive intervention is the explicit focus on automatic thoughts, ideas, assumptions, attitudes, rules, or beliefs, and the direct efforts to reshape or revise those mental objects.

Through a cognitive intervention, mental objects (automatic thoughts, assumptions, beliefs) may be altered in degree of believability, importance, or flexibility by additional ideas or contexts that were previously not being used or given value. Cognitive interventions are not designed to delete or control thoughts, or to insert "right" thoughts for "wrong" thoughts, but rather to create a greater range of choice and pliability in mental alternatives.

Detect and Evaluate Automatic Thoughts

This intervention is a basic and fundamental cognitive strategy (J. Beck, 1995; Greenberger & Padesky, 1995). Automatic thoughts are an evaluative part of our ongoing stream of consciousness, occurring spontaneously but potentially influenced by the current mood state. Under normal circumstances, such as when a person is not in distress, there is also an automatic reality testing where the accuracy or utility of thinking is quickly checked. When this critical examination fails, the person experiences emotional distress, which typically leads to more negative automatic thoughts.

In this intervention, the therapist helps the client learn about automatic thinking and how to bring negative automatic thoughts into awareness. To do this, specific situations need to be pinpointed, where the client can discern a change or shift in emotions. Then, automatic thoughts are distinguished from both situations, and emotions. The degree of emotion is typically rated on a subjective scale, such as from 0 to 100, to help the client have greater discrimination of degrees of difference, and to identify the more emotionally provocative automatic thoughts.

The next step in the intervention is to prompt reality checking of the automatic thoughts by using a series of questions or probes that focus on the evidence to verify the thought, the alternative interpretations available, or the implications to be addressed if the thought contains some truth (see J. Beck, 1995). Cognitive therapists often use a written illustration as they work through this exercise, using a piece of paper or a whiteboard. In sequential columns, the basic information is listed: situation, emotions, automatic thoughts, and the constructed response, which will either be reformulated cognitions or a coping action plan. Emotions that are subsequent to the constructed response may also be listed, to illustrate for the client how their emotions are affected by cognitive perspective.

Clinical Example

Debra was feeling depressed and lonely, so she decided to phone a close friend whom she had not seen in a while. During their brief conversation, she detected a detached tone in the friend's voice, and she thought she could hear the tapping of a keyboard in the background, as if her friend was working on her computer during their conversation. After hanging up the phone, she felt more sad, lonely, and miserable than ever. Her automatic thought record looked like this:

Situation	Emotion	Automatic Thoughts	Coping Response	Emotions
Conversation with Ella	Sad—80 Lonely—99 Miserable—90	Ella didn't even want to bother talking to me. She must not like me anymore. I have no friends. I'm a loser and a reject.	I never asked if it was a bad time for her. Maybe she had a work deadline. Just because she was distracted does not mean that she is no longer my friend. We've been friends for a long time, and I do still have other friends. I can try calling her again at a better time or maybe send her an email.	Lonely—60 Hopeful—40

Guided Discovery

Guided discovery involves asking a series of questions in a Socratic style dialogue, to draw out intermediate beliefs or those conditional rules and assumptions that arise from and reinforce distorted core beliefs about the self, others, and the future. Such assumptions and rules form a web of emotionally charged cognitions that guide and direct the person's behavior. These cognitions can be addressed with the same methods of critical reality testing that are used for automatic thoughts. To do this, the client first must detect the belief and bring it more fully into conscious awareness, including exploration of the emotions and behavioral responses that are tied to the rule or assumption. This process of questioning and exploring provides some important reality testing as such rules typically operate as a "given," "just the way things are," or "the way I was raised." This typifies the cognitive rigidity and lack of alternative ideas that the intervention is designed to address.

Clinical Example

Debra and her therapist had the following guided discovery dialogue about friendship.

Therapist: Debra, you were clearly distressed by this experience of Ella sounding detached when you phoned her. I'd like to explore further some of the associations your mind makes to such a situation. For example, how would you complete the following thought: If a friend is distracted when I call, then . . .

Debra: She isn't really there for me.

Therapist: So if someone is a friend, then they will always be there for you?

Debra: Yes.

Therapist: And is the reverse also true for you, that if someone isn't there for you, that means they are not a friend?

Debra: I guess so.

Therapist: Is this rule an absolute one, or are there any exceptions? Could someone have one or two "strikes" and still be your friend?

Debra: Well, I suppose so, but I don't like it.

Therapist: Have there ever been times that you were not able to be there for a friend, but you still felt very committed to the friendship, and were able to be there at some point in the future?

Debra: Oh, never, I'm always a "perfect" friend (laughs). No, really, I see what you're getting at. Maybe my rules for friendship don't have to be so strict.

Downward Arrow

This technique follows one particular thought with successive questions about the attached meaning. By following a trail of associated meaning, the client can articulate global conclusions that are reference points in the schema for self, others, and the future. These are the core beliefs that are highly believable, salient, and persistent over time. The downward arrow exercise helps bring the idea into the client's awareness in a verbal form that can be further discussed and modified.

Clinical Example

Bill reported having anxious and depressed feelings after eating lunch with his coworkers in the office cafeteria. The topic of conversation had been a variety of hobbies, and Bill saw his colleagues as being vastly more accomplished than he was. The downward arrow conversation went as follows:

Bill: I can barely cover my bases on the job and these guys all excel at work and accomplish something in their hobby as well.
Therapist: What do you think that means?
Bill: They are better than me.
Therapist: Better than you in terms of . . . ?
Bill: Being a competent human being.

Therapist: If that were true, and I'm not buying that it is, but if that were true, what would that mean?
Bill: That I am incompetent and defective.
Therapist: So when you are around highly competent coworkers, how much do you believe that you are incompetent and defective?
Bill: Just about 100%.
Therapist: And if it is 100% true that you are incompetent and defective, what does that mean?
Bill: I am ultimately a weak person.
Therapist: And does that mean anything else?
Bill: That I am unlovable and unworthy of associating with strong people.

Generate Options and Alternatives

The client's upsetting thoughts may be related to situations or circumstances that are true or unchangeable. The distress is not a function of the client's distorted view of reality, but rather a constricted view of the possible options for coping. The client and therapist work together to brainstorm a list of possible choices, or ideas to try to make a difficult situation more workable. To the extent that the client lacks skills or experience, the options should include a skill-building component.

Clinical Example

In the previous example of Debra, who was upset about her friend's distraction, the therapist helped her generate some ideas about ways she could respond to this situation. Together, they made a list of possible options for her to consider. The list looked something like this:

- Do nothing. Our friendship has room for her to be distracted.
- See how things go when we get together next and then decide.
- Call her and vent my feelings.
- Call her and schedule a time to discuss our needs and feelings about our friendship.

(continued)

Clinical Example (Continued)

- Call her to make some plans, but don't specifically bring anything up, just have a friendly contact.
- Write a "Dear Jane" letter to tell her how angry I am.
- Drop her as a friend. Don't call or write, and refuse to answer her correspondence.

Each of these options was discussed for its possible workability and likely result. Debra decided that she wanted to try calling Ella to schedule a time for discussing their mutual needs and feel-ings about the friendship. She felt this was most in keeping with her value of being a loyal friend herself. However, she was also uncomfortable because she had little experience with such direct communication. She was afraid that she would bungle the conversation or provoke Ella's anger. So her natural tendency was to avoid confrontation. Thus, Debra needed assistance in practicing assertive communication skills to help her overcome the avoidance barrier.

Scale on a Continuum

The problem at hand often *feels* like the *worst* problem ever because the proximal demands and the level of arousal activate extreme appraisals. Emotional reactions to having the problem can magnify the negative aspects of it, much like a pebble in one's shoe can feel like a boulder after a very short distance. This is especially true if the circumstances are highly salient to self-esteem and the client has little confidence in being able to cope. Scaling on a continuum recasts the perspective on the problem; this shrinks back the intensified distress and decreases the meaning or importance ascribed to a single action or situation.

Clinical Example

Shirley made a special effort to prepare a "healthy" birthday treat for her daughter's first-grade class. When she checked back in the afternoon, the snacks were mostly untouched and the teacher told her that the children had not been interested in a snack that day. Shirley then felt "horribly embarrassed," as if she could never show her face again at the school. She was convinced this was a failure at being a mother.

Prior to using the willingness exercise described above, Shirley's therapist used the cognitive scaling exercise to help her reduce the intensity of her embarrassment. The therapist asked her to make a continuum of possible motherhood failures, with a degree of importance attached from 0 to 100% (see the figure following). They brainstormed a list of possible failures, from minor importance to major importance by Shirley's estimation. The list included failure to wake your child up on time for school (25%), failure to check your child's homework (40%), failure to check with

Clinical Example

a doctor when your child is ill (70% or worse), failure to know your child's whereabouts (90%), failure to protect your child from known dangers or threats such as poisons (99%) and failure to love your child as 100%. In the context of this continuum, the disturbing situation of the failure of her snack to delight the class seemed much smaller and less important, rating in the end, only 15%.

Shirley's continuum of possible motherhood failures

0	15	30	45	60	75	90	100
	Unpopular snack		Neglect homework		Overlook illness		Fail to love

Redirect Attention

When anticipating a challenging activity that provokes some discomfort, the cognitive response often deteriorates into fruitless rumination. Rather than evaluating the truthfulness or usefulness of these thoughts, a somewhat different tactic is used. It is already evident that the thoughts are not useful, and there is little or no dispute of the accuracy of the observations.

Instead, the stream of consciousness produces avoidance behavior, sometimes identified by clients as "procrastination." It is clear that some important task or activity is not getting done, and this in turn is creating tension and worry; and perhaps very real negative consequences are looming. This intervention instructs the client to recognize the unproductive nature of the thoughts, and redirects attention toward more productive tasks. *Tic-Toc* is an acronym for "task-*interfering* cognitions," and "task-*orienting* cognitions" (Burns, 1989). By labeling the ruminations that accompany procrastination as "task-interfering," the debate can be curtailed, and the focus of energy shifted more directly toward "task-orienting" thoughts.

Clinical Example

Moritza, a high school senior, kept putting off the work of completing college applications. She would sit down at her computer and think, "I don't know where to start. There's too much to do. I can do it later. I don't feel like doing it now. Besides, I don't know where I want to go to college, or if I will be accepted." It was no surprise that she typically would find something else to do instead of working on the applications. However, her parents and school counselor were beginning to come up with more nagging questions about her progress, which further made her think "Everyone is getting mad at me. I'm probably not college material."

(continued)

Clinical Example (Continued)

Moritza's therapist explained that there was an important and specific task at hand, and it appeared that Moritza was having a lot of TICs when she needed more TOCs. This aroused her curiosity, and the therapist explained that TOCs were "task orienting cognitions," or thoughts that would help her get focused and directed on actually getting something done. TICs only interfered with her getting the task done. So her therapist offered some examples of TOCs, including "I can start anywhere, it's okay, just as long as I get started. It will be simple to just fill out the name and address parts. If I run into a snag, the counselor or my mom will help me. I need to get started now, even though I don't feel like it. And I won't know where I can go until I apply and get accepted. The first thing to do is just open the file with the application form and start filling in the blanks."

Assign a Realistic Probability

Once an idea or a possibility is present in our mind, emotions often follow the possibility, even if it is extremely remote or unlikely. If you think of a terrible catastrophe, you are likely to feel some sadness and anxiety at the mere thought or image. This reaction may then build in a cumulative fashion, much like an avalanche cascading down a mountain, getting larger and larger as more catastrophic thoughts and images are easily brought to mind.

Stopping this avalanche may take a systematic effort of assigning realistic probabilities to the ideas and images. Sometimes just stopping to think about

Clinical Example

Alice developed a fear of being bitten by a dog after she was randomly bitten by a pet walking with his owners. Her experience told her that being bitten was possible, and now every dog she saw carried the potential to harm her. The notion of experience salience was explained to Alice (having had an experience leads us to think it is likely to happen again). Then she was asked to place this experience in a context of realistic probability.

As homework, Alice gathered more information from dog-training experts and learned that many factors can increase or decrease the probability of a dog biting her. These could include the dog's breed, the dog's history of care (which would likely be unknown to her), as well as the dog's behavior at the time of contact with her, and the place of contact (whether she was in the dog's "territory"). Signals such as growling, staring, flattening of the ears and fierce barking would typically precede more aggressive behavior. Any and all of these factors could help her determine a realistic probability of a dog being aggressive toward her, and help her to plan an appropriate response rather than simply guarding herself against any contact with dogs whatsoever.

the realistic probability will easily bring the concept of remoteness to mind, and help the person realize the minimal likelihood of the apprehension. Other times, specific testing of ideas or gathering of information is needed to create a semblance of a realistic probability. If the client does not immediately have a sense of realistic probability, then further information may be needed to form a realistic judgment.

Conduct a Survey

A useful way to introduce flexibility into the client's thinking is to encourage informal surveys of the thoughts, beliefs, and practices of others. This can help the client reduce a fear (e.g., "would you laugh and ridicule someone who passed out in public?"), gain greater confidence in their own convictions (e.g., "would you disapprove of a 14-year-old being allowed to smoke pot?"), or normalize common reactions ("do you ever worry about doing well enough at your job?").

It is important to discuss who will be the respondents to the survey, as this will provide a context for the information gathered. For example, a drug dealer just might approve of the 14-year-old smoking pot. Gathering information, considering the sources, and deciding whether to revise one's own beliefs on the basis of this information are the essential ingredients for increasing flexibility and ability to think critically about one's perceptions and beliefs.

Clinical Example

Fritz, an assistant professor, was discouraged and embarrassed that his first submission of a research grant request had been rejected. This provoked significant doubts about his ability to succeed in his chosen field, and he began ruminating about ending up as a barista at the coffee shop. Conducting a survey on the typical frequency of this sort of outcome among colleagues in his current department felt too threatening to him, but he was willing to contact some of his mentors to inquire about their early career experiences. He was surprised to learn that virtually all of them considered this "par for the course," and thought that he had understood this because it was so common. About this time, he also attended a national conference where there was a panel discussion on early career development, and inquiry of the conference panelists revealed the same response— with only one exception, everyone else had the same experience.

Summary

Effective therapists do many different things, and have many tools at their disposal as the preceding examples show. One thing that we hope they will all do is remain sensitive to the needs of the client and choose wisely from the vast array of technical interventions. Having a broad repertoire of technical skills from which to select options is an important foundation for competent clinical practice (see Table 11.1).

Table 11.1 Common Clinical Procedures

Interpersonal and System Interventions

Family and cultural history: Summarize the members and cultural affiliations of the family. Major events and the impact of any secrets can be assessed, as well as learned rules and patterns of behavior. Develop a realistic picture of strengths and limitations.

Interpersonal developmental time line: Review personal developmental history to refine global self-perceptions of interpersonal skills and experiences.

Current interpersonal inventory: Note the network of current relationships with relevant dimensions such as degree of intimacy, frequency of communication, power and control, and connections to group affiliations.

Roles and role transitions: Spotlight the psychosocial roles of the client and the associated expectations, demands, and opportunities, and explore any transitions between roles or changes within a role.

Routines and rituals: Encourage individual and group routines and special rituals, often culturally sanctioned, to induce organization and stability, and provide opportunity for emotional expression.

Assertive communication skills: Practice when and how to express personal thoughts and feelings to maintain effective and respectful interpersonal relationships.

Family and collateral meetings: Designate group meeting to facilitate communication and effective role functioning for members of a system. Discussion might include exchange of information; assessment of primary concerns and progress issues; expression of feelings; and efforts to resolve specific problems, conflicts, or current stresses.

Balance autonomy and affiliation: Review adaptive choices to meet individual needs for autonomy and involvement in relationships, groups, and communities.

Affective Interventions

Mindfulness practice: Focus awareness on internal components of experience and observation without judgment or change.

Emotional deepening and validation: Attend, label, and explore emotions in a context of interpersonal understanding and acceptance.

Interoceptive exposure: Activate uncomfortable body sensations systematically to reduce avoidance and fear, produce habituation, and detect associated cognitions.

Willingness exercises: Release control attempts over emotional components of an experience to facilitate functional behavior.

Values assessment: Detect emotional investment in broad life objectives.

Metaphors: Describe vivid images that illustrate concepts of change in a memorable and emotionally nonthreatening way.

Imagery replacement: Construct pleasant images to prompt positive affect and more functional coping response.

Expressive monologue: Facilitate articulation of thoughts and feelings in relationship to past events or absent persons.

318

Table 11.1   (Continued)

Behavioral Interventions

Define target behavior and monitor baseline: Translate abstract intentions such as being happier or more confident into an operational definition of specific target behaviors that are relevant and meaningful. Track or monitor frequency and details of a target behavior or class of behavior prior to any specific attempts to change.

Activities for mastery and pleasure: Schedule activities to provide general activation and increase likelihood of contact with positive experiences such as pleasure or mastery. Increase understanding of the relationship between mood and behavior.

Graduated tasks: Break a complex activity into manageable components.

Systematic exposure: Confront an avoided, feared stimulus through repeated contact of increasing proximity or intensity.

Behavioral rehearsal and time management: Practice specific steps as a successive approximation toward desired skill or outcome. Apply the rehearsal of behavior in a real-time context.

Stimulus control: Increase or decrease the likelihood of a behavior or sequence of behavior by altering associated cues.

Behavioral relaxation: Use systematic tension reduction to disrupt and reduce physical and mental stress.

Generalization of behavior: Transport an established behavior or skill into a new or more challenging situation.

Cognitive Interventions

Detect automatic thoughts and evaluate the evidence: Increase awareness and reality checking of spontaneous cognitions, especially evaluative thoughts.

Guided discovery: Ask a series of questions to draw out a collection of intermediate beliefs or conditional rules that reinforce distorted core beliefs.

Downward arrow: Ask a series of questions to trace a specific thought back to a distorted core belief.

Generate options and alternatives: Brainstorm a range of possibilities for coping or construing a problem to reduce tension, increase flexibility, and foster hope.

Scale on a continuum: Recast perspective on a problem by placing in a context such as a scale of 0% to 100%.

Redirect attention: Label rumination as unproductive thought and redirect or orient the focus of cognitive attention toward a productive task.

Assign realistic probability: Reality check predictions against actual possibility and gather further information if needed.

Conduct a survey: Assess potential social consensus for a perception or belief.

Understanding, Facilitating, and Evaluating Change

12

Chapter

The overall purpose of any therapeutic intervention is to foster change that improves the client's life in some way. To accomplish this purpose, the clinician must understand the complexities of bringing about change, how to track and measure change, how to communicate key information about change as it is happening, and how to maintain change over time.

Learning Objectives

At the end of this chapter, the reader should be able to:

- Recognize four principles of therapeutic change based on the general principle of patient autonomy.
- Understand motivation to change as a process involving identifiable stages.
- Recognize clinical indications of five established stages and five proposed stages in the process of change.
- Explain key barriers to measuring change and practical strategies for overcoming them.
- Discern professionally sound ways to communicate about change with patients, care managers, and other involved parties.

Think for a moment about a personal change that you have attempted some time in your life. Perhaps you decided to lose weight or to improve your physical fitness, your social life, your academic performance, or the tidiness of your personal space. What motivated you to attempt this change? Did you achieve your desired results? What sort of steps did you take to accomplish your goals? How much energy and effort did the change require? Did you go through repeated attempts to change? How did you measure or evaluate your changes? Did others notice the change? Could you maintain the change over time? If you did not achieve the results you wanted (maybe you are still trying), what do you think stood in your way?

The most substantive part of therapy is the middle part, where the bulk of the work of change takes place. This is sometimes referred to as the "working through" phase of therapy. The ideas and goals that have been established in the treatment plan are now pursued in a systematic fashion and progress is made. Objectives for this phase of therapeutic intervention include keeping the treatment focused, incorporating new information as it becomes available, eliciting productive change, evaluating progress, and communicating effectively with all relevant parties. Tools that help therapists effectively navigate the middle phase of treatment include an awareness of principles and stages of change, understanding the processes that are relevant to each stage of change, and knowing ways to adjust interventions to the stage of change. Efficient interventions, whether they are brief or extended, depend on doing the right things at the right time and involving the right people and circumstances to support the process of change (Prochaska, DiClemente, & Norcross, 1992). Clinicians will also find it important to apply their assessment skills to measure change as the patient progresses through therapy. In addition, ongoing communications about change are an important part of the substantive work of therapy.

Understanding Change

Many patients come to therapy in pain from intrapsychic or interpersonal problems. They want relief as quickly as possible. These patients (and often their therapist) see the need and the possibility for the psychotherapeutic collaboration to immediately move toward change. This is especially true in the "short-term" or "time-limited" therapies as opposed to traditional long-term therapies. In the brief therapy models, the pressure of time limits often compel the therapist to use a more technical-mechanical approach to try to quickly move patients to change before the necessary base for change has been built. The therapist may, in effect, try to have patients run before they have learned to crawl and walk. Realistic expectations reflect an appreciation of the complexity of change as a process. Occasionally, change takes place in a fast and direct fashion. More often, change is circuitous, following a path of starts and interruptions, new problems, redirections, and unanticipated challenges (Prochaska & Norcross, 2003). Rather than being a discrete occurrence, change happens through both internal and external events accruing over time. How much time is needed will depend on the patient, the nature of the problems and the resources that are available to support and encourage the desired changes.

The tools of collaboration discussed in Chapter 10 are directly related to the process of change. Here we discuss specific tools related to change that enable the therapist to effectively manage the collaborative relationship and the therapeutic endeavor. As the consulting professional, a therapist can reasonably be expected to have a good understanding of how change usually occurs, and can facilitate the patient's understanding of change as a process that may not be linear or simple to execute. Even when rapport and general understanding between patient and therapist are excellent, a lack of understanding of change or miscommunications about change can foil the productivity of the therapy. An effective understanding of change processes enables the clinician to keep therapy moving along in a beneficial direction.

The Principles of Change

The first tool for successfully navigating the change process is to understand that there are certain principles of therapeutic change (Kleinke, 1994). These include the assertions that (1) the patient is the agent of change; (2) the agent (patient) determines the pace of change; (3) action is required for change to occur; (4) change involves emotional risk.

The Patient Is the Agent of Change

Beginning therapists, and some experienced hands as well, may approach an intervention by thinking of the changes they will "get" their patient to make. The therapist has a direct plan in mind and, sleeves rolled up, is ready to get going. The therapist sees a need to "make" the patient be more flexible, to make more effort at work, to confront anxiety-provoking situations, or enjoy more of life. The treatment plan may be sound in terms of overall goals and objectives, yet flawed in terms of identifying the agent of change. By thinking of what the patient must be persuaded to do, the therapist is reaching over a boundary and taking on the role of agent of change. In a sense, the effort of the therapist and the patient's behavior are viewed in a way that fuses the responsibility for action. This can create an unhelpful struggle for control of whatever change will or should occur. Often, such a control struggle will lead to frustration for one or both parties, and the therapeutic collaboration can suffer or disintegrate. Therapists may believe that their competence and reputation are at stake if patients cannot be "gotten" to make expected changes in a timely manner.

This potential control struggle can be averted by recognizing that the patient is the agent of change, and the therapist is the agent of facilitation, encouragement, and support. Any change that happens will be a function of the patient's doing. The choice to take action belongs to the patient, even if therapists do not fully appreciate this reality. Recognizing the patient's ultimate agency in the change process can open up many more possibilities for helping the patient align wishes, intentions, and actions. Just because the patient is the agent of change does not mean that he or she is immediately ready to take action, that action will be easy, or that change will occur if the therapist works hard enough. In helping the patient to become a more effective agent of change, the therapist may address several issues, including setting functional expectations for what or who can change, progressing through stages of change, developing a sensitivity to small increments of change, and clarifying boundaries with others concerning desired or expected changes.

Both patients and therapists may hold implicit assumptions about the therapist being the primary agent of change, thus compromising patients' agency in their own lives. These patients may have a long history of struggling with change and feel ineffective or incapable as their own agents. Such demoralization makes it even more likely that patients will struggle with directive efforts offered by therapists. Patients who are longing for relief from struggle seek strong therapists who offer the latest, most powerful technology. At the same time, these patients may remain in a passive mode, waiting for things to somehow change as a function of going to therapy or taking medication, or seeking a perfect intellectual understanding that will circumvent the potential for failed efforts. Commitment to the autonomy of patients and understanding of change processes and relevant techniques for facilitating movement toward change can keep the therapy focused in relevant ways, and help patients tap their internal capacity for change.

The Patient Determines the Pace of Change

It may be safe to assume that most if not all patients would prefer quick results. Can you imagine anyone really preferring the alternative of delayed or slow results, if a choice is possible? However, it is not safe to assume that most patients are ready or able to change at a rapid pace. Some can change quickly, some not. This pace is determined by a number of factors, the largest being the patient him or herself. As much as 55% of the patient's improvement in psychotherapy may be attributable to aspects particular to the patient such as his or her expectations, prior skills, and life circumstances (Lambert & Barley, 2002). The therapist can most influence the patient's pace by facilitating progress through the identifiable stages of change to be discussed.

Historically, it has been assumed that no patient could quickly change and that rapid change could only represent a superficial and incomplete resolution of underlying conflicts. Accelerated results were merely a transitory illusion of change that would soon be followed by new symptoms, commonly referred to as "symptom substitution." If depressed patients experienced a notable mood shift in a positive direction early in treatment, the symptom substitution theory predicted that they would soon develop new problems, perhaps compulsive eating or panic attacks. The new problems developed because underlying conflicts had not yet had time to be discovered and resolved; thus the patients lacked true readiness to change. New or substitute symptoms were still needed to express the unresolved conflict. We now have evidence that many forms of brief, focused therapy provide effective symptom remission and sustained effects over time (Chambless et al., 1998).

It is risky to overgeneralize the positive results of brief interventions to assume that anyone can quickly execute significant changes. The notable benefits obtained in studies of short-term interventions may contribute to an assumption that is probably just as faulty as inevitable symptom substitution. This opposing assumption is that all change will occur rapidly, and that anything beyond very brief therapy is unnecessary. Both assumptions impose a time frame on the patient, and do not account for the patient's agency in setting the pace of change, as well as differential readiness for the action of change and complexity of the overall change needed.

The challenge is to more precisely discern what factors most influence the pace of change in therapy. We have some basic understanding of which patient factors facilitate or impede the pace of change. Factors associated with positive change include an active involvement in the treatment process, a positive expectation for change through therapy, and social support for the desired change. Factors that may impede change include the severity and chronicity of the problems, lack of social support, the presence of secondary gain or benefits associated with the symptoms, hopelessness or pessimism about the possibility of change, and a passive or disengaged attitude about the process of change.

Action Is Required for Change to Occur
In many areas of health care, being a patient means following the directions of an authoritative caregiver. When the treatment objective is something concrete, such as the removal of a tumor, the provider gives explicit instructions for the preparations that the patient is expected to make (e.g., must arrive on time for a scheduled surgery having restricted all intakes of food and fluids for a pre-scribed period). At this point, the professionals take over the action of change and expertly administer the necessary medications and procedures. The patient cooperates and consents to the procedures, but may even be unconscious dur-ing most of this treatment. When the procedure is complete, the patient must resume an active role of attending to the matters of physical recovery.

Psychotherapy is a different sort of service, as the patient, being the agent of change, is the one who needs to take charge of the action for any change to occur. Just showing up physically for therapy is an important part of the process, but alone this action is not likely to cause any notable change. Defining the action that must take place is a bit of a challenge. Just talking or developing insights does not necessarily lead to behavior change (Kleinke, 1994; Yalom, 1980). At the same time, just executing some action may not produce needed or lasting change either. Doing things randomly and reactively may be a fundamental part of the problem. Sometimes the change needed is a reduction in harmful actions, such as cutting, purging, or using drugs. Here the action needed is not just to "do something," but to learn a more subtle process of responding differently to internal states and perhaps better master-ing the impulse to action. Changes in verbal behavior are often an important part of this change, as patients move away from reciting reasons for maladap-tive behavior and toward discussion of alternatives, priorities, and direction of action. The changes in verbal behavior then pave the way toward strategic choices in actions.

Change Involves Emotional Risk
What if you encourage a patient to embrace the challenge of change, and his fears are confirmed? What if you role-play to the best of your ability the skills of assertive communication and instead of getting the requested raise, the pa-tient gets fired from his job? What happens if you encourage the shy coed to go out for sorority rush, and she finds herself shunned? What if your patient fi-nally gives up drinking and discovers a deep unhappiness with most aspects of his life?

It may be that both patient and therapist expect effective treatment to prevent any undesirable feelings or events. This reflects an underlying assumption that the purpose of therapy is to master or control emotions and situations. The mastery approach maintains that if the patient is sufficiently rehearsed in the winning strategies, potentially difficult experiences will not happen. Yes, we all want our patients to get positive results, and we will help them acquire the needed skills and make calculated judgments in what they attempt. But we cannot control outcomes, and we especially cannot control the emotional experience that will take place as the patient undertakes new experiences. The assumption of this latter approach is that of a *coping* model for therapy. Under this model, the purpose of therapy is to expand the patient's range of coping with difficult emotions or situations, and to make purposeful choices.

The risk associated with change appears to be the risk of having to experience negative emotions such as embarrassment, anxiety, disappointment, or the stress of inadequately developed skills. Old problems may have developed as a compensation for even older problems, and when the former is removed, the latter may be revealed. Emotions encountered within the process of change may not all be as wonderful as the thrill of success.

Many people assume that the emotional risks of change constitute a negative experience, characterized as painful, frightening, and requiring great courage (Kleinke, 1994). A broader assumption is at work here, the assumption that experiencing a range of emotions is *inherently* an adverse event. At least some of the emotional risk associated with change may be the threat of unwanted emotions, thoughts, or outcomes. Emphasizing the aversive quality of consequences that may in fact be uncontrollable usually leads to control efforts, including impulsive or avoidant behaviors. Change involves the risk of encountering different feelings and experiences, and that is precisely why change is sought. This risk does not have to be labeled as "bad" even if it is uncomfortable or taxing. A person might feel frustrated, discouraged, or uncertain and yet not consider any of these emotions as particularly painful or frightening. Our therapy strategies can teach patients that it is possible to manage and redefine such risk in the pursuit of important goals. Coping well often means understanding, accepting, and managing a full spectrum of emotions.

A sports analogy illustrates this willingness to risk a range of thoughts, emotions, and experiences. Although all athletes would rather win than lose, no athlete has risen to the top of his or her sport by being unwilling to take the risk of losing. The player does not choose to play the game to feel frustrated with personal limits, embarrassed over mistakes, tired and anxious about tedious practice, or disappointed in losing to a rival team, but is willing to risk all these in the pursuit of higher performance. There is risk of emotional, cognitive, and physical discomfort, yet it is understood as a functional part of a desired objective.

Motivation and Stages of Change

There is an old joke that asks, "How many therapists does it take to change a lightbulb?" The answer is, "Only one, but the lightbulb has to *want* to change." In this section, we discuss the dimensional aspects of patient motivation within the construct of progressive stages of change. Whether short-term or time-unlimited, therapy occurs in a series of developmental stages. These stages, like life, are regular, identifiable, and predictable. For some patients change can be implemented more quickly than for other patients. For some patients there needs to be a greater focus in the therapy on the preparation for change before the change can occur.

The issue of motivation to change has long been recognized as crucial to successful therapy. Some highly motivated patients embrace change more quickly than other patients do and are apt to have a successful therapy experience. For other patients, change seems to progress at a glacial pace, if it happens at all, and their motivation appears to be low. The question of what precise factors mediate this varying level of motivation has hovered in the field of intervention for decades. However, a simple motivational continuum from low to high has yielded little in the way of understanding how patient motivation works.

An alternative approach that conceptualizes patient motivation to change as a process with identifiable stages has been gaining scientific support over the past few decades. The application of a stage concept to the process of change has had a tremendous impact on our understanding of this crucial variable. Most well known in the area of stages-of-change is the work of Prochaska and Di-Clemente (Prochaska & DiClemente, 1982, 1983, 1985, 1992; Prochaska et al., 1992). Originally derived from empirical research with patients in smoking-cessation treatment, this transtheoretical model has shown tremendous usefulness in understanding the process of change among patients dealing with addictions and other problematic behaviors. Variations of Prochaska and DiClemente's model can also be found in the writings of Brownell, Marlatt, Lichtenstein, and Wilson (1986), Dryden (1986), and Marlatt and Gordon (1985). There are five stages in the Prochaska et al. (1992) model of motivation to change: (1) precontemplation; (2) contemplation; (3) preparation; (4) action; and (5) maintenance.

Freeman and Dolan (2001) have expanded on the Prochaska and Di-Clemente model with an additional five stages that detail important clinical challenges that may be encountered in the precontemplation and maintenance stages (see Table 12.1). In breaking down the earlier stages, Freeman and

Table 12.1 **Expanded Stages of Change**

Prochaska, DiClemente, & Norcross	Freeman & Dolan
—	Noncontemplation
—	Anticontemplation
Precontemplation	Precontemplation
Contemplation	Contemplation
Preparation	Action planning
Action	Action
—	Prelapse (Redirection)
—	Lapse (Redirection)
—	Relapse (Redirection)
Maintenance	Maintenance

Source: "Revisiting Prochaska and DiClemente's Stages of Change Theory: An Expansion and Specification to Aid in Treatment Planning and Outcome Evaluation," by A. Freeman and M. Dolan, 2001, *Cognitive and Behavioral Practice, 8,* 224–234. Reprinted with permission.

Dolan's expansion articulates different cognitive perspectives that may precede attempts to change, each requiring a different therapeutic response. Similarly, the failure to sustain change can be broken down into distinct stages and dealt with according to the specific issues. Armed with this detailed perspective, the therapist can more precisely assess the patient's progress in developing the necessary motivation to move through the stages of change. Progress does not typically occur in a finite and direct path. The change process is more of a spiral through the stages than a straight line toward a cure. Each of these stages may be visited repeatedly throughout therapy, perhaps even in a single session. However, not every patient will experience every stage of the expanded version of the stages of change. For example, not everyone will progress through anticontemplation or relapse.

Noncontemplation
Noncontemplation is the stage of change in which an individual is not considering or even thinking about changing. Those in noncontemplation seem oblivious to a need to change, the effect that their behavior has on others, or the fact that their global level of functioning is considerably less than it might be if they were more attentive or cognizant of the need to change. Noncontemplators simply do not make a connection between their behavior and a negative situation until it is pointed out to them. They are, in a word, clueless.

Patients at this point are not actively avoiding, resisting, or opposing change. They simply have not considered it, and may be willing to work on change when it is made manifest or obvious by the therapist. The key statements by the patient are "I didn't realize that I need to change." In the noncontemplative stage, patients may enter treatment because of a circumstantial issue and not necessarily for personal reasons. They may or may not be willing to consider or think about their own problems, depending on the perceived relevance to the presenting concern.

Case Example

Brenda brought her 11-year-old daughter to a school performance clinic for evaluation of excessive anxiety related to homework and tests. As part of the assessment, Brenda was asked about how she assisted her child with homework. She reported a lengthy and detailed approach of carefully monitoring all assignments, sitting beside her child to actively participate in the completion of "our" homework, drilling her child in areas of perceived weakness, coaching her with extensive lectures on the importance of academic achievement, and providing workbooks for supplemental practice to assist her daughter in excelling to her highest level. Brenda believed her own behavior was part of a solution, and never thought of it as part of the problem until it was suggested that perhaps she might consider whether some of these actions induced the child's anxiety.

Anticontemplation

Anticontemplation is an active process of distinct opposition to the idea of personal change where problems are adamantly attributed to external sources. The emotional tone of this process may vary, from outright hostility or aggressively righteous indignation to smug condescension. Whatever the emotional tone, the essence of this response is a strong reaction to the notion of a need for personal change. Either overtly or covertly, the patient tells the messenger, "Screw you! I do not need or want to change."

Those who try to reason with the anticontemplator or to tell him about the impact of his behavior will be told, "You're crazy; You're overreacting; It's really your problem, not mine. You're imagining things, as no one else thinks this is a problem." Much time may be spent in complaining about unfairness and others who are really to blame for any obvious problems. Individuals who enter therapy in this stage are most often there due to duress, mandated by the court or pushed into therapy by family or significant others. They will typically spend the therapy time soliciting validation of their perspective, blaming others, or otherwise complaining about their unfortunate circumstances.

Case Example—Claire

When 15-year-old Claire came for therapy for a depressed mood, she reported, among other problems, significant conflict with her mother. Her mother was invited to attend the next session. The mother immediately took control and opened the session by emphatically stating "I am NOT the one who needs to change, and I have no intention of changing. I am the mother, and I should not have to change." She then proceeded to launch into a list of complaints and criticisms of her daughter's behavior, outlining the many ways in which she believed that Claire should change and be more submissive to her authority.

Case Example—Bob

Bob, age 16, was referred for treatment after being caught under the influence of alcohol and possibly other drugs at a school function. Bob denied any misuse of alcohol and stated that his only problem was that someone told the principal that he had been drinking. When confronted, Bob stated that he had no problem and that everyone did it so that he was being singled out unfairly. He became angry and felt that everyone was overreacting to what he characterized as "normal behavior."

Between the first and second session, Bob stole his older brother's ID so that he could purchase a keg of beer for a party. When confronted, Bob again became angry and said that this had nothing to do with his alcohol use and his only problem was in getting caught. Bob started yelling at his parents for their own drinking behavior. When his therapist suggested that all of these incidents involved his use of alcohol, he again stated that alcohol was not a problem and refused to talk about it any more.

Patients at this point are actively avoiding, resisting, or opposing change. They are most often unwilling to work on change and expend great energy displacing blame for their current difficulty. The key statements by the patient are, "I don't need to change," or, "Others should be nicer to me and then I would not have to change."

Precontemplation

In the precontemplation stage, a person begins to consider the consequences, purpose, and the possibility of change but the process is short-circuited. It is a metacognitive state wherein the patient is thinking about thinking about change. Patients at this point are not actively considering the implications of change nor are they significantly invested in resisting or opposing change. They simply have not considered it, or may be postponing or rationalizing the need for change. The key attitude of the patient is, "I'll get around to changing one of these days if and when I need to," or "This problem is not really all that bad."

Precontemplators might passively wait for motivation to strike, perhaps wishing for things to be different but never focusing sufficient attention to enter the contemplation stage. Not thinking about change is a way of coping with the potential stress that actual intentions might precipitate. Energy is required to make a change, and staying the same is easier. It may be the only option if patients lack the energy and supportive resources to initiate and sustain the change process. The precontemplation stage may be brief or it may be prolonged if nothing compels movement to the next stage. Patients may be vaguely aware that self-change is needed to solve a particular problem, but they do not pursue further self-examination in hopes that other circumstances will alleviate the need for such effort. In effect, patients hope that the problem will go away or become unimportant by one means or another, or that they will feel more empowered to change under different circumstances in the indeterminate future.

Case Example

Mary was a single, 32-year-old woman with significant debt. She sensed that she could do a better job with her finances, but minimized the potential consequences of this as a problem. She assumed that she would be getting a reasonable inheritance eventually and that she would also marry someone who would take care of her finances. Given these two assumptions, she did not really see a need to develop any other financial skills and or to label her current level of functioning in this domain as a problem. Thinking about the extent of her debts upset her so she just did not dwell on the subject. She did not want to try to change her spending habits because spending less money would mean a total meltdown of her personal and social life. She believed that she was incapable of such change and that it was really unnecessary and perhaps even damaging in the long run anyway. After all, if she did not spend the money to dress nicely and socialize in all the "right" places, she would not be able to meet the husband who was supposed to pick up the financial reins.

In precontemplation, the individual is unaware or underaware of problem behaviors and the associated consequences and has no intention to change any time in the foreseeable future. Precontemplators may wish for change to occur, but their idea of change is external or eventual.

Contemplation

Contemplation is the stage in which the person more deeply considers that an internal problem exists and gives serious thought to personal behavior change in the near future. However, the person has not yet made a significant commitment to action or established a realistic and effective plan.

Attempts to implement an action-oriented intervention at this stage may be ineffective or even detrimental, as efficient self-change depends on doing the right things (processes) at the right time (stage; Prochaska et al., 1992). In addition, effective change also requires having sufficient circumstantial or social support. Contemplation is thus a critical, systematic, and meaningful stage that requires sufficient energy and attention.

Case Example

Jessie, a 17-year-old female was referred to treatment after telling her parents that she was addicted to heroin and felt scared about her escalating use. Jessie had been using heroin since the age of 15. She admitted to snorting heroin on a daily basis and that her use had escalated from a couple of "lines" a day to 9 "bags" a day. She had been able to stop for a maximum of 2 days, but was unable to stop for a longer time than that. Jessie stated that she had a family history of addiction and that a maternal aunt died of a heroin overdose 2 years earlier. Her parents were supportive, but they found it difficult to follow through with treatment recommendations if Jessie objected to them. Jessie and her parents became tearful during the initial session as they talked about the death of her aunt. Jessie was unable to understand how she could sometimes hate her addiction yet remain so attached to it despite the obvious risks.

During sessions, it became obvious that Jessie did not have adequate coping skills for simple daily problems let alone the skill to get through the emotional, physical, and social turmoil of detoxification and recovery from heroin dependence. Jessie's strength was her intelligence which was evident in her honor student status in high school despite her addiction to heroin. This strength was also a source of liability in her contemplation of change, as it led her to (erroneously) believe that she had intellectual control over her substance use. She thought, "I'm smart enough to stop whenever I want. Maybe I will feel like stopping when I go to college."

Contemplation is a state of actively considering change. Patients presenting at this stage typically have discomfort and are seeking relief, but lack clarity in their intention to take on the tasks of change. The patient's motivation is beginning to build momentum, but could just as easily diminish at this point. Motivation can be enhanced through specific activities that help the patient evaluate the risks and benefits of changing versus not changing and begin to develop a concrete understanding of how change occurs.

The therapy goal of contemplation is to help patients consider what they might be able to do, what will be necessary for success, and why they might choose to make the effort. Some patients become stuck in the contemplation stage, substituting repetitive thinking for action, and in effect become "chronic contemplators" (Prochaska & Norcross, 2003, p. 520). Contemplators are evaluating their options and values in considering self-change, but may be vulnerable to intractable rumination.

Preparation/Action Planning
Preparation is the stage in which intentions and actions begin to converge. The intention to take action is immediate or close at hand, with significant action expected within days or weeks. Small but definite behaviors mark this stage, and these help solidify the intention for additional effort.

Case Example

Sam, a 19-year-old college student came to therapy stating, "I need to study and can't seem to do it all. When I was in high school I didn't need to study. I breezed right through without cracking a book. Now I'm getting Cs and Ds and can't seem to get it together to study and do the papers. I end up overwhelmed and then sit around and watch television even when I know that I need to be studying." Sam had begun to carry a textbook to class so he could review right before lectures started, but he needed a more comprehensive plan. He needed a road map that he could follow in changing his behavior so that he could attain better academic performance.

Patients at this point are actively planning change. They have made a thoughtful decision and are willing to work on the actions needed to fulfill their change agenda. They are looking for advice on what to do and how to do it, and will typically attempt to use suggestions the provider may offer. Motivation may increase at this stage, as change is more fully conceptualized as a series of possible behaviors. Motivation may also decrease at this stage, as the bulk of the action remains ahead, and the patient may cycle back to a previous stage of contemplation or precontemplation. Support and encouragement to change as well as a focus on specific small actions can facilitate the patient's successful negotiation of the preparation stage.

Action
The action stage is the key point at which observable changes in behavior, experiences, or interactions gain momentum. Patients are making changes within themselves to overcome a problem. Some patients will enter therapy at this point, having worked through the contemplation and preparation stages on their own, with the assistance of friends and other supports, or through previous and related treatment efforts. These are the patients who will respond rapidly to action-oriented techniques and progress quickly in therapy.

It is a fundamental mistake to assume that every patient entering therapy is at the action stage. Many patients are not really at this stage of readiness or level of motivation to change. This is often because they have not sufficiently addressed matters of contemplation and preparation, or they do not have sufficient energy or available resources to support the effort that will be needed. The patient who is not actually in the action stage may feel an urgent desire to change right away, but does not have a clear sense of what might be involved or how to deal with practical or psychological challenges in the execution of change.

Case Example

Jose, a 43-year-old Hispanic male was referred to outpatient treatment through the employee assistance program (EAP) at his place of work after requesting assistance with his substance abuse problem. Jose has been in mental health treatment for this problem several times over the past 15 years. He admitted that he was not ready for change at those times. However, he now felt that he was at the point in his life where he would probably die soon if he didn't change. Based on his previous experiences, he felt that he had a pretty good understanding of what it was going to take to turn his life around. At intake, he was diagnosed as chemically dependent with cocaine as his drug of choice. From the first session of therapy, Jose was able to remain abstinent for 45 days and attend daily 12-step support group meetings as well as participate in individual and group counseling. He reported that he was performing his work at an adequate level, and he had no current disciplinary or attendance problems. He followed his therapist's suggestion that he monitor his thoughts and behaviors in a journal so he could discuss them in his therapy sessions and generally engaged in a productive alliance with all providers.

Other people in the patient's life become most aware of changes at the action stage, and will react according to their own frame of reference. The reactions of others can either help or hinder the patient's continued effort. However, the efforts of the previous stages will pay off at this point, as those who have worked through consideration of others reactions' and made some preparations for handling this are best equipped to maintain their course of action.

Those patients who have attempted to go directly into the action stage without much contemplation or preparation may have the roughest challenge, as they are in effect attempting to leap a tall building in a single bound. With some sustained action and initial success, motivation can be expected to increase.

Prelapse
Prelapse is a stage with active and often overwhelming cognitions related to reversal of the changed behavior or pattern of behavior. There is longing for old times and circumstances, and a resurgence of thoughts and desires consistent with a return to previous functioning.

The patient is craving an old way of being, but this craving is based on an idealized memory of the experiences. The desire to return to old ways may be triggered by current stress, or it may be simply a spontaneous recovery of associations set in motion by an emotionally provocative memory. This is a crucial junction in the change process, as it may be the beginning of a spontaneous return to a previous level of functioning. However, specific targeted interventions can address this problem early, before an entire chain of behavior is reactivated.

Case Example

Ryan had a year of sobriety from alcohol and pot when the stress of Christmas holidays began to wear on him. Although he felt committed to sobriety and was happy with his progress, he began to long for the "good old days" of "partying" and having fun. He felt sorry for himself because he no longer had the camaraderie that he had experienced with drinking buddies. On the day of his office holiday party, he started having fond memories of past celebrations. As he sat in his office listening to the sounds of merriment down the hall, with champagne corks popping and beer bottles clinking with the offering of cheerful toasts, he began to ruminate that as a nondrinker, he could no longer enjoy holiday parties "like everyone else." He longed for the imagined happiness of his past. He underrecalled the negative aspects of this glorious past when a bottle of beer on Friday led to a weekend-long binge and trouble showing up sober on Monday. Labeling this identifiable change as a prelapse might help Ryan recognize how dangerously close he was to a behavioral reversal of change, sliding back toward his substance abuse in an effort to recapture an idealized past.

This is a crucial point in the change process. Active, directive disputation, problem solving, and review of cognitive and behavioral skills can short-circuit the prelapse before it leads to the next stage.

Lapse

Lapse is the stage where the skills needed to go from action to maintenance decrease or are ignored. This is not a full return to prechange patterns, but the stage is set for relapse to occur. The individual contemplates the reasons for changing *back* to old ways, and has behavioral slips in that direction.

Affect during the lapse may run the gamut, from panic to anger to resignation or even relief. What happens at this juncture is critical to whether the lapse is corrected, or progresses further into a broader relapse of old patterns of thought, affect, and behavior.

Case Example

Ryan is sitting alone in his office during the group holiday party, feeling socially alienated and sorry about his sobriety. He finally comes to the conclusion, "Screw it, if I want a beer, I'm going to have a beer." So he ambles down the

---

Case Example (Continued)

hall and amidst claps of welcome from his colleagues, he grabs a beer, which he found tasted "bitter and nasty." He looked around at his coworkers and noticed a range of drinking behavior, including two who were not drinking

alcohol at all, a few who he knew would stop after one or two drinks, and a couple of guys whom he labeled as "just like the old me," already on their 4th drink and likely to make a night or even a weekend of it.

Patients at this point are both working at change and starting to revert to previous patterns of action. They are not immediately opposing change but they have gotten careless about managing stress, staying focused, and accessing support for change. They may be going through a natural rejection of the new behavior or think that they are beyond the need to make a concerted effort.

Relapse

Relapse is the stage at which there is a return to the behaviors that caused the original referral that had been altered in the action stage. Relapse constitutes a crisis for most patients. Immediate intervention is crucial for the patient to continue to progress forward and not recycle back to precontemplation or anticontemplation. The patient may think, "I'm right back where I started from" and begin to recover the original behavior pattern.

Case Example

Ryan did not progress into the full relapse stage, which might have involved joining the guys who were like his "old" self. Even though he did not progress from lapse to relapse, he was vulnerable to doing so. If he had greatly enjoyed the drink, embraced his old self and old buddies, and continued to think of sobriety as overrated, he might have been more likely to progress into full relapse where he returned to all his old behaviors and made no effort to

change. Lacking the skill to distinguish prelapse, lapse, and relapse can increase vulnerability to relapse, as one slip may be magnified into huge failure, with concomitant guilt and resignation. In that case, Ryan might think, "Well, I've done it now. I've messed up, so I might as well enjoy myself." Such thoughts provide a gateway to spontaneous recovery of the old patterns, even if he doesn't really enjoy himself very much.

Redirection

Redirection is the process that must be implemented in the prelapse as well as possible lapse or relapse stages. Redirection involves the recognition that one is off track concerning change, that further effort is needed to avoid reversal of change, and that the reasons for making changes may need to be reviewed and updated. Further, the specific methods of getting back on track and overcoming the temptation or the lapse/relapse need to be specified. As noted, being able to distinguish each of these stages is quite helpful for both patient and therapist. Any indications of these stages are important to the change process, and merit attention and explicit discussion. It is important to consider and discuss what is happening when the patient wants to revert to old ways, and when small shifts in attitude or behavior are noted.

Case Example

Ryan did not automatically understand these stages of change. Fortunately, he was an active participant in his therapy, and he brought up his feelings of frustration and deprivation, and was forthcoming about his behavior, opening the door for labeling the stages of prelapse and lapse. He explored his reactions to the lapse of drinking a beer in some detail, noting that the majority of his associates were either nondrinkers or moderate drinkers. Thus, his belief that "everyone" was partying and drinking a great deal was inconsistent with the evidence from his own observations. A careful review of his past personal expe-

rience helped him remember that he did not typically drink in moderation, and that occasional use was neither an effective or satisfying option for him. Redirection efforts included this review of himself and his reasons for change, a reconsideration of his environment and his perceptions of others, recommitment to his specific goals (sobriety), and returning to use of behavior change methods including counterconditioning and stress management, as well as accessing social support from his spouse, new friends, and an online recovery discussion group.

Maintenance

Finally, in the maintenance stage, behavior change is stabilized into an enduring new pattern or lifestyle. One of the most significant challenges is avoiding relapse or reactivation of previous problematic behaviors.

Patients will present differently at the maintenance stage, as some actively recognize the importance of support and others may be prone to taking the stability of their changes for granted. Therapeutic goals are to (a) fine-tune and adjust changes, (b) support growth, (c) encourage stability, and (d) help patients become their own therapist.

Case Example

Ryan continued treatment for short periods (one to six sessions) over several years on an "as needed" basis. He completed his master's degree and found a

job where there was less drinking among coworkers. After working through a few additional lapses with redirection and no relapse, he became more confident in his

Case Example (Continued)

ability to maintain change on his own. For a long period, he was out of contact with his therapist. Eventually, he was in line for a managerial position, married, and raising two children. Ryan decided to return to regular therapy because he wanted a tune-up for dealing with the new stresses in his life. He was keenly aware that if he did not effectively manage these new stressors, the likelihood of a relapse would increase. As Ryan moved further into the demands of the business world and his adult life, he had less access to emotional support, and he found himself questioning his competence to succeed. At this point of maintenance, Ryan needed to focus on the strengths that had supported his sobriety over several years and generalize those skills to the challenges of his current job and family roles.

Although it might be tempting to view maintenance as a static stage with an absence of change, it is more accurate to consider it an ongoing effort with unique challenges. Patients actively maintain changes even in new contexts or situations and are sensitive to cues that indicate the potential for relapse. Patients appreciate their volitional role and understand change as a process that involves a variety of tasks and resources.

Facilitating Change

Although we are strongly encouraged as therapists to initiate action in the very first session, to "hit the ground running," not everyone is at the same stage of action readiness when therapy begins. Contrary to common assumption, simply presenting for therapy does not mean the patient has already progressed through contemplation and preparation for change. An individualized approach means working forward from the patient's current stage at the outset of therapy, and targeting the intervention to the patient's state of readiness for change. Providing a secure, supportive therapeutic environment that focuses on selected tasks and goals can help the patient find the energy to engage in the process, tolerate the emotional risks, and titrate the destabilization of moving from one stage to another.

Patients who enter therapy in a stage of readiness for action are most likely to have a successful outcome in therapy. A study of smoking cardiac patients found that the pretreatment stage of change was clearly related to outcome, as those who were not smoking at 12 months were those who began the study either in preparation or action (76%), versus those who were contemplating change (43%), and those who were precontemplators (22%; Ockene, Ockene, & Kristellar, 1988). Another large study of smokers followed over 18 months found that patients who could progress just one stage forward in a month more than doubled their likelihood of taking action on their own (Prochaska & DiClemente, 1992).

Many reasonable candidates for therapy fail to obtain the benefit because they drop out or terminate treatment prematurely, without any notable change or problem resolution. Although approximately 30% to 40% of patients terminate prematurely, we cannot reliably predict who will drop out and who will not. The variables that help predict psychotherapy outcome such as client characteristics or problem duration do not offer much in terms of accurately targeting potential drop-outs. However, one study correctly identified 93% of those who prematurely terminated by their pretreatment stage of change (Medieros & Prochaska, 1993). It is no surprise that those who dropped out of treatment were in the precontemplation stage. Those who terminated quickly but appropriately were those who entered treatment in the action stage, and these were fewer in number overall. Those who continued in treatment were those who entered in the contemplation stage. Thus, the patient who can complete a successful therapy in 6 to 10 sessions is one who enters treatment prepared to take action. The patient who attends some therapy but fails to benefit is likely to be stalled at the stage of precontemplation. Those patients who have more complex problems and less preparation for change will have a longer course of psychotherapy, extending from 6 months to years, if they can be engaged in a process of contemplation and planning action.

Is it important to use methods or processes that are targeted to specific stages? The empirical answer to that question is yes. Significant evidence accumulated from over 20 years of research in behavioral medicine and psychotherapy shows the differential effectiveness of different processes (Prochaska & Norcross, 2003), including a recent meta-analysis of 47 cross-sectional studies showing a large effect of different processes across the stages (C. S. Rosen, 2000). The results of this body of research offer psychotherapists an evidenced-based foundation for systematic and efficient use of psychotherapy methods and procedures to facilitate change.

Adjusting Intervention to Stage of Change

How do people move through the stages of change? The initial steps appear to be consciousness or awareness of a problem and whether the problem is biological (physical symptoms or impairments), psychological (emotional distress, cognitive impairments, behavioral dysfunctions), or social (interpersonal, role, family, or community impairment), or some combination of these dimensions. At the precontemplation stage (and its variants), little time or energy is invested in self-evaluation. If there are negative aspects to a problem, the individual does not react much to them. At this stage, the person is rather closed to new information, perhaps even downright hostile as noted, and will resist owning the problem or planning behavior changes.

The most helpful therapeutic stance for *precontemplation* is likely to be a supportive approach that draws patients into a consideration of their circumstances. Offering an opportunity to examine thoughts and feelings in an understanding and nondemanding atmosphere may help the patient move toward greater recognition that a possible problem exists. Providing the patient with normative information may also be useful, as a reference point for the patient's self-evaluation.

The greatest challenge at this stage is developing a rapport that fosters problem exploration and keeps the patient engaged in the treatment process. Just intellectually recognizing there is a problem, however, is not likely to be sufficient for progressing toward contemplation of change. Some emotional connection to the consequences of the problem is needed. The problem has to matter in some emotionally relevant way. Bringing this emotional component into awareness can be accomplished through a variety of affective techniques such as expressive dialogue or guided discussion of personal values, culturally relevant impacts, and socially normative alternatives.

Fortuitous life events that affect the patient, even through observation only, may help bring feelings into consciousness. The diagnosis or loss of a loved one to a serious illness may be a wake-up call to contemplation. Near-death experiences of the patient or others may precipitate caring enough about chronically maladaptive conditions. For example, a young soldier has a near-death experience in combat, and decides that his life at home will significantly change on his return. He is prompted to seriously consider his passive acceptance of his spouse's alcohol abuse and neglect of the children and home, and how inconsistent that is with his desired family life. This leads to planning the steps he will begin to take to change this unhappy and no longer acceptable situation.

The *contemplation* stage is marked by increased openness to information and self-evaluation. Interventions such as clinical assessment as well as psychoeducation, bibliotherapy, and exposure to the coping strategies used by others are helpful at this point. Empowered by more thorough information, the patient has the tools to evaluate options. A therapeutic stance of guiding the patient through information gathering and decision making is helpful, along with the use of truly exploratory Socratic questions. Attention to the patient's key values is central to moving this process along, as it is the effects most cared about that will spur the effort to action. It is also important to examine the sources of ambivalence about change as the patient also has a valued attachment to some aspects of the behavior in question. As noted, some patients—and some therapists—are prone to become stuck in the contemplation stage, endlessly considering issues and feelings, but not taking the next step of determining what direction is important in the patient's life. Both may believe, mistakenly, that continuous rumination about options can reduce anxiety or discomfort with the available options, and that keeping options open will result in a more satisfactory outcome in the long run. As patients evaluate what matters most and the impact on significant others, some sense of direction should emerge. This will help move patients into the next stage, of preparing to take action. Chronic contemplation can be identified as a specific choice of action that results in vague commitment and ongoing discomfort, rather than more effective choices.

In the *preparation* stage, patients formulate a plan for what to change and how to change it, with specific action steps beginning to take shape. The path of change may not be detailed down to the minutiae, but there are goals and priorities and some idea of how to achieve these objectives. The therapist continues to provide support and encouragement, and also coaches patients on specific methods or procedures that are apt to facilitate success. Small action steps are recognized and highly encouraged. In this stage, the therapist shares the methods of psychotherapy in ways that empower patients to see that change is possible and within their control. The therapist can help focus patients' efforts, and provide crucial reassurance that their actions are contributing to a productive purpose. Patients may be hesitant and overwhelmed at this point, and often need liberal doses of reinforcement for their initial change efforts.

In the *action* stage, therapists help maintain the affective and cognitive foundations of the earlier stages and provide technical support for the behavioral change efforts. They can help patients effectively apply techniques of counterconditioning, stimulus control, and contingency management, as well as manage thoughts or emotions that might get in the way of using the behavioral technology. Encouragement, accountability, and partnership all are important in the action stage. Patients are surrounded by advice on the action of change, and may be drawn off track by many distractions or misdirections. Others' suggestions may be helpful and right on target, or they may be poorly informed or downright sabotaging to the patient's intentions. Thus, an effective therapeutic stance is that of an informed (and patient) consultant who knows the particulars of the patient's situation and is keeping track of both progress and direction of change. The therapist can encourage persistence when the changes become difficult, tedious, or questionable. When one method doesn't seem to be working, the therapist can be helpful in offering alternative strategies if needed.

Maintenance begins when the change has been substantially implemented for a noted period of time, often 6 months or longer. *Prelapse, lapse,* and *relapse* are important at this stage as well as ways to cope with these stressors through redirection. Developing a new or adjusted sense of identity is also important for success in the maintenance stage. The patient incorporates the problem into his or her view of self, and the accomplished or ongoing change as desirable and real. Ryan, the patient described earlier in the stages of change, came to see himself as a person in recovery from alcohol and substance abuse. A smoker begins to think of himself as a nonsmoker. A patient with agoraphobia thinks of herself as a highly sensitive but functioning and mobile individual. The better-defined the change is, and the more clearly the patient can articulate a positive sense of identity to associate with the change, the more likely it is that change can be maintained without spiraling back to earlier stages.

The procedures most helpful at this stage include reviewing reasons to maintain the change, behavioral ways to maintain the change, and enhancing identification and contact with others who behave this way and who endorse the new identity. Risks at this stage include overestimating the stability of the behavior change, underestimating the need for any ongoing effort or sensitivity to potential to lapse or relapse, and under-utilizing productive interpersonal support.

Evaluating Change

Measuring Change

Measurement of change in psychotherapy is a somewhat controversial issue. Many clinicians do not use external measures of outcome or patient change in their clinical practice. In one survey (Hatfield & Ogles, 2004), only 37.1% of 874 responding psychologists said they used any form of outcome measure in practice. This is similar to other reports of 29% (Phelps, Eisman, & Kohout, 1998), and 23% of child and adolescent clinicians (Bickman et al., 2000). There are also many providers and consumers who think that measurement of change is an important component of a systematic approach to clinical practice. Thus, it is important to understand the factors that facilitate or hinder this action in practice.

According to the Hatfield and Ogles (2004) survey of a random sample of practitioner members of APA (American Psychological Association), training in the use of outcome assessment strategies was significantly related to practitioners' behavior. Presumably, training helps providers to know what measures to use, how and when to use them, and whether it is clinically useful to do so. Further, this survey explored both the uses and barriers to measuring change in clinical practice. The most important uses were in tracking progress since intake, measuring overall problem severity, evaluating specific problems, and tracking the maintenance of therapeutic gains over time. The barriers to outcome measurement were either practical or strategic. The practical reasons were things such as taking too much time or burdening the patient or therapist with paperwork, and the strategic reasons related to incompatibility with therapeutic approach or threat to professional integrity or confidentiality. Overall, the strategic reasons were less prominent than practical ones as a factor in practitioner behavior.

For the measurement of change to be a functional component of the treatment process, the methods need to meet basic assessment criteria of reliability and validity, as well as be suitable to the problem and treatment setting. The most commonly used methods involve well-standardized, easily administered symptom checklists that provide direct measures of specific problems. These include the Beck Depression Inventory (BDI-II; A. T. Beck et al., 1996), the Beck Anxiety Inventory (BAI; A. T. Beck, Epstein, Brown, & Steer, 1988), the Child Behavior Checklist (CBCL; Achenbach, 1991), and the SCL-90-R (Derogatis, 1983; Hatfield & Ogles, 2004). Patients can complete these inventories quickly and easily in a waiting area, or in the first few minutes of a meeting. Many other clinical instruments are potentially available for use in evaluating specific clinical problems and overall severity or tracking progress over time. These can frequently be located either through test vendors, or through a research literature review for a specific problem.

Other options for measuring patient change over the course of treatment include individualized tracking of target behaviors, changes in the global assessment of functioning, and reports of the patient or significant others concerning relevant psychological or emotional changes. These methods are discussed in depth in Chapters 7 and 8. Observational methods of charting change are particularly helpful because of the direct relevance to the main reasons for seeking therapy. Patients often come to therapy with a specific agenda of changing a behavior, solving a problem, or improving their functioning. Guiding a patient through self-assessment for evidence of change, or lack of change in the presenting problem is important both for patient satisfaction and feedback to the clinician on the usefulness of treatment.

Measuring specific target behavior can be useful in the process of tracking change because it is both observable and quantifiable. One option is to measure increases in functional behaviors such as regular exercise or social contacts. Another option is to measure decreases in harmful behaviors such as purging, cutting, or school or work truancy. It may not always be easy to identify a specific target behavior to track as context plays a role in whether a behavior is functional or dysfunctional. However, this can be taken into consideration when determining the target. Being present in the workplace is generally a functional behavior, but staying at work for excessive hours while obsessively checking is not adaptive. Thus, the behavior to track might include the number of days where work was completed within designated work hours, without repetitive checking. In most instances, a brief inquiry and patient self-report or self-monitoring is sufficient to measure and track the progress in these areas over time. Depending on the clinical context, other sources of information may be added to the patient's report to get the most reliable index of change. An example of this is the patient in drug treatment who submits a urine sample to be tested for substances as a corroboration of his or her self-report of abstinence.

Behavioral tools are relatively easy to use, require minimal time or paperwork to administer, and may enhance the integrity of the treatment by tracking progress toward overall objectives. At least one measure of symptoms and one target behavior to track for increases or decreases can easily provide a foundation of change measurement for routine practice. If the patient's desired outcome is to be less stressed and worried and to live a calmer lifestyle, we might use an anxiety checklist to track both problem severity and progress over time. In addition, we might ask the patient to monitor the frequency of tension-reducing activities such as exercise or meditation. Thus, the measurement of change can be streamlined in a way that is both workable and valuable to the clinical process.

Communicating about Change

An important feature of contemporary therapy is the frequent occurrence of direct communications about change between patient and therapist and possibly clinical and external third parties. Patients and therapists talk about the processes and methods of change and are likely to directly discuss expectations, responsibilities, and satisfaction with the rate and direction of change. Communications about change may take place either in a formal, written context, or in an informal or conversational exchange. The particular concerns of any communication vary with the intended audience, so we will give separate consideration to patients, external third parties, and clinical third parties.

Communicating with Patients about Change

Discussion of change is typically part of the agenda whenever the patient and therapist have contact. When a patient and therapist meet, the patient reports on changes experienced since the last meeting, for better or worse. If the patient does not spontaneously report such developments, the therapist will inquire and attempt to socialize the patient toward noticing and reporting changes.

The focusing of attention on noticeable differences helps the patient to recognize the process of change as it is happening. Noticing improvements also encourages a cognitive shift toward more constructive focus of attention. This discussion may involve changes in affect in specific situations or encounters, changes in overall mood, changes in thoughts, attitude, or mental activity, or changes in behaviors or actions. The data used to guide such discussion may come from the symptom inventories or self-monitoring records or diaries assigned as homework, or may come from the patient's recollection and self-report. Observations of others may also be part of the change data, as shared by the patient's report or perhaps directly communicated by the outside entity.

Over time, as the clinician gathers a database of experience and information, a repertoire of relevant questions can be developed. Some of those questions may become part of clinical routine, perhaps asking each patient, "What changes have you experienced since we last met?" As you get to know different patients, you can help them spot changes that are particularly relevant to their interpersonal and intrapsychic world. This discussion of change adds meaning and depth to differences that may be evident on symptom inventories or other measures of functioning. If you know that a given client has often responded passively to challenges or difficulties at work, it will be easier to notice and comment on a report of behaving more assertively with a work project. Or you may be able to help a patient see that certain discrete actions such as volunteering to chair a committee are important shifts in a more functional direction, even (or especially) when difficult feelings like anxiety are part of the experience.

The clinician's professional opinion on the evidence of progress and relevance of change is typically important in encouraging the patient's persistence and motivation in treatment. Sometimes it is required by third-party payers in the form of a treatment progress report, where specific clinical information is required. Thus, it is crucial to pay attention to the change taking place and provide feedback to the patient on your observations. Much of the time, the feedback is delivered in the course of discussion, but other structured communications may be useful or necessary. The structure of the communication will depend on the clinical context and vary in degree of complexity.

A simple structured communication might be a summary and perhaps charting of symptom index measures over the course of treatment, which is communicated informally to the patient in the course of ongoing treatment. You might use a whiteboard or graph paper and list changes in the Beck Depression Inventory over the course of several weeks of treatment, to show the client visually how much change has taken place (see Figure 12.1). By discussing this during a treatment session, you can talk about what steps, interventions, or changes accompanied the shifts in symptoms.

In the case illustrated in Figure 12.1, the initial slight increase in mood-related symptoms was related to specific stressors, including a major work project that coincided with children's health problems and other family challenges. The drop in symptoms noted between Sessions 11 and 14 was associated with some alleviation in the situational stresses, and continued use of specific coping skills. The client could see that as she continued to make the effort to resolve her stress and cope as effectively as possible, she began to feel considerably better, even though she still faced day-to-day challenges.

Communicating with Care Management and Other External Third Parties
When it is necessary to communicate with third-party care managers, a more complex and formal communication is typically required. For patients using

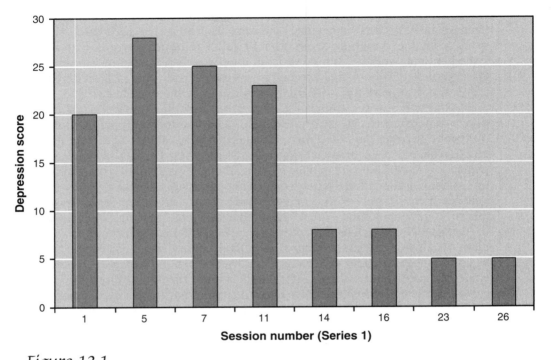

Figure 12.1

Mood over Time

some form of managed behavioral health care insurance coverage, this is a common requirement for accessing benefits, as of this writing. Most often, a specific form is provided by the managed care company for the clinician to complete, either on paper or by secured electronic submission.

Managed care progress reports typically require the clinician to report a diagnosis and ratings of the severity of stressors and overall functioning, as well as the presence of risk indicators such as self-harming behaviors or substance abuse, medications being used, communications with other primary care providers, and need for additional treatment. Thus beginning to gather this information at the onset of therapy will enable completing this important communication in a timely manner.

A care manager subsequently reviews this information and either provides approval for additional treatment, denies payment authorization based on the patient's insurance contract, or requests further discussion of the client's care with the clinician if warranted. Follow-up with the clinician is most likely when there are any questions about the patient's risk level, such as with suicidal intent, to ensure that treatment is of sufficient quality and intensity to meet the patient's needs.

Denial of authorization by an insurance carrier is primarily a denial of authorization of payment under the patient's contract for service. This does not mean that a patient is disallowed to continue treatment, but rather that the patient and therapist must determine an appropriate course of action that is in the patient's best interest, including alternative payment arrangements or use of alternative treatment or community support resources. Insurance carriers make decisions about authorizing payment for services; the patient and therapist make decisions about what services are needed and what the options and alternatives may be.

The most complex and formal communication with an external third party might be a written report that summarizes repeated observations, assessments, or the results of multiple test instruments across time. This written report may be distributed to one or more parties, and may or may not be released to the patient, depending on the circumstances. In the instance of a complex and formal written summary or opinion, this would most likely have been specified as an objective at the beginning of the treatment consultation, and appropriate informed consent obtained (e.g., the patient may have been remanded to treatment by an outside entity such as the court, and the formal report is required as a condition of the order).

Beginning clinicians are advised that this latter circumstance is a specialized application of clinical practice requiring appropriate training and supervised experience to effectively execute both the treatment and the corresponding communications. Any release of written clinical information should be done deliberately and carefully, to ensure that appropriate safeguards to patient confidentiality are maintained, and that appropriate ethical and legal responsibilities are addressed.

Communicating with Clinical Third Parties

Several clinical situations involve communications about patient change with third parties who are part of the treatment process. One is when the therapist is part of a treatment team, as often occurs in hospital, clinic, or school settings where other professionals are also working with the patient on a target health or mental health problem. Typically, the team will have a set time to discuss progress and relevant concerns of their patients, but this may not always be the case. If there is not a designated time for a team meeting, the clinician may need to initiate contact with other treating professionals to exchange information about the patient.

In all such cases, a written consent from the patient, or the patient's parent or guardian in the case of a minor, is required for such information to be disclosed or exchanged with any third party. This written consent may be woven into the routine intake procedure, for example when a patient is seen in a medical clinic such as pediatric diabetes clinic or adolescent eating disorders clinic. If the consent is not obtained on intake, a specific discussion of informed consent for this communication needs to be conducted with the patient, along with signed documentation of the discussion and consent.

Although the consent for this communication needs to be specifically structured, the information that is actually exchanged is typically less structured as the treating professionals simply discuss their observations, concerns, and notations of progress or change. This communication serves many purposes. These include helping establish common goals, sharing points of encouragement, identifying any obstacles to further change, and generally helping everyone be "on the same page" in providing consistent and coherent care.

Beginning clinicians are often hesitant to discuss a patient with other professionals who may take a very different perspective on the patient's problems, or perhaps be less than sensitive to psychological considerations. Such communications can be productively directed by keeping the focus on the patient's best interest and realizing that differences in perspectives are part of the reason for the exchange of information. Sharing features of the psychological case conceptualization with other involved clinicians helps them have a broader understanding of the patient and contribute to the patient's overall quality of care. The psychological perspective is a unique and valuable contribution to a multidisciplinary consultation.

Another circumstance involving communications with clinically involved third parties is interactions with family members or significant others of the patient. These communications can be crucial to the ongoing process of change, yet should always be guided by the priority of the patient's best interest. Both clinical skill and knowledge of the boundaries of confidentiality are needed to successfully execute such contacts. There are many possible circumstances where the clinician will receive inquiries about the patient's progress and potential for change, and not all of them merit a direct response. If there is any doubt, the superordinate ethical standard of privacy and confidentiality (APA, 2002; 4.00–4.07) should prevail, at least until the situation can be clarified.

Family members, including spouses or parents of majority age young adults, do not automatically have a right to information concerning the patient, unless the patient gives specific consent to disclosure. This is true even if the familial third party is paying the bill. The consent for disclosure should be obtained formally for adult patients, in the manner noted for other treating professionals. The patient may also provide informal consent by bringing a significant other along to a consultation, although it still must be ascertained that the patient is freely consenting and not being coerced by the significant other.

Where minor children are concerned, a delicate balance must be maintained between protecting the confiding relationship and keeping parents informed so that they can appropriately manage their parental responsibilities. A general guideline many child clinicians follow is that of making discussion of change and progress with parents a part of the treatment plan, and informing their youthful patients at the outset of treatment of necessary disclosure under any circumstances of harm, danger, high-risk behavior or illegal behavior.

When a patient brings someone into a therapy session such as a partner, family member, or friend, that person is referred to as a *collateral* participant in the patient's treatment. For a minor, it is usually preferable that at least one parent be involved as a collateral participant in treatment. When the collateral party enters the treatment room, it is made clear that he or she is not a patient, has no record of being a patient, and has no rights or privileges regarding information shared, or financial responsibility (unless as a financially responsible parent).

Sometimes, clinicians have the participant review and sign a formal *collateral consent* form. The collateral consent form specifically outlines that the person is participating in the therapy at the patient's request, and for the patient's benefit. If it appears that the collateral participant has a personal agenda for therapy, then it would most likely be appropriate to provide a referral to another provider, or to direct that agenda to designated family therapy sessions.

Clarity in structuring these contacts can help keep the patient's treatment focused, and prevent any disruption by the interests of others.

With an appropriate structure, there can be many benefits of having communications with significant others as collateral participants. Others often play an important role in either reinforcing or discouraging change. Sometimes they interfere with change because they do not have a clear idea about how to best direct their efforts. Family members may be frightened by emotional distress, and may worry that placing any demands on the patient will cause the person to worsen, snap, or have a nervous breakdown. Significant others may be confused about the reasons for psychological symptoms and engage in a pattern of coercion or negative communication with the patient as a result of their own frustration. They may be very stressed by the patient's problems, and pressuring the patient to use simple solutions, such as to "stop whining and get over yourself." The tension caused by the "hurry up and get over it" message may greatly exacerbate the overall distress of everyone. Family members may be reacting with anger or shame, compounding the patient's sense of demoralization.

In many clinical situations, significant others either underrespond or overrespond in assuming some portion of influence on the problem. "What have I done to cause this?" may be part of their inner struggle, when they are not a causative element. Alternatively, the defensive posture of "this is not my problem; you need to fix him/her" can exacerbate the patient's sense of interpersonal isolation. In such cases, collateral contacts can provide an opportunity to discuss realistic expectations for the pace and extent of change that is likely, and what specific attitudes and behaviors are likely to help or hinder the desired change.

With few exceptions, communications with collateral contacts are apt to have the greatest success when face-to-face discussion is used, rather than formal or written statements. Significant others benefit from sharing information, having their input taken into consideration, being involved as a relevant party, and becoming informed about the treatment and expectations for progress. In informal discussion, their understanding and reactions can be checked, and their concerns resolved or at least considered.

Written documents provide a much greater risk for misinterpretation or distortion in a way that may not be beneficial to the patient, and there is less opportunity to discern what further understanding might be needed. In situations where there are written communications to significant others, as in providing a copy of a psychoeducational evaluation to parents, it is important to offer an opportunity to explain and discuss what is contained in the report in language that the family members can understand (APA, 2002, 9.10).

Summary

Change in psychological and behavioral functioning is best conceptualized as a complex and cumulative process rather than a discrete occurrence at a single point in time. The patient always remains both the agent and the object of the change process, setting the pace and determining the extent of emotional risk allowed. In the cumulative process of change, there are as many as 10 different stages of an evolving complex of emotions, thoughts, motivations, and actions. If we are alert to the stages of change, interventions can be selected for their usefulness in facilitating progress toward the next step. Evaluating or measuring at least some behavioral and symptomatic aspects of the patient's functioning is important in demonstrating progress through the stages and toward a productive purpose. Throughout planning, facilitating, and measuring progress, there are ongoing communications with the patient about change. This communication may also include others involved in the treatment as third-party payers and managers of care, other treating professionals, or significant others who play a role in the change process as part of the patient's life. Our ability as clinicians to understand, facilitate, measure, and communicate about a patient's change affects the focus and direction of treatment, the patient's engagement, persistence, and motivation, and the successful use of external resources.

Impediments to Change

13
Chapter

Bringing about change is not a simple matter. Even when the clinician is prepared with the latest scientifically based methods, a comprehensive conceptualization, and an accurate understanding of the client's progress in the cycle of change, impediments may still need to be addressed during therapy. These obstacles to progress stem from several sources. Although it is tempting to attribute the obstacles exclusively to conflicts within the client, it is necessary to consider other possible explanations to effectively work through these clinical barriers.

Before reading the following discussion, ask yourself to think about what you believe most stands in the way of change. Are the barriers to change in the client, the therapist, the environment, or embedded in the problem? If clients claim that they simply cannot change a problem behavior (e.g., overeating), are the obstacles to change caused by the client's poor impulse control, the therapist's misdirected approach, an overabundance of food surrounding the client, or food addiction and bad genetics?

Learning Objectives

At the end of this chapter, the reader should be able to:

- Describe how the *client* can be a source of therapeutic impediment.
- Describe how the *therapist* can be a source of therapeutic impediment.
- Describe how the *environment* can be a source of therapeutic impediment.
- Describe how the *psychological disorder* can be a source of therapeutic impediment.
- Describe how the therapist can remain relatively unaffected by resistance.

Throughout this text, we have stressed the collaborative nature of the therapeutic effort. When there is change in the expected and agreed-on direction, when clients can do things that they did not previously attempt, when the client's life and efforts are moving in positive and desired directions, both the therapist and the client experience success and fulfillment. However, like true love, the course of therapy never (or rarely) runs smoothly. There will be relapses, stagnation, plateaus, backward movement, and even active resistance to change. This does not necessarily stop therapy, nor does it necessarily injure the therapeutic efforts. Detours may slow things down, but they can be used for positive effect. They are, in fact, expected and even to be sought after. After all, if the client can get back on track in the therapy after a slip, it suggests that they are building and honing life skills. It provides evidence for the client that a slip is not the end of the process or a failure. It simply tests clients' skills so that they can stay on track when therapy is over.

When therapy gets "stuck," it is tempting (and simplistic) to blame treatment difficulty (or lack of progress in therapy) on the client's noncompliance or resistance. With certain clients and client types, this is easy to do. Adolescents who generally do not choose therapy on their own, those remanded to therapy by the judicial system, or those sent to therapy by a family member may be prone to avoid or resist therapy. This is also true of clients with chronic and pervasive disorders, who have experienced life in a certain way over many years. After all, if they have been in therapy for many years and have not as yet resolved their myriad difficulties, then how can any one therapist be expected to help them?

Therapists may find it is convenient to judge some clients as untreatable. Seeing a client as untreatable lifts any demand or expectation that the therapist should work longer, harder, or more creatively with the client. Therapists often assume that when there is no therapeutic movement or when progress lags, it is because the client does not want to change or get well for conscious or unconscious reasons. Many issues, circumstances, and problems can slow or block progress in therapy, and only a few are due to the client's wanting to retain problems. Think of a "self-help" or "self-improvement" task that you have attempted. This might be losing weight, exercising more regularly, or completing unfinished, overdue paperwork. To what extent is the lack of follow-through due to a secret desire to remain fat, out of shape, or lag behind in your paperwork? To what extent is it due to more mundane factors such as personal comfort, time limitations, anxiety, or perfectionism, and to what extent is it some combination of these factors?

Impediments to change in therapy are costly to clients in terms of their ongoing pain and discomfort and the price they pay for continued dysfunction. The cost in human terms is compounded by the economic loss to the individual and to the economy. It has been estimated that the cost of depression to U.S. business is 30 to 44 billion dollars per year (Elinson, Houk, Marcus, & Pincus, 2004; Stewart, Ricci, Chee, Hahn, & Morganstein, 2003). This represents the combined expenses for psychological care, medications, and hospitalization, and the cost of lost wages due to decreased productivity and absenteeism. Obviously, the financial burden to agencies and institutions is monumental. Estimates of the costs of untreated mental health disorders indicate an additional

70 billion dollars of lost productivity per year (U.S. Department of Health and Human Services, 1999). Finally, the emotional and economic costs to families of delayed or limited change is incalculable. Therapists are not immune to the price of extended therapy in that noncompliance makes the therapy work more difficult and personally wearing. This can lead to decreased effectiveness and ultimately to therapist burnout.

Definitions of Resistance

In traditional psychoanalytic terms, resistance was primarily conceptualized as a negative patient variable, and a form of pathology embedded in a narcissistic, false, and pathological character that strove to maintain the status quo at any cost (Menninger, 1958; Stark, 1994). Campbell (2003) addressed the topic of resistance from a psychoanalytic position. He differentiated between id, ego, or superego resistances. He identified common themes of client resistance to therapy as involving distrust of the therapist, personal shame, grievances against others, depreciation, or fear of rejection. Typically, resistance may be manifested directly (e.g., tardiness or missing of appointments) or more subtly through omissions in the material reported in the sessions. Writing in 1914, Freud, quoted in Fine (1979) stated, "It may thus be said that the theory of psychoanalysis is an attempt to account for two striking and unexpected facts of observation which emerge whenever an attempt is made to trace the symptoms of a neurotic back to sources in his past life; the facts of transference and resistance" (p. 52).

There are many reasons for noncompliance other than the client not wanting to change or wanting punishment. Resistance is no longer being viewed as entirely negative or as only a patient variable. Several authors (Adelman & Taylor, 1986; Ellis, 1985; Gerber & Nehemkis, 1986; Meichenbaum & Gilmore, 1982; Milman & Goldman, 1987) have considered the adaptive nature of resistance. Many volumes have explored this important issue from a variety of perspectives (Ellis, 1985; Leahy, 2004, Wachtel, 1982).

Rather than use the term *resistance,* which has come to mean an action of the client, we have chosen to use the term *impediment to change* (Freeman & McCloskey, 2004). This implies that there are many roadblocks (Leahy, 2004) or speed bumps that do not have to stop progress, but may slow it down. No one impediment is more powerful or influential than any other. The impact that an impediment has on the therapeutic progress is related to the meaning to the client, how the impediment manifests itself, how the therapist deals with it, or a combination of all of the preceding factors.

Clinically, we can identify several explanations for the impediments to change that may appear to be the client's resistance or noncompliance. Impediments can appear in any combination or permutation, and the relative strength of any noncompliant action may change with the client's life circumstance, progress in therapy, relationship with the therapist, and so on. We can divide these impediments to therapy into four broad categories. The first set of impediments is problems coming from the client. In the second category of impediments are those roadblocks that emanate from the therapist and the therapeutic interaction. The third category includes factors related to the client's life situation, personal context, and significant others. The final factors come from the type, severity, and nature of the client's problem(s) or behavior. In the following discussion, we describe therapeutic interventions for reducing or ameliorating these problems and impediments to therapeutic change.

The manifestation of these impediments may take many forms. Some would appear more directly negative: verbal or behavioral evasion ("I forgot my homework for the session. So what?"), verbal hostility ("You are a lousy therapist and haven't helped me at all."), threats of physical aggression ("I'll get you if you turn me in."), or threats against the institution or agency ("I'll blow this place up."). Other impediments may be more subtle: frequent lateness for appointments, missing appointments, or extended silence in sessions. And yet other behaviors may appear positive, but still interfere with progress: trying to win the therapist over with praise ("You are the best therapist I have ever had."), gifts ("I saw this and thought how nice it would look in your office."), or statements of devotion ("I could never work with any other therapist.").

Roadblocks may be conscious, such as when the client chooses to withhold information and details from the therapist so as to appear healthier, smarter, and more competent (e.g., not reporting having failed a test, gotten a traffic ticket, or being unable to accomplish a homework task). The same material might also not be reported to the therapist because of "forgetting," a process that might be more unconscious ("Didn't I tell you about Jim breaking up with me? I thought that I did.").

A starting point for understanding the impediments to change is to conceptualize the client's actions as a normal and adaptive response to threat. Whether the behavior is viewed as an ego defense or as a response to unfamiliar demands, it is unreasonable to expect that an individual will move directly to change without some level of discomfort, avoidance, or reactance. In point of fact, an individual who moves too quickly to change may be impulsive, unstable, or labile. The client with a borderline personality disorder may move quickly from idealization of the therapist ("You are the best.") to devaluation ("You are worthless as a therapist."). Both extremes need to be identified and addressed directly within the therapy.

Many of our clients have been in therapy at some previous point. If the previous therapeutic experience has not been successful, it would be essential for the therapist to first assess what was done in the previous therapy in terms of the focus, direction, content, timing, cadence, and style of the therapy. What was the client's view of the therapist (both personally and professionally)? What strategies and techniques worked in the therapy and what was left undone or poorly done? How well did the client think that the therapy met their needs? What were, in the client's view, the most helpful and therapeutic experiences?

With that information in hand, the therapist can work to alter any and all the factors emblematic of the negative aspects of the previous therapy so that the present therapy is experienced as different and not more of the same old pattern. If the previous therapy was free-floating and unstructured, structure would offer a different therapeutic experience. If the content revolved around a particular issue, shifting to a variant of that issue, or even a different issue could be helpful. Different examples could be useful. The goal is to make the present therapy a new experience and opportunity for change. If the previous therapy was successful and fulfilling of the client's needs, but ended due to outside forces (loss of insurance or the therapist leaving the agency), the therapist can try to follow and use what worked before. For the previously "therapized" client, the current therapist must be creative in finding new directions or foci.

Bordin's Model of the Working Alliance

Bordin's model (1979) of the working alliance emphasizes the agreement about the goals and tasks of therapy and the establishment of a positive, interpersonal bond between client and therapist as being crucial to the success of therapy. Many of the identified impediments to therapy appear to be related to difficulties in the establishment of the working alliance. Lack of clarity in the definition of problems and related goals, lack of precision in the definition of the tasks of treatment, and confusion about the division of labor in treatment and the failure to establish a collaborative, goal-directed relationship can severely limit the effectiveness of treatment.

We have found it useful to separate the *working alliance* into its component parts and to deal with them in a more focused manner. We use the term working alliance or therapeutic alliance to mean the therapeutic goals and contract between therapist and client. This contract or treatment plan needs to be explicit and negotiated early in the therapy. In this way, the goals of therapy will be clear, as well as the direction of the therapy, the potential time line for therapy, the elements of the therapy, the strategies that might be used in the therapy, and the people who might be called on to contribute to the therapy (family members, significant others).

We use the term *therapeutic bond* to refer to the relationship between the therapist and the client. For some clients the relationship may be the central focus. For other clients, the alliance may be far more important. The focus on one does not, in any way, ignore or diminish the importance of the other. It may be a question of which will be the ascendant feature at a particular point in therapy. If a client were to come into an emergency facility with suicidal ideation or after a suicide gesture or attempt, the therapeutic relationship may be secondary to the need to act immediately and directly on helping the client toward safety. Clients who need emotional support to accomplish their goals may need far more of the therapeutic bond to provide the environment for change.

Impediments to Treatment and Change

Some impediments to treatment may not reside within the person of the therapist or of the client. Cultural, familial, social, and interpersonal factors may all contribute to difficulties encountered in the treatment setting. In addition, factors related to the health and medical well-being of the client may contribute to the degree of difficulty encountered in attempting to implement a structured, planned intervention. As an extension of Bordin's work, we identify four broad areas that may interfere with, or even halt therapeutic progress: client factors, therapist factors, environmental factors, and factors related to the problems or pathology that brings the individual to seek therapy.

Client Factors

These are cognitive, affective, or behavioral aspects of the client, and may even be seen as typical of their style. These characteristics may be clear, obvious, and overt and not easily missed. Or, these characteristics may be far more limited and evident only under stress, or when the individual experiences threat. They may include the following:

- The client lacks skills to comply with the therapeutic requirements or tasks.
- Previous treatment experience, often of failure, has produced negative expectations or cynicism.
- The client fears that others will be hurt or impacted in a negative way by the changes produced in therapy.
- There is secondary gain from maintaining symptoms, for the client or significant others.
- The client fears the experience of change or being "different."
- The client lacks compelling reasons to change.
- The client has a generally negative set toward therapy.
- The client has limited ability for self-monitoring of thoughts, feelings, and behavior.
- The client has limited or poor ability to monitor the responses and reactions of others.
- The client has a demanding or self-centered interpersonal style.
- The client has a low tolerance for frustration and expects progress to be effortless and rapid.
- The client perceives being in therapy as a loss of social status and feels stigmatized.

Therapist Factors

As active participants, therapists bring their own values, skills, and motivation(s) to the treatment endeavor. All therapists, no matter which gender or how many years of experience or training, potentially contribute to the therapeutic roadblocks. If you doubt this, you need only peruse the public record of state licensing board disciplinary actions for evidence of misdeeds by licensed psychologists. Not all the clinician-based roadblocks are at the level of misdeed.

Some are factors of experience and training. The therapist contributions to the impediments include the following:

- The therapist lacks skills.
- The client and therapist maintain congruent distortions.
- The client has been poorly socialized by the therapist to the expectations of the therapy or of a particular treatment model.
- The therapist is unable to build or communicate an active and effective collaboration or working alliance. Essentially, the therapist has not gotten informed consent and agreement with therapy goals.
- The therapist and the client are attempting to operate from an impaired or limited database.
- The therapist has therapeutic narcissism.
- The therapist's timing of interventions is poor.
- The therapist has limited skills but lacks experience.
- The therapy goals are unstated, unrealistic, or vague.
- The therapist fails to build and maintain the therapeutic bond.
- The therapist has a lack of understanding of the norms and of the developmental process.
- The therapist has unrealistic expectations of client.

Environmental Factors

We all live within a subgroup, a group, and a society. Each entity will have expectations and demands for conformity, allegiance, and contributions from the client. Sometimes these demands will be in conflict; other times they may be in direct opposition one to the other. The client's difficulty may come from the delicate balancing act of trying to meet the demands of many masters, and not being able to do it. These psychosocial stressors would, ideally, be coded on the *DSM-IV-TR* Axis IV. The demands of the environment could include:

- Environmental stressors that preclude change.
- Significant others (SOs) who foil or sabotage therapy.
- Agency or institutional reinforcement of pathology and illness through compensation and benefits.
- Cultural opposition to help seeking.
- The maintenance of system homeostasis.
- Gross family pathology.
- Unrealistic demands on client by self and family members.
- Unrealistic demands on client by institutions.
- Financial factors that may limit the opportunities for change.
- Lack of resources or support from the environment.
- Resources with conflicting agendas for the client.

Problem or Pathology Factors

Clients bring with them a plethora of factors. Some are related to the client's personal style as listed earlier. Other factors are indicative or diagnostic of the client's problems and pathology. These factors may be found in Axes I and II and be part of the criteria for disorders coded on these axes. These could include:

- Rigid cognitive style.
- Significant medical or physiological problems.
- Trust impairments.
- Impulsivity and poor executive control.
- Cognitive impairment, confusion, or limited cognitive ability.
- Social isolation or alienation.
- Symptom profusion.
- Extreme dependence.
- Ongoing self devaluation.
- Limited energy for change.
- Substance misuse.

Client Factors

Lack of Skill to Comply with the Therapeutic Requirements or Regimen

Therapists cannot assume that every client has developed the skills to effectively perform a particular behavior or sequence of behaviors. For many clients, their difficulty in therapy will parallel their inability to cope with life stressors. Both may be based on inadequately developed skills. These skill deficits may be broad (overall social skills) or more discrete (making eye contact while speaking to another person).

For many individuals, their present skill set has been adequate for getting by in familiar and highly structured areas of life experience. In a novel situation, however, they have far more difficulty and may avoid it, when possible, withdraw from it, or fail to meet its requirements. If they are overtly unsuccessful at coping, they may experience such a high level of discomfort that they will avoid future encounters. Because these clients may never have developed skills, or not developed them to the level necessary for adequate functioning, the therapist may need to teach particular skills to help them move along in therapy and thereby in life.

The assessment protocol must include an evaluation of the skill repertoire of the individual including behavioral skills (e.g., acting in particular ways when confronted with particular stimuli); cognitive skills (e.g., being able to evaluate or dispute thoughts); situational skills (e.g., being able to leave situations that are potentially damaging); and affective skills (e.g., being able to control emotion). If there are skill deficits, the therapy must include the necessary skill building. Whether this will be a major or minor component of the therapy depends on the goals of the therapy.

Jim was a 26-year-old graduate student in clinical psychology. He reported for the first day of his clinical practicum wearing a tee shirt, cutoff jeans, and sandals. When asked by the agency's director of clinical training (DCT) why he was dressed that way, Jim replied that it was a hot day and that this is what he generally wore to school. When the DCT informed Jim that the agency had a dress code for warm weather, Jim argued that he was the same person no matter what he wore and that dress codes were foolish and without value. When it was emphasized to Jim that the dress code was not open for discussion or debate, he demanded to know what the DCT expected him to wear. The DCT identified the sentence in the practicum student's manual that stated that practicum students were expected to dress "appropriately" and "professionally." Jim asked what that meant. The DCT informed Jim that he had to wear shoes, not sandals, long pants, a shirt with a collar and a tie, if he chose. Jim agreed and left for the practicum student orientation meeting.

The next day Jim appeared at the agency wearing black shoes, yellow socks, brown pants, a red shirt, and a green tie. On being informed of Jim's outfit, the DCT called him into his office and demanded, "What is this? What sort of outfit do you call this? Is this from a clown catalogue?" Jim seemed stunned. He stammered, "I did what you said. I am wearing everything that you said that I should."

The DCT stopped and considered the following: Was Jim's outfit the result of passive aggression or simply a lack of social skills? He decided on the latter. He asked Jim, "How did you choose this particular set of clothes to wear?" Jim responded, "I guess I just took what was on the top of the clothes pile or what was clean. What's wrong with this?"

The DCT replied, "There are too many colors. They clash. In the future, choose one or two colors and stay with them." In a particularly poignant and academic manner Jim asked, "Is there a book that I can read on how to dress?"

The next day, Jim came to the agency wearing black pants, black socks, black shoes and a black shirt. He sought out the DCT to show his adherence to one color.

Jim's dress issues were the result of a lack of skills. By the end of the year, with input from other students, Jim's dress was far more conventional.

Ideas about Therapy Based on Previous Therapy Failure

Clients entering therapy will carry with them, perhaps in an overriding way, their experience in a previous therapy or the cumulative impact of therapeutic experiences that they view as failures. When clients have cognitions of failing to make changes in thought or behavior, the therapist needs to help the client carefully examine their ideas of what succeeded in the past, what they see as failed, and what they would like to accomplish in the present work. It is essential that the therapist does not label the previous therapy as failing, but rather as clients' further attempts or steps taken toward succeeding. Examining the client's underlying assumptions and reactions to the previous therapy will be an important first step in building the new therapy.

An aspect of failure that inhibits many clients is their rumination about the previous therapist's reactions and if the previous therapist considered that the client did the therapy "right." Rather than trying to interpret the previous therapist's reaction, it would be far more adaptive to examine the client's views of others. If the client anticipates receiving harsh criticism, anger, expressions of disappointment, or other aversive responses from the therapist, it may be useful to bring the question into the here-and-now. Does the client expect criticism and failure in the present therapy? Do they wait for the inevitable criticism? Are they waiting for their pink slip firing them from therapy . . . again?

It is important for the therapist to respond to this impediment without being punitive or authoritarian and instead to work with the client to understand what blocked compliance. However, it is also important for the therapist to be alert for negative anticipation based on the client's previous experience with parents and teachers and to address these explicitly if they impede therapy. Homework is an area in which clients' negative expectations often emerge. Their fear is that if they fail to do it, they will be thrown out of therapy. Perfectionist clients often anticipate extreme reactions if they don't do homework perfectly, and it can be useful to address these anticipations early in therapy.

Usually it is possible to honestly present the client's task as a "no-lose" situation by pointing out incidents of noncompliance or unexpected results that provide opportunities for making valuable discoveries. The therapist might follow the first homework assignment with, "One of the nice things about this sort of approach is that whatever happens, we come out ahead. If you go ahead and do [the assignment] and it goes the way we expect, great! We're making progress toward your goals. If you unexpectedly cannot get yourself to do it or if it does not work out the way we expect, then we have an opportunity to look at what happened and at your thoughts and feelings to discover more about what blocks you from your goals. If it goes smoothly, we're making progress and if it doesn't, we're making a discovery." For many clients this greatly reduces the fear of failure.

Ellen, aged 35, came to therapy after having been in therapy for 3 years with her previous therapist. She had a list of therapists that went back to age 14. At that point, she was referred because of bulimic purging once or twice a week. The therapist had Ellen placed on an inpatient psychiatry unit for 3 weeks. Afterward, she was seen twice weekly for 3 years. Ellen's bulimia was reduced to once a month. She could control it but frequently thought about purging.

Over the past several years, she sought therapy to get rid of the thinking, and the monthly binge-purge experience. In seeking the present therapy, she started with the challenge, "No one has gotten me to stop this. Part of me is hopeful that this time I will be successful, but part of me believes that this will fail like all of the other times."

Fears That Others Will Be Hurt or Impacted in a Negative Way

Sometimes, clients fear that change will have a negative impact or cause damage to significant others. These clients view the result or consequences of their changing as a catastrophe and need not only to decatastrophize the potential, but to examine whether there are possible advantages to changing. In many cases, their negative view is either gained from a significant other or is more subtly reinforced. A client's family may see growing independence as a way of drifting away from the family. The family will then offer the view that the client's changes are damaging individuals ("You're killing me"), the family system ("Your actions are breaking up the family"), or will be damaging to the client ("You don't realize how good you have it now").

Clients can be helped to examine and discuss (a) the explicit and implicit messages that they get from others; (b) the content, feeling tone, and timing of these messages; (c) the implications of what others attribute to the client's change; and (d) advantages and disadvantages of change both within and without the system of significant others. As therapists, we should be careful not to try to challenge the "others" directly as the older (and more powerful) allegiances and alliances may come back to haunt us.

Marsha, aged 19, came to the college counseling center without an appointment. She was in tears and was seen immediately by a staff psychologist. Marsha opened up quickly and described a crying/screaming/threatening experience at her home. She had agreed with her parents to spend the first year of college at a local campus of the state university system and to live at home to "save money." Her plan for subsequent years was to then transfer to the main campus of the state university and live on campus.

Money is not the issue, she told the therapist. My folks have lots of money. We have a big house, my mom and dad both drive Mercedes, and we have a full-time housekeeper. "My mother is afraid that if I were to move out to go to college, she would never see me again. That I would graduate and move to the moon. She is very frightened of being alone. She fears that my dad will die, I'll be away, and then she'll have nobody."

"How does that make you feel" asked the counselor. "Guilty, bad, wrong, stupid, ungrateful, and uncaring" said Marsha. "If I go away to college, my mother will die. I just know that she will waste away and die."

Secondary Gain from Maintaining Symptoms

In some situations, clients may not change because of the gain that accrues from continuing their dysfunctional thinking or behavior. In the case of suicidal behavior or ideation, this can force family members to treat the client gently, not put any pressure on the client, avoid confrontation, and generally allow the client to do whatever the person wishes, rather than increase the suicidal potential. This gain may be gotten from family, friends, employers, or other individuals with whom the client has interaction.

The client needs to look at the primary loss that goes into achieving their secondary gain. When possible, the client needs to be helped to obtain their gain in other ways. If the gain is powerful enough, therapists may find themselves stymied in the head-to-head confrontation. The Socratic dialogue is most helpful at this point. This directive dialogue can help the client to find a perspective that is far more powerful at limiting the perceived gain than simply being told by the therapist to consider the liabilities.

Allen, aged 44, lived at home with his parents. He did not work and he slept until 11:00 A.M. each day. Allen had no responsibilities at home. His mother cooked all meals, cleaned up afterward, and washed his clothes. When his father tried to have Allen do things around the house (gardening, cleaning) Allen refused stating, "I'm not your slave."

When asked to contribute money to the house for food, Allen refused stating, "It's your job to take care of me. You abused me as a kid and now you have to pay it back." When pressed, Allen would run to the basement of the house, stand on a chair, place a rope around a beam in the basement and then around his neck and threaten to hang himself. His parents were so frightened of his possible suicide that they gave in to all his requests.

Allen sounds like a 13-year-old in the body of a 44-year-old. This being how the therapist saw the situation, the recommendation was for family therapy to help Allen but also to try to maintain the contingencies for his behavior at home by working with his parents as one would do with an adolescent.

Fear of Change or Becoming Different

For some clients, change means giving up ideas, beliefs of behaviors that they see as inimical to their survival. This may seem paradoxical because it is their thinking that keeps them stuck. In reality, these clients fear any change because of the unknown and therefore threatening element. The familiarity of their pain is preferable to the uncertainty of a new mode of thinking or behaving. More simply, they believe "The devil that you know is better than the devil that you don't know."

As with many fears, the first approach is to gather as much data as possible, including the client's perception of the effort needed to change, the possibility of successful change, the impact of change, the client's ability to cope with change, and the price that the client believes must be paid for change.

Henry, 52, came to therapy at the referral of his physician. He was told that he had to slow down and reduce the stress on his body (especially his heart) from his 16-hour workdays, 6 or 7 days a week. Henry rarely took vacations and spent very little time with his wife or children. This had been his pattern since he was 12. He worked a paper route, cleaned up in a meat market at the end of the day, and worked nights in his father's pharmacy while studying and graduating with a scholarship to college. At college, he went to classes, worked in the university library, and worked 2 nights a week in a local pharmacy.

His expressed concern was that everyone (his wife, the doctor) was trying to turn him into a "typical working slob." Who could be successful working 9 to 5? He credited his financial and professional success to his long hours of working without distraction. He did not know what it would be like to work less.

Therapy focused on his incrementally and experimentally reducing various activities. The goal was not to stop, but to evaluate what would happen if he turned down the intensity of his activity and allowed some time to relax and connect with others.

Lack of Compelling Reasons to Change

Clients may be experiencing some discomfort with the impact of their behavior, yet are still comfortable with the behavior. Often, clients see small parts of the problems but view these issues as "part of them," or as too small to bother with in therapy. There is no compelling reason to consider a personal change, and there may even be strong reasons the client wishes to avoid change. Clients may also come for therapy under protest. The therapy may be mandated as part of a legal penalty ("go to therapy or go to jail") or coerced by family members ("If you don't get help, I'm leaving you"). For child and adolescent clients, the referral will come from the school or parents ("You are in trouble and must change what you are doing, now").

In these circumstances, clients come to therapy with the message that the therapist is an agent of the referring (or coercive) individual, whether that individual is parent, spouse, judge, probation officer, guidance counselor, or teacher. This sets up a negative and possibly adversarial situation prior to the first therapy session.

Helping clients to identify the advantages and disadvantages of being involved in therapy can help generate motivation and reasons to consider change. A second technique would be to have the client examine and to entertain the possibility of some value to changing, no matter how small that possibility might be.

Clients often accept identifying the value, gain, profit, advantage, merit, desirability, or benefit no matter how minimal. The motivation can be extrinsic or intrinsic. The extrinsic motive may be to stay out of jail, to have a parent or probation officer "get off of their back," or to profit in financial ways. The goal of the intervention is to have the client agree to therapy for whatever period of time is appropriate or mandated. The question the therapist asks is, "How might this work to your advantage?" Or, "How can therapy work in your enlightened self-interest?"

A final technique is to work in therapy time modules. A therapy module can be from 1 to 10 sessions. This strategy removes the therapy from the realm of forever and makes it into a more proximal and workable time frame. The goals for each module are specified and limited.

Erik, aged 15, was brought to therapy by his parents in an attempt to help him be more cooperative at home. Erik did not want to be in therapy, had little to say in therapy, and believed that the therapist was part of the adult conspiracy to punish him for speaking his mind. Erik's first action was to shock the therapist by his language. Every other word Erik uttered seemed to be a four-letter one, interspersed liberally with other sexual references. Rather than challenging Erik ("Watch your mouth young man") or joining him ("Sure, I can see that coming here is a f_____g waste of your f_____g time and f_____g effort,") the therapist stated the obvious. "Speaking this way at home has the goal and effect of getting your parents upset and annoyed. It won't have that effect or impact on me." Erik eventually slowed down his attempts to upset the therapist when the therapist kept asking, "What can I do to help get your folks off your back?"

General Negative Set toward Therapy

Often clients seem to have a "bad attitude," or "a very negative view." What is labeled as attitudinal is often an issue of negative set. The negative set might be manifested directly as "Yes-but" behavior by being agreeable and then quickly disqualifying whatever the therapist says, or directly arguing with the therapist on issues both large and small.

When dealing with a client with a negative set, it is essential that the therapist refrain from being drawn in debates, arguments, or tautological discussions that do not enhance the therapy. Given the negative set, the therapist can help to develop a positive cognitive set in otherwise resistant clients. The protocol involves several steps.

First, use Socratic questioning rather than interpretation. This involves a process of guided discovery. By the careful placement of simple closed-ended questions, the client can be moved slowly toward a more positive view. While the temptation may be to use open-ended questions to keep the therapy moving, the closed-end questioning keeps stress low in the interview. The client only has to answer relatively easy questions. This may preclude having the client develop an opening for ongoing venting of their upset with the world.

In framing the questions, the therapist has to be careful to state them so that the answer is affirmative. The rule is that the therapist does not move ahead unless and until they receive an affirmative response:

Poor question: Do you want to be here?
Better question: Are there many other places you would rather be?
Poor question: Do you believe that they treated you (fairly; well; appropriately)?
Better question: I would guess that you believe that they treated you (unfairly; poorly; inappropriately) is that so?

If the client offers a negative response, immediately reframe it so that the new question will elicit a positive response:

Therapist: "Do you think that you had any responsibility for what happened?"
Client: "No. None."
Therapist: "So what happened was, in your view, due to what others did. Is that what you are saying?"

The basic idea is that the content of the interview with the negative client is secondary to the purpose of reducing resistance and increasing rapport. When this technique is used, clients will see the therapist as more on their side, more agreeable, and less threatening. Once the negative set is shifted, more traditional therapeutic tools can be used.

Maria came from a home where she was always questioned, and every choice that she made was challenged. She married Brad who (not surprisingly) questioned and challenged every choice that she made. She worked in an office at the university where her boss questioned and challenged every choice that she made. Her children, modeling their father, questioned and challenged every choice that she made or rule that she set or tried to enforce.

Her referral for therapy came from her family physician, who was treating her pharmacologically for depression. Despite her physician's encouragement, Maria came to therapy with a negative set which was voiced as, "There is nothing that anyone can do to help me. I'm beyond help. I can't do anything right. I have always been this way and I deserve what I get. That's what everyone says, my folks, my husband, even my kids."

The initial focus of therapy was to use the questioning with a positive response to help Maria to begin to relate more positively in therapy, to begin to chip away at the negative cognitive set, and have her see that there *might* be *possibilities* for change in her life.

Limited Ability for Self-Monitoring of Thoughts, Feelings, and Behavior
Individuals may see the flaws and foibles of others but be blind to their own. The difficulty or, in some cases, the inability to self-monitor will often cause major problems in life, and be a major stumbling block for therapy. Being either unaware of the need to self-monitor or unable to self-monitor can have a range of effects for the individual. These individuals may say or do things that others view as strange or bizarre. By virtue of not self-monitoring, they may find themselves in deep difficulty with work, or with interpersonal or intrapersonal issues. By not attending to their internal or external environments, they may, in the words of the popular saying, "be up to their eyeballs in alligators." The inability to accurately self-evaluate can lead to depressive affect and behavior that in turn distorts clients' ability to accurately self-monitor. When depressed, they do not self-monitor but rather self-devaluate with negative appraisals and attributions.

Clients who do not self-monitor their more grandiose movements may find themselves out on a limb by virtue of involving themselves in projects or schemes that are far beyond their ability to satisfy. Rather than self-devaluation, this client's reflections are more self-serving and preserving of their positive self-image, even if reality is underrepresented.

The broad goal of intervention is to help clients develop a productive self-monitoring style. A major part of that goal involves the development of an observant style. If an individual has surveyed the scene and still decides to move ahead with a project or action, we can assume that it is not necessarily their self-monitoring that is flawed, but their problem-solving ability.

Jim, the psychology student described earlier, had to self-monitor what he wore, not merely wearing what was available or clean. He had to plan ahead for those days that he was at the practicum site. What started as a way of avoiding problems became a more global attempt to fit into a new professional role.

Limited or Poor Ability to Monitor the Responses and Reactions of Others
Monitoring of others is a problem that often goes hand in hand with poor self-monitoring. These clients look at others, may even be preoccupied with them, but actually see little. Their response to others is based on images, projections, and distortions rather than a data-based assessment. Others appear to be brighter, more attractive, more skilled, and so on. All other relationships must be more rewarding than any they have or might have. Others, quite simply, are not seen in terms of their realistic human needs, limits, and vulnerabilities.

Interventions, both in the sessions and as homework, need to focus on practice in observing others. This may take place as an observer in a mall, restaurant, or store. Subtly and carefully observing others is good practice. Observing and estimating the specific response of significant others can be a useful homework assignment. Even gauging and predicting the therapist's reaction to certain stimuli can be used. Group work can be useful to help clients with this problem.

Gretchen had become convinced that she lived in a different social world than everyone else. She avoided going out very much because she expected people to look at her "funny" because she was alone in public. She believed that most people had lots of friends and relatives to share activities with and that it was abnormal to do anything alone. When she had to travel about on her own, she felt very conspicuous and perceived herself as a focus of attention, no matter how quietly she behaved. Examining her perceptions in the context of a therapy session had little impact on Gretchen's degree of conviction in her view of self and the world. Gretchen's therapist proposed an experiment to test some of these perceptions by meeting for a session at a coffee shop. They arrived separately, and the therapist observed Gretchen for the first 15 minutes as she ordered coffee and sat alone reading a book. Then the therapist joined Gretchen and together they discussed her experiences and observed others in the coffee shop. Gretchen wondered whether people were looking at her funny, but she had not actually seen anyone staring. The therapist offered a reliability check to this perception with her observation that Gretchen has drawn no particular attention from the other patrons. Gretchen surveyed the scene and observed an assortment of other people in the coffee shop, some in pairs, a couple of groups, and several people enjoying their beverage alone, disconfirming her notion that it was abnormal to go anywhere in public alone.

A Demanding Interpersonal Style

Highly demanding or self-centered interpersonal behavior may reflect a narcissistic personality style. This needs to be differentiated from a diagnosis of clinical narcissism, which is a more pervasive and severe impairment in interpersonal relationships. The narcissistic style causes these clients to be so self-involved that any attempt to have them look at others or at themselves is met with resistance. The reaction is typically framed as, "The problem can't be me," or "Why would you (or anyone) expect so much from me." What is problematic is that the demanding style is often reinforced by having others accede to their wishes or demands.

It is essential for the therapist to set clear limits early in therapy. Once set, these limits must be maintained until restated or purposely renegotiated and changed. The use of self-instruction and assessing with the client the value of the demanding style can be discussed.

By virtue of luck, personal charm, good looks, and a demanding style, Sal had become used to getting his needs met without question. He came to therapy as an alternative to jail after he was caught and convicted of selling stolen property. Sal maintained that he did not know that the property was stolen, but despite his charm, he was convicted. His style in therapy was to ask for favors: "Do I really have to come every week? After all, if I come every other week, the judge wouldn't know, right?" He smiled, complimented the office décor, the therapist's suit, and the therapist's credentials. He voiced how lucky he was to be seeing the therapist. When his charm did not work, Sal pouted: "How can you do this to me? From what I remember from school, therapists are supposed to meet their client's needs." When this did not work, Sal switched back to charm. When this did not work, Sal became sad because he was being "misunderstood" by the therapist.

Low Tolerance for Frustration and Unrealistic Expectations

Clients may have unrealistic expectations of therapy and possible therapy progress. When the expectations are not met, clients may blame themselves or the therapist for the lack of progress. They may respond to their frustration by withdrawing, withholding from the therapeutic collaboration, or terminating therapy.

If, at the outset of therapy, there are discrete goals and realistic change criteria, the progress of therapy can be assessed and monitored. Without these, the client can easily see no progress and may prematurely foreclose the effort.

Bill's expectation or demand was that the therapy should take no more than 10 sessions. He had read an article about therapy and it stated that more than 10 sessions was unnecessary. To support his argument, he pointed to the limited sessions that were being paid for by insurance companies. "After all," he said, "if these multimillion dollar companies have studied therapy and concluded that it should only take ten sessions, I expect that from you."

Therapy Perceived as a Loss of Social Status

For some individuals, being in therapy, for whatever reason, is a mark of lowered status. Being in therapy is the mark of being "sick," "disturbed," "weird," "a nut case," or "crazy." Given the belief that being in therapy equates with being flawed, it would follow that fighting therapy (or the therapist), leaving, or avoiding therapy makes one less flawed. This is especially true in working with children and adolescents who are invariably sent, brought, or threatened into therapy. They then see the therapist as another adult, which emphasizes their helplessness.

Clients can be helped to reframe their position as one of taking greater control. In fact, the goal of the therapy will be for them to take control over those areas and circumstances that are reasonable, and to work at coping with those situations that are less controllable. The therapy must be framed to raise their position rather than to indicate their helplessness or low position. It is in this regard that the therapeutic collaboration, the therapeutic bond, and a clear working alliance are essential.

Maria, described earlier, saw her client status as proving that there was something wrong with her. It was essential for her to fight the therapy and the therapist to prove that she would not submit in this arena, too. By reframing the therapy as a way for Maria to gain skills that she could use at home, with her folks, with her boss, and with her children, she could agree to be part of the collaboration. The metaphor that was helpful for Maria was that therapy was a cast and a crutch for a broken leg. Both would be useful until there was sufficient healing of broken bones. These would not be needed when her leg was strong enough to support her.

Therapist Factors

Lack of Therapist Skill

Just as clients come into therapy with a particular set of skills, so, too, do therapists. Because of limited experience with a particular client problem or population, the therapist may not be best equipped to work with a particular client. The therapist working within the context of an agency or hospital setting may call in colleagues for consultation on the case or seek supervision on a particular case or problem. It is incumbent on therapists to constantly develop, enhance, and upgrade their skills through additional training. Postgraduate courses, continuing education programs, seminars, workshops, or institutes are part of the professional growth of all therapists. If the therapist's skills are a poor match with the client's problem, transfer to another therapist is the ethical indication.

Students often have the disadvantage of seeing clients with extensive histories of psychological problems. This occurs at a time when the student is just learning about the range of problems and skills. However, the development of professional skills is a career-long endeavor, and students can expect to continually expand their fund of knowledge and range of skills. There is a spectrum of skill development efforts that professionals can use for the duration of their career, from student to seasoned practitioner. At one end of the spectrum is *information seeking*. This can involve reading of texts or other books, or searching the literature and Internet for information. Another tool is *self-supervision* where therapists review their session notes and tapes, and do their own supervision or consultation. *Peer consultation* can be useful when therapists meet with colleagues to support and instruct each other. A therapist confronted by a particular client type or client problem may seek *professional consultation* on an as-needed basis for a single meeting or for a limited number of consultation sessions. The therapist may also choose an *ongoing professional supervision* or consultation where the discussion is not limited but part of an overall professional growth experience.

For students, there is always required *ongoing professional supervision* that is part of professional training requirements and necessary to avoid unlawful practice without a license and potential risks to the client. Where the supervisor's experience is limited, *additional professional consultation* might be sought for a specific area of concern. For many psychologists, an *integrative approach* is used. This includes professional supervision, peer consultation, and self-supervision. Finally, therapists who are experiencing difficulty in dealing with a particular client, client type, or client problem, may find that *personal therapy* helps them cope, and consultation on risk management may be advisable.

Congruent Distortions Maintained by Client and Therapist

Therapists' blind spots may be very destructive to the therapeutic process in that they generally incline the therapist to accept the client's dysfunctional beliefs without question. If a client and therapist share a particular dysfunctional idea (e.g., "everything is hopeless and cannot change"; "all men or women cannot be trusted"), it will bode poorly for the therapy. This sharing of an idea or belief can result in the therapist buying into the client's hopeless ideas and beliefs, not testing these beliefs, and even encouraging them.

Therapists must be exquisitely tuned into their personal life issues. Without this awareness, they may be blindsided by a client's revelation or comment. Whether this awareness comes from personal therapy or self-examination is of lesser consequence. Whenever we accept the client's statements as being unassailable we as therapists surrender our ability to help. While it is always appropriate to empathize with the client, the therapist must be able to go further and ask, "What are we going to do about it?"

Sue, aged 27, sought therapy for her depression. She described her depression to her therapist Alicia as based on the fact that despite everything that she and her husband were doing, Sue could not get pregnant. She described her desperate wish for a baby, a desire that she stated went back to her adolescence.

"Being a mother has always been more important than school, degrees, jobs, or anything else."

In supervision, Alicia described her goals of helping Sue to (a) come to terms with her inability to conceive a child, (b) view herself as a woman despite her inability to conceive, (c) not be angry at her husband for his inability to help her conceive, (d) reduce her anger at her husband for not understanding the depth of her upset and trying to placate her. When the supervisor tried to gather more data from Alicia about everything that Sue had done, Alicia stated, "She's done *everything*!"

"So, the fertility clinic here at the university has written her off?" The supervisor asked.

"I guess so" replied Alicia. When the supervisor persisted, Alicia became angry and told him that she did not expect a man to fully understand Sue's loss. Alicia thought the supervisor was being sexist and ignorant of the issues, and that she (Alicia) did not want to continue the discussion of Sue. When the supervisor persisted and asked Alicia to stay with the issue just a while longer, Alicia said, "I can't." She began crying and after a period of soothing revealed the following. Her two children were adopted. This was not known to her peers or coworkers. Alicia was unable to get pregnant, an issue that ultimately caused stress in her marriage and contributed to the ending of that relationship. She had never questioned whether Sue had sought fertility treatment but went immediately to trying to soothe Sue.

When Alicia questioned Sue further, she discovered that Sue had never sought fertility treatment. Alicia and Sue shared the idea, "I cannot ever get pregnant," that might have been true for Alicia but not necessarily for Sue.

Failure to Adequately Socialize Client to Treatment

Clients who do not understand what is expected of them will have difficulty complying with the therapeutic regimen. It is essential that the therapist assess the level of understanding of the goals and guidelines for therapy generally and for the specific model throughout the therapy work. Often clients' very problems may impair their ability to listen and understand. Hundreds of self-help books are available but these rarely if ever explain the role of being a client. The therapist cannot assume that having read books about therapy provides adequate socialization to therapy generally, or to a particular model specifically. Further, there may be proactive interference because of ideas from readings or previous therapy. Clients who have been in therapy have, ideally, been socialized to that previous therapy model. They will continue to use the same strategies and approach to therapy and to life in general unless and until they are taught to respond differently.

Milt, aged 66, had psychoanalysis sessions 3 times per week for 14 years with the same analyst. When the analyst died, Milt spent the next year and half shopping for a new analyst to replace his lost friend. "He knew everything about me, I called him by his first name, sent him Christmas cards." After an unsuccessful search where Milt either interviewed therapists or started trial therapy, he decided that his analyst could not be replaced and that he would have to settle for a "lesser" therapy. This brought him to a therapist that had been recommended highly as an expert in the treatment of depression. After a two-session interview of the therapist, Milt decided to enter treatment. He reported that the reason that he sought therapy over 15 years earlier was to treat his depression. When asked if that was done in the analytic work Milt said, "No, but I liked going."

The new therapist was careful to not, in any way, question what was done in the previous therapy. When Milt came to each new session, he would start to engage in free association. When it was pointed out that this new therapy used a more focused approach, Milt heard that as critical of his previous therapy. Milt and the new therapist negotiated an agreement to put free association on the agenda as the first item. This would last for no more than ten minutes, and that was followed by agenda setting and a more focused approach to therapy. It is the therapist's job to make sure that the client is aware of the requirements, expectations, special circumstances, and goals of the therapy and to negotiate a satisfactory working alliance.

Inability to Build an Active and Effective Collaboration

Collaboration is an essential ingredient for all psychotherapy. If the client and therapist do not have a good working alliance, it would follow that the client may be less motivated to work with the therapist, do homework, follow the therapist's direction, or generally work toward making changes. The lack of collaboration, if not based on socialization difficulty or the skill of the therapist, may be due to the client's thoughts about cooperation or collaboration. Certain clients may actively thwart the therapist. This type of passive-aggressive behavior may be motivated by any of a variety of client ideation; issues of control, entitlement, fear, competition or displaced anger may all cause difficulty in the therapy. This client may be directly challenging or more covertly avoidant as in the classic "yes, *but*" response.

A therapist in training asked for advice in handling a client's noncompliance with behavioral experiments designed to reduce the client's perfectionism. The client's goals for therapy were to resolve some relatively minor marital problems, but the therapist saw the client's perfectionism and the stress and job dissatisfaction that resulted from it as more significant. Rather than discussing this issue with the client and reaching an agreement on the goals of therapy, the therapist had unilaterally begun working on perfectionism and this led to the noncompliance.

Collaboration involves both the therapist and the client and either of them can disrupt it. If the client feels that he or she has no voice in how therapy proceeds, either because this is indeed the case or because of his or her beliefs and expectations, this is likely to interfere with collaboration and produce problems with compliance. It is important for the therapist to actively solicit and value the client's input in setting agendas, determining the focus of therapy, and developing homework assignments, particularly with clients who tend to be unassertive. It is also important to be alert for any client thoughts that could block collaboration.

An Attempt to Operate from an Impaired or Limited Database

We have stressed that the basis for therapy is the assessment and general collection of data. The therapeutic conceptualization and treatment plan is then data based. If the therapy is focused on theory without data, the therapy will suffer.

The therapist may then make major conceptual leaps without a solid footing on which to base the interventions.

The therapist must always be searching for data and, as a function of the therapy, help the client to become an effective data collector. Questions such as, "What value does that have for you?" "What meaning do you give that?" "What exactly did he say?" or, "Let's go over the process step by step?" all direct the client toward collecting and evaluating the data instead of responding to bits and pieces of it. In working with individuals or couples, an effective data-gathering question subsequent to something being said or done within the session is, "What just happened right here?" This directs the client(s) to the here-and-now.

Homework, an important part of the overall therapy, is designed to help the client gather data.

Ray, aged 42 came to therapy as a facet of his ongoing difficulty with his wife. She had returned to school to pursue an associate's degree in nursing. When Ray and Judith married 20 years earlier, she dropped out of school to work at home and to raise their two children. They were now aged 17 and 15, and Judith felt that it was a good time for her to return to school.

Ray, on the other hand, was used to having his dinner ready for him when he came home from work and was very upset that Judith wasn't around. She was in classes, studying, and involved in clinical experiences. A crisis emerged when Judith informed Ray that she and several other students would be funded by the college to attend the state nursing conference a month hence. Ray came for therapy very upset. "What am I to do? I'll be home alone." For the 20 years of their marriage, the only time that Ray and Judith had spent a night away from each other was when she gave birth.

Ray's thoughts were like a runaway train. "She'll like going to the conference. Now she'll start going to all of these conferences. There are many throughout the year. She'll be away a lot." When asked if that was what Judith said, that she was going to go to one conference a month, and that she would be away a minimum of a weekend a month, Ray said no. "She's going to this conference." This observation immediately slowed the racing of his thoughts and the distress in his mood. Looking at the data had a marked impact on slowing his runaway emotional train.

Therapeutic Narcissism

An issue that can be a major impediment to change is what we term "therapeutic narcissism." This results from therapists being so taken with themselves and their therapeutic approach that they are blinded to the need for greater humanity, empathy, and depth.

Therapeutic narcissism may take the form of telling rather than asking clients how they feel. It may show up in several other ways: deciding what the client needs without consulting the client, believing that change should take less time than it does, setting goals for change that are distal and grandiose, or labeling clients as resistant for continuing to believe the dysfunctional ideas taught to them by parents and significant others. Therapeutic narcissists believe they are more powerful than they really are, smarter than they really are, that they know what the client is "really" thinking, that they never have to accept the germ of truth in a client's negative comments and that simply spending time in their aura should be therapeutic.

Pat was a psychology intern. He was very bright and very verbal. He claimed to be an advocate for a short-term rational emotive behavior (REBT) model of treatment that used debate and persuasion as a major therapeutic tool. What was clear about Pat's work was that it was short term. Most of his clients were seen for one session. In that session Pat would quickly identify the problem, enter a debate with the client and by the end of the session, the client would admit that Pat was right. The client rarely returned for another session. Pat's view was that if they did not return than they were either cured or not ready to hear the "truth."

Poor Timing of Interventions

Untimely interventions may cause clients to miss the importance or relevance of the therapeutic work, and thereby appear to be noncompliant. If the therapist, because of anxiety, tries to push or rush the client, the result may be the loss of collaboration, the missing of sessions, a misunderstanding of the therapeutic issues, or a premature termination of therapy, a possibly fatal issue with a hopeless client.

If the therapist misses an opportune moment for an intervention, it is far better to let it go and return when the moment is once again opportune. Trying to place an intervention when the timing is wrong may obscure the value and purpose of an otherwise excellent option. Given that problems and issues do not disappear in a day, there will be other times for the therapist to use that tactic.

Chris, a therapy intern, saw an opportunity to use a metaphor in the first session of the therapy. When he did, the client looked at him and said that he considered the therapist's statement condescending and inappropriate. Further, he thought that an apology was due him. Rather than enter into a power struggle with the client, Chris apologized if anything that he said upset the client.

The same metaphor, used several sessions later, was not only accepted but prompted the client to say that he had not been ready to see what the therapist was pointing out in the earlier session.

Lack of Experience

This impediment exists because everyone starting something new is inexperienced. This impediment is unintentional and a standard part of the mental health training system. The front-line therapists working with the most disturbed and problematic clients may be the therapists in practicum, internship, or residency settings. The key for the therapist with limited experience is ongoing supervision.

The attainment of the state license in psychology allows the psychologist to function independently. However, this typically requires at least 1 year of postdoctoral supervised experience. Even though the newly minted therapist may feel ready to practice independently, the practitioners overall professional judgment is developed over time within the more protected confines of supervision and regular consultation.

Unstated, Unrealistic, or Vague Goals

When the goals of therapy are unstated, unrealistic, or vague, the client may unknowingly resist the treatment. The client's problem list must be clearly and explicitly set out and then ordered in terms of the priorities of the therapy. This prioritization must be realistic rather than idealistic.

The client who does not understand and agree to what is expected will have difficulty complying with the therapeutic regimen. It is easy for therapists to overlook that clients have not understood and accepted their instructions and explanations. It is important for the therapist to repeatedly solicit feedback from the client and to encourage the client to raise any concerns and objections, so that therapist and client can develop a shared understanding of the client's problems which forms a basis for collaboration and so that it is clear that the client understands and accepts the homework assignments. Generally this proves to be sufficient, but when the client holds strong preconceptions about therapy, the therapist may need to compromise to some extent to facilitate collaboration. This issue also raises problems with informed consent. Clients must be part of the treatment planning process and informed as to the goals, strategies, and interventions of the therapy so that they can best comply rather than being noncompliant out of ignorance.

Inability to Build and Maintain the Therapeutic Bond

In the interest of providing technical interventions and producing rapid results, many contemporary therapists overlook the importance and primacy of the therapeutic bond. Just taking time to get to know the client and developing rapport, understanding, and a feeling of familiarity may feel entirely too passive or underproductive. The eager therapist wants to get going and do something to help the client. However, the client may feel very uncomfortable with this technique-oriented therapy and thus be a reluctant participant. There are many reasons the therapist may lapse in this particular endeavor, including an underestimation of the importance of the therapeutic bond, time pressure from managed care, difficulty relating to diverse clients, therapeutic narcissism, or difficulty in tolerating the emotional aspects of this professional role.

Brandon took a very businesslike approach with all his therapy clients. There is nothing inherently wrong with this strategy, except that Brandon tended to come across to clients as cold and mechanical. He had little to say to any individual client, and he focused on writing notes and directing "exercises" during each session. One client even remarked on a feedback form that Brandon seemed to have a "preprogrammed" approach to therapy that made the experience feel very impersonal. It was no surprise that Brandon had an extremely short turnaround time in his case-load.

Poor Understanding of Developmental Norms and Developmental Process

An understanding of developmental process including the works of Piaget and Erikson are essential ingredients in assessment, conceptualization, treatment planning, and interventions.

Starting with the notion of individuals developing schemas as templates for understanding and responding to the world, the therapist must focus on the stages of cognitive development (sensorimotor, preoperational, concrete operations, and formal operations) that can be observed most clearly in the pathological presentations of clients with personality disorders.

Although we expect that adults have achieved the stage of formal operations, this is not always the case. This will assist in the matching of therapeutic interventions to the client's level of cognitive development. Having a developmental focus also helps therapists understand the clients' evolution of schema in terms of their psychosocial development.

Allen, discussed earlier, was an adult only in years on earth. In every other way he was an adolescent. In fact, he was an oppositional-defiant adolescent. To try to treat him in individual therapy would be of limited value in that, like most adolescents, Allen saw his parents as the source of all his frustration. When Allen was asked why he stayed in such a stressful setting, Allen's response was, "What do you expect me to do, leave my home?"

Unrealistic Expectations of the Client

One of the subsets of therapeutic narcissism is having expectations of clients that are more in line with ideal change and out of the realm of reality. The clients, their families, and even the therapist may believe that a total change is what is needed for the client. Whether this is realistic based on the long-term nature of the client's problems must be an overriding part of the treatment plan.

Estelle, aged 45, came for therapy to "finally get her life together." She described over 30 years of therapy with many therapists in many different settings. She described episodes of severe depression, multiple hospitalizations, self-injurious behavior, suicide attempts, poor work history, poor school performance, few relationships, and estrangement from her family. She was supported by SSI (government subsidy) and lived in a room that she rented by the week.

Her therapy goals within a year were to have a job that she liked, earn enough money to buy a house, begin dating, establish a love relationship, possibly adopt "some" children, restore her relationship with her parents and sister, no longer be depressed, and no longer want to hurt herself. The therapist's statement, "We can start to work on all of these," set up an expectation that Estelle had the skills, the ongoing motivation, and the supports to do any of them. Before moving ahead, it would be prudent for the therapist to assess what is possible, what is probable, and what may not be realistic.

Environmental Factors

Environmental Stressors Precluding Change

Factors in the client's environment may maintain their psychopathology. There may be family schemas that mediate against the client making changes, even if the family has identified the changes as important. Without malice or intent, significant others may do things that maintain the client's dysfunctional and self-destructive behavior. Clients may get the messages of nonchange either overtly or covertly. Overtly, clients may be assaulted for going to therapy, assailed for talking of "private family matters with a stranger," or teased or stigmatized for being a "psycho" and needing to get their head "shrunk." Covertly, the message may be sent by the withdrawal of significant others while clients are in therapy. In some cases, the clients' change will make their continuation within their environment untenable.

Paul was a 25-year-old who had a 6-year heroin habit. He lived at home with his mother and three brothers. All in his family were heroin addicted. His mother would boil their "works" (paraphernalia) every night to prevent infection. Paul wanted to join the police department. He had done well in high school and had avoided the heroin so readily available at home. He knew that he could not join the police force as a heroin user. He had never been involved in any drug treatment program nor had he ever been arrested for possession or use of heroin. He had, on two occasions, stopped using heroin for periods of 3 and 6 months. When asked what got him started again, he replied that it was impossible to live in his home without someone offering him a "taste." Although his mother and brothers complimented him on stopping, they also offered him a taste when they scored a particularly good batch of narcotic.

Paul recognized that living at home clean would be too difficult for him and for his family. To meet his life's goal of being a police officer, he had to move away from his home environment.

Therapy Foiled or Sabotaged by Significant Others (SOs)

For many reasons, including expressions of power, the significant others of clients may sabotage therapy. This can be either directly or indirectly and include not providing transportation for the client or not making agreed-on funds available for therapy. Other forms of proactive sabotage include the behavior of the codependent partner who buys alcohol for the alcoholic, buys ice cream by the gallon for the obese client, or goes shopping for food for the client with bulimia. This is especially true with children and adolescents. If the parents, caretakers, and family members are not directly involved, they may actively sabotage treatment.

Steve, aged 16, was brought to therapy by his mother, Harriet. She announced in the first session that no therapist could deal with Steve. He did not want to come for therapy and was unwilling to take help that she could offer; she was generally pessimistic about Steve's future. Steve had voiced suicidal intent for sometime in the future, had no friends, and was overweight. This was all said with Steve in the room.

After an initial meeting, Harriet was asked to step into the waiting room while the therapist spoke with Steve. Harriet was visibly upset. "He's a minor, I'm his mother, and I have a duty to be here when you speak to him." With that said, Steve began screaming and cursing at her. She seemed embarrassed and shrugged and left the room, saying, "I think you now see what you'll be working with." With his mother out of the room, Steve calmed down. The therapist set a rule that Harriet was only to come in when invited by the therapist. When she began to protest, the therapist told her that unless she could agree to the therapist's conditions of therapy, he (the therapist) would not start to work with Steve. Harriet agreed.

Steve was seen for about a dozen sessions. He stated that he liked coming to see the therapist, was able to calm himself when at home and at school, and was feeling more hopeful. It was at this point that Harriet called and announced that she had decided that what Steve needed was family therapy and that she was immediately withdrawing him from work with the therapist. This was followed by a hushed call by Steve begging the therapist to be allowed to continue.

Five years later, the therapist received a call from Steve. He had graduated from a community college, was living across the country from his mother, had a job, and was feeling "good." He had called to tell the therapist that the dozen sessions that he had had given him hope. He had established an identity that was separate from the dictates of his mother, had a few friends, sought therapy again, and felt as though he was successful in his life.

Institutional Reinforcement of Illness with Benefits

For many clients, the changes sought in therapy lead to the undesirable consequence of losing funding or benefits based on having psychological problems. This might include Social Security Disability income, veterans' benefits, or workers' compensation and disability payments. The client is often reinforced for maintaining symptoms. Successful therapy would very quickly lead to a review by the relevant agency and a loss of benefits. This is not true of every client who receives such monetary benefits, as some are truly unable to function at a capacity that would resolve this dependence. Others, however, do have greater potential for change, but the risks of such change appear to outweigh the benefits.

Allen could be thought of as "retired." He did not have to work, received a check each month, had no expenses, could spend the day as he chose, and had no responsibilities. If he were able to work, have friends, and support himself, he would lose his retirement and have to follow the same course as most other adults.

Rose, a 76-year-old woman, lived in a home that she and her late husband bought 50 years earlier. It was now in need of major plumbing, electrical, and mechanical repairs. She could not afford them based on her Social Security check and public assistance. She could use the toilet in one bathroom but not the sink. She could bathe and use the sink in another bathroom, but not the toilet. Because of the changing neighborhood, she was frightened to shop at the nearby market. Her windows were nailed shut to prevent break-ins. When asked why she continued to live there, she pointed out that she could sell the house, but would then have to turn the money over to the city to reimburse the city for the public assistance. That would leave her no money, and no home. Her only recourse would be to live in a shelter.

Cultural Opposition to Help Seeking

The process of therapy, which involves trust, collaboration, self-disclosure, and change, may be difficult for individuals from cultures where these behaviors are more aberrant than common. An understanding of the cultural rules and schemas of a culture will help the therapist avoid these reasons for impasse.

Questions about cultural rules of an individual or of a family can often be addressed through supervision or consultation. Cultural issues that could impact the therapy might be related to the therapist's gender, age, or ethnicity.

Certain religious groups demand that the client find a therapist of their religious group inasmuch as therapists of other religious groups might not understand the client's behaviors. In many cases, the cultural issue may be reflective of the client feeling uncomfortable with a therapist of a different cultural group just as a therapist may be equally uncomfortable with a client of a different group.

Jena, aged 36, had converted from Christianity to Judaism to marry Michael. Her husband then joined a Chasidic group and Jena found herself in the midst of an ultra-Orthodox sect. In keeping with the cultural expectations, Jena had 5 children in 7 years. After her third child was born, Jena started to have severe headaches that, at first, were responsive to medication. Now, nothing seemed to help. They went to the rabbi, who after listening to her complaints, asked that all the mezuzahs (prayers on the doorpost of their home) be brought to him. He read each one and found that the scribe who had written them had made several errors. He predicted that once the errors were corrected, Jena's headaches would vanish. After the corrections were made, Jena had a brief period of relief, followed by a return of the headaches.

When she sought therapy from a Jewish therapist, the parameters of therapy were spelled out in a call from the rabbi for their group. He told the therapist what could and could not be discussed in therapy. Religion was not to be discussed, her role within the community could not be discussed, her relationship with her husband should not be questioned, and the requirements of being a Jewish wife could not be discussed. Rather than following his initial reaction to refuse the case, the therapist asked for and received the client's permission to include the rabbi as a consultant to the therapy. The rabbi agreed to be available. Using the rabbi as a consultant, the therapist was, in fact, able to deal with a number of relationship issues. Key among them was her husband's demand for more children. With the rabbi's consultation, this demand was removed inasmuch as having more children would cause damage to Jena, making her less able to be the mother and Jewish wife that she was expected to be.

Maintenance of System Homeostasis

A systems model of family and group dynamics suggests that systems will work (sometimes very hard) to maintain a balance or homeostasis. In its simplest form, it involves keeping things as close to where they are as possible. Change is seen as undesirable, and even dangerous, because the loss of homeostasis brings about anxiety and the resultant discomfort. Through direct and indirect maneuvering, families and other systems will seek to keep all members in the same approximate position, even if that position is one of discomfort, pain, or pathology. If, for example, the issue for a patient is being in a position of power, any event or interaction that places the person in a position that seems less than powerful will result in immediate action to restore the perception of power.

What occurs in many interactions (especially true in family and couples work) is that the participants know when the actions will reach the homeostatic point. If any member crosses that line, the system will be unbalanced. To avoid that, the members will withdraw from the interaction thereby using a homeostatic cutoff to keep things balanced.

Hillary, aged 40, was a single woman who lived with her physically disabled father. He was wheelchair-bound and spent the day in his room watching television. Hillary would prepare his breakfast, prepare his lunch, and always be home to prepare dinner. She would wash his clothes and clean the house. He would greet her each night telling her about how tasteless the lunch had been. He would often throw the food and dishes against the walls and then demand that she clean up. He insulted her and called her "lazy and stupid" or called her a "cow." Her response to his insults was to apologize and tell him that she would be more careful in the future. If he did not like what she prepared for dinner, he would throw the plate against the wall and demand something else.

She had learned many years earlier that there was no time for dating in her life because it interfered with her care of her father. When questioned about her caring for her father, her response was that she had to do it because if she didn't no one else would. She sought therapy close to her 40th birthday. She had decided that unless she did something else, she was going to die alone.

One of the therapeutic interventions was an attempt to extinguish her father's abusive behavior. What Hillary agreed to try was to continue to make him breakfast and lunch, but she would tell him that if he threw his dinner against the wall she would not replace it and there would be no food again until breakfast. That night he threw his dinner against the wall and screamed insults at her. When she cleaned up the food and told him that there would be no food until breakfast, he continued to scream insults at her. This continued for 2 more days. On the third day, he ate dinner without comment. He even asked for seconds. Hillary needed support for what she knew she needed to be doing. Over the course of the next few months, the same contingencies were used to have him stop insulting her.

Gross Family Pathology

Related to the issue of homeostasis is frank family pathology. In this situation, the level of emotional, cognitive, psychic, or behavioral functioning is diagnosed as disturbed. The pathology may take the form of global drug use, sexual acting out, antisocial behavior, boundary violations, or abusive behavior (sexual, emotional, and physical) overt control and manipulation or all of the preceding. Individuals coming from chaotic, dysfunctional, and pathological families can be said to come by their problems honestly.

It is no surprise when the therapist discovers during the client's evaluation that there is a significant family history of a particular symptom or disorder. Disorders that are known to be heritable (e.g., bipolar illness, depression, or schizophrenia) are often diagnosed by the presence of the family history. In other cases, the family pathology results in a physically, mentally, or psychologically abusive environment that the therapist must report to social welfare or legal offices.

Beyond the difficulties caused by the client's own measure of this disturbance, the family circumstances are an impediment to progress when the chaos or pathology of the family makes it difficult or impossible for the client to change. The family pathology contributes to the smaller scale impediments to change through missed appointments, problems in doing homework, difficulty in maintaining gains, or the maintenance of a negative set concerning therapy. Family problems may absorb an inordinate amount of therapeutic time, as the client is constantly dealing with crises and demands from others in the system.

The only way that some clients can escape the influence of their family is to physically leave the home or geographic area. For children, this is impossible, though the government may determine that it is in the best interests of a child or adolescent to be placed in a foster care or institutional setting.

Alex was referred by his high school guidance counselor because of academic difficulty and failure, truancy, and fighting in school. When the psychologist called Alex's mother and asked to meet with her, she claimed to be unavailable. When the psychologist insisted, she became angry and started cursing. When she was told that by not assuring that Alex went to school she was in legal jeopardy, she agreed to come in. She came for the session and was clearly intoxicated, whether on alcohol or some other substance. She informed the psychologist that Alex's father was incarcerated for assault with a deadly weapon, and several other offenses. He was eligible for parole some 10 years hence. It became clear that Alex came by his style honestly and was following in his parent's path.

Unrealistic Demands Compounded by Family Members

Clients can be confused or even paralyzed by their internal demands. These demands are complicated by hopelessness and inability to challenge this demanding internal dialogue. Such ruminations can cause clients to end up in a downward spiral. When the external voices of family, friends, and significant others are added to the mix, the client may be frozen in place or may even take a contrary position and do whatever is opposed to the demands of others. The therapist may be placed in the same role as these demanding others.

Claudia, aged 36, was the middle of five children, having an older brother and sister and a younger brother and sister. Her siblings had all graduated from prestigious universities and now held high-paying professional positions. All were married and all had families. Claudia saw herself as the "failure," "disappointment," "black sheep," and "disturbed one" of all of her siblings. She graduated from a community college and worked as a manager at a convenience store. Her internal dialogue regarding her failure was amplified whenever her parents would beg her to return to school and get a "real degree." "Then," they said, "she could get a real job." Being compared with her sisters who, her parents said, "are no smarter than you" was a constant source of distress.

Claudia viewed therapy as one more opportunity to fail. In fact, if she succeeded at therapy, it might mean that there would be both internal and external pressure to do even more.

Unrealistic Demands by Institutions

The major demands on clients from institutions and agencies come as a two-edged sword. One message is that change is desired, but the other message is that change must occur within a limited time frame due to reimbursement policies. Insurers and therapists voice the goal that there should be services provided for those in need. At the same time, Clients know that if they do not or cannot change within the limits of reimbursed services, they will be limited in the therapy that they will receive.

Henry had an insurance plan that provided for 10 therapy sessions per year. His long-term emotional difficulties needed a far more intensive approach. He reported that he barely got started in therapy when termination occurred. It was hard for Henry to use those 10 sessions very productively due to his anxiety about losing access to treatment.

Financial Factors May Limit the Opportunities for Change
Financial factors can impede therapy in several ways. Related to the previously noted point, once reimbursed services run out, therapy will end unless the patient has the financial resources to continue (or if the therapist can see the patient for a substantially reduced fee or for free). The financial issue can also be a factor in abusive relationships; abused partners may be afraid of leaving because of inadequate financial resources to support themselves and their families. They may then choose to stay in an abusive situation against the best interests of their personal safety or the safety of their family.

Marika was involved in a relationship with a man who would drink and then become verbally and physically abusive. He was one of a series of abusive relationship that Marika had over the years. To financially support her three children, she stayed with her partner. Unlike previous partners, he provided a home, food, utilities, and some companionship when not drinking. She resolved that it was better to be beaten than to lose whatever security she and her children now had.

Lack of Resources or Support from the Environment
Clients may come to see the therapist as their principal support person. They may experience few people in the world as accepting, understanding, caring, and thoughtful as the therapist. They then place all of their eggs in the therapist's basket. Therapy, however, is in many ways an unreal relationship, and it has never been intended to replace a nonprofessional social network. One of the goals of therapy with all patients is to help them build a broader, more useful, more accepting, more available, more generous, and more appropriate support network. Sometimes this can be done through recognized support groups such as Alcoholics Anonymous, parenting groups, or disability-oriented groups, or interest-based clubs such as a coin-collecting club or a bicycle riding club.

Rose, the elderly woman living alone in the crumbling home described earlier, had one person she saw regularly, her therapist. Each week, she drove the few miles to her provider's office for their weekly chat. These meetings provided Rose with a purpose in getting out of her house and the sense of a safe connection with someone in the outside world. There was little change in Rose's overall situation from week to week. Remaining stable and independent was her primary therapeutic goal.

Resources with Conflicting Agendas for the Client
Many institutions give clients mixed messages. They state that they are willing to support the individual because of the individual's disability. This support

might include medical coverage, living expenses, and housing expenses. Support, however, is predicated on the individual having a diagnosable medical or psychiatric disorder. The therapy provided under the institutional plans, whether through the federal government or through some agency, requires that the individual work to overcome the pathology. At that point, all financial support would cease. It would be reasonable for an individual who is reinforced for having severe psychopathology to want to maintain their support.

Leonard, aged 56, was a client in a community mental health setting. He had been receiving Social Security Supplemental Income (SSI) for at least 30 years. Though a college graduate, Leonard had a breakdown at age 24 and had to leave his job and continue to live with his parents. He was diagnosed as having a schizoaffective disorder. He claims that he never had delusions or hallucinations, nor does he have them at this point. He was, and still is, he says, extremely depressed. The diagnosis was adequate to get the government funding. The diagnosis has been used ever since despite the lack of his meeting criteria. When asked about this, Leonard smiles and replies, "When they ask me about having hallucinations and delusions, I just smile and shake my head. They always think that I am lying and that I am just not admitting to having them. I have never lied."

At this point in life, Leonard sees himself as retired. He sees no reason to be in therapy. He takes antidepressant medication for the depression.

Problem or Pathology Factors

Cognitive Rigidity
The personality rigidity of some clients foils their ability to productively benefit from therapy. With clients who are obsessive-compulsive, or paranoid, among others, their symptoms preclude their acceptance of the therapist's influence. They may question the therapist's motives or goals. They may be unable to break out of the rigid position that they see themselves as having to maintain to stay safe.

Significant Medical or Physiological Problems
It is essential for every client coming for therapy to have a complete medical evaluation as part of a comprehensive assessment and treatment plan. It is unethical and dangerous for the therapist to be treating what may appear to be psychological disorders that have a medical etiology. A client with hypothyroidism may appear depressed because of the slowed action and thinking. Conversely, hyperthyroidism might be confused with anxiety disorders.

Trust Impairments
Trust is a central issue in therapy. The trust must be bidirectional where the client trusts the therapist and the therapist can trust the client. Clients with problems of trust as a diagnostic part of the disorder will have problems in therapy. Traumatized clients may have recurring trust challenges, both internal and external to therapy. Dangerous, threatening or antisocial clients can create unsafe conditions that make it impossible to continue therapy. Trust is a primary goal, and until it begins to develop, little other progress is likely.

Autonomy Press
Autonomous individuals will be reluctant to come for therapy. Their view is that if they cannot help themselves, no one else can help them. The idea of coming to someone's office at a time set by someone else's schedule, to talk about personal matters, at best, is uncomfortable. Opening up to the possibility of feedback and influence from others is even more difficult. Their avoidance of therapy is seen as one way of maintaining their autonomy.

Impulsivity and Poor Executive Control
Clients who are impulsive, and this includes most children and adolescents, see therapy as restrictive and limiting. At best, it is out of line with how they generally respond, at worst the therapy is seen as an onerous and problematic requirement that they cannot meet. Their standard and accustomed manner of response is to act without thinking or self-monitoring rather than to self-monitor and to think about actions.

Cognitive Limitations, Impairment, or Confusion
Clients who are confused because of schizophrenia, bipolar illness, or neurological injury or deficit will have difficulty making use of therapy. They may have memory problems, difficulty in follow-through, difficulty with homework, and problems dealing with any abstractions. For some, verbal psychotherapy may be contraindicated, at least until their mental status improves sufficiently enough to engage in some verbal exchange.

   Clients may have limited cognitive ability as a result of limited intellectual ability or neurological deficit. Their processing will be limited by the lowered level of cognitive integration. Therapy goals will need to be adjusted according to their capacity for learning and abstraction.

Social Isolation or Alienation
Relative social isolation can impede therapy by virtue of the reduced opportunities for the client. Autonomous clients may have difficulties with this, as they are apt to tolerate and even seek jobs and situations where they can go about their business relatively unfettered by the needs and demands of others. But that also means that they will lack access to the support and stimulation of others. Other clients may be isolated due to some aspect of their family pathology (known drug abusers), their personality style (e.g., introverted), or a low social currency (e.g., physically unattractive).

Symptom Profusion
Anxious clients can overwhelm the therapist with graphic, elaborate, and detailed descriptions of their symptoms. Their idea is that if anything is left out, they run the risk that the omitted piece will be the essential piece that makes it impossible for them to be helped. If part of their symptom picture is gastrointestinal distress, they will regale the therapist with images of their distress. The therapist will quickly learn more about the client's gastrointestinal tract than is necessary. These clients actually take a fairly dependent approach to therapy by trying to spill all the details, expecting that the therapist will then organize all

the information and provide curative answers. In essence, clients avoid self-reflection by filling therapy time with excessively detailed symptomatic reports.

Extreme Dependence

Clients who are dependent often work to ensure that the therapist is totally and completely on their side. They may overwhelm the therapist with data, bring the therapist gifts, or praise the therapist for wit, insight, sensitivity, and perspicacity. The goal is closeness. Without the closeness, they believe that they will be injured or even destroyed. They are often frightened by goal-oriented therapy in that it means that in a relatively short time they will be without their helper.

Ongoing Self-Devaluation

Often termed low self-esteem or poor self-image, this involves devaluing everything that one does or the concomitant overvaluing what everyone else does (and therefore by comparison devaluing self). This often leads to "yes-but" behavior and to devaluing both the therapy and the therapist. This devaluation can be summed up by paraphrasing Groucho Marx's comment, "I would never join any club that would have me as a member." The therapist and the therapy are, by extension of working with the client, tainted.

Limited Energy for Change

Depression is a major contributor to this impediment. Individuals who are depressed will often have vegetative signs that include lowered energy. It then becomes difficult to cooperate in therapy because the major goal is to avoid any activity that requires action or energy. The level of energy within the session, for homework, or for interpersonal relationships is minimal. However, change requires some energy. Thus, the pace of these clients' change will be determined by the amount of energy that can be activated for working on change.

Substance Misuse

If substance-abusing clients come to sessions drunk or stoned, they cannot make use of the therapy. What may occur is state-dependent learning whereby they can only act in certain ways when under the influence of the substance. Clients who are semiaware or semirelated to the therapist will make little use of the therapy. When sober, they either will not remember what was said or done or will have distorted it due to the filter of the drugs.

Summary

Despite carefully gathering data, organizing the obtained information, using a structured and coherent approach to planning treatment and following a well-defined model of therapy, there are still potential impediments to effective, successful short-term therapy. Often, when treatment appears to stumble or falter, the responsibility for the difficulties is laid at the doorstep of the client. Traditionally, difficulties in treatment were viewed as the result of client resistance, either to the treatment or to change itself. Though convenient, such a view is unfair, and often inaccurate.

The variables that can, and often do act to impede the progress of therapy can be roughly divided into four categories; client factors, therapist factors, environmental factors, and problem or pathology factors.

Often, interactions of the variables in each of these categories can and will limit the speed and the efficacy of treatment. These difficulties may lie in a lack or absence of essential skills on the part of the client or the therapist, the lack of motivation for change on the part of the client, the lack of structure in the planning or goal setting of therapy, or unclear expectations on the part of both the client and therapist. The symptoms or pathology that prompted treatment in the first place present challenges to be specifically addressed as impediments or barriers to treatment. These pathology factors should not just be attributed to a client's preference for pathology.

Bordin's model of the working alliance emphasizes that the agreement as to the goals and tasks of therapy, as well as the establishment of a positive, interpersonal bond between client and therapist are crucial to the success of therapy. Many of the identified impediments to therapy appear to be related to difficulties in the establishment of the working alliance. Lack of clarity in the definition of problems and their related goals, lack of precision in the definition of the tasks of treatment, as well as confusion about the division of labor in treatment and the failure to establish a collaborative, goal-directed relationship can severely limit the effectiveness of treatment. Other impediments are related to the therapeutic bond. Lack of trust, interpersonal distance, therapeutic narcissism, overly technical or cold therapists, or extreme client dependence are disruptive forces that impede the emotional bond that is a foundation of therapy.

Some impediments to treatment may not reside within the persons of the therapist or client. Cultural, familial, social, and interpersonal factors can all contribute to difficulties encountered in the treatment setting. In addition, factors related to the health and medical well-being of the client may contribute to the degree of difficulty in a structured, planned intervention.

Effective Termination

14

Chapter

Termination refers to a point of ending in therapy. For one reason or another, contact between client and therapist is discontinued. Effectively managed termination is a beneficial step in creating a lasting impression of therapy as a positive experience. Likewise, if the process is poorly handled or insufficiently negotiated, closure can diminish benefits. In more extreme terms, a good termination can seal the success of therapy forever, but a bad termination can sour the best efforts.

Learning Objectives

At the end of this chapter, the reader should be able to:

- Understand the rationale, foundation, and main components of an effective termination strategy.
- List six different types of termination.
- Explain the professional standards of care for competent termination.
- Define client abandonment.
- List 10 applied skills for effective termination.

There are two major viewpoints on psychotherapy termination. One view is that termination is a logical conclusion that can be identified easily and intuitively when the pace of therapy slows or goals are reached. The other holds that termination is a crucial stage in the therapy process that merits explicit and careful attention. Both perspectives are relevant, but neither alone fully prepares therapists for the termination challenges of contemporary practice.

Rationale for a Termination Strategy

Beliefs about when and why therapy should end are typically influenced by an overall theoretical perspective on clinical psychopathology and the means and ends of intervention. To some, therapy should conclude only after the patient's internal resources have been substantially strengthened by experiences accumulated during a long-term relationship with a therapist. To others, therapy should conclude as soon as the patient experiences significant relief from targeted symptoms or problems. Both perspectives have empirical support, but we are only just beginning to develop evidence-based ways to determine the needed length of therapy. Practical contingencies often trump theoretical aspirations when it comes down to everyday decisions. At the same time, all therapist actions must fall within the bounds of ethical professional conduct. No practical situation trumps this responsibility, but many circumstances require difficult judgments.

Effectively navigating termination requires the clinician to blend clinical, practical and ethical or professional considerations into a sound strategy. Here are some hypothetical scenarios to illustrate why such a strategy is needed, and what can happen when this vital ingredient is missing.

Practice Scenario 1: Trainee Limits

Anna was finishing a graduate practicum at the university student counseling center. She felt highly attached to her clients and conflicted about terminating therapy at the close of the semester. It made her sad to think that these relationships would "just end" and she would not know what happened in the lives of her clients. As the time for termination drew closer, Anna avoided the topic. She hoped to continue with some of her clients, although pragmatically this was difficult and discouraged by the counseling center administration. New class and research responsibilities would have to be compromised to make time. The counseling center had defined office hours and very tightly allocated office space, making schedules almost impossible, unless she broke the rules and saw the clients after hours or at another location, without actual supervision. Anna began to ruminate about giving her favorite clients her home telephone number, and offering to correspond via e-mail or meet regularly for coffee. That way, they could stay in touch.

Practice Scenario 2: Personal Changes and Unprofessional Actions

Helen had been in intermittent treatment for depression for a dozen years at the same clinic, with several therapist transfers. Each of these former transfers had a reason that made sense to Helen. The most recent, however, occurred without Helen's realization. She had attempted to return after a hiatus of 6 months and found that her therapist was no longer working at that clinic. Further, she was informed that she could no longer be seen as a client in this practice due to changes in business policies, and no contact information was available for her former therapist.

At her support group meeting, Helen softly sobbed, "What is wrong with me that even my therapist didn't want to see me anymore?" Someone in the group told her that this therapist had relocated to a new office in a nearby county, and had transferred many patients with him. Helen then tried to contact the therapist at his new location, and was informed by staff that his practice was full and he was no longer accepting any new or transfer clients. The therapist did not return her call or make any attempt to contact her or assist with transfer of her care or records.

Practice Scenario 3: Managed Care

After a few years in independent practice, Kelly began to worry that he was burning out as a psychotherapist. He was vaguely depressed and demoralized, although he continued to believe that he was doing good, ethical work and helping his clients. He had been trained in both brief and long-term interventions. In ongoing practice, he found that it was difficult to terminate clients after only brief interventions, and challenging to keep long-term treatments oriented toward a goal. Many of his most difficult clients had treatment subsidized by managed care programs that approved only brief segments of therapy, from 8 to 12 sessions per authorization. Monitoring and repeatedly obtaining managed care approval was a recurring stress for him and his clients as it seemed they had to talk about possible termination every time they turned around.

Practice Scenario 4: Poor Boundaries

At her first session, Julie bluntly told her therapist, "I want to be sure that I don't get tangled up in therapy that goes on forever." When the therapist inquired about Julie's previous experience in therapy, she described a relatively helpful, positive interaction. However, she felt somewhat guilty about having "ducked-out" by simply failing to show for scheduled appointments and not returning the therapist's calls and attempts to reschedule. "He was really nice and supportive, but I was frustrated and did not know how to handle the situation. We spent a lot of time talking about his life, and it got to the point where I wasn't sure which one of us was the therapist and which was the client. I didn't want to hurt his feelings, but I felt trapped, so I just stopped. This time, I want to be sure the focus is on me."

Practice Scenario 5: Unfocused Therapy

Andrew was somewhat confused about when it was appropriate for him to initiate termination. As a postdoctoral clinician, he had a foundation of basic experience, but he still had numerous questions about how and when to draw therapy to an appropriate close. Many of his clients had resolved their initial target problem but still had daily hassles and issues to discuss. Andrew continued to see them in therapy, but the work was unfocused. There were no established goals that could be measured, or objectives that would indicate the completion of their work together. Much of the time he and the client seemed to be just chitchatting. Andrew felt uncomfortable about bringing up the subject of termination because he was afraid it would cause uproar with some clients, or that the client or his peers might construe this as client abandonment. So he kept scheduling sessions, avoided the subject, and decided that the client would ultimately decide when enough was enough.

Practice Scenario 6: Harassment of Therapist

Joan had been working for more than a year with Leigh, an emotionally labile, depressed young woman with aggressive and self-destructive tendencies. Leigh demanded that Joan write a letter of "fitness for duty" so that she could return to work after a mental health leave of absence. Leigh indicated that the letter should attest to her emotional stability, ability to work effectively with people who might be sick or otherwise vulnerable, and her ability to be honest and trustworthy handling the personal belongings of others.

Joan did not think that she could reasonably make these statements based on Leigh's history and current functioning, so she declined to write the letter. Leigh was outraged by this refusal and exploded with demands and threats, saying she would stalk Joan until she wrote the letter, or enlist the help of her gang-involved boyfriend if necessary. Joan was frightened and wondered whether she should just write a generically supportive letter, or continue to refuse and maybe obtain a gun for self-protection. Instead, she decided to schedule more frequent sessions with Leigh to discuss the letter, but keep pepper spray and a cell phone nearby at all times.

It may be helpful to pause at this point for discussion or reflection on how you would describe the problems being encountered in the vignettes described above. What are the different risks? Are there any potential ethical violations, and if so, what are they? What do you think the therapist could or should do to manage each situation?

These cases illustrate how therapy does not always conclude smoothly or easily. And these are but a few of the risky and rocky situations that can develop when the therapist lacks a steady hand in directing therapy toward an appropriate conclusion under varying conditions. The client may appear to make little if any progress. It may seem that the client will need therapy indefinitely. Or it may be that circumstances abruptly precipitate termination. The client and therapist might be uncertain of how much therapy is "enough." Strong emotions may make the ending particularly difficult. Conflicts and high emotions can significantly impact the judgment of either client or therapist, further complicating an already challenging task. Failure to address termination directly can leave both client and therapist struggling with confusion and increase the vulnerability to adverse outcomes. Therapy can become unfocused, unproductive, or even harmful if termination is not incorporated into the goals of treatment.

Without a strategy to effectively manage termination, the therapist is ill equipped to productively channel emotions or maintain a strong and reasoned professional course of action. Termination is to a clinician what the landing of an aircraft is to a pilot—a task that requires focused attention, skill, and planning, with an increased risk of adverse events or possible negative professional and legal consequences. Just as the pilot needs a flight plan, the clinician needs a treatment plan. Just as the pilot needs to land the plane at the appropriate time and location before running out of fuel, the clinician also needs to conclude therapy before running on fumes. Just as the pilot sometimes needs to deal with storms, winds, and inclement conditions, the clinician needs to deal with high emotions and other nonambient forces. Both want to achieve a safe and uneventful landing.

Effective Termination Strategy

Effective termination strategy is based on a foundation of clinical, ethical, and practical judgments. It is a "best practice" approach of creating positive closure in the greatest number of cases. This maximizes the usefulness of therapy overall, and minimizes possible stresses, especially the stress of a poor outcome for the client and an adverse professional or legal action for the provider. The judgments of a termination strategy are not separate or distinct, but blended together in a plan for termination that is under development and revision throughout therapy.

Main Components

The termination strategy has two main components: (1) ongoing communication and negotiation of the ending that is directly linked to the overall treatment plan, and (2) a reasonable plan of action that estimates when, why, and how termination will take place. Ideally, effective termination begins before intake, as the provider determines on the basis of his or her skills and competence those who will or will not be accepted for treatment. From there, termination issues are addressed in the first few meetings in the context of informed consent to service and orientation to the tasks of treatment (J. Beck, 1995; B. E. Bernstein & Hartsell, 2000; S. A. Kramer, 1986).

Any course of therapy, no matter how brief or lengthy, needs to have a beginning, middle, and end, and a plan for what will take place during each segment. As part of this fundamental structure, termination is acknowledged right from the beginning and a *plan* for termination is under consideration at all times. Creating a plan for termination can be considered a task of treatment that is best approached through collaborative discussion. This opens up a dialogue and establishes termination as part of the therapeutic work and not simply an eventual destination or a unilateral decision of either participant.

Types of Termination

According to Davis (2008), the quality of a termination can be characterized by the quality of interaction between the participants concerning the ending of their contract. The quality of interaction is determined by three elements: (1) direct communication about reasons for termination; (2) opportunity to express feelings, check perceptions, and assess satisfaction with the therapy and therapist; and (3) a clear disposition decision concerning any ongoing or potential future needs.

A better quality termination includes some direct communication about the decision to terminate, some assessment and expression of affect, including elements of satisfaction, dissatisfaction, or uncertainty, and a mutual understanding of a specified disposition, whether that disposition is final closure, transfer, open-ended follow-up, or some other specified plan. In poor terminations, there is little or no direct communication about the reasons and timing of termination, there may be no expressed affect or conversely an unproductive profusion of affect, and finally there may be confusion or misunderstanding about the disposition. The taxonomy of five types of termination is described by Davis (2008): prospective, flexible, complex, oblique, and unprofessional termination. A sixth category—premature termination—is included here because it is commonly discussed in the literature. These types of termination describe a spectrum of possible experiences, from the positive closure we ideally hope to capture to the conflicted or unprofessional termination that we aspire to minimize or avoid.

Premature Termination

Premature termination has been referred to as the ending of treatment without the sense of psychological closure that comes with having resolved problems or at least with an understanding of the reasons for ending therapy (Kleinke, 1994). In a research context, premature termination has been variously defined as failure to complete a predetermined number of sessions (Pekarik, 1992) or as attending only one to four sessions (Garfield, 1994). A problem with the term *premature* is that these many different definitions have created a category with multiple possible meanings. Prematurity is either judged from the clinician's perspective or is based simply on the client having chosen to attend only a few sessions.

Premature termination is considered a problematic waste of resources and potentially demoralizing to both clinician and provider (Reis & Brown, 2006). However, clients who drop out before an expected number of sessions are a heterogeneous group. The judgment of a termination as premature may be due to a mismatch of expectations between therapist and client, where the therapist is skeptical of quick fixes but the client prefers and expects brief therapy (Reis & Brown, 2006). To avoid the implications of a therapist bias toward long-term treatment, we prefer not to label any termination as premature. Instead, a more specific term can be selected from the other types of termination, based on the quality of the interaction rather than the assumptions of the therapist. A more qualitative description of termination allows us to better understand the interaction between provider and client and to recognize the client's stage of change as relevant to the length of therapy (see Chapter 12 on understanding change).

Prospective Termination

Prospective termination is the expected model for termination. Most often, the client's goals have been reached and provider and client agree that it is reasonable to draw therapy to a close. Sometimes prospective termination occurs without the client's goals being fully achieved, but termination is planned for some other reason such as a specific time limit. Prospective termination always includes some advance notice, even if that is only a few sessions or possibly just one. There is a shared decision-making process where various considerations are directly discussed by the provider and the client. Often there is some progression into the process of termination, such as spacing out sessions at greater time intervals until a final session is planned.

The decision to end therapy ideally includes agreement between provider and client, but total agreement is not necessary. Either party has veto power over the therapy relationship. The client has absolute veto power and can end therapy at any time for any reason. The clinician must operate within the bounds of professional duty and cannot end therapy without cause but can and sometimes must end therapy with cause, ethically and positively. The provider's actions are still positive and constructive because there is an identified reason, a clear disposition, and a process of direct communication with the client.

In prospective terminations, it sometimes happens that neither provider nor client is actually happy about ending, but they have identified, discussed, and understand the reasons for the action. There has been an opportunity for the client to express feelings and ask questions to resolve doubts or check perceptions. The therapist has made an effort to assess the client's satisfaction with both therapy and the therapist. Overall, the process of interaction and psychological integration is positive, even if there is a range of conflicted emotions. There is no specific expectation of permanent resolution of problems as a prerequisite for termination. Circumstances may bring about unexpected or forced termination, and the provider must handle it in an appropriate and skillful professional manner. A caring, dignified, and respectful approach to creating a transition out of therapy can engender positive closure even under less than ideal circumstances.

In terms of disposition, both client and provider know that therapy has ended. They are clear on how any ongoing or future client needs might be handled. Disposition often includes an option to follow up "as needed." Clients vary in their potential need for follow-up, depending on the nature and severity of their original problems and their access to treatment. In some situations, follow-up may not be likely or feasible because of personal changes, as people move and redirect their lives. When the provider is certain that he or she will not be available for follow-up beyond a certain point (e.g., moving in 6 months), then some discussion of follow-up alternatives is needed. If termination is forced by the limits of insurance, managed care, or other financial factors and the client is otherwise unready for termination, referrals and efforts to link the client to other resources are vital to a positive process. These are often the most difficult dispositions and are where the clinician is most apt to extend efforts to allow time for formal departure discussion and planning.

Flexible Termination
Flexible termination occurs when the client has improved but postpones further sessions or does not follow up in rescheduling. Regular meetings are

Case Example—Prospective Termination

Luke had worked with his therapist off and on for over 3 years when his employer abruptly changed insurance plans. His therapist was not in the preferred provider network of his new plan. Luke was going through some significant family stress, and he had been dissatisfied with several previous therapists so he was not enthusiastic about a transfer. The provider checked with the insurance plan and they approved payment for three sessions to allow time for closure and transition to a new therapist, if the client wished to continue therapy. There was no provision for payment beyond that point because there were plenty of other in-network providers in the geographic area.

Luke presented no imminent danger of harm to himself or anyone else. The three sessions were used to discuss Luke's current status and situation, his overall progress and the skills he had acquired, the financial implications of continuing with his current provider versus transferring to a new therapist, his options of continuing treatment or terminating with an option to begin with a new therapist, and his feelings about the current situation and the therapy process. Luke had an opportunity to ask questions, express his feelings, assess his strengths and accomplishments, get the therapist's help in weighing the options and making a decision, and be reassured of the therapist's support in providing records or information to new providers should Luke request that in the future. Luke expressed satisfaction with his progress and with the provider's efforts to offer formal termination discussion. Together they reviewed the list of alternative providers, and the therapist helped Luke identify three likely candidates. Luke decided that he would use this list for his plan to follow up on an "as needed" basis.

discontinued, but the formal process of closure is abbreviated and the option to return is open and left to the client's discretion. Usually the client has made some gains and the termination is generally positive and appropriate. The opportunity for follow-up is made clearly available, and it is assumed that the client will take advantage of this option if and when it may be needed.

Flexible termination may be appropriate and useful when the client has insufficient energy for active change but also does not want to definitively withdraw from the process either. There has been some improvement and the client is either saying, "That's enough for now. I'll be back later for more," or "This might be enough but I'm not sure." Circumstances often combine with initial improvements, tipping the client toward greater willingness to stop and resume when issues might be more pressing or change is more readily possible. The emotional tone of a flexible termination is usually positive, and the established relationship remains as a viable resource for the client, although the ongoing contract for sessions is discontinued.

Based on previous experience with Lucy (case example), the therapist interpreted the message to mean that Lucy was in less distress and wanted to terminate contact for some undetermined and perhaps indefinite length of time,

Case Example—Flexible Termination

Lucy was in therapy off and on for various health anxiety issues. Over time, she had made notable gains. Recently, she returned for help with a bout of obsessive thinking triggered by some unusual sensations in her chest. Over the course of six sessions, Lucy quickly activated her skills in managing thoughts about potential health problems, and she identified other contributing tensions, including work stress and family conflict. Although the various stresses continued, Lucy was coping better and worrying less. When a schedule conflict caused her to cancel an appointment, she left a message stating, "I'd like to cancel for now and get back with you after things settle down."

knowing she had the option of returning. In supporting Lucy's autonomy and self-directed use of resources, the therapist accepted this as a flexible termination and did not insist that Lucy complete a formal termination. The therapist left a follow-up message for Lucy stating, "I got your message. That's fine. I assume that you will let me know if or when you want to reschedule or resume sessions. If you want to come in to talk about this plan, don't hesitate to call me."

Complex Termination

Complex termination happens when communications about termination do not follow an ordinary course. Most clients can discuss termination and come to a reasonable resolution. However, some clients have extreme emotional reactions, or they may not be able to discuss termination in a reasonable way at all. Complex terminations are difficult and stressful for client and provider, and resolution is not readily established. These terminations require additional attention and care, as the risk for an adverse outcome is elevated.

Complex terminations can be triggered by several factors that interact and produce a bottleneck in communication. These factors include the client's interpersonal response biases, the provider's vulnerabilities, length of therapy, the client's progress, and the precipitating reasons for termination. The client's idiosyncratic cognitive profile and coping strategies are often the most significant factors in this equation, along with situations that produce significant secondary gain or advantages associated with the client's illness.

Clients with personality disorders or significant Axis II psychopathology are most likely to have a complex termination. These clients have a tendency to prolong or otherwise distort termination, and the clinician must create and maintain reasonable boundaries. Clients who are emotionally overwrought by termination need special assistance in coming to terms with these limits and in managing their emotional reactions. Gradually fading sessions or building toward termination help to mediate a highly reactive client's perceptions of termination as being too abrupt. Clients also sometimes terminate in abrupt, precipitous ways. Clinicians usually attempt to prevent abrupt departures by involving the client in a plan for termination early in therapy, and encouraging the client to discuss any impulses toward suddenly quitting therapy.

Consultation helps support the provider through what may be a difficult, even arduous process of making judgments and taking actions under stressful conditions, especially when there is overt conflict or the client becomes angry or accuses the therapist of wrongdoing. This high-risk situation recalls our metaphor of attempting to land an aircraft, but the original flight plan has been rendered impossible by thunderstorms or gale force winds. Redirection is necessary to protect the safety of all involved.

Case Example—Complex Termination

Gail was extremely emotionally reactive and prone to misinterpret the actions of her therapist. She often worried that she was "a pain" to the therapist and expected to be dumped or fired as a client. This was a significant pattern in Gail's life, as she was highly sensitive to potential rejection in both close and casual personal relationships. One of her primary coping strategies was to avoid humiliation or distress by impulsively rejecting people at the slightest sign of uncertainty. Gail's mood was depressed and her functional impairment varied from moderate to severe. She was hardly ready for termination.

Gail was making progress and had recently achieved the goal of visiting her children during the holidays. She then interpreted her therapist's attentive listening to the description of her achievement as an indication that she should terminate therapy. As they were wrapping up the session, Gail abruptly said, "Well, I guess this means we're done." With that, she quickly left the office without scheduling her next appointment. When the therapist phoned her about rescheduling, Gail acted surprised. "I thought when you were quiet for so long, that meant you were tired of listening to me. Now that I was able to see my kids, therapy must be over." Gail's therapist explained that termination should not occur in such an abrupt way, and asked Gail to work with her on developing a clear plan and set of goals for termination.

Oblique Termination

Oblique termination refers to a termination that is unilaterally enacted by the client without discussion, explanation, or response to follow-up contacts. The contextual cues offer little explanation and the therapist may be quite surprised by the client's disappearance. This termination is abrupt, although it may be preceded by lateness and cancellations. The "no-show" or "no call" and no further communication create an unsettled dimension. The communication is incomplete, and there is no message of client satisfaction or interest in following up at a future point. The behavior of the client is precipitous and evasive so the therapist cannot adequately glean the subtle or contextual cues for the client's reasoning. The emotional undertone suggests a negative component, but this is unconfirmed. This type of termination can occur at any point in therapy, but most often occurs after relatively few sessions. Possible reasons for an oblique termination may be a provider-client mismatch, client dissatisfaction with the provider or the process, ineffective or harmful therapy, some unique adverse reaction to therapy, poor communication skills among otherwise satisfied clients, or disruptive events in the client's life that are unknown to the therapist.

Case Example—Oblique Termination

Just as he got to his car after leaving his third therapy session, Rick received a text message from a family member alerting him to a family crisis. His father, who lived 400 miles away, had suffered a stroke. In the flurry of dealing with this crisis, he forgot all about his next therapy visit. The therapist, who knew nothing of the father's illness, left a voice message following Rick's "no-show," but never received a reply. Unbeknownst to the therapist,

Rick decided he was just too preoccupied with dealing with his father's situation to be in therapy, but might return if needed at some point. He viewed follow-up communications as rather annoying, trivial, and unnecessary and he was unsure what he wanted to say. So he did not respond to the therapist's two phone messages. He figured, "I'll call him if I need him. That's what he's there for."

Unprofessional Termination

Unprofessional termination occurs when the provider fails to uphold reasonable standards of conduct expected of a mental health provider. To label a professional's actions as unprofessional is a serious charge, potentially career altering or ending, and should not be done without a full understanding of all the information and relevant context. With this caveat in mind, we speak only of potential indications of unprofessional termination. Any final determination of unprofessional conduct must be done with all the facts pertinent to a particular case. Talking about clinical dilemmas among colleagues and peers is helpful, but care should be taken to do this in a professional manner.

Unprofessional termination involves actions that are exploitive or capricious and damaging or potentially damaging to the client. The duties of professional conduct require that the provider has a rationale for termination that falls within the scope of reasonable professional actions. The provider's personal limitations, difficulties, or commitments may be a reason for termination insofar as these circumstances impact the provider's competence and ability to provide safe and effective therapy. It is not unprofessional for the provider to have human needs and limits. It is unprofessional for the provider to terminate therapy to pursue personal gain directly from the client. It is unprofessional to impulsively or abruptly terminate therapy because of being frustrated or angry with the client. Further, it is unprofessional not to follow through in assisting the client with understanding the termination, considering alternative resources, and having access to his or her record of care.

Case Example—Unprofessional Termination

Jennifer's client Martina was starting a new custom jewelry business and wanted a partner. Not wanting to miss this ground-floor opportunity, Jennifer decided that the best thing would be to terminate therapy with Martina so that she could become her business partner. Both thought this was terrific, since "we already work so well together." The business failed, and both lost money. Martina became depressed and wanted to resume her therapy. Jennifer refused, saying that she was sick and tired of dealing with Martina's lazy, ineffective behavior. When Martina requested her records to take to another therapist, Jennifer said she would send them but never did. Martina was upset and angry over having lost her business, her investment, and her relationship with Jennifer so she filed a complaint of unprofessional conduct with the state licensing board.

Competence and Professional Standards of Care

What skills must the provider have to develop and use effective termination strategies? Ask yourself what you think a clinician needs to know to effectively navigate the procedures of ending therapy. You've worked hard to build your skills for assessment, conceptualization, alliance, and intervention. What more does it take to be competent in handling termination? Can you identify any particular subskills for this important task?

A provider's competence in handling the many challenges of termination begins with an adequate foundation of ethical reasoning and familiarity with professional standards of care (Davis, 2008). Contrary to the common belief that providers should initiate termination only under the rarest circumstances, current standards of care support and even demand termination in a surprisingly broad range of situations. Whereas termination based on reasonable professional judgment and procedure is an ethically sound and appropriate action (Fisher, 2003), both clinical acumen and sound ethical and legal judgment are needed to navigate the conditions of today's clinical practice. To develop this sound judgment, therapists need to have a clear grasp of the relevant expectations as delineated by ethical codes and guidelines.

Although each mental health discipline of psychology, social work, counseling, and so forth has its own official ethics code, the underlying principles are essentially the same fundamental principles of beneficence and nonmaleficence, responsibility, integrity, justice and respect for individual autonomy (American Psychological Association [APA], 2002; Beauchamp & Childress, 2001). The principle of respect establishes that the practitioner must appreciate the client's right to autonomy and self-determination. The practitioner makes recommendations, but it is the client's right to choose whether to accept the recommendations or the therapy. Clients have the right to terminate therapy at any point without notice. Unless it can reasonably be determined that the client poses imminent risk of physical harm to self or others, the practitioner need only take reasonable action to confirm the client's intentions. If the client does pose specific risks, the provider must take whatever actions are indicated under state laws to protect against harm, such as contacting a significant other or involving mental health crisis outreach.

Beneficence and *nonmaleficence* are principles that refer to the practitioner's striving to provide benefit and avoid harm in working with clients. This is interpreted to mean that the practitioner only provides services that are actually beneficial to the client. If a therapist likes an intervention and believes it to be helpful, that's great. But the therapist has to remain somewhat of a skeptic, because if the client does not actually benefit, then continuing the intervention is unethical. This point can be easily lost in dealing with painful issues when the client is distressed and the benefits are not exactly clear. Nevertheless, it is still up to the provider to ensure that the therapy is actually providing benefit. Similarly, if the client appears to be harmed by the therapy, it should be stopped. Client perceptions of the benefit or harm of therapy should be checked regularly and any perception of harm taken very seriously. These judgments of benefit and harm are often difficult to make and are explored in greater detail later.

The contractual and professional nature of psychotherapy as a service distinguishes this relationship from other personal attachments. The provider is both ethically and legally bound to adhere to the principles of responsibility, integrity, and justice in professional relationships, even though the provider is still free to take the personal risk of being irresponsible, or discriminatory in other nonprofessional matters. To competently handle termination matters, the provider must be reliable, honest, and fair.

Every state has specific statutes (laws) as well as rules and regulations that define the legal parameters of health-related practice, with the intended purpose of protecting the best interests of the public. As licensed professionals, mental health providers are expected to adhere to professional standards of conduct as a function of the state laws that grant the license to practice. It is common for a specific professional ethics code to be adopted within the practice rules and regulations of that discipline to establish a legally enforceable set of expectations for professional conduct. Thus, the professional ethics code is more than just a good idea or a suggested guideline. When it is incorporated into the rules of practice, it takes on the force of law, and it defines expected standards of practice within the professional role.

Across the different mental health disciplines of psychology, psychiatry, social work, advanced practice nursing, pastoral counseling, counseling, and marriage and family therapy, there is much similarity in the ethical codes for professional conduct and the provision of therapeutic services. The actual texts of the different ethics codes are a great resource for understanding basic professional role expectations in both routine and challenging circumstances (see American Association for Marriage and Family Therapy [AAMFT], 2001; American Association of Pastoral Counselors [AAPC], 1994; American Counseling Association [ACA], 2005; APA, 2002; National Association of Social Workers [NASW], 1999). Together, they illustrate a common standard of care within the professional practice of mental health care.

Ethical Responsibilities Specific to Termination

If therapy is interrupted, providers are expected to make reasonable efforts to facilitate access to alternative service (AAMFT, 2001, 1.11; AAPC, 1994, III.A; ACA, 2005, A.11.a; APA, 2002, 3.12). Interruptions might be either anticipated or unanticipated. Providers are also expected to make reasonable efforts to provide orderly and appropriate resolution of responsibility for client care in the event that their employment or contract ends, with paramount consideration given to client welfare (APA, 10.09). Dealing with interruptions usually means offering the client information for locating other providers or types of service, or providing a reference back to their managed care contractor for information on their provider network. It does not mean one must schedule an appointment and go with the client to be sure the contact is made and that the client likes the new provider.

In some cases, a conflict of interest or potential conflict of interest might require termination with proper referral. A conflict of interest is any situation that might "interfere with the exercise of professional discretion or impartial judgment" (NASW, 1999, 1.06 (a)), or "(1) impair their objectivity, competence, or effectiveness in performing their functions," or "(2) expose the person or organization with whom the professional relationship exists to harm or exploitation" (APA, 2002, 3.06).

Providers are generally expected to "terminate therapy when it becomes reasonably clear that the client/patient no longer needs the service, is not likely to benefit, or is being harmed by continued service" (APA, 2002, 10.10 (a)). If the provider cannot provide professional help and offers clinically appropriate referrals that are subsequently refused, the provider is directed to discontinue the relationship (ACA, 2005, A.11.b).

Providers are prohibited from terminating therapy for the pursuit of sexual intimacies with clients, relatives, or significant others of current therapy clients (APA, 2002, 10.05; 10.06). Termination for the purpose of pursuing other social or financial relationships with the client may be expressly restricted (NASW, 1999, 1.16 (d)), or restricted by the calculated risk of impairing the provider's objectivity, competence, or effectiveness, or of exploiting or harming the client (APA, 2002, 3.05).

In preventing exploitation or harm, providers also have a right to self-protection. Nonpayment of agreed-on fees for services can be an acceptable reason for termination (ACA, 2005, A.11.c). However, it is wise to ensure that the financial arrangements have been made clear to the client, that the clinical and other consequences of nonpayment have been discussed, and that the client does not pose an imminent danger to self or others (NASW, 1999, 1.16 (c)). If the client threatens or otherwise endangers the provider or creates jeopardy of harm, or another person with whom the client has a relationship creates these conditions for the provider, termination is permitted (ACA, 2005, A.11.c; APA, 2002, 10.10 (b)).

To complete termination in an ethical and professional manner, clinicians provide notice and offer termination counseling prior to ending contact, suggest alternative service providers as appropriate (APA, 2002, 10.10 (c)), and discuss the benefits and risks of options for the continuation of service (NASW,

1999, 1.16 (f)). The exception to this provision would be preclusion by actions of the client or third-party payers (APA, 2002, 10.10 (c)). The intent as we understand it is to provide communication that fosters the client's informed self-determination, if that is not deterred by the client's own threatening or noncooperative behavior. Providers are not ethically required to provide termination sessions that are not approved by the third-party payer (insurance or managed care). Many providers, however, do offer at least a single termination session even if it is not reimbursed, as a good risk management strategy. Investing a bit of uncompensated time to support the client's resolution is usually well worth the effort.

When termination or interruption of services can be anticipated, it is appropriate to notify clients promptly and seek resolution in accordance with the clients' needs and preferences (NASW, 1999, 1.16 (e)). Pretermination counseling should include: (a) advance notice of termination when possible; (b) discussion of the reasons for termination; (c) an opportunity for clients to ask questions about termination; and (d) referral information as appropriate (Fisher, 2003).

Client Abandonment

Many providers are confused about when or how they can appropriately initiate termination. Traditionally, mental health clinicians have taken an extremely conservative position based on the assumption that completion of treatment meant a long-term course of therapy that could only end when the client felt ready to depart. If a therapist ended therapy, it was considered abandonment, an egregious professional error. Thus it may not be unusual to encounter colleagues with circumscribed views on ethically appropriate reasons for termination. "Once a patient, always a patient," is the admonition, implying that once a client is accepted, therapy becomes a noncancelable contract.

This adage of always a client has been mistakenly interpreted to mean that the practitioner is perpetually responsible for the client and cannot ethically end treatment. The client is cast in the role of decision maker to the extent that therapy cannot end if the client vetoes the action. Further, client resistance to termination has been taken to mean that therapy must continue or the provider will be guilty of abandonment. Together, the threat of abandonment and the demands of the "in perpetuity" principle create a bottleneck for reasonable determination of when it is appropriate for the provider to initiate, recommend, or even insist on termination.

Many conscientious and compassionate providers unnecessarily fear making an inadvertent blunder due to a blurry concept of abandonment. The professional ethics codes offer no direct guidance on this issue because they do not discuss abandonment. The laws governing clinical practice offer little additional insight either, as one does not find any specific statute that spells out parameters of abandonment.

Abandonment is a legal concept that has been applied mainly in medical malpractice cases where direct harm occurs from the physician's failure to complete necessary treatment such as chemotherapy. When this concept is extrapolated to psychotherapy, completion of treatment has been equated with the client's readiness to quit. But the completion of psychotherapy is not readily definable and is highly related to the goals and productivity of the therapy, concepts that are also difficult to precisely establish (Weiner, 1998).

In its literal meaning, abandonment refers to deserting or forsaking a duty. A practical definition in the context of psychotherapy is the absence of a clinically and ethically appropriate process of termination of the professional relationship (Younggren & Gottlieb, in press). What is a clinically and ethically appropriate process of termination? It is one that meets the professional standards of care and fulfills the duties expected of a mental health professional.

To meet professional standards, the provider is expected to exercise a level of care and judgment that is comparable to an average provider within the same discipline. A dereliction of the duty occurs when there is willful neglect or action that falls below general community standards for reasonable or prudent action. Practice statutes require conduct that is moral, professional, and honorable as defined by community standards of care. Abandonment can occur if the provider fails to fulfill the identified duties at the level of community standards and causes direct harm to the client as a result. Providers owe a duty to their clients primarily in three areas: (a) to protect against known, imminent physical harm; (b) to create and maintain a professional record of services; and (c) to conduct practice in a professional manner. Thus, a standard-of-care model defines an appropriate termination as one that addresses these three duties.

Termination and Protection from Harm

Practitioners are generally expected to assess for the imminent risk of physical harm, and to take steps to protect any identifiable potential victim, including the client (Fulero, 1988; Sales, Miller, & Hall, 2005). Terminating therapy without assessing for any imminent risk of harm to self or others can be abandonment if there is subsequent harm. If a client has a history of self-harm, previous suicide attempts, or violence toward others, the average provider would be expected to recognize the need for assessing this risk before discharging the client. Because emotional crisis can increase a client's potential for impulsive and potentially violent actions, it is generally unwise to terminate anyone at the peak of a crisis. The exception to this would be if the client is directly threatening to harm the practitioner (APA, 2002, 10.10 (b)). Termination may appropriately occur at some point before a crisis is completely resolved, but imminent risk of harm has subsided or further steps to reduce the risk of harm have been taken (e.g., hospitalization).

Termination and Record Keeping

The construction, maintenance, and disposal of client records is regulated by state and federal laws (e.g., Health Insurance Portability and Accountability Act; HIPAA) that are designed to protect privacy and preserve the client's timely and effective access to this personal information. Failure to provide appropriate access to the client's record can be construed as potentially harmful to the client. Practitioners can avoid most if not all risks of abandonment of client records by following record-keeping guidelines. This duty does not have a direct relationship to decisions of termination, but it does apply to professional actions posttermination. Client records must be maintained in a secure and accessible location for an extended period after therapy ends. State laws usually define the minimum length of time that secure records must be kept. The essence of the duty is to make reasonable efforts to provide client access to records and not to simply abandon the record in an unsecured, inaccessible, or unknown location.

Termination and Professional Conduct

The third duty pertains to behaving in a manner that engenders public trust. General standards for professional conduct require the provider to behave in an orderly, predictable, ethical, and fair manner when offering services. If the client is directly harmed by the clinician's failure to provide agreed-on services, this can be construed as abandonment. Providers are expected to do what they said they would do and provide clients with a means of communication throughout treatment. This includes establishing when and how to reach the provider, what to do in case of an emergency, and what alternative resources might be used if the provider is unavailable. This is not an obligation to be available "on demand" to respond to the client's whims and impulses, or to continue therapy with an unresponsive, uncooperative, or hostile client.

A provider who cannot complete treatment, for whatever reason, has a duty to assist the client in locating other resources. If further treatment is not necessary, steps can be taken to draw the work to a close. Termination is in fact an appropriate fulfillment of one's professional duties when there is a conflict of interest, the client no longer needs therapy, is unlikely to benefit, or the provider cannot offer services of a sufficient quality to be beneficial to the client. The client does not have to agree or even like the termination, although it is certainly preferable to seek reconciliation of opinion. The practitioner is not obliged to continue services until the client feels ready to accept the termination or until an unresponsive client improves. In fact, there may be a greater risk of harm to the client by continuing unproductive or ineffective therapy. Continuation of therapy is contraindicated when there is no benefit or there is potential harm to either client or provider.

If termination occurs because the practitioner has been fired, downsized, or laid off from work, the practitioner is not obliged to continue working without pay to avoid accusation of client abandonment. What providers must do, however, is take reasonable steps to manage termination in a professional way that protects the client's best interests as well as addresses their own personal and professional risks.

Applied Skills for a Sound Strategy

As noted, an effective termination strategy has two main components; an ongoing dialogue and a plan of action. Effective implementation of this strategy requires certain applied skills. The clinician not only must know what is required for appropriate termination, but must also know how to do it consistently with skill and expertise. Successful, positive termination is not random, but rather a function of systematically using the following applied skills (Davis, 2008).

Talking about Termination

Practitioners need sufficient technical skill and cognitive effort to be effective in the role of therapist. They also need strong professional communication skills to ensure that therapy begins *and* ends on a positive note. Communications about termination should ideally occur at multiple points throughout the process of professional consultation, from intake and orientation to treatment planning, progress assessment, and finally to deciding on a point of closure. To be ready to talk about termination with confidence and authority, the clinician also should undertake much preparation before the client ever arrives. This includes defining the limits of practice, setting a basic policy on termination, and having a general plan to deal with limits, disruptions, or unexpected events.

The most important aspect of communicating about termination is to make certain that it happens. Avoidance of the subject should not be the default approach. Beginnings and endings are important, much as the takeoff and landing of an aircraft are times of particular attention to fundamental tasks. The topography of communication about termination (e.g., the frequency, length, detail) will vary according to the client's particular involvement in therapy. In uncomplicated situations, discussion about termination may be minimal but strategically placed. In more complex clinical situations, the communications about termination may be more frequent, or may require more thought, consultation, and attention to detail in progress notes.

For some clients and therapists, termination may be more difficult to talk about than sex or money. This underassertiveness can have many components, including the avoidance of uncomfortable feelings, awkwardness with the subject, lack of clarity on reasons for termination, or a fear of abandonment. Finding the right time to broach the subject and knowing what to say and how to say it are all skills we expect the therapist to develop.

At the heart of difficulty with termination communications may be distorted beliefs about strong emotions. Both client and therapist may fear that talk of termination will produce hurt feelings that cause the other to feel rejected. Either may fear the other will become angry or critical, especially if the termination issues include elements of disappointment or lack of progress. Or it may be that worry about emotional reactions is not a distortion. Talk of termination really will precipitate a firestorm of client affect, so the therapist avoids the subject. Recognizing this tension is the first step in its remediation, followed by efforts to bring the topic into the discussion. Further information on thoughts and beliefs that impede termination communications, as well as specific conversational targets, can be found in Davis (2008).

These communications seal the success of therapy. The provider always hopes to create a sense of psychological order and productivity at termination, regardless of the reason. The client's autonomy, right to self-determination, and responsibility to make personal decisions are always respected and encouraged. Discussion of the client's accomplishments, as well as strengths and opportunities ahead, can reinforce a sense of dignity and value associated with participating in therapy, even if the contact is quite brief. Doing this in a warm, respectful, and encouraging way can also create a more positive experience with the provider and with psychotherapy.

Therapists who are having trouble with personal reactions to termination should check their internal agenda. Some examples of troublesome personal reactions include being overly directive, disrespecting the client's autonomy, feeling out of control or highly uncomfortable, personalizing the client's desire to end therapy, or feeling unable to let go. Clients might express fears of having a relapse, doubt their ability to solve problems without the input of the therapist, fear disappointing the therapist, or are unhappy with the circumstances surrounding the termination. These reactions can be examined within open and supportive discussion as part of considering the decision to end or continue therapy.

Develop a Practice Profile and Informed Consent Policy on Termination

A practice profile spells out the provider's approach to psychotherapy in terms of competencies, philosophy of practice, and pragmatic aspects of service. Having clarity in this profile aids in concrete tasks such as creating marketing and informed consent materials. Although it is not absolutely necessary, it is useful to develop a written profile that specifies the types of service and populations served, the major methods used, and the structure of the practice. Having a written statement creates a framework of consistency for ongoing decisions about the boundaries of one's clinical practice. If these boundaries are clear and specific rather than vague or ambiguous, the provider can better manage both professional risk and personal stress. The written practice policy also ensures having an adequate informed consent agreement with each client. Providers who are working in a setting where the practice policy and informed consent forms have already been developed and written by someone else will still want to articulate their own statement of personal competencies, philosophy, and pragmatic limits. Providers will also want to review their practice profile from time to time to evaluate the need for updating or correcting any information.

Informed consent discussions usually begin at intake. Brief but explicit discussion of termination at this stage can greatly enhance smooth consideration of this issue throughout therapy. Details of the provider's policy on termination need to be clarified and preferably written into the statement of informed consent for psychotherapy, including what to expect in terms of who initiates termination as well as when and how termination might occur. Specific mention of billing or scheduling issues as triggers for termination may be explained here, even if these points are repeated in other parts of the informed consent document. Details of these policies may vary according to the provider, agency, or practice setting. The following is an example of a termination policy that is similar to those outlined by Davis (2008).

Example: Termination Policy

Termination of services typically occurs by mutual agreement when treatment goals have been met, or when maximum benefit has been reached. However, you have the right to terminate at any point. If possible, it is best to discuss therapy termination prior to ending contact. Please feel free to raise the issue at any point, especially if you have concerns about the benefit of your therapy or are wondering if or when it should end. If I think you might be better served by other resources, including a more intensive level of care, I may initiate termination. I will consider therapy terminated if you do not contact me within 90 days of our last contact, have missed 2 appointments without notice, have a repeated pattern of cancellation, or if you otherwise do not comply with our agreed plan of payment. You may contact me to resume therapy at any point, and I will accommodate your request if possible. If you would like my assistance in locating additional treatment or alternative resources, please feel free to contact me.

An important part of this statement is the outline of a general plan for responding to common clinical situations as well as oblique terminations, thus establishing parameters of closure. This nonpejorative approach emphasizes client autonomy and self-direction and accepts the client's right to terminate without notice yet offers the opportunity to return or obtain assistance in locating other services. Assuming that clients terminate for many reasons, the therapist creates a simple structure that acknowledges the possibility of this action, and encourages follow-up if the client wishes to do so. At the same time, the client is informed of the possibility of a therapist-initiated termination.

Respect and Plan for Personal Limits

Clinicians overall are becoming much more attuned to the importance of attending to personal needs and limits (see Chapter 15). Therapist limits have important and direct implications for termination plans and practices. Sometimes events in the provider's life trigger a termination. They move, change jobs, bear children, get sick, experience role overload, decide to shift career focus or retire. Therapists also have limits to their competence and may have insufficient skills to address the client's problems, personal biases that skew their ability to work effectively with certain persons or groups, or may simply be minding their own business when a conflict of interest lands in their lap. These circumstances are not always predictable or clear at the outset of therapy.

Competence or Conflict of Interest

Therapists must recognize when personal limits are interfering with the effectiveness of treatment and take steps to resolve the situation (APA, 2002, 2.0; 3.06), possibly terminating therapy. Many times, the therapist can take some action to remedy the situation and protect the therapy relationship, but this is not always feasible. Dr. Green is not likely to sell his house so that he can continue providing therapy to Mr. Smith, who has just become his new next-door neighbor. Or, let's say the deal falls through and Mr. Smith doesn't move next door but has a fundamental religious conversion and is "born again." Dr. Green may still need to terminate therapy because he cannot work effectively with religiously enthusiastic individuals due to his personal experience of emotional and sexual abuse in a religious context. An overdeveloped work ethic can be dangerous in clinical practice as well. Although most if not all therapists possess a sincere desire to help, no one possesses the skills and energy needed to treat all of the patients all of the time. All practitioners need to know the scope of their competence, and be prepared to terminate treatment if their personal or professional limits have been reached.

Relocation

When closing or relocating a practice, providers will make provisions to either finish therapy or transfer clients without abruptly withdrawing service. All provider-initiated terminations require some notice, explanation, or pretermination counseling. Whether the clients transfer with a provider depends on individual circumstances and the options available. Providers first need to establish whether client transfer is possible for the provider. Can they accept the client for continuation in the new practice situation? Clinics or group practices do not "own" clients; they have the right to leave one location and obtain service elsewhere, provided they fall within the practice profile of the new setting. Suppose Dr. Green leaves the medical center and opens a private practice. His client, Mr. Smith, simply continues to work with Dr. Green in his new office. If Dr. Green moved from Florida to Montana, however, it would not be feasible to continue working with Mr. Smith. Likewise, if Dr. Green stayed in town but moved from the medical center to a job at the Veterans Health Administration hospital, Mr. Smith could transfer with Dr. Green only if he qualified to receive services at the VA clinic. Whether clients end treatment or transfer to a new setting or a new provider will depend on their assessment of the relative need for further therapy versus the costs of establishing a new professional relationship.

Providers are advised to check for any state-specific rules or regulations concerning the relocation or closing of their practice, such as providing notice to former patients. It may be that some form of public notice is required, such as a posted notice in the clinic or a newspaper. The intent of such a rule is not to create one more annoying task for the provider, but to alert clients to the change and allow the courtesy of access to treatment records. We hope that clinicians want to offer an opportunity for clients to obtain a sense of closure, to communicate with the provider or the provider's representative if they wish to do so, and to correct any potential distortions or misinterpretations that the client might draw in the absence of any explanation for the provider's change in venue. It is most helpful to leave contact information at the former site of clinical practice and to check back periodically to assist staff in redirecting inquiries.

Ending Practice

Eventually, all therapists end their practice. Ideally, this will be a well-executed process at the end of a productive career. Nevertheless, all clinicians must anticipate the possibility of a more precipitous end or significant interruption that could temporarily or permanently close a practice. Current standards of practice require that provisions are made either in the therapist's will or as stipulated in a business associates agreement to name a qualified professional who will handle the closing of practice, transfer of clients, and orderly management of confidential records in the event of the therapist's unavailability such as by accidental death, illness, relocation, or professional unavailability (APA, 2002, 3.12; 10.09). Just as it is wise to establish a contingent guardian for one's children, so it is important to have a qualified contingent professional to oversee the closure and possible transfer of a practice if the clinician could not carry this out. Those working in an agency or group practice are most likely to establish this agreement within their employment setting. Those working more independently or in solo practice need to take additional steps to establish a designated person for this important task. It is important to clarify the terms of such an agreement with the designated person to minimize any potential confusion or distress for clients.

Uncertain Situations

Therapist illness or other personal compromise is a nebulous area that requires advance plans. If you are sick or distracted, the feasibility of being sufficiently available needs to be weighed against the level of care needed by clients and the scope of your practice. It may be necessary to reduce or restrict your practice, which could mean terminating some clients or services while continuing with others. Here are a few examples of therapists who all have an active clinical practice, but are facing personally demanding circumstances:

- Archie has long-term complications from diabetes and has to undergo kidney dialysis three times per week, as well as monitor his activity level and avoid contact with those who might carry contagious illnesses.
- Betty is in her first trimester of uncomplicated pregnancy, but is unsure about whether she and her husband want to hire out infant care or provide full-time parent care.
- Calvin, an only child and sole care manager for his elderly parents who both require assistance with nursing home and assisted-living arrangements, learns he has serious complications from Crohn's disease. He not only needs immediate hospitalization, but will also require multiple surgeries at unpredictable intervals, with extended hospital stays.
- Dionne, a horseback riding enthusiast, is thrown from her horse on a trail ride, suffers a head injury with loss of consciousness and several broken ribs, and is hospitalized for several days.
- Elvira reaches a professional crescendo when she learns that her large-scale research grant proposal has been funded; she has agreed to advise three additional students beyond her already full cohort; she has a new course to prepare; she has just been elected to an office in her professional association; she has committed to chair two symposia at an international conference; and her spouse receives a promotion that requires extensive out-of-town travel increasing her family responsibilities.

What should each of these therapists do, if anything, about their clinical practice? Should patient contact be terminated? Of course, the first answer is "It depends."

Although it can be difficult for therapists to acknowledge that their own needs and circumstances constitute legitimate reasons for termination, these situations might all require termination. Therapists have an ethical responsibility to make appropriate arrangements in the event of their compromised availability or effectiveness. Decisions about what is appropriate are guided by the client's readiness to end therapy, and the availability of both parties relative to the level of care needed by the client. Some clients will move toward ending therapy if the current provider will no longer be available, others will readily accept transfer, and others may take a "wait and see" position.

Of the preceding therapist scenarios, Calvin and Elvira closed their clinical practice in response to changes in their circumstances. Facing immediate and prolonged medical interventions for his Crohn's disease, Calvin was physically unavailable to see his patients. His continuing responsibility for helping his parents combined with his medical situation reasonably absorbed all of his mental and physical energy, and the resolution of both of these situations was unpredictable in terms of length of time. He had a solo clinical practice, so a designated colleague took possession of the clinical records and assisted him in contacting current patients to explain the circumstances and assist each one in a decision regarding further care.

Elvira greatly enjoyed her clinical practice, but had to reassess her overall academic, clinical, and personal responsibilities. There were simply not enough hours in the day to meet her role obligations. She tried for a time to jigger her schedule to continue her practice, but soon realized that even if she was physically present, she did not have the energy to be sufficiently mentally and emotionally present for her clients. She closed her practice more slowly than Calvin, first declining any new referrals and informing current clients of her practice closure with 6 weeks' notice. Most of her clients found this sufficient time to reach completion of their current treatment, with one exception. This client had long-standing problems and wanted to transfer to an established, full-time community provider who would be available long term.

Archie continued practice at a community mental health agency where he could specifically limit his hours, and alternative providers were readily available in the event of a worsening of his medical condition. He was also diligent in his self-care, doing what he could to protect his clients from unplanned terminations due to his illness.

Betty continued practicing throughout the duration of her pregnancy, and made individual arrangements with each client for the period of interruption for her delivery and maternity leave. She also established a backup plan similar to that of Calvin for the possible transfer of her clients should she experience any unexpected medical complications and be rendered immediately unavailable. She informed all new clients of her pregnancy, and did not accept any new referrals in her last trimester. During her maternity leave, she decided to return to practice on a limited basis, and to assess her family and work situation over a longer period. She arranged part-time office hours for continuing clients only, and did not accept new referrals until she had clarified her new practice profile. In forming her plans, Betty consulted frequently with her colleague, Barbie, who had return to work full time after maternity leave. Barbie continued her practice with the assistance of a full-time nanny and backup babysitters.

Dionne, the horseback rider, thankfully had a rapid recovery without any long-term deficits, not even a fear of getting back on a horse. Her assistant canceled all her appointments for the duration of her hospitalization, but no decisions were made until the extent of her medical condition was known. As a provider in an independent practice, she also had a designated colleague who was ready to help her assistant with patient management in the event she was incapacitated. Prior to returning to practice, she was medically evaluated for any cognitive or physical impairment that could impact her overall competence to practice.

As these examples illustrate, therapist needs and limits have direct implications for termination. Therapy must be terminated if the provider cannot assure competent, available service; advance provision for abrupt cessation of service is a professional obligation to reduce the risk of client distress or harm.

Link Termination with Treatment Plans and Goals

Ending is not just a final decision in therapy; it is part of the overall goals for what therapy is expected to accomplish. The point where therapy ends is a mutually negotiated decision that begins with the initial plan. Completion or discontinuation of the treatment plan is the most likely trigger for termination. The clarity of the plan for termination thus begins with the clarity of the plan for treatment. A client may have no idea when therapy should reasonably come to an end, but a therapist cannot afford this same naiveté. If the therapist has only a vague idea when the therapy should be concluded, it is likely that the treatment plan is similarly vague. Difficulty knowing when to end treatment can be addressed with more specific goals and objectives. A time line might be useful when the treatment objective is to assist in coping with an ongoing stressor or development issue.

In dealing with a stressful work environment and mercurial boss, the treatment plan might be to extend therapy over a course of 6 months at which point the patient's yearly work evaluation would be complete, and need for further treatment could be reassessed. Or the treatment plan might be tied to a specific behavioral goal such as completing a medical evaluation (for the health-anxious client) or a stable mood state such as minimal depressive symptoms for at least 8 weeks.

Early in therapy, you can ask useful questions about treatment objectives that pinpoint termination goals and orient the client to think about possible points of completion. In the middle section of therapy, ongoing review of benefits and progress toward goals is important to keep the interaction focused and avoid unhelpful digressions. As therapy progresses in time, the question of ending versus continuing may be easy or may become more challenging. Clarifying the intended point of termination may be difficult, but particularly so if the purpose of therapy has been lost, forgotten or changed. Throughout therapy, the provider will want to include termination considerations in the client's progress notes.

Early on, the provider can connect therapy goals with termination by asking the client, *"What do you want to accomplish before we end our work together?"* Or the provider might ask, *"When we have reached the close of therapy and consider the effort a success, what changes have been made?"* To bring the consideration of time limits into the discussion, the provider might offer the following question: *"What is your top priority for the first 10 sessions?"* Or perhaps, *"If we have only 10 sessions, what are the most pressing concerns you want to address?"* The client's global objectives can be assessed by asking, *"Time limits aside, what would you hope to gain before stopping therapy?"* These questions can be brought up again as improvements are made or time limits approach and the question of termination needs to be reevaluated.

Other primary considerations that have an impact on termination can also be discussed at this point. Simply asking, *"Are there any barriers to your participation in therapy?"* can open up a dialogue about factors that might precipitate early discontinuation.

These questions can lead directly into an orientation to productive use of therapy. The provider might ask, *"Would you like to know how to make the most out of each session and get the best results?"* Presuming that the client will answer yes to this question, the provider has a logical opening for brief socialization to the therapy process. The provider summarizes the key aspects of the discussion of therapy goals and closes with a statement of positive expectation for the work ahead and its eventual outcome. The closing statement might sound something like this: *"I think I can help you with (reducing your worry and finding more joy in life). Let's work together as we've discussed and see what kind of progress we can make in the weeks ahead. If our initial approach works as expected, that's great; we'll keep going toward your goals. If it doesn't, we'll figure out what changes to make to keep you moving in the direction you want to go until you get there. How does this sound to you?"*

In a closing statement like this, the provider establishes confidence in helping the client toward specific ends and an expectation that therapy will end on a positive note. At the same time, it establishes that initial plans are not a guarantee of results and should be evaluated for effectiveness along the way. The agreement to therapy is not a commitment to striving for the sake of striving, it is an agreement to pursue certain results as long as there is a reasonable expectation that they can be obtained.

Assess Progress, Benefit, and Potential Harm

Assessment of progress, benefit, and potential harm are all routine aspects of conducting therapy. Bringing termination into these considerations is a fairly logical step, particularly when it is time to request managed care approval of additional sessions, or when it is apparent that the goals of the original plan have been met. Pragmatic considerations require that client and therapist not only ask, "What kind of progress are we making?" but also consider, "What kind of progress are we making given the time we have available?" as well as "Are we ready to stop yet?" and "Do we need to stop?"

There are several possible benchmarks for tracking progress and readiness for termination (see Table 14.1). Standardized measures such as symptom rating scales or structured interviews are wonderful for capturing major improvements, but alone may not always be feasible or sensitive enough for tracking on a session-by-session basis. It is always important to be alert to signs of the patient's possible interest in and psychological readiness for termination. This may be communicated by direct statements such as "I think I'm ready to stop therapy for now," by obvious progress in symptom resolution or tasks accomplished, or by more indirect hints or suggestions such as missing appointments, arriving late, or engaging in a mainly peripheral discussion. Clinicians might use any of the following benchmarks to assess progress and benefit of ongoing therapy as well as readiness for termination (Davis, 2008).

Table 14.1 **Benchmarks of Client Benefit/Progress and Termination Readiness**

- *Subjective sense of purpose and accomplishment linked to therapy sessions:* Either one or both parties have a sense that what they are doing has a valid purpose and that they are getting somewhere. Clients make spontaneous statements such as "This is really important," or "What we did today really helped." Readiness for termination will be suggested by a subjective sense of having sufficiently addressed key issues.

- *Productive alliance:* Client and therapist feel as though they are working as a team. Positive affect is expressed and the client shares important thoughts and feelings. Readiness for termination is mainly indicated by a diminished intensity of desire for contact.

- *Stabilization or restabilization following contact:* Some clients use therapy to focus their reality testing and stabilize overall functioning. Readiness for termination is evident when the client can perform these functions on a more independent basis.

- *General symptom reduction:* The number and scope of symptoms diminishes and a range of positive affect is more apparent. Readiness for termination is indicated by the client's subjective sense that functioning is returning to "normal".

- *Focused symptom improvement:* There may be discrete improvement in a focused area despite other persistent difficulties, as noted by decreases in specific features of a symptom cluster. Readiness for termination is indicated by the client's assertion that this change is sufficient, in the absence of any imminent risk of self-harm.

- *Functional or behavioral changes, including improvements in role adjustment or performance:* Important behavior changes are achieved such as returning to work, completing a feared medical test, or attaining a positive evaluation. Movement toward these changes is noted in affective, cognitive, and behavioral increments across sessions. Readiness for termination is indicated by the client's assertion of goal attainment and satisfaction.

- *Improved family or other system functioning:* Attention is focused on relevant issues, and incremental improvements in organization, affective expression, problem solving, and communication are evident. Readiness for termination is apparent when the needs of the system are being met and homeostasis is restored.

- *Noting benefits in one or more of these areas is vital to an ethical practice:* If there is no benefit in any of these areas over a sustained period of time such as 6 to 8 weeks, then ethically the provider is obligated to consider termination.

There are no clear benchmarks of harm other than specific physical harm. It is potentially harmful to interfere with clients' efforts to seek other services (e.g., telling the client not to seek a second opinion). It may be harmful to fail to suggest other options when treatment is not working. It is also harmful to cause more problems than you are helping to solve. Any of the benchmarks of progress happening in reverse should be cause for concern as a potential indication of harm: The client does not think therapy is worthwhile or getting anywhere; the alliance is strained or hostile and there is desire to withdraw from contact; the client significantly destabilizes after contact; symptoms are getting significantly worse in relationship to treatment interventions; functional behavior or role performance deteriorates; or family and system functioning degenerates. The worst harm would be if the client becomes suicidal and takes action as a result of therapy, a development that would potentially constitute malpractice. Indications of *possible* harm do not necessarily mean that therapy should be immediately terminated. Efforts should be made to address the problem first. If these efforts to remediate the problem are not sufficient, the provider may want to seek consultation before proceeding with termination.

Modify the Treatment Plan

Altering the treatment plan and renegotiating the goals as therapy progresses is a necessary part of keeping therapy focused and determining a suitable point of termination. As old problems are resolved, even older problems may surface to take their place. For various reasons, termination may come up for consideration sooner or later than originally planned. Reviewing the conceptualization and treatment plan can revive stalled therapy, crystallize new objectives or pinpoint the remaining tasks. There is nothing inherently wrong with extending a treatment contract, and in fact, this probably happens quite often. The therapist bears primary responsibility for negotiating and updating an acceptable and workable plan and regularly attending to the progress, benefit, and readiness for termination. These efforts can head off an oblique, complex, or unprofessional termination and increase the likelihood of a positive conclusion.

Pinpoint Typical Reasons for Termination

Let's consider in more detail some typical reasons therapy comes to a close. Reasons for termination vary according to degree of predictability, certainty, salience, and amount of advance notice. These precipitants generally are related to practical, ethical, financial, emotional/motivational, and clinical conditions that are necessary for safely and effectively conducting therapy. As we look at these reasons, keep in mind that both patient and therapist perspectives are relevant.

The client and therapist might agree on the reason for termination, they might negotiate an agreement based on their review of relevant information, or they might be at an impasse if they disagree on the reason for termination. The following are some common reasons for terminating therapy. These include goal attainment, financial issues, practical circumstances, client actions, and provider-client match. Further discussion of reasons for termination is provided by Younggren and Gottlieb (in press).

Attainment of Initial Goals

Therapy most often ends when the goals have been reached and the client no longer needs the service. Client and therapist are relatively satisfied with the outcome, and there is little disagreement or conflict over the decision to end sessions. Client and therapist formed an agreement to work toward a specified purpose, and that purpose has been achieved. The client's goal might be a specific behavior such as driving alone on the interstate. Goals might also be states of functioning, such as "able to work regularly"; or "living a more relaxed or joyful life," with some form of operational measures such as nonclinical levels of symptoms to demarcate when the goals can be considered reasonably ac-complished. Particularly when a client enters therapy to resolve a crisis, the main goal for therapy may simply be to resolve the crisis. The client may be ready for termination as soon as the immediate distress is diminished.

Financial Issues

Providers are ethically obligated to establish an agreement for billing arrange-ments and compensation at the outset of therapy. If foreseeable circumstances may limit services because of financial constraints, the provider must address this as early as possible (APA, 2002, 6.04). The client's financial situation is an important parameter of therapy that must be objectively addressed. When fi-nancial limits are reached, it is appropriate to terminate treatment, to renegoti-ate the contract if possible, or to assist the client in transferring to lower cost alternatives.

The client's mental health insurance coverage might require preautho-rization or limit the number of reimbursable visits. This creates a financial limit for most clients. Providers usually keep track of the number of sessions because it is the provider's responsibility to obtain preauthorization and to advise the client on changes in the payment structure that occur if authoriza-tion is denied. These circumstances could be considered more of a termina-tion alert, as the client might be willing to continue therapy without insurance coverage. However, this should not be assumed. The issue needs to be promptly recognized and included in a session agenda so that provider and client can decide together how they wish to proceed. Thus, the provider ap-proaches the session with awareness that termination is a possible outcome, and is prepared to provide pretermination counseling. In discussing the op-tions, the provider needs to clarify the financial parameters of treatment con-tinuation and assess the client's willingness to agree to those new terms. If maximum insurance benefits have been reached and the client wants to con-tinue, can the client assume financial responsibility for additional service? If the client has a change in insurance plan that shifts more of the cost to the consumer, does the client understand and accept this arrangement? If not, then termination or transfer is indicated.

Outstanding charges or the lack of a timely payment by the client are po-tential triggers for termination that should not be ignored. Providers who dele-gate business tasks to administrative staff need to provide enough supervision to ensure timely attention to preauthorization, insurance claims processing, and aging accounts receivables. They must also make certain that clients are aware of the situation, understand their responsibility and are willing to comply with the financial agreement.

The most emotionally stressful situation may be when the client has an unpaid balance that must be addressed. In this circumstance, an ounce of pre-vention is worth a pound of cure. Timely payment behavior can be shaped from the beginning of therapy to prevent the accumulation of an unpaid balance. Providers should be sensitive to the possible exploitation of either themselves or the client in the making and continuing of financial arrangements. There are many reasons a client might not comply with fee arrangements, and it is in-cumbent on the provider to investigate the causes. It may be a simple misunderstanding of when and how to make payment or of not having received an accurate or understandable billing statement. There may be contributing marital or family communication problems because the client delegated the task of bill payment to spouse, parent, or an accounting service, and there is a snag in the third-party understanding, agreement, or execution of this task. Sometimes clients do not intend to pay the charges because they are unhappy with the service, felt pressured into continuing therapy, think that the provider charges too much, or have overall financial difficulties. Any of these reasons are important to identify as soon as possible so that appropriate remedies can be implemented. If lack of payment precipitates termination, it is important that the client understands this reason and has a chance to make prompt payment, particularly if the provider intends to implement formal collection proceedings (APA, 2002, 10.10, 6.04 (e)).

Practical Circumstances

Practical circumstances have a significant impact on the client's assessment of the cost-to-benefit ratio for therapy. There are many costs to the client beyond just the fees, and it is imperative to be sensitive to these circumstances. Time, energy, and emotional or social support are also needed to effectively participate in therapy. Costs are relative to the level of available resources and are perceived by the client in that context. Timing is also important, as the relative perception of cost shifts when resources improve.

The clients' assessment of the cost-benefit ratio is integrally linked with their relative stage of change for the most pressing problems. The motivation for change affects the client's perception of the overall costs of therapy. At the same time, motivation for change is impacted by the overall costs and available energy. Some of the most significant aspects of therapy rest in helping clients to assess their motivation for change and effectively titrate their efforts (see Chapter 12). It may be positive and appropriate to terminate therapy when the client does not have the resources to move forward in the change process.

Clients with high role demands are often challenged to allocate time for therapy. Despite the benefit of taking time to attend to emotional needs, those with limited flexibility may experience significant stress in making and keeping appointments, getting time away from work or home responsibilities, and having to make up missed work or arrange coverage. This stress might lead the client to choose a different provider with a more convenient location or adaptable hours, or perhaps postpone therapy.

Emotional costs are also important in the client's cost-benefit assessment. Therapy takes emotional energy and there must be an adequate available supply. It may be appropriate to postpone or terminate therapy until the client has more energy to focus on the tasks of treatment. If simply being in therapy causes the client to lose emotional support or suffer increased discord with significant others, costs escalate. The cost may be too high if the client is getting the cold shoulder, being interrogated, or is ridiculed for "seeing all those quack nut doctors."

Physical distance does not prevent therapy, but it adds to cost and other risk considerations. There are several contextual elements to consider in determining whether it is reasonable to proceed if therapy requires the client to commute a significant distance. *Significant distance* is relative to the norms of the area and the specialized nature of the service. A general measure of significant travel is more than an hour of transit time each way. In areas with a low density of providers or a lack of specialized services, there may be no other option but to commute an hour or more. In most instances, clients will self-select the service providers who are most convenient or whose location falls within the clients' ability to manage transit time.

There are two types of circumstance where authoritative provider judgment is needed. The first is when there is an already established therapy relationship and the client relocates to another geographic area. Reluctance of either party to terminate may result in efforts to continue therapy in some abbreviated or truncated fashion. Whether this constitutes a reasonable course of action depends on several factors, including the client's overall clinical needs, level of functioning, emotional stability, the new distance, and the availability of alternative resources. If the client's needs suggest that greater access to a provider is necessary, it is incumbent on the original provider to prompt the client to establish a new therapy relationship by firmly insisting on termination. Despite advanced technology, attempting to maintain therapy via long-distance telecommunication or e-mail is fraught with legal, ethical, and clinical risks. The lack of face-to-face interaction blunts the overall impact of the interaction (Nickelson, 1998). The client is less likely to benefit and the risks of incompetent service or other potential harm are increased (Fisher, 2003). The legal and regulatory implications of client and therapist being in two different states at the time of contact are murky at best. Without a current license to practice in that jurisdiction, the therapist could be violating clinical practice laws in the client's state.

The second type of situation occurs when the client avoids more proximal providers. Reasons usually include a concern for privacy, a desire to work with a particular specialist, or a lack of confidence in local resources. These may all be legitimate concerns, but each should be carefully considered in light of other information. A stable client who is well known in a small town might travel a couple of hours to a larger town on a regular basis, combining business, various health care consultations, and visits with family in the distant location. Compare this with an unstable client who tends to mistrust any provider and travels great distances in search of someone who will fulfill what are essentially unrealistic expectations. Unstable clients present many risks, and these may be multiplied when significant distance is involved. Not the least of these risks is the difficulty of managing any emergency contacts when physical proximity is limited.

Client Actions

Clients sometimes abandon their therapy, or they take actions that require termination. A client who stops scheduling appointments may have terminated therapy. But this is not always clear, as some clients get distracted or have symptoms such as anxiety or depression that interfere with the responsible action of following up. It is not unusual for a client to fail to show for a scheduled visit or not schedule a follow-up, yet this is always taken in the context of the client's usual behavior, current issues, and overall progress. It is important to have a practice policy on no-shows and broken contacts so that the provider can establish a boundary around client-initiated terminations. Sometimes a simple prompt is useful in refocusing therapy. At other times, the client's failure to follow up is an indication of the intent to terminate. If the client could benefit from more therapy, the therapist can encourage the client to return. In our managed care environment, it is now common practice to work with clients in repeated segments of therapy where there may be multiple points of "soft" closure rather than a single point of final termination.

It is always useful to seek more information on the client's intention and to attempt a closing consultation. This may be impossible if the client does not respond to reasonable follow-up inquiries. With clients who repeatedly cancel and reschedule, the provider will establish the limits on what is tolerable before declining to reschedule another appointment, as some sort of predictable participation is a necessary condition for progress.

Client actions that are dangerous to the provider create conditions where it is unsafe and unproductive to continue the work. Termination is the appropriate response when the client makes threats to the provider or the provider's significant others (e.g., the client described early in the chapter, who threatened to stalk and harm her provider for not writing a fitness-for-duty letter). Other examples include threats to sue the provider or take any sort of legal action, or any criminal behavior that targets the provider such as stealing or damaging office property.

Provider-Client Match

Termination may be appropriate if the client and provider are not well matched, if the provider does not have the right skills for dealing with the problem at hand, or if the client has not established a clear plan for working with a single provider. Multiple providers working with a single client usually function in an integrated manner, each contributing in a specific way as part of a team. A client might work with a nurse practitioner for medication management, a psychologist for individual therapy, and a family counselor for marital issues. Working with multiple providers at the same level of intervention (e.g., individual therapy) is counterproductive.

Clients often interview several therapists before settling with one, or talk to someone for a second opinion. If clients schedule a second or third session, they should be encouraged to focus on one therapeutic relationship and to terminate the other, or to explicitly plan a brief and directed consultation. The provider must be careful not to discourage clients' autonomy or right to seek multiple opinions. It is important to discuss the therapeutic issues with clients and try to reduce any confusion or conflict while helping them come to a decision that best meets their needs (APA, 2002, 10.04).

Providers want to encourage arrangements that help clients build trust and emotional involvement in therapy, basic ingredients for effective work. When a client consults a new provider, whether by choice or necessity, the current therapist helps the client negotiate the process of termination, if that is appropriate. The second provider will proceed with sensitivity and caution, but may need to either help the client with the termination decision or redirect the client back to the original therapist. The biggest quandary for relatively stable clients who simply want to explore a different approach, or who should make a change for other circumstantial reasons is the interpersonal anxiety associated with leaving or "firing" the established therapist. Talking this through will help most clients sort out their feelings and come to a reasoned decision. Although the client has the right to terminate without notice, it is helpful to encourage some closing communication with the discontinued provider, either in a session, with a phone or e-mail message or in a letter, depending on the client's preference.

When providers determine that they do not have the appropriate skills to help a client or be effective in therapy, they should redirect the client to other resources as soon as possible. Often this mismatch becomes evident relatively quickly, during the first session or first few sessions. A mismatch can also become apparent later in therapy as new information becomes available or as the client's concerns shift. Providers who, after giving thoughtful consideration to the option of treating a client, do not feel appropriate for the job should handle termination tactfully and respectfully but remain firm in their professional judgment. The client's preferences, while they are important, cannot determine the scope of the provider's competence.

Six Essential Steps

All professional actions should be systematic and follow a consistent process. The following six essential steps will guide clinicians through implementing termination. These six steps will ensure that the provider has followed a clinically and ethically appropriate process:

1. *Recognize triggers for termination.* These were described in this chapter.

2. *Review the clinical and emotional context.* Begin preparation for termination by anticipating the client's potential emotional and behavioral responses. Bear in mind that individual responses will reflect each person's clinical history and status, emotional propensities, coping strategies, and current stress level.

3. *Identify any legal, ethical, and contractual limits.* Next, assess whether any legal, ethical, or contractual circumstances affect termination. Some of these circumstances are absolute in that the provider has little room for judgment or negotiation. Others have some relative degrees of freedom or room for discretion. A systematic series of questions ensures attention to each critical issue:

   • Are there any legally or ethically compelling reasons for termination?

   • Are there legally or ethically compelling reasons to delay or postpone termination?

   • Are there contract issues that have to be considered?

4. *Consider risks and strategies for risk management.* No termination is completely risk-free, although most risks can be sufficiently managed, especially when approached with forethought and strategic effort. Different areas of risk include adverse outcomes in clinical, emotional, and profes-

sional domains. The client gets worse, there is emotional distress to the client or provider, or the provider might be subject to legal action or professional discipline. The magnitude of any of these risks can range from mere inconvenience to major fiasco. A combination of risks may also be more than just a simple sum as a single risk may exponentially escalate the magnitude of the other risks. It is worthwhile to consider overall risk exposure along a continuum of potential for adverse outcomes to establish an appropriate level of intensity for mediating efforts. It is hazardous to consider anything a minor risk, yet some risks need more vigilance and planning on the part of the provider.

5. *Provide pretermination counseling.* Pretermination counseling occurs over the course of one to three sessions that mark the end of a particular segment of therapy. There are two main objectives for this pretermination discussion. The first objective is to provide notice of termination and discuss the circumstances. In this discussion, it should be possible to evaluate the client's needs, preferences, and options. The second objective is to provide a forum for the client to express feelings, to check perceptions, or ask questions about the termination and to receive any helpful feedback or practical information to facilitate the transition. There may be times when client actions or the third-party payer's limits preclude pretermination counseling (APA, 2002, 10.10 (c)). Encouraging participation in a termination session is generally useful, but extreme or repeated efforts to contact the client are not usually necessary or advisable.

6. *Establish the disposition and note in client's record.* Disposition can be established during the pretermination consultation, which might extend beyond the final face-to-face meeting if follow-up contact by telephone is necessary. Notes on the termination discussion, with reference to each of the preceding steps, are entered into the client's record, including the closing outcome. Any further telephone contacts should also be noted, as well as possible written correspondence. Creating an adequate record of each step taken is both an opportunity for the provider to reflect on the work and draw a sense of closure as well as a basic professional task. If the client or any other providers ever have questions about what transpired, the record will reflect the degree of professional integrity that was maintained.

Prevent and Defuse Volatile Situations

Many risky or contentious clinical interactions can be averted by regularly following the six outlined steps. When snags or difficulties are encountered, it is helpful to seek peer consultation for ideas and emotional support in managing those challenges. This helps the provider to ensure that his or her decisions are consistent with the community standard of care. What's more, it is powerful proof that the provider intended to maintain a high standard of care by making this effort. Professional consultation on issues of risk management is essential for any volatile, conflicted or potentially legally contentious situation. It is especially important to obtain consultation that is both professionally qualified and confidential for matters of legal threat.

Several other general strategies are useful for managing emerging risks. A practitioner who believes that a client is not benefiting from treatment still should not terminate the service during an acute phase of a crisis when there is any risk of self-harm. Instead, the provider has a duty to address the client's immediate safety prior to examining the suitability of termination, and to provide a reasonable referral. The provider is not obligated to retain the client until a new therapy relationship is settled, as it is unethical and highly risky to continue unproductive therapy with an unstable client.

If a client intentionally misrepresents basic information needed for therapy such as presenting a false identity or fabricated clinical symptoms, termination is warranted. The basic trust required for psychotherapy has been compromised, and the therapist has significant cause to suspect the patient's motives. Because the therapeutic enterprise is based on trust (APA, 2002, Principle B) any action that substantially disrupts this foundation becomes a reason for termination.

Similarly, many therapists would consider the therapeutic alliance irreparably compromised if the client tried to engage the therapist in a fraudulent action. Requesting that the therapist make untrue statements such as an inappropriate diagnosis for insurance purposes, billing insurance for missed appointments as if the services were rendered, or making statements of fact that are not true to gain disability reimbursement, entry into jobs or military service, child custody, or any number of possible situations are attempts to conspire with the therapist in commission of fraud, which could result in professional censure or possible loss of licensure as well as other legal charges. If the client attempts to use therapy or the therapist, the therapist must refuse to cooperate.

The psychologist's ethics code allows for therapy termination if the provider is threatened or otherwise endangered by the patient or someone associated with the patient (APA, 2002, 10.10 (b)). This standard of conduct is broad enough to allow for judging a range of possible circumstances where the best and most reasonable action is clinical termination. It also provides the clinician with a means of defending such action should the patient make retaliatory charges of unethical behavior. What constitutes a threat or endangerment can include verbal or physical threats (Fisher, 2003). Termination under these adverse conditions can occur precipitously, without pretermination counseling or referral, and may include efforts to seek protective services from legal authorities if appropriate (APA, 2002, 10.10 (c); 4.05 (b) (3)).

If a patient or the patient's significant other threatens to file a lawsuit or professional complaint, it would obviously be preferable to try to resolve the dispute prior to legal action. It is important to take all complaints seriously, and attempt to fix the problem. If this is not possible, termination is indicated (Younggren, 2004). If the patient has taken any formal legal action against the therapist, then therapy should be immediately terminated with no further communication and personal legal counsel obtained. As noted, consultation is an essential step in managing any termination related to verbal, physical, or legal threats.

Follow-Through and Follow-Up

If time allows, it can be helpful to reduce the frequency and increase the time interval between sessions. This creates an opportunity for the client to practice new skills or continue self-directed efforts with decreasing input from the therapist. Termination is more gradual and natural, with sessions fading out over time. There is time to process the client's remaining concerns and diffuse the initial emotional responses. Clients as well as therapists may experience some emotional discomfort even with a reasonable and appropriate termination. It is easier to end therapy when goals have been met, the client is satisfied and ready to end treatment, and the therapist feels a sense of mastery in the finished work. However, not all terminations feel complete. It is harder to end therapy without time to process whatever regrets, frustrations, or anxiety might be associated with the termination. Discussing any feelings such as these is an important part of termination follow-through.

The fading approach also helps to reinforce a coping versus mastery objective in therapy. This is an opportunity to review with the client the specific actions, skills, or changes that have been useful, and to prepare the client for coping with potential challenges ahead. The client might be encouraged to systematically schedule times for "self-therapy," during which he or she reviews issues, checks symptoms, pinpoints problems, plans homework activities, anticipates challenges, and schedules the next self-therapy session (J. Beck, 1995). Self-therapy might include adaptive homework such as weekly exercise, regular social contacts, scheduled activity for pleasure and accomplishment, or a "booster" visit with the therapist.

A common termination dilemma occurs when the client makes a bid for some sort of personal contact or relationship after therapy. It is quite natural to want to extend a positive interpersonal experience, so this should not be a total surprise nor is it necessarily a bad sign. Because therapy is a personal service, mental health professionals have a special obligation to be clear about personal and professional boundaries to avoid any appearance of impropriety. The decision of whether to allow posttermination contact should be based on sound professional judgment. Some therapists might disallow or discourage any contact following termination. Others might encourage contact, but frame it clearly as a follow-up professional contact in a professional setting. Having contact of a social nature once therapy has terminated ventures into a fuzzy area, where it is not clear if the contact is therapy or friendship or something else.

Any sexual contact is explicitly prohibited for at least 2 years following the final professional contact, and even thereafter is apt to be highly questionable behavior (see APA, 2002, 10.08). Other social contact is less clearly defined in the code of conduct (APA, 2002), allowing room for professional and personal judgment, or misjudgment as the case may be. Key aspects of this judgment involve spotting reasonably foreseeable risks and taking action to avoid, minimize, or manage any risk of harm to the other person. According to Younggren and Gottlieb (2004), the patient's history, diagnosis and level of psychological functioning as well as the nature and length of the therapy are all important in determining how the practitioner should manage possible contacts outside a formal therapy setting.

Summary

Effective termination does not just happen; it is based on a sound strategy. The two main components of a termination strategy are ongoing dialogue about termination and a reasonable plan of action. The positive quality of a termination is determined to a large degree by how well the client and therapist communicate about this important decision. Terminations do not all look alike and it is helpful to identify the good and bad variations. Six types of termination describe a spectrum of different endings. Premature termination is an unclear label that often refers to ending therapy without a sense of closure or completion. Premature termination may reflect a therapist bias toward long-term over short-term treatment. Prospective termination is planned in advance and includes a clear rationale and an opportunity to process thoughts and feelings about termination. Prospective termination is typically mutually agreeable and uncomplicated. Flexible termination is used when conditions require an interruption of therapy or when the client is unsure about the need for further treatment. Complex termination involves difficulties in the planning and communication about termination and strong affect associated with ending sessions. Complex termination may be connected to personality disorders or secondary gain. Oblique termination is an abrupt termination that is unilaterally enacted by the client with highly ambiguous or potentially negative emotional tones. Unprofessional termination involves provider actions in ending therapy that fall below a reasonable standard of care.

The clinician's competence in termination is based on having a clear grasp of professional standards, role expectations, ethical guidelines, and clinical needs of individual clients. Applied skills are needed to implement the termination strategy and achieve positive closure under the varying circumstances in clinical practice. These skills include the ability to communicate effectively about termination, to characterize one's practice and form a policy on termination, to plan for one's limits and potential vulnerabilities, to incorporate termination into the treatment plan and goals, to systematically monitor and evaluate client progress, to modify the treatment plan in response to new information, to follow a systematic course of action when implementing termination, to manage the risks of volatile situations, and finally, to create a productive transition and manage the outer limits of follow-up contacts without compromising professional standards or harming the client.

PART

IV

WHAT EVERY CLINICIAN
NEEDS TO KNOW

Self-Care and Ethics: Applying the Techniques of Positive Psychology

15

Chapter

Psychologists dedicate their careers to advancing the well-being of others and caring for their clients. Like many other professionals, however, they do not always practice what they preach. The profession is working hard to encourage psychologists to be mindful of self-care and to support those whose self-care falters. This chapter identifies sources of potential burnout and offers suggestions for self-care and for care of colleagues. We highlight sensitive topics and challenging aspects of therapy that are difficult to navigate with clear minds, and even more difficult under fatigued, burned out, or impaired conditions. We explore clients' and therapists' vulnerable thoughts and feelings including anger, pity, sexual attraction, and identification, and their resultant behaviors. We want to help new clinicians be alert for these aspects of therapeutic relationships that they might not otherwise expect, and to think about the best ethical practices for managing these risks. We offer suggestions for self-monitoring, self-care, pitfalls to avoid in therapy, and effective coping strategies that emphasize the principles of positive psychology. Finally, we extend these principles to the important matter of caring for colleagues.

Learning Objectives

At the end of this chapter, the reader should be able to:

- Describe the symptoms of therapist burnout.
- Identify at least three deterrents to confronting burnout or impairment in oneself or for colleagues. Consider how to address these obstacles ethically.
- List at least five symptoms of therapists' problems in reacting to clients.

- List 10 self-care practices for therapists.
- Describe how to care for colleagues.
- Explain how positive psychology relates to burnout.

In this book, we have explored why people become clients, and how to assess and treat a wide variety of difficulties ranging from mild distress to pervasive personality problems or antisocial behavior. We have considered methods to encourage and instill change, monitor progress and outcomes, and recognize difficulties in this process. This chapter aims to help readers turn this knowledge inward to prepare for self-reflection, self-evaluation, and self-care. To get yourself thinking about this topic, answer the following questions: What have you done for yourself today? What activities have you engaged in this week that have helped you relax, laugh, and feel good? How regularly do you do these things? Every day? Every week? Every month? Do you consider your self-care, recreation, and work balanced?

Too often, the person in therapy least cared for is the therapist. Yet, clinical psychologists serve as role models to many constituencies, such as students, colleagues, workshop attendees, and clients. It would seem that psychologists and therapists should practice what they preach or help others achieve across the biopsychosocial domains. Many of them do. However, therapists like all human beings (including their clients), are susceptible to the stressors and challenges of major and minor life events. Some have better coping strategies than others, some have had better role models than others, and individuals' ability to effectively self-monitor and achieve self-change varies considerably. Most everyone can think of times where they have responded to stressful situations in less than optimal ways. Can you think of times when you have responded to stressors (persons, situations, or events) in ways that have left you feeling embarrassed, guilty, regretful, or more stressed? We hope that these examples have been exceptions rather than the norm. Yet, when you are vulnerable, and the impact of the stressors seems unmanageable, increasingly irrational and inappropriate responses often lead to personal and professional problems. Psychologists who are burned out might have clouded judgment or skewed perceptions that could lead to unethical or unprofessional behavior. Alternatively, assuming a knowledge base of ethics is in place, ongoing practice of self-care and maintenance of mental health should increase the likelihood that ethical standards are followed and American Psychological Association's (APA) aspirational ethical principles are upheld.

Students are encouraged to learn the ethical obligations professionals have in recognizing and responding to self- and colleague-impairment. Understanding the burnout syndrome and ways to assess this phenomenon is deeply important for students in training, and following degree completion. Lack of self-care can lead to burnout, and it, in turn, may to lead to unethical or unprofessional behavior. Therapists suffering from burnout might be impaired or exhibit problematic behavior.

Understanding psychologist burnout, psychological morbidity, high-risk therapist behaviors, and management of personal reactions to clients builds awareness of stressors, and ways to deal with them through self-care. The positive psychology movement has provided new ways to look at self-care and the prevention of burnout and impairment. Positive psychology prescribes self-care practices to increase happiness, optimism, satisfaction, creativity, and moderators of stress for clinicians. Increasing positive thoughts, feelings, and behaviors (self-care) may help decrease burnout, and maladaptive, and perhaps, unethical behaviors in professional practice.

Ethics, Impairment, Personal Problems, and Burnout

The *Ethical Principles of Psychologists and Code of Conduct* (APA, 2002), Standard 2.06 titled "Personal Problems and Conflicts," offers the following guidelines:

> (a) *psychologists refrain from initiating an activity when they know or should know that there is a substantial likelihood that their personal problems will prevent them from performing their work-related activities in a competent manner.*
>
> (b) *When psychologists become aware of personal problems that may interfere with their performing work-related duties adequately, they take appropriate measures, such as obtaining professional consultation or assistance, and determine whether they should limit, suspend, or terminate their work-related duties. (p. 1064)*

On first sight, these standards seem quite clear, but professionals also must recognize that many individuals who become patients or clients do so only after negative consequences arise in their personal or professional life. Insight about your own emotional or affective, cognitive, or behavioral dysregulation or interpersonal problems may be lacking at the onset of difficulty. How then are psychologists supposed to self-evaluate their competency or impact of personal stressors if their judgment is impaired due to stress, distress, or poor coping with life events? When does having a few "bad days" turn into having problems? Since the APA Ethics Code of Conduct is intended to be a guide that relies heavily on "professional judgment of psychologists" compared with others "engaged in similar activities in similar circumstances, given the knowledge the psychologist had or should have had at the time," (APA, 2002, p. 1060) there is a need to look elsewhere to answer this complicated question or set of questions.

We begin with a discussion of *impairment* and *problematic* behavior as they pertain to our professional roles. Judgment was discussed in Chapter 8, with regard to biases and heuristics in clinical decision making, and a review of this information would be helpful. The core competencies, and therefore, core curriculum expected of professional psychologists are detailed in Chapter 2 and also warrant a review.

Impairment

The difficulty in identifying impairment stems partly from the profession's difficulty in defining the term. The psychology literature defines impairment in many ways, ranging from specific behaviors to broad individual characteristics that hamper professional performance. A review of the literature (Barnett & Hillard, 2001) summarizes distress and impairment as existing along a continuum, and referring to sexual misconduct, substance abuse, emotional, and mental health issues. Barnett and Hillard also equate impairment to disorders diagnosable on Axis I, II, or III of the *Diagnostic and Statistical Manual of Mental Disorders* (*DSM-IV;* American Psychiatric Association, 1994).

Without knowing exactly what impairment is, how can we know if someone is impaired? Furthermore, how can we help someone who might be impaired? Similar questions were asked of intern supervisors in counseling centers known to be active in addressing supervisees' competence problems (Gizara & Forrest, 2004). These experts also had difficulty defining impairment. Their institutional policies also did not provide clear operational definitions of impairment to help them make this determination. Analysis of interview content (Gizara & Forrest, 2004), revealed conceptual themes about impairment suggesting that impaired interns engaged in professionally harmful or deficient and persistent patterns of behavior. Supervisors related that impaired intern behaviors represented *diminished functioning* (change in performance), and *deficient skills* (broadly defined). Skills deficits included basic skill sets (e.g., interviewing, delivery of therapeutic intervention), interpersonal difficulties due to lack of self-awareness, and lack of professional responsibility. Skill deficits represented the majority of examples provided.

Students' attitudes toward impaired peers in clinical psychology training programs were solicited in an e-mail survey (Oliver, Bernstein, Anderson, Blashfield, & Roberts, 2004). The operational definition of "student impairment" (Lamb et al., 1987) was described as interference in professional functioning in one or more of the following areas: (a) an inability and/or unwillingness to acquire and integrate professional standards into one's repertoire of professional behavior; (b) an inability to acquire professional skills to reach an acceptable level of competency; (c) an inability to control personal stress, psychological dysfunction and/or excessive emotional reactions that interfere with professional functioning (p. 598).

The definition was summarized to study participants to describe impaired or problem students as those who "experience difficulties associated with interpersonal problems, substance abuse, Axis II disorders, and so forth and are consequently unable to meet the expectations of their programs" (p. 142). Reflecting on this definition, students stated that impairment was most frequently evidenced by depression and other mood disorders, personality disorders or traits, anxiety disorder, eating disorders, substance abuse problems, burnout, lack of timely preparedness, and interpersonal boundary concerns. Impairment among student-colleagues and professionals negatively impacts others within the profession, and those served by the impaired, therefore others' perceptions provide important insight into shaping a definition.

At times, impairment has been confused with disability, as defined by the American Disabilities Act. This term confusion is problematic because many disabilities would not negatively impact professional performance or delivery of service. Because surveys suggest that it is unclear whether professionals and students define impairment the same way, the term *professional impairment* was suggested to focus on specific difficulties that may "impede or interfere with professional responsibilities" (e.g., deficient knowledge, limited clinical skills, inadequate technical skills, poor judgment, and disturbing interpersonal attributes; Oliver et al., 2004, p. 146). Others (Gizara & Forrest, 2004; Kutz, 1986) suggest that impairment should be reserved for describing diminished functioning, while those whose performance has not decreased, but rather has never achieved sufficiency or proficiency should be deemed "not competent." "Unqualified" might also be appropriate for this latter category. "Problematic" behaviors seem to be less well attended to in the literature and likely refers to questionable behaviors that are borderline inappropriate. Problematic behaviors that might warrant concern by trainers, supervisors, or colleagues often precede impairment. If poor judgment leads to poor skill delivery, but does not quite cause harm, perhaps the clinician's behaviors are problematic. Likewise, students or professionals whose behaviors are interpersonally distasteful, abrasive, or distancing among colleagues, but not among clients, might be considered problematic within an academic or professional setting, but not grounds for discontinuance of practice. Practitioners who seem hostile, labile, or irresponsible in ways that are not illegal or unethical might be labeled as problematic and would likely benefit from early intervention or approach by colleagues or superiors. Problematic might describe subclinical or prediagnostic impairment.

A clear operational definition for impairment is lacking in the psychology literature. Definitions vary from specific to broad, from focus on legal definitions to ethical considerations, from diagnostic categories to syndromes. The seminal review article by Forrest, Elman, Gizara, and Vacha-Hasse (1999) concludes that the field of professional psychology defines impairment broadly, with a focus on diminished role functioning of a qualified professional resulting from distress, burnout, or substance use, and sometimes resulting in unethical, incompetent, and compromised professional behavior. Burnout may be a common cause of impairment, yet it is another poorly understood construct.

Burnout

Burnout has been defined as a "psychological syndrome in response to chronic interpersonal stressors on the job" (Maslach, Schaufeli, & Leiter, 2001, p. 399). There are three major components to burnout: *emotional exhaustion,* feelings of *depersonalization* (detachment from the job), and self-perception of lack of *accomplishment* or ineffectiveness on the job. Maslach et al. (2001), pioneers and forerunners in the field of burnout theory and research, suggest that stress is captured by the construct of emotional exhaustion and refers to feeling depleted of one's emotional and physical resources, and extended beyond one's perceived or real resources. Cynicism or depersonalization is characterized by negative feelings and detachment from one's job, representing the interpersonal context dimension of burnout. Personal accomplishment or perceived lack thereof, represents one's self-evaluation of job efficacy.

Qualitative investigations and case studies on burnout originated with a focus on professionals in human services and health care workers, whose job focus was on their relationships with service recipients and coworkers. Thus, the importance of the relationship competency described earlier in this book (Chapter 2) is highlighted again in the context of the burnout syndrome, in which impairment in this domain of professional functioning is a key defining factor. Early writings on burnout were anecdotal and conceptual, beginning in the 1970s. Empirical studies on burnout emerged in the early 1990s, approximately 15 to 20 years after the initial introduction of the concept, partially due to the development of objective measures of the tripartite phenomenon. Today, the Maslach Burnout Inventory-Human Services Survey (MBI-HSS; Maslach & Jackson, 1981) and the Maslach Burnout Inventory-Educators Survey (MBI-ES; Maslach, Jackson, Leiter, & Schaufeli, 1996) are two resources for psychologists' assessment of burnout in clients and perhaps themselves. Other versions exist for professionals outside human services and health care workers and educators. Interestingly, these measures do not generate a burnout "score" or rating; instead, the three constructs remain distinct factors of the overall concept of burnout. Yet, these tools have allowed investigators to quantitatively research contributing factors, influences and consequences of burnout. This research led to more refined theory and understanding of the constructs of burnout and their relationships to each other. Further explanation of emotional exhaustion, depersonalization, and personal accomplishment follows.

Although emotional exhaustion and/or job-related stress is a core component of burnout, stress and exhaustion alone do not constitute burnout. It is the impact the stress and exhaustion have on one's attitude, work effort and performance, and interactions with others that represent the construct of burnout. Someone who is burned out might be stressed and exhausted, and therefore, puts little effort into her client's sessions, cares little about getting paperwork done, and has trouble feeling energized about her job for an extended period. This is different from the transient stress people may feel because they are running late for work or have an impending deadline to meet, and therefore, are short-tempered or tired on a given day.

Emotional exhaustion prompts actions that emotionally and cognitively distance the professional from the work, perhaps as a coping mechanism (Maslach et al., 2001). Working with terminally ill patients is intense work that some professionals might deem depressing or hopeless. Likewise, some professionals might maintain this impression of working with inner-city, abused children of drug-addicted parents. These professionals are not likely to choose careers in working with these populations; this does not constitute burnout. In comparison, professionals who choose to work with such clients or patients might find times within their careers when they have a series of difficult interactions with patients, or have become invested in clients whose ultimate outcomes differ dramatically from what was aspired. Burnout theory suggests that when many successive or simultaneous situations, or even one significant one such as this occurs, and the professionals' coping resources are taxed or not buffering the job stress, they might inadvertently withdraw from other clients, colleagues, or their job responsibilities to protect themselves from further disappointment, hurt, or frustration.

Undergraduate and graduate students alike often refer to themselves as burned out toward the end of an academic term, year, or completion of a major milestone (degree, practicum, internship, and dissertation). Can you think of times in your professional or academic history when you felt drained and exhausted, despite getting adequate sleep? At that time, maybe you cared less about completing work in an ideal fashion than just completing it? Have there been times when you postponed returning phone calls to classmates or coworkers, or have avoided other responsibilities related to school or work because you didn't feel like you had the energy? Perhaps you can think of time when your frustration tolerance was particularly low, and you found yourself to be irritated with your professors or colleagues for what others might perceive as minor wrongdoings or delays? While answers to these questions don't necessarily indicate that you were burned out, certainly further self-reflection would be indicated. Distancing seems to be an immediate reaction to exhaustion, according to studies on burnout that reveal a strong relationship between exhaustion and depersonalization, across settings (Maslach et al., 2001).

The preceding questions do not ask about irregularities in your eating habits, mental acuity, or gastrointestinal functioning-vegetative symptoms often associated with depression, which are less likely to be experienced by persons who are burned out. In fact, professionals understand burnout and depression to be different phenomenon (Bakker et al., 2000). Research distinguishes burnout from depression in that it is job-related, situation-specific, and limited to the work context, whereas depression impacts and is experienced in all aspects of one's life (Maslach et al., 2001). Persons who experience burnout may not have ever experienced depression or other psychopathology. This underscores the importance of professionals' and students' ability to recognize the key aspects of burnout within themselves and others, because it presents differently than the depression clinical psychologists are used to identifying. Although different from depression, burnout may still constitute impairment in professionals who suffer extreme symptoms and manifest inappropriate behaviors consistent with this phenomenon.

The concept of personal accomplishment or job-related self-efficacy is related to emotional exhaustion and depersonalization in a more complex way (Maslach et al., 2001). It appears that there are reciprocal interactions between exhaustion and personal accomplishment, and personal accomplishment and depersonalization. Chronic job-related stress might lead to decreased personal accomplishment, and decreased personal accomplishment might lead, therefore, to increased depersonalization and exhaustion. Furthermore, if professionals are detached from their work and work relationships, it is unlikely that they will experience feelings of personal accomplishment. The three constructs of burnout possibly develop simultaneously, rather than sequentially, but more research is needed to ferret out these relationships. Experts in the field suggest that work overload and social conflict contribute most significantly to emotional exhaustion and depersonalization, whereas lack of relevant resources likely contributes most significantly to decreased personal accomplishment (Maslach et al., 2001).

The concepts of burnout and the burnout syndrome are complex. Many practicing professionals are likely to have experienced or will experience some degree of burnout during their academic pursuits, professional practice, or career at large. Yet, when do these experiences cross the line from "normal and transient" to "dysfunctional" and "interfering" with professional judgment and work, and therefore, ethically concerning? When does socially acceptable burnout turn into impairment? Or, as some suggest based on a review of the literature (Forrest et al., 1999), is there no difference between the two? While exact equations or recipes do not exist to answer these questions, a look at the prevalence of burnout and impairment in student and professional practice might raise awareness to the possibilities.

How Common Is Burnout and Impairment in Training and Professional Practice?

General statistics on the incidence and prevalence of burnout and impairment in training programs and professional practice are difficult to quote with certainty due to limited reports of this information and variations in methodology to gather such data. Studies mostly focus on specific subgroups of mental health professionals and psychologists such as those who work with traumatized or maltreated children or adults (e.g., Azar, 2000; Collins & Long, 2003; Sabin-Farell & Turpin, 2003; Salston & Figley, 2003; Stevens & Higgins, 2002), substance abuse counselors (e.g., Mack, 2004; Shoptaw, Stein, & Rawson, 2000), older adults (e.g., Spear, Wood, Chawla, Devis, & Nelson, 2004), or those practicing outside the United States (Brown, Prashantham, & Abbott, 2003). Studies examining correlates and factors related to burnout and impairment might underestimate the prevalence and incidence of these phenomena due to self-selection biases. Many of those who participate might be willing to do so because they are not feeling particularly stressed or burned out. However, several review articles and studies have attempted to summarize more general findings from objective sources.

Based on the four studies of rates of impairment in training that were conducted between 1982 and 1991, more than two-thirds of all surveyed programs reported having at least one impaired student within the 5 years prior to study participation (Forrest et al., 1999). Furthermore, data suggest that all programs identified at least one impaired student each year for the 5-year period (Forrest et al., 1999).

In a more recent professional competence survey of 71 representatives of graduate programs in clinical, school, or counseling psychology, almost half of the respondents reportedly had at least one student with limited clinical skills. Personality and emotional problems were frequently the cause of this problem (Procidano, Busch-Rossnagel, Reznikoff, & Geisinger, 1995). A large majority of respondents (89%) had experience with at least one student who exhibited nonacademic or professional deficiencies (Procidano et al.). Similar statistics were provided by department heads of American Psychological Association-accredited professional psychology training programs, suggesting that two to three impaired students per program were identified within a 5-year period (Schwebel & Coster, 1998).

Self-reports of professional psychology students' perception of impairment or burnout are limited. However, an exploratory study of over 1,000 clinical psychology graduate students (mostly female) showed that approximately 75% of these students, most of whom were in PhD programs, had received psychotherapy for various reasons (personal growth, impairment, family issues, adjustment, etc.) at some time either during or prior to graduate studies. A closer look at statistics related to impairment revealed varied reasons for seeking therapy. Over half the respondents sought therapy for depression, or "adjustment or developmental issues." Another 20% of the sample sought therapy for problems with spouse or significant other, or for other interpersonal issues. Finally, just under 10% sought therapy for suicidal ideation; eating disorders; physical assault, abuse, or sexual abuse; or substance abuse (Holzman, Searight, & Hughes, 1996). Respondents rarely told their supervisors they were in therapy. Assuming the findings are generalizable, these results suggest, therefore, that training directors' reports of impairment, burnout, or students' "problems" might underrepresent the frequency in which students experience such difficulties. This disparity also highlights the possibility that not all experiences of depression or other mental health concerns by students and professionals result in impairment or diminished functioning by practitioners, despite the frequency with which these phenomena apparently occur.

In professional practice, early studies show that many professional psychologists experience psychological distress, and continue to work while doing so (Guy, Poelstra, & Stark, 1989; Pope et al., 1987). In fact, in a study of 456 practicing psychologists, approximately 60% reported that they continued to work despite being too distressed to function effectively (Pope et al., 1987). You can probably think of a time when you or some friends were so stressed out that you had trouble paying attention in class, or maybe didn't perform as well on an exam because you were distracted, so these statistics seem reasonable. When considering the changes in judgment, attention, concentration, and memory people tend to experience under distress, it is frightening to think of the potential negative impact psychologists could have on their clients as a result.

In a survey study of 304 Tennessee psychologists, respondents estimated that 19% of their colleagues had psychological conditions (including substance abuse) that rendered them impaired in their practice (Floyd, Myszka, & Orr, 1998). Respondents reportedly had concerns that at least one or two colleagues were impaired at the time of survey. When asked to think about the past year, psychologists estimated that nearly 30% of their colleagues suffered impairment in that time frame. While people knew of more psychologists with substance abuse problems, impairment was perceived to result more frequently from psychological problems. Respondents' reported (in order of frequency) overwork, personality disorders, emotional or mental illnesses, and health or age effects, as other problem areas for colleagues.

In parallel to the students' self-reported experiences with therapy, which provides another perspective of incidence of psychological problems or impairment, a survey of 425 members of the Counseling Psychology division (Division 17) of the American Psychological Association was conducted on personal experiences with depression and treatment (Gilroy, Carroll, & Murra, 2002). Slightly more than half of this sample identified themselves as being employed in private practice. More than half of the respondents identified themselves as depressed. Of the 114 who recall receiving formal diagnoses during therapy, approximately one-third were diagnosed with dysthymia, one-third with adjustment disorder with depressed mood, and about 10% had a major depressive disorder or bipolar disorder; almost half of the sample reported experiencing some form of suicidal ideation or behavior (Gilroy et al., 2002). Although some of the depressed participants perceived their depression as having a positive impact on their clinical work by increasing empathy and effectiveness, the majority thought their depression impacted their work negatively. Feeling depressed led these counselors to have reduced energy, be less productive, feel distracted, experience decreased patience and confidence, be less emotionally available, and feel burned out (Gilroy et al., 2002). Of course, these findings may not be generalizable due to limited sample sizes and the self-selection process inherent in survey studies.

How Does the Profession Handle Impaired or Burned-Out Trainees and Professionals?

Even though professional deficiencies and impairment can be difficult to identify and ameliorate (Procidano et al., 1995), clinical training programs (graduate programs, predoctoral and postdoctoral internships) frequently need to address these issues with students. The Ethics Code (APA, 2002) mandates self-identification of diminished functioning and self-referral for assistance in recovering from such difficulties. Yet, many barriers prevent students and professionals from seeking assistance from their training programs or colleagues for personal problems.

Students might fear losing their careers or being stigmatized by professors and classmates if they admit to personal deficiencies or impairment. Professionals might also fear stigmatization or have difficulty identifying or admitting their own need for help. Also, avoiding dual relationships can be challenging in professionals' search for a therapist or supervisor to help them remediate deficiencies or impairment. Practitioners in rural areas or those who are highly visible in professional organizations might encounter this difficulty most often.

For students, programs often limit the time for degree completion, and leaves of absence or remediation work could delay meeting program milestones. Admitting deficiencies, therefore, if others have not identified them, can present a dilemma for the student whose decision making might already be impaired. Professionals may similarly have financial burdens that present obstacles to them taking a temporary break from providing client services to allow time for self-care and remediation. Other reasons students or professionals might not seek help include self-doubt, unrealistic expectations for what one should be able to handle, and what others expect of them. Training programs and personal philosophical orientations, practices, and social climates might foster outreach, or might prohibit it.

As the literature review on personal therapy during training has revealed, in many situations self-identification and self-referral for personal problems do not occur. Training programs have at least some responsibility for aiding students in identifying problematic behaviors and impairment, and developing remediation plans. When remediation plans are unsuccessful, termination is often the only outcome.

Few studies or articles detail the types of remediation plan used for students (Forrest et al., 1999), and even fewer can be found for practicing professionals (Koocher & Keith-Spiegel, 1998). Training programs often recommend personal therapy, repeat practicum, extra or repeated coursework, leave of absence, increased supervision, tutoring, growth groups, or students leaving their programs (Forrest et al., 1999). While personal therapy was the most common remediation action taken in Forrest's review, this intervention is somewhat controversial among training program philosophies and directors, based on ethical guidelines. Recommending personal therapy is controversial because trainees might be resistant to seeking treatment; the trainees' privacy might be compromised or they might perceive it to be so; mandating personal therapy may be considered a boundary violation in the student-supervisee relationship; therapists have conflicting roles in servicing the student and communicating with the program about progress; program involvement may interfere with the therapeutic relationship; and therapy does not guarantee remediation of trainee deficiencies (Forrest et al., 1999).

Based on the limited literature, it is advisable for remediation plans to be goal-focused and problem-solving oriented. The identified problems and the proposed solutions or remediation plans should be obviously linked. Steps for remediation should be detailed and behavioral so that progress and change can be monitored and students and training supervisors have objective understandings of what is expected. Students and trainers would also benefit from prospectively outlining consequences of successful and unsuccessful completion of these plans. While these recommendations make intuitive sense, little is offered in the literature to document the frequency of clearly delineated policies, procedures, remediation plans, or outcomes.

The frequency of student dismissal is an outcome that has been empirically surveyed. According to a review of several studies, most programs reportedly have separated or dismissed at least one student within a 3-year time period as a last resort for any of the following reasons: inadequate clinical skills, deficient interpersonal skills, supervision difficulties, unprofessional demeanor, personality disorder, emotional problems, and academic dishonesty. These statistics underscore the prevalence of such difficulties even at the training level. Much like the profession as a whole, much work is needed to improve remediation procedures, documentation, and report of outcomes.

Practicing professionals, especially those in private practice, are often not directly accountable to supervisors or administrators. They are responsible to society, the profession, and the clients to maintain their own competence and well-functioning. This presupposes a high degree of self-monitoring, and allows limited opportunity for identification of impairment by others beyond their service recipients. Formal remediation programs for impaired psychologists are rare, although colleague assistance programs are increasingly available on a state-by-state basis.

If not by self-referral and intrinsic motivation, then how do professionals enter into remediation for impairment or personal problems? If not self-motivated, professionals might be sanctioned by state licensing boards to engage in therapy, additional supervision, or suspension of providing services, if found guilty of problematic, illegal, or unethical behavior. Other actions taken by state boards, depending on the severity of misconduct or consequence to impaired or unethical behavior may include educative or warning letters, reprimanding letters, directives to take specific corrective action as dictated by the regulatory board, or even revocation of licensure. Notice, however, that these actions occur based on *behaviors* and *evidence* of impairment or misconduct, rather than on the proactive approaches that are more easily taken in training programs *before* damage occurs. Ideally, identification of professional impairment occurs by self or colleagues before consumers are affected.

The Ethics Code (APA, 2002) provides guidelines outlining the responsibility of professionals to confront colleagues directly before pursuing official means of intervention for impairment. Standard 1.04 "Informal Resolution of Ethical Violations" states:

> When psychologists believe that there may have been an ethical violation by another psychologist, they attempt to resolve the issue by bringing it to the attention of that individual, if an informal resolution appears appropriate and the intervention does not violate any confidentiality rights that may be involved. (p. 1063)

If the preceding actions do not resolve the situation, Ethical Standard 1.05 (Reporting Ethical Violations) states "psychologists take further action appropriate to the situation. Such actions might include referral to state or national committees on professional ethics, to state licensing boards, or to the appropriate institutional authorities" (p. 1063).

For recipients of services (clients, patients, students), the procedures are probably less well known by the public, and actions are most likely pursued through lawyers or the help of other psychologists. Such actions are probably less likely to occur due to the individuals' own personal problems that sent them to a psychologist in the first place! There are few formalized ways to address problematic behaviors in practicing professionals before the behaviors become evidence of impairment.

The legal and ethical mechanisms described are in place to protect the public from unlawful, incompetent, and unethical actions by psychologists (Koocher & Keith-Speigel, 1998). The relationship between law and ethics is complex, but neither tolerates impaired functioning. Unlike privacy afforded in graduate training programs that protects students from having other students know about their personal situations, actions taken by legal and ethical bodies in the profession of psychology are often public and published. Thus, self-regulation is critical to self-preservation, as are support and encouragement for and of others. Self-regulation and support are the best forms of prevention. Awareness of due process procedures and policies outlined by the APA in their Ethics Code (2002), and in state licensing guidelines is also important. These documents inform professionals and consumers about the consequences for professionals engaging in misconduct or whose impairment is negatively impacting clients. This information, much like that for trainees, can motivate or inhibit colleagues and consumers from reporting impaired psychologists.

Therapists' Reactions to Clients: Normal to Problematic and What to Do about It

In your past week, what emotions have you experienced? Have you been excited? Elated? Anxious? Nervous? Compassionate? Empathic? Fearful? Concerned? Worried? Angry? Aggressive? Responsible? Embarrassed? Competitive? Avoidant? Aggravated? Frustrated? Relaxed? Talkative? Overwhelmed with love or attraction for someone? Have you had intrusive thoughts of self-assured success or defeat? Jealous thoughts? Fantasies about what life would be like if . . . ? All these are commonly experienced emotions, feelings, and thoughts. Yet, are they positive or negative? Appropriate or not? The answer depends largely on the frequency, intensity, and circumstances in which they are experienced, and the resultant behavior.

It is appropriate to feel somewhat anxious about a job interview or traveling to a new place, but if that anxiety prevents you from presenting yourself as well as you might have otherwise, or if it interferes with your ability to arrive at the destination of choice, the anxiety might be considered excessive or problematic. The behaviors that result might be displays of insecurity or negatively affected communication or physiological functioning, for example, loss of train-of-thought, stuttering, distraction, avoidance, sweatiness, or heart palpitations. For others, the intensity of anxiety in these situations might be uncomfortable, but their coping strategies might prevent their anxiety from negatively affecting their behaviors or outward appearance. These individuals may continue to function without consequence.

Thus, in discussing therapists' reactions to clients, it is important to recognize that like any other person, therapists will experience a wide range of emotions in response to their clients' stories, symptoms, appearance, personalities, therapy behaviors (compliance, participation, honesty), and other variables. This is normal and expected. The key, however, is being self-aware of the thoughts, feelings, and behaviors one has in relation to each client, and populations as a whole so that self-monitoring occurs; supervision or assistance can be sought, if needed; and appropriate therapist-client relations and boundaries are maintained. Sounds easy and obvious, right? The following illustrations are actual situations that have occurred for trainees or professionals in the field, with identifying information disguised for protection. Consider how you might think, feel, and act if you were in the position of the trainee or therapist.

Clinical Example: Mina and Her "Rescue"

Mina is a third-year doctoral student in clinical psychology. She has succeeded in school through undergraduate training, but always felt pressured to achieve a doctoral degree due to her parents' academic achievements. In her doctoral training, Mina struggled with certain aspects of the curriculum, and with balancing school, personal life, and her part-time job. She had several meetings with faculty to address her disorganization, lack of follow-through, and academic difficulty that put her in jeopardy of not progressing in the program. She experienced feelings of depression and intermittent anxiety.

In her practicum, she assessed a 20-year-old female, Rachel who had a similar background. Rachel had failed conversational Italian and was seeking an evaluation of a possible learning disability to validate her appeal to the college to expunge her grade because it resulted from a self-reported language

(continued)

Clinical Example: Mina and Her "Rescue" (Continued)

disability. After extensive history taking and testing, Mina concluded that while the tests did not actually confirm a language disability, they did not entirely disconfirm this claim either. Also, Rachel appeared to have some organizational difficulties and stressors that might ave interfered with her successful performance. Considering Rachel's family pressure to graduate with honors, and the unlikely chance that this would result if the grade remained, Mina felt inordinate pressure to produce results consistent with Rachel's pleas for help. Mina felt badly for Rachel and the feelings she expressed about her parents'

reactions. Since the data was unclear, Rachel felt conflicted and inclined to highlight (possibly embellish) the difficulties Rachel experienced with recommendations to give her a waiver exam and accommodations for a reexamination that would dismiss her previous grade. After all, testing was imperfect and therefore, how could she say for certain that Rachel's self-assessment *wasn't* accurate?

Points to Ponder: *What would be appropriate steps for Mina to take on concluding her evaluation? How could she identify the potential for her emotions to dictate her professional judgment and behavior?*

Clinical Example: Lola and the Hug

Lola was a third-year doctoral student who had little clinical experience prior to beginning her graduate studies. Her previous career was as a resource room teacher in an elementary school. During Lola's practicum training year in a community mental health setting, she had few returning clients and little success with the few ongoing cases she had. She was overwhelmed by her sense of responsibility for her clients' well-being, and her need to recall didactic information to apply it in clinical situations. She often felt stressed and exhausted by these perceived demands, until she was assigned to work with a 10-year-old boy, Brad, who was having behavioral problems at home. The child's mother had four other younger children and was often stressed and upset about Brad's poor behavior, which often led her to frustration and angry outbursts instead of the scheduled behavioral plan she was to follow. After

the fourth session, Brad's mother reported success with the behavior plan during their vacation week. Lola was so pleased by the mother's report that she jumped up in session, hugged her and overzealously expressed her joy. For the first time in this placement, Lola felt like she had succeeded in her therapeutic efforts and that she was competent to practice what she had been learning. In contrast, Brad's mother was too stunned to respond to her hug, did not hug her back, and canceled their next session.

Points to Ponder: *What were some of the possible antecedents that led to Lola's hug? Consider her thoughts, feelings, beliefs, and behavior; consider those of the mother. Whose needs were served by Lola's hugging the client? What are some other possible ways that Lola could have expressed her satisfaction to Brad's mother? What cues could have helped Lola identify her vulnerability to acting inappropriately with this client?*

Clinical Example: Andy and the Never-Ending Client Commitment

Andy had worked as a clinical psychologist for 10 years. His income was generated from private practice, adjunct teaching, consultation, and executive job coaching. In the summertime, Andy was referred a new client from a previous client. Joanie, a 42-year-old administrative assistant, had a long-standing history of severe depression that she attributed to genetics (maternal side) and to being raised by an uncaring, demeaning, alcohol-abusing mother and mostly silent father. Andy identified early in the assessment process that Joanie lacked specific adaptive coping skills and had maladaptive and dysfunctional thoughts and belief patterns, for which he outlined a specific cognitive behavioral approach to treatment. Joanie, however, seemed more interested in venting and whining about her problems each session, was help-rejecting of suggestions made by Andy, and was noncompliant with homework. Andy monitored Joanie's depression and anxiety with standardized self-report questionnaires, and found that she had not improved at all in four sessions. Joanie committed only to biweekly sessions, and canceled her appointments fairly often. Andy often found himself either bored during her sessions, in which he would find his mind wandering during her complaint monologues, or he found himself angry and irritated by her unwillingness to make efforts to change her situation. She argued that others were the cause of her problems, or that she simply did not have time to do Andy's homework between sessions even if she did think they would be helpful. Quickly, he became less active in the sessions and discontinued assigning homework or practice exercises. Joanie claimed that she felt better after her sessions, despite her lack of improvement according to the outcome measures or her display of affect. Andy's client census was low, and despite his frustration with her, and his wish prior to sessions that she would not actually present for therapy, he continued to allow her to be enrolled as a client and scheduled regular sessions with her.

Points to Ponder: *Andy expresses feelings of frustration, anger, and boredom with Joanie. How do these feelings possibly affect his practice of therapy with her? What are the potential consequences to her as a client? What are some of the other motivating factors for Andy to continue to work with Joanie? What are some of the behaviors Andy exhibits that might be apparent to Joanie or that he needs to recognize as signs that he is not functioning optimally?*

Clinical Example: Mitchell and the Therapeutic Gift

Mitchell, aged 48, had been a private practicing clinical psychologist for 20 years. Single and never married, he maintained a home office in a somewhat rural area. He had a part-time secretary who mostly took messages

(continued)

Clinical Example: Mitchell and the Therapeutic Gift (Continued)

and processed billing for him. Among his various clients, Mitchell began seeing a 36-year-old mother, Anna, who had three children (ages 4, 6, and 9) and whose husband of 11 years had just announced that he was leaving her for someone else. Mitchell described this woman as competent, educated, resilient, and very attractive. She was reportedly a dedicated mother, wife, and respected colleague in her part-time position as a project manager for a pharmaceutical company. Her goal for therapy was to focus her efforts on constructing her future life around her children's well-being, financial security, and eventual comfort of a new romantic relationship.

Mitchell was intrigued by Anna's rationality, pragmatism, and goal-oriented approach to life. He found himself thinking about her between sessions when he drove by basketball courts that reminded him of stories she told about her children's love of sports. He appreciatively noticed women who wore glasses and accessories similar to Anna's distinct style. On one occasion, he purchased a three-dollar key ring that had a clever saying on it that he thought captured what could be Anna's motto for life, "Don't wait for chance—Create happiness around you!" He rationalized to himself that the key chain would be a therapeutic reminder for her to maintain her positive attitude. He found himself self-disclosing his own coping practices and mantras that helped him through

specific difficult times in the past, which he detailed for her.

As time progressed, Mitchell's availability for sessions with Anna seemed to push later and later into the evening, and beyond the hours when his secretary was present. He allowed a 30-minute break prior to her session that allowed him to "rejuvenate," by showering and freshening up. Often, she held the last session of the evening, and her time allotment extended beyond the standard 60 minutes as she talked and talked about her problems, efforts, solutions, and goals. Anna was grateful for the support and help. She was focused exclusively on her own challenging situation of managing three children, an emotional divorce, increasing work responsibilities, and reestablishing her independence, and therefore, didn't think twice about the change in her session time. She assumed he gave all of his clients this extra attention.

Points to Ponder: *Mitchell had been in private practice for 20 years and therefore, had much experience in the practice of therapy with no reported history of inappropriate or unethical behavior. How could Mitchell have identified his stray from appropriate professional practice? What reactions to Anna did he have that should have been signs for him to monitor his behavior more closely? If Mitchell avoided or denied his emotions or feelings toward Anna, what behaviors might he have recognized as potentially problematic?*

Promoting Self-Awareness

Can you imagine yourself in any of the preceding situations? Depending on the amount of experience you have had as a therapist, the answer to the question is sure to vary. Whereas these scenarios each differ, there are common themes among them. These themes can be tied back to some of the core principles of cognitive-behavioral theory and practice.

First, therapists need to use their own feelings as cues to potential problematic situations. This is a key concept for self-awareness and professional problem solving.

Second, the link between thoughts, feelings, beliefs, and actions is clear both for the individual therapist, the individual client, and the interactions between them. The concept of Bandura's (1977) reciprocal determinism (the idea that a person affects his or her environment, which in turn, affects the person's thoughts, feelings, and behaviors) is illustrated in these examples. Because of the power differential of the therapeutic relationship, the therapist is responsible for being the authority and operating in a competent, nonboundary violating, professional manner.

Third, considering the earlier discussion of how personal problems, psychological distress or impairment, or burnout can impact therapists' judgment, personal and clinical decision making, self-awareness of stressors and their impact must be attended to at all times, so that global difficulties will be less likely to cause inappropriate behavior at an individual client level. Fourth, therapists must be aware of their ethical and legal obligations to their clients, the community, and the profession. If self-monitoring reveals that there is potential for ethical or illegal misconduct, therapists or students-in-training must be aware of their avenues for prevention of such behavior. These include consultation, supervision, self-care, and appropriate management of thoughts, feelings, and behaviors that will allow for best-practice behaviors toward clients, or appropriate termination and referral of clients if this cannot be achieved. Mitchell could have recognized his boundary slide when he was spending more and more time thinking about his client. He could have taken steps to address these thoughts by seeking consultation, beginning his own therapy, or self-monitoring his behaviors more consciously.

Overall, a problem-solving approach to self-awareness and clinical decision-making (Felgoise et al., 2002; A. M. Nezu & Nezu, 1989; A. M. Nezu et al., 1997) is advocated in monitoring thoughts, feelings, and actions related to professional practice and client care. Recognizing feelings as cues (such as Andy's feelings for his client), challenging your own thoughts and beliefs, and identifying behaviors that are adaptive or maladaptive in clinical situations and relationships are imperative (e.g., delaying termination or holding longer sessions). Identifying potential problems, goals, and relevant obstacles to those problems will be important for prevention and intervention, should it get to that point. Generating alternative solutions for handling potentially problematic situations, and making rational and systematic decisions about how to handle the situations based on the generated solutions is critical. Perhaps most importantly, implementing the solutions and monitoring the consequences of your behaviors, decisions, and solutions will be critical to the overall outcome of your professional conduct in the specific situations addressed. If the outcomes are unsatisfactory, or the alternatives are unlikely to reach the goals, troubleshooting and seeking professional help are part of all therapists' professional responsibility, as described earlier.

Self-Assessment of Burnout, Distress, and Daily Hassles

Given the popularity of burnout, distress, and daily hassles as topics in the public domain, self-assessments of these constructs are widely available. A simple

Internet search will yield many publicly available self-assessment tests that are free of charge and self-scoring. Alternatively, the checklists and questionnaires you learn about in your studies of clinical psychology are appropriate for self-assessment as well. The following three web sites can help you start this self-evaluation:

1. www.mindtools.com/pages/article/newTCS_08.htm. This link provides a burnout self-test and articles on related topics, such as stress management. Unless otherwise stated, James Manktelow authored many of the articles listed (August, 2003).
2. www.healthyplace.com/site/tests/psychological.asp. This link offers many psychological self-tests for education and screening.
3. Stamm, B. H., & Figley, C. R. (1996). Compassion Satisfaction and Fatigue Test. Available on the World Wide Web: www.isu.edu/~bhstamm /tests.htm.

Identifying and Confronting Inappropriate or Problematic Behaviors in Peer-Trainees or Colleagues

If we have established that identifying potentially problematic reactions to clients is important, yet preventing misconduct or inappropriate behavior can sometimes be difficult for professionals, how does this compare with doing the same for our colleagues or peers in the profession? If the preceding examples presented clearly identifiable targets for change or intervention, then shouldn't it be that easy to identify the problems in our colleagues or peers? We would argue, yes . . . and no. Yes, if information is provided in the same forthright manner, it should be easy to identify problematic situations for professionals who are knowledgeable and aware. However, the answer is often no because information is seldom so easily obtainable from trainees, either because supervisees are fearful of sharing information that could affect their evaluations, or lack of self-awareness prevents sharing pertinent information that would allow others to identify problematic situations. Audio- or videotapes for review would help, but trainees still would need to share the thoughts and feelings that guided the behaviors in question, and that is not always easy for students to do. Many professionals practice therapy independently and do not take advantage of or seek peer supervision, consultation, or client feedback. There would be few forums for other professionals to gain access to scenarios like the ones previously described unless therapists sought help in these situations. It is possible, however, that therapists could learn of the problematic behaviors through the clients themselves, should they seek out other therapy or assistance relating to such matters.

Now, imagine that Mina, Lola, Andy, and Mitchell have inadvertently shared the scenarios with you, either through consultation, casual conversation, or their supervision of you! However, they are unaware of the potential problems that could arise. How would you give them this feedback? What are some of the reasons that you might not give them this feedback, even if you thought it is warranted?

Why might Mina's, Lola's, Andy's, or Mitchell's supervisors, supervisees, or other peers or colleagues not confront them, despite the Ethics Code's (APA, 2002) explicit principle that explains professionals' responsibility to do so? Try to recall if you have ever had to give feedback to friends or family members about something they have said or done that was unacceptable or concerning to you? What skills were necessary for you to do so?

Confronting problematic behavior is seldom if ever an easy task. Providers of negative feedback must have acute communication skills, assertiveness skills, confidence in their own appraisal of situations but reservation about the limits of their perspective, and feelings of physical, emotional, and interpersonal safety to communicate such information. They must choose an appropriate context for offering feedback and approach the task with an attitude of tact and respect. Also, the perceived risks cannot outweigh the potential benefit or responsibility identified by the feedback provider. Supposing an individual had all the necessary strengths and skills listed, there are still obstacles. Many of these were reviewed earlier, which brings this chapter's discussion almost to a full circle: to the operational definitions of impairment and problematic behavior; few options for remediation or self-help specific to professional issues; somewhat vague ethical guidelines and principles; and potentially severe consequences for trainees or professionals if behaviors are determined to be significant. The effort or emotional conflict or discomfort felt by the observer of the inappropriate behavior may be consciously or unconsciously a deterrent for getting involved in such situations. Principles of social psychology such as bystander apathy and diffusion of responsibility may also come into play. Readers are encouraged to role-play or rehearse how they would address these issues with their peers, colleagues, or supervisors, should the situations ever arise.

When Reactions to Clients Lead to Inappropriate or Unethical Behavior

Unseasoned practitioners or trainees may think that it is unlikely they would find themselves in situations such as those described, where their judgments are clouded or their actions are faulty. Seasoned professionals might be able to identify with some of these experiences, or recall their vulnerability. They realize that no-one is error-proof and belief in the idea of invulnerability increases the risk of mistakes. In fact, anyone could put themselves at risk for engaging in inappropriate or unethical behavior, when in unfavorable circumstances. When self-care is poor, and burnout is high, it is likely that judgment, decision making, and boundaries are compromised. We challenge you to think about how you behave, think, and feel when you are burned out, or are neglecting self-care. Are your judgments clear? When you lack sleep, do you find yourself less inhibited or attentive? Pulling together the concepts of self-care, burnout, and risks for unethical behavior, we encourage you to think about how clinicians find themselves in situations like the ones we have described.

Personal therapist characteristics are known to be risk factors for troubled outcome. Koocher and Keith-Speigel (1998) published a book that we highly recommend: *Ethics in Psychology: Professional Standards and Cases* (second edition). In review of hundreds of case studies, ethics, law, decision making, standards and best practices, they illustrate the challenges professional psychologists (practitioners, scholars, educators, etc.) face in daily practice, and discuss ways to prevent inappropriate, unethical, and illegal conduct.

Koocher and Keith-Speigel (1998) discuss several categories of risk factors for inappropriate behavior or conduct either as a result of poor judgment, or as a result of poor self-monitoring or coping with reactions to clients. The likelihood that therapists or students will engage in role blending, crossing professional boundaries, and maintaining conflicts of interest is often increased by the behaviors and circumstances of "risky therapists," "risky career periods," "risky work settings," and "risky clients" (pp. 174–176). The research summarized by Koocher and Keith-Speigel is vast, but several highlights are important to the purpose of this chapter on self-care and prevention of negative consequences from impairment, personal problems, and incompetence.

Risky therapists are described as those who demonstrate poor boundaries (Koocher & Keith-Speigel, 1998) by actions that cross the expected limits for professional behavior. Such therapists are prone to excessive, unnecessary, and often inappropriate self-disclosure. Gift-giving and acceptance of gifts raise serious questions and concerns about clients' well-being and best interests, and whose needs (therapists' or clients') are being served. Therapists with poor boundaries, inexperience, and poor judgment are most likely to engage in gift-giving or gift-accepting practices when they are not in the clients' best interest, or when the therapist does not even know to evaluate the consequences of such actions.

Risky therapists may have personal problems themselves that lead them to seek "adoration, power, or social connection" (Koocher & Keith-Speigel, 1998, p. 174) through their professional work. Certain theoretical orientations might also be likely to draw persons with these risky characteristics into training. Or perhaps, practice within certain theoretical orientations is less well defined, and therefore allows for boundary violations (Koocher & Keith-Speigel). Further exploration of clinical judgment and boundary management is offered by Barnett (1998) or Zur (2007).

Risky career periods are explained by Koocher and Keith-Speigel (1998) as potentially occurring at any time. Misconduct or inappropriate management of thoughts, feelings, and behaviors toward clients is easily understandable, though not acceptable, during early training, especially if supervision or role-modeling was poor, or when students have had minimal experience handling complicated reactions and issues. The midcareer time frame is considered risky due to the increased likelihood that psychologists might experience more personal problems across the biopsychosocial domain during that time in their lifespan. Lastly, late-stage career professionals might be considered risky due to the potential for distance from the standards of the practice, and inflated beliefs about their own competence and judgment as a result of passage of time.

Risky work settings include those in which professionals are practicing psychology in isolation from other psychologists or mental health professionals (Koocher & Keith-Speigel, 1998). Home offices have also been considered a potential risk source or factor because of the automatic information known by the client about the therapist, and the possibly intimate and personal nature of such a setting (Koocher & Keith-Speigel). Nontraditional settings or those with multidisciplinary teams might also create less clear boundaries. Physicians and patients have different expectations of appropriate boundaries than do psychologists and patients or clients. Also, psychologists are more exposed to patients in vulnerable states, such as various levels of undress, fear, or consciousness due to medication or procedures conducted. Patients might attribute their survival or ability to cope with such circumstances entirely to therapists' participation in their care, as differentiated from those who were poking and prodding them for physical care.

Risky clients probably need less description than the other categories described. Clients who have poor boundaries, low self-esteem, neediness, high dependency, or experiences of abuse, victimization, or abandonment in their past or current circumstances might present opportunities for risky therapists or naive therapists to engage in misconduct, knowingly or not. Risky clients might look to the therapist as a replacement for lost persons in their lives, or for them to serve in roles they have not been able to fill outside the professional relationship (Koocher & Keith-Speigel, 1998).

Preventing Psychologists' Problems from Becoming Professional Problems: Identifying the Warning Signs

Koocher and Keith-Speigel (1998) discuss the fact that therapists can be caring, compassionate persons who experience a wide range of emotions in personal situations and in reaction to clients, and still these same individuals are ethical and professional in maintaining appropriate boundaries with consumers of their services and expertise. They note that the literature suggests that individuals who engage in inappropriate, unethical, or impaired practice either due to personal problems, incompetence, or other reasons, often lack insight about their judgment and actions and rationalize their behaviors as actions intended to be in the best interest of their clients (p. 197). Table 15.1 provides a list of warning signs and signals of boundary crossings that may result from extreme emotional, cognitive, or behavior reactions to clients. It is offered by Koocher and Keith-Speigel (1998), and encompasses works described by Epstein and Simon (1990, as cited by Koocher & Keith-Speigel, 1998, p. 198).

Crossing boundaries by engaging in sexual intimacies with clients is a significant problem that often seems so far out of the realm of possibility to students in training because the rationale for why this is not acceptable makes sense. Estimates of the frequency of such conduct are hard to guess or obtain due to the low report rate of such occurrences. However, even if estimates are as low as recent reports suggest (0.9% for male therapists, 0.2% for female therapists; Borys & Pope, 1989), psychologists are still violating the professional role by engaging in sexual intimacies with clients. Koocher and Keith-Speigel (1998) explain that many instances of sexual attraction will diminish and do not result in inappropriate conduct. However, for some, these feelings will escalate into unacceptable behavior. Table 15.2 describes 10 warning signs of sexual attraction toward clients (Koocher & Keith-Speigel, 1998, p. 203).

The warning signs and signals provided by Koocher and Keith-Speigel (1998) are helpful in differentiating potentially problematic thoughts, feelings, and behaviors from those that are typical and expected in therapy. Self-reflection

Table 15.1 **Warning Signs and Signals of Boundary Crossings That May Result from Extreme Emotional, Cognitive, or Behavior Reactions to Clients**

1. Actively seeking opportunities to be with a client outside the professional setting.

2. Anticipating with excitement, a certain client's visitation.

3. Expecting that a client should volunteer to do favors for you (e.g., get you a better deal from his business).

4. Viewing a client as in a position to advance your own position and fantasizing how that would play out.

5. Wishing that a client were not a client and, instead, in some other type of relationship with you (e.g., your best friend or business partner).

6. Disclosing considerable detail about your own life to a client and expecting interest or nurturing in return.

7. Trying to influence a client's hobbies, political views, or other personal choices that have no direct therapeutic relevance.

8. Allowing a client to take undue advantage without confrontation (e.g., missing many appointments).

9. Relying on a client's presence or praise to boost your self-esteem.

10. Giving in to a client's requests and perspectives on issues from fear that he or she will otherwise leave therapy.

11. Feeling entitled to most of the credit if a client improves, especially if marked achievement is attained while under your care.

12. Viewing clients as the central people in your life.

13. Greatly resisting terminating a client even though the indicators are clear.

14. Believing that you are the only person who can help a particular client.

15. Noticing that the pattern of interactions with a client is becoming increasingly irrelevant to the therapeutic goals.

Offered by Koocher and Keith-Speigel (1998); encompassing works described by Epstein and Simon (1990, as cited in Koocher & Keith-Speigel, 1998, p. 198).

and self-awareness are critical aspects of the self-monitoring process as well. As noted, therapists with personal problems and their own diagnosable mental illness or difficulties should pay extra attention to their vulnerabilities and behaviors. Balancing one's life between personal and professional roles and responsibilities and engaging in adaptive coping skills and stress management should help therapists maintain healthy lifestyles and appropriate boundaries. Therapists who ensure they have adequate social and emotional resources (professional or not), physical or stress outlets, opportunities for spiritual grounding or exploration (if interested), and opportunities for meaningful interpersonal and environmental experiences should have less need to seek comfort or personal affiliation through their clientele. For readers who identify themselves as lacking in one or more areas mentioned, self-help resources are provided for addressing stress, emotional reactions, and personality characteristics that might present challenges to working with others. Of course, persons need to identify

Table 15.2 **Warning Signs That a Clinician Is Sexually Attracted to a Client**

1. Thinking often about the client while not in session.

2. Having recurring sexual thoughts or fantasies about the client, in or out of session.

3. Dressing or grooming in an uncustomarily conscious fashion on the client's appointment day or looking forward to that client's sessions above all others.

4. Attempting to elicit information from the client to satisfy personal curiosity, as opposed to eliciting information that is required to achieve therapeutic goals.

5. Daydreaming about seeing the client socially as a "date."

6. Becoming mildy flirtatious or eliciting discussions of sexual materials during therapy when not therapeutically relevant.

7. Indulging in rescue fantasies or seeing yourself as the only person who can heal this person.

8. Believing that you could make up for all the past deficits, sadness, or disappointments in the client's life.

9. Becoming sexually aroused in the client's presence.

10. Wanting to touch the client.

Source: Ethics in Psychology: Professional Standards and Cases, second edition (p. 203), by G. P. Koocher and P. Keith-Spiegel, 1998, New York: Oxford University Press. Reprinted with permission.

when self-help materials are not sufficient and professional help should be sought.

Self-Help References

Appendix A lists self-help materials that authors reviewing such materials recommend highly; we have used some of these works in therapy with our clients. Norcross et al. (2000), provide thorough annotated bibliographies on over 15 mental health topics in the *Authoritative Guide to Self-Help Resources in Mental Health,* developed on the basis of five national survey studies conducted on over 2,500 psychologists who are members of either the Clinical Psychology or Counseling Psychology divisions of the American Psychological Association. O'Halloran and Linton (2000) provide annotated references to self-care resources for counselors who experience stress on the job. While their focus is on burnout and secondary traumatic stress from working with traumatized individuals, we selected references that seem to have broader application to psychologists working with a variety of persons.

The references appended to this chapter are by no means exhaustive, given that self-help books are published in extremely high volume—estimated at about 2,000 a year (G. M. Rosen, 1993). Readers are cautioned that self-help may be independently beneficial when burnout and distress have not led to impaired functioning, or problems are still within grasp of self-management. Otherwise, professional help may be warranted, and these resources may be best used as supplements. The discussion provided in this chapter and some of the self-assessment references will aid in self-reflection and self-evaluation to make this determination, if relevant.

Positive Psychology

To this point, this chapter has mirrored the historical emphasis in the field of clinical psychology, with the focus on problems, impairment, dysfunction, and weaknesses and the alleviation of such. Clinical psychology has traditionally looked at psychological health as the absence of maladies or concerns, and the goals of intervention have been to reduce negative traits, thoughts, feelings, behaviors, belief systems, and interpersonal and social relationships. Although many therapies also tout goals to increase positive thinking, feeling, and behaving; adaptive belief systems; and interpersonal relationships, they are usually secondary goals of the therapeutic process and seldom the reason clients seek therapy. In fact, the *Diagnostic and Statistical Manual of Mental Disorders* (*DSM-IV*) does not provide codes for positive change targets, nor do insurance companies pay for clinical psychologists to provide guidance in increasing adaptive behaviors and competencies. In the past 10 years, however, there has been a major movement toward *positive psychology* as a science examining happiness, well-being, human potential, and social strengths. From the research focused on positive psychology, investigators aim to reconstruct the approach to maximizing individual potential and well-being by focusing on building strengths and resiliency factors, rather than just minimizing disability and deficits. Clinical psychologists and other researchers have begun to reexamine concepts such as burnout (Maslach et al., 2001) from the vantage point of positive psychology research, and are learning more about job engagement and positive approaches to alleviating negative syndromes such as those addressed earlier. The discussion that follows provides only a cursory overview of key concepts in this field. Yet, the hope is that readers will be inspired to learn more about this field and the topic areas as a means for self-enhancement, self-care, and self-discovery.

Happiness and Subjective Well-Being

Happiness and subjective well-being refer to positive feelings and positive states. Understanding these states is at the core of positive psychology (Seligman, 2002). There is some debate in the field as to whether happiness should be defined by "the good life in terms of pleasure seeking and pain avoidance," also known as the *hedonic* tradition, or "the good life in terms of achieving one's full potential," called the *eudaimonic* tradition (Carr, 2004, p. 41). Seligman (2002) describes positive emotions as occurring in the past, present, and the future. Past positive emotions relating to happiness include "satisfaction, contentment, fulfillment, pride and serenity" (Carr, 2004, p. 2). Present happiness is said to include momentary pleasures and more enduring gratifications (Carr, 2004). Future happiness is associated with positive emotions such as optimism, hope, confidence, faith, and trust (Carr, 2004).

Pleasures, as described in Seligman's (2002) view of positive emotions, are derived through the senses and through positive experiences that result in positive emotions. Gratifications are dependent on engagement in activities that result in achieving flow through signature strengths (Carr, 2004). *Flow* and *signature* strengths are key concepts to positive psychology.

Flow

Mihaly Csikszentmihalyi coined the term flow, and defined it as "a particular kind of experience that is so engrossing and enjoyable that it becomes . . . worth doing for its own sake even though it may have no consequence outside itself. Creative activities, music, sports, games, and religious rituals are typical sources for this kind of experience" (Csikszentmihalyi, 1999, p. 824). However, flow experiences can occur during studying, reading, dancing, writing, driving, or doing anything that one intensely loves to do. Persons who are experiencing flow are said to lose their sense of time, be completely engrossed in the activity generating this state, and experience a sense of ecstasy or excitement that can almost seem too powerful or great . . . as if they are outside of themselves (Csikszentmihalyi, 1999). Flow is said to require skill, concentration, and perseverance, and is thought to lead to subjective well-being. Csikszentmihalyi (1999) suggests that people are not necessarily experiencing happiness while they are in flow experiences because they are not thinking about their feelings or emotions at that time. Rather, the positive feelings such as happiness may be the result of experiencing flow. Csikszentmihalyi (1999) states that "People are happy not because of what they do, but because of how they do it" (p. 826).

The take-home message from this discussion of flow and happiness is that trainees and psychologists need to find what makes them fully engaged and engrossed to the point that they have positive outlets and escapes, so to speak, from their ordinary stressors and hassles. Activities, whether work-related (writing or reading), personal, or social, that activate flow experiences and stimulate cognitive, spiritual, or physical channels may be those that help balance oneself in a meaningful way that could buffer against burnout, psychological distress, and eventual impairment, and increase enjoyment from participation in everyday work and personal experiences.

Strengths

In addition to engaging in flow, possessing human strengths such as courage, future-mindedness, optimism, interpersonal skill, faith, work ethic, hope, honesty, perseverance, and self-determination, has been discovered to provide buffers against mental illness and distress (Seligman & Csikszentmihalyi, 2000). Examining human strengths is thought to help make people stronger and more productive (Seligman & Csikszentmihalyi, 2000), and also helps them cope with life better. Examining individuals' strengths is another key focus of positive psychology, and is pertinent to the topic of self-care.

Signature strengths, are defined as strengths individuals have that are core attributes of themselves; whose use are cause for excitement; that promote rapid learning when used; that are desired to be used often with resulting feelings of positive emotions when they are used; and could be used in many situations (Seligman, 2002). Signature strengths are determined by self-assessment according to the Values in Action Classification System (C. Peterson & Seligman, 2001), which examines 24 possible strengths. Based on a review of Seligman's work, Carr (2004) suggests that signature strengths are important in romantic relationships, familial relationships, work settings, and leisure activities. Use of signature strengths is thought to be related to the experience of flow. Trainees and professionals may increase self-care and positive affectivity if they can identify their signature strengths, use them, and initiate experiences that will lead to self-efficacy, happiness, and satisfaction.

Other Key Concepts in Positive Psychology

Other personal characteristics are frequently considered in examination of positive psychology and the study of human strengths. Such topics include quality of life, expectations, the roles of emotional intelligence, giftedness, creativity and wisdom, positive motives and traits, positive self (self-esteem, self-efficacy, coping), and positive relationships (Carr, 2004). Although discussion of these detailed topics is beyond the scope of this chapter, much can be learned from delving into these topics. Yet, to remain focused on self-care, happiness, flow, and signature strengths were chosen as focal points for discussion.

Happiness: Who Experiences It and How Can You Acquire More of It?

A review of the empirical and theoretical literature suggests that positive affectivity, which results from positive experiences, pleasures, and gratifications, is "associated with greater job satisfaction and marital satisfaction and may be enhanced through regular physical activity, adequate sleep, regular socializing with close friends and striving for valued goals" (Carr, 2004, pp. 39–40). These conclusions suggest that trainees and professionals seeking a fuller and more positive personal and work life might benefit greatly from learning about positive psychology research outcomes and predictors of happiness for the population-at-large, and professionals, specifically. Furthermore, studies reveal that persons reporting high degrees of happiness are generally extraverted and optimistic, and have high self-esteem and internal locus of control. Carr (2004) summarizes the recommendations and conclusions drawn from empirical studies (Argyle, 2001; Buss, 2000; Diener, Suh, Lucas, & Smith, 1999; Lykken, 1999; Myers, 1992; Seligman, 2002) on happiness and positive emotions to suggest the following:

> *We can optimize our sense of well-being by taking some of the following courses of action. With respect to relationships, mate with someone similar, communicate kindly and clearly and forgive faults; maintain contact with extended family; maintain a few close friendships; co-operate with acquaintances; and engage in religious or spiritual practices. With respect to the environment, secure physical and financial safety and comfort for yourself and your family, . . . live in a geographically beautiful environment where there is fine weather and where there is pleas-*

ing music and art. With respect to physical well-being, maintain good health and engage in regular physical exercise. With respect to productivity, use skills that are intrinsically pleasing for tasks that are challenging; achieve success and approval at work that is interesting and challenging; and work toward a coherent set of goals. With respect to leisure, eat quality food in moderation; regularly rest, relax and take holidays in moderation; and engage in co-operative recreational activities with groups of friends. (pp. 40–41)

Although Carr's (2004) summary of the research findings and suggestions seems general and unencumbered by barriers, the recommendations make sense. Too often, we may overcomplicate our understanding of human behavior and the approaches we take to optimizing our lives. As such, Carr's synopsis is deemed relevant and valuable to the discussion of self-care. We recommend that trainees and professionals seek out the literature Carr draws on to explore areas that seem most pertinent or that could be used for introspective focus. Carr also reviews suggestions and advice to decrease negative affectivity, negative feelings, and dysfunctional thoughts, schemas, and beliefs. However, since much of clinical psychology focuses on these goals and approaches, they are not reiterated here.

A small survey of program and clinical training directors on the National Council of Schools and Programs of Professional Psychology listserve, conducted for this chapter on self-care, showed that many psychologists in leadership roles in Clinical PsyD programs are practicing what Carr suggests. Box 15.1 summarizes the responses. This is great news because if graduate training and program directors model good self-care behavior, the hope is that students will practice good self-care behavior as well.

Box 15.1

Responses by program and training directors, in order of frequency, to survey question, "What practices do you in engage in for self-care or care-for your colleagues?"

1. Exercise/physical fitness alone or in interactive sports
2. Connections to friends and family, those who make you laugh, stay close to good people
3. Cultural events—music, movies, concerts, plays, things that are thought provoking and emotionally satisfying
4. Hobbies—pleasure reading
5. Maintaining a religious connection, regular worship
6. Meditation, mindfulness, taking breaks
7. Clear boundaries on work (no nights/weekends), and balance at work; seeking supervision for different cases
8. Getting adequate sleep
9. Maintaining a good diet
10. Engaging in personal psychotherapy

Self-Assessment of Happiness, Strengths, Well-Being, Quality of Life and Emotions

Numerous scales are available to measure happiness, strengths, and psychological and subjective well-being, quality of life, and emotions. Carr (2004) provides useful reference lists of measures available for research and self-testing on all these variables. Among those that measure happiness are the following: "The Satisfaction with Life Scale" (Diener, Emmons, Larsen, & Griffin, 1985), "The Extended Satisfaction with Life Scale," (Alfonso, Allinson, Rader, & Gorman, 1996), and "The Depression-Happiness Scale" (Joseph & Lewis, 1998). The "Values in Action Inventory of Strengths" is a popular measure used to evaluate signature strengths as defined by Seligman and his colleagues (C. Peterson & Seligman, 2001), which also can be accessed through a public website (www.positivepsychology.org/viastrengthsinventory.htm).

Self-Help and Self-Exploration References on Positive Psychology

Appendix B provides additional resources to aid trainees and professionals in maximizing their positive well-being and minimizing possible precursors to distress, burnout, and impairment. The reference lists provided focus on positive psychology topics and are gleaned from the same resources as the previous lists.

Summary

Throughout this chapter, numerous suggestions have been made to increase psychologists'-in-training and professionals' awareness of burnout, impairment, personal reactions to clients, and professional and ethical issues relating to these topics. Trainees and professionals need to be mindful of setting clear boundaries with clients and other professionals. Maintaining career vitality and good self-care practices ought to also help minimize the likelihood of burning out. Social support and good mentorship and supervision serve as buffers to prevent personal problems from developing into professional problems and risky behaviors. Suggestions have been made as to how trainees and professionals can be more self-aware and self-reflective of thoughts, feelings, and behaviors that might be cause for concern when responsible for others' well-being, or for their own well-being.

Cognitive and behavioral strategies that have been discussed throughout this book are revisited in discussion of self-care. Self-monitoring through journaling, self-talk, and reflection of how one's behaviors impact others in personal and professional domains is advisable. Seeking peer consultation or professional supervision is critical to ongoing growth and development of professional skills, and prevention of boundary violations, ethical infractions, or misconduct. Supervision or consultation can and should be instrumental in reviewing thoughts, feelings, behaviors, and biases that could be working in favor of or against the care of clients. Use of video- or audiotapes, role-plays, on-site observation, and review of case materials can augment actual caseload discussion, and should be used when possible. Learning clinical decision making, and problem-solving skills as applied to personal and professional competence is strongly advised.

There are ways to gain mentoring and supervision outside one's own training program. Students and professionals can benefit greatly from observing professionals in practice and listening to clinical and ethical decision making by seasoned and responsible professionals they encounter in the field, at workshops or presentations or through readings. Maintaining affiliation with peer and advanced trainees and professionals through listserves and professional organizations offers means to discuss, problem-solve, and explore issues that are less likely to be found in textbooks or didactic exercises. Topics addressed in these forums might include how one manages personal stress and life demands, emotional reactions to clients, and grey areas of professional practice.

Trainees' and professionals' use of personal psychotherapy for growth, development, or intervention was also discussed in this chapter. For those who do not undertake therapy, but want to address personal matters less formally, a sampling of self-help assessments and intervention resources has been provided. This abbreviated list offers direction for those who have recognized the need for pursuit of self-care in response to reading this chapter, or as a handy guide for future reference. Many of the strategies and techniques discussed throughout this chapter have also been applied and defined in reference to caring for colleagues, addressing colleagues with perceived personal or professional difficulties, and attending to impairment and incompetence in the field, both in training and in the public professional domain. Lastly, the movement of positive psychology was introduced and key concepts highlighted to encourage developing professionals to initiate flow experiences, enhance their signature strengths, and maximize the positive aspects of their personal styles.

Trainees and professionals need to maintain a sense of balance in their lives that allows for healthy self-care and attention, and development of meaningful relationships and personal experiences that enhance positive feelings, develop a strong sense of personal and professional self, and keep themselves in tune to how external situations are impacting their behaviors, thoughts, and feelings, and vice versa:

www.mindtools.com/pages/article/newTCS08.htm

www.healthyplace.com/site/tests/psychological.asp

www.isu.edu/~bhstamm/tests.htm

www.positivepsychology.org/viastrengthsinventory.htm

Appendix A: Self-Help for Stress Management and Relaxation

Benson, H. (1985). *Beyond the relaxation response.* New York: Berkley.

Brock, B. (2003). Beyond burnout: When the counselor needs help. *Addiction Professional, 1*(4), 18–22.

Davis, M., Eshelman, E. R., & McKay, M. (1999). *The relaxation and stress reduction workbook* (4th ed.). Oakland, CA: New Harbringer.

Halberstam, J. (1994). *Everyday ethics: Inspired solutions to real-life dilemmas.* New York: Penguin.

Harris, R. (2001). *Twenty minute retreats: Revive your spirits in just minutes a day with simple self-led exercises.* New York: Pan Books.

Hittleman, R. (1995). *Richard Hittleman's 28 day yoga exercise.* New York: Random House Value.

Kabat-Zinn, J. (2005). *Wherever you go, there you are: Mindfulness meditation in everyday life.* New York: Hyperion.

Madders, J. (1997). *The stress and relaxation handbook: A practical guide to self-help techniques.* London: Vermilion.

McGoldrick, M. (1998). *You can go home again: Reconnecting with your family.* New York: Replica Books.

Self-Help for Managing Emotions and Reactions to Clients

Ellis, A., & Tafrate, R. C. (2000). *How to control your anger before it controls you.* New York: Citadel.

Kleinke, C. (2002). *Coping with life challenges* (2nd ed.). New York: Waveland Press.

McKay, G., & Dinkmeyer, D. (2002). *How you feel is up to you: The power of emotional choice.* San Luis Obispo, CA: Impact.

Nay, W. R. (2004). *Taking charge of anger: How to resolve conflict, sustain relationships, and express yourself without losing control.* New York: Guilford Press.

Weisinger, H. (1985). *Dr. Weisinger's anger work-out book.* New York: Quill.

Self-Help Books Addressing Major Life Events

Beck, A. (1989). *Love is never enough.* New York: Harper Paperbacks.

Frankl, V. (2006). *Man's search for meaning.* New York: Beacon Press.

James, J. W., & Cherry, F. (1988). *The grief recovery handbook: A step-by-step program for moving beyond loss.* New York: Harper & Row.

Larson, D. G. (1993). *The helper's journey: Working with people facing grief, loss, and life-threatening illness.* Champaing, IL: Research Press.

Trafford, A. (1982). *Crazy time: Surviving divorce.* New York: Harper & Row.

Warren, S., & Thompson, A. (1999). *Dumped: A survival guide for the woman who's been left by the man she loved.* New York: Avon.

Appendix B: Self-Help and Self-Exploration References on Positive Psychology

Baldwin, C. (1990). *Life's companion: Journal writing as a spiritual quest.* New York: Bantam Books.

Carr, A. (2004). *Positive psychology: The science of happiness and human strengths.* Hove, England: Brunner-Routledge.

Covey, S. (2004). *The 7 habits of highly effective people.* New York: Free Press.

Nezu, C. M., & Nezu, A. M. (2004). *Awakening self-esteem: Spiritual and psychological techniques to enhance your well-being.* New York: New Harbringer.

Prochaska, J. O., Norcross, J. C., & DiClimente, C. C. (1995). *Changing for good.* New York: Avon.

Seligman, M. (2006). *Learned optimism: How to change your mind and your life.* New York: Vintage Press.

Seligman, M. (2000). *Authentic happiness.* New York: Free Press.

References

Achenbach, T. M. (1991). *Manual for the Child Behavior Checklist/4–18 and 1991 profile.* Burlington: University of Vermont, Department of Psychiatry.

Ackerman, S. J., & Hilsenroth, M. J. (2001). A review of therapist characteristics and techniques negatively impacting the therapeutic alliance. *Psychotherapy, 38*(2), 171–185.

Adams, D. W. (1995). *Education for extinction: American Indians and the boarding school experience.* Lawrence: University Press of Kansas.

Adelman, H. S., & Taylor, L. (1986). Children's reluctance regarding treatment: Incompetence, resistance, or an appropriate response? *School Psychology Review, 15,* 91–99.

Alfonso, V., Allinson, D., Rader, D., & Gorman, B. (1996). The Extended Satisfaction with Life Scale: Development and psychometric properties. *Social Indicators Research, 38,* 275–301.

Allport, G. W. (1954). *The nature of prejudice.* Cambridge, MA: Addison-Wesley.

American Association for Marriage and Family Therapy. (2001). *AAMFT code of ethics.* Available from www.aamft.org.

American Association of Pastoral Counselors. (1994). *Code of ethics.* Available from www.aapc.org.

American Board of Professional Psychology. (n.d.). *About us.* Retrieved February 12, 2007, from www.abpp.org/aboutus.htm.

American Counseling Association. (2005). *Code of ethics.* Available from www.counseling.org.

American Educational Research Association, American Psychological Association, & National Council on Measurement in Education. (1985). *Standards for educational and psychological testing.* Washington, DC: American Psychological Association.

American Heritage dictionary (3rd ed.). (1994). New York: Houghton Mifflin.

American Psychiatric Association. (1952). *Diagnostic and statistical manual of mental disorders.* Washington, DC: Author.

American Psychiatric Association. (1968). *Diagnostic and statistical manual of mental disorders* (2nd ed.). Washington, DC: Author.

American Psychiatric Association. (1980). *Diagnostic and statistical manual of mental disorders* (3rd ed.). Washington, DC: Author.

American Psychiatric Association. (1983). *Diagnostic and statistical manual of mental disorders* (3rd ed., rev.). Washington, DC: Author.

American Psychiatric Association. (1994). *Diagnostic and statistical manual of mental disorders* (4th ed.). Washington, DC: Author.

American Psychiatric Association. (2000). *Diagnostic and statistical manual of mental disorders* (4th ed., text rev.). Washington, DC: Author.

American Psychological Association. (1997, August). *Archival description of clinical health psychology as a specialty in professional psychology* (Minutes of the council of representatives meeting). Washington, DC: Author.

American Psychological Association. (2000a). Guidelines for psychotherapy with lesbian, gay, and bisexual clients. *American Psychologist, 55,* 1440–1451.

American Psychological Association. (2000b). *Report on the task force on test user qualifications.* Washington, DC: Author.

American Psychological Association. (2002). Ethical principles of psychologists and code of conduct. *American Psychologist, 57*(12), 1060–1073.

American Psychological Association. (2003). Guidelines on multicultural education, training, research, practice, and organizational change for psychologists. *American Psychologist, 58,* 377–402.

American Psychological Association. (2004). Guidelines for psychological practice with older adults. *American Psychologist, 59*(4), 236–260.

American Psychological Association. (2006). *Disaster response network: A pro-bono service of the American Psychological Association and its members.* Retrieved February 12, 2007, from www.apa.org/practice/drn.html.

American Psychological Association. (n.d.-a). *Division 4: American psychology law society.* Retrieved February 12, 2007, from www.apa.org/about/division/div41.html.

American Psychological Association. (n.d.-b). *Division 12: Society of clinical psychology.* Retrieved February 12, 2007, from www.apa.org/about/division/div12.html.

American Psychological Association. (n.d.-c). *Division 22: Rehabilitation psychology.* Retrieved February 12, 2007, from www.apa.org/about/division/div22.html.

American Psychological Association, Division of Clinical Psychology. (1995). Training in and dissemination of empirically validated psychological treatments: Report and recommendations. *Clinical Psychologist, 48,* 3–27.

Anastasi, A. (1988). *Psychological testing* (6th ed.). New York: Macmillan.

Aponte, J., & Crouch, R. (2000). The changing ethnic profile of the United States in the twenty-first century. In J. Aponte & J. Wohl (Eds.), *Psychological intervention and cultural diversity* (pp. 1–17). Needham Heights, MA: Allyn & Bacon.

Aponte, J., & Wohl, J. (2000). *Psychological intervention and cultural diversity* (2nd ed.). Needham Heights, MA: Allyn & Bacon.

Argyle, M. (2001). *The psychology of happiness* (2nd ed.). London: Routledge.

Atkinson, D. R., & Hackett, G. (1995). *Counseling diverse populations* (2nd ed.). Boston: McGraw-Hill.

Atkinson, D. R., Morten, G., & Sue, D. W. (1998). *Counseling American minorities* (5th ed.). New York: McGraw-Hill.

Azar, S. T. (2000). Preventing burnout in professionals and paraprofessionals who work with child abuse and neglect cases: A cognitive behavioral approach to supervision. *Psychotherapy in Practice, 56*(5), 643–663.

Bakker, A. B., Schaufeli, W. B., Demerouti, E., Janssen, P. M. P., Van der Hulst, R., & Brouwer, J. (2000). Using equity theory to examine the difference between burnout and depression. *Anxiety Stress Coping, 13*, 247–268.

Bandura, A. (1977). *Social learning theory*. Englewood Cliffs, NJ: Prentice Hall.

Bardos, A. N. (2001). General Ability Measure for Adults (GAMA). In W. I. Dorfman & M. Hersen (Eds.), *Understanding psychological assessment* (pp. 43–58). New York: Kluwer Academic/Plenum Press.

Bardos, A. N., & Powell, S. (2001). Human figure drawings and the draw-a-person: Screening procedures for emotional disturbance. In W. I. Dorfman & M. Hersen (Eds.), *Understanding psychological assessment* (pp. 275–294). New York: Kluwer Academic/Plenum Press.

Barnett, J. E. (1998). Should psychotherapists self-disclose? Clinical and ethical considerations. In L. Vandecreek, S. Knapp, & T. Jackson (Eds.), *Innovations in clinical practice: Vol. 16. A source book* (pp. 419–428). Sarasota, FL: Professional Resource Press.

Barnett, J. E., & Hillard, D. (2001). Psychologist distress and impairment: The availability, nature, and use of colleague assistance programs for psychologists. *Professional Psychology: Research and Practice, 32*(2), 205–210.

Barr, W., & Cole, M. (2007). *Division 40: Clinical neuropsychology*. Retrieved February 12, 2007, from www.div40.org.

Beauchamp, T., & Childress, J. (2001). *Principles of biomedical ethics* (5th ed.). New York: Oxford University Press.

Beck, A. T., Epstein, N., Brown, G., & Steer, R. A. (1988). An inventory for measuring clinical anxiety: Psychometric properties. *Journal of Consulting and Clinical Psychology, 56*, 893–897.

Beck, A. T., Freeman, A., Davis, D., & Associates. (2004). *Cognitive therapy of personality disorders* (2nd ed.). New York: Guilford Press.

Beck, A. T., Rush, J., Shaw, B., & Emery, G. (1979). *Cognitive therapy of depression*. New York: Guilford Press.

Beck, A. T., Steer, R. A., & Brown, G. K. (1996). *Manual for Beck Depression Inventory: Vol. 2 (BDI-II)*. San Antonio, TX: Psychology Corporation.

Beck, J. (1995). *Cognitive therapy: Basics and beyond*. New York: Guilford Press.

Belar, C. D., & Deardorff, W. W. (1995). *Clinical health psychology in medical settings: A practitioner's guidebook*. Washington, DC: American Psychiatric Association.

Bernal, G., Bonilla, J., & Bellido, C. (1995). Ecological validity and cultural sensitivity for outcome research: Issues for the cultural adaptation and development of psychosocial treatments with Hispanics. *Journal of Abnormal Child Psychology, 23*(1), 67–82.

Bernstein, B. E., & Hartsell, T. L. (2000). *The portable ethicist for mental health professionals: An A-Z guide to responsible practice*. New York: Wiley.

Bernstein, D., & Borkovec, T. (1973). *Progressive relaxation training: A manual for the helping professions*. Champaign, IL: Research Press.

Berry, J. W. (1995). Psychology of acculturation. In N. R. Goldberger & J. B Veroff (Eds.), *The culture and psychology reader* (pp. 457–488). New York: New York University Press.

Berry, J. W., & Sam, D. L. (1997). Acculturation and adaptation. In J. W. Berry, M. H. Segall, & C. Kagitcibasi (Eds.), *Handbook of cross-cultural psychology* (pp. 291–326). Needham Heights, MA: Allyn & Bacon.

Beutler, L. E., & Clarkin, J. F. (1990). *Systematic treatment selection: Toward targeted therapeutic interventions*. Champaign, IL: Research Press.

Beutler, L. E., Machado, P. M., & Alstetter Neufeldt, S. A. (1994). Therapist variables. In S. L. Garfield & A. E. Bergin (Eds.), *Handbook of psychotherapy and behavior change* (4th ed., pp. 229–269). New York: Wiley.

Bickman, L., Rosof-Williams, J., Salzer, M. S., Summerfelt, W. T., Noser, K., Wilson, S. J., et al. (2000). What information do clinicians value for monitoring adolescent client progress and outcomes? *Professional Psychology: Research and Practice, 31*, 70–74.

Biernat, M. (2003). Toward a broader view of social stereotyping. *American Psychologist, 58*, 1019–1027.

Bordin, E. S. (1979). The generalizability of the psychoanalytic concept of the working alliance. *Psychotherapy: Theory, Research, and Practice, 16,* 252–260.

Borys, D., & Pope, K. S. (1989). Dual relationships between therapist and client: A national study of psychologists, psychiatry, and social workers. *Professional Psychology: Research and Practice, 20,* 283–293.

Bowers, L. (2000). *The social nature of mental illness.* New York: Routledge.

Boyd-Franklin, N. (2003). *Black families in therapy: Understanding the African American experience* (2nd ed.). New York: Guilford Press.

Brewer, M. (1991). The social self: On being the same and different at the same time. *Personality and Social Psychology Bulletin, 17,* 475–482.

Brewer, M., & Brown, R. J. (1998). Intergroup relations. In D. T. Gilbert & S. T. Fiske (Eds.), *The handbook of social psychology* (4th ed., Vol. 2, pp. 554–594). New York: McGraw-Hill.

Brofenbrenner, U. (1994). Ecological models of human development. In T. Husen & T. N. Postlewaite (Eds.), *International encyclopedia of education* (2nd ed., Vol. 3). Oxford: Pergamon Press/Elsevier Science.

Brown, N. C., Prashantham, B. J., & Abbott, M. (2003). Personality, social support, and burnout among human service professionals in India. *Journal of Community and Applied Social Psychology, 13,* 320–324.

Brownell, K. D., Marlatt, G. A., Lichtenstein, E., & Wilson, G. T. (1986). Understanding and preventing relapse. *American Psychologist, 41,* 765–782.

Brugha, T. S. (Ed.). (1995). *Social support and psychiatric disorders.* New York: Cambridge University Press.

Burns, D. (1989). *The feeling good handbook: Using the new mood therapy in everyday life.* New York: Morrow.

Buss, D. (2000). The evolution of happiness. *American Psychologist, 55,* 15–23.

Campbell, R. J. (2003). *Campbell's Psychiatric dictionary (8th ed).* New York: Oxford University Press.

Cardemil, E. V., & Battle, C. L. (2003). Guess who's coming to therapy? Getting comfortable with conversations about race and ethnicity in psychotherapy. *Professional Psychology: Research and Practice, 34,* 278–286.

Carkhuff, R. R. (2000). *The art of helping in the 21st century* (8th ed.). Amherst, MA: Human Resource Development Press.

Carr, A. (2004). *Positive psychology: The science of happiness and human strengths.* Hove, England: Brunner-Routledge.

Caspar, F. (1997). Plan analysis. In T. D. Eels (Ed.), *Handbook of psychotherapy case formulation* (pp. 260–288). New York: Guilford Press.

Caspar, F., Rothenfluh, T., & Segal, Z. V. (1992). The appeal of connectionism for clinical psychology. *Clinical Psychology Review, 12,* 719–762.

Castonguay, L. G., Goldfried, M. R., Wiser, S., Raue, P. J., & Hayes, A. M. (1996). Predicting the effect of cognitive therapy for depression: A study of unique and common factors. *Journal of Consulting and Clinical Psychology, 64*(3), 497–504.

Cautela, J. R., Cautela, J., & Esonis, S. (1983). *Forms for behavior analysis with children.* Champaign, IL: Research Press.

Chambless, D. L., Baker, M., Baucom, D., Beutler, L., Calhoun, K., Crits-Christoph, P., et al. (1998). Update on empirically validated therapies, Vol. 2. *Clinical Psychologist, 51*(1), 3–16.

Chambless, D. L., & Hollon, S. D. (1998). Defining empirically supported therapies. *Journal of Consulting and Clinical Psychology, 64,* 497–504.

Chaplin, J. P. (1985). *Dictionary of psychology* (2nd ed.). New York: Dell.

Cockersham, W. C. (1999). *Sociology of mental disorders* (5th ed.). Upper Saddle River, NJ: Prentice Hall.

Collins, S., & Long, A. (2003). Working with the psychological effects of trauma: Consequences for mental health-care workers—A literature review. *Journal of Psychiatric and Mental Health Nursing, 10,* 417–424.

Cone, J. D. (1995). Assessment practice standards. In S. C. Hayes, V. M. Follette, R. M. Dawes, & K. E. Grady (Eds.), *Scientific standards of psychological practice: Issues and recommendations* (pp. 201–224). Reno, NV: Context Press.

Cone, J. D. (1998). Psychometric considerations: Concepts, contents, and methods. In A. S. Bellack & M. Hersen (Eds.), *Behavioral assessment: A practical handbook* (4th ed., pp. 22–46). Boston: Allyn & Bacon.

Conn, S. R., & Rieke, M. L. (1994). *The 16PF technical manual* (5th ed.). Champaign, IL: Institute for Personality and Ability Testing.

Cormier, W. H., & Cormier, L. S. (1991). *Interviewing strategies for helpers.* Pacific Grove, CA: Brooks/Cole.

Crocker, J., Major, B., & Steele, C. (1998). Social stigma. In D. T. Gilbert & S. T. Fiske (Eds.), *The handbook of social psychology* (4th ed., Vol. 2, pp. 504–553). New York: McGraw-Hill.

Crowther, M. R., & Zeiss, A. M. (2003). Aging and mental health. In J. S. Mio & G. Y. Iwamasa (Eds.), *Culturally diverse mental health: The challenge of research and resistance* (pp. 309–322). New York: Brunner-Routledge.

Csikszentmihalyi, M. (1999). If we are so rich, why aren't we happy? *American Psychologist, 54*(10), 821–827.

Davis, D. (2008). *Terminating therapy: A professional guide for ending on a positive note.* Hoboken, NJ: Wiley.

Davis, D., & Hollon, S. (1999). Reframing resistance and noncompliance in cognitive therapy. *Journal of Psychotherapy Integration, 9*(1), 33–55.

Derogatis, L. R. (1983). *SCL-90: Administration, scoring and procedures manual for the revised version.* Baltimore: Clinical Psychometric Research.

Diener, E., Emmons, R., Larsen, R., & Griffin, S. (1985). The Satisfaction with Life Scale. *Journal of Personality Assessment, 49,* 71–75.

Diener, E., Suh, E., Lucas, R., & Smith, H. (1999). Subjective well-being: Three decades of progress. *Psychological Bulletin, 125,* 273–302.

Dryden, W. (1986). Eclectic psychotherapies: A critique of leading approaches. In J. C. Norcross (Ed.), *Handbook of eclectic psychotherapy.* New York: Brunner/Mazel.

Dubin, W. R., & Fink, P. J. (1992). Effects of stigma on psychiatric treatment. In P. J. Fink & A. S. Tasman (Eds.). *Stigma and mental illness* (pp. 1–10). Washington, DC: American Psychiatric Publishing.

Duckworth, J. C., & Anderson, W. P. (1995). *MMPI and MMPI-2 interpretation manual for counselors and clinicians* (2nd ed.). Bristol, PA: Taylor & Francis.

D'Zurilla, T. J., & Nezu, A. M. (1982). Social problem solving in adults. In P. C. Kendall (Ed.), *Advances in cognitive behavioral research and therapy* (Vol. 1, pp. 202–274). New York: Academic Press.

D'Zurilla, T. J., & Nezu, A. M. (1999). *Problem solving therapy: A social competence approach to clinical intervention* (2nd ed.). New York: Springer.

Edwards, D. J. A., Dattilio, F. M., & Bromley, D. B. (2004). Developing evidence-based practice: The role of case-based research. *Professional Psychology: Research and Practice, 35*(6), 589–597.

Eels, T. D. (Ed.). (1997). *Handbook of psychotherapy case formulation.* New York: Guilford Press.

Egan, G. (1998). *The skilled helper: A problem-management approach to helping others.* Pacific Grove, CA: Brooks/Cole.

Elinson, L., Houck, P., Marcus, S. C., & Pincus, H. A. (2004). Depression and the ability to work. *Psychiatric Services, 55,* 29–34.

Ellis, A. (1962). *Reason and emotion in psychotherapy.* New York: Lyle Stuart.

Ellis, A. (1985). *Overcoming resistance: Rational-emotive therapy with difficult clients.* New York: Springer.

Engel, G. L. (1977). The need for a new medical model: A challenge for biomedicine. *Science, 196,* 129–136.

Erickson, C., & Al-Timimi, N. (2001). Providing mental health services to Arab Americans: Recommendations and considerations. *Cultural Diversity and Ethnic Minority Psychology, 7,* 308–327.

Exner, J. E. (1993a). *The Rorschach: A comprehensive system: Vol. 1. Basic foundations* (3rd ed.). New York: Wiley.

Exner, J. E. (1993b). *The Rorschach: A comprehensive system: Vol. 2. Interpretation* (3rd ed.). New York: Wiley.

Felgoise, S. H., Nezu, C. M., & Nezu, A. M. (2002). Problem-solving therapy for treatment of anxiety: The case of Sandra. In R. A. DiTomasso & E. Gosch (Eds.), *Comparative treatments of anxiety disorders* (pp. 73–109). New York: Springer.

Fine, R. (1979). *History of psychoanalysis.* New York: Continuum.

Finlay, K. A., & Stephan, W. G. (2000). Improving intergroup relations: The effects of empathy on racial attitudes. *Journal of Applied Social Psychology, 30,* 1720–1737.

First, M. B., Gibbon, M., Spitzer, R. L., Williams, J. B., & Benjamin, L. (1997). *Structured Clinical Interview for DSM-IV Axis I disorders (SCID-I), clinical version.* Washington, DC: American Psychiatric Press.

First, M. B., Spitzer, R. L., Gibbon, M., & Williams, J. B. W. (1997). *Structured Clinical Interview for DSM-IV Personality Disorders (SCID-II).* Washington, DC: American Psychiatric Press.

Fisher, C. B. (2003). *Decoding the ethics code: A practical guide for psychologists.* Thousand Oaks, CA: Sage.

Fiske, S. T. (1998). Stereotyping, prejudice, and discrimination. In D. T. Gilbert & S. T. Fiske (Eds.), *The handbook of social psychology* (4th ed., Vol., 2, pp. 357–411). New York: McGraw-Hill.

Fitchett, G., Burton, L., & Sivan, A. (1997). The religious needs and resources of psychiatric inpatients. *Journal of Nervous and Mental Disease, 185*(5), 320–326.

Floyd, M., Myszka, M. T., & Orr, P. (1998). Licensed psychologists' knowledge and utilization of a state association colleague assistance committee. *Professional Psychology: Research and Practice, 29*(6), 594–598.

Foa, E. B., & Kozak, M. J. (1997). *Mastery of obsessive-compulsive disorder: Client workbook.* Albany, NY: Graywind.

Follette, W. C. (1996). Introduction to the special section on the development of theoretically coherent alternatives to the DSM system. *Journal of Consulting and Clinical Psychology, 64*(6), 1117–1119.

Follette, W. C. (1997). A behavior analytic conceptualization of personality disorders: A reponse to Clark, Livesley, and Morey. *Journal of Personality Disorders, 11*(3), 232–241.

Follette, W. C., & Hayes, S. C. (1992). Behavioral assessment in the DSM era. *Behavioral Assessment, 14*(3/4), 293–295.

Forrest, L., Elman, N., Gizara, S., & Vacha-Haase, T. (1999). Trainee impairment: A review of identification, remediation, dismissal, and legal issues. *Counseling Psychologist, 27*(5), 627–686.

Frank, J. D., & Frank, J. B. (1991). *Persuasion and healing: A comparative study of psychotherapy* (3rd ed.). Baltimore: Johns Hopkins University Press.

Franklin, M. D., Schlundt, D. G., & Wallston, K. A. (in press). Development and validation of a religious health fatalism measure for the African-American faith community. *Journal of Health Psychology.*

Fredrickson, B. L. (2001). The role of positive emotions in positive psychology: The broaden-and-build theory of positive emotions. *American Psychologist, 56*(3), 218–226.

Freeman, A., & Dolan, M. (2001). Revisiting Prochaska and DiClemente's stages of change theory: An expansion and specification to aid in treatment planning and outcome evaluation. *Cognitive and Behavioral Practice, 8,* 224–234.

Freeman, A., & Leaf, R. C. (1989). Cognitive therapy applied to personality disorders. In A. Freeman, K. M. Simon, L. F. Beutler, & H. Arkowitz (Eds.), *Comprehensive handbook of cognitive therapy* (pp. 403–433). New York: Plenum Press.

Freeman, A., & McCloskey, R. D. (2004). Impediments to effective therapy. In R. Leahy (Ed.), *Roadblocks in cognitive behavior therapy: Transforming challenges into opportunities for change* (pp. 24–48). New York: Guilford Press.

Fulero, S. M. (1988). Tarasoff: 10 years later. *Professional Psychology: Research and Practice, 19*(2), 184–190.

Gaddy, C. D., Charlot-Swilley, D., Nelson, P. D., & Reich, J. N. (1995). Selected outcomes of accredited programs. *Professional Psychology: Research and Practice, 26,* 507–513.

Gaertner, S. L., & Dovidio, J. F. (2000). *Reducing intergroup bias: The common ingroup identity model.* Philadelphia: Brunner/Mazel.

Galinsky, A. D., & Moskowitz, G. B. (2000). Perspective-taking: Decreasing stereotype expression, stereotype accessibility, and in-group favoritism. *Journal of Personality and Social Psychology, 78,* 708–724.

Garfield, S. L. (1994). Research on client variables in psychotherapy. In A. E. Bergin & S. L. Garfield (Eds.), *Handbook of psychotherapy and behavior change* (4th ed., pp. 190–228). New York: Wiley.

George, L. K. (1999, October). *Multidimensional measurement of religiousness/spirituality for use in health research: A report of the Fetzer Institute/National Institute on Aging Working Group.* Kalamazoo, MI: John E. Fetzer Institute.

Gerber, K. E., & Nehemkis, A. M. (Eds.). (1986). *Compliance: The dilemma of the chronically ill.* New York: Springer.

Gilroy, P. J., Carroll, L., & Murra, J. (2002). A preliminary survey of counseling psychologists' personal experiences with depression and treatment. *Professional Psychology: Research and Practice, 33*(4), 402–407.

Gizara, S. S., & Forrest, L. (2004). Supervisors' experiences of trainee impairment and incompetence at APA-Accredited internship sites. *Professional Psychology: Research and Practice, 35*(2), 131–140.

Golden, B. A., & Felgoise, S. H. (2005). Clinical health psychology. In A. Freeman, S. H. Felgoise, A. M. Nezu, C. M. Nezu, & M. A. Reineke (Eds.), *Encyclopedia of cognitive behavior therapy* (pp. 114–117). New York: Springer.

Greenberg, J., Solomon, S., Pyszczynski, T., Rosenblatt, A., Burling, J., Lyon, D., et al. (1992). Why do people need self-esteem? Converging evidence that self-esteem serves an anxiety-buffering function. *Journal of Personality and Social Psychology, 63,* 913–922.

Greenberg, L. S., Rice, L. N., & Elliott, R. (1993). *Facilitating emotional change: The moment-by-moment process.* New York: Guilford Press.

Greenberger, D., & Padesky, C. (1995). *Mind over mood: Change how you feel by changing the way you think.* New York: Guilford Press.

Greenwald, A. G., & Banaji, M. R. (1995). Implicit social cognition: Attitudes, self-esteem, and stereotypes. *Psychological Review, 102,* 4–27.

Groth-Marnat, G. (1990). *Handbook of psychological assessment* (2nd ed.). New York: Wiley.

Guy, J. D., Poelstra, P. L., & Stark, M. J. (1989). Personal distress and therapeutic effectiveness: National survey of psychologists practicing psychotherapy. *Professional Psychology: Research and Practice, 20,* 48–50.

Hafen, B. Q., Karren, K. J., Frandsen, K. J., & Smith, N. L. (1996). *Mind/body: The effects of attitudes, emotions, and relationships.* Boston: Allyn & Bacon.

Hamilton, M. (1960). Hamilton Rating Scale for depression. *Journal of Neurology, Neurosurgery, and Psychiatry, 23,* 56–61.

Handelsman, M. M., Gottlieb, M. C., & Knapp, S. (2005). Training ethical psychologists: An acculturation model. *Professional Psychology: Research and Practice, 36*(1), 59–65.

Hanh, T. N. (1987). *The miracle of mindfulness.* Boston: Beacon Press.

Hansen, N., Pepitone-Arreola-Rockwell, F., & Greene, A. (2000). Multicultural competence: Criteria and case examples. *Professional Psychology: Research and Practice, 31,* 652–660.

Hatfield, D. R., & Ogles, B. M. (2004). The use of outcome measures by psychologists in clinical practice. *Professional Psychology: Research and Practice, 35*(5), 485–491.

Hayes, S. C., & Follette, W. C. (1993). The challenge faced by behavioral assessment. *European Journal of Psychological Assessment, 9,* 182–188.

Hayes, S. C., Strosahl, K., & Wilson, K. (1999). *Acceptance and commitment therapy: An experiential approach to behavior change.* New York: Guilford Press.

Haynes, S. N. (1992). *Models of causality in psychopathology: Toward synthetic, dynamic and nonlinear models of causality in psychopathology.* Boston: Allyn & Bacon.

Haynes, S. N. (1998). The changing nature of behavioral assessment. In A. S. Bellack & M. Hersen (Eds.), *Behavioral assessment: A practical handbook* (4th ed., pp. 1–21). Boston: Allyn & Bacon.

Haynes, S. N., & O'Brien, W. H. (2000). *Principles and practice of behavioral assessment.* New York: Kluwer.

Hays, P. (2001). *Addressing cultural complexities in practice.* Washington, DC: American Psychological Association.

Helbok, C., Marinelli, R., & Walls, R. (2006). National survey of ethical practices across rural and urban communities. *Professional Psychology: Research and Practice, 37*(1), 36–44.

Helms, J. E. (1990). *Black and White racial identity: Theory, research, and practice.* Westport, CT: Greenwood Press.

Helms, J. E., & Cook, D. A. (1999). *Using race and culture in counseling and psychotherapy: Theory and process.* Boston: Allyn & Bacon.

Hergenhahn, B. R. (1992). *An introduction to the history of psychology* (2nd ed.). Belmont, CA: Wadsworth.

Hershey, J. M., Kopplin, D. A., & Cornell, J. E. (1991). Doctors of psychology: Their career experiences and attitudes toward degree and training. *Professional Psychology: Research and Practice, 22,* 351–356.

Hewstone, M., Rubin, M., & Willis, H. (2002). Intergroup bias. *Annual Review of Psychology, 53,* 575–604.

Higgins, E. T., & King, G. (1981). Accessibility of social constructs: Information-processing consequences of individual and contextual variability.

In N. Cantor & J. F. Kihlstrom (Eds.), *Personality, cognition and social interaction* (pp. 69–121). Hillsdale, NJ: Erlbaum.

Holtzworth-Munroe, A., Jacobson, N., DeKlyen, M., & Whisman, M. (1989). Relationship between behavioral marital therapy outcome and process variables. *Journal of Consulting and Clinical Psychology, 57,* 658–662.

Holzman, L. A., Searight, H. R., & Hughes, H. M. (1996). Clinical psychology graduate students and personal psychotherapy: Results of an exploratory survey. *Professional Psychology: Research and Practice, 27*(1), 98–101.

Hornsey, M. J., & Hogg, M. A. (2000). Assimilation and diversity: An integrative model of subgroup relations. *Personality and Social Psychology Review, 4,* 143–156.

Horton, A. M., Jr. (1979). Behavioral neuropsychology: Rationale and presence. *Clinical Neuropsychology, 1,* 20–23.

Horvath, A. O., & Greenberg, L. S. (1994). *The working alliance: Theory, research, and practice.* New York: Wiley.

Horvath, A. O., & Symonds, B. D. (1991). Relation between working alliance and outcome in psychotherapy: A meta-analysis. *Journal of Counseling Psychology, 38,* 139–149.

Horvitz, A. V., & Scheid, T. L. (Eds.). (1999). *A handbook for the study of mental health: Society, contexts, themes, and systems.* New York: Cambridge University Press.

Idler, E. (1987). Religious involvement and the health of the elderly: Some hypotheses and an initial test. *Social Forces, 66*(1), 226–238.

Idler, E. (1999, October). *Organizational religiousness: Multidimensional measurement of religiousness/spirituality for use in health research—A report of the Fetzer Institute/National Institute on Aging Working Group.* Kalamazoo, MI: John E. Fetzer Institute.

Iwamasa, G. (1996). On being an ethnic minority cognitive behavioral therapist. *Cognitive and Behavioral Practice, 3,* 235–254.

John E. Fetzer Institute. (1999, October). *Multidimensional measurement of religiousness/spirituality for use in health research: A report of the Fetzer Institute/National Institute on Aging Working Group.* Kalamazoo, MI: Author.

Johnston, J. M., & Pennypacker, H. S. (1993). *Strategies and tactics of behavioral research* (2nd ed.). Hillsdale, NJ: Erlbaum.

Joseph, S., & Lewis, C. (1998). The Depression-Happiness Scale: Reliability and validity of a bipolar self-report scale. *Journal of Clinical Psychology, 54,* 537–544.

Kamphaus, R. W., & Frick, P. J. (1996). *Clinical assessment of child and adolescent personality and behavior.* Boston: Allyn & Bacon.

Kanfer, F. H., & Schefft, B. K. (1988). *Guiding the process of therapeutic change.* Champaign, IL: Research Press.

Kaschak, E. (1992). *Engendered lives.* New York: Basic Books.

Kassinove, H., & Tafrate, R. C. (2002). *Anger management: The complete treatment guidebook for practitioners.* Atascadero, CA: Impact.

Kazdin, A. E. (2003). *Research design in clinical psychology* (4th ed.). Boston: Allyn & Bacon.

Kazdin, A. E., & Kagan, J. (1994). Models of dysfunction in developmental psychopathology. *Clinical Psychology: Science and Practice, 1,* 35–52.

Keijers, G. P., Schaap, C. P., & Hoogduin, C. A. (2000). The impact of interpersonal patient and therapist behavior on outcome in cognitive-behavior therapy. *Behavior Modification, 24,* 264–297.

Kleinke, C. L. (1994). *Common principles of psychotherapy.* Pacific Grove, CA: Brooks/Cole.

Koerner, K., & Linehan, M. M. (1997). Case formulation in dialectical behavior therapy for borderline personality disorder. In T. D. Eels (Ed.), *Handbook of psychotherapy case formulation* (pp. 340–367). New York: Guilford Press.

Koocher, G. P., & Keith-Spiegel, P. (1998). *Ethics in psychology: Professional standards and cases* (2nd ed.). New York: Oxford University Press.

Kozak, M. J., & Foa, E. B. (1997). *Mastery of obsessive-compulsive disorder: A cognitive-behavioral approach—Therapist guide.* Albany, NY: Graywind.

Kramer, R. M. (1999). Trust and distrust in organizations: Emerging perspectives, enduring questions. *Annual Review of Psychology, 50,* 569–598.

Kramer, S. A. (1986). The termination process in open-ended psychotherapy: Guidelines for clinical practice. *Psychotherapy: Theory, Research and Practice, 23*(4), 526–531.

Kring, A. M., Davison, G. C., Neale, J. M., & Johnson, S. L., (2006). *Abnormal Psychology.* New York: John Wiley & Sons.

Kunda, Z., & Sinclair, L. (1999). Motivated reasoning with stereotypes: Activation, application, and inhibition. *Psychological Inquiry, 10,* 12–22.

Kunda, Z., & Thagard, P. (1996). Forming impressions from stereotypes, traits, and behaviors: A parallel-constraint-satisfaction theory. *Psychological Review, 103,* 284–308.

Kutz, S. L. (1986). Defining "impaired psychologist." *American Psychologist, 41,* 220.

Lah, M. I. (2001). Sentence Completion Test. In W. I. Dorfman & M. Hersen (Eds.), *Understanding psychological assessment* (pp. 135–143). New York: Kluwer Academic/Plenum Press.

Lamb, D. H., Presser, N. R., Pfost, K. S., Baum, M. C., Jackson, V. R., & Jarvis, P. A. (1987). Confronting professional impairment during internship: Identification, due process, and remediation. *Professional Psychology: Research and Practice, 18,* 597–603.

Lambert, M. J. (1986). Some implications of psychotherapy outcome research for eclectic psychotherapy. *Journal of Integrative and Eclectic Psychotherapy, 5*(1), 16–45.

Lambert, M. J., & Barley, D. E. (2002). Research summary on the therapeutic relationship and psychotherapy outcome. In J. C. Norcross (Ed.), *Psychotherapy relationships that work* (pp. 17–32). New York: Oxford University Press.

LaRoche, M. J., & Maxie, A. (2003). Ten considerations in addressing cultural differences in psychotherapy. *Professional Psychology: Research and Practice, 34,* 180–186.

Layden, M. A., Newman, C. F., Freeman, A., & Byers-Morse, S. (1993). *Cognitive therapy of borderline personality disorder.* Boston: Allyn & Bacon.

Lazarus, A. A. (1989). *The practice of multimodal therapy: Systematic, comprehensive, and effective psychotherapy.* Baltimore: Johns Hopkins University Press.

Lazarus, R. (1999). *Stress and emotions.* New York: Springer.

Leahy, R. L. (2004). *Roadblocks in cognitive behavior therapy: Transforming challenges into opportunities for change.* New York: Guilford Press.

Levant, R. (2004). The empirically validated treatments movement: A practitioner/educator perspective. *Clinical Psychology: Science and Practice, 11*(2), 219–224.

Levin, J. (1999, October). *Private religious practices: Multidimensional measurement of religiousness/spirituality for use in health research—A report of the Fetzer Institute/National Institute on Aging Working Group.* Kalamazoo, MI: John E. Fetzer Institute.

Linehan, M. (1993). *Cognitive-behavioral treatment of borderline personality disorder.* New York: Guilford Press.

Llewelyn, S., & Kennedy, P. (2003). Introduction and overview. In S. Llewelyn & P. Kennedy (Eds.), *Handbook of health psychology* (p. 9). Chichester, West Sussex, England: Wiley.

Lykken, D. (1999). *Happiness: The nature and nurture of joy and contentment.* New York: St. Martin's Press.

Lyubomirsky, S. (2001). Why are some people happier than others? The role of cognitive and motivational processes in well-being. *American Psychologist, 56*(3), 239–249.

Mack, S. (2004). *Predictors of occupational burnout among substance abuse treatment clinicians.* Unpublished doctoral dissertation, Philadelphia College of Osteopathic Medicine.

Macrae, C. N., & Bodenhausen, G. V. (2000). Social Cognition: Thinking categorically about others. *Annual Review of Psychology, 51,* 93–120.

Mahoney, M. J. (1991). *Human change processes: The scientific foundations of psychotherapy.* New York: Basic Books.

Mahoney, M. J., & Norcross, J. C. (1993). Relationship styles and therapeutic choices: A commentary. *Psychotherapy: Theory, Research and Practice, 30,* 423–426.

Major, B., Quinton, W. J., & McCoy, S. K. (in press). Antecedents and consequences of attributions to discrimination: Theoretical and empirical advances. In M. F. Zanna (Ed.), *Advances in experimental social psychology* (Vol. 34). New York: Academic Press.

Maluccio, A. N. (1979). *Learning from clients.* New York: Free Press.

Marin, G., & Marin, B. (1991). *Research with Hispanic populations.* Newbury Park, CA: Sage.

Marin, G., Marin, G., Otero-Sabogal, R., Sabogal, F., & Perez-Stable, E. (1987). *Cultural differences in attitudes toward smoking: Developing messages using the theory of reasoned action* (Tech. Rep.). (Available from Box 0320, 400 Parnassus Ave., San Francisco, CA 94117)

Marlatt, G. A., & Gordon, J. R. (1985). *Relapse prevention: A self-control strategy for the maintenance of behavior change.* New York: Guilford Press.

Marshall, W. L., Serran, G. A., Moulden, H., Mulloy, R., Fernandez, Y., Mann, R. E., et al. (2002). Therapist features in sexual offender treatment: Their reliable identification and influence on behavior change. *Clinical Psychology and Psychotherapy, 9,* 395–405.

Martin, D. J., Garske, J. P., & Davis, M. K. (2000). Relation of the therapeutic alliance with outcome and other variables: A meta analytic review. *Journal of Consulting and Clinical Psychology, 68,* 438–450.

Martin, J. R. (1997). Mindfulness: A proposed common factor. *Journal of Psychotherapy Integration, 7*(4), 291–312.

Maslach, C., & Jackson, S. E. (1981). The measurement of experienced burnout. *Journal of Occupational Burnout, 2,* 99–113.

Maslach, C., Jackson, S. E., Leiter, M. P., & Schaufeli, W. B. (1996). *Maslach burnout inventory* (3rd ed.). Palo Alto, CA: CPP Books.

Maslach, C., Schaufeli, W. B., & Leiter, M. P. (2001). Job burnout. *Annual Review of Psychology, 52,* 397–422.

Masten, A. S. (2001). Ordinary magic: Resilience processes in development. *American Psychologist, 56*(3), 227–238. Retrieved September 3, 2001, from http://pantheon.yale.edu/~mp274/div53/.

Matthews, A. (1997, March). A guide to case conceptualization and treatment planning with minority group clients. *Behavior Therapist,* 35–39.

Mayne, T. J., Norcross, J. C., & Sayette, M. A. (1994). Admission requirements, acceptance rates, and financial assistance in clinical psychology programs: Diversity across the practice-research continuum. *American Psychologist, 49,* 806–811.

McDaniel, S. H. (1995). Collaboration between psychologists and family physicians: Implementing the biopsychosocial model. *Professional Psychology: Research and Practice, 26,* 117–122.

McGoldrick, M., Gerson, R., & Shellenberger, S. (1999). *Genograms: Assessment and intervention.* New York: Norton.

McLeod, J. (1990). The client's experience of counseling and psychotherapy: A review of the research literature. In D. Mearns & W. Dryden (Eds.), *Experience of counseling in action* (pp. 66–79). London: Sage.

Medieros, M., & Prochaska, J. O. (1993). *Predicting premature termination from psychotherapy.* Unpublished manuscript.

Meichenbaum, D., & Gilmore, J. B. (1982). Resistance from a cognitive-behavioral perspective. In P. L. Wachtel (Ed.), *Resistance: Psychodynamic and behavioral approaches* (pp. 133–156). New York: Plenum Press.

Menninger, K. (1958). *Theory of psychoanalytic technique.* New York: Basic Books.

Merriam-Webster online dictionary. (2007). Retrieved February 12, 2007, from www.m-w.com.

Miller, W. R., Taylor, C. A., & West, J. C. (1980). Focused versus broad-spectrum behavior therapy for problem drinkers. *Journal of Consulting and Clinical Psychology, 48,* 590–601.

Millon, T. (1994). *Millon Clinical Multiaxial Inventory-III: Manual.* Minneapolis, MN: National Computer Systems.

Milman, D. S., & Goldman, G. D. (1987). *Techniques of working with resistance.* Northvale, NJ: Aronson.

Morrison, J. R. (1995). *The first interview: A guide for clinicians-Revised for DSM-IV.* New York: Guilford Press.

Mueser, K. T., Glynn, S. M., Corrigan, P. W., & Baber, W. (1996). A survey of preferred terms for users of mental health services. *Psychiatric Services, 47,* 760–761.

Murray, H. A. (1943). *Thematic Apperception Test manual.* Cambridge, MA: Harvard University Press.

Myers, D. (1992). *The pursuit of happiness.* New York: Morrow.

Myers, D. G. (2006). *Social psychology* (9th ed.). New York: McGraw-Hill.

National Association of Social Workers. (1999). *Code of ethics*. Available from www .socialworkers.org.

Nelson, E. A., & Dannefer, D. (1992). Aged heterogeneity: Fact or fiction? The fate of diversity in gerontological research. *Gerontologist, 32*, 17–23.

Nezu, A. M. (1987). A problem solving formulation of depression: A literature review and proposal of a pluralistic model. *Clinical Psychology Review, 7*, 122–144.

Nezu, A. M., & Nezu, C. M. (Eds.). (1989). *Clinical decision making in behavior therapy: A problem solving perspective*. Champaign, IL: Research Press.

Nezu, A. M., Nezu, C. M., Friedman, S. H., Faddis, S., & Houts, P. S. (1998). *Helping cancer patients cope: A problem solving approach*. Washington, DC: American Psychological Association.

Nezu, A. M., Nezu, C. M., Friedman, S. H., & Haynes, S. N. (1997). Case formulation in behavior therapy: Problem-solving and functional analytic strategies. In T. D. Eels (Ed.), *Handbook of psychotherapy case formulation* (pp. 368–401). New York: Guilford Press.

Nezu, A. M., Nezu, C. M., & Lombardo, E. R. (2001). Cognitive-behavior therapy for medically unexplained symptoms: A critical review of the treatment literature. *Behavior Therapy, 32*, 537–583.

Nezu, A. M., Nezu, C. M., & Lombardo, E. R. (2004). *Cognitive-behavioral case formulation and treatment design: A problem solving approach*. New York: Springer.

Nezu, A. M., Nezu, C. M., & Perri, M. G. (1989). *Problem solving therapy for depression: Theory, research, and clinical guidelines*. New York: Wiley.

Nezu, C. M., & Nezu, A. M. (1995). Clinical decision making in everyday practice: The science in the art. *Cognitive and Behavioral Practice, 2*, 5–25.

Nezu, C. M., & Nezu, A. M. (2003). *Awakening self esteem: Spiritual and psychological techniques to enhance your well-being*. Oakland, CA: New Harbinger Press.

Nezu, C. M., Nezu, A. M., & Gill-Weiss, M. J. (1992). *Psychopathology in persons with mental retardation: Clinical guidelines for assessment and treatment*. Champaign, IL: Research Press.

Nickelson, D. W. (1998). Telehealth and the evolving health care system: Strategic opportunities for professional psychology. *Professional Psychology: Research and Practice, 29*, 527–535.

Nilsson, J. E., & Anderson, M. Z. (2004). Supervising international students: The role of acculturation, role ambiguity, and multicultural discussions. *Professional Psychology: Research and Practice, 35*(3), 306–312.

Norcross, J. C. (2002). Empirically supported therapy relationships. In J. Norcross (Ed.), *Psychotherapy relationships that work* (pp. 3–16). New York: Oxford University Press.

Norcross, J. C., Santrock, J. W., Campbell, L. F., Smith, T. P., Sommer, R., & Zuckerman, E. L. (2000). *Authoritative guide to self-help resources in mental health*. New York: Guilford Press.

Norcross, J. C., Sayette, M. A., & Mayne, T. J. (2002). *Insider's guide to graduate programs in clinical and counseling psychology* (2002–2003 ed.). New York: Guilford Press.

Nutkowicz, M. S. (2003). *Borderline personality disorder in older adulthood: Assessment and treatment*. Unpublished dissertation, College of Osteopathic Medicine, Philadelphia.

O'Brien, R., Linehan, M., Dowd, T., Kohlenberg, R., & Nezu, A. M. (1999, November). *Cognitive vs. behavioral, cognitive and behavior, cognitive/behavioral: You are what you think (behave)*. Panel discussion presented to the 33rd Annual Convention of the Association for the Advancement of Behavior Therapy, Toronto, Ontario, Canada.

Ockene, J., Ockene, I., & Kristellar, J. (1988). *The coronary artery smoking intervention study*. Worcester, MA: National Heart Lung Blood Institute.

Oetting, G. R., & Beauvais, F. (1990–1991). Orthogonal cultural identification theory: The cultural identification of minority adolescents. *International Journal of the Addictions, 25*, 655–685.

O'Halloran, T. M., & Linton, J. M. (2000). Stress on the job: Self-care resources for counselors. *Journal of Mental Health Counseling, 22*(4), 354–365.

O'Leary, K. D., & Wilson, G. T. (1975). *Behavior therapy: Application and outcome*. Oxford: Prentice Hall.

Oliver, M. N. I., Bernstein, J. H., Anderson, K. G., Blashfield, R. K., & Roberts, M. C. (2004). An exploratory examination of student attitudes toward "impaired" peers in clinical psychology training programs. *Professional Psychology: Research and Practice, 35*(2), 141–147.

Orlinsky, D., Grawe, K., & Parks, B. (1994). Process and outcome in psychotherapy: Noch einmal. In A. Bergin & S. Garfield (Eds.), *Handbook of psychotherapy and behavior change* (4th ed., pp. 270–376). New York: Wiley.

Otto, M., Jones, J., Craske, M., & Barlow, D. (1996). *Stopping anxiety medication: Therapist guide*. San Antonio, TX: Psychological Corporation.

Otto, M., Reilly-Harrington, N., Kogan, J., & Winett, C. (2003). Treatment contracting in cognitive-behavior therapy. *Cognitive and Behavioral Practice, 10*, 199–203.

Oyserman, D., Gant, L., & Ager, J. (1995). A socially contextualized model of African American identity: Possible selves and school persistence. *Journal of Personality and Social Psychology, 69*, 1216–1232.

Parham, T. A. (2001). Psychological nigrescence revisited: A foreword. *Journal of Multicultural Counseling and Development, 29,* 162–164.

Patel, C. (1993). Yoga-based therapy. In P. M. Lehrer & R. L. Woolfolk (Eds.), *Principles and practice of stress management* (2nd ed., pp. 89–138). New York: Guilford Press.

Paul, G. (1969). Behavior modification research: Design and tactics. In C. M. Franks (Ed.), *Behavior therapy: Appraisal and status.* New York: McGraw-Hill.

Pekarik, G. (1992). Relationship of client's reasons for dropping out of treatment outcome and satisfaction. *Journal of Clinical Psychology, 48,* 91–98.

Persons, J. B., & Tompkins, M. A. (1997). Cognitive-behavioral case formulation. In T. D. Eels (Ed.), *Handbook of psychotherapy case formulation* (pp. 314–339). New York: Guilford Press.

Peterson, C., & Seligman, M. (2001). *Values in Action Inventory of Strengths (VIA-IS) manual.* Philadelphia: University of Pennsylvania, Department of Psychology.

Peterson, D. R. (1976). Need for the doctor of psychology degree in professional psychology. *American Psychologist, 31,* 792–798.

Peterson, D. R. (1982). Origins and development of the doctor of psychology concept. In G. R. Caddy, D. C. Rimm, N. Watson, & J. H. Johnson (Eds.), *Educating professional psychologists* (pp. 19–38). New Brunswick, NJ: Transaction.

Peterson, D. R., Eaton, M. M., Levine, A. R., & Snepp, F. P. (1982). Career experiences of doctors of psychology. *Professional Psychology: Research and Practice, 13,* 268–277.

Peterson, R. L., McHolland, J. D., Bent, R. J., Davis-Russell, E., Edwall, G. E., Polite, K., et al. (Eds.). (1992). *The core curriculum in professional psychology.* Washington, DC: American Psychological Association.

Pettigrew, T. F. (1998). Applying social psychology to international social issues. *Journal of Social Issues, 54,* 663–675.

Phelps, R., Eisman, E. J., & Kohout, J. (1998). Psychological practice and managed care: Results of the CAPP practitioner survey. *Professional Psychology: Research and Practice, 29,* 31–36.

Pope, K. S. (1989). Therapists who become sexually intimate with a patient: Classifications, dynamics, recidivism and rehabilitation. *Independent Practitioner, 9,* 28–34.

Pope, K. S., Tabachnick, B. G., & Keith-Speigel, P. (1987). Ethics of practice: The beliefs and behaviors of psychologists and therapists. *American Psychologist, 42,* 993–1006.

Prochaska, J. O., & DiClemente, C. C. (1982). Transtheoretical therapy: Toward a more integrative model of change. *Psychotherapy: Theory, Research and Practice, 20,* 161–173.

Prochaska, J. O., & DiClemente, C. C. (1983). Stages and processes of self-change of smoking: Toward an integrative model of change. *Journal of Consulting and Clinical Psychology, 51,* 390–395.

Prochaska, J. O., & DiClemente, C. C. (1985). Common processes of change for smoking, weight control, and psychological distress. In S. Schiffman & T. Wills (Eds.), *Coping and substance abuse* (pp. 345–364). New York: Academic Press.

Prochaska, J. O., & DiClemente, C. C. (1992). Stages of change in the modification of problem behaviors. In M. Hersen, R. M. Eisler, & P. M. Miller (Eds.), *Progress in behavior modification* (pp. 184–214). Sycamore, IL: Sycamore Press.

Prochaska, J. O., DiClemente, C. C., & Norcross, J. C. (1992). In search of how people change: Applications to addictive behaviors. *American Psychologist, 47,* 1102–1114.

Prochaska, J. O., & Norcross, J. C. (2003). *Systems of psychotherapy: A transtheoretical analysis* (5th ed.). Pacific Grove, CA: Brooks/Cole.

Procidano, M. E., Busch-Rossnagel, N. A., Reznikoff, M., & Geisinger, K. F. (1995). Responding to graduate students' professional deficiencies: A national survey. *Journal of Clinical Psychology, 51*(3), 426–433.

Psychological Corporation. (1997). *WAIS-III-WMS-III technical manual.* San Antonio, TX: Author.

Reed, P. G. (1987). Spirituality and well-being in terminally ill hospitalized adults. *Research in Nursing and Health, 10*(5), 335–344.

Reich, W., Jesph, J., & Shayk, M. A. (1991). *Diagnostic instrument for children and adolescents-revised: Child and Parent* (Version 7.2). Seattle: University of Washington.

Reich, W., Shayka, J. J., & Taibleson, C. (1991). *Diagnostic Interview for Children and Adolescents Revised-Parent version (DICA-P); DSM-III-R version.* St. Louis, MO: Washington University, Department of Psychiatry.

Reis, B. F., & Brown, L. G. (2006). Preventing therapy dropout in the real world: The clinical utility of videotape preparation and client estimate of treatment duration. *Professional Psychology: Research and Practice, 37*(3), 311–316.

Reisner, A. D. (2005). The common factors, empirically validated treatments, and recovery models of therapeutic change. *Psychological Record, 55*(3), 377–400.

Rosen, C. S. (2000). Is the sequencing of change processes by stage consistent across health problems? A meta-analysis. *Health Psychology, 19,* 593–604.

Rosen, G. M. (1993). Self-help or hype? Comments on psychology's failure to advance self-care.

Professional Psychology: Research and Practice, 24, 340–345.

Roth, B. (1997). Mindfulness-based stress reduction in the inner city. *Advances, 13*(4), 50–58.

Rozensky, R. H., Sweet, J. J., & Tovian, S. M. (1997). *Psychological assessment in medical settings.* New York: Plenum Press.

Rudd, M. D., & Joiner, T. (1998). The assessment, management, and treatment of suicidality: Toward clinically informed and balanced standards of care. *Clinical Psychology, 5,* 135–150.

Ruiz, A. S. (1990). Ethnic identity: Crisis and resolution. *Journal of Multicultural Counseling and Development, 18,* 29–40.

Ryan, J. J., & Lopez, S. J. (2001). Wechsler Adult Intelligence Scale-III. In W. I. Dorfman & M. Hersen (Eds.), *Understanding psychological assessment* (pp. 19–42). New York: Kluwer.

Sabin-Farrell, R., & Turpin, G. (2003). Vicarious traumatization: Implications for the mental health of health workers? *Clinical Psychology Review, 23,* 449–480.

Sackett, D., Rosenberg, W., Gray, J., Haynes, R., & Richardson, W. (1996). Evidence-based medicine: What it is and what it isn't. *British Medical Journal, 312,* 71–72.

Safran, J. D., McMain, S., Crocker, P., & Murray, P. (1990). Therapeutic alliance rupture as a therapy event for empirical investigation. *Psychotherapy, 27,* 154–165.

Safran, J. D., & Muran, J. C. (Eds.). (1995). The therapeutic alliance [Special issue]. *In session: Psychotherapy in practice* (Pt. 1).

Safran, J. D., & Muran, J. C. (2000). *Negotiating the therapeutic alliance: A relational treatment guide.* New York: Guilford Press.

Safran, J. D., & Segal, Z. V. (1990). *Interpersonal process in cognitive therapy.* New York: Basic Books.

Sales, B. D., Miller, M. O., & Hall, S. R. (2005). *Laws affecting clinical practice.* Washington, DC: American Psychological Association.

Salovey, P., & Turk, D. C. (1991). *Clinical judgment and decision-making.* Elmsford, NY: Pergamon Press.

Salston, M., & Figley, C. R. (2003). Secondary traumatic stress effects of working with survivors of criminal victimization. *Journal of Traumatic Stress, 16*(2), 167–174.

Santrock, J. W. (1999). *Life-span development* (7th ed.). Boston: McGraw-Hill.

Scherer, M., Blair, K., Banks, M. E., Brucker, B., Corrigan, J., & Wegener, S. (n.d.). *Rehabilitation psychology.* Retrieved February 12, 2007, from www.apa.org/divisions/div22/Rpdef.html.

Schiepek, G., Fricke, B., & Kaimer, P. (1992). Synergetics of psychotherapy. In W. Tschacher, G. Schiepek, & E. J. Brunner (Eds.), *Self organiza-tion and clinical psychology* (pp. 239–267). New York: Springer.

Schneider, B. A. (2001). Rorschach inkblot technique. In W. I. Dorfman & M. Hersen (Eds.), *Understanding psychological assessment* (pp. 77–106). New York: Kluwer Academic/Plenum Press.

Schober, C., & Felgoise, S. H. (2002, December). *Problem-solving, job stress, and burnout in administrative assistants.* Poster presented to the European Academy of Occupational Health Psychology, Vienna.

Schwartz, G. E. (1982). Testing the biopsychosocial model: The ultimate challenge facing behavioral medicine? *Journal of Consulting and Clinical Psychology, 50,* 1040–1053.

Schwebel, M., & Coster, J. (1998). Well-functioning in professional psychologists: As program heads see it. *Professional Psychology: Research and Practice, 29,* 284–292.

Segal, Z., Williams, J., & Teasdale, J. (2002). *Mindfulness-based cognitive therapy for depression: A new approach to preventing relapse.* New York: Guilford Press.

Seligman, M. (2002). *Authentic happiness.* New York: Free Press.

Seligman, M., & Csikszentmihalyi, M. (2000). Positive psychology: An introduction. *American Psychologist, 55*(1), 5–14.

Serran, G., Fernandez, Y., Marshall, W. L., & Mann, R. E. (2003). Process issues in treatment: Application to sexual offender programs. *Professional Psychology: Research and Practice, 34*(4), 368–374.

Seymour, R. B., Smith, D. E., & Chambers, T. (2003). *Journal of Psychoactive Drugs, 35*(3), 410.

Sharma, V., Whitney, D., Kazarian, S. S., & Manchanda, R. (2000). Preferred terms for users of mental health services among service providers and recipients. *Psychiatric Services, 51*(2), 203–209.

Shea, S. C. (1988). *Psychiatric interviewing.* Philadelphia: Saunders/Charcourt Brace.

Sheldon, K. M., & King, L. (2001). Why positive psychology is necessary. *American Psychologist, 56*(3), 216–217.

Shoptaw, S., Stein, J. A., & Rawson, R. A. (2000). Burnout in substance abuse counselors: Impact of environment, attitudes, and clients with HIV. *Journal of Substance Abuse Treatment, 19,* 117–126.

Silva, F. (1993). *Psychometric foundations and behavioral assessment.* Newbury Park, CA: Sage.

Simmons, Z., Felgoise, S. H., Bremer, B. A., Walsh, S. M., Hufford, D. J., Bromberg, M. B., et al. (2006). The ALSSQOL: Balancing physical and nonphysical factors in assessing quality of life in ALS. *Neurology, 67,* 1659–1994.

Skinner, B. F. (1953). *Science and human behavior.* New York: Free Press.

Spear, J., Wood, L., Chawla, S., Devis, A., & Nelson, J. (2004). Job satisfaction and burnout in mental health services for older people. *Australian Psychiatry, 12*(1), 58–61.

Stark, M. (1994). *Working with resistance.* Northdale, NJ: Aronson.

Sternberg, R. J. (1999). *Cognitive psychology* (2nd ed.). Philadelphia: Harcourt Brace.

Sternberg, R. J., & Detterman, D. K. (Eds.). (1986). *What is intelligence? Contemporary viewpoints on its nature and definition.* Norwood, NJ: Ablex.

Stevens, M., & Higgins, D. J. (2002). The influence of risk and protective factors on burnout experienced by those who work with maltreated children. *Child Abuse Review, 11,* 313–331.

Stewart, W. F., Ricci, J. A., Chee, E., Hahn, S. R., & Morganstein, D. (2003). Cost of lost productive work time among U.S. workers with depression. *Journal of the American Medical Association, 289,* 3135–3144.

Strauss, A., & Corbin, J. (1994). Grounded theory methodology. In N. K. Denzin & Y. S. Lincoln (Eds.), *Handbook of qualitative research* (pp. 273–285). Thousand Oaks, CA: Sage.

Strickland, B. (2000). Misassumptions, misadventures, and the misuse of psychology. *American Psychologist, 55,* 331–338.

Stuart, R. B. (2004). Twelve practical suggestions for achieving multicultural competence. *Professional Psychology: Research and Practice, 35,* 3–9.

Sue, D. W., Bingham, R. P., Porche-Burke, L., & Vasquez, M. (1999). The diversification of psychology: a multicultural revolution. *American Psychologist. 54*(12), 1061–1069.

Sue, D. W., & Sue, D. (1999). *Counseling the culturally different: Theory and practice* (3rd ed.). New York: Wiley.

Sue, S. (1998). In search of cultural competence in psychotherapy and counseling. *American Psychologist, 53,* 440–448.

Sweeney, J. A., Dick, E. L., & Srinivasagam, N. M. (1998). Biological assessment. In A. S. Bellack & M. Hersen (Eds.), *Behavioral assessment: A practical handbook* (4th ed., pp. 418–436). Boston: Allyn & Bacon.

Swim, J., & Mallett, R. (2002). *Pride and prejudice: A multi-group model of identity and its association with intergroup and intragroup attitudes.* Manuscript submitted for publication.

Szasz, T. S. (1984). *The myth of mental illness: Foundations of a theory of personal conduct* (rev. ed.). New York: Harper & Row.

Szasz, T. S. (1988). *The myth psychotherapy: Mental healing as religios, rhetoric, and repression.* Syracuse, NY: Syracuse University Press.

Szasz, T. S. (1997). *The manufacture of madness: A comparative study of the inquisition and the mental health movement.* Syracuse, NY: Syracuse University Press.

Tajfel, H., & Turner, J. C. (1986). The social identity theory of intergroup behavior. In S. Worchel & W. G Austin (Eds.), *Psychology of inter-group relations* (pp. 7–24). Chicago: Nelson-Hall.

Tanaka-Matsumi, J., Seiden, D., & Lam, K. N. (1996). The culturally informed functional assessment (CIFA) interview: A strategy for cross-cultural behavioral practice. *Cognitive and Behavioral Practice, 3,* 215–233.

Tausig, M., Michello, J., & Subedi, S. (2003). *A sociology of mental illness* (2nd ed.). Upper Saddle River, NJ: Prentice Hall.

Teyber, E. (2006). *Interpersonal process in therapy: An integrative model* (5th ed.). Pacific Grove, CA: Brooks/Cole.

Thompson, C. E., & Carter, R. T. (1997). *Racial identity theory: Applications to individual, group, and organizational interventions.* Mahwah, NJ: Erlbaum.

Thorndike, R. L., Hagen, E. P., & Sattler, J. M. (1986). *Stanford-Binet Intelligence Scale: Technical manual* (4th ed.). Chicago: Riverside.

Thorp, S. R., & Lynch, T. R. (2005). Depression and personality disorders—Older adults. In A. Freeman, S. H. Felgoise, A. M. Nezu, C. M. Nezu, & M. A. Reinecke (Eds.), *Encyclopedia of cognitive behavior therapy* (pp. 155–161). New York: Springer.

Tolkien, J. R. R. (1986). *Tolkien reader.* New York: Ballantine Books.

Triandis, H. (1995). The self and social behavior. In N. R. Goldberger & J. B. Veroff (Eds.), *The culture and psychology reader* (pp. 326–365). New York: New York University Press.

Triandis, H. (1996). The psychological measurement of cultural syndromes. *American Psychologist, 51,* 407–415.

Turner, J. (1987). *Rediscovering the social group: A self-categorization theory.* London: Blackwell.

Turner, J., Brown, R. J., & Tajfel, H. (1979). Social comparison and group interest in in-group favouritism. *European Journal of Social Psychology, 9,* 187–204.

Turner, S. M., DeMers, S. T., Fox, H. R., & Reed, G. M. (2001). APA's guidelines for test user qualifications: An executive summary. *American Psychologist, 56*(12), 1099–1113.

Tversky, A., & Kahnemann, D. (1974). Judgment under uncertainty: Heuristics and biases. *Science, 185,* 1124–1131.

U.S. Department of Health and Human Services. (1999). *Mental health: A report of the surgeon gen-*

eral. Washington, DC: Author. Available from www.surgeongeneral.gov/library/mentalhealth /home.html.

Vandello, J., & Cohen, D. (1999). Patterns of individualism and collectivism across the United States. *Journal of Personality and Social Psychology, 77,* 279–292.

Wachtel, P. (Ed.). (1982). *Resistance: Psychodynamic and behavioral approaches.* New York: Springer.

Wade, C., & Tavris, C. (2000). *Psychology* (6th ed.). Upper Saddle River, NJ: Prentice Hall.

Wampold, B. E. (2001). *The great psychotherapy debate: Models, methods, and findings.* Mahwah, NJ: Erlbaum.

Wechsler, D. (1989). *Wechsler Preschool and Primary Scale of Intelligence—Revised.* San Antonio, TX: Psychological Corporation.

Wechsler, D. (1991). *Wechsler Intelligence Scale for Children manual* (3rd ed.). San Antonio, TX: Psychological Corporation.

Wechsler, D. (1997). *WAIS-III administration and scoring manual.* San Antonio, TX: Psychological Association.

Weinberger, J. (1995). Common factors aren't so common: The common factors dilemma. *Clinical Psychology: Science and Practice, 2*(1), 45–69.

Weiner, I. B. (1998). *Principles of psychotherapy.* New York: Wiley.

Whites' majority steadily shrinking. (2004, March 18). *Tennessean,* p. 1A.

Wilkenson, G. S. (1993). *Wide Range Achievement Test-III.* Wilmington, DE: Jastak Associates.

Wilner, K. B. (2004). *An investigation of anger-management techniques for essential hypertension patients: A case study.* Unpublished doctoral dissertation, Philadelphia College of Osteopathic Medicine.

Wohl, J. (2000). Psychotherapy and cultural diversity. In J. Aponte & J. Wohl (Eds.), *Psychological intervention and cultural diversity* (2nd ed., pp. 75–91). Needham Heights, MA: Allyn & Bacon.

Wolsko, C., Park, B., Judd, C. M., & Wittenbrink, B. (2000). Framing interethnic ideology: Effects of multicultural and color-blind perspectives on judgments of groups and individuals. *Journal of Personality and Social Psychology, 78,* 635–654.

Woolger, C. (2000). Wechsler Intelligence Scale for Children (WISC-III; 3rd ed.). In W. I. Dorfman & M. Hersen (Eds.), *Understanding psychological assessment* (pp. 219–233). New York: Kluwer.

Worchel, S. (1999). *Written in blood: Ethnic identity and the struggle for human harmony.* New York: Worth.

World Health Organization. (1948). *The International Classification of Disease.* Geneva, Switzerland: Author.

World Health Organization. (1992). *ICD-10.* Geneva, Switzerland: Author.

Wright, J. H., & Davis, D. D. (1994). The therapeutic relationship in cognitive-behavioral therapy: Patient perceptions and therapist responses. *Cognitive and Behavioral Practice, 1,* 25–45.

Yalom, I. D. (1980). *Existential psychotherapy.* New York: Basic Books.

Younggren, J., & Gottlieb, M. (in press). Termination and abandonment: History, risk and risk management. *Professional Psychology: Research and Practice.*

Younggren, J. N. (2004, May 1). *Legal and ethical risks and risk management in professional psychological practice sequence II: Risk management in specific high risk areas.* Workshop sponsored by the APA Insurance Trust and the Tennessee Psychological Association, Nashville, TN.

Younggren, J. N., Davis, D., Hjelt, S., Gottlieb, M., & Schoener, G. (2007, August 17–20). *Termination and abandonment: Ethics, law, and risk management.* Symposium presented at the annual convention of the American Psychological Association, San Francisco.

Younggren, J. N., & Gottlieb, M. C. (2004). Managing risk when contemplating multiple relationships. *Professional Psychology: Research and Practice, 35*(3), 255–260.

Zur, O. (2007). *Boundaries in psychotherapy: Ethical and clinical explorations.* Washington, DC: American Psychological Association.

About the Authors

Arthur Freeman is Visiting Professor of Psychology at Governors State University, University Park, Illinois, Clinical Professor of Clinical Psychology at Philadelphia College of Osteopathic Medicine, Chief Psychologist and Director of Training at Sheridan Shores Care and Rehabilitation Center in Chicago, and President of the Freeman Institute in Fort Wayne, Indiana. He was the founding chair of the APA accredited program in clinical psychology at Philadelphia College of Osteopathic Medicine. He completed his early graduate work at New York University, and his doctoral work at Teachers College—Columbia University. He studied with Albert Ellis, and later completed a postdoctoral fellowship at the Center for Cognitive Therapy at the University of Pennsylvania under Dr. Aaron T. Beck.

Dr. Freeman has published over 60 professional books, two trade books, and more than 60 other professional contributions. His publications have been translated from English into nine languages. He is a diplomate in Clinical Psychology and Behavioral Psychology from the American Board of Professional Psychology, a diplomate in Adlerian Psychology, and a fellow of the American Psychological Association, of the American Psychological Society, and of the Academy of Clinical Psychology. He is a past president of the Association of Behavioral and Cognitive Therapies (ABCT) and of the International Association of Cognitive Psychotherapy. He has lectured in more than 30 countries over the past 30 years. He is licensed to practice psychology in Pennsylvania, Indiana, and Illinois. In 2000, he was given an award for Distinguished Contributions to the Science and Profession of Psychology by the Pennsylvania Psychological Association. As a perennial traveler and teacher around the globe, he prefers to relax at home where he enjoys cooking for his extended family, playing with his grandchildren and reading stories to them, searching for bargains on eBay, adding to his collections of old cars and old cameras, listening to Barbra Streisand and other music of the 1950s, and every now and then, cutting the rug with a little swing dancing.

Stephanie H. Felgoise is Associate Professor and Vice-Chair of the Department of Psychology, and Director of the PsyD Program in Clinical Psychology at the Philadelphia College of Osteopathic Medicine. She completed her doctorate in clinical psychology at Hahnemann University where she worked with Drs. Arthur and Christine Maguth Nezu. Her predoctoral internship was in clinical and community psychology at the University of Medicine and Dentistry of New Jersey-Robert Wood Johnson Medical School, where she acquired specialty training in marital and sexual health under Dr. Sandra Leiblum, in addition to other areas of behavioral medicine. She completed a postdoctoral fellowship in Health Psychology and Research and was Research Assistant Professor at the Medical College of Pennsylvania-Hahnemann University, also under Drs. Arthur and Christine Maguth Nezu.

Dr. Felgoise has been active in the leadership of the Association for Behavioral and Cognitive Therapies (ABCT) for the past 15 years as a committee member for Awards and Recognitions and Local Arrangements, Associate Program Co-Chair (1999), and Chair for Membership Committee (2001–2004) and Nominations and Elections Committee (2005–2007). She is also a member of several other national organizations, and attends the conventions of ABCT and the National Council of Schools and Programs of Professional Psychology (NCSPP) annually. She has coauthored numerous journal articles and book chapters and, with Drs. Arthur and Christine Maguth Nezu, coauthored a problem-solving therapy treatment manual for persons with cancer and their significant others, based on research supporting its use. She is also coeditor of the *Encyclopedia of Cognitive and Behavioral Therapies,* with Drs. Art Freeman, Art Nezu, Christine Maguth Nezu, and Mark Reineke. Her career focus is behavioral medicine and clinical health psychology. Her research has focused on social problem solving, coping, adjustment, and quality of life in caregivers of, and adults with cancer, amyotrophic lateral sclerosis, irritable bowel syndrome, infertility, and more recently, children and adolescents with Long QT syndrome and their parents.

Dr. Felgoise is licensed to practice clinical psychology in Pennsylvania and is a diplomate of the American Board of Professional Psychology in Clinical Psychology. Her private practice serves individuals and couples with clinical health and general clinical psychology challenges. Her favorite relaxation practices include spending time with her two young children, Benjamin and Elizabeth, husband Glenn, mini schnauzer Roxy, and also with her parents and two sisters and their families. She enjoys movies, the arts, classical music, travel, sudoku puzzles, and many forms of exercise and sports, especially lap swimming. Self-care practices incorporate her preferred recreational activities, and also time spent in communication with close friends and family, season ballet tickets with friends, healthy eating and consumption of dark chocolate, eating lunch with colleagues rather than at her desk at least twice weekly, periodic personal days for individual time, and annual vacations to Ft. Lauderdale, Florida, with her family.

Denise D. Davis is the Assistant Director (Arts and Science) of Clinical Training for the Vanderbilt University Psychology Departments Integrated Graduate Program in Clinical Science, where she teaches core courses in psychotherapy, professional ethics, and cultural diversity. She completed her doctorate in Clinical-Community Psychology at the University of South Carolina, and a research postdoctoral fellowship at Indiana University School of Medicine followed by a clinical postdoctoral fellowship at the Center for Cognitive Therapy at the University of Pennsylvania under Dr. Aaron T. Beck. She is a Founding Fellow of the Academy of Cognitive Therapy.

Dr. Davis has served several years as an Ethics Consultant to the Tennessee State Board of Examiners (BOE) in Psychology, and completed a 3-year term as a practicing member of the BOE, including a year as Vice-Chair of the Board. She is a past president of the Indiana Psychological Association and a past Grassroots Legislative Chair for Tennessee. She was a founding editor of the journal *Cognitive and Behavioral Practice* (volumes 1 through 4), coauthor of two editions of *Cognitive Therapy of Personality Disorders* (A. T. Beck, Freeman,

Davis, & Associates, 1990, 2004) and author or coauthor of more than 25 articles and book chapters. Current projects include a forthcoming authored book titled *Terminating Psychotherapy: A Professional Guide for Ending on a Positive Note,* to be published by John Wiley & Sons. She is presently serving on a committee of the newly formed Tennessee Colleague Assistance Foundation (TCAF) to develop a formal colleague assistance program with prevention and rehabilitation components. She is licensed to practice clinical psychology in Tennessee and she has practiced in various independent and institutional settings for 25 years. Her favorite relaxation and self-care activities include modern dancing, quilting, attending her son's basketball games, cooking, reading, traveling with friends, and mindfully enjoying the beauty of nature.

Author Index

Subject Index

DATE DUE

Demco, Inc. 38-293